Dangerous Anarchist Strikers

Studies in Critical Social Sciences Book Series

Haymarket Books is proud to be working with Brill Academic Publishers (www.brill.nl) to republish the *Studies in Critical Social Sciences* book series in paperback editions. This peer-reviewed book series offers insights into our current reality by exploring the content and consequences of power relationships under capitalism, and by considering the spaces of opposition and resistance to these changes that have been defining our new age. Our full catalog of *SCSS* volumes can be viewed at https://www.haymarketbooks.org/series_collections/4-studies-in-critical-social-sciences.

Series Editor
David Fasenfest (York University, Canada)

Editorial Board
Eduardo Bonilla-Silva (Duke University)
Chris Chase-Dunn (University of California–Riverside)
William Carroll (University of Victoria)
Raewyn Connell (University of Sydney)
Kimberlé W. Crenshaw (University of California–LA and Columbia University)
Heidi Gottfried (Wayne State University)
Alfredo Saad-Filho (Queen's University, Belfast)
Chizuko Ueno (University of Tokyo)
Sylvia Walby (Lancaster University)
Raju Das (York University)

Dangerous Anarchist Strikers

Steve J. Shone

Haymarket Books
Chicago, IL

First published in 2023 by Brill Academic Publishers, The Netherlands
© 2023 Koninklijke Brill NV, Leiden, The Netherlands

Published in paperback in 2024 by
Haymarket Books
P.O. Box 180165
Chicago, IL 60618
773-583-7884
www.haymarketbooks.org

ISBN: 979-8-88890-342-1

Distributed to the trade in the US through Consortium Book Sales and Distribution (www.cbsd.com) and internationally through Ingram Publisher Services International (www.ingramcontent.com).

This book was published with the generous support of Lannan Foundation, Wallace Action Fund, and the Marguerite Casey Foundation.

Special discounts are available for bulk purchases by organizations and institutions. Please call 773-583-7884 or email info@haymarketbooks.org for more information.

Cover design by Jamie Kerry and Ragina Johnson.

Printed in the United States.

Library of Congress Cataloging-in-Publication data is available.

Contents

Introduction   1

PART 1
Women in Action

1 Virginia Bolten: Myth and Reality   13
   1   The Origins of Anarchism in Argentina and Uruguay   13
   2   Virginia Bolten: the Myth   25
   3   Virginia Bolten: the Reality   41

2 Helen Armstrong: Champion of Labor, Women, and the Poor   68
   1   The Trials   72
   2   Meetings and Talk of Revolution   78
   3   Immigrants and British Subjects   82
   4   Forgotten Women   87
   5   Poverty and Women's Pay   100

3 Elizabeth Gurley Flynn: a Star Who Ceased to Twinkle   116
   1   Before and after Spokane   123
   2   Elizabeth and the IWW   129
   3   The Chicago IWW Trial   143
   4   The Workers' Defense Union and the ACLU   144
   5   Sacco and Vanzetti, the LDC, and the ILD   149
   6   Flynn the Communist   158

PART 2
Internationalists

4 Tom Barker: a Wobbly Who Wobbled   171
   1   New Zealand   172
   2   Australia   189
   3   Chile   219
   4   Argentina   222
   5   Europe, Conferences, and the Twelve   225
   6   Russia   230

7	New York City	240
8	England	245

5 Kōtoku, Shūsui: the Ringleader 252

    1   Kanno, Suga, "Wife," and Other Wives 265
    2   Kōtoku's Trajectory toward Anarchism 272
    3   Sugamo Prison and Six Months in the United States 285
    4   Ashio Copper Mine 299
    5   Kōtoku and the Japanese Language 301
    6   Kōtoku the Atheist 303
    7   Kōtoku's Chinese Influences 305

Conclusion 311

Bibliography 319
Index 385

Introduction

The purpose of the present work is to explore the ideas of five thinkers associated with the following political perspectives: anarchism, syndicalism, the Industrial Workers of the World (IWW, the Wobblies), industrial unionism, the general strike, and militant labor union activism in general, direct action, creating One Big Union, anxiety about "the social question," support for people and soldiers of "enemy" nations, and opposition to military conscription, to the First World War, and to the sending of Western troops at the end of that conflict to interfere disruptively in the Soviet Union. Although to some extent all these concerns have attracted the interest of various radical thinkers, the five discussed here exemplify support for many or most of these overlapping topics, making them collectively a suitable topic for discussion.

The logic underlying the approach outlined above is that existing definitions of concepts such as "anarchism" and "syndicalism" suggest an appropriateness to certain ways of explaining the categories in question, resulting in some quite negative consequences. When many students of "anarchism" have attempted to define their topic, they have focused their understandings mainly on a group of European thinkers no longer alive – in particular, Pierre-Joseph Proudhon, Mikhail Bakunin, Peter Kropotkin, and Max Stirner, and maybe Emma Goldman, but never Lucy Parsons – and have then in some cases included others in terms of their relationship or non-relationship to the lives or ideas of the latter as it were "proven past masters" of the phenomenon. Often, it would seem, when the writers in question first, as undergraduates, encountered anarchism, they learned about Proudhon, Bakunin, Kropotkin, and Stirner, and maybe Emma Goldman, but never Lucy Parsons, passed their examinations with flying colors, and then as they developed into serious scholars, they nonetheless continued to understand the subject of their research in the same way. In some cases, this attitude, which for the sake of argument might be called "Anarchism Limited," has led to its advocates dismissing other, quite similar thinkers, including those, for example, who lived in North or South America or Australasia as not being anarchists at all. Moreover, advocates of Anarchism Limited, whether intentionally or not, have often tended to be the persons presiding over relevant journals and conference sections, making their long-held views clear, while academics in and of other hemispheres and their contributions have tended to be left out. Thus, in his review of one of the present author's previous works, *American Anarchism* (Shone 2013) and of A. Terrance Wiley's, *Angelic Troublemakers: Religion and Anarchism in America* (Wiley 2014), Carl Levy (2019) apologetically titles his piece "American

Anarchisms?" even as he accurately explains in significant detail some of the arguments to be found in those two books.

It has been frustrating to have written about the Chicago anarchists and then be told that they were "not anarchists," or that the subject of another project, Lysander Spooner (Shone 2010), was not an anarchist but a libertarian. Of all political ideologies, anarchism is a way of thinking that benefits least from the application of any type of ideological correctness by a scholastic politburo. Unfortunately, introductory textbooks about the topic have often in the past followed the direction of Anarchism Limited. For example, David Miller's *Anarchism* (1984) proceeds as follows under the heading, "What is Anarchism?" to situate the important thinkers firmly in Europe as follows:

> We may trace the origins of anarchism to the outbreak of the French Revolution in 1789. Although it is possible, by searching diligently enough, to find precursors of anarchism as far back as the ancient Greeks – and perhaps even the Chinese – this shows only that there have always been men willing to challenge authority on philosophical or political grounds. This might be described as the primitive anarchist attitude: but for anarchism to develop beyond a stance of defiance into a social and political theory that challenged the existing order and proposed an alternative, such wholesale reconstruction needed to become thinkable. This reorientation of thought was the work largely of the Revolution, which, by challenging the old regime in France on grounds of basic principle, opened the way for similar challenges to other states and other social institutions.
>
> MILLER 1984, 3

Later, he speaks of anarchism as a movement that is both European in character and no longer active, "with France acquiring pride of place again in the early 1900s (with the Syndicalist movement), and Spain witnessing the finale with the anarchist-inspired union movement that fought and perished in the Civil War" (Miller 1984, 4). Even though it was translated by Steven T. Byington and published by Benjamin R. Tucker, who were both themselves important American anarchists, Paul Eltzbacher's *Anarchism: Exponents of the Anarchist Philosophy* (1908), a potential early compendium, contained chapters on the following thinkers alone: William Godwin, Proudhon, Stirner, Bakunin, Kropotkin, and Tolstoy, along with one about Tucker himself, with Byington (1908, xi) in his preface mentioning another American anarchist, Lysander Spooner, in a single sentence.

Over the last thirty years, historians and scholars of other disciplines have been discussing and activating a new "transnational" approach to their research, no longer situating phenomena within the boundaries of the nation-state, generating new information that promisingly at times has eschewed prior, more restricted explanations that had given support to nationalistic propaganda (Ngai 2012). With respect to the history of anarchism, there has been substantial discussion of a similar paradigm shift (Bantman and Altena 2017), although the recognition of a need to move beyond deficient explanations of anarchist developments in a particular place has to some extent been championed by researchers who previously proffered explanations in terms of Anarchism Limited. Since the present author was never an advocate of Anarchism Limited, this present study should not be seen as an example of a "transnational turn." Nevertheless, discussion of anarchism and syndicalism and the allied beliefs mentioned above in the first paragraph as they apply to the countries discussed here, to Argentina, Uruguay, Chile, New Zealand, Australia, Japan, Canada, and the United States, is approached in a fashion of unabashed recognition that anarchism is a global phenomenon, even as repeated reference is naturally and reasonably made to the ideas of Goldman, Kropotkin, Stirner, and others who have had substantial influence worldwide.

The cluster of topics referenced above seems a potentially less confusing approach to explaining the links and disagreements between the thinkers who are examined in this book, Virginia Bolten, Helen Armstrong, and Elizabeth Gurley Flynn, and Tom Barker, and Kōtoku, Shūsui. The three radical thinkers discussed in the first three chapters are all women. To some extent, that choice reflects a continuation of the author's desire to further contribute to the restoration of the ideas of much-forgotten anarchist, feminist, and other allied exponents of liberty who have been to various degrees lost to an academic environment that has tended (and continues) to stress the achievements of men to the exclusion of those of women. In *Women of Liberty* (2019), the author presented the ideas of Mercy Otis Warren, Louise Michel, Victoria C. Woodhull, Tennie C. Claflin, Lois Waisbrooker, Itō, Noe, Elizabeth Cady Stanton, Margaret Sanger, Mollie Steimer, and Rose Pesotta.

Indeed, the academic environment within the discipline of political science, dominated now for many decades by its own rather unwise "behavioralist" paradigm shift in favor of a mainstream "rigorous" quasi-mathematical approach to the collection and dissemination of "data," has left the political theory subfield isolated and to some extent under attack from advocates of statistical and/or econometric "rational choice" methods who see little use for what they claim is the "normative" (and thus allegedly unscientific) research of their rivals, whose influence continues to decline as do the numbers of their faculty and classes offered. In many ways, the study of politics has been excised from the discipline that bears its name.

Dissatisfaction with the dominance of statistical and rational choice theory approaches prompted the birth of a "perestroika" movement in 2000, its advocates borrowing the name that refers to the reforms in Russia's political system frequently identified with Mikhail Gorbachev, and the appearance of a number of its supporters at the 2001 American Political Science Association (APSA) meeting in San Francisco and at later conferences, resulted in increased attention to the issue. An earlier wave of dissatisfaction created another group in 1967, the Caucus for a Critical Political Science (CCPS), which is now associated with the New Political Science section of the APSA. However, notwithstanding the limited success of "perestroika," not only has the discipline continued to be dominated by quantitative approaches, but graduate methodology classes have also persisted in emphasizing particular lines to be taken in the conduct of research. A paper presented at the 2001 conference by Peregrine Schwartz-Shea (2001) examined political science doctoral program degree requirements, finding that quantitative methods were heavily favored, and Schwartz-Shea and Yanow (2002) analyzed fourteen texts used in graduate research methods classes, concluding that twelve of the books, some of which are still used in newer editions today, "convey symbolically, if not explicitly, that words must be converted into numbers to be useful or even suitable for truly scientific research. Such silencing is what leads us to see positivist presuppositions in these texts, even when such a position is not taken explicitly" (Schwartz-Shea and Yanow 2002, 470). At the discipline's academic conferences in the succeeding years, there has been greater attention to alternative methods of inquiry, but in college departments there is much less evidence of curricular reform.

Meanwhile, political theory classes have continued to present the history of political thought by promoting an historical string of almost exclusively male and Western thinkers, some of whom present negative or inaccurate views about women or the potential of women to achieve equality with men. Collectively, the political science environment does little to incorporate more representative research outlooks consistent with the values of the twenty-first century, which are much more likely to be found in occasionally taught Women and Politics classes or far away in Women's Studies departments not dominated by the same methodological bias, and therefore providing contradictory information that to some extent is difficult for students to integrate with the mainstream perspectives of the political science discipline. Moreover, the focus on quasi-empirical methods has prioritized work related to countable aspects of voting, campaigns, and public opinion, producing a positive perception of the apparent evidence of democracy somehow validated by these "results," in the absence of much explanation as to why voting, rather than, say, equality of opportunity for women, is an indication of democracy or even bothering to say why voting matters at all or has any practical effect on those who vote.

Mainstream journals in the US that are administered by the APSA or its regional affiliates have approached the criticism that they need to say more about women by focusing on, for example, biographies of First Ladies, or asking why women are less likely to run for elective office, or study of "the gender gap in political knowledge" based on information from phone survey data (Sanbonmatsu 2003, 370), and similar research that, while of value in itself and for those for whom it is of interest, continues, intentionally or by chance, to reinforce the behavioralist "counting" template and its implied message that the discipline is exclusively a quantitative form of science. Writing about the situation a decade ago, Yanow and Schwartz-Shea pointed out:

> [T]he discipline, as seen through its teaching and journals, was in large measure not open to research questions answerable through other than quantitative measures.
> YANOW AND SCHWARTZ-SHEA 2010, 742

Despite improvements, then, particularly with respect to participation at conferences, and with graduate student methodological training most likely the aspect that lags farthest behind, and despite the fact that beyond the reaches of the APSA's intellectual canopy, there is much greater openness to different approaches, there remains a continued need to speak up in favor of more reform. Interpretivist studies of little remembered women are required to make political science whole and can address not only their actions and writings and accomplishments, but their feelings and understandings of their own identities as women, since inclusion of such elements would send a message to female students of political science that the discipline concerns their lives as much as it does those of men. An expanded political science would include the encounters of women in the past, presenting the information in the form of actually scientific historical information, rather than as the results of a model relying on a simplified number of variables or applying an equation that is presumed to fit the shape of the data being investigated. Additionally, with respect to political theory, an expansion of the subfield should allow better presentation of the arguments and life stories of female thinkers who risked disapprobation or imprisonment to achieve social change, and who by the sacrifices they made gave opportunity to others, opportunities that today are once again threatened by socially conservative enemies.

Virginia Bolten (c. 1876–1960), the subject of Chapter 1, an anarchist who lived in Argentina and Uruguay, and was active in labor disputes and protests in both countries, has attracted much scholarly interest in recent years. However, there is considerable disagreement about the details of her life, and a number of unexplained questions persist, such as why the main written work attributed to her, an extant journal named *La Voz de la Mujer*, makes no reference to her in any of its issues, and why, if she was, as some scholars insist, born in Argentina, she would have been deported to Uruguay, which she was, apparently several times. The chapter looks at the content and role of anarchist newspapers, of which there were many in southern South America, and reinterprets the significance of Bolten's contributions to radical thought using the writings and events that have been correctly attributed to her, replacing Virginia's laudatory mythical significance with a more realistic appraisal, one that confirms, notwithstanding the confusion, that she is entitled to be considered a major contributor to anarchist thought.

Chapter 2 discusses Helen Armstrong (1875–1947), a major leader of the Winnipeg General Strike of 1919, which is today considered one of the most important events in the history of Canada, a person who opposed the First World War and its aftermath in the Soviet Union, viewing its new communist regime as a positive change. The role of Helen, the rambunctious leading light of the Women's Labor League, was for a long time ignored as strike events were interpreted through the activities of her male collaborators, including her husband, George Armstrong, a distortion that to some extent remains. Many labor union leaders were imprisoned, and many of their speeches and publications, some of which endorsed the idea of One Big Union, made them subject to arrest, a standpoint caused by the pervasive sense of wartime emergency and fear of Wobbly industrial activity embodied in the imposition of government via orders-in-council, which was authorized by a War Measures Act, undermining many attributes of a society that enjoyed some agreement about what might constitute democracy. Among her other concerns, Helen Armstrong emphasized the need for a minimum wage and allowances for those who could not find employment, focusing on the difficulties encountered by many women workers who could not live on the salaries they earned, and, like her husband and many labor leaders in Winnipeg, she opposed conscription.

Elizabeth Gurley Flynn (1890–1964) constitutes the focus of Chapter 3, a woman who became an IWW leader when she was still in her teens, appearing in many hard-fought strikes around the United States, drawing much attention when she was involved in a strike in Spokane, Washington in 1909, and from time to time being imprisoned for her ideas. At one point the author of a tract titled *Sabotage*, she became a little less militant, working under the aegis of other groups, including the Workers' Defense Union, the Labor Defense Council, and International Labor Defense. Flynn was one of the founders of the organization which became the American Civil Liberties Union (ACLU), and she lobbied to free anarchists scheduled for deportation, working for several years to prevent the executions of Nicola Sacco and Bartolomeo Vanzetti, anarchists who, despite their extensive support and doubts about their guilt were eventually put to death. Gradually, she became more and more sympathetic to a communist point of view, and in *United States v. Flynn et al.* (1955), her conviction for violating the Smith Act was upheld, leading to a two-year period of imprisonment in the Federal Women's Reformatory at Alderson, West Virginia. In 1961, she was chosen as the leader of the Communist Party, USA, a transformation that is difficult to explain.

Both the thinkers discussed in Part 2 are internationalists, not only in the general sense of that word, that they each believed in the commonality and common dignity of human beings, but also in the respect that anarchists, Wobblies, and socialists have generally sought to achieve working class solidarity and to at least lessen the negative consequences of capitalism, and often to eliminate capitalism completely. Tom Barker (1887–1970) was an anarchist who eventually became a socialist who worked to promote labor unionism on four continents and who tried to create a global One Big Union for sailors. Kōtoku, Shūsui (1871–1911), as he is known in Japan, with his family name being given first, was a liberal who became a socialist and finally an anarchist. An opponent of govenmental imperialism and ecological mismanagement, he studied and translated the works of Western thinkers and sought to apply what he learned from other cultures to the development of Japan.

Chapter 4 describes the life of Tom Barker, who caused trouble wherever he went. In New Zealand, as an IWW leader and the editor of its local paper, the *Industrial Unionist*, he was involved in substantial union activities, including the failed 1913 general strike, before moving on to Australia, where, as the editor of *Direct Action*, he opposed conscription, being charged with violating the War Precautions Act. His arrest prompted accusations of industrial terrorism against his allies, the "Sydney Twelve," accused of firebombing businesses as they sought Barker's release. The Twelve would remain imprisoned for a long time, the last of them for five years, almost entirely on the basis of charges that were mostly proven eventually to be completely false. Deported to Chile, Barker worked with the Valparaiso branch of the IWW and its leader, Juan Onofre Chamorro, before being expelled again, this time at gunpoint, to Argentina, after Chile passed a residency law that excluded agitators like him.

He then spent time in Buenos Aires' La Boca dock area, where he operated the Marine Transport Workers Industrial Union (MTW), a global operation that represented sailors and longshoremen and affiliated with the Federación Obrera Regional Argentina (FORA). Moving on to the United States, he worked for five years to organize and promote Bill Haywood's Kuzbas Autonomous Industrial Project in Siberia. Having all but disappeared from radical memory for many years, he was eventually rediscovered living a more peaceful life back home in his native England, yet still occasionally able to foment disturbance, as on the day in 1958, when, at his suggestion, the Red Flag was flown over the St. Pancras Town Hall.

Kōtoku, Shūsui is the topic of Chapter 5. Eventually executed by the Japanese government for his beliefs, his political commitments changed progressively until he became known as one of the most dangerous anarchists in the world. A journalist who often expounded on the views of political philosophers about whom he knew rather little, remedying this disadvantage when spells of imprisonment gave him the opportunity to catch up on his reading, he somewhat questionably connected his own Western-influenced ideas with those of classical Confucian and Taoist ideas. With colleagues, he translated some of the works of Kropotkin, Marx and Engels, Tolstoy, and August Bebel, and he crafted eloquent appeals on behalf of farmers who were victims of a major environmental disaster. Though many of his socialist allies were Japanese Christians, eventually he became a fierce critic of that faith, claiming that Jesus had never lived, an opinion that had some influence in China. In public, he supported women's rights, although scholars have suggested that in his relationships with women and in his private life in general, he behaved less graciously than in his writings. An opponent of the Russo-Japanese War and of imperialism in general, he spent six months in northern California, building connections to various anarchist, Wobbly, and socialist thinkers, and when the Japanese government decided to eliminate him in an act of judicial murder known as the High Treason Incident, radicals around the world attempted to save him and protested his fate.

The five thinkers stand out due to their radical activism on behalf of ordinary workers and involvement in labor strikes and also due to their exposition of anarchist ideas. Armstrong, a strike leader who was in favor of the formation of One Big Union in Canada, is best described as a socialist, although at meetings and as an organizer of the Winnipeg General Strike of 1919 she engaged in especially disruptive activities which mirrored the actions of IWW members in the United States, New Zealand, and Australia, and the dominion's minister of labor, Gideon Robertson, portrayed the strike as being a Wobbly attempt to stage a coup. Additionally, she is an appropriate subject for the present study because her participation in strikes and her related unionizing activity have been neglected by scholars in the past. Flynn and Barker were Wobblies who advocated anarchism and eventually drifted toward socialism. Kōtoku traveled in the opposite direction, and though Bolten was less critical of Batllism in Uruguay at times when it came closer to her own views and she was then seen by some as having become an "anarcha-Batllista," she was a lifelong anarchist.

The research that undergirds this book has been greatly facilitated by the existence of newspaper and other information archives that did not exist in the past. Of particular help were Anáforas, the communications database of the Universidad de la República Uruguay; the Biblioteca del Congreso Nacional de Chile, a service of the Chilean National Congress; Chronicling America, a facility provided by the US Congress; the Diccionario Biográfico de las Izquierdas Latinoamericanas, a resource of el Centro de Documentación e Investigación de la Cultura de Izquierdas (CeDInCI) in Buenos Aires, Argentina; La Hemeroteca Digital, the online library of the Biblioteca Nacional de España in Madrid, Spain; Papers Past, an equivalent service of the National Library of New Zealand; Trove, the research database of the National Library of Australia; and the University of Manitoba's extensive Digital Collections.

The author is grateful to Bill Carter, Jenny B. Clark, David Fasenfest, and Howard Price for their helpful comments and valuable suggestions for improvement that have allowed him to refine many of the arguments presented in this volume. All errors should, of course, be attributed to the writer himself.

PART 1

Women in Action

∴

CHAPTER 1

Virginia Bolten: Myth and Reality

Interest in the life and thought of Virginia Bolten, the anarchist feminist labor union activist who lived in Argentina and Uruguay in the late nineteenth and early twentieth century, continues to blossom, with many scholars in those countries, in Brazil and elsewhere, publishing articles and book chapters about someone who is generally portrayed as a fascinating heroine. However, while that assessment seems ultimately to be appropriate, many continuing questions remain as to who Bolten really was, including when and where she was born, and consequently whether or not she participated in a strike of seamstresses in 1889 and a march in 1890 in Rosario, a city located on the Paraná River in the Argentinian province of Santa Fe, events for which she is often given acclaim. Some sources misspell her last name, while others assert that she was an Argentinian, rather than the more likely view that she was originally from Uruguay, with the former researchers not explaining or even considering why, if she had been an Argentinian, she would have been deported from that country as an undesirable alien, which she was. Virginia is often afforded substantial credit for being one of the editors and writers of the Buenos Aires publication, *La Voz de la Mujer*, yet none of its nine issues, all of which are extant, claim any association with her or reveal her authorship. Many of her defenders say she was associated with another newspaper based in Rosario, one which bore the same name, but no copies of this putative alternative *La Voz* exist today. Recent scholarship has achieved significant success in suggesting errors in the conventional wisdom, and has raised another issue, that she was perhaps for a long time a practicing Catholic, a surprising detail considering her promotion of scientific explanations at the expense of religious ones, and her extreme political ideas and strident advocacy of their revolutionary import, which are revealed in articles that she clearly does appear to have scribed.

1 The Origins of Anarchism in Argentina and Uruguay

The Paris Commune began on March 18, 1871, enduring for approximately two months until it was crushed by the soldiers of the national government, the French Third Republic. Ever since, its ideal of an autonomous revolt by ordinary citizens with the goal of instituting a direct democracy has been venerated by anarchists and those of similar perspectives around the world. Also prized is the modernization of the city that the Communards instituted during the brief period of their control of Paris, undermining the power of the Catholic Church, a secularization project that to some extent has survived, long after the deaths of 25,000 Parisians, a figure that includes those subsequently executed for their roles in the rebellion; some of its leaders, like Louise Michel, with whom Virginia Bolten would later be compared as "la Luisa Michel rosarina," were not killed, but deported to New Caledonia; others were imprisoned in France (Shone 2019, ch. 2).

To a significant degree, the demise of the Paris Commune was the cause of immigration from France and other European countries to Argentina and Uruguay. In Europe, both anarchists and members of Karl Marx's International, also known as the International Workingmen's Association, who supported and had often participated in the Commune, saw South America as a place where they might encounter relative freedom. As migrants, they brought with them a familiarity with radical and revolutionary ideals and a commitment to try and achieve them. In the 1880s, these influences were strengthened by the arrival of many immigrants from Spain and Italy bearing similar philosophies, including, in Buenos Aires, the prominent Italian anarchist thinkers, Errico Malatesta (1853–1932), who moved his newspaper, *La Question Sociale*, from Italy to Argentina, where he lived from 1885 to 1889 before moving to the United States; and Ettore (Héctor) Mattei (1857–1915), who started publishing *El Socialista: Organo de los Trabajadores* in Argentina in 1887. Both Malatesta and Mattei were influenced by the philosophy of the Commune and by the ideas of Peter Kropotkin (1842–1921), who had openly supported the Commune and the libertarian principles that it embodied, proclaiming that "[t]he Government evaporated like a pond of stagnant water in a spring breeze, and on the 19th the great city of Paris found herself free from the impurity which had defiled her, with the loss of scarcely a drop of her children's blood" (Kropotkin 1909, 3). Mattei, an accountant who had been forced by suppression of his radical activities to leave Livorno in Italy, continued them in France and Spain before eventually arriving in Buenos Aires in 1884. Sections of the International Workingmen's Association that were set up in Argentina starting in the 1870s were often dominated by those influenced by Mikhail Bakunin rather than by the followers of Marx or of Kropotkin (De Souza 2019, 32; Rama 1990, xviii; Turcato 2014).

In Argentina and Uruguay, the diffusion of anarchist ideas and manifestos in a variety of small publications such as *La Justicia Humana* and *El Perseguido*, many of which did not last for very long, drew the critical attention of governments and police. By the end of the decade, their provocation led to the imprisonment of some writers, prompting others to leave the country; some of those in Argentina chose to move nearby, across the Rio de la Plata estuary to Montevideo, where their writings encountered less hostile scrutiny and reaction than at home (Nettlau 1972, 18–20, 22–23; Simon 1946, 38–39; Zaragoza 1996, 79–80).

A. Gobley, whose first name is now unknown, had spent time imprisoned in Fort Quélern in France, where some of the non-executed and non-deported Communards served their sentences, with another important anarchist, Elisée Reclus. Gobley was a hatmaker, whom Segall (1972, 347), describes as having improbable commercial success that did not undermine his commitment to radical activities: "Citoyen prospère ... il demeurait toujours un militant décidé" [A prosperous citizen ... he was still a determined activist]. Gobley spent much of his life in Argentina, and information about some of his activities in South America can be found in extant letters written by Reclus to Victor Buurmans, the Belgian socialist who was another former Fort Quélern prisoner. Moving from Montevideo, where he was exposed to yellow fever, to Rio de Janeiro, and finally, in 1878, to Buenos Aires, where one of his sons attended university, Gobley's experience is additionally not typical of anarchists who relocated to the area, since he remained there, while many others returned to Europe. To some extent, this was because, from 1881 onward, Communards received amnesty from the government back home (Cappelletti 1990, 30; Fleming 2019, 120; Lopes 2009, 162; Rama 1990, xiv–xv; Reclus, letter to Burrmans of August 17, 1871 in Reclus 1914, 70, 1943, 110; Reclus, letter to Buurmans of June 2, 1873 in Reclus 1914, 129, 1943, 127; Reclus, letter to Buurmans of February 17, 1878 in Reclus 1914, 200–201, 1943, 147, Reclus 1914, 200, fn 3, 1943, 147, fn 2; Zaragoza 1996, 79–80).

Another anarchist, the poet and lawyer, Pietro (Pedro) Gori (1865–1911), was present in Argentina from 1898 to 1902, influencing many with his oratorical eloquence in front of large audiences, including Alberto Ghiraldo, another poet, who edited the radical Buenos Aires newspapers, *El Obrero Panadero* and *Ideas y Figuras*. In his speeches, such as one called "La Donna e la Famiglia," which he gave at the Teatro Iris in Buenos Aires on November 25, 1900, Gori (1927) allotted attention to feminist ideas, criticizing traditional forms of legal marriage, and promoting a protectionist perspective that enjoyed rather more support in this era than it would later on, of limiting the extent to which women should be allowed to work at night; such feminist views would rapidly become associated with, and at the same time clash with expanded anarchist perspectives that were developing at the same time. In his lectures at the University of Buenos Aires, Gori described the extent to which mental illness, rather than defects in character, produced a negative effect on human behavior, emphasizing the anarchist view that almost all crime is social, and should thus be responded to in a more humane way than just by punishment, a perspective shared by many anarchist and feminist thinkers such as Mikhail Bakunin, Alexander Berkman, Voltairine de Cleyre, Samuel Fielden, Emma Goldman, Peter Kropotkin, Louise Michel, Lucy Parsons, Pierre-Joseph Proudhon, Margaret Sanger, Elizabeth Cady Stanton, Benjamin R. Tucker, Lois Waisbrooker, and Victoria C. Woodhull. The presence of anarchist, including syndicalist, ideas in Argentina, Uruguay, and other South American countries led to the formation of many labor unions and their participation in a wide range of strikes. In Buenos Aires, the Federación Obrera Regional Argentina (FORA) [Argentine Regional Workers Federation] was formed in 1901 with the original name, Federación Obrera Argentina (FOA) [Argentine Workers Federation], the title being revised in 1904. It had the support of many workers, but immediately its anarchist leanings became subject to conflict with members of socialist and Marxist perspectives. Many strikes followed the FORA's creation, with some success being achieved as painters and longshoremen managed to reduce the length of their working days. A threatened strike by fruit workers caused the Argentinian Congress [Congreso de la Nación Argentina] to pass the *Ley de Residencia*, or Residence Law (an important development which is discussed below), and forced much union activity to cease. Then, in December 1902, the government declared a State of Siege, forcing the FOA to close down for two months (Baer 2015, 63; Cappelletti 1990, 32, 37; Carlson 1988, 126–127; Lavrin 1995, 265; Nettlau 1972, 31–35; Simon 1946, 39–40; Yerrill and Rosser 1987, 22–23; Zaragoza 1996, 440).

As among anarchists elsewhere, there existed in Argentina and Uruguay a bifurcation between communitarian (or anarcho/a-communist) approaches that might have origins in familiarity with the writings of Kropotkin, and, on the other hand, more individualistic understandings with roots in the ideas of the German, Max Stirner, and his book, *The Ego and Its Own*, the main surviving source of his beliefs, in which Stirner failed to concede any authority at all save that of the person in question. The many publications that now appeared across southern South America allowed a range of perspectives, some at times mutually contradictory, to appear, although in some cases only one issue would be published, with their authors and editors possibly subject to prosecution for expressing their ideas. Thus the immigrants from Europe who had migrated hoping to be able to persist with their radical standpoints or implement them in a more open environment found in Argentina, to a greater extent than in Uruguay, that the type of oppression that they had hoped to evade remained nevertheless a phenomenon with which they would have to contend.

Certain revolutionary themes often associated with the history of anarchism and much recounted by its advocates around the world occurred with some regularity in the many radical Argentinian and Uruguayan newspapers of the period. Unsurprisingly, one was the celebration of, and commiserations about, the crushing of the Paris Commune (Bellucci 2003; Shone 2019, ch. 2). Other topics included the execution of the Chicago martyrs and various happenings related to local area strikes, marches, and deportations, and admiration for other putative heroes such as Alfred Dreyfus, Sébastien Faure, and Émile Zola.

In Chicago, Illinois, on May 4, 1886, the day after several strikers from the McCormick Reaper Works had been shot by police, there was an attempt to close a large public meeting in Haymarket Square where more than two thousand people assembled to protest. Someone threw a bomb, killing a police officer, Mathias J. Degan, following which, eight anarchists were arrested and charged with murder. After a trial of very questionable legitimacy, all eight were found guilty, with four of them being hanged, an event considered outrageous by anarchists and many others and viewed increasingly as judicial murder (Avrich 1980, i-ii, 1984; DeLamotte 2004, 4–5; Shone 2013, ch. 5). Not surprisingly, anarchists refused to forget this outrageous event and from time to time those in southern South America met to recall it. On March 18, 1888, a gathering of radicals at the Vorwärts club in Buenos Aires, the home of socialists of German extraction, memorialized the events at Haymarket, and six anarchists who attended that demonstration were arrested by the police and spent the night in jail. A later Haymarket commemoration in that city, on May 1, 1904, led to more confrontation with the police, and a sailor named Juan Ocampo was killed. In Montevideo, on May 1, 1911, more than ten thousand union workers honored the Chicago anarchists and called for the recognition of May 1 as "Workers' Day" (Cappelletti 1990, 30, 38; Fernández 2010, 35–36; Zaragoza 1996, 103).

Also of consequence to anarchists and to those of similar viewpoints in Argentina and Uruguay were items related to Émile Zola's account of poor, struggling coalminers in northern France in his novel, *Germinal; or, Master and Man* (also translated just as *Germinal*) (Zola [1894] 2005). Zola himself was of considerable interest, and in 1902, a new Montevideo-based journal, dedicated to the French author and named *Pro-Zola* appeared, the publication apparently being one of the many of which only a single installment would be printed. Like the Haymarket Tragedy, the Dreyfus Affair was another appalling miscarriage of justice, the details of which many remained unwilling to allow to disappear. In France, a series of trials based on false evidence led to Alfred Dreyfus being imprisoned for treason, events much explained, because Dreyfus was Jewish, as an example of Anti-Semitism, an outrage that would not be fully resolved until four years after *Pro-Zola* emerged. Zola's article, "J'Accuse." had done much to draw attention to the harm done to Dreyfus, a

French artillery officer wrongly accused of working for Germany. In an article in *Pro-Zola*, Emilio Frugoni, who would in 1910 become the founder and leader of the Uruguayan Socialist Party, and would for decades edit its newspaper, *El Socialista*, offered an analysis of the significance of Zola's response in the Dreyfus Affair (Miller 2008, 206; Rama 1957, 164; Zaragoza 1996, 168). That commitment, which he considered to buttress the political steadfastness of Zola's novels, identified him as someone whom South American radicals should very much want to admire:

> Dreyfus, salvado como un símbolo de fraternidad universal por sobre las corrientes tempestuosas de una infamia política, dio á Zola la ocasión de sacrificarse por ideas que eran las vuestras, … y es por la semilla de rendención arrojada al fecundo surco de la idea desde las páginas de «Germinal» y de «Los Cuatro Evangelios,» que os honrais á vosotros mismos honrando la memoria del insigne escritor.
>
> FRUGONI 1902, 7

> [Dreyfus, saved as a symbol of universal brotherhood over the stormy currents of political infamy, gave Zola the opportunity to sacrifice himself for ideas that were yours, … and it is for the seed of surrender thrown into the fertile furrow of the idea from the pages of *Germinal* and *The Four Gospels*, that you honor yourselves by honoring the memory of the famous writer.][1]

In a speech in 1902 at the Vida Nueva Club in Montevideo, lawyer, poet, and playwright, Víctor Pérez Petit, praised Zola for defending Dreyfus, saying that "Emilio Zola es tal vez el hombre que ha demostrado tener más carácter en este siglo" (Petit 1902, 11). [Emilio Zola is perhaps the man who has shown the most character in this century].

The March 18 1910 issue of *La Nueva Senda*, the anarchist Montevideo-based newspaper, dedicated itself to commemorating the Paris Commune (including an article written by its current editor, Virginia Bolten, which is discussed below). Other contributions explained the demise of the Commune and its significance for workers elsewhere. A piece titled "La mujer en la Comuna" ["The Women in the Commune"] identified some of the major actors: Louise Michel, André Léo, and "Elisa Dmitrieff" [Elizabeth Dmietrieff]; as was noted above, Bolten would become thought of as "la Luisa Michel rosarina" (Cawen

---

[1] Here, and throughout the book, the author provides a translation of the text.

2017, 229; Dalmau i Ribalta 2016, 27–28; see also Shone 2019, ch. 2). That issue of *La Nueva Senda* also included an excerpt from Zola's *Cuentos a Ninon*, a Spanish translation of *Contes à Ninon* (1864), in which soldiers, tired of killing and haunted by memories of it, decide to bury their weapons and depart the conflict: "Nuestros sueños estan turbados por las almas de aquellos á quienes hicimos morir" (Zola 1910, 3). [Our dreams are troubled by the souls of those we put to death.]

Perhaps surprisingly, another periodical, *Germinal*, which operated during 1897 and 1898, while being one of the most radical of the anarchist publications of the time, was also the advocate of the most individualistic form of anarchism and, while Zola's novel suggests many different radical approaches for workers to consider embracing, the *Germinal* newspaper's adoption of an antiorganizational approach familiar to Italian anarchists that extends at least as far as the ideas of Stirner, seems contradictory, and the slant is not, after all, one of the alternatives that Zola considered, unlike the perspectives of Bakunin, Proudhon, and Marx, which were embodied in the narrative (Shone 2022, 14; Zaragoza 1996, 507). Indeed, the complaint to be found in *Germinal* that organization and cooperation with others necessarily fail, since "las ideas de unos pocos prevalecen sobre la mayoría" (Zaragoza 1996, 249) [the ideas of a few prevail over the majority] sounds like Stirner's argument in favor only of transitory, voluntary, strictly self-interested participation in communal activity, for "the society is sacred, the union your own; the society consumes you, you consume the union" (Stirner [1907] 2005, 313). Moreover, perhaps the *Germinal* philosophy goes beyond Stirner, seeing even brief associations with like-minded others as being problematic, an approach that has no similarity with the perspective of Zola himself. Zaragoza (167) points out that the *Germinal* paper never credited Stirner as an influence. Perhaps, then, as he also notes (262), *Germinal* can be better understood in terms of its tactics, provoking other groups to reassess their own programs for change. Also paradoxical was the fact that the publication worked in tandem with the "Germinal Bar," a Buenos Aires hostelry where radicals could drink, dance the tango, and otherwise socialize with those of similar beliefs. Zaragoza (420) notes that "Se escribieron milongas y tangos anarquistas que los socialistas repudiarían como arte rastrero y de mal tono." [Anarchist milongas [a less formalized kind of tango that has its roots in Buenos Aires] and tangos were written [so] that the socialists would repudiate [them] as creepy, bad-toned art.] Indeed, as Morse notes, the choice of that form of dance was hardly coincidental:

> Anarchists did not limit their radicalism to the written word. They were pivotal in the development of the tango, the quintessential expression

of Argentine working-class culture before World War II. Anarchist dissidence even impacted language: lunfardo, the Argentine argot (slang) born of the prisons and ghetto streets, was closely linked to the tango and was part of the anarchist counterculture.

MORSE 2009, 4

Similarly, coffee houses such as *El Polo Bamba* in Montevideo, which was open to purveyors of intellectual and radical opinion from 1885 to 1913, and the *Café de los Inmortales* in Buenos Aires, frequently served as places where anarchists and other bohemians could exchange ideas and hear news that was relevant to their own perspectives. Other newspapers named *Germinal* operated in Spain, as well as in Paraguay, where it was quickly closed down (Delgado 2010, 169–170; Rosenthal 1995, 334; Siracusa 2014, 56–57). The influence of anarchism in the area also extended to other artistic, dramatic, and social activities. For example, the Cuadro Dramático of the "Nueva Humanidad" school provided activist performances, including those by a children's choir in the Corrales Viejos area of Buenos Aires, which is now known as the Parque de los Patricios. Similarly, speeches by Gori, such as a presentation he gave to tannery workers in 1900, were sometimes supplemented by drama performed by children, and reportedly he also used cinematic projections to supplement some of his talks (Porrini 2013, 368, fn 9; Valobra 2019, 89).

No less individualistic and no less radical, *El Perseguido* [The Persecuted], was run by Baldomero Salvans, who was originally from Spain, and who had been deported from Brazil in 1893 as a consequence of his anarchist beliefs, having been accused by the authorities in Rio de Janeiro of dynamiting a textile plant in Spain, a charge that may or may not have been true (Albornoz and Galeano 2019, 321; Leal 2006, 157, fn 21, 158, 160). *El Perseguido* identified its authors as being "the vagrants, the malefactors, the rabble, the scum of society, the sublimate corrosive of the present social order" (Moya 2004, 22). Nonetheless, they saw themselves as disciples of Kropotkin and as anarcho/a-communists. They advocated, following the institution of a general strike, a program of violence against the government that included the burning down and looting of buildings, a stance that attracted supporters and kept the paper solvent. Unsurprisingly, they denounced the deportations from Brazil and Argentina of anarchist writers for expressing their opinions. However, *El Perseguido* also shunned the connections being made between anarchism and the local labor unions, which caused it to lose subscribers. Lasting for six years, from 1890 to 1896, the paper can be viewed as one of the more successful, even though it did not survive. In meetings with rival socialists that were held at the Vorwärts club in 1891, the anarchists of *El Perseguido* challenged the socialists' rather more accommodating tactics of seeking permission from the police for demonstrations and petitioning the government for reform; instead, they advocated unauthorized street protests and the use of violence. Like its less uncompromising rivals, the newspaper also reported on the social turmoil of the 1890s, including widespread hunger and its corollary, which was that some people were migrating back to Europe (Albornoz and Galeano 2019, 325; Poy and Gaido 2011, 491–492; Yerrill and Rosser 1987, 12–13, 17; Zaragoza 1996, 36–37, 131–132).

Not every anarchist paper experienced the same inadequate result, though it may have been disappointing for some anarchists to achieve eventual reconciliation with more moderate perspectives. *La Protesta Humana*, a Buenos Aires-based publication which began in 1897, changing its name in 1903 to *La Protesta*, continues to this day. *El Perseguido* had folded in 1896, but *La Protesta Humana* continued the reporting of the miserable circumstances that were affecting many poorer residents (Prieto, Cordero, and Muñoz 2013/2014, 220, fn 2; Rago 1997, 282; Zaragoza 1996, 37). In an 1897 editorial, it noted:

> La crisis obrera en la Argentina va adquiriendo cada día proporciones más alarmantes. El vendabal [vendaval] de la miseria arrecia con furia por toda la República, haciendo sentir sus estragos en el mísero hogar del proletario, arrancando de él seres anémicos en un tiempo llenos de vida, transportándoles en fúnebre torbellino al imperio de la muerte, del mismo modo que el pampero arranca de cuajo á los débiles arbustos.
> "La crisis obrera" 1897, 1

> [The workers' crisis in Argentina is acquiring more alarming proportions every day. The gale of misery rages with fury throughout the Republic, making its ravages felt in the miserable home of the proletarian, tearing from it anemic beings at one time full of life, transporting them in a funereal whirlwind to the empire of death, in the same way that the pampero uproots the weak bushes.]

Moreover, the whirlwind was raging across southern South America, doing damage beyond national borders:

> El vendeval [vendaval] de la crisis arrecia. No es solo en la Argentina donde en la ciudad y en el campo popula jadeante, extenuado, aterido de frio, y vacío el estómago el ejército de los sin trabajo, la legión de los que sin casa ni hogar mendiga asilo y ocupación, algo con que alimentar un día más el mecanismo digestivo que les anima. La crisis, la falta,

de trabajo manifiéstase con igual ó mayor prepotencia en las Repúblicas que nos rodean. Del Uruguay emigran los obreros á millares por que alli la vida es imposible. En la Paraguay la escasez es aterradora. En Chile se reunen más de ocho mil obreros reinvindicando su derecho á la existencia y aclamando la revolución social

"La situacion" 1897, 1

[The gale of the crisis is getting worse. It is not only in Argentina where in the city and in the countryside, the panting, exhausted, cold-blooded and empty stomachs are the army of the jobless, the legion of homeless, begging for asylum and occupation, anything to feed the digestive mechanism that animates them for one more day. The crisis, the lack of work, manifests itself with equal or greater arrogance in the republics that surround us. Thousands of workers emigrate from Uruguay because life is impossible there. In Paraguay the shortage is terrifying. More than eight thousand workers are gathered in Chile, claiming their right to exist and acclaiming the social revolution.]

Toward the end of 1902, in response to union calls for a general strike, when the Argentine government declared a State of Siege, it had also passed the Anti-Alien Act, the law often referred to as the Residence Law, which gave itself the power to deport any immigrant who threatened national security or the public order, giving them only three days to leave. This would become the basis for deporting Virginia Bolten to Uruguay for her anarchist activities. In Uruguay, deportees encountered less hostility, with José Batlle y Ordoñez, who became president for the first time in 1903, even welcoming them, and during his two four-year terms, the second of which began in 1911, he supported many of the same issues as the labor unions, and allowed newspapers to write from an anarchist or socialist perspective, an approach that may ultimately have persuaded Bolten (1905h; see also Vidal 2012, 79) to sometimes support him and his political agenda, although on other occasions, and in general, as an anarchist, she would demur (Alexander with Parker 2005, 20, 21; Cappelletti 1990, 38; Carlson 1988, 127; Cawen 2017, 228–230; Peterson 2015, 129–130; Prieto, Fernández Cordero, and Muñoz 2013/2014, 210; Vidal 2012, 77).

One of the most radical newspapers of the era was *El Rebelde*, also an advocate of individualistic anarchism, which published Kropotkin's article, "Lo que entendemos por revolución" ["What We Understand by Revolution"], in two parts in the publication's first two issues, those of November 11 and November 27, 1898 (Kropotkin 1898a, 3, 1898b, 3; Suriano 1997, 441). Other periodicals in the Spanish-speaking world have borne the title *El Rebelde*, but the one discussed here was published in Buenos Aires between 1898 and 1903, until some of its editors migrated back to Madrid after they became victims of prosecution for what they wrote and of the Residence Law. These included José Reguera, who wrote a substantial number of the pieces that were printed, the father of whom, Manuel Reguera, was often listed as the director of *El Rebelde*, as "M. Reguera"; in earlier editions, he was identified instead by the pseudonym "J. Mayorka" (Domínguez 2012/2013, 42, 2018, 260; Stavisky 2020, 998).

José had come to Argentina from Spain in 1899, and he returned in December 1902, escaping Buenos Aires by way of Santos and Rio de Janeiro in Brazil, and with his wife, Victoria, and infant son, Abel, boarding the Southampton, England-bound ship, the *Clyde*. Another *El Rebelde* leader obliged to return to Spain at this time was Julio Camba Andreu who, with Antonio Apolo, restarted the publication from Madrid. Deported to Italy, one of the first victims of the Residence Law, was Santiago Locascio, who had been involved with the *Germinal* newspaper. A strong advocate of the individualistic perspective, Locascio was one of the original staffers on *El Rebelde* and a frequent named contributor of its content; he was also publishing another Buenos Aires paper, *Nueva Era* (Albornoz and Galeano 2016, 33; Baer 2015, 52, 207 fn 8; Cunha 2018, 144–145; Dalmau i Ribalta 2011, 101; Stavisky 2020, 998; Suriano 1997, 448 fn 72; Tarcus 2021).

Like other anarchist papers of its time, in South America and elsewhere, *El Rebelde* referred to the Haymarket Tragedy. Also lauded was the example of Sébastien Faure, the paper spelling his first name as "Sebastián," the latter being the atheist anarchist colleague of Louise Michel who, prior to Zola, had protested the treatment of Dreyfus. One issue of *El Rebelde* provided a classic anarchist definition of mainstream politics, outlining it as follows: "Es el arte de engañar hábil e inicuamente a las masas populares, a aquellos que todo lo producen y que en cambio de su producción, sólo reciben las migajas de la masa de sus explotadores" ("¿Que es política?" 1902, 2; see also Suriano 1997, 423). [It is the art of cleverly and wickedly deceiving the popular masses, those who produce everything and who, in exchange for their production, only receive the crumbs of the table from their exploiters.] In contradistinction, like *El Perseguido* and *La Protesta Humana*, *El Rebelde* attempted to depict much more accurately the grim social reality of life in Argentina for ordinary people. In both its Buenos Aires and Madrid incarnations, the publication advocated and attempted to justify violence as a means of responding to and undermining the status quo, a verbal assault rarely matched by any action on the part of its writers, but one disliked and reacted to strenuously by authorities (De la Rosa 2010, 82; Diez 2007, 300; Yeoman 2020, 186 fn 370; Zaragoza 1996, 420).

Even relatively short-lived periodicals could have a significant effect, and the issues they discussed may remain of interest today. For example, the Montevideo newspapers, *El Surco*, which consisted of six issues released from June to September 1909, and *La Nueva Senda*, which ran from September 1909 to May 1910, provided the reader with content that Vidal (2017, 110–111) describes as being representative of the thought of "nuevos trabajadores-intelectuales" [new worker-intellectuals], which in both papers included the ideas of Juana Rouco Buela (later, when she lived in Brazil, known as Juana Ruocco), and in *La Nueva Senda* contained contributions from Virginia Bolten. *El Surco* included an article by Gori called "La cuestión social y los anarquistas" (Gori 1909, 3) in which he distinguished anarchists from other radicals offering false promises and fake solutions:

> ¿Se dejará embaucar el proletariado con las tantas promesas de los partidos políticos, radicales, semi-socialistas ó socialistas legalitarios? O, más bien, ¿prestará fe á los anarquistas, á nosotros que á nuestra vez, del examen del problema del trabajo y de la libertad, hemos sacado elementos que nos paréce haber encontrado la palabra justa de la solución? Esperemos.
> GORI 1909, 3

[Will the proletariat allow itself to be fooled by the many promises of political parties, radicals, semi-socialists or legal socialists? Or, rather, will it give faith to the anarchists, to us who, in our turn, by examining the problem of work and freedom, have brought out elements that seem to us to contain the right answer for the solution? Let's hope.]

Here, Gori included also his characteristic anarcho/a-feminist condemnation of legal marriage prompted and excused by personal and financial interests, arguing that the continuation of the institution in anything like its present form given its unhappy and oppressive nature would lead to more adultery, wife murder, and infanticide (3).

The lavishly illustrated Buenos Aires magazine, *Caras y Caretas*, in general a much more mainstream publication, nonetheless went to pains to document the activities of anarchists, and at times attempted to rationalize them. On July 29, 1900, Italy's King Umberto I was assassinated by Gaetano Bresci, an anarchist and acquaintance of Malatesta (Pellicer 1900, 14; Rogers 2008, 148). The next month, in an article in *Caras y Caretas*, writer Eustaquio Pellicer caricatured the suspicions of the Argentine police with respect to the nature of anarchism locally, showing the authorities operating in such a pernicious atmosphere that they might foolishly identify the actual Malatesta as being "un cunado suyo que tiene muy mala cabeza" (Pellicer 1900, 14) [a brother-in-law of his who has a very bad head.] Pellicer attributed some of the blame for the inherent superficiality in trying to tarnish Buenos Aires radicals with foreign regicide on other "news" sources, sarcastically praising the local press for this achievement:

> Vive uno en la mayor ignorancia de los peligros que le rodean, y si no fuese por los periódicos, que todo lo averiguan y de todo nos precaven, no sabemos lo que sería de nosotros.
> PELLICER 1900, 14

> [One lives in the greatest ignorance of the dangers that surround him, and if it were not for the newspapers, which find out everything and warn us about everything, we do not know what would become of us.]

Six months later, in its January 19, 1901 number, *El Rebelde* ran an article reprinted from *La Questione Sociale* about Bresci ("Bresci" 1901, 1), in which the writer expressed the hope that the "assassin's" actions would in the future be better understood: "Entre tanta nauseabunda reacción nos consuela la esperanza de que la historia verdada se pronunciara por Bresci y por su ideal" (1901, 1). [Amid so much nauseating reaction, we are consoled by the hope that true history will pronounce itself for Bresci and for his ideal.] But how often, we might wonder, are history and the news *ever* "true"?

2 Virginia Bolten: the Myth

Groundbreaking research by Prieto, Fernández Cordero, and Muñoz (2013/2014) has cast doubt on many of the claims made about the life and achievements of Virginia Bolten. Even though there remain many reasons to remember, discuss, and celebrate her commitment and vivacity, it is surely better to do so with a better-informed and inevitably more skeptical attitude about who she was. Claims that she was "nacque nel 1870" (Pandolfi 2021) [born in 1870] have permitted a range of authors to assert that she was politically active in 1889 and 1890, but Prieto, Fernández Cordero, and Muñoz (2013/2014, 209) demonstrate that, in fact, 1876 is a much more reliable date for Virginia's date of birth. They write:

> La primera referencia fehaciente a la presencia de Virginia Bolten en Rosario proviene del Segundo Censo Nacional, realizado en mayo de 1895. Manuel Manrique y Virginia de Manrique fueron censados en un inquilinato de la calle Mendoza. ... Virginia, nacida en San Luis, tenía 19 años y no declaró ocupación.
> PRIETO, FERNÁNDEZ CORDERO, AND MUÑOZ 2013/2014, 209

> [The first reliable reference to the presence of Virginia Bolten in Rosario comes from the Second National Census, carried out in May 1895. Manuel Manrique and Virginia de Manrique [Bolten's apparent married name] were registered in a tenancy on Mendoza Street ... Virginia, born in San Luis, was 19 years old and did not declare [her] occupation.]

Of course, her claim to have been born in San Luis, the capital city of San Luis Province in Argentina, also muddies the waters because this does not seem likely to be the case either, since, if she had been, and had therefore been an Argentinian citizen, she would not later have become liable for deportation, as she was. Consequently, the veracity of her replies, including her claim on this occasion also to be a Catholic, can be questioned, since there is no substantial incentive for a person interviewed by a census taker to tell the truth if they do not suspect their deception will be found out, and a person from another country – in this case, it seems, from Uruguay – might have a motivation to instead say that she was a native, especially to avoid any chance of deportation. As an anarchist involved with radical labor union activity, perhaps Virginia had more reason to lie about her origins than most. Additionally, whether or not Bolten and Manrique were married is another matter for debate. For example, Carlson (1988, 128) attempts to answer these questions when she writes: "It is known that Virginia Bolten founded, with Pietro Gori, an organization of socialists and anarchists dedicated to the dissolution of conventional marriage and other authoritarian concepts, and that she lived openly for years with her lover, the anarchist Manrique." But the feminist questioning of the institution of marriage that is found in the extant *La Voz* is associated with Pepita Guerra, whose name, perhaps a pseudonym, appears on it, while any association of Bolten with that paper is unproven (Molyneux 1986, 135–136). Evidence that Bolten participated in the baptism of her first child leads Prieto, Fernández Cordero, and Muñoz to suggest she did not even become an anarchist and move away from Catholicism until later in her life, when she was living in Montevideo (Prieto, Fernández Cordero, and Muñoz 2013/2014, 210):

> En el casillero de algunos anarquistas dice "ateo" o "librepensador" ¿el casillero en blanco de Virginia y Manuel indica que fueron tomados por tales por el censista o que declararon serlo? Podemos colegir lo segundo: su primera hija, María Milagra Zulema, fue bautizada en la fe católica en la localidad santafesina de Cayastá el 23 de octubre de ese mismo año.
> PRIETO, FERNÁNDEZ CORDERO, AND MUÑOZ 2013/2014, 209

> [In the answer field for some anarchists it says "atheist" or "freethinker": does the blank box for Virginia and Manuel indicate that they were taken as such [as Catholics] by the census taker or that they declared that they were? We can choose the second option: their first daughter, María Milagra Zulema, was baptized in the Catholic faith in the town of Santafesina, Cayastá on October 23 of that same year.]

Virginia and Manuel appear to have had nine children, although, as with all information about Bolten, there is always some doubt as to its accuracy. The offspring commenced with the daughter mentioned above, María Milagra Zulema Manrique Bolten, born in 1895, whose baptismal certificate was located by Prieto, Fernández Cordero, and Muñoz. María was followed by a son called Urano Líber Manrique Bolten, born on November 25, 1896; alternatively, Fernández Cordero (2019) gives 1898 as being the birthdate, and says that Urano was a daughter. Then came a daughter, Acracia Manrique Bolten, followed by Hume Mayo Manrique Bolten, a son who was born in 1903, Themis Manrique Bolten, a daughter born in 1905, Helios Manrique Bolten, a son born in 1908 who did not die until 2004, Ildara Ácrata Manrique Bolten, a daughter born in 1911, and Esmirna Olga Manrique Bolten, a daughter born in 1916 who died in 2000 (Fernández Cordero 2019; Prieto, Fernández Cordero, and Muñoz 2013/2014, 209, 210, 212; "Helios Manrique Bolten" 2021; "Urano Liber Manrique" 2019; "Urano Liber Manrique Bolten" 2021; "Zulema Manrique" 2019).

The research of Prieto, Fernández Cordero, and Muñoz raises even more questions. While the authors found Virginia's baptism certificate in the Capilla Santiago Apóstol in Baradero, a city in the Buenos Aires area, which indicated her actual date of birth to be December 26, 1876, the date of her baptism is indicated in the documents to have been December 29, 1880 (Prieto, Fernández Cordero, and Muñoz 2013/2014, 209). While it seems quite likely that Bolten was born at the later date (1876), there is no way to absolutely verify this, nor that her family were telling the truth, since, at the time Virginia was four years old, not the most common time for someone to be baptized, and the fact that she was now present in Baradero provides no evidence on the basis of which it might be convincingly denied that she had been born in Uruguay.

In the light of the discoveries made by Prieto, Fernández Cordero, and Muñoz, Marifran Carlson's story of Bolten's life seems particularly questionable, notwithstanding its likely reliable description of her as a "Uruguayan":

> Gori encouraged women students who had already committed themselves to the anarchist cause before they came to Buenos Aires. One of these was the Uruguayan activist Virginia Bolten, who had helped to organize a successful strike of seamstresses in Rosario in 1889; ... Gori introduced Virginia Bolten to anarchist intellectual circles in Buenos Aires and helped her to found the first women's anarchist newspaper, *Women's Voice*.
> CARLSON 1988, 126–127

It seems much more likely that Bolten was not associated with *La Voz* at all, the title of which Carlson translates a little loosely here, suggesting a popular magazine dedicated to more traditional women's pursuits. Furthermore, Virginia may well not have participated in the seamstresses' strike and the 1890 march and demonstration at the Plaza López at all because, as Prieto, Fernández Cordero, and Muñoz document, she was likely only fourteen and fifteen respectively when they occurred. It is uncertain whether or not those claims are true, and they write:

> De todos modos, es posible que participase aunque, según el acta de bautismo y el censo, tenía entonces sólo 14 años.
> PRIETO, FERNÁNDEZ CORDERO, AND MUÑOZ 2013/2014, 210

> [Anyway, it is possible that she participated although, according to the baptismal certificate and the census, she was only 14 years old at the time.]

Alicia Simeoni gives a similarly now questionable account when she writes of "la historia de cuatro mujeres, una de ellas Virginia Bolten, quienes al ser despedidas de una hilandería del barrio Refinería de Rosario decidieron sacar un periódico, La voz de la mujer, el primero que en Latinoamérica englobó las ideas comunistas-anarquistas y feministas" (Simeoni 2007) [the story of four women, one of them Virginia Bolten, who, when they were fired from a spinning mill in the Rosario Refinery neighborhood, decided to publish a newspaper, *La Voz de la Mujer*, the first in Latin America that included communist-anarchist and feminist ideas.]

Dalmau i Ribalta writes about the meetings of radicals in Rosario who met at a café called "La Vieja Bastilla," one of the outcrops of which was the 1890 May Day demonstration, and claims that "Conocemos los nombres de los participantes en esas reuniones y entre ellos figuraba ... la dirigente obrera Virginia Bolten, conocida como "la Luise Michel rosarina"'" (Dalmau i Ribalta 2016, 27–28) [We know the names of the participants in those meetings and among them was ... the labor leader Virginia Bolten, known as "la Luise Michel rosarina."] Bellucci writes with similar confidence:

> En 1890, en una manifestación de resistencia efectuada el Primero de Mayo, en la Plaza López, La Bolten encabeza una gruesa columna de hombres y mujeres portando estandartes con leyendas alusivas a la fecha: Primero de Mayo – Fraternidad Universal.
> BELLUCCI 2003

> [In 1890, in a resistance demonstration held on May Day, in the Plaza López, Bolten heads a thick column of men and women carrying banners with legends alluding to the date: May Day – Universal Fraternity.]

However, for Prieto, Fernández Cordero, and Muñoz, Virginia's presence at the May Day event is not only questionable due to the doubt about when she was born, but because the only sources for the claim are probably what people had said, with a surprising absence of her name or description evident in newspapers that covered the event: "[N]o hemos podido encontrar referencias directas en la prensa, ni tampoco indicios que podrían llevarnos a inferir su participación efectiva" (Prieto, Fernández Cordero, and Muñoz 2013/2014, 210). [We could not find direct references in the press, nor indications that could lead us to infer her effective participation.]

Calzetta (2014, 13) also associates Bolten with the periodical in which no actual mention of her can be found when she writes that "Pepita Guerra y el grupo editor del periódico *La voz de la mujer*, Virginia Bolten, Teresa Caporaletti, Juana Quesada, Iris Pavón, Lucce Fabri o Herminia Brumana ... son eslabones de una serie" [Pepita Guerra and the group editor of the newspaper *La voz de la mujer*, Virginia Bolten, Teresa Caporaletti, Juana Quesada, Iris Pavón, Lucce Fabri or Herminia Brumana ... are links in a series] – but it is a series that owes much to the aspirations of those who delineate its existence, rather than to clear evidence. Similarly, Macoc insinuates Bolten's association with others, despite the absence of the needed evidence:

> De particular importancia ha sido la experiencia de "La Voz de la Mujer," periódico feminista que surgió hacia fines de la década de 1890. Desde allí, las mujeres anarquistas –entre las que podemos contar a Virginia Bolten, Maria Calvia y Teresa Marchisio (redactoras) y militantes como Pepita Gherra, Ana López, entre otras, pudieron expresar sus idearios feministas.
>
> MACOC 2011, 158–159

[Of particular importance has been the experience of "La Voz de la Mujer," a feminist newspaper that emerged towards the end of the 1890s. From there, anarchist women – among whom we can count Virginia Bolten, Maria Calvia and Teresa Marchisio (editors) and militants such as Pepita Gherra, Ana López, among others, were able to express their feminist ideals.]

Additionally, Bellucci writes:

> De su [Bolten's] trayectoria han quedado los testimonios recogidos por los periódicos "La Protesta Humana" y "La Protesta" y, en especial, la publicación "La Voz de la Mujer," (1896–1897), que se convierte en el primer manifiesto libertario dirigido por mujeres para mujeres, siendosostenido económicamente con el aporte de su trabajo como aparadora de calzado.
>
> BELLUCCI 2003

[From her [Bolten's] trajectory we have the testimonies collected by the newspapers "La Protesta Humana" and "La Protesta" and, especially, the publication "La Voz de la Mujer," (1896–1897), which becomes the first libertarian manifesto led by women for women, being financially supported by the contribution of her shoemaking work.]

Millán, too, subscribes to the theory as follows:

> Entre 1896 et 1897, la revue-journal *La voz de la mujer* paraît à Buenos Aires. Elle est dirigée par Virginia Bolten, la fondatrice du groupe Les Libertaires, qui propose des alternatives de résistance aux femmes travailleuses.
>
> MILLÁN 2012, 40

[Between 1896 and 1897, the newspaper *La Voz de la Mujer* appeared in Buenos Aires. It is directed by Virginia Bolten, the founder of the group Les Libertaires, who proposes resistance alternatives to working women.]

In a recent article, Pandolfi (2021) also continues the story of Bolten's involvement with the paper when she writes: "Quella di Virginia Bolten, fondatrice de *La Voz de la Mujer*, fu una vita di lotta ispirata agli ideali anarchici" [The life of Virginia Bolten, founder of *La Voz de la Mujer*, was a struggle inspired by anarchist ideals]. Unfortunately, the testimony provided by *La Voz* itself is that there is no evidence that Bolten participated in its creation.

The view that *La Voz* was the handiwork of Bolten has its roots in the work of pioneering researchers such as Gonzalo Zaragoza and Ángel Cappelletti, who are among those best known for assembling the catalog of feminism and anarchism in Argentina and Uruguay, and Bolten is repeatedly associated with some of the names that stand out from that accounting. Zaragoza writes:

> El 8 de enero de 1896 lanzan su propio periódico, *La Voz de la Mujer*. Colaboran en él Virginia Bolten, Pepita Gherra, Teresa Marchisio, Irma Ciminaghi y Ana López.
>
> El periódico desaparece en marzo de 1897 pero reaparecerá en Rosario 1900, bajo la dirección de Virginia Bolten, enérgica propagandista, de profesión obrera aparadora, a quien los socialistas califican de grosera, soez y violenta.
>
> ZARAGOZA 1996, 440

[On January 8, 1896 they launched their own newspaper, *La Voz de la Mujer*. Virginia Bolten, Pepita Gherra, Teresa Marchisio, Irma Ciminaghi and Ana López collaborate.

The newspaper disappeared in March 1897 but it would reappear in Rosario 1900, under the leadership of Virginia Bolten, an energetic propagandist, of a working-class profession, whom the socialists describe as rude, vulgar and violent.]

In her prior research, one of the Prieto, Fernández Cordero, and Muñoz (2013/2014) authors, Laura Fernández Cordero, contributed to the argument that "Casi como en respuesta Pepita Gherra, Luisa Violeta y Virginia Bolten salieron con La Voz de la Mujer (1896–97)" (Fernández Cordero 2006/2007, 245). [Pepita Gherra, Luisa Violeta and Virginia Bolten came out with *La Voz de la Mujer* (1896–97).] Of course, this was written before the research revealed in Prieto, Fernández Cordero, and Muñoz (2013/2014) contributed to a more accurate understanding. More recently, however, Fernández Cordero (2015, 310), conceding that her initial statement was likely wrong, has indicated support for another theory, that while "nothing indicates that she [Bolten] participated in" the surviving Buenos Aires edition of *La Voz de la Mujer*, "she is undoubtedly responsible for the version ... that was published in Rosario, which has unfortunately been lost." In similar fashion, Alonso (2021) claims that "Virginia, in fact, was a member of the group Las Proletarios together with Teresa Marchisio and María Calvia, who were responsible for editing the Rosario version of La Voz de la Mujer (1899–1900)." However, the fact that there are no extant copies of the alleged Rosario publication, along with disputability of claims that Bolten was connected with the known version, can also be interpreted in a different fashion, by arguing that she had nothing whatsoever to do with *La Voz de la Mujer* beyond maybe just being a reader or an admirer or someone who had similar beliefs. There is nothing "undoubted" about the existence of an alternate version of *La Voz* in Rosario around the turn of the century. In the hands of Cives (2019, 46), the argument that "Pepita Guerra" was the *nom de plume* of Bolten, "Pepita Gherra – seudónimo de Virginia Bolten" (46) is merged with the theory of a Rosario *La Voz*:

> En diciembre de 1899, junto a Teresa Marchisio y María Calvia fundan el grupo "Las Proletarias," quienes, a su vez, reeditan *La Voz de la Mujer* (1899–1900), fundado unos años antes en la ciudad de Buenos Aires.
>
> CIVES 2019, 46 fn 87

> [In December 1899, she, together with Teresa Marchisio and María Calvia, founded the group "Las Proletarias," who, in turn, republished *La Voz de la Mujer* (1899–1900), founded a few years earlier in the city of Buenos Aires.]

However, the only citation given by Cives for this argument is to the paper of Prieto, Fernández Cordero, and Muñoz (2013/2014), in which not only do the authors *not* claim that "Pepita Guerra" was Bolten, but make no mention anywhere in the article to Guerra's name. De Souza notes the difficulty here, as well as its consequences for the literature about Bolten:

> A falta de análises mais profundas dessa fonte [*La Voz de la Mujer*] permitiu que as concepções equivocadas circulassem entre os pesquisadores, como é o caso da afirmação de que a libertária Virginia Bolten teria sido uma de suas redatoras. Entretanto, fazendo uma leitura atenta do periódico percebe-se que a mulher citada não assina nenhum artigo

nos nove exemplares disponíveis para pesquisa. Nem tampouco seus pseudônimos aparecem no periódico. A afirmação da participação da libertária é feita por trabalhos que se desenvolveram nos anos 1980–1990 e ainda não teve uma revisão adequada.

DE SOUZA 2019, 17; 2019, 31 is similar

[The lack of deeper analysis of this source [*La Voz de la Mujer*] allowed misconceptions to circulate among researchers, as is the case with the claim that the libertarian Virginia Bolten would have been one of its editors. However, after a careful reading of the journal, it is clear that the woman mentioned did not sign any article in the nine copies available for research. Nor do her pseudonyms appear in the journal. The affirmation of the libertarian participation is made by works that were developed in the years 1980–1990 and that have not yet had an adequate revision.]

In fact, the errors persist to the present day, perpetuated by recent authors who add their footnotes to problematic material inherited from the past. De Souza (2019, 168) herself praises "[a] edição do *La Voz de la Mujer de Rosário*" [the Rosário edition of *La Voz de la Mujer*], although there is no evidence that this putative alternate version of the paper, to which Bolten might have contributed or for which she might have edited articles, ever existed. In another contribution to the research, written with Angela Maria Roberti Martins, de Souza provides some possible evidence for a later Rosario resurgence of *La Voz*:

A "Louise Michel" de Rosário, como Bolten ficou conhecida, publicou em diversos periódicos anarquistas a partir do ano de 1899; teve participação ativa no jornal *El Rebelde* onde apareceu pela primeira vez em 1899 anunciando a versão rosarina do *La Voz de la Mujer*. Pertencia ao grupo Las Proletarias juntamente com outras duas militantes do anarquismo.

MARTINS AND DE SOUZA 2018, 233

[The "Louise Michel" of Rosário, as Bolten became known, published in several anarchist periodicals commencing the year 1899; she took an active part in the newspaper *El Rebelde* where she first appeared in 1899 announcing the Rosarian version of *La Voz de la Mujer*. She belonged to the group Las Proletarias along with two other militants of anarchism.]

However, Martins and de Souza provide no citation here for this questionable argument beyond giving the year 1899, although in a later article, de Souza (2019, 31) cites *El Rebelde*, #20, referring to Laura Fernández Cordero's book,

Amor y anarquismo (2017), as the source for the additional information. There, Fernández Cordero writes:

> No caben dudas de que Bolten y el grupo Las Proletarias eran responsables de publicar la versión rosarina de *La Voz de la Mujer*. Sus iniciales rubrican el aviso de aparición del periódico en agosto de 1899 (*El Rebelde*, n° 20, 1899).
> FERNÁNDEZ CORDERO 2017, 49; PRIETO, FERNÁNDEZ CORDERO, AND MUÑOZ 2013/2014, 211 makes the same claim

> [There is no doubt that Bolten and the group Las Proletarias were responsible for publishing Rosario's version of *La Voz de la Mujer*. Her initials sign the announcement of the appearance of the newspaper in August 1899.]
> *El Rebelde*, #20, 1899

However, there are problems here. Issue #20 of *El Rebelde* was dated September 3, 1899, not August. The only issue in August 1899 was #19, dated August 14, 1899. The actual notice to which de Souza and Fernández Cordero refer appears in a later edition, #21, which is dated September 17, 1899, where the piece is signed "v.b. por la grupo," without giving Bolten's full name, though the initials may well refer to her. The confusion about where the information was posted likely arises from the fact that the note itself is dated as "Rosario de Sta. Fe, Agosto 30 de 1899" ("Compañeros de "El Rebelde"" 1899; Prieto, Fernández Cordero, and Muñoz 2013/2014, 211).

Fernández Cordero also writes that "además, en una nota de enero de 1900 se menciona una reunión en la que el periódico *La Voz de la Mujer* fue representado por Bolten" (Fernández Cordero 2017, 49) [also in a note dated January 1900 it mentions a meeting in which the newspaper *La Voz de la Mujer* was represented by Bolten.] Possibly, Fernández Cordero is referring to edition #28 of *El Rebelde*, which was dated January 7, 1899, apparently an error, the correct date being, it would seem, January 7, 1900. This paper did carry an article by Juan Bautista Perez, itself contradictorily bearing the date November 1899, which was titled "La emancipación de la mujer," but it contained no reference to Bolten or to *La Voz* (Perez 1900, 1–2); on page 4 of the same misdated issue, *La Voz de la Mujer* is included in a list of publications without any further detail being given. In edition #5, dated January 8, 1899, correspondence with "M. Manrique," presumably a reference to Bolten's partner (or husband), Manuel Manrique González, is reported (on page 4), a fact that confirms only a common political interest, without reference to *La Voz*.

Prieto, Fernández Cordero, and Muñoz (2013/2014, 211) make a number of additional arguments in favor of there being a later, Rosario edition of *La Voz*. For example:

> Se la menciona en la edición del 10 de diciembre de ese año, en una pequeña nota donde se felicita al grupo editor del segundo número de *La Voz de la Mujer*
>
> La Protesta Humana, n°64, 10/12/1899 (211)

> [It is mentioned in the edition of December 10 of that year, in a small note where it congratulates the editorial group of the second issue of *La Voz de la Mujer*.]
>
> La Protesta Humana, #64, 12/10/1899

However, the December 10 1899 edition of *La Protesta Humana* was numbered #73, and #64 was dated August 6, 1899. In edition #64, there is no mention of *La Voz de la Mujer*, although there is another announcement about anarchist activities in Rosario:

> En Rosario de Santa Fé se ha constituido un nuevo grupo anarquista denominado Libres Pensadores.
>
> "Progresando" 1899b, 3

> [In Rosario de Santa Fe, a new anarchist group called Free Thinkers has been formed.]

The December 10 edition (#73) does contain the note to which Prieto, Fernández Cordero, and Muñoz refer. In its entirety, the piece reads:

> De Rosario de Santa Fé hemos recibido el núm. 2 de *La Voz de la Mujer*, nuevo propagandista de los ideas anarquistas que un grupo de activas compañeras han principiado á publicar en eso localidad. Le deseamos larga vida al nuevo colega y mientros tanto felicitamos al grupo de compañeras que con tanto teson contribuyen á la emancipación de la parte más esclavadel género humana: la mujer. Dirigir la corresponcia á Virginia Bolten. – Calle Uruguay, 846. – Rosario de Sta. Fé.
>
> "Publiaciones recibidas" 1899

> [From Rosario de Santa Fe we have received the number 2 of *La Voz de la Mujer*, a new propagandist of anarchist ideas that a group of active

comrades have begun to publish in that locality. We wish the new companion a long life and in the meantime we congratulate the group of comrades who with so much determination contribute to the emancipation of the most enslaved part of the human race: women. Address mail to Virginia Bolten. – Calle Uruguay, 846. – Rosario de Sta. Fé.]

Although the note suggests that a new version of *La Voz* may be being produced, and that Bolten is in some way associated with it, by itself, it adds little to the main argument that a second version did exist, and does not indicate who the authors may be except by inference that it might be Virginia because she was the one who told the paper about it. It is surprising that, given the notoriety of the original, Buenos Aires-based *La Voz*, no comment is included here to distinguish the new version from the old or to remind readers that the "new" version walks in the shoes of a profoundly significant previous contributor to women's liberation.

Prieto, Fernández Cordero, and Muñoz continue by pointing out the following source:

> En la nota dedicada a la apertura de la Casa del Pueblo de Rosario es mencionada entre los oradores que participaron del acto de inauguración.
> *La Protesta Humana*, n° 76 (211)

> [In the note dedicated to the opening of the Casa del Pueblo in Rosario, she is mentioned among the speakers who participated in the opening ceremony.]
> *La Protesta Humana*, # 76

On the one hand, this additional source seems to confirm a connection between Bolten and *La Voz*:

> Se ballan presentes los grupos *Libre pensadores, Ciencia y Progreso, Libertario, Amor Libre*, el periódico *La Voz de la Mujer*, representado por la compañera Virginia Bolten, se lee la adhesión de *Tribuna Libre*, de Córdoba, y toma la palabra el compañero Marí que después de deplorar justamente la ausencia de algunas agrupaciones anarquistas, presenta al compañero Ros llegado de Buenos Aires en representatión de *La Casa del Pueblo* para tener una conferencia.
> "Progresando" 1899a, 4

[The groups *Libre pensadores, Ciencia y Progreso, Libertario, Amor Libre*, the newspaper *La Voz de la Mujer*, represented by comrade Virginia Bolten, are present, the accord with *Tribuna Libre*, from Córdoba, is read, and comrade Marí takes the floor, and after justly deploring the absence of some anarchist groups, he introduces comrade Ros who has arrived from Buenos Aires on behalf of *La Casa del Pueblo* to hold a conference.]

On the other hand, the article notes only a connection, whatever that may mean; it does not say that Virginia wrote anything or edited anything that has appeared in *La Voz*. Moreover, it does not indicate whether it is referring to the actual *La Voz* known to exist or to the putative one of which not a trace has been found. The piece continues by referring to "la compañera Virginia Botten" [sic] (1899a, 4) [the comrade Virginia Botten [sic]], which may be a misprint, but it might also suggest a lack of familiarity with who Virginia was. So, again, nothing is really decided based on this reference. As Prieto, Fernández Cordero, and Muñoz note (2013/2014, 211), an allusion in the April 1, 1900 issue to *La Casa del Pueblo*'s conference on the situation of women again mentions Bolten, as "la estimada compañera Virginia Bolten" [the esteemed companion Virginia Bolten] who spoke "con la soltura de frase que la caracteriza" (En el Rosario de Santa Fe 1899, 4; Prieto, Fernández Cordero, and Muñoz 2013/2014, 211) [with the ease of phrase that characterizes her.] Such references confirm that Bolten was active in anarchist and feminist activities at the time and that she was an eloquent speaker, but there is no mention in the article in question to *La Voz de la Mujer*. In another citation given by Prieto, Fernández Cordero, and Muñoz, to a brief note in *La Protesta Humana* #82, there is, as the authors point out, a reference to Virginia being unable at the present time to publish *La Voz* due to a lack of funds. Although this may be viewed as a better proof of the existence of a new version of the publication, the fact that Bolten's last name is here given as "Botlen," a misprint not mentioned by Prieto, Fernández Cordero, and Muñoz (2013/2014, 211), also adds room for doubt:

> El periódico *La Voz de la Mujer* que redacta la activa amiga Virginia Botlen [sic] no aparece por falta de recursos. Si algunos compañeros lo desean ayudar – que débese ayundarlo – pueden escribir al Rosario de Santa Fe, calle Uruguay núm. 846.
> DESDE EL ROSARIO. 1900, 4

[The newspaper *La Voz de la Mujer*, written by my active friend Virginia Botlen [sic], does not appear due to lack of resources. If some comrades want to assist – and you should help them – they can write to Rosario de Santa Fe, calle Uruguay núm. 846.]

Similarly, Manzoni (2009, 2, fn. 3) writes that "En 1901 (Rosario) y 1902 (Montevideo) aparecieron ejemplares homónimos, vinculados a Virginia Bolten, pero no está claro si se trataba del mismo periódical" [In 1901 (Rosario) and 1902 (Montevideo) homonymous copies appeared, linked to Virginia Bolten, but it is not clear if it was the same newspaper], again implying without any convincing evidence that it did exist, though conceding that nothing is known about its content. More cautious in her detailed oft-cited article, Molyneux (1986, 130) more judiciously refers to claims that *La Voz* later reappeared in Rosario or Montevideo as being only possibilities amid "reports" that cannot be verified.

For one reason alone, her expulsion from Argentina due to the Residence Law, it is highly likely that Virginia Bolten was born in Uruguay, although the precise location remains unknown. She was quite possibly deported several times, along with or separately from her partner (or husband) (Molyneux 1986, 130; Prieto, Fernández Cordero, and Muñoz 2013/2014, 214; Simon 1946, 41, 42). However, the idea that Bolten was originally from Argentina appears in a number of places in the research material. For instance, Simeoni (2007) writes of "Virginia Bolten nacida en San Luis, ... que fueron despedidas de una hilandería ubicadas en barrio" [Virginia Bolten born in San Luis, ... fired from a spinning mill located in the neighborhood]. The inconsistency goes unnoticed by Cawen (2017, 229), who writes that Bolten and her partner were victims of the Residence Law even as she claims that "Virginia Bolten nació en la ciudad argentina de San Luis, en 1890 se radicó en Rosario y junto a su esposo se vinculó a los grupos ácratas" (229) [Virginia Bolten was born in the Argentine city of San Luis; in 1890 she settled in Rosario and, together with her husband, became involved in anarchist groups.] She continues that "En febrero de 1905, Bolten fue deportada a Uruguay, pocos días después que su marido y unos treinta compañeros" (229) [In February 1905, Bolten was deported to Uruguay, a few days after her husband and some thirty of her companions.]

Prieto, Fernández Cordero, and Muñoz, disagreeing with Virginia's friend Ruoco, also make the claim that Bolten was not Uruguayan, noting only that, unlike her, her brother and one of her children were born in Montevideo, but providing no additional information:

> En la autobiografía que la española-argentina Juana Rouco edita en 1964, al recordar a Bolten como compañera en el exilio montevideano, afirma

que era uruguaya. No lo era, en sentido estricto, pero es cierto que la mayor parte de su vida transcurrió en Montevideo.

PRIETO, FERNÁNDEZ CORDERO, AND MUÑOZ 2013/2014, 212

[In the autobiography that the Spanish-Argentinean Juana Rouco publishes in 1964, remembering Bolten as her companion in exile in Montevideo, she affirms that she was Uruguayan. She was not, strictly speaking, but it is true that most of her life was spent in Montevideo.]

Baer (2015, 54, 189) perhaps provides a better understanding of the underlying situation when he describes the removal of Ramón Palau, another of the anarchists deported under the Residence Law. He comments:

Palau ... did not regard his return [to Spain] as permanent ... and planned to go back to Argentina. Like many other immigrants there [in Argentina], Palau had not applied for citizenship despite his long residence. Many immigrants found the process of becoming a citizen cumbersome, and, since civic participation was almost meaningless in a fraudulent political system, citizenship brought few benefits prior to the residency law.

BAER 2015, 54

Bellucci suggests a more likely scenario with respect to the citizenship issue, given the fact that Bolten was deportable and in fact deported:

De Virginia Bolten, pese a su protagonismo arrollador en las filas libertarias de finales del siglo XIX hasta las primeras décadas del siguiente, se carece de información precisa que permita reconstruir su historia de su vida y la de su activismo proselitista. ... De nacionalidad uruguaya, pero reside gran parte de su vida en Rosario.

BELLUCCI 2003

[About Virginia Bolten, despite her overwhelming role in the libertarian ranks of the late 19th century to the first decades of the next, precise information is lacking that allows reconstructing his history of her life and that of her proselytizing activism. ... A Uruguayan national, but she resides for most of her life in Rosario.]

Other sources spell Virginia's last name incorrectly. For example, Lavrin (1995, 264) refers to "[t]he women anarchists of the period – Virginia Bolton, Teresa

Marchisio, Irma Ciminaghi, and others"; in the index to Lavrin's book, she is also named as "Bolton" (1995, 463). Listing some of the more important anarchists in Uruguay as of 1908, Alexander with Parker (2005, 14) give her name as being "Virginia Belton." Also, because Arturo Lozza (1985) claimed that "Virginia Bolthen" was one of the speakers in Rosario on May 1, 1890, the misspelling adds additional doubt to the possibility of her actual presence then (Prieto, Fernández Cordero, and Muñoz 2013/2014, 210).

From Bordagaray comes an argument that research up to the point at which she is writing, a little more than a decade ago, has been flawed in a different way:

> La reconstrucción de los itinerarios de vida de varias militantes ácratas ha tenido un impulso en los últimos años. ... en el caso de Salvadora Medina Onrubia de Botana, Virginia Bolten y Juana Rouco Buela y ... Herminia Brumana. Sin embargo, en estos casos, el interés ha estado más concentrado en sus creaciones artísticas, las que trascienden sus agencias en el movimiento libertario o anarquista.
>
> BORDAGARAY 2011

> [The reconstruction of the life itineraries of various militant anarchists has had a boost in recent years. ... in the case of Salvadora Medina Onrubia de Botana, Virginia Bolten, and Juana Rouco Buela and ... Herminia Brumana. However, in these cases, interest has been more concentrated in their artistic creations, those that transcend their agency in the libertarian or anarchist movement.]

In the present context, "creaciones artísticas" might refer to a certain personality cult that exists with respect to Bolten and others, heroines of a beguiling bygone age who had the courage to stand up for themselves, those of temperaments now of interest to researchers, and deservedly so. Nonetheless, perhaps the implied criticism is a cogent one here, that to understand Virginia Bolten in the most appropriate way, we should be examining those of her writings that can be accessed today to supplement the esteem of admirers content to focus mainly on her received reputation. Furthermore, additional focus on her "agencia" [agency] may achieve a more accurate estimate of the degree to which she contributed to anarchist thought.

3 Virginia Bolten: the Reality

Even though the trailblazing research of Prieto, Fernández Cordero, and Muñoz has shown the extent to which the story of Virginia Bolten that was told in the past (and continues to be circulated) may often be inaccurate and is to some extent mythic, there are a number of Bolten's articles that remain extant, and which give the reader a good sense of why she is so lauded, showing what her opinions were, and suggesting what kind of person she was. Prieto, Fernández Cordero, and Muñoz (2013/2014) have collected and published those writings, the content of which which will be discussed in what follows in the present chapter. In addition, an article written by Bolten which was titled "Nuestras agitaciones" and published in the fortnightly, feminist-run, anarchist Montevideo paper, *La Nueva Senda*, which is not included in the Prieto, Fernández Cordero, and Muñoz compilation (Bolten 1909b), is described here.

In articles in *Caras y Caretas* in 1902 concerning two contemporary labor disputes, titled "El movimiento obrero: La huelga en Barracas" [The Labor Movement: The Strike in Barracas] and "En Zárate," which contained many photographs, one of the shots, titled "Comisión de mujeres huelguistas" [Commission of Women Strikers] ("En Zárate" 1902, 42), was of Bolten along with some of her confederates, and another, titled "La oradora, Virginia Bolten" (43) [The speaker, Virginia Bolten], showed her alone, although the commentary that accompanied the pictures indicated that she was one of the leaders of the Zárate strike, which had been a response to the imprisonment of 25 workers, who were soon released ("En Zárate" 1902, 44; Rogers 2008, 148–149). An article in the Montevideo paper, *Vida Nueva*, congratulated the strike leaders for this early success, also confirming for historians of the present day, Virginia Bolten's involvement:

> La actitud cobarde de las autoridades no ha logrado ahogar el movimiento obrero en esa población, donde la huelga continúa. En Zárate, la simpática población en que todos los obreros pjrofesan sincero amor á la lucha, no solo sigue la huelga de estivadores, sino, que también han abandonado el trabajo los obreros de la fábrica de papel y los panaderos. Los compañeros Basterra y Camba, y la compañera Virginia Bolten han dado varias conferencias á los huelguistas.
> "Argentina" 1902, 6

> [The cowardly attitude of the authorities has not succeeded in stifling the labor movement in that town, where the strike continues. In Zárate, the pleasant town in which all the workers profess sincere love of the

struggle, not only does the strike of stevedores continue, but also the paper factory workers and the bakers have left their jobs. Comrades [Felix B.] Basterra and [Julio] Camba, and Comrade Virginia Bolten have given various lectures to the strikers.]

In an earlier issue of *Caras y Caretas*, dated August 11, 1901, an article appeared titled "El anarquismo en el Río de la Plata" (1901, 25, 27) [Anarchism in the Río de la Plata], which is also the title given by Laura Fernández Cordero (2019) in the entry for Bolten in the *Diccionario Biográfico de las Izquierdas Latinoamericanas*. Prieto, Fernández Cordero, and Muñoz (2013/2014, 210) had changed the title slightly to "El anarquismo del Río de la Plata" [Anarchism of the Río de la Plata]. Molyneux (1986, 130) refers to the article, but does not give its title and lists only the date of the issue as being 1901. Even in the case of some of the most successful and generally accurate portrayers of the life of Bolten, small errors and omissions can become evident. In "El anarquismo en el Río de la Plata" (1901, 25), a number of local anarchist publications are listed, including *La Voz de la Mujer*, as well as the names of important anarchists whose ideas are reflected in these writings, including those of Kropotkin, Malatesta, Reclus, and Gori:

> En el Rosario, desde 1895, han sido publicados: «La Verdad», «La Federación Obrera», «La Libre lniciativa,» «La Nueva Humanidad,» redactado por el médico doctor Arana; y «La Voz de la Mujer», homónimo del de Buenos Aires, escrito por Virginia Bouten.
>
> "El anarquismo en el Río de la Plata" 1901, 28
>
> [In Rosario, since 1895, have been published: "La Verdad," "La Federación Obrera," "La Libre lniciativa," "La Nueva Humanidad," written by the medical doctor Arana; and "La Voz de la Mujer," same name as [the one in] Buenos Aires, written by Virginia Bouten.]

Here, the spelling of Virginia's last name as "Bouten," together with the sense that she was the writer of one or other version of *La Voz* raise questions discussed earlier in this chapter, although the piece can be used to support the argument that a Rosario edition did exist. But the choice may be better understood as being between her association with (1) the edition that existed and in which there is nothing written by her, and there is no other reference to her, and (2) the later, Rosario, edition that may not have existed at all. The article also mentions "María Calvía, iniciadora del grupo «Los Proletarios» y colaboradora de «La Voz de la Mujer,» y Virginia Bouten y Teresa Marchisio, directora y compañera de redacción, respectivamente, delmismo periódico" ("El anarquismo en el Río de la Plata" 1901, 28) [María Calvía, initiator of the group "The Proletarians" and collaborator of *La Voz de la Mujer*, and Virginia Bouten [sic] and Teresa Marchisio, director and partner writing, respectively, for the same newspaper.] Nowhere, however, does it refer, as Molyneux (1986, 130) claims, to "two beautiful women who edit *La Voz de la Mujer*." A photograph of Virginia is appended, and gives her name correctly (and contradictorily) as "Virginia Bolten" ("El anarquismo en el Río de la Plata" 1901, 28), indicating that she was the editor of *La Voz de la Mujer*, which might be considered as validation of her association with the publication, or it might be viewed as confirming confusion about some of the aspects of anarchism in the River Plate area on the part of the *Caras y Caretas* writers and editors; photographs of Calvía and Marchisio bearing the same attribution are also affixed (28).

In Montevideo in 1909, Bolten established *La Nueva Senda* with Juana Rouco Buela and Maria Collazo; issues #5 and #6 of that periodical, which lasted from 1909 to 1910, indicate Bolten's "Direccion" and some of her writing appeared in this publication. *La Nueva Senda*'s somewhat liberal tone causes Ehrick (2004, 61) to remark that the paper "reflected the rather grim state of working class women's activism in Montevideo during this era." For example, Cawen discusses an article called "A las mujeres" that appeared in the January 7, 1910 issue of *La Nueva Senda* ("A las mujeres" 1910), when Bolten was now officially in charge of the publication, although she points out that Rouco Buela's autobiography, *Memoria*, indicates that the new director following her withdrawal was in fact Collazo (Cawen 2017, 225, fn 28; Martins and De Souza 2018, 237; Prieto, Cordero, and Muñoz 2013/2014, 216). But, considering "A las mujeres" to reflect Bolten's thinking at the time, although the name of its author is not affixed to the article, she comments that, "dirigido a las madres obreras, no se hizo hincapié en su "emancipación" sino que su autor procuró hacerles tomar consciencia del costo social que tenía que abandonaran los hogares" (Cawen 2017, 225) [directed at working mothers, their "emancipation" was not emphasized, but rather the author tried to make them aware of the social cost they would have to bear if they abandoned their home life], and thus the focus hardly centered around the need for mothers to avoid domestic drudgery.

In the case of a subsequent publication, *Nuestra Tribuna*, which operated in Montevideo from 1922 to 1925, and was directed by Juana Rouco Buela, there has been similar criticism that the radical feminism revealed there lacked attention to issues considered more important to women at other times and in other places. Lavrin writes:

> Early in the decade Juana Rouco Buela's *Nuestra Tribuna* advertised three books dealing with sex and planned parenthood. Apart from a couple of articles on free love, however, this newspaper added no new dimension to the discussion of birth control and sexuality.
>
> LAVRIN 1995, 133

Fortunately, as Lavrin (1995, 393, fn 21) notes, there were a few exceptions, such as a 1924 article titled "La mujer" by Luisa Capetillo:

> Tal es la mujer latina, en todos los paises de habla castellana, especialmente. La mujer, compañera del hombre, á la que la Naturalaleza la dado el derecho de crear y educar las generaciones, la que forma el corazón y el cerebro de los futuros libertadores del mundo, es una esclava. Esclava maniatada al capricho de su dueño, sin voluntad, sin conocimiento de las más elementales nociones de fisiologia y de ciencia social.
>
> CAPETILLO 1924, 4

[Such is the Latin woman, in all Spanish-speaking countries, especially. The woman, the companion of man, to whom Nature has given the right to create and educate the generations, the one who forms the heart and brain of the future liberators of the world, is a slave. She is a slave tied to the whim of her owner, without will, without knowledge of the most elementary notions of physiology and social science.]

For Fernández Cordero, despite Ruoco's friendship with María Collazo and Virginia Bolten, there was much more involvement in the publication by other authors, for example by Vicenta González and Rosalina Gutiérrez, and the content is therefore, while consistently feminist in its character, quite pedestrian (Fernández Cordero 2015, 315–316, 2017, 283). For Cano (2006, 890), *Nuestra Tribuna* has a journalistic tone.

La Nueva Senda had followed the setting up by the same founders, together with Teresa Capolaretti, in Buenos Aires in 1906, of *Emancipación* ("Collazo, Maria" 2020). Virginia seems also to have been involved with *Regeneración*, on the mastheads of which it says, "Toda la correspondencia a nombre de Virginia Bolten, Rodriguez Larreta 9" [Address all correspondence to Virginia Bolten, Rodriguez Larreta 9]. However, none of the articles in *Regeneración* bear her name.

Reports in *La Rebelión* indicate that Virginia spoke at a conference on December 27, 1902 at the Salón Silva del Cerro to imaugurate the Cerro Social Studies Center, Cerro being a neighborhood of Montevideo ("Movimiento

Social: Montevideo" 1903). Her planned appearance at a "propaganda" meeting at the same location on January 18 1903 was announced by the same issue of the paper ("En el Cerro" 1903). On May Day the same year in Montevideo, Bolten spoke at a protest opposing Argentina's Residence Law (Bellucci 2003). In Montevideo, Bolten and Gori were involved in the activities of the influential Centro Internacional de Estudios Sociales de Montevideo (CIES) [the International Center for Social Studies], which operated between 1897 and 1928; this organization, situated in the center of the city near the seat of government and the university, was dominated intellectually by anarcho/a-communist people and their ideas, which is indicative of the greater tolerance for radical ideas evinced by Uruguay as opposed to Argentina (Simon 1946, 51). The CIES is the building where, in August 1905, a workers' congress will inaugurate the the Federación Obrera Regional Uruguaya [Uruguayan Regional Workers Federation] (FORU), modeled on the Federación Obrera Regional Argentina (FORA) [Argentinian Regional Workers Federation], to which, for a time, most of the important unions would be affiliated. The FORU would engage in many aspects of labor union activity such as campaigning for an eight-hour day and a minimum wage, but also cultural exploits of many different kinds, and be dominated for a number of years by anarchist, rather than socialist perspectives, with assistance from Virginia Bolten, who had participated in the initial congress, and be influenced also by the work and writings of Juana Rouco Buela and María Collazo (Alexander with Parker 2005, 13; Cawen 2017, 214–215, 229–230; Muñoz 2020, 15; Rosenthal 1995, 334–335; Simon 1946, 51; Vidal 2014, 5, 7, 7 fn 22, 10; Viera 2013, 64–65; Yanes Torrado, Marín Suárez, and Cantabrana Carassou 2017, 78, 79).

At the FORU's Third Congress in 1911, the members passed a resolution opposing compulsory vaccination, "pues ve en ella una medida coercitiva de la libertad individual, sin entrar a discutir si es beneficiosa o no" (Rama 1968–1969, 32–33) [since it sees in it a coercive measure of individual freedom, without discussing whether it is beneficial or not.] This is an argument that continues to find favor in many countries as governments attempt to fight infectious diseases using compulsion. During this FORU Congress, on May 1, 1911, many attendees, considered to have been between 10,000 and 12,000 persons, marched from the International Center to the Maciel Pier where many speeches were given, including one by Virginia Bolten. As noted above, participants indicated their solidarity with the Chicago martyrs, and they also denounced Argentina's Residence Law, the reason why some of them now lived in Montevideo.

The fact that anarchists, unions, and others in Montevideo saw that the conditions faced by streetcar workers imposed by foreign owners were exploitative and the provision of local transportation service was inadequate, led to development of an alternative view of how the city should develop, which resulted in a general strike organized by the FORU in May 1911 that lasted for a few weeks. The same process of a strike by streetcar workers that turned into a general strike was repeated in 1918. (Fernández 2010, 35–36; Rago 1997, 282–283; Rosenthal 1995, 320, 337–338, 341). For Rosenthal, these developments have something to say about the role of anarchism in Uruguay:

> Rather than viewing anarchism as an impractical short-lived movement that was co-opted by Batlle, it may be more useful to evaluate the culture of anarchism in Montevideo as it developed in cafes and union halls and to look at its long-term impact on thought and public behaviour in the city. Perhaps the most enduring legacy of the anarchists is that in the early years of this century they forced the debate over the future of their city out of the private clubs and corporate offices and into the newspapers and the streets.
> ROSENTHAL 1995, 341

The previous month, in April of 1911, Bolten was involved with setting up in Montevideo the *"Asociación Femenina "Emancipación""* ("Emancipation" Women's Association), a coordinating group that was intended to coordinate resistance to the influence of religious organizations and, like Virginia herself, was opposed to giving the vote to women (Alonso 2021; Ehrick 2004, 62, 63). Although Batlle y Ordóñez, who had just begun his second term as president (1911–1915), also wanted to separate church and state, and his party organization's daily newspaper, *El Día* gave space to anarchist, socialist, and internationalist perspectives, the approach of *Emancipación* was not necessarily supported by every radical in Uruguay, with the consequence that Bolten's ideas during this period of her life have been considered a form of "anarcha-Batllism" (Cappelletti 1990, 75; Cawen 2017, 230). However, this commitment should be qualified by noting that Bolten was never afraid to give her opinion and to criticize aspects of *El Día*'s support for Batlle's polices and those of the more moderate Claudio Williman, who was president between Batlle's terms, from 1907 to 1911, when labor unions and anarchists were affected negatively (Vidal 2012, 85). Peterson notes:

> Even the highly regarded writer, orator, and militant Virginia Bolten – veteran of libertarian struggles in Uruguay and Argentina and perhaps the most famous anarchafeminist in the Rio de la Plata region – also expressed sympathy for batllismo although she never abandoned radicalism.
> PETERSON 2015, 130

On the other hand, Vidal (2014, 16–17, fn 54) portrays Virginia's actions more in terms of her inconsistency: "Virginia Bolten es un ejemplo del cambio de posición, desde la convocatoria a la huelga, el sabotaje y la destrucción de maquinaria, hasta la necesidad de la organización o, años más tarde, su integración al grupo batllista Avanzar" [Virginia Bolten is an example of the change of position, from the call for strikes, sabotage and the destruction of machinery, to the need for organization or, years later, her integration into the Batllista group Avanzar].

For much of her life, Bolten was involved in radical activities in both Uruguay and Argentina, moving backwards and forwards across the River Plate, even though she had been deported from Argentina in 1905 not long after her partner, and she may have been deported on other occasions (Alonso 2021; Cawen 2017, 228). Pandolfi writes:

> Tornata in Argentina fu molto attiva nel Comitato femminile di sciopero del FORA (Federación Obrera Argentina – Federazione operaia argentina), ma la sua fama si perse con il graduale sopravvento del partito socialista sul movimento anarchico. Tanto che nel 1913 *El Socialista* la accusò esplicitamente di aver tradito il movimento operaio.
>
> PANDOLFI 2021

> [Back in Argentina, she was very active in the women's strike committee of the FORA (Federación Obrera Argentina – Argentine Workers' Federation), but her fame was lost with the gradual gain of the socialist party over the anarchist movement. So much so that in 1913 *El Socialista* explicitly accused her of having betrayed the workers' movement.]

Virginia's article, "Preguntas y respuestas" (Bolten 1900b) ["Questions and Answers"], signed "Virginia Boltén," is identified by Prieto, Fernández Cordero, and Muñoz (2013/2014) as having been published in issue #96 of *La Protesta Humana*, on October 10, 1900, and other scholars, citing them, have repeated that citation. However, the article in question is not to be found at that location, but at page 3 of *La Protesta Humana* #83, dated April 29, 1900. In her thoughtful piece, designed to explain "He ahí lo que somos y lo que no somos" (1900b) [Here is what we are and what we are not], Bolten outlines many of the inaccurate prejudices that others nurse about anarchists, opinions she obviously views as mistaken. In contradistinction, using "libertarios" [libertarians], as others have often done, to refer to anarchists, she outlines the details for achieving a much more positive grasp of the concept, and attempts to show why women's rights are central to an anarchist perspective. Critics, she notes, are often suspicious of the motives of those who wish to redistribute the fortunes of the rich, thinking anarchists wish to misappropriate that money so that they can transform themselves into a new aristocracy. But, Bolten responds, to argue this is to miss the point that wealth permits and entitles a life of luxury, while people who are poor and must work hard to survive are denied appropriate access to the good things in life. This hidden reality of capitalist exploitation, the denial of humanity and physical and mental comfort to the majority of the population through the societal agency of prosperity, is the real target here, and the only way to avoid remaining "el burro de carga" (1900b) [the workhorse] in such a system is to rebel.

Bolten also addresses the criticism that anarchists are anti-family. Denying the charge, she argues that, while the family at present is a flawed institution based on exploitation and pursuit of personal interest, anarchists are actually in favor of spontaneous relationships developed within an environment where women are fully educated about the nature of society and able to make a free choice about how they live their lives (1900b).

Why, then, do anarchists oppose government? Here, Bolten argues that government actions reveal a class basis, which allows ordinary working people to be exploited by more comfortable members of society, while their protests, questioning the fairness of this stratification, are violently crushed: "nos embrutecen por la patria, nos matan por la patria, nos apalean por la patria" (1900b) [they brutalize us for the homeland, they kill us for the homeland, they beat us for the homeland]. She also demonstrates her dislike of religion, rejecting it in favor of science, pointing out the lack of judgment involved in assigning a particular religion to a child at birth, and seeking to prevent them from ever disputing the validity of their non-choice, rather than, as a matter of fairness, allowing people exposure to the tenets of all religions so that they might decide whether any of them matched their own needs and perspectives. Nonetheless, anarchists will tend to reject all religions because they constitute one of the means by which the class basis of society is enforced:

> No abracemos ninguna religión: porque sabemos que son todas ellas, la farsa inventada por los ambiciosos para embrutecernos. ... Amamos la ciencia; que es la verdad: la religión es lo desconocido, la ilusión; por lo tanto somos sus enemigos mortales; la religión, siendo todo misterios, va contra la proclamación de nuestra luz.
> BOLTEN 1900b

[Let us not embrace any religion: because we know that they are all of them the farce invented by the ambitious to brutalize us. ... We love science; which is the truth: religion is the unknown, the illusion; therefore we are its mortal enemies; religion, being all mysteries, goes against the proclamation of our light.]

More specifically, in a short piece with the title "Dios" (1908b) ["God"], Virginia attacks the nature of Christianity and mocks what she sees as its preposterous and unscientific claim of a virgin birth, anticipating some of the theological arguments for the existence or non-existence of God, and claiming the weakness of a Panglossian Christianity, scoffing at the assumption that while human beings are responsible for their sins, as well as the wars, accidents, natural disasters, and illnesses that torment them, somehow it is still quite logical to believe that "hay un dios todo poderoso, justo y puro" (1908b) [there is an omnipotent being, an all-powerful, just, and pure god], and that "no se mueve una paja sin su consentimiento" (1908b) [one doesn't move a straw without his consent]. In an attempt to rectify this contradiction, modern theologians and their opponents have considered that perhaps God is not omnipotent after all and can not in advance prevent the various living hells endured by humankind (Lawrence 2020; Mackie 1955; Plantinga 2008). Bolten, in contradistinction, makes the argument that failure to deliver on this promise over many centuries means that "su omnipotencia nos resulta impotencia; su poderío debilidad, porque sólo reina en cerebros débiles y enfermos" (Bolten 1908b) [his omnipotence is impotence to us; his power weakness, because he only reigns in weak and sick brains].

On October 20, 1901, Cosme Budislavich, an immigrant from what is now Croatia, was shot by the police during a strike in Rosario at a sugar refinery called Refinería Argentina de Azúcar. When demonstrations to protest the killing were banned, the workers called a general strike, and large protests were held on October 24 and 25. Today, a square in Rosario (Plaza Cosme Budislavich) commemorates his sacrifice. A speech Bolten made in repudiation of the killing was printed in the local newspaper, *El Municipio*, on October 25; even as she participated in that protest, she bravely and characteristically expressed her dissatisfaction that such dissent had officially been banned (Bolten 1901; Prieto, Fernández Cordero, and Muñoz 2013/2014, 210; Stavisky 2017, 168, 170). In the report, where she was identified as "Virginia Bolthen," Bolten continues many of the arguments that she had made in "Preguntas y respuestas," also making reference to the Chicago anarchists, and suggesting that crime is social, which, as noted above, was a belief shared by many other anarchists, including Gori. She speaks of "el yugo de la escuela que nos impone determinados estudios, el yugo de la religión que nos impone determinada creencia, el yugo de los patronos que consumen nuestras energías y absorben por un jornal miserable nuestra vida, el yugo del matrimonio que nos ata a un hombre a perpetuidad" (Bolten 1901) [The yoke of the school that imposes certain studies on us, the yoke of religion that imposes a determined belief on us, the yoke of employers who consume our energies and absorb our lives for a miserable wage, the yoke of marriage that binds us to a man in perpetuity.] This expansive version sounds much like the anarchism of Max Stirner, displaying an unwillingness to let the life of the individual be bounded beyond personal choice, yet it is an argument articulated on behalf of poor workers and their labor union, rather than the lonely antiorganizationalist. These apparently contradictory motivations are, of course, present in a number of the anarchist publications that flourished in Argentina and Uruguay at the time; indeed, they are an aspect of many anarchist perspectives. Here, Virginia presents marriage as a form of legal prostitution, an argument shared by a number of feminists and anarchists, such as Tennie C. Claflin, Voltairine de Cleyre, Louise Michel, Lois Waisbrooker, Mary Wollstonecraft, and Victoria C. Woodhull. Thus, she complains in her speech, "Dicen por ahí que la ley nos concede d[e]rechos: sí, el de la prostitución legal p[or] medio del matrimonio, y el d[e] morirnos de hambre abrazadas a nuestros hijos" (Bolten 1901). [They say that the law grants us rights: yes, that of legal prostitution through marriage, and that of starving while embracing our children.]

The same bifurcation is again to be seen in another piece, "La organización se impone" (Bolten 1910b) ["The Organization Prevails"], but Virginia this time abandons the fork in the anarchist footpath that leads to antiorganizationalism, Stirner, isolation, and probable failure, writing "Se desprecia la organización por considerarla formada por el egoísmo personal, sin ver que, también se es egoísta el encerrarse en el mayor grado de individualismo" (1910b) [The organization is despised when considering it formed by personal selfishness, without seeing that it is also selfish to lock oneself up in the highest degree of individualism.] So, compromise with others, the concession always emphatically rejected by Stirner, rather than "el individualismo exagerado" (1910b) [the exaggerated individualism], is a requirement for success:

> No es suficiente llamarse progresista o anarquista, es preciso estar con el progreso, luchando por su triunfo; no es bastante pensar anárquicamente, es necesario extender los conocimientos, hacer prosélitos, divulgar las teorías y buscar el medio de llevarlas a la práctica, de otro modo no se hará jamás la tan deseada transformación de la sociedad.
> 1910b

[It is not enough to call oneself a progressive or anarchist, you have to be with progress, fighting for its triumph; it is not enough to think anarchically, it is necessary to spread knowledge, proselytize, disseminate theories, and seek the means of putting them into practice, otherwise the much desired transformation of society will never be achieved.]

In another article in *El Obrero*, one that bears the title "¿Por qué se lucha?" (Bolten 1905d) ["Why Do You Fight?"], Bolten continues the theme of exploitation of ordinary, hard-working but poorly paid people at the expense of a more comfortable class whose idleness and happiness increase reciprocally in proportion to the exploitation of others. Martins and de Souza explain:

> Os burgueses são aqui representados como parasitas, figuras que nada produzem, mas que tudo roubam; são enxergados e descritos por Virginia Bolten como aqueles que nada fizeram pelo bem-estar da humanidade, suas relações com trabalhadores giravam em torno da opressão e da arbitrariedade. Essas atitudes burguesas, segundo a articulista, eram apoiadas pelo Estado e pela Igreja, os braços do capitalismo e da exploração.
> MARTINS AND DE SOUZA 2018, 235

[The bourgeois are here represented as parasites, figures who produce nothing but steal everything; are seen and described by Virginia Bolten as those who did nothing for the well-being of humanity, their relations with workers revolved around oppression and arbitrariness. These bourgeois attitudes, according to the columnist [Bolten], were supported by the State and the Church, the arms of capitalism and exploitation.]

If anything, Virginia's criticism here is even more harsh:

> El productor elabora desde la más rica tela al grosero algodón y cáñamo; desde las más hermosas obras de arte y de ciencia, más acabada, a la limpieza pública y privada y sus callosas manos arrancan de las entrañas de la tierra, desde el carbón hasta el oro, la plata y toda clase de metales; él ha de pulir y hermosear las piedras preciosas y labrar los utensilios de coquetería de nuestros señores y señoras de gran tono.
> BOLTEN 1905d

[The producer refines from the richest cloth to coarse cotton and hemp; from the most beautiful works of art and science, most finished, to public and private cleaning, and his calloused hands pluck from the bowels of the earth, from coal to gold, silver and all kinds of metals; he has to polish and beautify the precious stones and to carve the snobbish utensils of our high-class lords and ladies.]

A related argument to be found in this piece is that all aspects of community life, including science and the arts have been contributed to by many different participants and thus it is inappropriate for anyone to claim ownership of any particular invention, innovation, or perspective, even if they supplied its final segment (1905d). Here, Bolten's perspective brings to mind Kropotkin's dictum that "There is not even a thought, or an invention, which is not common property, born of the past and the present" (Kropotkin [1906] 2011, 7). Therefore, he continues, buying a home in a city like Paris is to some extent to appropriate the labor of all those who have contributed to the cultural and architectural environment that makes an individual want to live in that place (Kropotkin [1906] 2011,6–7, [1927] 1970, 153, 212–213). It follows from this situation, Bolten argues, that almost everyone has a right to make use of social wealth and facilities, the sole exception being those who have contributed nothing to it. Unhappily, the present predicament is that the laziest, least productive people tend to be the ones with the best access, and thus those who enjoy lives of luxury:

> [S]on los que no han hecho nada, pero que, por una dolorosa arbitrariedad son los únicos que gozan de todas las comodidades y placeres de la vida y luego, para colmar la medida de la injusticia, se erigen en nuestros jueces, pretendiendo ser a nosotros superiores.
> BOLTEN 1905d

> [[They] are the only ones who enjoy all the comforts and pleasures of life and then, to complete the measure of injustice, they become our judges, pretending to be superior to us.]

Bolten continues this theme of a society divided by class in an article called "Las dos clases" (Bolten 1906) ["The Two Classes"], in which she emphasizes the psychological consequences of being one of the subjugated, someone who works excessively, but lacks enough to eat, someone who has a family, for whom poverty renders the experience a burden rather than an enjoyment. Once again, she emphasizes how different life is for those who benefit from the way society is organized, and whom she views as being responsible for the misery of the lower class:

La otra clase, los grandes, los que no trabajan y gozan de todos los placeres de la vida, amplia, intensa. Son los zánganos que han de rendir cuenta de todas las lágrimas vertidas, de toda la sangre derramada y de la desesperación que han provocado con su único y despótico proceder.
1906

[The other class, the great ones, those who do not work and enjoy all the expanded, intense pleasures of life. They are the drones that must account for all the tears shed, for all the blood spilled and the despair that they have caused with their distinctive and despotic behavior.]

On page 3 of issue #84 of *La Protesta Humana*, which was dated May 13, 1900, there is a series of notes about what is going on in the anarchist universe, and these records collectively bear the title, "Varias" ["Various"]. None of these items designate their writers, or indicate whether they have the same or different authors. However, Prieto, Fernández Cordero, and Muñoz (2013/2014) list "Varias" as one of Bolten's extant writings, including only the section that contains Virginia's name, although there is no indication in that edition of the paper that she wrote the segment. The piece in question relates happenings on May 1, 1900, in Rosario, where, following speeches that inspired some of the local anarchists, it was decided to go on a march, bearing a flag that proclaimed "¡Viva la Revolución Social!" (Bolten 1900c) ["Long live the Social Revolution!"] Reportedly, two hundred people were involved in this spontaneous demonstration, including Bolten and her partner Manrique, with supporters chanting "¡Viva la Anarquía!" (1900c) ["Long live anarchy!"] among other similar sentiments.

It is highly likely that Bolten wrote that section of "Varias," because of a letter titled "Comunicado" ["Announcement"] that appeared in issue 88 of *La Protesta Humana*, dated July 8 of the same year. That piece, which is also listed among the writings assembled by Prieto, Fernández Cordero, and Muñoz (2013/2014), was itself signed "Virginia Bolten, Rosario de Santa Fe, julio 1900" (Bolten 1900a) and in it she complained that her earlier account of the May 1 demonstration had been disputed in an issue of another Buenos Aires publication, *L'Avvenire*. In response, she suggested that anyone who doubted the accuracy of the information she had provided should consult the reports in the mainstream newspapers, Rosario's *La Capital* and Buenos Aires' *La Prensa*, which matched her own account (1900a).

In the River Plate area, there were several publications during Bolten's life that bore the title, *El Obrero*, and many more that had similar names. From 1890 to 1892, there was a Marxist *El Obrero* based in Buenos Aires, which featured editorials written by Germán Avé Lallemant. Also in that city in 1896, Alberto Ghiraldo edited another newspaper of the same name. Based in Rosario, *El Obrero Panadero*, which first appeared in 1895, was edited by a Communard from France, Artur Dupont, and later run by the baker, Francisco Berri, who would, like Bolten, be deported and move to Montevideo, in his case in 1903; in 1900, *El Obrero Panadero* changed its name to *El Obrero*. There was also a paper called *El Obrero en Calzado* [The Worker in Footwear], an organ of the Federación Obrera del Calzado, that operated in Montevideo from 1905 to 1906. In Paysandú, Uruguay, there was another *El Obrero*, which was in operation from 1898 to 1899. Other, similar titles were published in Montevideo during this period, including *Boletín Oficial del Círculo Católico de Obreros*, *El Amigo del Obrero*, *El Defensor del Obrero*, *El Obrero Sastre*, *El Obrero Zapatero*, *El Partido Obrero*, *El Trabajo*, *Federación de Trabajadores*, *La Lucha Obrera*, *La Voz del Empleado*, and *La Voz del Obrero*, In Salto, Uruguay, there was another *El Trabajo* and a paper called *Tribuna del Obrero*. Following her deportation in 1905, Bolten started writing articles for local radical publications that included a different *El Obrero*, this version based in Montevideo and edited by Alfonso Grijalbo, with which Berri would also become involved, a publication not surprisingly dedicated to criticizing the crackdown on anarchists in Argentina that had resulted in Bolten, her partner, Manrique, and Berri relocating to the city (Baer 2015, 63; Cawen 2017, 229; Dalmau i Ribalta 2016, 27; Prieto, Fernández Cordero, and Muñoz 2013/2014, 214; Suriano 1997, 447–448; Walter 1980, 7; Zubillaga and Balbis 1986, 98–112; Zubillaga and Tarcus 2020).

In a short piece called "¡Trabajadores!" (Bolten 1905f) ["Workers!"] that appeared in that *El Obrero* on May 20, 1905, Bolten advocates a new society that, once again, would value scientific knowledge rather than religion, which she dismisses as "un cuento pasado de moda" [an old-fashioned tale]. As in other articles that Virginia would write for this paper, she advocates here the use of violence to achieve political change, in particular anything that would improve the predicament of workers (Prieto, Fernández Cordero, and Muñoz 2013/2014, 215). Such is the anger in Bolten's writing at this point that Peterson (2015, 134) argues she would be unable to continue at such intensity for very long, and suggests that this may account for her soon becoming somewhat accommodating toward the ideas of Batllism. However, in "¡Trabajadores!" can be found only her characteristically anarchist style, as she advocates creation of a completely new type of society: "No olvidéis que el principio de la autoridad es una llaga social muy arraigada; buscad sus cimientos, cortad la base: no son los efectos los que hay que destruir, son las causas" (Bolten 1905f) [Do not forget that the principle of authority is a deeply rooted social wound; seek its foundations, cut the base: it is not the effects that must be destroyed, it is the causes].

In "Oíd, vosotros!" (Bolten 1909c) ["Hey, you!"], Virginia complains about the deportations from Argentina, where she points out that the intellectual atmosphere is being polluted as "se prohíbe el desembarco de hombres que se cree de ideas avanzadas" (1909c) [the landing of men believed to be of advanced ideas is prohibited], and she also dismisses voting as a means of achieving democracy, a skepticism shared by other anarchists such as Mikhail Bakunin, Luigi Galleani, Peter Kropotkin, Lucy Parsons, Lysander Spooner, Benjamin R. Tucker, and, after she changed her mind, by Lois Waisbrooker. Here, Virginia warns that the oppression she is seeing on the other side of the river will have the effect of making ordinary people become more willing to endorse violent revolution:

> La sangre de los inocentes, las lágrimas de la niñez desamparada, la desesperación de las madres, amantes y hermanas, formarán la montaña que os aplastará, destrozando el andamiaje levantado por vuestras leyes represivas.
> 1909c

> [The blood of the innocent, the tears of helpless childhood, the despair of mothers, lovers, and sisters, will form the mountain that will crush you, destroying the scaffolding erected by your repressive laws.]

She rejects the idea that what appears to be progress, the transformation of government from monarchy to a seemingly more democratic system, with a constitution that allows people to vote, will make any significant improvement to what is experienced by the masses:

> Todos los gobiernos, llámense como se quiera, cumplen su misión: la de imponerse. La república no es menos arbitraria que la monarquía cuando no se obra en consonancia con los deseos de los que mandan. Rusia, España y la Argentina son tres naciones diferentes en apariencias, iguales en el fondo: lo mismo se sostiene por la fuerza arrancada a los pueblos en su ignorancia.
> 1909c

> [All governments, whatever they call themselves, fulfill their mission: to impose themselves. The republic is no less arbitrary than the monarchy

when it does not act in accordance with the wishes of those who rule. Russia, Spain, and Argentina are three different nations in appearance, the same in the background: the same is sustained by force torn from the nation in their ignorance.]

Indeed, although modern political scientists tend to conceive of democracy excessively in terms of universal suffrage, anarchists have preferred to differ. When Luigi Galleani was living in Paterson, New Jersey, the Italian anarchist who was eventually deported from the United States served as the editor of *La Questione Sociale*. Galleani ([1925] 1982, 72) believed that to vote for a candidate was to give up the power that naturally belonged to the individual. Similarly, for Lysander Spooner, voting in the United States is little more than a symbolic reward for financing an oppressive government for which no one alive today has ever given consent (Shone 2010, 55–56, 68; Spooner [1867] 1971, 5–6). While Benjamin R. Tucker (1926, 83) warned that voting was one of the methods that government employs to control its citizens, Bolten dismisses "el sufragio una bonita farsa en que algunos ríen y otros comen, mientras la mayoría se encoge de hombros" (1909c) [the suffrage a pretty farce in which some laugh and others eat, while most shrug their shoulders]. Fortunately, she argues, though they may lack many other opportunities, those most exploited in society, the "[p]roletarios del universo" (1909c) [proletarians of the universe] as a group do possess the ability to bring governments of any type to a standstill. Here, she is endorsing the classic anarchist responses of the general strike and rebellion.

In 1905, anarchists in Buenos Aires (and some from Montevideo who had been deported from Argentina) were irate about goings-on in Russia, particularly the Bloody Sunday massacre in St. Petersburg, and other killing and suppression of radicals. On both sides of the River Plate, anarchists gathered, with "the Uruguayan anarchist Virginia Bolten" (Moya 2004, 26, 2008, 62) contributing to the condemnations. Street demonstrations in Buenos Aires and Montevideo at the end of January and the beginning of February 1905 made the Argentinian government nervous, and they proclaimed a State of Siege, banning outdoor protests, arresting and deporting anarchists (Bolten 1905c; Moya 2004, 26–27, 2008, 62).

In an article in *El Obrero* titled "La mazorca" (Bolten 1905c) ["The Spike"], Bolten compares the Argentine government and its violence to that of the Czar in Russia, pointing out that the behavior of "Rusia Argentina" (Bolten 1905c; Moya 2004, 26) was not a new experience for anarchists and other advocates of liberation; in another piece in *El Obrero* she used the title, "En la rusia Americana" (Bolten 1905b) ["In American Russia"] to refer to Argentina. No, they had not forgotten past injustices: the example of Montjuich Prison in

Barcelona, where Francisco Ferrer was executed by the Spanish Government and the Catholic Church, had been committed forever to their memory:

> Las persecuciones no nos hacen temblar ni retroceder, hoy más que ayer, estamos aquí en la brecha, decididos más que nunca a conquistar nuestros derechos pese a quien pese y cueste lo que cueste.
> BOLTEN 1905c

> [The persecutions do not make us tremble or retreat; today more than yesterday, we are here in the rupture, determined more than ever to conquer our rights regardless of whomever or whatever it may cost.]

Far from being cowed by persecution, Bolten argues that it will be considered a challenge: "El mayor abono en el campo de los principios de emancipación, es la sangre de los mártires y las lágrimas de la niñez." (1905c) [The greatest fertilizer in the field of emancipation principles is the blood of martyrs and the tears of childhood.]

Bolten's commitment to fundamental change is one of the ways in which she resembles the Communard, Louise Michel, and helps explain the application to her of the name "la Luisa Michel rosarina." As was noted earlier, the March 18, 2010 issue of *La Nueva Senda* was dedicated to commemoration of the Paris Commune, and in one of the articles there, titled "Enseñanzas del pasado" ["Lessons from the Past"], Bolten, this time identified as Virginia Boltén (1910a), emphasizes the French insurrection's significance, arguing as many others have done in favor of being aware of one's history in order to be able to learn from mistakes that were made in the past. However, evoking the significance of historical awareness should not be seen as Virginia wanting to glorify past events for their own sake, but only to be able to avoid repeating the miscalculations that may have undermined previous efforts to attain greater liberty:

> La Comuna de París es un movimiento histórico que los revolucionarios recuerdan no para imitarla, sino, para superarla, no para caer de rodillas por sus actos, actitudes o determinaciones, sino, para tener en cuenta en sus luchas diarias el valor del pasado ante el porvenir.
> BOLTEN 1910a

> [The Paris Commune is an historical movement that revolutionaries remember not to imitate, but to overcome, not to fall to their knees

because of their actions, attitudes or determinations, but, to take into account in their daily struggles the value of the past over the future.]

She warns that even the Communards were willing to settle for a rebellion that failed to challenge many of the institutions of the previous regime:

> Ayer la Comuna colosal, poderosa labró su muerte por sostener la propiedad, el estado y el principio de autoridad, mañana sabrá hacer un auto de fe, quemando todo lo que represente desigualdad económica y social.
> BOLTEN 1910a

> [Yesterday the colossal, powerful Commune carved out its death by upholding property, the state, and the principle of authority, tomorrow it will know how to make an auto-da-fe, burning everything that represents inequality, economic and social.]

Here, once again, an immoderate commitment to the most violent of revolutions, at least in so far as impelled by her rhetoric, is the characteristic standing out most notably from Bolten's analysis.

In a piece published a few years earlier in *El Obrero* on June 3, 1905, called "A los obreros en huelga" (1905a) ["To the Workers on Strike"], Virginia addresses the tactics that she believes should be used by employees engaged in attempts to improve the conditions under which they toil. She advocates workers threatening to strike and if necessary, actually walking out of their jobs to accomplish industrial reform, which is a characteristic anarchist strategy. The employment in question, Bolten describes in terms of exploitation, identifying the denial of rights, slavery, chains, sacrifice, humiliation, and being despised and discontented or despairing, and the only solution she sees is rebellion, whatever the cost, avoiding settling for minor improvement, even if this means accepting death:

> [P]ero no olvides que sólo el [camino] de la rebelión te dará el triunfo. Todas las libertades o mejoramientos, por insignificantes que fueron han costado sacrificios, perseverancias y virilidad.
> BOLTEN 1905a

> [But do not forget that only that [path] of rebellion will give you the triumph. All the freedoms or improvements, however insignificant they were, have cost sacrifices, perseverance, and virility.]

Again, the argument is couched in terms of violence: "¡O vencer o morir! el que se acobarda muere; el que se impone, haciendo uso de su fuerza, ha triunfado!" (1905a) [Either win or die! He who cowers dies; the one who prevails, making use of his force, has triumphed!]

In the twenty-first century, the idea of "Virginia Bolten" is an attractive subject for South American scholars and graduate students and many others, and given the extent to which her actual uncompromising rhetoric as expressed here in "A los obreros en huelga" is celebrated, rather than the more widely surmised but allegorical reputation, which, as discussed earlier in this chapter, combines truths, untruths, and many doubtful claims about her life, there seems to be a potential problem for contemporary anarchists. That is so particularly for those who have sought to emphasize the actual characteristics of anarchist thought, and resist the denigrating caricature acquired from its mainstream opponents that its advocates are merely crazy bombers and angry assassins who wish to achieve absolutely no government at all, rather than what anarchists often are, purveyors of extensive intellectual content who deserve to be read and listened to again. To the degree that Bolten is essentially, rather than just symbolically, advocating violence and maybe wanting as much brutality as possible, in service of her sometimes rather understated political goals, it becomes necessary to consider the extent to which her inclusion in the canon (albeit, of course, that anarchism by its very diverse and contradictory nature could never really constitute a canon) will scare away others of potentially similar views who would never commit to bloodshed in anything like the magnitude in which they value liberty. Ironically, in "Preguntas y respuestas" (Bolten 1900b), Virginia, too, had attempted to explain to the uninitiated and to those opposed to what they misunderstood as being anarchism what the word really meant.

A significant idea to be found in Bolten's writings is that what passes for society is fundamentally flawed and out-of-date, and in dire need of being overthrown. Unfortunately, she comments in her article, "Una Idea" (Bolten 1905g) ["An Idea"], which appeared in *El Obrero* in 1905, although it is possible to understand the true situation, most people do not really analyze the reasons for their discomfort, thus making it difficult to progress. Consequently, to achieve change, it will be necessary to educate the great, passive, ignorant masses about the reasons why their lives are so unsatisfactory. Without such remediation, society will be unable to visualize the need for necessary changes due to the widespread "falta de desarrollo cerebral, el que por desgracia tiene toda la actitud de una epidemia, efecto natural causado por la indolencia que hace delegar nuestros deberes esperando que otros piensen por uno, y el gran respeto que se inculca al pueblo a todo lo viejo" (Bolten 1905g) [lack of brain development, which unfortunately has all the posture of an epidemic, a natural effect caused by indolence that makes us delegate our duties hoping that others will think for us, and the great deference for everything old that is instilled in the people.] Meanwhile, government operates as though it is the culmination of a well-run society that caters to the will of its citizenry, when actually people struggle amidst "toda la expoliación y latrocinio de un estado social absurdo y equivocado, que no tienen razón de ser como entidad social" (Bolten 1905g) [all the plundering and robbery of an absurd and mistaken social state, which has no reason for existing as a social entity.] Consequently, she writes:

> Nuestro deber es decir al pueblo: Tú tienes derecho a la vida amplia, a la verdadera vida, imponente a esa máquina que te quita fuerzas; el amor que te degenera te regenerará; pero, para esta saludable transformación solo es preciso que pienses, que estudies, que ames inmensamente y que aborrezcas con toda la fuerza de tu amor. Cuando hayas hecho esto, sigue tu conciencia, obra en justicia, proclama tus derechos, se libre y emancipado y habrás dejado de ser niño pueblo, serás hombre!
> BOLTEN 1905g

> [Our duty is to say to the people: You have the right to a wide life, to true life, imposing on that machinery that takes away your strength; the love that degenerates you will regenerate you; but, for this healthy transformation [it] is only necessary that you think, that you study, that you love immensely, and that you hate with all the force of your love. When you have done this, follow your conscience, act in justice, proclaim your rights, be free and emancipated and you will have stopped being a child people, you will be a man!]

Starting in the second half of the nineteenth century, the idea of "the social question" occupied the thoughts of many contemporary thinkers who were not anarchists, including Benjamin Disraeli, Henry James, John Stuart Mill, and William Morris, who, notwithstanding the inability of many ordinary people to rectify or even analyze their own lives, recognized a pressing need to improve society as a whole and reallocate its resources in a way that would prevent an upcoming disaster as what were perceived as dangerous radical challenges became apparent in a world that was rapidly changing (Howerth 1906). In *The Princess Casamassima* ([1886] 1980), Henry James juxtaposes the painful and wasted lives led by ordinary people as a result of the failure to address "the social question," but rejects the violent response endorsed by anarchist characters Hyacinth Robinson, Paul Muniment, and Princess Casamassima as being cruel and inappropriate. Inability to overcome one's disadvantage is expressed through the character of Rosy Muniment, who is introduced to the reader as "a narrow bed in a corner and a small object stretched upon it" (James [1886] 1980, 85). She is a person who cannot walk, who spends her life lying on a bed in a room she never leaves. Her brother, Paul, takes care of her needs, but society, at present, does not care to do this. Paul introduces Rosy to Hyacinth, the male anti-hero, saying, "You mustn't mind her being in bed – she's always in bed" (85). As things were, she had no meaningful future. It can be argued that, in the twenty-first century, despite piecemeal improvements staggered across the developed world, the "social question" remains largely unrectified as the masses struggle with poverty, living unnecessarily wasted lives; the predominant unfairness that troubled anarchists and non-anarchists alike essentially remains.

In a different way, being one of those who threatened the rival solution, Errico Malatesta, who gave his newspaper the title of *La Question Sociale*, attempted to find the best way, from a rather different perspective, to bring about societal transformation. As Turcato (2014) notes, "For ... Malatesta, socialism meant the discovery of the "social question": formal equality and freedom were a mockery in the presence of material inequality and submission to capitalists." For another anarchist, Alexander Berkman, it is also clear that the lack of social improvement rests on the failure of the majority to perceive the connection between their own conditions and the need for revolution:

> It is a Herculean task to rouse Apathy to the sordidness of its misery. Yet if the People would but realize the depths of their degradation and be informed of the means of deliverance, how joyously they would embrace Anarchy! Quick and decisive would be the victory of the workers against the handful of their despoilers. An hour of sanity, freed from prejudice and superstition, and the torch of liberty would flame 'round the world, and the banner of equality and brotherhood be planted upon the hills of a regenerated humanity. Ah, if the world would but pause for one short while, and understand, and become free!
> BERKMAN [1912] 1970, 225–226

In Australia in the 1890s, the labor union activist Rose Summerfield (1892, 10; Shone 2022, ch. 1), who eventually relocated to a commune in Paraguay, emphasized in speeches her commitment to a new labor unionism that would educate the masses and achieve a transformation such as the one described above by Bolten.

Virginia Bolten addresses the problem also in "Los gobiernos y la cuestión social" (1905h) ["Governments and the Social Question"], where she argues that, by its very nature, government is unable to facilitate substantial social change, and thus the problems attendant upon the social question can never be alleviated from the top downward. This reality applies, she continues, even if someone in power wishes to permanently improve the conditions experienced by working people, because that person is perforce bound, due to the fact of his or her authority, to undermine even desired change:

> Donde quiera que exista un mandatario hay gobernados, por lo que pone de relieve la antítesis de libertad, desde que hay quien mande es preciso obedecer y esto implica la abdicación de la personalidad, por lo tanto, la no libertad.
> 1905h

> [Wherever there is a president, there are governed, so it highlights the antithesis of freedom; since there is someone who commands, it is necessary to obey, and this implies the abdication of the personality, therefore, non-freedom.]

While it might be considered an improvement, as modern thinkers recommend, to have a constitution, particularly from the perspective of more affluent citizens, and especially if people in the government follow its prescriptions, the reality is that the business world is always to a significant extent able to influence public policy, and it does this by advancing its own private interests, which require it exploit the poor in order to remain profitable, even as the middle class cheers the supposed development of democracy. Moreover, she continues, once those private interests are threatened, the freedoms enjoyed at present by the majority are bound to be pushed back (1905h):

> Es pues urgente, hoy más que nunca en esta capital, recordar al obrero que lucha para que no se considere favorecido por los que, tal vez muy pronto y en defensa de sus intereses, siempre contrarios a los de las masas extreman ciertas medidas de represión, más o menos disimuladas, por lo cual es preciso que nos encuentren en nuestros puestos, sin confiar en palabras y hechos insignificantes.
> 1905h

> [It is therefore urgent, today more than ever in this capital, to remind the worker who fights so that he does not consider himself favored by those

who, perhaps very soon and in defense of their interests, always opposed to those of the masses, exert certain measures of repression, more or less disguised, for which it is necessary that they find us at our posts, not taking for granted insignificant words and deeds.]

As Vidal (2012, 79) points out, while Bolten and other anarchists welcomed the relative freedom of Montevideo where they could express their ideas without being arrested and were sympathetic to Batlle's plans to reform Uruguay's labor laws, they were unsure whether such relative progress would continue and thus they were often reluctant to offer their support. That specific local predicament appears to be the context within which Bolten's more universal, philosophical argument in "Los gobiernos y la cuestión social" is couched.

"Los gobiernos y la cuestión social" may also reflect the influence of Malatesta. In a pamphlet titled "Programma e Organizzazione della Associazione Internazionale dei Lavoratori," some of the editorial staff of *La Question Sociale*, including Malatesta, during the time the publication was located in Italy, had made a similar argument:

> Affirming that the emancipation of the workers must be the workers' own doing, the International showed that it understood that no ruling class has ever surrendered its privileges, no matter how much a proper understanding of its own interests might prompt it to do so – it never develops any such understanding by itself – and foresaw all the revolutionary needs that complicate resolution of the social question.
> "Program and Organization of the International
> Working Men's Association" [1884] 2014

When her freedom did in fact lessen in Uruguay, during the less tolerant, more mainstream government of Claudio Williman from 1907 to 1911, and the party newspaper, *El Día*, became more critical of labor unions and radical policies, Bolten also increased her negative tone (Vidal 2012, 85). In an article called "Alerta!" (1908a) ["Alert!"] she criticizes the change of policy which has now led to some persecution of militants. Within the space of three years, from 1905 to 1908, *El Día* has followed a similar trajectory, changing from "liberal acérrimo" (1908a) [staunch liberal] to "reaccionario intransigente" (1908a) [uncompromising reactionary], though to some extent doing it in a deceptive way, "intercalando de cuando en cuando algún artículo imparcial para no perder la venta y la popularidad, mientras sostiene por otro lado la legalidad de lo ilegal" (1908a) [inserting from time to time an impartial article so as not to lose the sale and the popularity, while on the other hand sustaining the legality of the illegal]. Now, without passage of labor reform, dissidents are prosecuted, and anarchists are denied entry into Uruguay.

In an issue of *El Surco*, dated August 10, 1909, an author identified only as "Otta" lamented the execution of Francisco Ferrer (an event which would actually not occur until two months later, on October, 13, 1909), commenting that, while there was "[u]n foco apagado" [a light had been turned off], the authorities would nonetheless be unable to prevent others from continuing to shine (Otta 1909, 4). In the following number, the mistake was corrected ("Francisco Ferrer" 1909, 3). Juana Rouco Buela's Spanish background and the fact that some of the other anarchists in Montevideo had also come from Spain meant that there was substantial familiarity with the work of Ferrer, and many viewed the Catalán educator as an intellectual guide. On October 17, 1909, Bolten and Rouco Buela spoke at a demonstration to publicize his murder, an event then followed by a confrontation outside the Spanish embassy that would lead to Buela being accused of rioting, as a result of which she was forced to withdraw from the day-to-day administration of *La Nueva Senda*. The atheist poet, Ángel Falco y Leoncio Lasso de la Vega, who worked at the CIES, described in verse the escape of Juana Rouco Buela from the demonstration, dressed as a man to avoid arrest (Calzetta 2014, 18; Fernández 2010, 40–41; Martins and De Souza 2018, 237; Rama 1968–1969, 31; Rago 1997, 285; Rosenthal 1995, 334; Vidal 2014, 14–15).

A month later, in an article in *La Nueva Senda* titled "Nuestras agitaciones" (Bolten 1909b) ["Our Agitations"], a signed editorial that is not included in the Prieto, Cordero, and Muñoz 2013/2014 listing of Bolten's writings, Virginia writes about the Ferrer rally in Montevideo, saying that it was no longer possible to remain silent about the matter (1909b). Although the protesters were known to include persons from different ideological backgrounds, she notes that "únicamente á varios anarquistas militantes" (1909b) [only several militant anarchists] were arrested. Similarly, she points out that even though, when she had addressed the crowd, Buela's comments had been no more radical and had expressed no more advocacy of violence than the contributions of others, Juana had been the one targeted for imprisonment (1909b).

In "¿Quiénes son?" ["Who are They?"], Bolten (1905e) addresses the changes in people's perceptions that must develop for a revolution to be successful. In a Marxian sense, perhaps she is addressing the "false consciousness" that prevents the victims of society from understanding their own predicament and which, as suggested above, is a factor that exacerbates the difficulties involved in trying to solve the "social question." People work hard, produce goods and services, and generate wealth, yet maybe they themselves lack enough food to eat, and may be reduced to begging for assistance to survive. Enlightenment takes place when they finally see "que su adorada patria los había convertido en carne de cañón, desconociendo la personalidad y el poder que representan; que su patrón solo ha sido explotador que disfruta con el dinero amasado con su sudor y su sangre" (1905e) [that their beloved homeland had turned them into cannon fodder, ignoring the personality and power they represent; that their employer has only been an exploiter who enjoys the money amassed with sweat and blood.] In this article, "[l]os humildes de ayer, los rebeldes de hoy" (1905e) [the humble of yesterday, the rebels of today] discover also that religion is a form of false consciousness, one that turns its faithful away from finding solutions to their exploitation. Instead, Virginia maintains, they should seek "en la ciencia lo que no puede dar les la religión, en la humanidad lo que le ha negado la patria" (1905e) [in science what religion cannot give them, in humanity what the country has denied].

This theme is continued in a later article, "Para los niños" (1911) ["For the Children"], where Bolten, here identified by her initials, views the lessening of a child's pain by charitably glossing over the negative aspects and mischaracterizing its causes as being a form of false consciousness, instead arguing that it is better for a child to have its family's poverty acknowledged and as a result to suffer unhappiness. The reality, she writes, is that such children lack not only toys but also the attention of loving adults, which is due to the economic realities that oblige poor parents to struggle on at a deficient level; not telling the truth about this is to compound the problem, compromising the dignity of poor offspring (1911).

In her brief article, "¿Justicia?" (1909a) ["Justice?"], Virginia discusses the nature of law and justice, mentioning both Diogenes and Themis. Diogenes was the Cynic philosopher who, rejecting the accoutrements of luxury, lived in a bathtub and wore a torn cloak, and is believed to have walked around ancient Athens with a dog, carrying a lantern that he kept alight in the daytime. Just as the historical Diogenes claimed that the significance of his lamp was that he was looking for an honest man (although he never found one), Bolten's Diogenes rejects two versions of the flawed law of the state. The first of these is the self-serving law of men and women she sees in Argentina and Uruguay, where those who enforce the rules as laid down in lawbooks can adopt the role of executioners:

> No; no es un libro donde encontraré lo que busco ... un libro no puede estar siempre fielmente interpretado, además ... ya no sirve para hoy, puesto que ha sido formulado para ayer, yo busco la justicia eterna, siempre la misma, sin artículos ni jueces.
> 1909a

[No; It is not a book where I will find what I am looking for ... a book cannot always be faithfully interpreted; furthermore ... it is no longer useful for today, since it has been formulated for yesterday, I seek eternal justice, always the same, without articles or judges.]

Bolten's Diogenes also discards law that favors the rich, enabling a corrupt legislator to kill his unfaithful mistress and get away with it, rationalizing her death in the light of her dishonesty; Virginia favors instead the universal law, "[l]a verdadera justicia" (1909a) [true justice], that is symbolized by Themis, the ancient goddess of justice, the bearer of a bronze sword, after whom she would name one of her daughters, Themis Manrique Bolten:

> Extraña es en verdad tu justicia, que da derechos de vida o muerte de unos sobre otros; es cierto que, es delito la mentira y la falsedad, pero, ¿se evita con un crimen? Yo busco a Themis sin espada que puede caer sobre un inocente; sin balanza, que puede inclinarse al peso del oro; busco la única capaz de evitar el mal, pero que no castiga, la que no permite que los "señores" compren sus queridas, con el dinero robado a sus hermanos para luego matarlas porque ... pagan.
> 1909a

[Strange indeed is your justice, which gives rights of life or death to some over others; it is true that lying and falsehood are a crime, but is it avoided with a crime? I seek Themis without a sword that can fall on an innocent; without scales, which can incline to the weight of gold; I look for the only one capable of avoiding evil, but that does not punish, the one that does not allow the "gentlemen" to buy their mistresses, with the money stolen from their brothers and then kill them because ... it pays.]

Bolten's reference to Diogenes exemplifies her role as a dissident pessimist, determined to achieve the most significant improvements to a society corrupted by wealth: one that, though it is governed by what appears to be law and reason and justice, actually ignores the plight of the large majority of ordinary people, those who are condemned to be exploited and labor for inadequate rewards in a place where it is difficult even to complain without being victimized by those who have power. It is clear from the writings now known to be her work that she is a consistent anarchist whose ideas fit together well with the prognoses of others who have penned or spoken or acted under that attribution. Consequently, those who admire or sympathize with an anarcho/a-feminist perspective have identified Virginia Bolten appropriately as a champion of their own values, and she is entitled to continue to receive their endorsement.

CHAPTER 2

Helen Armstrong: Champion of Labor, Women, and the Poor

The Winnipeg General Strike of 1919, an effort by labor unions to achieve collective bargaining that received significant support from workers' organizations in other provinces, lasted for only six weeks, ending in a crushing defeat as elements of the city power structure, together with members of the dominion government conspired to overcome it, while much of the press of the time caricatured the work stoppage as a Bolshevik conspiracy. Today, the strike is routinely described as being a major event in Canadian history. However, there continues to be debate about the motives of its leaders, and about who those leaders were, since earlier accounts tended to ignore the role of women such as Helen Armstrong, the wife of George Armstrong, one of the strikers imprisoned for his involvement, about whom Francis (2010, 228) says, "But his wife Helen had played a more central role in the General Strike than he did."

Amidst a rate of inflation higher than that at which wages were increasing, the first element of the confrontation was a walkout on May 1 1919 by building trade workers seeking union recognition, followed by a similar move on May 2 by the metal trades employees. On May 6, Winnipeg's Trades and Labor Council, an organization that had been set up in 1894 to weave together, educate, and provide protection for labor unions, asked its membership to vote on a sympathetic strike action. As a result, 24,000 workers, including city, post office, and retail employees, went on strike beginning on May 15. Soon, they were joined by telegraph and telephone workers, making communication difficult (Berzish 2010; Francis 2010, 185; Greening 1965, 77–78; Isitt 2003, 54; MacKinnon 1977, 626–627; Smith 1994b, 6–7; "Winnipeg Strike Collapse: Causes of Men's Defeat" 1919, "Winnipeg Strike Spreads Further" 1919).

When provincial and city leaders ordered workers to go back to their jobs, many refused to abandon the cause. Consequently, on May 26, postal employees and telephone operators were fired; many of them would never be rehired. Municipal workers were ordered on pain of dismissal by Mayor Charles Frederick Gray, to sign an "anti-sympathy strike" pledge which caused many, including those in the treasurer's office, the light and power department, firefighters, and street sweepers, to return to work ("All Postal Workers in West Ordered to Strike" 1919; "Civic Employees Returning to Work Repudiating Sympathetic Strike" 1919).

City police officers, who had themselves voted to participate in the stoppage, but agreed with the Strike Committee that they should stay at work, were required to sign an undertaking that would have limited their own capacity to be unionized or go on strike, a threat that most of them rejected, causing most officers to be fired, on June 9. With the assistance of the Citizens' Committee of One Thousand, a recently set-up local anti-union organization dominated by business owners and attorneys, they were replaced by about 250 "special police," some of whom had political views vastly different to those who had withdrawn their labor, and, indeed, to the officers who had now been fired; many of them again became unable to return to their positions (Berzish 2010; Lewycky 2019, 7; McCallum 1998, 39; "Most Orderly Strike on Record" 1919; "Strike Parade in Defiance of the Mayor's Proclamation is Abruptly Discontinued" 1919; "Threats of Terrorism" 1919). On June 10, when the special constables began to take control, there was immediately a confrontation between them, and a group of strikers and the ensuing argument led to some violence ("Winnipeg Strike Flames Anew" 1919). On June 11, the headline on page one of the *Western Labor News*, the publication of the strikers, greeted the engagement of the specials with the words "Police Replaced by Thugs" ("Police Replaced by Thugs" 1919).

By the end of May, newspapers were reporting that the metal trades workers had accepted an offer by the rail employees' union to mediate the issue of collective bargaining. On May 24, strike and Trades and Labor Council representatives met with the Citizens' Committee of One Thousand and talked terms for ending the dispute. In a letter dated May 27, the Manitoba premier, Tobias Norris, encouraged the companies who employed them, the Vulcan Iron Works, the Manitoba Bridge and Iron Works, and the Dominion Bridge Company, to take the opportunity, and they agreed to participate. On June 16, these employers proposed somewhat conciliatory terms to their employees, though not a complete form of collective bargaining, and without giving recognition to the Metal Trades Council, but in so doing averted the likelihood that the strike would be joined by railroad workers ("Canadian Labor War Spreading Over Entire Country" 1919; Dupuis 2014, 79; Francis 2010, 208; Masters 1950, 100–101; "Metal Trade Employers are Ready for Mediation" 1919; "Night Meeting Fails to Settle Winnipeg Strike" 1919; "Winnipeg Strike Over" 1919).

Unfortunately, as more reasonable interpreters of the disagreement focused on the actual issues and the overtures proceeded toward agreement, exaggerated reports that what was happening constituted Bolshevism prompted the dominion government to dispatch acting minister of justice, Arthur Meighen, and minister of labor, Gideon Robertson, to Winnipeg. In a speech at the beginning of June, Robertson identified "the plan of One Big Union promoters to destroy labor organizations ... socialism has chosen the One Big Union as its path toward world domination" ("Says O.B.U. Men Try to Destroy Organized Labor" 1919). In discussing the One Big Union (OBU), he referred to ongoing plans being proposed in Canada, and also in other countries, including Australia, New Zealand, the US, and the UK, to develop a single, massive union that would represent all industrial workers. Robertson nursed an inherent conflict of interest about that because although he was also a labor unionist, he was committed to the philosophy of the traditional "international" craft-based approaches, advocates of which felt threatened by arguments in favor of implementing the OBU. In telegrams, Robertson emphasized the interconnections between the strike leaders, supporters of OBU, and, ostensibly, the Industrial Workers of the World (IWW), claiming that these factions intended to take over the economy and government of Winnipeg, and he called on the prime minister, Sir Robert Borden, to arrest the leaders of the strike (Botelho-Urbanski 2019; Devine 2009, 30; Dupuis 2014, 79; Francis 2010, 208; Johnson 1919, 656; "Strike Heads Sought to Control Civic, Provincial and Federal Ships" 1919).

The General Strike Committee rejected the metal trades employers' current offer, and an article in the *Western Labor News* dated June 17, warned:

> The right of collective bargaining, recognition of the Metal Trades' council and the Building Trades' council, and the reinstatement of all strikers must be conceded before the strike can be settled.
> "On Getting Together" 1919

Early that same day, June 17, Robertson's plan was put into effect, with police searching the offices of various labor organizations, including the Labor Temple, the Ukrainian Temple, which served immigrants in the North End of the city, and the *Western Labor News*. They went to the leaders' homes, where they broke down doors and emptied cabinets onto the floor, arresting a number of people, including George Armstrong, Roger E. Bray, Abraham A. Heaps, Rev. William Ivens, John Queen, and R.B. "Bob" Russell, who were taken to the Stony Mountain Penitentiary, an atypical destination for those merely accused of a crime, but the warden, W.R. Graham, was told that the decision had been made by Robertson and A.J. Andrews, K.C., who would be the prosecutor in the subsequent trials. Additionally, Richard J. "Dick" Johns was arrested in Montréal. Meighen doubted the arrests were justifiable as a response to union agitation, but Andrews gave the impression to him that they had been conducted pursuant to immigration violations ("Ask Release of Winnipeg Strike Men" 1920; Bercuson 1971, 164–165; Francis 2010, 208–209; Greening 1965, 79; Kramer and Mitchell 2010, 165, 178; Masters 1950, 102; Mitchell and Naylor 1998, 209–210; Szach 2009; "Who is Responsible for the Outrage?" 1919).

Three days later, George Armstrong, Bray, Heaps, Ivens, Queen, and Russell were released on bond, having agreed to play no further part in the strike. News of the arrests had spread quickly, and the Toronto area Trades and Labor Council issued a resolution calling not only for those arrested to be let out of jail, but for Robertson to be fired. Other arrestees remained imprisoned, and additional strike participants would later be tried, or attempts would be made to deport them, any legal authorization for which the Toronto resolution argued should be reversed ("Ask Immediate Resignation of Labor Minister" 1919; "Captives Released" 1919; Francis 2010, 208–209; "Who is Responsible for the Outrage?" 1919).

A parade by the Winnipeg strikers that took place on June 21 turned violent as police were stationed on the streets and some of the demonstrators took offense at a streetcar driver believed to be opposed to the labor unions, blocking the vehicle's movement and then overturning it, smashing its windows and setting fire to its seats. Mayor Gray declared the gathering over, some protestors threw bricks and rocks, and police, who included specials and, on horseback, the Royal Northwest Mounted Police (RNWMP), attempted to end the march with their clubs and eventually by firing their guns. Two participants, Steve Szczerbanowicz and Mike Sokolowski, would die from bullet wounds attained from the police barrage, and perhaps as many as a hundred others would be wounded in what became known as "Bloody Saturday." Almost as many of those present were arrested (Bercuson 1971, 171–174; Botelho-Urbanski 2019; Gutkin and Gutkin 1997, 243–244; "Krwawe zajścia uliczne: Wojsko strzela do tłumów" 1919; "L'Émeute à Winnipeg" 1919; Lewycky 2019, 11–12; 38–39, 44–45; "Mike Sokolowski Innocent" 1919; Mortin 1979; "Winnipeg Rioters are Shot by Police" 1919).

As Mitchell (1996, 135–136, 137, 146, 148, 149, 2004, 10–11, 14, 2019, 73) notes, skepticism about the appropriateness of the arrests and planned prosecutions was expressed by some of those in government, and neither the province nor the dominion authorities agreed to accept responsibility for holding trials, so when a preliminary hearing was held, it was driven by prominent attorneys such as Andrews, Isaac Pitblado, Travers Sweatman, and J.C. Coyne, people who were also leaders of the Committee of One Thousand, although funding of the subsequent prosecutions would be provided by the Canadian people via the War Appropriation Act to the tune of $196,000. Mitchell writes:

> The Department of Justice also paid $12,832.09 to the Winnipeg based McDonald Detective Agency for work associated with the prosecution. This federal largesse allowed Andrews to secure two juries almost certainly tainted by pre-trial investigations ordered by Andrews through

>   the McDonald detective agency for work contracted by the Committee
>   during the strike.
>   MITCHELL 2004, 14

Indeed, the attorneys in question, in addition to serving their political goals, benefited from various fees accrued from participating in the trial process. Pitblado, for instance, was estimated to have received $26,990 ("Liberal Members Contest Budget in Wednesday Debate" 1921; Mitchell 2004, 24).

1 The Trials

The first court trial, which took place in November 1919, concerned Bob Russell, who, although opposed to the strike, had participated in a conference of Western Canada unionists that took place in Calgary earlier in the year (a meeting that will be discussed later in the chapter). A tremendous amount of radical materials was assembled because part of the prosecutor, Andrews' plan was to use it as evidence for the claim that the strikers were involved in illegal activity. For example, it was found that Russell possessed and had read a copy of Marx and Engels' *Communist Manifesto*. Seven counts, including one of seditious conspiracy, were heard by the jury. Andrews also read out reports from Winnipeg area newspapers, many of which presented the actions of the strike leaders in a negative way. A man in the audience was removed from the courtroom for booing Andrews' evidence and cheering the remarks of Russell's counsel, Robert Cassidy, K.C. ("Dramatic Incident at Trial of Russell" 1919; Greening 1965, 80–81; Knowles 2019; MacKinnon 1977, 629; "Project Early End of Winnipeg Strike" 1919; "Russell is Witness in Own Behalf" 1919; "The Winnipeg Strike Trial: Evidence of Eleven Witnesses Heard" 1919; "Winnipeg Strike Head Found Guilty by Jury" 1919).

The judge in the case, Justice J.T. Metcalfe, barred Cassidy from making two arguments key to Russell's defense: that the purpose of the strike was to establish collective bargaining, and that the strikers, including Russell, had wanted to bring an end to the work stoppage. Without this evidence, the trial seemed to be, and continues to look today to have been less than fair, and it resulted in conviction on all seven charges, for which Metcalf awarded a sentence of two years' imprisonment, about half of which Bob would serve (Mitchell 1996, 159; Walker 2004, 91; "Winnipeg Strike Leader Released" 1920; "Winnipeg Strike Leader Sentenced" 1919).

The convictions were then appealed to the Manitoba Court of Appeal on the basis of the admissibility of the various radical documents that had been seized. Both the ones that were in Russell's possession and those found to be owned by other strike leaders were ruled by the Chief Justice of Manitoba, William Egerton Perdue, to have been used appropriately, a standard that tended to make conviction more likely and to confirm Andrews' repeated arguments in the original trial that there had been a "conspiracy," activity which the Court of Appeal felt fell beyond the protective legal boundaries granted to regular labor union activity (Cahill 1996, 302–303; Fudge and Tucker 2010, 347–348; Lefeaux 1921, 8; MacKinnon 1977, 629–630).

Russell's final chance to overturn his convictions took the form of a Petition for Leave to Appeal, which was submitted to the Judicial Committee of the Privy Council, in London. However, that body, citing the fact that there had been a jury trial and that the appeal had been heard by the Manitoba Court of Appeal, did not see the issues that were raised as warranting its own interference in the province's legal rulings. Lawyers for the Canadian government had paid A.J. Andrews $2,500 to prepare materials that would bring that result to fruition ("Favor Second Winnipeg Strike" 1920; Lefeaux 1921, 8–10; Mitchell 2004, 43).

The second trial, *R. v. William Ivens, et al.* (also known as *R. v. the Winnipeg 7*), took place from January 22 to April 7, 1920, a long process partly because four of the strikers (Heaps, Ivens, W.A. "Bill" Pritchard, who had been arrested in Calgary, and Queen) chose to defend themselves, unlike George Armstrong, Bray, and Johns, who relied on legal help. Unsurprisingly, the foci of their arguments were the right to free speech and the outlandishness of the way thousands of books, papers, and letters had been amassed, many of them having no association with the persons on trial, about one thousand of the documents being selected to make the claim the accused were guilty of subversion. That process led to some repetition of the political arguments that had been heard in the Winnipeg area over the previous few years. The prosecution was again spearheaded by Andrews, who presented a picture of a systematically organized plot stretching across meetings in Winnipeg at the Walker and Majestic Theatres, followed by the Western Labor Conference in Calgary (events that are discussed later in the chapter). With the advantage of hindsight and knowledge of actual details, including those released by the Winnipeg Strike Defense Committee, Andrews' analysis seems to obscure the real, much more haphazard, process of presenting arguments and voting on motions that is common in labor union types of assemblies. The most serious charge was again one of seditious conspiracy, and much attention was given to the nature of any "revolution" that had been promoted (Greening 1965, 82; Kramer and Mitchell 2010, 243; Lefeaux 1921, 4; MacKinnon 1977, 630; Masters 1950, 120). Moreover, Andrews' approach was disingenuous and calculated to be unfair to the strikers. If there was a conspiracy at the time, his own activities, and those of Isaac Pitblado and other attorneys who worked with him, and of their vehicle, the Committee of One Thousand, are more suitably identified as a plot, one designed to undermine the customary democratic processes to which Canadians are entitled.

Pritchard, a Socialist Party of Canada (SPC) member from Vancouver who had participated in the Calgary conference, had come to Winnipeg during the strike to offer his assistance, and had been arrested in Calgary when making his way back to Vancouver (Naylor and Mitchell 2019, 279). In his defense at the trial, he cast himself as another in a line of those persecuted as heretics, mentioning Copernicus' discovery that the sun, rather than the earth, lay at the center of the universe, a belief frightening to existing authorities, and thus one that would cause his follower, Giordano Bruno, in 1600, to be burned at the stake (Defense Committee 1920b, 5). At other times, he noted, Galileo had been imprisoned for his opinions, and Michael Servetus, who was tortured and burned to death along with some of his books for disputing an opinion of John Calvin, were likewise victims of their ideas (Defense Committee 1920b, 9, 12), The strike leaders' present predicament was similar, since they also were promoting truths unacceptable to those in authority:

> When Pritchard comes along and, out of the paucity of knowledge which he may possess, drives the knife of research into our economic life, and with his little knowledge of economics tells you that the industrial situation today has developed to that point; has become so intense; has become so complex; its mechanism has grown to such a degree that no longer can industry guarantee a living wage to all its workers and at the same time guarantee interest upon bonds.
> DEFENSE COMMITTEE 1920b, 9

Meanwhile, he continued, mocking the prosecution's decision to employ the reading materials seized in the homes of the accused as evidence of their seditious conspiracy:

> If you were sitting upon a case for stealing a horse, what would you think of the prosecutor who told you that the horse thief was a follower of [American atheist and First Amendment defender Robert] Ingersoll? Has that anything to do with the theft of a horse? Has it any thing to do with the case at all?
> DEFENSE COMMITTEE 1920b, 11

The reality, Pritchard continued, reprising a theme that he and his colleagues had presented in the meetings at which they were now portrayed as having plotted a totalitarian takeover of the Canadian government, was that the contemporary economy could not any longer be run on the basis of ideas that clearly no longer worked:

> And have you seen them fight like tigers, as I have seen them at the dock gates in Manchester, fighting for the chance to get a temporary job at 11 cents an hour? We have seen a repetition of Liverpool and Manchester on the docks at Vancouver. Then you wonder how it is that out of those conditions there may be here and there a man of anarchistic thought in a Trades and Labor organization. But the system of economics, which, as I pointed out in the early part might explain some of these things, just as old Galileo with his telescope discovered the four moons of Jupiter, and the learned thinkers of that day said that he must have made those four moons and put them into his telescope, so they turn around on us today and they say: "Yes, you have discovered the Laws that govern production and exchange of commodities in a modern society, but you must have invented these things to find them so." Gentlemen, we may have to explain them, but to those who understand, we don't need to explain them so much, as these things are driven home to them every day in the week by the conditions they are surrounded with here, there and the other places.
> DEFENSE COMMITTEE 1920b, 65

Nonetheless, he continued, those who have power, those who benefit from continuing an economic system that perpetuates the misery of working people, will refuse to recognize the logic of a new approach. No one should be afraid of revolution, Pritchard told the jury, which is really just recognition of a need for improvement, the need to grow (Defense Committee 1920b, 65, 72).

Armstrong, Ivens, Johns, Pritchard, and Queen were convicted of seditious conspiracy and received imprisonment of a year, Heaps was acquitted, and Bray was sentenced only to six months on the lesser charge of being a common nuisance (Lewycky 2019, 127; "Strike Leaders Sentenced" 1920; "Winnipeg Strike: Leaders of Last Year's Trouble Sent to Prison" 1920).

Edward James McMurray, a solicitor who was working for the arrested strike principals, recommended that Fred Dixon, like many of his union colleagues a British-born participant, who had edited the strike bulletin of the *Western Labor News*, and was now, in *R. v. Dixon* (1920), accused of a somewhat lesser charge, seditious libel, follow the strategy of another editor, Joseph Howe, in the latter's trial, *R. v. Howe* (1835), and document the freedoms of speech and press that had historically been permitted. In the bulletin, there had appeared a similar argument, with an ironic title, to the one Pritchard had made at his trial:

> [T]here is no use shutting our eyes to the fact that modern industry is no longer a matter of private concern. Under these conditions the next step forward is for the public to control industry. Whether this can be done effectively without collective ownership is a matter for debate. Personally we cannot see that it can.
> "A Crime to Strike" 1919

Dixon followed McMurray's advice, using the information he found in the 1909 book, *The Speeches and Public Letters of Joseph Howe*. His well-prepared performance, directed at the members of the jury, led to his acquittal, making him, along with Heaps, one of the only two Winnipeg strikers who were tried to avoid conviction. In court, the liberal Dixon, a supporter of collective bargaining and women's rights, and an admirer of the ideas of Henry George, but not a socialist, distinguished his activities from those of George Armstrong, against whom he had run for elective office, and disassociated himself from the One Big Union. The prosecutor, Hugh Phillips, K.C., had argued that even the title of one of the articles Dixon had published in the bulletin, "Kaiserism in Canada," was seditious (Cahill 1996, 281, 286, 293, 295–296; "Dixon Begins Appeal to Jury" 1920; "Dixon under Arrest on Sedition Charge" 1919; Dupuis 2014, 22; Gutkin and Gutkin 1997, 37–43; Larsen 2017, 41; Mills 1980, 36, 39–42; Naylor 2016; Stubbs 1954, 102, 107, 108, 111; "Try to Link Dixon with 'Red' Coterie" 1920).

In the aftermath of the conflict, the labor environment changed. Many employees who had embraced their own needs and welfare lost their jobs and often then found it difficult to be hired elsewhere. A party, reported to have included a thousand guests, was held in the Armstrongs' home at 159 Edmonton Street on March 1, 1921, to celebrate the release of George Armstrong, Ivens, Johns, Queen, and Pritchard. The union leaders and their allies would continue to lobby to achieve their radical goals, but the unsatisfactory conclusion of the strike pushed others in the direction of a more moderate approach ("Causes of the Winnipeg Strike: Royal Commission Appointed" 1919; "Informal Reception Tendered: Five Released Strike Leaders" 1921; Masters 1950, 135). At the height of the industrial action, some commentators had observed a conflict between the values of North America and those of the "European" immigrants in Winnipeg who had promoted their allegedly alien revolutionary goals. An editorial in the *Chicago Tribune* cemented this perspective with a desire to crush social difference and dissent:

> The Winnipeg strike was inspired by ideas that, as far as America is concerned, are fundamentally false. These ideas may have some application in European countries, where economic conditions are entirely different, but to assume that they could apply to the United States or Canada was equivalent to assuming that Buddhism or Mohammedanism would be acceptable to the great majority of Americans as a philosophy of life.
>
> The most significant and encouraging aspect of the Winnipeg strike was the method by which the middle class demonstrated their independence. We had an outbreak of a similar kind in Seattle, and Ole Hansen by the use of the police and the military succeeded in crushing it in short order.
>
> "The Winnipeg Strike" 1919

But it may be asked, to whom does "we" refer? Not, it would seem, to poor workers, union members, open-minded elements of the community, Buddhists, Muslims, those with "European" ideas, etc., but rather to an elite minority who would rule a North American "democracy" scarcely worthy of its name. The Committee of One Thousand was not legitimately a vehicle of the "middle class," but the tool of wealthy capitalists and the attorneys who served that interest along with their own. An editorial in the *Western Labor News* emphasized this point:

> We have heard much noise about the Committee of one thousand. But what about the committee of thirty-five thousand? There they stand, with their relatives, men[,] women, boys, girls – over half of the population of Winnipeg. What charge can be laid against them?
>
> For years they have labored to feed, clothe, house and otherwise serve the whole community, a small section of which has fleeced from them the greater part of the wealth they have produced. A large number of those strikers have served years in France fighting for Liberty and Democracy.
>
> "The Committee of 35,000" 1919

2 Meetings and Talk of Revolution

The sense that the Winnipeg Strike of 1919 was something more than an industrial dispute about improving working conditions owes much to the series of meetings held in the months that preceded it. The first of these gatherings took place at the Walker Theatre in Winnipeg on December 22, 1918, an assembly that was advertised as being "Under auspices of Trades and Labor Council" (Defense Committee 1920a, 10). The revolutionary rhetoric was considerable, and many of the future strike leaders who would be arrested, Bob Russell, George Armstrong, Fred Dixon, William Ivens, Dick Johns, Sam Blumenberg, and Michael Charitinoff were among the participants. Reasonably, they protested the imposition of government via orders-in-council, which had been adopted due to the wartime emergency situation, calling it "a distinct violation of the principles of democracy" (Defense Committee 1920a, 11; Naylor 2016). Immediately following the declaration of war, the Borden government had passed the War Measures Act, which read:

> The Governor in Council shall have power to do and authorize such acts and things, and to make from time to time such orders and regulations, as he may by reason of the existence of real or apprehended war, invasion or insurrection deem necessary for the security, defence, peace, order, and welfare of Canada.
>
> KEALEY 1992, 285

Subsequently, these "orders and regulations" had allowed suppression of speech and written materials and even communication using any of fourteen languages, outlawed organizations such as the IWW, and allowed arrest for all kinds of activities, some only distantly related to the war. At the Walker Theatre, speakers called for the release of everyone jailed for their political opinions, the Rev. Ivens defending protest as a tactic of many of the very best members of society, saying their freeing was required by Christian charity. Like many other radicals at the time, the speakers celebrated the Russian Revolution and the ideas that it represented to them, unaware of the repression and violence that would characterize its development, and blasted the Canadian government for opposing it and for thereby serving the interests of global capitalism (Balawyder 1967, 12–13; Bercuson 1971, 83, 84, 85; Defense Committee 1920a, 10–17; Francis 2010, 90–91; Kealey 1992, 285; Kramer and Mitchell 2010, 94–95; Masters 1950, 4).

The Walker Theatre meeting had been at least partly sponsored by the Socialist Party of Canada (SPC), and it was followed by an SPC gathering at

Winnipeg's Majestic Theatre on January 19, 1919 at which some of the same persons, including George Armstrong, Blumenberg, Johns, and Russell again defended the Russian Revolution and pressed for complete freedom of speech in Canada, talking about the theory of surplus value and explaining other elements of Marxist economics, topics that Armstrong and Blumenberg had been advocating in public meetings for several years. Speaking first at the Majestic Theatre conference, George Armstrong said:

> The greater the wealth in capitalist society the larger is the percentage of its population in absolute poverty, and it could not be otherwise, as the wealth of this society is but the expression, or estimate, of the surplus value wrung from the hides of the workers.
> DEFENSE COMMITTEE 1920a, 18

The clear theme of this meeting was that it was obvious that capitalism could not be reformed and that it needed to be replaced (Defense Committee 1920a, 18–20; Francis 2010, 95; Masters 1950, 29).

Most of the arguments of the Walker Theatre and Majestic Theatre rallies reappeared at the Western Labor Conference, which opened at Calgary's Labor Temple on March 13, 1919, with many of the same Winnipeg leaders being present, including Helen Armstrong, whose active participation, which is described later in the chapter, came with her official delegate role. The proceedings resulted in a formal statement as follows:

> Be it resolved, that this Conference places itself on record as being in full accord and sympathy with the aims and purposes of the Russian Bolshevik and German Spartacan Revolutions and be it resolved that we demand immediate withdrawal of all Allied troops from Russia.
> DEFENSE COMMITTEE 1920a, 30; LEWYCKY 2019, 78

The additional support indicated for "Spartacan Revolutions" is a reference to the Spartacist uprising (*Spartakusaufstand*), a brief insurrection in Germany in favor of a revolution similar to the one occurring in Russia. Its repression included the murders of the *Spartakusbund*'s leaders, Karl Liebknecht and Rosa Luxemburg, whose graves, as noted in Chapter Four, were visited by Tom Barker in 1920. Another Calgary resolution threatened a general strike if the Allies failed to withdraw their troops from Germany and Russia (Bercuson 1971, 92; Defense Committee 1920a, 30; Francis 2010, 215–216; Masters 1950, 31–32).

At least in theory, an important event that occurred at the convention was the formal setting up of the One Big Union (OBU), with a request for affiliated organizations to pay two cents for each of their members, financing that could be used for its promotion. As a means of counteracting unemployment, the conference sought a thirty-hour week, to which it referred as a Six-Hour Day, a resolution that, like the call for the OBU, was passed unanimously. Again, the conference advocated freedom of speech and the release of all political prisoners (Berzish 2010; Defense Committee. 1920a, 28–31; Smith 1994a, 5). The Calgary meeting would subsequently often be blamed for the more negative aspects of the Winnipeg Strike. For example, C.L. Johnson wrote at the time:

> It was, however, to the Calgary convention of extreme Socialists held in March last that the Citizens' Committee in Winnipeg this year pointed as the source and origin of the present general sympathetic strike which began on May 15, and deprived the chief city of Western Canada of street cars, telephones, milk and bread and ice deliveries, postal service, fire protection, and everything else needful in the life of the community which could be cut off by orders from the headquarters of organized labor.
> JOHNSON 1919, 654–655

How, then, is the Winnipeg strike of 1919 to be explained? There has often been disagreement. The *New York Times* swallowed whole the propaganda of the *Winnipeg Citizen*, the newspaper of the Citizens Committee of One Thousand:

> The revolution in Winnipeg, a city of 200,000, was the outcome of a Bolshevist movement started at Calgary last March, under the direction of the I.W.W. organization in New York City, at which a "Red Five" Executive Council was chosen. These men are named and described by The Winnipeg Citizen.
> "Bolshevism in Winnipeg: "One Big Union" Assumed Entire Control of City But Was Ousted by a Bourgeois Committee" 1919

In the *Chicago Tribune*, Arthur M. Evans opined as follows, touching most of the necessary bases of a conspiracy theory missing facts:

> A comparatively few revolutionaries who came to power through alien support while the fighting men were in France, are running the show.
> The one big union idea, which proposes to toll the bell for trades unionism, to overthrow the present industrial system, and establish the soviet form of communism and class control, is the real issue. It is getting support through funds, paid organizers, and propaganda from coteries in the United States.
> EVANS 1919

Evans' article raises questions about the use of rhetoric in news stories: for instance, why say "coteries" instead of "persons with similar interests," and, who, exactly, is an alien? Many of the First World War veterans supported the strike ("Winnipeg Strike: Returned Soldiers in Separate Camps" 1919). Similarly, the *Toronto News* of May 23, 1919 concluded that:

> Winnipeg is in the hands of the IWW's [sic] and Bolsehvists [sic] who are bent upon prostituting organized labor to their own aggrandisement, upon overthrowing the established order of civilization and upon creating a proletariat dictatorship which would be as tyrannical as any autocracy ever seen.
> *Toronto News* cited by DUPUIS 2005

This type of interpretation of the strike was repeated in many newspapers across Canada and the United States, promoting a viewpoint disputed today based on the profusion of much more factual reportage which is available to contemporary historians. Nonetheless, the oratory employed by the union leaders who participated in the conference at Calgary, and the meetings at the Walker and Majestic Theatres, suggests a rival explanation, of routine union advocacy possibly being assumed in tandem with diverse and not necessarily consistent elements of Marxism, anarchism, syndicalism, and/or the philosophy of the OBU (Dupuis 2005; "Winning Denies Any Knowledge of Soviet" 1919).

For one of the imprisoned architects of the strike, Pritchard, revisiting the events, the only ideological basis for what happened lay in the need to achieve fair compensation for employees' labor:

> The strike was what we said it was – a labor dispute between the building workers and the building masters, and the iron workers ... and the iron masters. It was a strike called in an attempt to establish the Principle of Collective Bargaining, a principle, by the way, which was established in Canada shortly after the strike.
> PRITCHARD 2019, 283

Similarly, Smith writes:

> Winnipeg employers who worked with the federal government to help crush the Strike saw it not as an ordinary Strike but as a revolution, but, while many Strike leaders subscribed to a variety of radical beliefs, they

> were trying not to overthrow established authority, but to win collective bargaining rights.
>
> SMITH 1994a, 3

At the time, an editorial in the *Manitoba Free Press* dismissed the strike as "a wanton, unnecessary assault upon the community by unwise labor leaders who were drunk with a sense of power and really imagined that they could force this community to yield to their dictatorship by the application of force" ("The End of the Strike: The Facts" 1919). But perhaps dissatisfaction with social conditions requires a weary, emotive response that will spur the disadvantaged and exploited to become engaged. Maybe more "reasonable" approaches to political participation in the absence of direct action will yield only the same low wages and a largely meaningless right to vote.

Notwithstanding the damage done to the Winnipeg community by the failure of the 1919 strike to achieve its ends, and its objectives, about which various analysts have differed in their portrayals, it is clear that many of its leaders were well-known to, and respected by the electorate, and the 1920 elections saw George Armstrong, Ivens, and Queen, though they were presently still in jail, returned as Members of the Legislative Assembly (MLAS) in Manitoba's parliament, which has been unicameral since 1876. Dixon, who, as noted above, had been acquitted of all charges, was reelected as an MLA. Heaps was sent back to the Winnipeg city council in 1921, and would eventually serve in the Canadian House of Commons (Dupuis 2014, 130; Francis 2010, 234; Greening 1965, 83; Kramer and Mitchell 2010, 321; Masters 1950, 147, 149; Mitchell and Naylor 1998, 215).

3 Immigrants and British Subjects

Just as immigrants from Europe and Russia, including disproportionate numbers of poor, Jewish, anarchist, and persecuted persons, were arriving in southern South America at the same time, so a similar wave of the same groups came to Canada, including to Winnipeg. As elsewhere, some of them held radical ideas and, also as elsewhere, many were looked down upon by the local population and some were viewed as being dangerous, which a small number were. Visits to Winnipeg by the leading anarchist, Emma Goldman, in 1907 and 1908 led to the city becoming one of the places from which her publication, *Mother Earth*, was distributed (Burrows 2008). Arriving in 1907, she disparaged the influence of Catholicism in the city as follows:

> The dirty crows – as a certain French artist named the priests – who infest the streets and cars of Montreal are not as numerous in Winnipeg, but the horrors of their creed are as dominant here as there – the creed that has for centuries gone about killing, burning and torturing is still holding the Canadian people in power, befogging their minds as in ages past.
> GOLDMAN 1907, 133

Margrét Jónssdóttir Benedictsson, the editor of *Freyja* [Woman], a monthly Icelandic language feminist magazine published in Selkirk, Manitoba, and her anarchist husband Sigfús Benedict Benedictsson, both members of Manitoba's Icelandic immigrant community, were involved in distributing *Mother Earth* as well as another contemporary anarchist publication, *Lucifer, the Light-Bearer*. Margrét, a suffragist admirer of Elizabeth Cady Stanton, first lectured on women's rights in Winnipeg on February 2, 1893. Disagreements between the couple led to Margrét leaving her husband and Winnipeg in 1910 and the end of *Freyja* (Burrows 2008; Crippen 2004, 65; Jonasson 2022; Weir 2007, 74–75).

Noting the potentially multicultural character of Winnipeg, Goldman recognized that conditions in the city were at present a long way short of what they might become:

> Men and women from every nook in the world gather at Winnipeg, the land of promise. They are soon made to realize, however, that the causes which drove them from their native shores – oppression, greed and robbery – are quite at home in this new, white land.
> GOLDMAN 1907, 133

However, just as the First World War and the growing lack of acceptance of Goldman's ideas in New York in the years that preceded it would eventually lead to her deportation to Russia with other anarchists on the *Buford* in 1919, so many other immigrants from Eastern Europe in Winnipeg came to be seen as suspicious once news of the Russian Revolution undermined what had started to be a growing tolerance of cultural difference in Manitoba and elsewhere in Canada (Devine 2009, 35; Shone 2013, 164).

In the case of the arrested Winnipeg strikers, ethnic origin explains much of the way they were treated. George Armstrong, like Helen, born in Ontario, and the British-born strikers were released on bail and had not faced deportation, an advantage accruing to "British subjects" that, as described in Chapter Four, had applied in New South Wales to most of the unionists accused of responsibility for "Barker's fires." In Canada, bail and rights under *habeas corpus* for those who were not British subjects were more generally resisted or refused.

The manner in which many newspapers in Canada and the United States were reporting the Winnipeg Strike prompted the government in Ottawa to toughen restrictions on immigrants. More specifically, this happened because there was direct contact between attorney A.J. Andrews, who was in charge of the prosecutions, and the Minister of Justice, Arthur Meighen. Andrews had falsely told Meighen that the Winnipeg police refused to arrest strikers, even if they were assaulting other citizens. Sections 41 and 42 of the existing Immigration Act of 1910 allowed deportation of persons of foreign origin if they were opposed to public order or the existence of government, a restriction particularly apposite in the case of anarchists and allied radical groups. Now, the Act to Amend the Immigration Act was passed on June 5, 1919, and amended the next day to include British subjects, the change prompted by the role of many of the Winnipeg strikers, who had been born in the UK (Berzish 2010; Defense Committee 1920a, 4–5; Kealey 1992, 313; Kramer and Mitchell 2010, 131, 142, 143, 182, 203; MacKinnon 1977, 628; Masters 1950, 103–104; Molinaro 2015, 149–150; "Winnipeg Strike Over" 1919).

Around the time that George Armstrong and those "British subjects" (Bray, Heaps, Ivens, Queen, and Russell) were arrested in Winnipeg, so were five others: Solomon Pearl (also given as Moses) Almazoff, Samuel "Sam" (also given as Max) Blumenberg (also given as Blumberg), Michael (also given as Matthew) Charitinoff (also given as Charitonoff), Oscar Schoppelrie (also given as Schappelrie, Schiapparell, and Choppelrie), and Mike Verenczuk (also given as Berenezuk). Almazoff, Blumenberg, and Charitinoff were Jewish, as was Heaps, who, born in Leeds in England, currently enjoyed protection from deportation. In the Edinburgh newspaper, the *Scotsman*, a Reuters report said that "Four persons of Russian nationality were also taken into custody," possibly implying the existence of a Bolshevik conspiracy, but maybe referencing different arrestees ("Winnipeg Strike: Many Leaders Arrested" 1919). When the six others were released on bail on June 20, 1919, the five "foreigners" remained at Stony Mountain jail, subject to deportation without trial and without any right to consult a lawyer, potentially on the basis of the fittingness of their political beliefs to those of the local elite ("Aliens' Release Asked by Labor" 1919; Avery 2006, 230–231 fn 81; "British Born Men Given Freedom but Must Stay Inactive" 1919; "Five Men to Come Out" 1919; Francis 2010, 209–210; Kealey 1992, 292–293; "Kronika Miejscowa" 1919; Masters 1950, 102; "No Bail will be Allowed in Case of Red Leaders" 1919; "The Charge" 1919). Subsequently, it was found that Mike Verenczuk, a Canadian soldier who had fought at the battle of the Somme, had been mistaken for Boris Devyatkin, at whose house he was staying, and eventually he was freed (Fairplay 1919; "Five Men to Come Out" 1919; "Kronika Miejscowa" 1919; Reilly and Reilly [1986] 2019).

At the time, a letter writer to the *Western Labor News* summarized this aspect of the way the prosecutions were being handled:

> In our concern for the interest of those well known men connected with the labor movement, i.e., Armstrong, Ivens, Queen, Russell, Heaps, and Bray, it seems to me we have perhaps been a little neglectful of those others, less well known, who were arrested at the same time and who are still in Stony Mountain Penitentiary. I refer to Almazoff, Charitinoff, Blumenberg, Verenchuk, and Schoppelrei. The position of these brothers is far worse than that of the so-called "leaders." Not because they are denied bail but because they are to be "tried" ... by a committee of State employees under the newly amended Immigration Act.
> FAIRPLAY 1919

A special board of inquiry chaired by a magistrate, R.M. Noble, was set up to determine the fates of the four remaining "aliens," Almazoff, Blumenberg, Charitinoff, and Schoppelrie, at the proceedings of which the accused were allowed legal representation, and they went to court to question the legality of the process as a whole. A court granted a *habeas corpus* petition on behalf of Almazoff, a decision that had applicability to the circumstances of the other three. However, the Court of Appeal upheld the legality of the board process (Avery 2006, 230–231 fn 81, 227; "Board Orders Deportation of Blumenberg" 1919; "Grants Habeas Corpus Writ in Test Trial Case" 1919; "Noble Mentions Bolshes at Blumenberg Hearing" 1919).

In 1915, Blumenberg, who was born in Romania, appeared in a one-person play at the New Grand Theater titled "War – What For?" advertisements for which appeared in the local radical paper, the *Voice*, at the same time as solicitations for his cleaning and dying firm, "The Electric Cleaners," were placed in the *Winnipeg Evening Tribune*. On behalf of the local branch of the SPC the same year, when George Armstrong was running as an SPC political candidate, Blumenberg spoke at the Globe Theatre on "The Balkan States from a Socialist Viewpoint." He lectured in 1916 at the Colonial Theatre on "Unemployment, Cause and Remedy" and "The Socialist Movement of Germany and the War" ("Blumenberg to Lecture" 1916; "S.P. of C. Election Funds" 1915; Untitled 1916). He later fell out with the SPC and was no longer a member when arrested. In February 1918, George Armstrong and Sam participated together in a discussion titled "The Programme of the Socialist Party of Canada and its Relation to the Bolsheviki." Blumenberg's business would be attacked by angry First World War veterans in January 1919, the same month they struck the SPC's Winnipeg headquarters, concerned about both people of foreign origin and socialists, and irritated by the Majestic Theatre meeting's endorsement of the Spartacist uprising in Germany (Avery 2006, 223; Basham 2000, 59; Defense Committee 1920a, 21; "Five Men to Come Out" 1919; Idiong 1997; Kramer and Mitchell 2010, 22; "Socialist Party and Bolsheviki" 1918). Blumenberg was viewed as deportable due to comments he made at the meetings at the Walker and Majestic Theatres. However, the technical reason for the board's approval of his deportation was that he had given untrue statements when he was admitted to Canada, a fact that he conceded was true (Bercuson 1971, 85; "Board Orders Deportation of Blumenberg" 1919). As someone who was very active in the local community and expressive of the concerns of many of his fellow-residents, it seems cruel to exclude him from the city that had long served as his home based on a technicality. The decision is reflective of the many prejudices of those on the other side in the Strike, the Citizens' Committee of One Thousand, and their xenophobic comments which would appear during that time in the *Winnipeg Citizen*. It would not have been much of a surprise if his deportation had been upheld because, at the Walker Theatre gathering, he wore a red tie (Masters 1950, 4).

At a meeting of the Young Jewish Labor League, Solomon Almazoff, a college student, had asked William Ivens questions which an informant, a former operative of the RNWMP, Austrian-born Harry Daskalud (also given as Daskaluk), claimed demonstrated Almazoff was in favor of violence to advance his beliefs, although he actually had said the opposite. Daskalud's poor command of the English language meant there was inadequate evidence to justify Almazoff's deportation to Russia, where he told the board of inquiry he would be executed, and he was acquitted, although he decided to move to the US and left Canada ("Almazoff is Released by Probe Board" 1919; "Almazoff Says He is Opposed to Bloodshed" 1919; Avery 2006, 230 fn 78; Fairplay 1919; "Five Men to Come Out" 1919; Francis 2010, 210; "Mountie Tells Court Almazoff Urged Revolt" 1919; "Won't Re-Open Almazoff Case" 1919). About two weeks prior to the decision, Almazoff had been denied bail because a copy of *Novy Mir*, a newspaper edited by Leon Trotsky in New York, had been found in his possession. Prosecutors claimed that an order-in-council made possession of the publication a crime, another sign of the excesses to which government by decree can lead ("Possession of Trotzky Paper Prevents Bail" 1919).

Michael Charitinoff, who had been imprisoned for editing a suppressed monthly Ukrainian language paper, *Robochyi narod*, and who had been at the Walker Theatre meeting, was ordered deported due to irregularities in the manner of his entry to Canada, although he was eventually allowed to stay ("Five Men to Come Out" 1919; Lewycky 2019, 127–128; Mitchell and Naylor 1998, 209–210; "*Robochyi narod*" [1993] 2001). Noble, the chair of the panel, demonstrated the underlying concern in that era about tolerating freedom of expression, demonstrating a curiously ironic understanding of "liberty":

> "My firm belief is that the soil of this continent is not at all fertile for these ideas," he said. "The United States and Canada have always been considered countries of liberty. It is my opinion that this continent is not ripe for revolution and upsetting of constituted authority, which, it is my belief, is the object of this propaganda."
> "Charitinoff's Deportation is Ordered" 1919

Oscar Schoppelrie, who was born in the US, was a Canadian First World War veteran who was deported to the US on the grounds that he had arrived in Canada illicitly. During the board's proceedings, he claimed that his misidentification as a Canadian citizen, which was the issue at the center of the illegal entry charge, was not made by himself, but by the military recruitment service. However, he was not allowed to present any evidence that this was the case ("Board Orders Alien Deported" 1919; "Board Orders Deportation of Blumenberg" 1919; "Five Men to Come Out" 1919; Francis 2010, 210; "Schoppelrei to be Deported This Week" 1919).

4   Forgotten Women

Although the Winnipeg General Strike of 1919 has attracted much interest and investigation by researchers, it has increasingly been pointed out that the involvement of women and of female leaders such as Helen Armstrong has been consistently underemphasized, and some attempts have been made to undo the damage caused to understanding of this major event in the labor history of Canada. As Molgat points out:

> Women figure neither in their accounts of the events leading up to the strike, nor in their accounts of the strike itself, where Norman Penner and Mary Horodyski, for example, have uncovered considerable strike action by women. Only David Bercuson has even attempted to address the involvement of women, and he unfortunately completely misrepresented it.
> MOLGAT 1988, 6

Her latter point is that in Bercuson's *Confrontation at Winnipeg* (1971), the Labor Café organized by Armstrong and run by other members of the Women's

Labor League (WLL), the prime purpose of which was to feed female strikers, is described by that author as having been set up to provide meals for men (Molgat 1988, 53, fn 94). To conclude thus would have been to ignore reports about the Café that said, for instance: "The plan is to feed the girl strikers free of charge. The men can also get lunch there. They may either give a donation or pay for their meal" ("Women Open Eating House in Strathcona Hotel, Cor. Main and Rupert" 1919). Similarly, Horodyski complains:

> For all that has been written on women's actions during the Winnipeg general sympathetic strike of 1919, it could be concluded easily that females were not there at all, that they passed the six weeks holidaying at Lake Winnipeg. The historiography of the strike has been male-centered, and like all history which refuses to include women and renders them invisible, it has been severely biased and incomplete.
> HORODYSKI 1986

Although greater awareness of the inaccuracies inherent in traditional explanations dates back, as can be seen above, to the 1980s, the male-oriented accounts persist in being influential, and some attempts to redress the gender balance have achieved little in the way of actual progress (Gutkin and Gutkin 1997, xiii, 2; "The Winnipeg General Strike" 1994; Zoratti 2015). Sampert comments:

> "The Wild Woman of the West" [Helen Armstrong] was a Winnipeg trailblazer overlooked for years by those studying the 1919 General Strike. Happily, her story is now being told as historians recognize women too often are left out of the history books, despite the important roles they play.
> SAMPERT 2019

But the account is still not being told with much completeness. For instance, Anna Penner writes:

> Shortly after midnight on the morning of 17 June, a frantic woman phoned the Chief of Police, Chris Newton. The North-West Mounted Police had permission to arrest her husband, George Armstrong, who was one of the leaders of the strike. The police chief said he could do nothing, there was a warrant.
> PENNER 2000–2001

Even in 2000, it was not considered important to mention Helen Armstrong's name. Indeed, a recent 200 page book about the Winnipeg General Strike (Lewycky 2019, 17–18, 187–188) mentions Helen Armstrong only twice, in a total of three brief paragraphs. Consequently, one of the purposes of the present chapter is to give an account of Helen Armstrong that employs much of the distinctive detail that can be obtained from newspapers and other published writings of her era, scripts that are frequently mentioned in works that seek a more balanced portrayal of the strike, but which often unfortunately fail to cite those sources with any degree of specificity.

Helen Armstrong was born in Toronto in 1875, the daughter of tailor and labor leader, Alfred Fredman Jury, and Emma Hart, who had five other daughters and four sons; she worked in the tailor shop for a time. Originally called Ellen Ann and Nellie, she later changed her name to Helen. Born in England, Jury had served as the local president of the Amalgamated Society of Tailors in Maidstone, the county town of Kent, an area not far from London. He and his wife emigrated to Canada, soon settling in Toronto, where he joined and became president of the Tailors Operatives Union. Like his daughter, he was known as someone never afraid to give his opinion. An agnostic, Alfred encountered outrage when he was scheduled to participate in a political science student-organized debate with a socialist called Phillips Thompson at the University of Toronto; eventually, the encounter had to take place off campus. Helen married carpenter George Armstrong in 1897, and they moved to Winnipeg in 1905, where they had three daughters, Helen, Mary, and Mabel, and one son, Frank (Andrew 2019; Forster 2011, 39, 40; Gutkin and Gutkin 1997, 225; Horn 1999, 5; Kealey and Burr 2003; Kelly 2016; Levi 2006, 164; Molgat 1988, 40–41, 52, fn 86; Reilly and Reilly [1986] 2019; Sampert 2019).

From 1894 until 1918, the main forum for information about the activities of labor unions and women's groups in the Winnipeg area was the *Voice* newspaper. However, in the year before the great strike, it was replaced by the *Western Labor News*, which assumed a more radical posture and became interested in revolutionary and quasi-revolutionary activity around the world, including accounts of the IWW's suppression as it was taking place in the United States. This progression toward more insurrectionist concerns can also be observed from accounts of meetings of the city's Trades and Labor Council in 1918 and 1919 (Bercuson 1971, 95–96; Masters 1950, 20; Molgat 1988, 1; Rea 1973, 5). Insofar as the newspaper change allowed expression of a fuller representation of women's potential, the new approach meant that many details of the work of Helen Armstrong and other feminists, frequently through the medium of the Women's Labor League (WLL), were now reported. As Molgat notes, the predecessor, the *Voice*, had hardly been on the cutting edge of the women's movement:

> The humour was almost misogynist. *The Voice*'s editorial pages might be promoting equal political rights for women and encouraging women to organize, but in its general content the paper was only rarely able to see beyond an image of women as domestic, pure, manipulative and not very bright.
> MOLGAT 1988, 113

Nonetheless, its successor may still not be regarded as having adequately addressed the deficit. Strong-Boag writes:

> Even such radical publications as ... *The Western Labor News* (Winnipeg) ... devoted few pages to female labour. ... As yet far too little is known about the influence of radical leaders and associations such as ... the Women's Labor League.
> STRONG-BOAG 1979, 153

The editor of the *Western Labor News*, its title being chosen to include the qualification of "Western" because another *Labor News* already existed in Hamilton, Ontario, was the Rev. William Ivens, one of the strike leaders who would be arrested in 1919 (Bercuson 1971, 77; Ryder 1920, 20; "Trades Council" 1918b). Ivens seems not to have been the first choice, because a report in the *Voice* indicated that "It being impossible to locate the whereabouts of Percy Chew, the committee submitted the names of Rev. W. Ivens and [J.] G. Soltis as suitable for the editorship of the paper, leaving it for the council to make the choice" ("Trades Council" 1918b). John Gabriel Soltis was an organizer for the Cooks and Waiters' Union, which merged with a guild of hotel workers, at which point he became the secretary of the International Alliance of Hotel and Restaurant Employees. He wrote an article titled "Taxation and the Working Class," which appeared in the *Voice*. ("Efficiency and Character of Hotel Workers" 1917; "Local News" 1917; Soltis 1918). There were 55 votes for Ivens and 19 for Soltis ("Trades Council" 1918b).

Arthur Percy Chew (1887–1967), often identified as "A. Percy Chew," was born in Prestwich, near Manchester in England, and was a member of the SPC, under the label of which he wrote articles with a strong Marxist tone that were published in the *Voice* in 1909 and 1910 (Chew 1909a, 1909b, 1909c, 1909d, 1909e, 1909f, 1909g, 1910a, 1910b; McCormack 1977, 60). In that sense, the *Voice* had been quite a radical paper. For instance, in one article, titled "Social Fungi," Chew wrote:

> We Socialists contend that if the workers have sufficient intelligence to construct and operate a railway, they are qualified to own it also. The owning part is the easiest in the proposition.
> The average workingman is essentially a moral creature; far more so than his capitalist master.
> CHEW 1909d

Like Helen Armstrong, Chew is one of the many area activists about whom information has been forgotten, but although some details are unclear, it seems likely he lived in Winnipeg at least from 1909 to 1914. He gave lectures, and through the medium of the paper engaged in debates with others about important contemporary topics such as the ideas of Henry George and the Single Tax Movement and of Thomas Robert Malthus (Bowman 1914; Farmer 1911, 1912; "Sunday Meetings" 1914; Thomas 1917). On other occasions, his whereabouts appear also to have been uncertain; for example, the *Voice* reported in December 1910 that he had relocated to "Manchester, England, where he intends to reside." Later, he moved to the United States, living in Washington, DC, and he died in St. Petersburg, Florida ("Arthur Percy Chew" N.d.; "Locals" 1910). Although two of the 1919 Strike leaders, Bob Russell and George Armstrong, were SPC members, Lewycky (2019, 87) notes that others in their party "saw the Strike as merely an effort to reform capitalism, while they sought its collapse." Many of Chew's pieces in the *Voice* suggest that he was an advocate of the latter position.

During the Strike, on June 7, a report of uncertain origin appeared in the *Scotsman*, reporting the visit to Winnipeg of James Alexander "Jimmy" Duncan and another "Bolshevik" labor organizer from Seattle ("Sudden Change for the Worse" 1919). Actually, Duncan, who was born in Fife, Scotland, was the secretary of the Seattle Central Labor Council (CLC), an affiliate of the American Federation of Labor (AFL), a group which was in general opposed to industrial unionism and the OBU, although Duncan, who was more sympathetic to that cause, openly criticized the leadership of Samuel Gompers, and attempted to change the perspective of other members, seeking to improve the organizational strengths of the AFL in order to be better able to compete with the IWW. He worked to free IWW members who had been imprisoned following the Everett Massacre of 1916 on "Bloody Sunday" in Washington state, and in 1918, on behalf of the Seattle CLC, he sent a letter threatening a strike if Thomas Mooney, who was accused of particpation in the San Francisco Preparedness

Day explosion of 1916 and imprisoned for 22 years before finally being pardoned, was not released (De Shazo 1925, 31, 31 fn 1; Duncan 1918; Friedheim and Friedheim 1964, 149, 154–155; Golin 2020). However, the report in the *Scotsman* accused Duncan of advising "Ivens and his colleagues" to starve people in Winnipeg by "forbidding the delivery of bread and milk" ("Sudden Change for the Worse" 1919). Such was the influence of Citizens' propaganda.

Although many of the activities in which Helen Armstrong involved herself in Winnipeg can be understood simply in terms of her concern for the poor and especially for disadvantaged women, details of her participation among the 237 delegates at the Western Labor Conference, in Calgary on March 13–15, 1919, suggest a person who was far more radical. Indeed, as was noted earlier, one of the ways that the Winnipeg General Strike developed in succeeding months has been interpreted in the light of the more extreme and allegedly "Bolshevik" goals of the Calgary proceedings. Delegates committed themselves to the idea of One Big Union, seeking to jettison the traditional craft-based "international" structure of labor organizations as they advocated the dictatorship of the proletariat and, at the instigation of Helen, who was one of only three female participants in the conference, demanded the withdrawal of Western troops from what was becoming the Soviet Union (Isitt 2003, 44–45; McCallum 1998, 15–16). Molnar writes:

> Syndicalist and industrial union impulses came together at the Western Labour Convention at Calgary, in March 1919, to form the One Big Union. The new organization expressed traditional socialist doctrine: the abolition of production for profit, the overthrow of capitalism, and the creation of an economic system based upon need. Trade unions, postulated the Conference, must organize along industrial lines, "so that by virtue of their industrial strength the workers may be better prepared to enforce any demands they consider essential to their maintenance and well being."
>
> MOLNAR 1987, 122

As a representative of the WLL, Armstrong noted that on other occasions she had "sat in meetings, hundreds of times the only woman – the only woman" (McCallum 1998, 15–16). Kelly (2016) points out that Helen was also "the only woman who stood up and spoke her piece at that historic gathering in Alberta." As noted above, seeing restoration of freedom of speech as a major issue, the conference demanded the release of all whom it referred to as "political prisoners," including members of the military who had been imprisoned for breaches of discipline, and it threatened a general strike that would begin on June 1. Without industrial action, Helen Armstrong argued, freedom of speech, press, and assembly, and the release of political prisoners would not be achieved:

> I am here to ask you to push this thing with your industrial power to get those boys out of prison. If you pass the resolution and simply leave it[,] it will be the same.
> "Western Canada Labor Conference Held at Calgary, Alberta, March 13, 14, 15, 1919: Report of Proceedings" 1919

She linked the withdrawal of troops to the speech issue and the need for a strike, as she asked, "I would like to know if withdrawing the troops from Russia will be included in the strike vote" ("Western Canada Labor Conference Held at Calgary, Alberta, March 13, 14, 15, 1919: Report of Proceedings" 1919), hearing that the different aspects would all be included in the same vote. However, the WLL was unsuccessful in persuading the other delegates to allot a female organizer for the Western provinces, a position Helen may have seen as suitable for her own skills (McCallum 1998, 25). She noted how necessary such an appointment would be, saying "how the women have had to suffer because organizers up and down the country for the last thirty years holding mass meetings and public meetings never invited the women workers" (Armstrong, quoted by McCallum 1998, 29).

Although Armstrong, unlike her husband, was not among the strike leaders arrested and tried for their activities, she did spend some brief time in 1919 in jail. On June 5, encouraged by Helen to prevent vendors of the *Winnipeg Evening Tribune* from making sales, two women, Ida Krantz (in different places given as Kraatz or Krants) and Margaret Steinbauer (or Steinhauer), accomplished this task, tearing up some of the papers of two sellers, whose names were identified as Miss H. Creak and Mrs. Moone. McCallum (1998, 44) points out the contempt that Armstrong displayed for other women who had volunteered to sell copies of the Citizens Committee's anti-Strike publication, the *Winnipeg Citizen*. In court, having been detained by a Constable Hughes, Krantz and Steinbauer were each fined $5, with Armstrong being arrested for counseling them to break the law. Following the preliminary trial, it was not immediately possible for Helen to be bailed out, although two days later she was allowed to leave having personally funded the bail of $2,000 along with two sureties of $1,000 to guarantee her future behavior ("Bail Refused to Mrs. Armstrong et al[.]" 1919; "Cases in Court" 1919; Forster 2011, 42; Gutkin and Gutkin 1997, 243; Horodyski 1986; Kramer and Mitchell 2010, 142; "Mrs. Armstrong Committed for Trial" 1919; "Mrs. Armstrong Gets Bail" 1919; "Mrs. Armstrong is to Face Charge"

1919; "Mrs. Armstrong Released on Bail" 1919; "Mrs. Armstrong to Stand Trial" 1919). Forster (2011, 39) argues that "Police considered jailed activist Helen Armstrong such a danger during the 1919 Winnipeg Strike that she was denied bail for days before being released." Similarly, Horodyski comments:

> This refusal must have been a special measure designed to keep Winnipeg safe from the activities of Helen Armstrong, as other women who had been held for trial on riot charges were granted bail.
> HORODYSKI 1986

In its newspaper advertisements, the Citizens' Committee now carped that this type of activity was, despite the denials of its leaders, directly connected to decisions made in Calgary earlier that year:

> Take note that the Mrs. Armstrong who seconded this resolution is the Mrs. Helen Armstrong who is now engaged in deluding the women and girls who are out on strike in Winnipeg today that there is nothing disloyal in the movement into which they have been drawn – that the present strike has no connection with the Calgary Labor Conference or the One Big Union – that revolution, so openly advocated at Calgary, is remote from the thought of the leaders of the strike in Winnipeg, who, such a short time ago, boasted of the establishment of the workers' soviet rule in this city.
> "These Are the Friends of Our Enemies" 1919

In September, Helen participated in one of the nine "Protest Sunday" demonstrations that were held in Winnipeg area locations to demand the freeing of currently imprisoned strikers. In a speech at the city rink, she said she was going to bring the matter up with the Prince of Wales, who was scheduled to visit Winnipeg the following week, and would hand him a petition that asked for the prisoners' release ("9 Meetings Held as Protest for Labor Leaders" 1919; "Will Ask the Prince to Use His Influence" 1919). The next month, on October 23, 1919, Helen and George Armstrong were delegates to the dominion-wide 35th annual Trades and Labor Congress, which that year took place in Hamilton, Ontario amid an atmosphere of disagreement between supporters of traditional "international" or craft-based unions and advocates of the idea of OBU. At the time, George was out on bail waiting for his trial on a charge of sedition, and before the other 900 participants he continued to promote the idea that the new government in Russia constituted a positive change that would benefit ordinary people, and again called for Canadian and other hostile forces to be withdrawn from that country. In typical fashion, concerned about the needs of the disadvantaged, Helen argued at the gathering that while she supported efforts to keep children in school until they were eighteen, the low pay received by many parents undermined any potential for achieving that goal while so many were obliged to rely on having teenagers employed at an earlier age to supplement their limited funds (Gutkin and Gutkin 1997, 190, 245; Kealey 1984, 36–37; "Labor Congress Has Auspicious First Session" 1919; "Labor Men Asking Six Hour Day and a Five Day Week" 1918).

The Women's Labor League (also referred to as the Woman's Labor League) was set up in Winnipeg in 1910, although the arguably more successful organization at winning the vote in Manitoba elections for women was the Winnipeg Political Equality League, which was founded in 1912. Somewhat surprisingly, then, one of the active members of the Winnipeg Political Equality League, Mrs. Luther Holling (Cleverdon [1950] 1974), wrote a letter to the *Winnipeg Evening Tribune* supporting the restrictions contained in the War-Time Elections Act, in which she said:

> At this time in our nation's crisis, it comes home to me forcibly the responsibility resting on the women of Manitoba respecting our federal franchise. I as a woman citizen of Manitoba believe unquestionably in my right to register my Dominion vote, yet if that right at this crisis carries with it the danger through women's vote of conscription being lost, and the lives of our brave lads at the front being endangered, then I, who have long looked for this great privilege, gladly resign it to the end that there shall never be a shadow of a doubt that woman's vote may in any shape or form dishonor our land or endanger our boys at the front.
> HOLLING 1917

It is not hard to find reasons to criticize Holling's perspective, which appears to see voting not in the way that she writes, as a "right," but rather as a "privilege" permitting those who possess it to endorse decisions made by the government, even if, as was the case with the First World War, those decisions seriously disrupt and put an end to many human lives, and consequently cause many people to view them as controversial. The WLL, on the other hand, opposed the provisions of the War-Time Elections Act, which limited the numbers of women who could vote in federal elections and took away the vote from many foreign-born men. Introduced in the House of Commons by Arthur Meighen in 1917, the Act's larger political goal was to secure continued popular support for Canadian involvement in the First World War, conscription of Canadians, and appreciation of the sacrifices made by veterans of that conflict. However, the Act aimed to achieve that support by disenfranchising voters considered most likely not to be in favor of the war: women who had little connection to men of draft age, men and women born in other countries, especially in places where their former governments might be thought hostile to Canada or to the British Empire, conscientious objectors, and men exempt from military service for religious reasons. Additionally, the Act would weaken support for the government's opposition, the Liberal Party (Campbell 2019; "Election Bill Before House Will Bar Alien Born Voters from Polls" 1917; "Liberals Plan Party Advantage: Caucus on Bill" 1917; Molgat 1988, 38–39).

Promoters of the War-Time Elections Act assumed a jingoistic posture that viewed disenfranchisement as the natural response any patriot was bound to approve. For example, Isaac Campbell, a prominent Winnipeg attorney who had previously represented Manitoba as Vice-President of the Canadian Bar Association, gave an address in December 1917 in Winnipeg in which he stated that more people should have been stripped of their vote because they failed to openly state their opposition to Germany ("Campbell Says Laurier Avoids Main Question" 1917; "Memorable Manitobans: Isaac Campbell (1853–1929)" 2018; Thompson Dorfman Sweatman LLP 2012, 6).

The Women's Labor League took a different tack, its executive opposing any disqualification, pointing out that if women who were not spouses, daughters, or mothers of veterans were going to lose their votes, then the same sanction should be applied to men who similarly had no family connection with the troops, a response that was unanimously approved at a September 18, 1917 meeting of the WLL membership at the Winnipeg Labor Temple (Watt 1917). From Armstrong came a request to be honest about the political motives that underlay passage of the War-Time Elections Act:

> Either give every woman the right of franchise or none. It is just another evidence of the Borden outfit gone military mad and they ought to come out plainly and say military service is the qualification for the ballot. What a spectacle for a moribund, last gasp group of incompetents to dare to legislate away the ballot of Canadian citizens!
> HELEN ARMSTRONG, quoted by GUTKIN AND GUTKIN 1997, 230

At a gathering attended by more than five thousand Winnipeg residents on December 10, 1917, the Liberal leader and former prime minister, Sir Wilfrid Laurier, made clear his opposition to conscription and pointed out that Canadian immigrants viewed as "Germans" by those who wished to take away their votes, were often Slavs from Austria-Hungary ("Laurier is Heard by Huge Crowd" 1917). Although the WLL attempted to register as many women as possible to vote during the official registration period of June 11–15, 1917 ("Winnipeggers to Register Names June 11 to 15?" 1917), many Canadians were prevented from voting due to the restrictions imposed under the new Act. For instance, because all those naturalized after March 31 1902 were no longer allowed to vote, Theodore Stefanik, a former Winnipeg city alderman, was excluded because he had become a citizen on April 17, 1902 ("Theo. Stefanik Loses Vote under New Franchise Act" 1917). Three years later, electoral registration in Winnipeg plummeted, raising a question as to what extent this might have been caused by the negative psychological or political effects of the War-Time Elections Act ("60,000 Electors Fail to Register" 1920).

The WLL appears not to have been much involved in political activity from 1911 until early 1917, partially explaining the greater success of the Winnipeg Political Equality League. However, when Helen Armstrong became WLL president, it swiftly assumed much significance in the life of Winnipeg society. The WLL quickly affiliated with the Trades and Labor Council, receiving three delegates to that organization's meetings and cementing connections regarding shared concerns about women's labor issues, as well as a seat on the Minimum Wage Board. Following her inspirational speech to the Women's Trades and Labor Auxiliary at the Labor Hall in Fort William (today the Thunder Bay area of Ontario, then known as the Twin Cities of Fort William and Port Arthur), in June 1918, the group changed its name also to the WLL. Under its new label, it provided refreshments for the local 1919 Labor Day celebration. To what extent there were other WLL branches is uncertain, although there was a cluster in Nova Scotia that was connected to local coal miner strikers to whom the Winnipeg group sent financial assistance. There appear also to have been local subgroupings within the Winnipeg WLL, including Elmwood, a district that lies to the east of the Red River, a Central section, and a St. James-Brooklands-Weston branch in the western suburbs. A group with the same name existed in England from 1906 to 1918, one of its presidents (until 1911) being Margaret MacDonald, the wife of future UK Labour prime minister, Ramsay MacDonald, although there seems not to have been any connection between that organization and the one in Winnipeg (Collette 1989, 1, 8, 34; Farmer 1919; Gutkin and Gutkin 1997, 225, 235; Molgat 1988, 38–39; "Protest Parade" 1919; Reilly and Reilly [1986] 2019; Sangster 1984, 109, fn 7; Thompson 2020, 135; "Women's Labor League" 1918a, 1918b).

One of Armstrong's most significant achievements took place at the time she first became involved with the WLL. This was the creation of the Retail Clerks' Union. The union went on strike at the two Woolworth's stores located in Winnipeg, where the mostly female employees earned as little as $6 weekly. Seeking a salary of $8 a week, Helen persuaded the Trades and Labor Council to fund subsistence payments for the strikers. Although this battle, like the general strike of 1919, was unsuccessful, and some of the Woolworth's employees were replaced, a fate that would be replicated in 1919, it demonstrated a way of responding to labor exploitation that would ultimately achieve significant social change. The same year, Helen was also involved in creating a union of stenographers (Gutkin and Gutkin 1997, 226–227; Kelly 2016; Molgat 1988, 39; "Stenographers Working in Offices" 1917). Not only was this an obvious focus for Armstrong given her interests and concerns, but as Lowe (1982, 18) points out, in Canada, "[g]enerally the feminization of machine-related clerical jobs was completed by the end of the 1920s." Also, he writes, "[a]s clerical jobs acquired a "female" label they replaced domestic work as the major female job ghetto" (16), requiring attention be given to the levels at which future wages would be paid. In 1919 and 1920, there was a significant attempt made to bolster the Office Workers' Guild, although there is no record of Helen having being involved in that endeavor. Rather, C.E. Weller, a man who chaired its organizing committee and then became its president seems to have been the most important campaigner for that local union's development, a process that included inviting prominent citizens to speak at its meetings. A woman named Miss E.A. McInnis was appointed as its secretary-treasurer. Although by 1920 some sightless women in Winnipeg had been trained as stenographers, there was a reluctance among employers to utilize their services ("Office Workers' Guild Perfects Organization" 1920; "Office Workers to Form a Union" 1920; "Seeks Work for Sightless Typists" 1920; Untitled 1919, 1920a, 1920b, 1920c; "'White Collar' Wearers Urged to Organize" 1920).

In 1918, Armstrong, aware that domestic workers had been organized in Calgary and in some US cities, was the prime mover in the creation of the Housemaids and Hotelworkers' Union, scheduling an inaugural meeting at the Labor Temple that was attended by at least forty housekeepers and hotel chambermaids. At a subsequent assembly, she was chosen as president, and the union expanded, holding picnics and dances, and it decided to lobby for a ten-hour day ("Housemaids Lay Plans for Union at Initial Meet" 1918; "Housemaids Pick Union Officials" 1918; "Housemaids' Picnic" 1918; "Housemaids to Ask for a 10-Hour Day" 1918; "Housemaids' Union Formed" 1918; "Housemaids Want 10 Hour Day" 1918; "Successful Dance Held" 1918; "Winnipeg Housemaids to Form Union at Meeting to be Held Thursday" 1918).

During the general strike of 1919, as noted above, another of Helen's major achievements was operation of the "Labor Café." Providing food for strikers is a tactic that has worked well for labor unions when they are on strike. For example, in her activities on behalf of the International Ladies' Garment Workers' Union (ILGWU) in the 1930s, Rose Pesotta provided meals during strikes in which she was involved in Los Angeles and Montréal, achieving worker solidarity that led to concessions from employers, though the latter's compliance did not last for long (Shone 2019, 297–298, 300). In Winnipeg, the Labor Café migrated between three locations, moving from the Strathcona Hotel to the Oxford Hotel, and eventually to the Royal Albert Arms Hotel, and its main purpose was always to feed women for free, along with providing for men on a less generous basis. The young, single women on strike were the least likely to have alternative resources to replace the pay they were sacrificing for the cause, and the WLL also helped them to make rent payments (Gutkin and Gutkin 1997, 68, 228, 238; Horodyski 1986; "No Girl Need Want for Food" 1919; Reilly and Reilly [1986] 2019; Smith 1994a, 6; "Thursday Evening Session" 1919; "Winnipeg Strike Spreads Further" 1919; "Women's Labor League" 1919; "Women Open Eating House in Strathcona Hotel, Cor. Main and Rupert" 1919).

Directed by Helen Armstrong, the Women's Labor League was involved in many policy issues and it, and she, often committed themselves to a particular point of view on matters in question, and sometimes in cases of mutual disagreement, she would threaten to resign her position (Gutkin and Gutkin 1997, 235–236). At this time, Winnipeg went from public transportation using horse-drawn buses to a streetcar system known as the Winnipeg Electric Railway, which was operated by a single company. By 1915, the system was unable to keep up with suburban expansion, which required the laying of tracks, an expensive task, and the city responded by licensing individuals for $20 per vehicle to operate jitneys (motor buses) anywhere except on the routes of the streetcars. By the middle of 1917, many of the more than 600 jitneys were organized into regular routes charging a fixed fare of a nickel per ride, and operated by an association, the Jitney Owners' and Drivers' Association, which was protected by labor interests such as the Trades and Labor Council. The Winnipeg city council and its Market, License and Relief Committee wrestled with designing a mandatory bond to protect injured passengers or bystanders that the drivers would be able to afford. However, the Winnipeg Street Railway Company and its lawyer, Edward Anderson, argued that it would operate most efficiently as a monopoly, and that this would best protect property values ("600 Jitneys in City This Year, Organizer Says" 1917; Cassidy 2021; "Jitney Drivers to Form Union; to Call Meeting." 1916; "Jitneys" 1915; "To Bond Jitneys" 1917). A controversial petition ostensibly organized by the company, which requested the city close down their rivals, appeared in 1918, but it was later revealed that people were being asked only to show their support for improving service, and their signatures were then employed as a means of advocating removing the jitneys from Winnipeg. When it renewed the Street Railway Company's license in 1918, the city agreed not to continue those of any of the jitney operators, and their service ended on April 30 of that year, even though representatives of the drivers had presented a legitimate petition to the council, reportedly signed by twenty-three thousand people who wanted to keep the jitneys ("Assert They are Tricked on Petition" 1918; Cassidy 2021; "Civic Committee Retires" 1918). Not surprisingly, given its relationship with the Trades and Labor Council, the Women's Labor League had preferred to continue with the jitneys, and when they were closed down, the organization formally condemned the decision. When Helen ran unsuccessfully for city council in 1923 to represent Ward 2, she indicated that, when the Street Railway Company's contract was up for renewal in 1927, she would wish to transfer the streetcar system to municipal ownership ("Candidates State Position on Vital Issues" 1923; Gutkin and Gutkin 1997, 248; "Mrs. Helen Armstrong Will Be Candidate" 1923; Untitled 1918).

5 Poverty and Women's Pay

A major issue for Helen Armstrong was the poverty experienced by women who spent much of their time toiling for employers, but who still could not afford to take care of their basic needs and family responsibilities. In this respect, she resembles the complaints made by labor union activist Rose Summerfield in Australia about working conditions for women in Sydney, and by contraception advocate Margaret Sanger, who reported how the children of Lawrence, Massachusetts were undernourished and lacked clothing (Shone 2019, 239–240, 2022, 32–33). In a letter to the *Voice*, Helen pointed out that even though female factory workers in Winnipeg might need to walk to work in winter temperatures of thirty degrees below zero, unlike their male employers, their salaries did not allow them to purchase fur hats and coats (Armstrong 1918; Gutkin and Gutkin 1997, 227). Women employees were at the time expected to survive on $5 a week, which could lead to them getting into debt they would be unable to service. Such poverty wages prevented many women from living independently, putting them under the control of their parents or pressuring them to marry unwisely. WLL members, including Armstrong and Gertrude Puttee, contended that an adequate wage should be at least double the amount that women often received. Helen told an investigator that "It is impossible for a girl to live in a decent and healthy manner under $10 a week" ("Part of McGrath's Report Tabled" 1918). Perhaps surprisingly, school principal May Pitblado, the second wife of the rich attorney Isaac Pitblado, who would be involved in crushing the Winnipeg Strike, also felt that women needed to earn $500 a year (Christie and Gauvreau 1996, 120; "Part of McGrath's Report Tabled" 1918; Ramsden and Kramer 2022).

Consequently, one of the issues in support of which Armstrong and the WLL campaigned was establishing a minimum wage for women in Manitoba. Often Helen spoke before a meeting of union workers and asked them to pass a resolution demanding passage of such a law, which was achieved in 1919, although many problems continued to exist afterwards, with employers finding ways to avoid paying as much as they were required ("Unions Demand Minimum Wage" 1918). Moreover, Helen needed to counteract the view that, unlike women, men needed higher salaries so they could take care of their families, while younger women, ubiquitously described at the time as "girls," were working only until they found a husband, at which time they would "retire" to become a housewife (Gutkin and Gutkin 1997, 228). A tactic Helen often employed in trying to convince others of the need to improve women's remuneration was to demonstrate how difficult it would be to live on the amounts that many Winnipeg area employees received.

When a commission system was instigated to determine appropriate wage rates for women, the WLL and the Trades and Labor Council protested that it was an inadequate way to accomplish progress, one that made it easier for employers to perpetuate exploitation, instead recommending that all women be paid at least $12 a week, proffering a draft of suggested legislation that both organizations had unanimously approved. As on other occasions, Armstrong took the complaint to levels others might, in the interest of achieving polite compromise, not have considered. At an engagement with the provincial legislature's Law Amendments Committee on February 6, 1919, Helen claimed that the Minimum Wage Board's members deliberately held as many meetings as possible so that they could draw the $10 fee they were paid for their services, suggesting that the payment in such circumstances amounted to a bribe from employers in return for favorable wage determinations:

> "Can you imagine gentlemen," she asked, "the inconsistency of the board members collecting $10 for a few hours work, that work consisting of deciding that a working girl can live on $10 or even $9 a week? I tell you what, labor considers this fee a mere bribe so that the manufacturers can get what they ask of the board."
> "Labor Asks $12 Wage Minimum for Women:
> Commission Scheme is Condemned" 1919

Although everyone participating in the WLL meeting which had developed the proposed legislation had voted to adopt it, there were some members who did not approve of an earlier attack by Armstrong on the Minimum Wage Board, which she had signed as WLL president and which had been published in two local newspapers, the *Winnipeg Evening Tribune*, and the short-lived *Western Star* ("Booze Project Splits Women's Labor League" 1918; "Labor Asks $12 Wage Minimum for Women: Commission Scheme is Condemned" 1919; "Women's Wage Law Under Discussion" 1918).

When a new system of fixed rates for female employees was published in July 1919, two categories of workers and, accordingly, minimum pay mandates were revealed: "experienced" women would receive at least $12.50 a week, while so-called "adult learners" would start at $10.50 a week ("Regulations Govern Women Employees" 1919). Soon afterwards, five restaurants in Winnipeg revealed that they may not have been paying waitresses the full $12.50 rate, and that, in an effort to challenge the authority of the law, they were reducing the pay of all female workers to $6 a week on the grounds that they received tips and ate meals at work when they were scheduled, and thus were alternatively remunerated ("Restaurants to Fight Minimum Wage Order" 1919). Although such reductions were illegal, it would prove difficult over the next decade to obtain underpayment compensation, and in 1929 Armstrong told of seamstresses who had been temporarily laid off once they qualified for the full rate of pay, and then offered a new position as a lower-paid trainee ("Minimum Wage Law Violated, Labor Men Say" 1929).

Another issue that caused conflict between Helen Armstrong and some of the women she represented was allowing the sale of alcohol, which had been outlawed in 1916, with all legal bars supposedly closed by the Manitoba Temperance Act, which followed a provincial referendum supporting Prohibition, in which women, recently enfranchised, had participated. However, many small bars that were putatively legal because they sold or claimed to sell only 2% proof beer proliferated in Winnipeg because the 1916 Act stated that "any liquor which contains more than two and a half per cent (2½ per cent) of proof spirits shall be conclusively deemed to be intoxicating," a requirement intended to be incidental to the overall ban, but which, in the absence of a clarifying court case, was used to justify allowing the 2% establishments to stay open (Liquor, Gaming and Cannabis Authority of Manitoba N.d.; "Two-Per-Cent. Beer Sales May Be Prohibited" 1916).

Helen Armstrong and the WLL took the position that lower alcohol beer and wine should be re-legalized, but this statement was not necessarily accepted by other groups with which they were generally allied. Some of the group's own members felt that Helen had steamrollered through a resolution to that effect at a meeting when many members were absent. Additionally, meetings of the Telephone Operators Union and the Hotel and Houseworkers' Union, groups that were generally natural allies of Armstrong, the latter having been founded by Helen, who served as its first president, resoundingly rejected the

WLL policy ("Booze Project Splits Women's Labor League" 1918; "Hotel and Houseworkers are Opposed to Liquor" 1918; "Labor Women in Clash as Booze Issue Re-Opens" 1918).

Another example of the conflict that sometimes afflicted the Women's Labor League is that when the Winnipeg-area Local Council of Women announced that it planned to associate with the WLL's ally, the Political Educational League, which had also strived to establish a minimum wage for women, the WLL voted to no longer work with them because its members remembered the Local Council of Women having picketers arrested and providing "scabs" during an earlier 1918 strike (Christie and Gauvreau 1996, 120–121; Gutkin and Gutkin 1997, 235; "Split in Ranks of Women's Societies over "Scab Troop"" 1918; "Trades Council" 1918a). Indeed, although the Local Council of Women, which had been founded in 1894, and was an organization of many social groups that believed it served the interests of women, consistently making recommendations for changes in the law, the WLL never affiliated with it, likely partly because it was felt that it catered to women of a different class, and arguably gave more affluent ladies opportunities to correct the non-conforming behavior of the lower-class, for example, by making sure that their children were not among a movie theater's audience any later than 9.00 p.m. (Heads 1997, vi; Jones 2003, 104; Spencer 2010, 21; "Want Woman as Juvenile Court Judge" 1916). For instance, it advocated appointment of a female police officer in Winnipeg, a woman to the Board of Censors, and a female judge on the juvenile court. There had previously been a female detective in the city, but she had been let go. Notwithstanding its primary focus, the Winnipeg Local Council of Women was more conservative than the WLL, and supported Canada's involvement in the First World War. Although one of its members, Harriet Dick (often at the time referred to as Mrs. John Dick), played a major role in passage of the 1916 Mothers' Allowances Act, the association generally had less radical goals than Helen Armstrong, and it lobbied to preserve the restrictions on alcohol use imposed by the Manitoba Temperance Act ("Ask Appointment of Policewoman to Local Force" 1915; Heads 1997, 144, 151–152; "To Fight Against Re-Introduction of "Demon Rum"" 1919; "Want Woman as Juvenile Court Judge" 1916). The Local Council of Women also favored buying Canadian-made products ("Country Before Politics Urged" 1925; "Want Control of Storage Plants to Precede Pledges 1917").

Another area of conflict occurred between members of the Women's Labor League in 1917 in connection with opposition to military conscription. Like her husband George, fellow 1919 strike leaders, Heaps, Dixon, John Queen, and his wife, Katherine Ross Queen, a feminist campaigner for access to birth control (who was generally in the manner of the time referred to as "Mrs. Queen"),

Helen voiced her feelings openly at public meetings, some in Winnipeg's Market Square, condemning Canada's involvement in the First World War. At a large gathering of women at the Central Congregational Church in late August 1917, Helen and Katherine spoke in an unsuccessful attempt to approve a motion against conscription, during which the latter revealed that three of her brothers had already been killed in the war. A pro-war rally at the Walker Theatre the following December led to Armstrong's first arrest, for participating in a demonstration outside the building with fellow-WLL member Laura Watts; this time, however, she was held only for a matter of hours (Bercuson 1971, 43; Goldsborough 2020; Gutkin and Gutkin 1997, 229, 230, 233; "Some of the Women" 1917; "The Trades and Labor Council" 1917a).

Nonetheless, as a group, the WLL was by no means supportive of the criticisms being aired about the government, and made a point of saying that it opposed "the tactics" of the campaign against conscription, and censured its member, likely referring to Armstrong, who had "taken a prominent part against conscription," indicating that she "was acting on her own behalf and not for the league" ("Women's Labor League Scores Draft Foes" 1917).

Some planned "Anti" gatherings were canceled in advance by government order (Forster 2011, 40; Waters 2010), a response Armstrong regarded as a violation of freedom of speech:

> I know how my blood fairly boiled with indignation to think that in the country where I was born and raised, and my children born and raised, and their forefathers before them, that we were denied the right and privilege of voicing our opinion either in a hall we had paid for or on the public market square, where we have held meetings for the past ten years.
> ARMSTRONG 1917b

Despite the obvious reasonableness of her defense of civil liberties, the above remark, which was not completely true because her parents had been born in England, indicates a tendency Armstrong displayed sometimes of listing more claims than were necessary, some having more merit than others, as she tried to connect with her audience. Except for her husband George, none of the strikers who would be imprisoned in 1919 were born in Canada, but as she of course agreed, all of them shared the right to speak. So why would the Armstrongs' longer association with their nation be an additional qualification that strengthened their case? Surely it would be only Canadians with overwhelmingly different viewpoints who thought thus, those who would soon form the Citizens' Committee of One Thousand, the strikebreaking champions of the moneyed elite who had foreign-born workers arrested based merely on their stereotypical perceptions of cultural differences, and for whom with much justification she came to have contempt. That population would largely overlap with local supporters of the War-Time Elections Act, which took away the national election voting rights of many women and foreign-born citizens of Canada.

On July 1, 1917, the Anti-Conscription League met at the Market Square. An earlier meeting had taken place at the Grand Opera House on June 3, and noise made by a group of three hundred soldiers who disapproved of the protest made it difficult for the speakers to be heard. A subsequent gathering scheduled for June 17 was prevented from taking place on the orders of Police Chief Donald MacPherson, who believed conflict between the different parties present might lead to violence ("Police Prohibit "Antis" Meeting" 1917; "Prussianism in Winnipeg" 1917). With respect to the July 1 event, the *Winnipeg Evening Tribune* took exception to the fact that handbills advertising the meeting had been produced in the languages "of Canada's enemies." The report further specified the leaflets were in "German, Austrian, Russian, and Polish" ("Antis Ask Aliens to Meeting" 1917). Either the reporters thought "Austrian" was a language, or they were referring to one of the Slavic tongues spoken by some citizens of what was then Austria-Hungary.

Although opposing mandatory military service, Helen Armstrong was sympathetic to the conditions encountered by soldiers and veterans, and believed that conscription would be unnecessary if the government were willing to compensate soldiers more adequately, for example by paying disabled veterans a pension of $100 a month (Armstrong 1917a; Gutkin and Gutkin 1997, 233):

> It is more than I can understand how anyone, the "capitalist class" especially, that remains at home or have the well-paid positions and the least dangerous in the service, have the nerve or dare ask a man to go out and risk his life and when he returns calmly request him to hand in his uniform and in exchange hand him out a miserable pittance that will reduce a once self-respecting citizen, making a good, comfortable living, and enjoying all that home and family means to such a man, a miserable pauper, dependent on either charity or friends.
> ARMSTRONG 1917a

With respect to immigrants, Armstrong demonstrated her same concern for the welfare of anyone who might be discriminated against or disadvantaged. Like Tom Barker, the subject of Chapter Four of the present work, she eschewed the views of those who saw persons from countries the British Empire had been fighting against as an enemy. Reportedly, she responded "I don't care what a man is if he is whole under the skin and a worker. The only enemy alien we have in Canada is the capitalist and the strike breaker" (Knowles 2019). On another occasion, Helen visited foreign-born railroad workers incarcerated for breach of contract at the Stony Mountain prison and demanded improvements in the conditions under which they were housed (Gutkin and Gutkin 1997, 229). At the Calgary conference, she complained about the continued imprisonment at the same penitentiary of those who had violated military rules:

> I may say while we sit here and talk about these things, we can't realize what it means until you go to the pen and see. I have been down, took parcels Christmas time, and walked home with parcels, you couldn't give these boys anything. They had them marching up and down in snow up to their knees all dressed up in those fancy suits they provide, like cattle herded around and we are sick and tired sending in petitions.
> "Western Canada Labor Conference Held at Calgary, Alberta, March 13, 14, 15, 1919: Report of Proceedings" 1919

However, because the conditions experienced by immigrants to Canada in the early 1920s were often challenging, Armstrong also argued for restrictions on the numbers of people allowed to emigrate. This was not in any way a contradiction of her desire to help people who came from other countries, but a natural extension of her concern for the welfare of the poor, particularly if they were women. At a meeting of the Trades and Labor Council, she and fellow member James Winning noted the imminent deportation of migrants back to England, families who had lived in Manitoba for two or three years, but had been unable to survive economically in their new terrain. At the same time, Canada's immigration policy was to encourage and welcome more and more people, regardless of the possible circumstances under which some immigrants would then live ("Labor Repeats Protest Against Immigration" 1923). In an appearance at the Trades and Labor Council three months earlier, as part of a delegation from the WLL, Armstrong emphasized that, in view of the extent of unemployment in Canada at present, many new immigrants would be unable to obtain jobs. When another speaker, William H. "Bill" Hoop, stated that the economy would likely soon improve, Helen reportedly responded "that women were being confined on the prairies without medical attention, and that thousands were dying" ("Labor Bound to Face Steady Immigration Next Fifteen Years" 1922), a claim that lacked much specificity. In a later venture at the Trades and Labor Council in December 1923, Helen Armstrong and Bill Hoop presented a joint report that concluded that British immigrants were continuing to come to Canada notwithstanding their awareness of the unemployment situation, and that harvesters originally from the UK were awaiting repatriation, while some of them were refusing to go. Although most agricultural workers coming from the UK in 1923 were quickly assigned to work on farms, occasional applications for financial assistance from recent arrivals spawned reactions of outrage from the Winnipeg political class (Goldsborough 2018b; "Labor Objects to Immigration" 1923; "Newly Arrived Harvesters Apply for Relief" 1923).

Notwithstanding Armstrong's general concern for immigrants and the conditions faced by ordinary workers in laundries and other businesses that demanded high intensity labor, there was a widespread attitude at the time that found it difficult for the majority to relate to people of Chinese origin and include them among general categories. Hence the Winnipeg chief of police, Donald MacPherson, formally asked the city's Market, License and Relief Committee to ban "white girls" from working in Chinese restaurants. He also singled out women-run businesses such as the low alcohol bars that existed at the time and barbershops as places needing additional supervision to prevent "immoral conditions" ("Opposes Chinese Hiring White Girls" 1919). Consequently, for a different reason, it is not surprising that the WLL and the Trades and Labor Council, seeking to improve working conditions for women, would see the "127 Chinese laundries and 56 Chinese restaurants in the city" as part of the problem and seek to readjust the racial balance, achieving "more work for girls who are employed under proper working conditions in white laundries" ("Committee to Help Unemployed Gets Job Without Least Delay" 1922). In this era, labor activists in Australia made similarly negative rationalizations about Chinese and other "foreign" workers, and many unions there did not allow them to become members. The founding of "cooperative laundries" in that country, while it sought improvement of conditions faced by women, had the effect of taking work away from ethnic minorities, especially those with roots in China (Shone 2022, 33, 79).

Under the Mothers' Allowances Act rules, women seeking assistance were first required to possess no more than $200, and the amount they did have was then taken from them by the government and returned when their claim came to an end; subsequent revisions changed the $200 to $1,000. Not only did applying for support mean that women temporarily forfeited all their money, but if they owned a home, liens were placed on their property to prevent them from obtaining a second mortgage, rendering them entirely dependent on the province. As a member of the Mothers' Allowance Commission in 1920, Harriet Dick petitioned the Manitoba government to expand the scope of the Act, allowing women with disabled or dying husbands to qualify for the program ("Cases of Disability of Wage Earners May Be Under Scope of Mothers' Allowance Act." 1920). Representing the Commission at a meeting of the Child Welfare Congress the next year, Dick suggested instituting a "delinquents farm" where men who had deserted their wives might be imprisoned. Perhaps concerned that recipients of Mothers' Allowance retained a modicum of human dignity, G.B. Clark, a member of the Winnipeg Social Welfare Commission – a body that oversaw the operation of Mothers' Allowance and various other programs for the homeless, the poor, and the mentally ill, reporting to the city council, which appointed its members – told the conference that they should be relocated to special government-run facilities to stop them "moving from one house to another" ("Declares State Should Assume Care of Fatherless Children" 1921.) Starting in October 1922, the Trades and Labor Council petitioned the provincial government to add coverage under the 1916 Act to more women who were currently ineligible, specifically those with only one child, those who had been deserted by their husbands for more than five years, and women whose husbands were incarcerated or otherwise unable to provide support ("Disputes Act is Sought by Labor Council" 1922; Jones 2003, 163–164; "Labor Bound to Face Steady Immigration Next Fifteen Years" 1922; "Labor Urges Changes in Humane Laws" 1923; Winnipeg City Council 1920, 15). It is hardly surprising, therefore, that activists such as Helen Armstrong and Harriet Dick attributed great importance to, and directed much of their activity toward this policy area. In 1919, Helen was appointed as the WLL representative to the Winnipeg Mother's Allowance Committee, which interacted with the Social Welfare Commission. For Armstrong, moreover, the basis of the benefit, a means of humiliation of women and their children, must have seemed particularly offensive. Gavigan and Chunn write:

> [A]fter the First World War, the limited government provision of allowances to destitute, widowed, and later to abandoned mothers [was] in recognition solely of their role in the social reproduction of future citizens, and not as women *per se*. This form of state financial assistance was means-tested, ... contingent on closely scrutinized "fit and proper" behaviour, and enforced, if need be, through disqualification and/or criminalization.
> GAVIGAN AND CHUNN 2007, 770

In March 1923, the WLL and a number of other organizations addressed what they saw as the inadequate funding of the Mothers' Allowance program, and a meeting was held at Helen's home, producing a resolution that in part concluded that "It would seem that the government has started its economies, as usual, on the allowances for the protection of the most helpless members of societies" ("Women's Labor League Objects" 1923). A week later, Armstrong chaired a meeting at Winnipeg's Central Congregational Church at which the WLL and a number of other social organizations urged the provincial government to maintain its level of funding under the Mothers' Allowance Act. That request was approved unanimously by representatives of the Trades and Labor Council, the Red Cross, the Local Council of Women, the Woman's Christian Temperance Union, and the Ladies' Auxiliary of the Great War Veterans' Association ("Labor Repeats Protest Against Immigration" 1923; "Strong Protest is Made over Allowance Cut" 1923). The issue had specific resonance for the Ladies' Auxiliary, who had pointed out at a general meeting scheduled on the same day as the gathering at Armstrong's home, that some of the recipients who faced a reduction in what for many of them was their only source of income, were widows of men who had died fighting for Canada ("Government Warned Against Reducing Mothers' Allowance" 1923). At the same time, members of William Ivens' Labor Church passed a resolution noting that the amounts paid to Mothers' Allowance recipients had been reduced four times in the previous year, and that the Mothers' Allowance Commission was now no longer able to serve everyone legally entitled to be given help ("Labor Church Protests Cut in Allowances" 1923). As noted above, the Local Council of Women concurred in the need to improve the finances of the Commission so that it could do its job adequately, albeit noting that "the members of this council recognise and appreciate the effort of the members of our government in endeavoring to reduce expenditures to a minimum" ("Local Council Protests Cut in Mothers' Allowance Act" 1923), a proviso unlikely to have been shared by Armstrong and her colleagues, Rev. Ivens, or the Ladies' Auxiliary. In a meeting chaired by Armstrong the following May, the WLL met to discuss the provincial government's plans to consolidate the Mothers' Allowance Act with the Child Welfare Act, which women's groups saw as being likely to dilute the present rate at which care of the disadvantaged would be available. When the new law was passed in 1924, its provisions proved to be inadequately funded, which achieved exactly the consequence that activists had feared ("Labor League Meets" 1923; Lewycky 2019, 146; "Supplementary Estimates for $120,057 Passed" 1924). Kelly (2016) notes that Armstrong's interest in this area of policy continued into the 1930s.

At a Winnipeg Trades and Labor Council meeting in January 1923, Armstrong launched an offensive against the Social Welfare Commission, a body that included both city aldermen and persons from other walks of life, calling for it to be investigated and reorganized, saying that the way it operated including forcibly breaking up families. She also complained that when women were sent out on a job interview by Manitoba's employment service, they were forced to pay the costs of transportation even if they were not hired (Gutkin and Gutkin

1997, 248; "Woman Claims Welfare Board is Home Wrecker" 1923). However, at a public meeting of the Commission the previous month at which Helen had presented examples of destitute persons being treated inappropriately, Alderman William Boad "Billy" Simpson, a member of the Commission and a fellow unionist, asked her, "What would you do with a man who won't work?" Reportedly she responded, "I would send him to the prison farm: he would have to work there. I would flog a man myself if he wouldn't work" (Goldsborough 2018a; "Social Board Hears Reports of Privations" 1922), a somewhat less than inspirational demonstration of her commitment to community dignity.

Another issue for the Women's Labor League was the size and weight of bread sold in retail establishments, with the WLL agitating for loaves to be of a standard twenty-ounce size. At a Winnipeg city council meeting in March 1918, Helen Armstrong issued a threat to profits of the bakeries, which preferred to make a sixteen-ounce product, backing a protest by people who would then make their own loaves at home. A week later, the WLL criticized Winnipeg's government for not reacting quickly to the standardization demand, and the city did impose a twenty-ounce mandate on all bread. When the city of Brandon, Manitoba, ordered the same size restriction, it was argued at the city council meeting which instituted the rule that it would enable customers to know the exact weight of what they were buying ("All Loaves of Bread Must Weigh 20 Ozs" 1917; "Civic Committee Retires." 1918; "Women's Labor League" 1918a). To understand why issues related to bread were so important to people at the time, perhaps it is necessary to know that a committee of the Winnipeg Trades and Labor Council determined that "a fair estimate of the consumption of bread is two loaves per day for three people" ("The Trades and Labor Council" 1917b). The diets of poor workers relied to a greater degree on the intake of such staples than they do today.

In 1917, Manitobans had dealt with a sugar shortage that prompted retailers to limit sales to one or two pounds, a restriction that was overcome by grocery shoppers who visited many different stores. In 1923, ten-pound sacks of sugar were available for $1.35, and for Armstrong, the WLL, and the Trades and Labor Council, the issue was now the commodity's high cost and that of some other products such as tea. They wanted sugar to go back to its old retail price of 95c. Ironically, the solution from some perspectives lay again in limiting purchases, and Helen sought a boycott of sugar, hoping to drive the prices down. She contended that "if every housewife in Winnipeg was to do without sugar for one day, prices would be forced to drop" ("Women Resent Duty on Raisins" 1923). To publicize the dispute, the WLL sent a telegram to the Canadian premier, W.L. Mackenzie King. Of allied concern to Helen was the fact that due to an increase in the duty on California raisins, raisins were now costing 25 cents, rather than

21 cents a pound ("Labor League Meets" 1923; "Winnipeg Women Ask Federal Probe into Sugar Prices" 1923; "Women Gather Sugar Stocks in Pound Lots" 1917; "Women Resent Duty on Raisins" 1923).

In the years when she was most active, there were not many locations and even fewer matters of public concern at which the presence of Helen Armstrong might not at one time or another be observed. At a meeting of the city's Fire, Water, and Light Committee in 1917, she was present as a member of a four-person delegation from the WLL, and she spoke out about the long hours firefighters were obliged to spend away from their families, the dangers inherent in their busiest activities, and the overall negative effects of their employment on wives and children. The committee discussed the possibility of changing the way fire protection was organized in the city. Although Winnipeg had a single platoon of firefighters who could be called out at any time, the discussants were aware that Minneapolis had experimented with a system of two teams, each only on call for a twelve-hour shift ("The Firemen's Union and the Proposed Compromise" 1917). Armstrong was also involved in the setting up by Mrs. B.W. Bellamy of the Medicine Hat, Alberta, Typographical Union's "Woman's Auxiliary" of a similar group that was connected to the union's Winnipeg local ("Labor Convention Asks Six-Hour Day for Miners" 1918; "Western Canada Conference of Typographical Unions" 1917).

Despite Helen Armstrong's frequently feverish activity, it is believed she and her husband George moved to Chicago in 1924 for a while so he could work in a construction job (Forster 2011, 42). Consequently, by 1925 it was necessary to hold a large gathering to reconstitute the WLL, an event at which fifteen members joined the organization, and perhaps the most important change was the appointment of Edith Hancox as recording secretary ("Women's Labor League is Again Organized" 1925). Hancox, who would later serve as the WLL's president, was an important contributor to advancing the interests of women and of the unemployed ("The Winnipeg General Strike: 100 Years Later" 2019). In a January 1921 meeting at Roblin Hall in Winnipeg's Agricultural College, she pointed out that it was more difficult for unemployed women than for men to live on the city's available $7 weekly emergency relief payment, at the same time arguing that the alternative that was offered to women, doing domestic work, was "oppressive and humiliating" ("Speaker Terms Domestic Work as "Humiliating"" 1921). The next year, following the city's ending of relief payments to single men and childless couples, she spoke at a council meeting as a representative of the Manitoba Association of Unemployed, working with the formerly imprisoned strikers, John Queen and Bob Russell, to try and restore the benefit. At a council meeting on January 2, 1923, together with Helen Armstrong, an audience of the unemployed, and a man named

William Boothman who emptied a packet of tea on the city clerk's desk, Hancox heard some of the aldermen rationalize that indigents from other cities were seeking to relocate to Winnipeg, and that consequently the caseload was too great. In a later appearance the following August, she pointed out that the latest street sweeping technology had left some older men who used to do that type of work without any employment. At the end of the year, together with another formerly jailed strike leader, R.E. Bray, Edith complained about the system of contracting supplies of groceries granted to relief recipients and suggested that unemployed men should be given payments of $15 a week. Again, she argued that persons receiving benefits were being assigned unsuitable work, for example the men sent to labor in the city's woodyard. In an earlier city hall meeting, she had pointed out some of those assigned to the woodyard but due to their poverty lacking shoes, had been forced to walk a significant distance barefoot to get to that place of work. Edith made practical suggestions to the committee such as giving the unemployed shoes to wear, and finding them work sweeping chimneys, but some of the unemployment committee members felt that in making her points, Hancox was resorting to personal attacks. That perception was one often attributed also to Helen Armstrong when she tried to illustrate the many ways that ordinary people were poorly served by those elected to "represent" them. In November 1924, Hancox appeared at another Winnipeg council meeting to point out that harvesters had been stranded in the city without employment or remuneration ("Council Will Support Claim of Unemployed" 1923; "Free Admission Parlor Closed by Magistrate" 1924; "Old Men Lose Cleaning Jobs" 1923; "Relief Body is Criticized" 1923; "Speakers for Jobless Men Invade Council with New Griefs." 1923; "Unemployed Ask Continuance of Relief Grants" 1922). Edith was clearly another of the women whose role in past events was for a long time little valued and little remembered. During the strike, on June 1, 1919, along with two of its leaders imprisoned for their activity, William Ivens and Fred Dixon, Hancox, who was referred to in the *Western Labor News* report of the event as "Mrs. Hancocks," spoke before a large crowd in Victoria Park, mocking the Committee of One Thousand ("7,500 Pack Labor Church" 1919; Reilly and Reilly [1986] 2019; Thompson 2020, 127). When Hancox ran for election to city government in Ward 2, a multi-member district, in 1923, she, like Armstrong, indicated her desire not to renew the contract of the Street Railway Company ("Candidates State Position on Vital Issues" 1923).

Occasionally, at times when she was less involved with battles of political leadership, though it is hard to imagine she was ever not entangled in activism to some extent, references to Helen Armstrong would appear in newspaper columns and letters. A contribution to the New Zealand newspaper, the

Taranaki Herald, in 1910, cited a "Helen Armstrong," its author referencing as its source the *Chicago Tribune*, although the *Tribune* contains no mention of Helen that year. Nonetheless, the sentiments expressed seem compatible with Armstrong's views:

> All women can do nowadays ... is to take the workaday world as they find it and learn how men do things. Later on they may mould the world according to their own ideas instead of being moulded by it contrary to their natures. They may put into the office some of the cosiness and charm they give to a home. They may do away with the city grime that consorts so ill with their dainty frocks. They may put an end to street noises. They may even instil some of their sympathy and goodness into business deals and political campaigns.
> "Woman's Quiet Influence" 1910

Kelly (2016) notes that, during one of Armstrong's discourses, "she departed from the history of suffrage to praise the new labour-saving machines that would one day free women from the drudgery of housework." Again, she seems to have been expressing an appreciation of a longstanding historical process that would finally result in gender equality.

An editorial in the *Winnipeg Citizen* on June 9, 1919, ever demonstrating its hostility to the strikers, portrayed Helen as having been mentally ill in the past, implying that she may not have recovered:

> Another local leader is Mrs. Helen Armstrong who, according to her own word, has spent some years of her life in an insane asylum. Her husband, George Armstrong, another notorious "Red," is one of the local leaders, who drew down upon himself the wrath of returned men both over the conscription issue and latterly when returned soldiers went on a rampage against a Bolshevist meeting which sent greetings to the Soviet government of Russia, and the Spartacans in Germany.
> "The Winnipeg Revolutionary Strike" 1919

An advertisement in the same paper a week later made a similar point, saying, "Passing over the personality of the female agitator Mrs. George Armstrong [Helen], who on her own admission spent several years in a lunatic asylum, and who therefore cannot be counted on to be extraordinarily well balanced" ("A Few Frank Words Concerning Agitators" 1919; Dupuis 2014, 88). Gutkin and Gutkin (1997, 241–242) note that "the diagnosis of insanity has served as a classic means to denigrate insubordinate females." Kelly suggests that Helen was merely depressed at the time and notes that the Brandon Mental Hospital record of her stay indicates a diagnosis far less extreme than lunacy (Gutkin and Gutkin 1997, 247; Kelly 2016).

Reportedly, after the Armstrongs relocated to Chicago in 1924, Helen worked with Jane Addams at Hull House, a connection that resulted from earlier correspondence between the two feminist activists. The ongoing Jane Addams Papers Project includes a reference to a Mrs. Armstrong who appeared at Hull House, but little more appears to be known about her in that context (Forster 2011, 42; Hajo N.d.).

In 1935, a letter was sent from Regina, Saskatchewan, to the editor of the *Winnipeg Free Press* from a person signing herself "D. Helen Armstrong." In view of its content, and the fact that it was sent to a Winnipeg paper, it seems likely that its author and the subject of the present chapter are the same person. She wrote:

> I should like to chide your contributor who wrote in the last issue declaring that women ought never to have been granted the franchise. I fear that this gentleman, like others of his sex, judges all women by the sort he notices. The sensible women never did get attention, while tinted fingernails, and loud voices were around, but that doesn't necessarily mean that women are pin-headed.
>
> ARMSTRONG 1935

During the Second World War, writing to the same newspaper, this time from Winnipeg, in a somewhat incoherent letter, she complained about currency restrictions that were preventing her and her husband from visiting their daughters in the United States. If they were to go, she pointed out:

> Our daughters must pay for our tickets, our meals, berth and spending money, if necessary, and then to add insult to injury they must keep us while there and provide pocket money. What a grand idea our government has of a visit.
>
> ARMSTRONG 1943

Another reader soon responded, taking a different tack:

> With my two children, virtually a prisoner, I live here as a pauper. Beyond the pittance which the British government allows my husband to send it is impossible to get any money out of England and for three years I have been waiting for a passage, bespoken and paid for in 1940 to get out of

> Canada. Of great moment as these facts are to me, I have no quarrel with either government. They are not planning "visits." They are both struggling to win this war in order to free millions of starving men women and children.
>
> Storm in Teacup 1943

Of course, there was a global conflict going on, which would make many people forgive the government for the various inconveniences. However, Helen Armstrong, who was actively involved in the most important strike in the history of Canada, never saw a reason to suspend her activities or to be happy at having to do so. Eventually, Helen and George relocated to California where their daughters now lived, Helen dying in Baldwin Park in Southern California in 1947, and George surviving for almost another decade until his death in Concord in Northern California, in 1956 (Gutkin and Gutkin 1997, 192; Kelly 2016).

As is often acknowledged, Helen Armstrong was a key figure in the Winnipeg Strike of 1919, and her absence or diminution in many of the accounts that have sought to document that important event is an unfortunate omission that has still not been completely rectified. However, if the happenings of the era, spanning before, during, and following the six weeks of labor stoppage, are included in the way that the experience is explained, perhaps considering the Strike as a system of ideas and attempts at societal reform spread over a period of twenty or more years of unresolved conflict and suffering by workers under an exploitative system of poverty deliberately imposed by governments who chose to focus on far less appropriate goals, then Armstrong's achievements are significantly much greater: then, the record is that she stood at the center of the Strike, as Winnipeg's champion of labor, women, and the poor.

CHAPTER 3

Elizabeth Gurley Flynn: a Star Who Ceased to Twinkle

At the age of nineteen, the profile and noteworthy visage of Elizabeth Gurley Flynn burst out onto the national scene as an energetic leader and prominent and articulate tribune of the Industrial Workers of the World and its working-class oriented politics. Not only was she a radical, but her arrival was also immediately viewed as a new direction for the Wobblies in the United States, who had hitherto been led only by men. Her future friend, Mary Heaton Vorse, would describe how Elizabeth appeared to a man who saw her in New York a few years earlier: "he found a beautiful child of fifteen, the most beautiful girl he had ever seen. A young Joan of Arc is what she looked like to him with her dark hair hanging down her back and her blue Irish eyes ringed with black lashes. That was how she entered the Labor movement" (Vorse 1926, 175).

Spokane, Washington was in 1908 a central location for recruiting mining, agricultural, lumber, railroad construction, and other workers for the Pacific Northwest region, and itinerant personnel would visit there to obtain a position, many of which were relatively dangerous and located in distant locales where employees would have to live in camps, but from which they could quickly be fired with no recourse. The Wobblies viewed the city-licensed employment agencies, which provided information about and, for a fee, access to available work as exploiters, and they retaliated by holding meetings and delivering speeches outside these businesses, a response the "job sharks" did not like. After the city passed a revised ordinance directed at the IWW that became effective on January 1, 1909, banning public speaking in much of the city, one of the IWW leaders, James P. Thompson, was arrested, although in his case, the judge, S.A. Mann, declared an aspect of the amended law invalid because it allowed exceptions to be made for the Salvation Army and other religious groups, which its predecessor had not included. Future cases were decided on the basis of the earlier ordinance, No. A1324, with Mann often ruling that the IWW members' speech was protected by the First Amendment. He also tried to prevent the police from beating up suspects ("Bloody Shirt; Two Teeth Knocked Out" 1909; "Here is the "Disorderly Conduct"" 1909; "Jail is Crowded with I.W.W. Men" 1909; "Judge Mann Dismisses Free Speech Case" 1909).

The local version of the Wobbly newspaper, the *Industrial Worker*, called for opponents of the restrictive legislation to come to town "and fill the jails of

Spokane." Many of the organization's supporters followed that injunction and arrived in the city, and within a few weeks, hundreds of them had been arrested (Hermida 2016; Kershner 2009; Kizer 1966, 110–112; Myers 2020). Following an activist success she had achieved in Missoula, Montana, and a recent marriage to John Archibald "Jack" Jones, Flynn was asked by the Wobblies to come to Spokane, where there was much public support for the IWW. As in Missoula, it was her intention to fight against a law prohibiting street demonstrations although, because she was pregnant, she did not herself demonstrate outdoors as she had done in the past. Referred to as "Gurley" or even "Girlie" by some of her Wobbly cohorts, she did, however, address a crowd at the Turner Hall, the meeting house of that city's German-American Society and historic location for radical gatherings. Additionally, she took charge of the *Industrial Worker*; such was the atmosphere in the city, that publication's editors had generally been arrested, as she was on November 30, 1909, when out walking, although she resisted this fate initially by tying herself to a lamppost (Baxandall 1987a, 7; Camp 1995, 17; "'Conspiracy' Cases Before Judge Stocker" 1909; "Elizabeth Gurley Flynn Sentenced for Conspiracy" 1909; Engle 2003, 134; Kornbluh 1964b, 95; Panzner 1964, 100; Vapnek 2015, 30–31).

Police raided the *Industrial Worker* premises, arresting everyone they found there and seizing the December issue, as well as anyone found selling the paper elsewhere (Kershner 2009; Vapnek 2015, 31). Another raid on the IWW office generated the seizure of eight boys aged between 11 and 16 who had been serving as newsagents, who were imprisoned for a night and subjected to two intensive sessions of interrogation, followed by the filing of charges of juvenile delinquency. Attempting to rationalize this decision, the prosecutor, Fred C. Pugh, argued that "The teachings of the I.W.W. are radical and many of them unAmerican, and for these small boys to live in an atmosphere where loyalty to the flag is sneered at, certainly does not put the ideas into their heads that will make them good citizens" ("Officials Try to Force Confessions" 1909). However, increasingly some residents of Spokane felt that actions such as Pugh's and their rationalization were more "unAmerican" than the speechmaking and journalistic articles of the IWW, a factor that led to donations to her cause and an eventual change of city policy (Vapnek 2015, 33).

Elizabeth spent a night in jail before being released on bail. The experience was enlightening, and reporting it had much propaganda value. At the time, the organ of the Montana Socialist Party, the *Montana News*, summed up her experience with a certain amount of hyperbole:

> The police have been itching to get Miss Flynn. She was thrown into a cell with prostitutes, insulted by the police, who came with their vile

familiarity in the night, and abused terribly by the prosecuting attorney, Pugh. She is in a pregnant condition, and the greatest fears are entertained for her safety, the first child lost owing to her overwork on the platform.

"Elizabeth Gurley Flynn Sentenced for Conspiracy" 1909

In jail, Flynn found herself incarcerated with prostitutes whose services were apparently being utilized and organized at a profit by the officers who ran the jail ("Crimes and Criminals" 1910). Like the newssellers and other Wobbly activists and supporters, Flynn was pressured to provide information to police, a process she later described as being subjected to the "third degree" (Engle 2003, 135). She spent the night in the women's section of the jail with two of the ladies of the night, and her presence apparently caused one of her cellmates to leave for a while to take care of a customer, an action that might have taken place in the cell if she had not been there (Engle 2003, 111, 135; Flynn 1973, 109). She derived much publicity from the fact that, in the morning, the head prison officer whose last name was Bigelow, while bringing her breakfast, woke her by touching her cheek. Elizabeth claimed to be outraged: "My anger blazed up and I said, "Take your hand off me; I didn't come here to be insulted"" (Flynn 1909). She continued:

> It certainly is a shame and disgrace to this city that a woman can be arrested because of union difficulties, bonds placed so high that immediate release is impossible, thrown into a county jail, where sights and sounds, horrible, immoral and absolutely different from her ordinary, decent mode of life can be forced on her. Her privacy invaded while trying to steal some sleep by a brute of a man in a jail that hasn't attained the ordinary standard of civilization that requires a matron for the care of women prisoners.
>
> FLYNN 1909

On December 6, Flynn was convicted on the charge of conspiracy by a jury who deliberated for only twenty minutes and she was sentenced to three months' imprisonment. She was released the next day on a $5,000 bond, part of which was contributed by her attorney, Fred H. Moore and part by local supporters. Other backers, such as the Western Federation of Miners, provided funds for an appeal. At this point, the Wobblies were even receiving donations from supporters in Australia and New Zealand. The following Sunday, she was already active again, speaking on the topic of "The Principles of the Industrial Workers of the World" in a meeting at Spokane's Odd Fellows' Hall. On December 30, she spoke at the city's Apollo Hall, sending invitations to that event to police officer Bill Shannon, as well as to Judge Mann, who had been involved in assigning her case prior to the trial, and was understandably viewed as sympathetic to the Wobbly's free speech claims. Around the same time, IWW supporters mailed threatening letters to various local officials including Mann, some of which were postmarked in Chicago, home of the Wobblies' headquarters. Elizabeth next made a trip to Hoquiam, Washington to give a talk at the International Union of Shingle Weavers' convention. Then she gave a presentation at the Pavilion in Coeur D'Alene, Idaho, where she gave a two-hours long account of her experiences in nearby Spokane. Subsequent engagements in mid-January included gatherings at a labor hall in Hillyard, on the east side of Spokane, and again at the Turner Hall ("'Conspiracy' Cases Before Judge Stocker" 1909; "Elizabeth Gurley Flynn Will Speak on Sunday" 1909; Engle 2003, 136; "Gurley Flynn Sends Bid to Bill Shannon" 1909; "Intense Interest in Elizabeth Flynn Trial" 1909; "Mayor and Chief are "Marked Men"'" 1909; "Miners Give $500 to Gurley Flynn" 1909; "Miners Rally to Aid of Women [sic]" 1909; Myers 2020; "Sidelights from Other Cities in Washington" 1910; "Speech Fight Appeals Grow" 1909; "Woman Sues the Mayor" 1910).

Correspondents struggled to find words to describe the nineteen-year-old activist, alternating between the name she chose, and one they felt was more appropriate: "Miss Flynn, or rather Mrs. Jones in private life" corrected one report ("Elizabeth Gurley Flynn Sentenced for Conspiracy" 1909). Later, she would laud an organizer of a demonstration in Paterson, New Jersey, Henrietta Rodman, an English teacher at Wadleigh High School for Girls in New York City, who had battled school district officials to protect the rights of married teachers and of married women to be teachers, including allowing them not to use their married names at work (Carter 2017, 129; Flynn 1973, 172; Vapnek 2015, 50). The British paper, *Justice*, as it reported news of Flynn's initial ninety-day sentence, also gave her opinion of marriage:

> Woman does not care much for individual rights. If she did she would take advantage of present rights which are not now denied her. Why does not woman keep her own name after marriage? No law prevents her. It is only her acknowledgement of possession by man for a woman to take his name. Women who have outgrown the idea that they belong to their husbands have no excuse for clinging to the symbol of ownership.
> FLYNN, quoted in "The Fight for Free Speech in America" 1910

In this respect, Flynn displayed a similar view to Elizabeth Cady Stanton, with whose contributions to feminist thinking she was familiar (Flynn 1973, 56, 277;

1987, 222), that the woman who adopts their husband's name upon marriage "as she changes masters ... has so little self-respect that she does not see the insult of the custom" (Shone 2019, 229; Stanton [1895] 1999, part i, 73). Referencing the contents of a notebook and a 1905 speech titled "Woman," resources which are today located in the Elizabeth Gurley Flynn Papers collection at New York University, Vapnek comments:

> Flynn believed in the ideal of "free love," framing "mutual desire" and "mutual affection" as "the only justification for a man and woman being together." In an early speech, she critiqued marriage as no better than "legalized prostitution," but she hesitated to violate contemporary standards of female respectability.
> VAPNEK 2018, 17

Indeed, in the handwritten text of a speech titled "Men and Women" (1915) today now situated in the same library, Elizabeth asked, "Do I believe in free love? What is the other alternative? Slave-love? Then I believe in *free* love at all costs" (Camp 1995, 12). She explained as follows:

> When you consider these reasons for marriage, these hypocrisies, deceits, woman's dependency on a man, especially after she has borne him children, then we are at no loss to understand why marriage in the majority of cases loses all semblance of love and becomes legalized prostitution, why most marriages are unhappy, at no loss whatsoever for no institution could remain pure amid such vile surroundings.
>
> *Sexual enslavement* then follows economic enslavement, and is but a gentle way of saying prostitution, whether it be for one night or one whole life. The woman who bears her children faithfully every year or so, who "submits herself to her husband" in a truly Christian way, whose life is that of a breeder of children, may be President Roosevelt's ideal, to guard against race-suicide. To me she is a miserable sex slave and my ideal is far different.
> FLYNN 1987, 102

Moreover, as she argued in another early essay, "Education and the School System" (1906) that she later delivered to a church congregation, sounding like Jean-Paul Sartre or Max Stirner or, indeed, the subject of Chapter 1, Virginia Bolten, that women (and men) are heavily influenced by what they are taught in school, learning what others value and being told how to behave:

> Without my gleanings from Marx, George and Proudhon, Thomas Paine and Ingersoll, Walt Whitman and Emerson and Thoreau, Shelley, Byron, even Ibsen and Bernard Shaw and many more such literary teachers, what sort of crude ideas would I have? Does the school training open the door of Knowledge? I would emphatically say no. Instead of giving you the key to the realms of booklore and then letting you alone to explore for yourself, they must pick and choose for you.
> FLYNN 1987, 82

Nonetheless, throughout her life, newspapers and magazines would often add what they thought of as being Flynn's appropriate married name to the one she preferred to use. As she noted many years later in testimony in her Smith Act trial, "I married in 1908, separated from my husband shortly thereafter, and have always used my own name" (Flynn 1952b). Like Cady Stanton, she was aware of the connection between married women's names and how seriously they would be taken, and whether or not they might be dismissed as spinsters or as other failures who had been unable to hold on to their husbands.

As in the case of Tennie C. Claflin, the sister of Victoria C. Woodhull (Shone 2019, 138–141), the attractiveness of Elizabeth Gurley Flynn earned her much media attention, but many of the terms that were used have grown increasingly irritating as norms have changed. Thus what was intended merely to be descriptive, such as "Elizabeth Gurley Flynn Jones, girl conspirator" ("Spokane Convicts I.W.W." 1910), unless read mistakenly as designating her a comic book superhero, has been rendered from today's perspective an insult, while "Mrs. Gurley Flynn, woman agitator of the I.W.W." ("Miners Give $500 to Gurley Flynn" 1909), although it still makes reference to the fact that Elizabeth had succeeded in finding a husband, seems less flawed. In "Miss Gurley-Flynn Jones, the would-be Spokane heroine" ("Union Combinations" 1910), she appeared as both single and married in the same phrase. In a story about the death of Jack's second wife, a Philadelphia paper recounted with a degree of bewilderment details of his earlier relationship as follows:

> John A. Jones and Elizabeth Gurley Flynn, the former I.W.W. agitator and campaigner, were married in 1908. Many stories have been told of their married life, the most unusual feature being that she retained her maiden name and always addressed Jones as "Comrade."
> "Artist's Bride Drowns from Honeymoon Launch" 1920

Elsewhere, she was referred to as "Mrs. J. A. Jones, known among socialists and in the industrial movement by her maiden name, Elizabeth Gurley Flynn," as though her alias were secret (""Conspiracy" Cases Before Judge Stocker" 1909). At other times in this first era of her political life, she was identified by newspapers as "Elizabeth Gurley Flynn, the I.W.W. agitator" ("Trenton Ban on Elizabeth Gurley Flynn." 1913), "Elizabeth Gurley Flynn, one of the best known women labor agitators in the world" ("Good Speakers at State Labor Convention" 1917), "the youthful Socialist orator of New York" ("Little Local Stories" 1908a), "a pretty little socialist of New York, East Side" ("Girl Leads Labor War" 1909), "The Girl Orator of the Bowery" ("Little Local Stories" 1908b), "The Anarchistic Joan of Arc" (1908b), and "the schoolgirl Socialist" ("Down and Out: Agitator Jones is a Little Shy on Cash" 1908). As Flynn would later reflect, the naming affront reflected the current nature of society:

> Even the clothes of women hampered them – the long skirts that touched the ground, the big unwieldy sleeves, the enormous hats. You were still "a girl" if your skirt was above your shoe tops.
> FLYNN 1973, 56

In Flynn's appeal, which was heard in February 1910, the jury met for a much longer time than in the original case, ranging in reports from 17 to 24 hours, the discrepancy possibly explained by the fact that at one point the judge sent the jury back to deliberate some more. It declined, as Barrett (1999, 40) writes somewhat colorfully, "to send that pretty Irish girl to jail merely for bein' big-hearted and idealistic, to mix with all those whores and crooks down at the pen." Despite her acquittal, her codefendant, C.L. "Charley" Filigno, whose last name was frequently misspelled in accounts, the person who had sent a telegram to Elizabeth when she was in Missoula asking her to come to Spokane and participate in the conflict, was found guilty of conspiracy a second time and sentenced to six months on a chain gang, a development that was not ideal from Flynn's perspective any more than it was for Charley. Interviewed in Coeur D'Alene, Idaho, on February 24, 1910, she commented:

> Personally I would much preferred that we had both been convicted or both cleared as that would be more on the issues of the case. It is not ourselves personally that we seek to vindicate, but the principle of free speech. As it stands now I feel that the element of sympathy for a woman played an important part in the decision.
> "Gurley Flynn Visits City" 1910

Fortunately, an agreement made soon afterwards with the Spokane mayor, Nelson S. Pratt, to allow the IWW to speak in public in future included also the release of Filigno, a positive result that turned out to be quite atypical of the Wobbly experience (Camp 1995, 24; "Detective is Expert on Writing" 1910; Kizer 1966, 112; "Spokane Convicts I.W.W." 1910; "Sympathy Helped Clear Gurley Flynn; Filigno Will Appeal" 1910; Vapnek 2015, 33; "Victory at Spokane" 1910). However, the accord also put an end to the criminal defamation suit she had filed against Pratt claiming that, in a letter he wrote, which was published in a local newspaper, he had lied about her and damaged her reputation. In that missive, Pratt had referred to "the wild and hysterical inferences and conclusions drawn by Miss Flynn," calling her "a hysterical and lawbreaking conspirator," and claimed that "Miss Flynn's charge against" the head of the jail in which she had briefly been incarcerated "refutes itself and discloses the prejudice and hysterical character of her" account of that experience ("Woman Sues the Mayor" 1910). Women who asserted their rights were often described as "hysterical." As discussed in Chapter 2 of the present volume, similar references were made to the alleged mental health problems of Helen Armstrong. The strength of Elizabeth's reputation as a speaker and as an organizer in Spokane has subsequently added to the extent of scholarly interest in her life story and in the nature of the arguments she made (Bartram 2018, 5).

1 Before and after Spokane

Though Barrett above portrays the jury that acquitted Flynn in terms of its admiration for "that pretty Irish girl," Elizabeth was, notwithstanding her political opinions and ancestry, not Irish, and was born in Concord, New Hampshire on August 7, 1890, although she qualified that fact by making her intellectual commitments clear:

> By birth I am a New Englander, though not of Mayflower stock. My ancestors were "immigrants and revolutionists" – from the Emerald Isle.
> FLYNN 1973, 23

Elizabeth's mother, Annie Gurley, was originally from Galway, where she had lived with her grandmother Gurley and spoken Gaelic until she was seventeen, arriving in the United States in 1876. She belonged to New York City's Irish Feminist Club, and she had attended lectures by Susan B. Anthony, Frederick Douglass, and Charles Stuart Parnell (Baxandall 1987a, 3; Camp 1995, 5; Flynn 1973, 29; Langston 2002, 79). Annie never forgot her Irish heritage, the worst details of which she imparted to her daughter:

> The awareness of being Irish came to us as small children, through plaintive song and heroic story. The Irish people fought to wrest their native soil from foreign landlords, to speak their native Gaelic tongue, to worship in the church of their choice, to have their own schools, to be independent and self-governing. As children, we drew in a burning hatred of British rule with our mother's milk. Until my father died, at over eighty, he never said "England" without adding, "God damn her!"
>
> FLYNN 1973, 23

There is conflicting evidence about the birthplace of Elizabeth's father, Thomas Flynn, which, notwithstanding his ancestry and commitment to Irish nationalism that he shared with his wife, does not appear to have been anywhere in Ireland. This is partly because at different times he claimed to have been born in a number of places, a tendency that indicated something of his character. A quarry worker, poet, and occasional candidate for political office, he had attended Dartmouth College and was a strong advocate of labor unionism. Elizabeth had two younger sisters, Anna Katherine (Kathie) and Lucy Sabina (Bina), and a brother, also called Thomas (Baxandall 1987a, 4; "Biographical Note" 2021; Camp 1995, 4; Flynn 1952b).

In 1906, at the age of fifteen, when Elizabeth first lectured in public, she talked about women and socialism, referring to the writings of Susan B. Anthony and to August Bebel's book, *Woman and Socialism* (a work that is also, at times, translated as *Women and Socialism*, which is the name Flynn used). As noted in Chapter 5, it was partially translated into Japanese by Kōtoku, Shūsui and Sakai, Toshihiko, and it had also influenced the development of Kōtoku's thought (Flynn 1952b, 1987, 174). When she became an IWW organizer, Flynn had read Edward Bellamy's *Looking Backward 2000–1987* (Bellamy 1887), a critique of contemporary society which, somewhat prophetically, she described as having "appealed to me as practical and feasible" (Flynn 1973, 47). For other readers, the ideal society delineated in *Looking Backward*, where there is extensive surveillance of people, and those refusing to work are imprisoned and fed only bread and water (1887, ch. XII), as were some of the Wobblies convicted in Spokane, appears oppressively totalitarian or even Stalinist, which critics of Flynn's later perspective as the leader of the Communist Party, USA, might feel was an aspiration she had in some ways always secretly nurtured (for a discussion of Bellamy and its demurrers, see Shone 2022, 67–70). Elizabeth refers to Bellamy's book as "a biting criticism of capitalism," but it can be viewed also as a blueprint for destroying the very liberty that, as a Wobbly, and in the future as one of the founders of what would become the American Civil Liberties Union, she would spend much of her time trying to defend.

Jack Jones had wanted Elizabeth to cease her activism interests when their second, first surviving, baby, whom they called Fred Flynn, was born on May 19, 1910, but she had no intention of doing this, so they argued and then she left him and went back by train to her mother's home in New York City where she give birth. Leaving Fred in the care of her family, she resumed her political activities. Despite their attempts to get together again, in 1920 Jones finally filed for divorce on the grounds of desertion. That same year, he married Anna Mitchell, who was drowned in a honeymoon cruise accident on Lake Michigan, and her body was found near Racine, Wisconsin. Later, he was married a third time, to Lailah Cooper. At the Dill Pickle Club on Chicago's North side, from 1914 onwards, Jack reigned over a forum for alternative politics and culture where budding revolutionaries and local college professors gathered to talk and watch plays. Eventually, Lailah would donate the club records to the University of Chicago library ("Artist's Bride Drowns from Honeymoon Launch" 1920; Barrett 1999, 73–74; "Bride Drowns; "Dill Pickle" Chief Saved" 1920; Camp 1995, 25; "Chief of Dill Picklers Sues Socialist Wife" 1920; Helquist 2015, 132; "John Archibald Jones" 1940; Vapnek 2015, 34).

Flynn became involved with the Italian editor of an anarchist newspaper, Carlo Tresca, who started to work with her on some Wobbly campaigns. He moved in with her family in the Bronx in 1913. Ultimately, Carlo's presence there while she was away on IWW assignments undermined their relationship, and he had a liaison with her sister, Bina. To hide the resulting pregnancy, Bina spent some time in Italy, and when he was born, the baby, Peter, was quickly assigned to foster parents. Notwithstanding her commitment to "free love," Elizabeth was upset by news of Tresca's dalliances with Bina and with other women, but when, many years later, on January 11, 1943, he was assassinated in the street in Manhattan, she indicated that she forgave him for his indiscretions. In the meantime, she had not spoken to Bina for a decade (Baxandall 1987a, 22; Camp 1995, 113; Fones-Wolf 1996, 284; Isserman 1988, 322; Lynn 2016, 307; Vapnek 2018, 21–22).

Although later in life Elizabeth Gurley Flynn continued to have relationships and sexual interludes with men, greater scholarly interest has accrued to her friendship with Marie Equi, with whom she lived much of the time for most of the years from 1926 to 1937 in Portland, Oregon, during an extensive section of her life in which she experienced substantial self-doubt, emerging with a rather different political philosophy that was to some extent a reflection of the views of Equi. Back in 1915, when Flynn was acquitted of incitement in Paterson, New Jersey, Equi had sat at the defense lawyers' table ("Gurley Flynn Free; Plans to Keep On Talking" 1915). In her analysis of Elizabeth's life, Helen C. Camp writes:

> Equi's open acknowledgement of a number of lesbian unions has inevitably led to speculation about the nature of her relationship with Flynn. Nancy Kruger, who made a study of Equi's career, has stated "it is certain they had an intense emotionally involved relationship" – a judgment confirmed by Flynn herself – but neither she nor any other researcher had found positive evidence of an erotic attraction. Kathie Flynn was worried about Elizabeth's living with Marie because she thought it would hurt her sister's reputation.
> CAMP 1995, 129–130

However, by omitting the initial clause of Krieger's conclusion, it may be asked, has Camp changed the meaning of what Krieger intended to convey when she wrote:

> Although there is not definitive evidence the two were lovers, it is certain they had an intense, emotionally-involved and occasionally stormy relationship.
> KRIEGER 1983

At one point, Vapnek, in her book about Flynn, appears to indicate that Flynn and Equi were involved sexually:

> After her relationships with Tresca and Equi ended, Flynn had a string of intense but temporary relationships with younger men. She hid these romances, knowing that sex outside of marriage was much less acceptable for a woman than a man.
> VAPNEK 2015, 4

On the other hand, she is more equivocal when she writes elsewhere as follows:

> While we may retrospectively label Flynn and Equi's relationship as lesbian, it might better fit the model of "romantic friendship," which often included shared political commitments.
> VAPNEK 2018, 23

Similarly, there is no clear commitment on the question in the following source:

> Equi was an outspoken, open lesbian, and it seems plausible that she and Gurley had a love affair during this time. In fact the Flynn family was so

> disturbed about their relationship that both her sisters Bina and Kathie came to Portland to try to tear her away. But it was not lesbianism that bothered her family as much as it was that Flynn seemed imprisoned by Equi and unable to make a jail break.
>
> BAXANDALL 1987a, 31

Baxandall continues:

> Flynn's friendship with Marie Equi is less decipherable. Were they lovers? Equi was an obvious lesbian; Flynn's family believed they were lovers and plotted to free Flynn. Equi seemed not to have wanted her to leave and warned that Flynn would die if she left.
>
> BAXANDALL 1987b, 268

In her book, *The Alderson Story: My Life as a Political Prisoner* (1963a), Flynn, possibly influenced by her new communist perspective or by her communist publisher, describes the lesbianism she encountered during her stay in the Alderson federal prison in West Virginia very negatively, in a way that, irregardless of its sexual or non-sexual nature, appears to conflict sharply with her firm and supportive friendship with Equi, as she calls lesbians "perverts":

> Some [prison] officers were greatly disturbed by the prevalence of lesbianism, especially as it spread to younger inmates. They talked to them, but their efforts were usually fruitless. They were laughed at as "prudes." ... Old and young, first-termers, many there for offenses not involving moral turpitude, most of whom had never met or heard of such people in their lives, were thrown in with tough, seasoned criminals and perverts, addicts, prostitutes, dope peddlers, and the like. They were often terrified of the perverts and with good cause. This was especially true in the dormitories, I was told, where conversations and actions were unrestrained, once the doors were locked. These dormitories were seedbeds of degeneracy. What happened to one young girl there, an officer described to me as "actual rape." These dormitories should be made over into individual rooms. And those known to be lesbians should be isolated from the young and first offenders. Prisons are not a cure but schools for every sort of evil.
>
> FLYNN 1963a, 162

It is hard to understand this passage in any light other than disingenuousness. Of course, given the mainstream views of the time, opinions that have only lessened today and certainly not disappeared, it would hardly be an unusual approach for Elizabeth to take if she sought to deflect any connection between herself and homosexual behavior, regardless of whatever was the truth. Moreover, the distorted perceptions that many more conservative persons nurtured about the characteristics of lesbian behavior, nonsensical as they may have been, would make a deceptive approach to her descriptions of life in a women's prison seem logical. Still, Vapnek's (2018, 14) statement that Flynn "refused to conform to heterosexual gender norms" seems particularly ironic given Elizabeth's declared hostility to people she thought were gay. Helquist writes:

> Flynn's family was also worried that Equi's lesbianism would damage Flynn's reputation. Popular culture in the 1930s favored sinister depictions of lesbianism in novels and magazines with dire outcomes for women who strayed into forbidden sexual territory. In bohemian circles curiosity about same-sex love and experimentation with it prevailed, motivated partly by sexologists' talk of lesbianism. But mainstream Americans feared lesbian seduction. They worried especially about immoral practices rumored to take hold in women's schools and in the cities.
>
> HELQUIST 2015, 228

Like the other commentators mentioned above, Helquist is unable to give a clear answer to the question of the nature of Flynn's relationship with Equi:

> If Equi wrote love letters to Flynn when they were apart ... none have been located. (Many of Equi's papers were lost or destroyed after her death). Flynn's feelings for Equi, at least those evidenced in her journal and correspondence with others, suggest more of a respectful collaboration, a sense of obligation, and an appreciation for her care and assistance rather than a romantic or sexual attraction. But Flynn was mindful of her own stature, reputation, and legacy, and she may have chosen to keep secret her sentiments for a woman known to be a lesbian. ... Given Equi's lesbianism and personal setbacks and Flynn's need for care and comfort after her troubled relationships, they may very well have enjoyed a meaningful intimacy together that included sex.
>
> HELQUIST 2015, 222–223

2   Elizabeth and the IWW

Elizabeth Gurley Flynn became a member of the IWW in New York City at the age of sixteen in 1906, having heard details of the recently founded group from the radical Irish republican James Connolly, who was a friend of her mother (Baxandall 1987a, 7). By 1907, she was also involved with the Socialist Women of Greater New York, and she and another member, Anna B. Touroff, solicited essays on "Women and the Socialist Movement" for a competition in which the best one would receive a prize of $100. As Touroff later revealed in a report she made as a delegate to the International Socialist Congress meeting in Copenhagen [København] in 1910, the New York organization had been set up in 1905 with the goal of educating working women about socialism. However, having discovered that Bebel's *Woman and Socialism* and Engels' *Origin of the Family* were too demanding for many of the audience, they decided instead to generate alternate texts by developing them using the medium of the essay competition. Unfortunately, the group found that examination of the entries into the contest showed that few working women had been participants, and there was also disagreement about who the winners should be ("Socialism and Women" 1907, 5; Touroff 1910, 3–6). Elizabeth was soon promoted by the IWW to being an organizer and before she arrived in Spokane to participate in the conflict described above, she was involved in action in the Minnesota Iron Range and then in Missoula, Montana. In accepting this new role, she joined an organization that contained not only Connolly, but also Arturo M. Giovannitti, an immigrant from Italy, and Joseph James "Smiling Joe" Ettor, which would intentionally stand up for the rights of many impoverished workers who had come to the United States from Europe. In September 1907, she represented New York City Local 179 at the Wobblies' national convention in Chicago where she met anarchist Lucy Parsons, traveling there by train (Flynn 1973, 78–79; "Proceedings of the Third Annual Convention, Industrial Workers of the World, Held at Chicago, Ill." [1907] 2011; Vapnek 2015, 20–22, 25).

When she arrived in the Mesaba Range in northern Minnesota to act for workers in their dispute with the Oliver Iron Mining Company, a subsidiary of U.S. Steel, Elizabeth met and quickly married fellow-organizer Jack Jones, in January 1908. She became pregnant, but the child, whom they named John Vincent, died soon after its premature birth (Camp 1995, 20). The Western Federation of Miners, a radical industrial union committed to the philosophy of One Big Union, locally represented most of the poor European immigrants mentioned above. In fact, their leader, an Italian immigrant called Teofilo Petriella had established three groupings of its members, who often spoke the language of their home countries, Finnish, Italian, and the languages of the

Slavic areas of the southern Austro-Hungarian Empire but were not fluent in English. Among the Wobblies who arrived were members who could speak Finnish, Italian, Serbo-Croatian, and Macedonian (Flynn 1939b). Working conditions at the mining company were dangerous, and the economic difficulties experienced by those who worked there were no better:

> The unmarried man can hardly afford to buy a decent suit of clothes, while the miner with a family cannot get along at all. For the most common necessities of life, many of them are compelled to go into debt against the coming pay day. And in case of sickness or loss of employment their debts remain unpaid. Evictions are not rare.
>
> The work is hard, dangerous and tiresome. The glacial deposit consisting, to dispense with geological terms, of fine sand, clay, gravel and rock which did not decay as fast as neighboring formations, has a disconcerting tendency to cave in, shift and slide about, especially when permeated with the moisture characteristic of the country.
>
> "Unpolished Story of Cause and Struggle of Minnesota Miners" 1907

The two-month long strike, which began on July 20, 1907, featured little violence, although some employees were briefly imprisoned. This was partly because the governor, John Albert Johnson, promoted discussion between the various parties, and declined to send troops to crush the strike. However, eventually, the effect of the company's use of "scab" labor caused the miners to return to work. An editorial in the Duluth area paper, the *Labor World* noted that:

> Probably the most convincing evidence of the desperation of the Steel Trust to get men was when 176 were shipped to Hibbing Sunday form [sic] New York. They were hired in the big city by an agent of the great corporation, who probably knew as much about hiring miners, as we do about running the Steel Corporation.
>
> "They Still Trifle with Human Rights up on the Mesaba Range" 1907

Many Finnish employees, vewed as troublemakers by the company and blamed for the stoppage, were blacklisted, regardless of any role they had taken in the dispute (Betten 1967, 340–343; Cartwright 2020; "Governor Johnson Will Not Order Troops to the Range" 1907; Kaunonen 2018; "To Reclaim Them" 1908; Vapnek 2015, 26, 63).

Elizabeth returned to New York because her mother, Annie, was sick. Following his arrest for supposedly dynamiting a house and brief incarceration in the village of Aurora, Minnesota, three weeks following their marriage ("Socialist Held as Suspect at Biwabik" 1908), Jack lingered near the Mesaba area in Duluth for a while, which prompted some criticism in the press:

> John Archibald Jones, formerly of the Mesaba range where he held the position of chief emancipator of the "slaves" up to the time Petriella arrived and euchered [euchred] him out of his job is on his uppers in Duluth and will be forced to go to work if he soon does not succeed in getting another graft.
>
> "Down and Out: Agitator Jones is a Little Shy on Cash" 1908

The situation was not exactly seen in a positive light by Jones, who told a Duluth paper:

> "God help me if the steel corporation finds out where I am or what I am doing," he said. "I cannot get work anywhere on the range, for orders have been given to keep me out. My work in endeavoring to organize the men into the Industrial Workers of the World has been strongly opposed and there is now no room for me up there."
>
> "Will Try Again to Organize the Mesabi Miners" 1908

At the end of March 1908, Elizabeth gave talks on "Industrial Unionism" at the Guild Hall in Providence, Rhode Island and on "working class interests" at Arbeiter Hall in Detroit ("Girl to Discuss Labor Problem" 1908; "Local News" 1908). The next month, she returned to Arbeiter Hall, where she spoke for ninety minutes on the subject of "Labor versus Capital," telling those in attendance that "The capitalist is for himself. The history of the steel corporation is a history of stolen inventions" ("Says Steel Trust Stole Inventions" 1908). In October of the same year, she again attended the annual Wobbly convention, which was held at Brand's Hall in Chicago; the only other female delegate was Dolly Reed Walsh, the wife of Wobbly songwriter and Spokane protester, John H. "Jack" Walsh. Elizabeth and Jack Jones traveled like hobos by freight train from New York to Chicago (Forbes 2021, 73, 117–118, 129; "Leaders of the Unemployed" 1908; "New York Joan and Husband Beat Freights All Way to Chicago" 1908).

In the early Fall of 1908, Jack Jones was sent by the IWW to be an organizer in Missoula, Montana, in a free speech fight that preceded the one in Spokane. Flynn was soon dispatched to join him, giving them an opportunity to work out the relationship problems that already divided them, and she later commented that this "was the first and only time we actually lived and worked together for any length of time" (Flynn 1973, 103). Here, as would be the case in Spokane, the IWW target was the local labor contractors, and again the city attempted to stop the Wobblies from speaking before large gatherings on the street. When they refused to comply, many arrests were made, including that of Flynn, who had been selling newspapers and was charged with "causing a disturbance." However, the ensuing trials came to be seen by officials as an expensive undertaking. As a result, Missoula authorities changed their minds, released their prisoners, and did not continue with any pending prosecutions. Again, as it would in Spokane, this looked like an IWW victory, but did not predict much of what would happen in the organization's future (Flynn 1973, 103; "Missoula Police Wage Brutal War on Free Speech" 1909; Vapnek 2015, 26–29).

Missoula, home to the University of Montana, was a place that Flynn liked, and one where local faculty provided her with additional support. When Flynn and Jones had moved on to Spokane in the conflict described at the beginning of the chapter, Elizabeth came back to Missoula to generate support from like-minded individuals. On October 2, 1909, she gave a speech in the basement of the Harnois Theater, a building that would serve as an opera house before eventually being torn down in 1968. "We need volunteers," she said there, "to go to jail" ("Woman Would Fill City's Prisons" 1909). In 1917, when she was again working on the Iron Range in Hibbing, Minnesota, where some striking miners had been charged with murder, she again came to Missoula to generate additional support, speaking at the Eagles' Hall on February 10 ("Elizabeth Flynn Speaks Saturday" 1917; Flynn 1973, 103; Harmon 2020).

The apparent success of the IWW's schemes in Missoula and then Spokane led to additional pursuit of the tactic that had developed in the latter city of attempting to overwhelm the jail system, the police, the courts, and municipal revenues. Contemporaneously with what was going on in Spokane, the fight against US Steel moved on to New Castle, Pennsylvania, a city to the north of Pittsburgh, where, unfortunately, as in the 1906–1907 dispute in the Mesaba Range, the action failed because the employer was able to replace the workers who withdrew their labor with new ones. However, the Wobblies were ultimately successful in 1909 at a nearby plant, the Pressed Steel Car Company in McKees Rocks, a suburb of Pittsburgh, which manufactured railroad cars. There, the workers, often of Balkans origin, succeeded in obtaining a pay increase, but a number of the strikers were killed or injured before the settlement was achieved, and some were evicted from their homes, which were owned by the company. A battle between strikers and police, which took place on the evening of August 22, 1909, was started when strikers ordered state troopers to get out of a streetcar. At least eleven men among the strikers and police were killed, as were some horses, and houses and streetcars were damaged, following which workers held responsible for the deaths were tied to police horses and dragged through the streets. The dispute in the area generated a new IWW organization, the "Pittsburgh-New Castle Industrial Council," which started to produce a new publication based in New Castle, *Solidarity*, which proved so offensive to authorities that everyone involved in printing it was arrested ("Desperate Riot at McKees Rocks" 1909; "Dragged at Horses [sic] Heels." 1909; "Fatal Strike Riot" 1909; Harding 1909; "Investigation of Strike Asked" 1909; Martin 2007, 516, 518, 522; "Riot Victims Buried" 1909; "Sheriff Refuses to Evict Strikers" 1909; "Strikers Fire on Constables" 1910; "Troopers Hold Rioters in Awe after Carnage" 1909).

In 1912, a 3.5% wage cut imposed upon impoverished textile workers laboring in unsafe conditions at the American Woolen Company, many of whom were of immigrant origin, "twenty-five different nationalities speaking forty-five different dialects" (Flynn 1939b), in Lawrence, Massachusetts led to a strike that attracted the attention of the Wobblies, leading to the dispatch of Elizabeth along and Bill Haywood, and, prompted by Haywood, Margaret Sanger, who was able to use her skills as a nurse to assist the employees' children, who were often found to be malnourished. Sanger was able to document their poor condition and lack of access to adequate food and clothing. One positive result that derived from the interest of others in this dispute, which became known as the Bread and Roses Strike, was an investigation by the US House of Representatives' Rules Committee, and eventually passage of federal child labor legislation in 1916 and 1918. At Lawrence, Flynn met Carlo Tresca, with whom she began her long relationship (Sanger 1931, 78–79, [1938] 1999, 82; Shone 2019, 239–240; US House of Representatives 1912, 227).

In the dispute, IWW organizers, Joe Ettor and Arturo Giovannitti were arrested on January 31, 1912 in the death of a striker called Anna "Annie" Lopizzo on the grounds that their incitement of the Lawrence strikers made them responsible for her death during a riot in which a police officer had been stabbed, an event with which they otherwise had no connection. Along with Joseph "Joe" Caruso, they were charged with murder, and refused bail. At the time, Ettor pointed out he was two miles away from the place where Lopizzo had died. They would spend seven months in jail ("Arrest of Two Awes Strikers" 1912; "Ettor, Giovannitti and Caruso Acquitted" 1912; Flynn 1939b; Haywood 1929, 247, 249, 253; "International Notes" 1913).

Flynn noted that the false charges that were used to undermine the efforts of the Wobblies to obtain fair treatment for the mill workers had obliged them to focus much of their time on obtaining the release of their own leaders:

> Instead of our being free to move on to bring a little economic freedom to another group of oppressed workers, we were made to use our time and funds in Essex county, fighting for our boys.
>   Capitalism smiled, and is still smiling at our dilemma. It sees us tied up for a time at least, and perhaps 'cured' for good, as it thinks.
>   But they are wrong. It will work the other way, I think. If agitators are suppressed, and our leaders are not left free to go on helping downtrodden toilers according to our ideals, then may come revolution!
>   FLYNN, quoted in BURTON 1912

In the two-months-long trial of Ettor, Giovannitti, and Caruso, which took place in Salem, Massachusetts, once again the right of free speech was raised in the context of Wobbly involvement in industrial activity. J. P. S. Mahoney, the attorney for Ettor, asked the jury:

> Are you going to strike a blow at the betterment of the human race by taking away a leader of the people? This case strikes at the foundation roots of government in the matter of assembly and free speech. In Massachusetts, which has lighted the fires of free speech and reform, which has been the advance guard of progress, if free speech is to be trampled on, what can we expect from the rest of the world![?]
>   MAHONEY, quoted in "Desperate to Get Ettor" 1912

Additionally, from the cage in the courtroom in which the accused were seated, Ettor shouted out that they were being tried not for anything they had done but because of their political opinions. Apparently impressed by this argument, the jury acquitted the defendants, who later gathered together with supporters at a meeting in the local Salvation Army Hall that was chaired by Elizabeth Gurley Flynn. Following his release, Ettor had immediately inquired, "Where is Gurley?" Fred H. Moore, who had defended Flynn in Spokane, and who would later represent anarchists Nicola Sacco and Bartolomeo Vanzetti, was another of the defense lawyers in Salem. Recognizing that the attention given to the trial by labor unionists across the United States and even in Europe, where there had been many demonstrations in Italy on behalf of Ettor and Giovannitti, was considerable, the latter having been born in Italy and edited the Wobblies' Italian-language newspaper, *Il Proletario*, the IWW scheduled additional appearances for Elizabeth in a forthcoming tour of Pennsylvania, Ohio, and Minnesota ("Ettor Addresses Jury" 1912; "Ettor and His Companions are Freed by Jury" 1912; "Ettor, Giovannitti and Caruso Acquitted"

1912; "Ettor Interest Mounts Higher" 1912; "Murder Trial in Progress at Salem" 1912; "New York Shudders in Fear of Salt and Pepper Attack" 1913).

1913 found Flynn heavily involved in a strike by silk workers in Paterson, New Jersey, where she assumed the mantle of previous speakers Enrico Malatesta and Luigi Galleani, anarchists who had come to the city to stimulate direct action, and she was charged with the familiar refrain of having incited the workers to violence (Flynn 1973, 154; "Flynn Woman Acquitted, To Keep Up Work" 1915; "International Notes" 1913).

Following their opposition to company plans to make workers operate three or four looms instead of the current practice of each being responsible for two looms, four employees at the Doherty Silk Mill were fired. This caused its 800 workers, who were mostly immigrants, to go out on strike because they saw the company's change, the "speedup," as an opportunity to produce the same amount of silk with less people. Following a mass meeting about a month later, on February 25, 1913 with IWW emissaries, Elizabeth, Tresca, and Patrick Quinlan, who was originally from Limerick in Ireland, almost all the silk workers in the Paterson area were out in support and they campaigned not only against the change in looms policy, but also for an eight-hour day and a minimum wage of $12 a week. Following their arrests, the three Wobblies spent the night of the meeting in jail, and upon their release the next day were told by the Paterson police chief, John Bimson, that agitators from outside the city were not welcome there (Baxandall 1987a, 11; Camp 1995, 51; Flynn 1914, 1973, 171; Haywood 1913, 783–784; "Haywood's Battle for Patterson [sic] Silk Mill Workers" 1913; "International Notes" 1913; Kornbluh 1964a, 198, 199; "Paterson Silk Strike" 1913; "Six Strikers Denied Free Speech" 1913).

Flynn's trial was postponed because she asked that it take place before a "foreign" jury, which the New Jersey Supreme Court agreed to on June 13, and it commenced on June 21 before veniremen from Jersey City rather than Paterson. Much journalistic attention was given to the fact that she was to be defended by two prominent New York female attorneys, Jessie Ashley and Inez Milholland ("Jury from Next County" 1913; "Retains Miss Milholland" 1913; "Start Trial of Woman Leader of Silk Strike" 1913; "Suffragist Lawyer Defends Girl Strike Leader in Patterson [sic] Trial" 1913; "Woman Agitator in Silk Strike on Trial at Paterson" 1913). However, the defense attorneys participating in the trial process were not Ashley and Milholland, but Jacob Kushner, Gustav A. Hunzicker, and Henry Marelli ("Miss Flynn on Trial" 1913; "Start Trial of Woman Leader of Silk Strike" 1913), although in the proceedings that took place on July 1, the *Newark Evening Star* reported that "Miss Jessie Ashley, a Socialist woman lawyer, of New York, appeared today to aid the three lawyers in defending Miss Flynn" (Police Frame-Up, Defense in Trial of Miss Flynn 1913).

The charge of incitement centered around Flynn's suggestion during the February 25 speech that strikers should "go in a body through the streets to each of the mills and drive them out, club them out, kick them out. Do this if it takes your entire force" ("Retains Miss Milholland" 1913). Other trial reports give a condensed version of these words, which were not written down by police at the time, a matter that was discussed in the trial. On the witness stand, Elizabeth emphasized that she had actually warned the striking millhands not to be violent or to do anything that could be interpreted as violence:

> I told them that the police were ready to arrest any of them who used violence and that we would be playing only into their hands if we used anything else but persuasive and tactful methods.
>
> FLYNN, quoted in "Says She Did Not Incite Riot" 1913

In their evidence, police officers revealed that Elizabeth had shared the platform on the day in question with Quinlan, Tresca, and local Wobbly, Adolph Lessig, and that Flynn had spoken for four or five minutes, being interrupted when a photographer took her picture. After being arrested, Flynn and Tresca were warned by police officers that they should leave the city and escorted to the train station ("Start Trial of Woman Leader of Silk Strike" 1913). In his summation, Marelli characterized the police witnesses as "lying cops who had memorized the words that they had put into the mouth of Miss Flynn" ("Jury Gets Case of Miss Flynn in Paterson Strike" 1913).

The jury was unable to reach a unanimous decision and, following 28 hours of deliberation, it was dismissed. Reportedly, there was a tie 10 to 2 in favor of conviction. Although the prosecutor, Michael Dunn, said a new trial would begin the following week, that did not happen, and Flynn was not retried until November 27, 1915. Quinlan, on the other hand, who had earlier been convicted, received a prison sentence of two to seven years and a fine of $500 ("Quinlan is Given Long Sentence" 1913; "Quinlan to Prison" 1913).

In the Paterson strike, as was often the case, some attention was given to Flynn's appearance. During the jury selection, it was reported that Elizabeth, "the most picturesque leader of the silk strikers," was "quietly dressed in a white silk shirtwaist and a blue skirt" ("Start Trial of Woman Leader of Silk Strike" 1913). In her autobiography, she notes that at the time, "a Paterson newspaper accused me of wearing an expensive imported linen dress to a strikers' meeting," though actually her mother had made it (Flynn 1973, 30). On another occasion, when she attempted to conceal her identity by wearing fashionable clothes and glasses, she was nonetheless identified by the police (172). On the other hand, at a women's meeting, she saw that, although the attendees worked in a silk factory, "the women clad in shoddy cotton dresses" (166) would be unable to purchase any of the material they produced.

On March 30, 1913, while arrangements for Flynn's trial were being negotiated, Tresca evaded capture by the police as fellow IWW leaders Bill Haywood, who was splitting his time between Paterson and another work stoppage in Akron, Ohio, and Adolph Lessig were arrested on their way to address a meeting at the Lafayette Oval on the outskirts of the city, a gathering Bimson had prohibited. They were eventually convicted of disorderly conduct and sentenced to six months in prison, with a requirement for hard labor being added to Haywood's sentence. At the time, Haywood suggested meeting in Haledon, an adjacent city, where the mayor was a socialist, and afterwards some public striker gatherings were held there (Flynn 1914, 1973, 161, 165; Russell 1913, 789–790; "W.D. Haywood is Indicted" 1913).

At the beginning of May, after three months of the stoppage, the Paterson strikers learned that the mill owners were now operating in other cities, including West Hoboken, Weehawken, Union Hill, and North Bergen. As they waited for trial, Elizabeth and Carlos went to those locations and were able to persuade most of the employees to stop work. On May 25, Elizabeth spoke to an assembly of 25,000 strikers (Meagher 2013, 28; "Ten Thousand More Join in Silk Strike" 1913).

In a strategy organized by journalist John "Jack" Reed, on June 7, 1913, the Wobblies took their strike to New York City, and Margaret Sanger led a march along Fifth Avenue in Manhattan to Madison Square Garden, where they presented a dramatization of recent events that has come to be known as the "Paterson Strike Pageant." More than a thousand strikers and a collection of actors and artists based in the city participated in this piece of performance art, which in some ways resembles the anarchist productions in South America mentioned in Chapter 1 of the present volume, where a speech might be accompanied by a children's choir (Edmund 2017, 15–16; Flynn 1973, 161, 168; Kornbluh 1964a, 201; Vapnek 2015, 49).

Details of the pageant suggest that it did not stray much beyond the events that had taken place, and neither did it involve revolutionary advances in dramatic creativity. Rather, although strikers had composed new music to accompany the presentation, it proceeded stuffily through depictions of silk employees at work, the announcement of a strike, the closed mill, violent encounters with police, funerals at which the Wobbly principals recreated their speeches, children relocated to other locales, and a final meeting; participants sang the Funeral March, the Red Flag, and the Internationale (Chaplin 1948, 140–142; Flynn 1973, 168–169; Haywood 1929, 263–264; Kornbluh 1964a, 202). While Haywood viewed the pageant as a significant achievement, it failed to raise much money, and others saw it as having damaged the strike because it diverted workers away from Paterson to Manhattan, creating a vacuum which allowed the mill owners to bring in more "scabs" (Edmund 2017, 17, 47; Flynn 1973, 169; Vapnek 2015, 49).

As the pageant portrayed, the silk mill owners had employed their own private police force, who had killed two of the strikers, Modestino Vallanio and Vincenzo Madonna, and injured Antonio Bischeu, who was sitting outside his home, observing the strikers as they jeered the gumshoes. Though three of these detectives were arrested they did not go to trial. Madonna's funeral was an enormous event, with fifty thousand strikers marching to the burial site where they heard speeches by Flynn, Tresca, and Haywood (Flynn 1973, 168; Kornbluh 1964a, 200; "Le Forche" 1913a, 1913b; "Many Hurt as Strikers Riot" 1913; "Riots Mark Paterson Strike" 1913; "Second Red Funeral in Paterson Strike" 1913).

The strike ended officially on July 22, 1913, when the general strike committee of the silk workers voted to allow each shop to return to work at a moment when many of them were feeling the effects of not having had a paycheck for five months. At a meeting in Haledon on July 20, Flynn and Haywood stated their opposition to this decision, with Elizabeth saying that it should have been ratified by all the strikers as a whole ("Ending of Paterson Strike Angers I.W.W." 1913). Drawing attention to the different perspectives of the generally English-speaking workers who wanted to go back to work, and who were willing to consider a new nine-hour day to be a reasonable improvement in conditions, and, on the other hand, their often non-English-speaking colleagues, who, like the IWW leaders, wished to continue the fight, she said:

> I believe the ones who have lived and suffered through this strike are not the ones who are going back to work. From the beginning of this strike we have urged you [to] stand together, fight together and win together or lose together. A shop by shop settlement is a repudiation of this principle.
> FLYNN, quoted in "Ending of Paterson Strike Angers I.W.W." 1913

Although the strikers were thus obliged to return to work, Flynn and other New York City-based Wobblies would return to Paterson to continue to spread their perspective. At that point, the city had not concluded processing the indictments against her and other leaders. In response to their continued visits, trial of Tresca for inciting a riot was reactified in June 1914, but the jury brought in from Hudson County quickly found him innocent (Flynn 1973, 171; Vapnek 2015, 49). At the same time, like Haywood, Elizabeth involved herself contemporaneously in other Wobbly pursuits. On April 5, 1915, she spoke at the Public Library in Washington, D.C. about "Unemployment, a Menace to

Society," and following a tour of the Western states, she was in Chicago on June 1 to talk about the "Revolutionary I.W.W." and the next evening about "Women in the Labor Movement" ("Socialists to Hear Elizabeth Gurley Flynn" 1915; "Two Flynn Dates" 1915).

Toward the end of 1915, amid concern that the silk workers would again go out on strike, police chief Bimson met with the city mayor, Robert F. Fordyce, and other officials on September 3 and decided that once again, Wobbly meetings would not be allowed in Paterson. That evening, Flynn arrived to speak at a gathering at Institute Hall and was greeted by police who told her that agitators from outside the city would not be participating. Other planned speakers were Tresca, Giovannetti, Lessig, and Abraham Greenstein, a goldsmith who was the secretary of the Jewelry Workers' Union. When the engagement was quickly moved to another location, a small meeting room located at 41 Bridge Street, police also closed it down there. Given the choice between being taken to the station or being arrested, Flynn agreed to leave on the next train home (Avrich 2004, 310; Flynn 1973, 171; *Labor and the War: American Federation of Labor and the Labor Movements of Europe and Latin America* 1918, 63; "Paterson Ceases to be Field for Labor Agitators" 1915; "Police Prevent Meetings and Bar Agitators from Paterson, N.J." 1915).

On November 11, Elizabeth did what she had been warned by Bimson not to do, which was to attempt to speak at another meeting in the city. This was a gathering of the Women's Free Speech League, organized to protest the police decision. It was held in the Auditorium Hall, but she and Tresca were denied entrance. Following that event, Flynn's incitement charge, which related to her speech on February 25, 1913, was also reactified, and she appeared in court on November 27, 1915, Jessie Ashley again volunteering her legal services. Like Carlo Tresca the previous year, she was quickly found not guilty, in Elizabeth's case after the jury apparently deliberated for a little more than an hour, though Flynn would later say that "I was acquitted in a few minutes" (Flynn 1973, 172). Reportedly, one of the jurors remarked that "This isn't Russia" ("Flynn Woman Acquitted, To Keep Up Work" 1915), an ironic statement in the light of Flynn's later prominence in the Communist Party, USA ("Bar Gurley Flynn, Even as a "Guest"'" 1915; Flynn 1973, 172–173;"'Free Speech is on Trial – Not I" Says Elizabeth Gurley Flynn" 1915; "Flynn Woman Acquitted, To Keep Up Work" 1915; "Gurley Flynn Free; Plans to Keep On Talking" 1915).

Here, as in the past, Flynn characterized her Wobbly battles as issues of free speech, an appeal that attracted the support of persons with a wide range of political perspectives. When she was talking with Chief Bimson at the Bridge Street location, where at first she refused to leave, she referred to evangelist Billy Sunday, an outside agitator of a different sort, who was allowed to rally support in Paterson and other strike locations where the IWW was involved, an activity for which, unlike herself, he was financially compensated ("I.W.W. Leader Charges Billy Sunday Broke Unions" 1915; "Paterson Ceases to be Field for Labor Agitators" 1915; "Says Sunday Is Paid to Oppose Workers" 1915).

As discussed in Chapter 4, the notion of "sabotage" was a potential key strategy that might be employed by the Wobblies, and the debate about its meaning and purpose was contributed to by Flynn, who in 1914, during the Paterson conflict, wrote *Sabotage: The Conscious Withdrawal of the Workers' Industrial Efficiency* (Flynn 1917a), which was first published in 1915 as a pamphlet by the IWW, and which was also translated into Italian, Lithuanian, and Hungarian, and came to be mistakenly viewed as a comment about the First World War (Baxandall 1987a, 27).

The fact that Tom Barker, the subject of Chapter 4, and Elizabeth Gurley Flynn spoke of sabotage made them look dangerous, but often, as noted in connection to Barker, the concept was chiefly understood as one of disrupting the operation of businesses in order to exert pressure that would benefit unionized employees; this was "scientific" sabotage, the intelligent exercise of force where it could best achieve gains. For example, painstakingly following a works rulebook, ostensibly a sign of cooperation with one's employers, could be subtly turned into a vehicle for wasting time and in turn lessening profits. Davis explains:

> The essence of the Wobbly advocacy of sabotage was to encourage the creativity of the workers in the discovery of different tactics. When moulded to the particularities of specific industries, these tactics could be applied directly on the job with maximum effect ... and with a minimum danger of company retaliation against individual workers. ... The relationship of these tactics to the overall Wobbly strategy is forcefully summed up by Elizabeth Gurley Flynn: "Sabotage is to the class struggle what guerrilla warfare is to the battle. The strike is the open battle of the class struggle, sabotage is the guerrilla warfare, the day-to-day warfare between two opposing classes."
>
> DAVIS 1983, 94; the quoted passage is from FLYNN 1917a, 4

In 1912, Giovannitti had translated Émile Pouget's brief work, *Sabotage* ([1898] 1912) from the French. Flynn's version shares many of Pouget's ideas, though it is not a translation, and offers her own perspective. Thus Cain (1993, 116) is incorrect to speak of "a more recent translation of Pouget's work by the American IWW leader Elizabeth Gurley Flynn." Pouget's line of reasoning, which he also had presented in journals in 1896 and 1897, had an influence on the recently founded *Confédération Générale du Travail* (CGT), the national labor union federation in France of which he would become the leader (Lay 1999, 122–123).

Flynn's *Sabotage* was a response to a speech by another Wobbly, Frederick Summer Boyd, who advocated sabotage during the Paterson strike, a perspective which, while not acceptable to others who heard what he had to say, seemed at the time to her, when the Wobblies were characterizing their activities in terms of a right to free speech, to be legitimate, and so she wrote her own lecture endorsing sabotage, which is what appeared in the pamphlet. White (2022, 97) writes that Flynn had actually given that speech to defend Boyd, but does not indicate where it would have taken place. Unfortunately, in its written form, the speech became viewed by prosecutors as "evidence" in Wobbly trials, and was even used in that way much later, in 1952, when Elizabeth's activities as a Communist party leader were being investigated (Andersen 2020, 61, 63; Camp 1995, 54–55; Flynn 1917a, 9, 1973, 162–163).

At the time of its writing, while many socialists who supported the Paterson strike disliked the concept of sabotage, Flynn explained that the Wobblies and the silk workers were keeping an open mind and wanted to hear all viewpoints:

> We had a discussion in the executive committee about it, and one after the other of the members of the executive committee admitted that they used sabotage, why shouldn't they talk about it? It existed in the mills, they said. Therefore there was no reason why it should not be recognized on the platform. It was not the advocacy of sabotage that hurt some of our comrades but denial of their right to dictate the policy of the Paterson strike.
> FLYNN 1914

The next year, in a speech at Oak Hall on Oak Street in Chicago, Flynn said:

> The I.W.W. is for sabotage. That means working slack instead of fast. It means interfering with the quality of goods. It is an attempt of [sic] the part of the workers to limit production in proportion to pay.
>
> Employers sabotage. They adulterate food. They mix tin and lead solutions into silks to make the product weigh more and look more valuable than it really is.
> "Women Pickets Asked by Girl Leader" 1915

However, Elizabeth did not stick to this position for very long, and in 1917, faced with the reality that it could be utilized in future trials, as it had been already in a case in Everett, Washington, she tried to persuade Haywood to junk the publication. His unwillingness to do that was one of the causes of Flynn's gradual disassociation from the Wobblies (Andersen 2020, 64; Camp 1995, 76; Vapnek 2015, 66–67, 2018, 19). Another reason for conflict between Flynn and Haywood took place when she returned to Minnesota's Mesabi Range in 1916 where another strike against US Steel was taking place. Haywood blamed Flynn and Ettor and their attorneys for making a deal whereby three non-English-speaking miners originally from Montenegro who were held in jail in Duluth would plead guilty and receive a short sentence for manslaughter, while some of the IWW organizers, Carlo Tresca, Sam Scarlett, and Joe Schmidt, who were leading the strike and had, in virtue of their inflammatory speeches, again been charged with murder, would be released and those ridiculous charges dropped. In fact, in court, the three miners ended up being convicted of second degree murder and received potentially much longer indeterminate sentences. Haywood said that he would never have accepted such a agreement in the first place (Flynn 1917b; Camp 1995, 74; Haywood 1929, 292; Vapnek 2018, 19; White 2022, 76–77).

Vapnek (2015, 47) argues that "Flynn advocated "sabotage" as a tool for workers to use in their ongoing struggle with employers. She defined sabotage as "the conscious withdrawal of the workers' industrial efficiency."" However, although Flynn did define it thus, she also included language that would inevitably be taken by others as being more violent and dangerous and as encouraging lawbreaking. She began the piece by claiming as follows:

> I am not going to attempt to justify sabotage on any moral ground. If the workers consider sabotage is necessary, that in itself makes sabotage moral. Its necessity is its excuse for existence. ... it is necessary to accept the concept of the class struggle.
> FLYNN 1917a, 2

Here, familiarly, Flynn indicates the primacy of class war, one of the dogmas of Wobbly ideology, and infers from it a right of the proletariat to rule ... so long, that is, that the workers wish to be in charge. They might not want to, but anyway morality will consist of whatever they decide to do. In this context, that means the withdrawal of efficiency, which, like Tom Barker, she sees as being either doing less work and limiting an employer's profits, or damaging the product of a person's labor, to similar effect (Flynn 1917a, 5–8; Kornbluh 1964c, 37). Although Elizabeth gives a number of ways that such industrial sabotage can be achieved, such as telling a restaurant customer about the poor quality of the lobster in his or her salad (Camp 1995, 56; Flynn 1917a, 14), she cautions:

> I have not given you a rigidly defined thesis on sabotage because sabotage is in the process of making. Sabotage itself is not clearly defined. Sabotage is as broad and changing as industry, as flexible as the imagination and passions of humanity.
>
> FLYNN 1917a, 29

Ultimately, sabotage might consist of doing or saying anything at all, and this would always be sanctioned by the morality automatically warranted by class, and so perhaps she is not aware at the time of writing the article of the drawback that her argument may be used to prosecute almost any activity engaged in by the Wobblies or by herself in her later life, which sometimes it was.

References to the use of industrial sabotage had occurred in January 1913 during a brief strike by hotel and restaurant workers in New York City in which Flynn and Tresca, who were living together in the city, Ettor, and Giovannitti were all involved. Use of "scab" replacements quickly put an end to the walkout, and Ettor recommended sabotage on the part of waiters and cooks obliged to return to work, saying they should "make the food of the capitalists the most dangerous thing in the world for them" ("'Poison Threat' has about Passed Away" 1913), with Giovannitti in response to the outrage that comment had created explaining that the term might just refer to adding excessive amounts of condiments to food that they served. At the same time, Flynn was busy collecting negative reports concerning the presence of rats and other unsanitary conditions in the city's hospitality businesses (Camp 1995, 44–46; "Ettor Here To-Night Giovannitti Says" 1913; "'Poison Threat' Has About Passed Away" 1913).

3   The Chicago IWW Trial

On September 5, 1917, agents of the federal Justice department arrived simultaneously at 48 IWW offices, seizing documents, books, and typewriters. On the basis of what they found, and also on the basis of a clear intention to disable the organization along with many other radical groups in time of war, a case was submitted to a grand jury which approved the arrests, and then 101 Wobblies, down from 166 as some of the cases against the accused were dismissed or dropped, were tried for conspiracy to undermine various federal laws and presidential orders. The case opened in Chicago, where the prosecutor was Frank K. Nebeker, the IWW defense attorney was George F. Vanderveer, and the judge was Kenesaw Mountain Landis ("10,000 Crimes are Charged to the I.W.W." 1917; Foner 2023, 39; George 1918, 10; Parfitt 2016; Renshaw 1968, 65–69; "Sab. Cat Yowls" 1918).

With respect to the New York-based Wobbly leaders, Flynn, Tresca, Ettor, and Giovannetti, notwithstanding the fact that they were indicted and had traveled to Chicago give themselves up, they found that their cases were among the ones that had been dropped, quite possibly because the federal government was aware of tactical differences between them and Haywood that had recently limited their IWW activities. Nonetheless, Giovannetti complained that he had been excluded from the proceedings. Haywood and fourteen other leaders were sentenced to twenty years, and every defendant received some spell of imprisonment (Camp 1995, 76–77; Chaplin 1948, 237; Haywood 1929, 313; Parfitt 2016; Renshaw 1968, 68; White 2022, 116–117). Use of the concept of sabotage, and correspondence with like-minded persons in Russia allowed Nebeker to define the Wobblies as the "Bolsheviki in America" ("I.W.W. Here and Russ Bolshevik Shown as Allies" 1918). Another seized document had optimistically declared that "This promises to be the banner year for the One Big Union. … All aboard for the greatest year in the history of labor" ("I.W.W. Here and Russ Bolshevik Shown as Allies" 1918), but the Chicago trial signified the worst year for the IWW, which would only barely survive. However, the Civil Liberties Union, of which Flynn was one of the founders, which would become the American Civil Liberties Union (ACLU), successfully campaigned to have the imprisoned Wobblies released, which all of them were by 1923 (Camp 1995, 104–105; Foner 2023, 41; Renshaw 1968, 68).

4 The Workers' Defense Union and the ACLU

Moving away from IWW involvement, Flynn continued her activism on behalf of free speech, through the medium of a new organization, the Workers' Defense Union (WDU), including campaigning for the release of Haywood and for that of Eugene V. Debs, jailed for ten years for giving an anti-war speech to fellow Socialist Party members in a park in Canton, Ohio, a conviction unanimously upheld by the US Supreme Court in *Debs v. United States* (1919), using the test of "clear and present danger," but later commuted by President Warren G. Harding at the end of 1921 to the time he had then served. Like Helen Armstrong, Elizabeth also opposed the dispatch of Western soldiers to Russia at the end of the First World War (Shields 1986, 15, 19). Meanwhile, the imminent deportation of Emma Goldman sponsored speculation about which woman might assume the leadership of radical thought in the US. Would it be Flynn or M. Eleanor "Fitzi" Fitzgerald, the long term assistant of both Goldman and fellow-deportee, Alexander Berkman? (Shone 2013, 160; "Who Will Wear Emma's Crown?" 1919).

At Rutgers Square in Manhattan (now called Straus Square) on April 6, 1919, the same day that Debs commenced his prison sentence, Elizabeth addressed a large meeting which called for a general strike. Arguing that there were 2,000 political prisoners in the US, she said that the country lagged behind other nations in providing amnesty. "For as long as one member of the working class is in jail we're all slaves," she said. "We must free ourselves" ("Soviet Republic Here Certain, 'Reds' Predict" 1919). Working with the WDU and ACLU in the coming years, freeing others became a major part of her political activity (Camp 1995, 104–105).

Thus, Elizabeth's involvement in the Pittsburgh area in a 1919 strike at the Allegheny Coal and Coke Company, a subsidiary of the Allegheny Steel Company, a US Steel affiliated business, was as a leader of the WDU, rather than the IWW. Frances "Fannie" Sellins was an official of the United Mine Workers of America (UMWA) who, on August 26, saw another picketer, Joseph Starzeleski (in various reports also spelled as Strazalecki, Strezelecki, Strzelecki, Strselecki, Spicenkit, and Spicenkt), being beaten and killed at the entrance to the mine in the borough of Brackenridge. When she attempted to intervene, she was shot and killed by security guards employed by a private detective agency or by deputy sheriffs, who were also present. The guards, who were protecting access by "scab" replacements, fired into the strikers, and Sellins' skull was also crushed by gun butts. Reportedly, news of Sellins' death reduced Flynn to tears ("Arrests Follow Riot at Mine" 1919; "Big Legal Fight over Killing During Strike" 1922; "Capitalist Courts Condone Murder of Men and Women" 1919; "Contending Parties in the Steel Strike are Optimistic" 1919; "Deputies Indicted for Killing Woman in Strike" 1922; Holleman 2022; "Organizzatrice Operaia Uccisa" 1919; Shields 1986, 24–25, 27).

The inquest into the deaths of the two strike demonstrators concluded on September 26 that they died "from gunshot wounds inflicted by persons unknown to the jury while an attack was being made on deputy sheriffs" ("Mrs. Sellins was Shot During Riot" 1919). The panel also added that "We deplore and criticise the foreign agitators who instill anarchy and Bolshevistic doctrines into the minds of the un-American and uneducated" ("Mrs. Sellins was Shot During Riot" 1919). An autopsy following exhumation of Sellins' body found that she had been shot in the back, which union officials hoped would make prosecution of the killers more likely. However, the sheriff, William S. Haddock, and the coroner argued that the wound in question may have been added after exhumation to produce that effect. In a letter, Haddock argued that this had taken place "to discredit those in authority, and for the further purpose of furnishing anarchistic, dangerous and revolutionary agitators and organizers propaganda to be used in the steel strike against the state and national governments" ("Mutilation of Body to Assist 'Reds' Alleged" 1919).

In 1922, two deputy sheriffs, Edward Mannison and D. J. Riley (also given as Reilly) were finally tried for the murders. In the case of Mannison, the judge directed a verdict of not guilty on the grounds of insufficient evidence, and the jury, after fifty minutes of discussion, found Riley also not guilty ("Big Legal Fight over Killing During Strike" 1922; "Deputies Indicted for Killing Woman in Strike" 1922; "Deputies on Trial." 1923; "Deputy Sheriffs Not Guilty in Slaying Miss Sellins" 1923; "Free in Murder Case" 1923).

Notwithstanding her work in defense of free speech, Flynn remained subject to being silenced and arrested even after she had moved beyond the more radical strains of Wobbly advocacy. Accused of possessing seditious literature in Philadelphia on March 6, 1921, she was arrested before she could deliver a speech at the New Garrick Hall. She was also charged with violating state law by being the organizer of a radical movement. On July 12, the superintendent of Philadelphia police, William B. Mills, assigned 200 officers to prevent further distribution of militant writings ("Elizabeth Flynn Held" 1921; "Elizabeth Gurley Flynn, 8 Others, Seized as Radicals" 1921; "Elizabeth Gurley Flynn Arrested in Philadelphia" 1921; "Gurley Flynn Arrested" 1921; "Philadelphia to Clean-Up "Reds"'" 1922).

In 1917, the Espionage Act had been passed, making it illegal to spread false information about the war with Germany or to try and limit military enlistment. The 1918 Amendments to the Espionage Act, also known as the Sedition Act of 1918, greatly increased the definition of speech that would not be allowed when the US was at war, including scornful and belittling criticism of the federal government. This restrictive legislation had rendered Debs' expression of personal opinion about the war in question a crime. Although it was now 1920, and the First World War was over, the Civil Liberties Union that was formed that year as an organization that sought to protect the freedom of speech authorized by the First Amendment but undermined by the Espionage and Sedition Acts, also found that its own written materials were subject to government censorship and banned from the mail. In addition to Flynn, its founders included Jane Addams, who was mentioned in the previous chapter, and Oswald Garrison Villard, the editor of the *Nation*. Like Elizabeth, Goldman, Berkman, Sanger, and many others had been arrested for expressing their points of view. At times, Flynn would deliver a lecture with the title "Freedom of Speech," as she did, following a Sunday service on December 2, 1923, at St. John's Church in New Haven, Connecticut (Foner 2023, 41; Johnson 2020, 204).

On June 4, 1924, a dinner was held in honor of Flynn by the Liberal Club of Chicago at the city's Central YMCA to celebrate her work for the ACLU in defense of free speech. At the gathering, she stated that, although many essential liberties had been taken away from Americans during the First World War, most ordinary people failed to see the significance of her activism, which made it difficult to restore what had been lost, whether the casualties were strikers, Wobblies, syndicalists, foreign born residents, or the Ku Klux Klan, all of whom had a stake in the success of the ACLU's campaigns (Frankenstein 1924).

Of course, the ACLU's practice of protecting the speech of all persons and organizations has been seen by its members as obliging them to act on behalf of the Klan and other racists. Though this is easily justifiable and not at all inconsistent, it may seem strange to find Flynn elsewhere seeking to undermine the influence of the Klan. Indeed, the same paradox would reoccur in a different form when the group adopted a resolution on February 5 1940 that tentatively barred from leadership positions those who were supporters of totalitarianism. In practice, the only member to whom this policy was applied was Flynn, who was then a member of the Communist Party USA's National Committee, and she was on May 7 the same year expelled from the board of the ACLU because her beliefs were felt by some members to be too extreme, not only as reflected in her party membership, but due to the content of articles she had written for the *New Masses*, explaining why she refused to resign, and for the *Daily Worker*, where she had criticized colleagues (Bangarth 2002, 509–510; "Board Acts to Oust Communist Member" 1940; Camp 1995, 129–130; "Exit Miss Flynn" 1940; Lamont 1968a, 13, 17; Schutzer 1969, 376). As might be expected, she defended herself, describing the new policy as a mistake.

> I do not concede the right of the board to exclude me for my political beliefs and affiliations. The Nazi-fascist stuff in the resolution is just window dressing, as there are no fascists or Nazis on the board. Its inclusion adds insult to injury. Nor do I accept the arbitrary characterization of the Soviet Union. Admiration for the USSR as a workers' country certainly does not label me a totalitarian.
> FLYNN 1940, 11; LAMONT 1968b, 157

Following the removal of the resolution in 1968, she was reinstated to the board in 1976 (Bangarth 2002, 509 fn 25). This took place after Flynn's death, when the reversal could do little damage.

At a February 9, 1921 conference in New York City of the National Association for the Promotion of Labor Unionism Among Negroes, an organization started among others by A. Philip Randolph, who in 1925 would form the Brotherhood of Sleeping Car Porters, Flynn, representing the WDU, commented that "As for the Ku-Klux Klan driving out foreigners, it ill-behooves those who came here on Monday to call those who came here on Thursday foreigners" ("Speakers Call on Labor to Destroy the Ku-Klux Klan" 1921). At that meeting, Randolph called for the use of the weapon of a general strike, and at a 1919 gathering also in Manhattan at the Church of the Ascension, James Weldon Johnson, one of the leaders of the National Association for the Advancement of Colored People (NAACP), recommended that black people should make use of their economic power and strike to improve their position in the local community. In that conversation, Flynn pointed out that black people, like other workers, had in the past been treated as "children, but as soon as they rose to demand the rights of grown-up people they became very fiends, a menace to civilization and fit subjects for Americanization" ("Offers the Strike as Negro's Weapon" 1919).

An important aspect of Elizabeth's work was seeking to prevent radicals who had not been born in the US from being deported amid circumstances under which the federal government was seeking to expel as many of them as possible. Like Emma Goldman, who would later herself be imprisoned at Ellis Island and then deported, Flynn sometimes successfully sent letters to the Commissioner of Immigration for the Port of New York, Frederic C. Howe, a man of progressive ideas, asking that people be allowed to stay. For example, from Duluth on July 24, 1916, Elizabeth mailed a request that an IWW colleague, Bulgarian born George Andreytchine, be released from custody, which eventually he was ("Goldman Wrote 'Dear Fred Howe'; Had Friend Freed" 1919; "Jailer of 'Reds' at Ellis Island Their Samaritan" 1919).

In an article published in the *Masses* in 1916, Flynn revealed her internationalist perspective that contributed to some of her interest in preventing deportations. Like Tom Barker and Helen Armstrong, the subjects of other chapters, she eschewed patriotism in all its deceptive forms:

> The majority of our workers are foreigners, one or two generations removed, and with their European home-ties and American environment, internationalism becomes the logical patriotism of a heterogeneous population.
>
> America – not as a melting-pot, that produces a jingoistic, mercenary, one-mold type, but as a giant loom weaving into a mighty whole the sons, the poetry, the traditions, and the customs of all races, until a beautiful human fabric, with each thread intact, comes forth – would stretch forth a myriad hands of brotherhood to the four quarters of the globe.
>
> FLYNN 1916

Seeking to move beyond the ACLU's focus on persons denied speech in the United States, Flynn became a member of the National Committee of the Labor Defense Council (LDC), which was set up by the Communist Party of America, a previous name of the Communist Party, USA, in September 1922 to provide funding for legal representation to workers affiliated with a number of unions and left-wing parties, including the IWW. In 1925, the LDC was replaced by the International Labor Defense (ILD), a Comintern-affiliated group with which Haywood was involved, and which provided a global approach to the same issues the LDC had addressed. Flynn also joined the ILD. Although she had not then immediately joined the Communist Party, she did become a member secretly in September 1926, an affinity that would work against her, as indicated below, in the Passaic strike. From the start, the activities of the ILD were favorably reported in the communist newspaper, the *Daily Worker* (Camp 1995, 111, 121; "International Labor Defense (1925–1946): Organizational History" N.d.; "Organizational History" N.d.; Vapnek 2015, 83). However, the belief that she did not become a communist until much later is reflected in the comment of someone who worked with her at the time, former ACLU director, Roger N. Baldwin (1956, 414), who writes that "her book of memoirs stops far short of her Communist conversion in 1937." It was as an LDC and then ILD leader that she involved herself in the campaign to free anarchists Sacco and Vanzetti, an enterprise that would take up a substantial amount of her schedule. Although she remained immersed in activities that were consistent with her previous work, the ILD period is thus a stepping stone to a more controversial sphere of operation that characterized the rest of her life, and which, as noted above, caused her expulsion from the ACLU.

5   Sacco and Vanzetti, the LDC, and the ILD

Nicola Sacco and Bartolomeo Vanzetti were anarchists originally from Italy, accused of the April 15, 1920 robbery and murder of Alessandro Berardelli, a shoe factory paymaster, who with another employee named Frederick Parmenter, was at the time carrying more than $15,000 of the company's payroll money on a street in South Braintree, Massachusetts (Shields 1986, 28; Shone 2013, 204; Topp 2005, 1; Young and Kaiser 1985, 23). The case and the possible execution of the two anarchists attracted much public attention, with their defense at first being organized by fellow Italian immigrants, and then by other anarchists, but eventually involving many radicals, including Elizabeth Gurley Flynn who, working for the WDU and the Sacco-Vanzetti Emergency Committee, organized a major protest campaign and would later note her intense interest in their fate, writing that "In 1924 I spoke seven times on May Day, for Sacco and Vanzetti" (Flynn 1939b). Organized meetings at New York and Boston at first suggested little interest in the clause, but as Flynn (1973, 302) notes, "it eventually spread around the world." Many others attempted to save Sacco and Vanzetti from execution, including anarchists Rose Pesotta, who led a protest march in Boston, and her husband, Frank Lopez, who was also known as Albert Martin, and the journalist, John Nicholas Beffel (Flynn 1973, 298–300; "John Beffel Dead; Aided Sacco Defense" 1973; Leeder 1993, 96; "Sacco-Vanzetti Defense Body is Ended; Reports" 1927; Shone 2019, 289–290). On November 25, 1921, at the Central Opera House in Manhattan, a meeting was held to demand an appeal of the convictions, the speakers including Flynn, Tresca, and Giovannitti ("$18,000 Here to Aid Sacco and Vanzetti" 1921). At the same location three and a half years later, on March 5, 1925, following a recent meeting with Sacco and Vanzetti, Flynn appealed for a unified strategy, telling the audience:

> We have no faith in the capitalist courts, but we have much faith in the working class. If the working class falls us we are lost.
> "New York Backs Sacco-Vanzetti in Life Fight" 1925

By the end of the campaign, organized protest gatherings such as the one that occurred at the opera house on May 21, 1926, would bring out communists, anarchists, immigrant and Italian groups, the ILD, and the ACLU (Pollack 1926). Flynn later recalled her visit with Mary Heaton Vorse and attorney Fred H. Moore to talk to Sacco, who was being held in the Dedham, Massachusetts jail. Already aware of "Elizabetta," having listened to her speak at the Lawrence strike, Nicola outlined his anarchist ideals: "No government, no police, no judges, no bosses, no authority; autonomous groups of people – the people own everything – work in cooperation – distribute by needs – equality, justice, comradeship – love each other" (Flynn 1973, 303).

During the years of the Sacco-Vanzetti protests, Elizabeth continued to concern herself with other issues. In the 1920s, Pennsylvania used its law against criminal syndicalism to prosecute a number of strikers. In 1924, six steel workers belonging to the Workers' Party's South Slavic Federation were arrested in Farrell, Pennsylvania for having violated that state law, an approach to fighting labor unionism which Ahmed A. White explains as follows:

> In practice, it mattered little that the targets of these laws seldom, if ever, actually advocated such conduct as means of social change, or that key terms in the statutes, like sabotage, were only vaguely and ambiguously

defined. What mattered instead was the ability to use these laws to outlaw the advocacy of social change itself, a purpose for which the statutes' ambiguities were well-suited and its targets' legal innocence was irrelevant.

WHITE 2007, 652

One of the six in Farrell was convicted. In response, the Cleveland chapter of the LDC held a meeting at the Royal Hall in that city on May 9 1924 in support of the workers at which Elizabeth Gurley Flynn spoke on the topic of "The Great Anti-Labor Frameups." The next evening, she addressed supporters at the Athletic Hall in Warren, Ohio. A week later, the LDC's Detroit section held a meeting at McCollester Hall at which Elizabeth spoke about the leader of the Workers' Party of America (which became the Communist Party), Charles Emil "C.E." Ruthenberg and the criminal syndicalism case, *People v. Ruthenberg* (1924), in which, somewhat like Debs, he had been convicted largely on the basis of his use of communist ideas at a 1922 party conference in Bridgman, in Berrien County, Michigan. Ruthenberg was currently awaiting an appeal ruling from the state Supreme Court, which would not ultimately be favorable ("Cleveland Workers Hear Ruthenberg Speak at May Day Celebration" 1924; "Elizabeth Gurley Flynn, Noted Fighter, Will Speak in Cleveland" 1924; Flynn 1973, 261; Foner 1991, vol. 9, 141; "Gurley Flynn Speaks for Labor Defense in Detroit Sunday" 1924; Johnson 1957, 162–165; "Meeting in Warren, Ohio" 1924; *The Shame of Pennsylvania* 1928, 3, 16).

Despite her various other commitments, Flynn continued to speak out against fascism and the Ku Klux Klan, talking at the Civic Club in New York City, on April 13, 1924, about the dangers of both these groups, and also, perhaps surprisingly, leveling similar criticisms at the American Legion. On May 29, she spoke to a meeting of the Chicago Federation of Labor about the vulnerability of workers born in other countries, who, in the United States, rapidly became victims when there was a strike. Again, she criticized the Klan, US-based fascists, and the Legion, each of whom she described as seeking to divide ordinary people and undermine their labor union activities. Similar topics were addressed on June 3, when she spoke to Chicago's Liberal Club at the YMCA on La Salle Street and, the next day, appeared at a gathering of the International Workers of the Amalgamated Food Industry, an industrial union, on State Street. On June 13, representing both the LDC and the ACLU, she spoke at the Labor Lyceum in Toledo, Ohio, about the "Menace of the Klan and Fascism," making reference to the Farrell case, and again including the American Legion in a list of anti-labor organizations. A few nights earlier, she had spoken on the same topic in New York to another session of the International Workers of the Amalgamated Food Industry, again mentioning Farrell and the Legion, and also relating the subject to the recent arrest of Tresca ("Elizabeth Gurley Flynn Warns of Fascist Menace" 1924; "Fascism is Real Menace in U. S. Labor Movement" 1924; "Miss Flynn Hits Klan Menace at Federation Meet" 1924; "Toledo Workers to Hear Gurley Flynn Speak Friday Night" 1924). On the subject of the Klan, she said, "We may laugh at the Klan, but they may very well have some serious purpose underneath which will overtake us when we are not expecting it" ("Elizabeth Gurley Flynn Warns of Fascist Menace" 1924).

On September 22, 1924, Flynn was on hand when manicurists, hairdressers, and other beauty parlor workers met at the Stuyvesant Casino in Manhattan's East Village to form a new union, the Independent Beauty Parlor Workers (Lowell 1924; "Manicurists Join Hairdressers in Organizing Union" 1924). Toward the end of 1925, Flynn and the ILD were involved in another strike by silk workers in New Jersey. At the Hillcrest Silk Mills in Hudson County, the employer cut wages by 20% and, as in Paterson a decade earlier embarked upon a plan to make workers newly responsible for three or four looms. When the 250 strikers declined to return to work following a settlement offer that retained the multiple loom proposal, the owners announced that they would relocate the business to High Point, North Carolina. In response to routine police violence levied against the strikers, it was decided to hold mass protest meetings to make political authorities aware of what was happening and press them to intervene. As part of that strategy, two months into the work stoppage, Flynn and Tresca addressed a large gathering. Meanwhile, "scabs" were being hired by the mill at higher rates of pay than what was offered to those on strike ("Indications of Business Activity" 1925; "New York United Textile Union Protests Police Interference in Hillcrest Silk Mill Strike" 1925; "Priest Fails to End Silk Strike in Jersey; Owners to Move Mills to North Carolina 1925; "Silk Strikers Draw Crowds at Mass Meeting" 1925; "Silk Strikers Insist upon Full Demands" 1925; Strikers Find National Plot to Herd Scabs" 1925). At the same time, Flynn, Tresca, and Giovannitti involved themselves in a New York City area unionization drive by the Journeymen Tailors' Union, speaking at a large meeting on October 14 1925 that was held at the Bohemian National Hall in Manhattan ("Tailors of N. Y. Organizing to Battle Bosses" 1925).

In the light of the ILD's international focus, attention was, in the Spring of 1925, drawn to perceptions of starvation in western Ireland, with radicals providing a picture of cattle and sheep in the counties of Donegal and Mayo having died, and area peasants being reduced to eating leaves. Flynn, Debs, and writer Upton Sinclair became members of the Irish Workers' and Peasants' Famine Relief Committee. On April 15, Flynn was one of the speakers at the Central Opera House to spread the word about what she believed was happening in

Ireland. At the same time, other commentators, including the *New York Times* and representatives of the new independent government of Ireland advised that the outcry was somewhat exaggerated, and that remedies were being intoduced in response to the admittedly widespread general existence of poverty in the area and to recent potato and turf crop failures (Grant 2011; "Irish Peasants Facing Plague Thru Starvation" 1925; "Many Join with Workers Party in Relief for Irish" 1925).

At the beginning of 1926, as Sacco and Vanzetti awaited the result of their appeals, Flynn embarked on a January and February speaking tour of the Upper Midwest on behalf of the imprisoned anarchists ("Flynn Starts East on Sacco-Vanzetti Tour" 1926; Helquist 2015, 216). On June 4, a mass meeting was held at the Moose Auditorium in Cleveland, Ohio, at which Flynn and James P. Cannon, the secretary of the ILD, were among the speakers ("Gurley Flynn, Coyle and Hayes to Speak at Cleveland Protest" 1926). On November 26, at Madison Square Garden in New York, Flynn, in her role as ILD chair, also chaired the meeting at which she emphasized the significance of the struggle, which had now failed:

> Sacco and Vanzetti have refused to appeal for a commutation of their death sentence to life imprisonment. They realize that they are no longer individuals but that they have come to symbolize the martyrdom of the masses. They say now, after six and one-half years of incredible suffering, always in the shadow of the electric chair, 'give us liberty or give us death!'
>
> They know that their deaths at the hands of the state of Massachusetts will be something of far more importance than the death of two Italian workers. It will be the American labor movement that will go to the electric chair together with Sacco and Vanzetti.
> "Huge Meeting Lauds Fight on Frame-Up" 1926

Elizabeth was also one of the speakers at a large ILD protest meeting a week later to demand a new trial for the imprisoned anarchists, which was held at the Ashland Auditorium on the west side of Chicago ("'Free Them All!' is Slogan at I.L.D. Meeting" 1926; "Huge Meeting Lauds Fight on Frame-Up" 1926; "Review Spirit of Fight to Save Sacco, Vanzetti" 1926; "Sacco-Vanzetti Conference in Intensive Drive" 1926).

Flynn remained the secretary of the Sacco-Vanzetti Emergency Committee, being involved in many of the 1926 protests until, in March 1927, illness forced her to resign and, as noted above, she moved to Portland, Oregon, where she would spend much of her time with Marie Equi; Sacco and Vanzetti had been executed on August 23, 1926. Reportedly, she had experienced a heart attack, or possibly the problem was an enlarged heart (Baxandall 1987a, 31; "Elizabeth

Gurley Flynn Ill" 1927; "Sacco-Vanzetti Defense Body is Ended; Reports" 1927). In September 1926, when the ILD held its second annual conference, the illness of the group's previous president, Andrew T. McNamara, had led to his replacement by Flynn, and the next month it was announced that she would undertake a national tour with goal of adding many more members to the ten thousand it presently claimed. However, in 1929, she would resign from her ILD position ("248 Delegates Set 300,000 Members as Goal For Second Year of Activity of I.L.D." 1926; "Add 10,000 New Members, Labor Defense Plan" 1926; Camp 1995, 118; Craton 1927; "Elect Engdahl Head of I.L.D." 1929; "Flynn Goes West to Speak on International Labor Defense Tour" 1926; "Flynn in Nation Wide Tour for Labor Defense" 1926).

On November 23, 1926, Elizabeth spoke at an ILD meeting at the Labor Lyceum in the Hill District of Pittsburgh, until 1930 a forum for Jewish union and socialist activism, where she talked about the strike in Passaic, which is described below, but she also found time to criticize Queen Marie of Romania, that nation's last queen, a member of British royalty who had been born in England and who had married King Ferdinand I of Romania. The queen was visiting the United States to secure financing (Cannon 1926; "Gurley Flynn Speaks in Pittsburgh, Will Expose Queen Marie" 1926; Lewis 1926b). Marie was a natural target for Flynn and the ILD, and an article in the *Daily Worker* referred to her as "this symbol of workers' oppression and persecution" ("Visit of Queen Here Won't be a 'Royal' Success as ILD Exposes Regime and City Officers Balk" 1926). An ILD statement documenting the reasons for focusing on the queen portrayed her as follows:

> Queen Marie is the representative of an autocracy which hounds to death and prisons the best workers and poor farmers of Roumania. Under the government she represents, no trade unions are permitted to exist and fight for the rights of the working man and woman. Under her government, no workers' papers are permitted to be published, to give expression to the demands of the people. Under her government, workers and poor farmers are not permitted to hold public meetings, or to organize into labor organizations of any kind. Under her government hundreds of workers have been murdered in cold blood by the bestial secret police called the "Siguranza." [Siguranza is also spelled Siguranță.] Hundreds of workers, men and women, are rotting in prison only because they defended the interests of workers.
> "Workers are Murdered and Imprisoned by the Thousands in the Land of the Queen Marie" 1926

An ILD protest meeting, reportedly with a crowd of 300, some handing out leaflets, took place when the queen visited the First Roumanian Congregation, Shaari Shomayim, an Orthodox Jewish synagogue in Chicago on November 21, 1926. Three protesters, Sophia Greenspoon, Sarah P. Berlin, and Eleanor Sadowska were arrested on charges of disorderly conduct. An earlier protest parade on Michigan Boulevard had led to three local ILD members, George Maurer, Margarite Miller and A. Zuris, also being arrested ("Queen Marie Visits Roumanian Synagog While in Chicago" 1926; Lewis 1926a).

The ILD was especially concerned about conditions in Romanian prisons and the executions, official or "accidental," of political opponents, in particular the fate of Pavel Tkatchenko, a communist activist with past involvement in revolutionary pursuits in Russia and Ukraine, who had been reported as missing. Later, information was received that he had been shot while trying to escape Romanian authorities, although at the time he was wearing heavy chains. A few weeks earlier, another ILD meeting had taken place at Union Square in New York to raise the issue of Tkatchenko's treatment and probable death ("Mighty Protest in N.Y Against Roumania Terror" 1926; "Siguranza Admits Murder of Workers' Leader in Roumania" 1926).

Events elsewhere in Eastern Europe also attracted the concern of the ILD and Flynn, along with that of Debs, Sinclair, and other radicals, who, for instance, considered that Lithuania's leaders had been changed as a result of a coup by Fascists in December 1926, removing the previous president, Kazys Grinius. Of distinct concern was the belief that four communists believed to have been involved in labor activism in the United States, Karl Pojella, Kasis Gedris, Josef Greifenberger, and Rafael Tchorny, had been summarily executed ("Lithuanian Fascist Atrocities Rousing World Wide Protest; Authors Send Cable" 1927). With Roger Baldwin and three others, she submitted a letter to the *Nation* that criticized the government of Hungarian prime minister István Bethlen and the country's regent, Admiral Miklós Horthy, which, having replaced a short-lived communist regime, had stopped a newspaper, *Vilag*, and other media from being published, and imprisoned *Vilag*'s editor, Charles Feleky, and other journalists for criticizing its leaders (Baldwin et al. 1926).

One of the most important campaigns in which Elizabeth participated during this period was the Passaic Strike of 1926–1927. At the Botany Worsted Mills in Passaic, New Jersey, near Paterson, where the well-known silk strike described above had taken place, textile workers who produced woolen products went on strike on January 25 1926 in response to a 10% reduction in their pay, and a walkout soon followed at other mills. The pay cut was ordered notwithstanding the fact that the Botany Worsted Mills' employees had generated an average of $3,160,212 profit per year for the seven years that ended in December 31, 1923, shortly after which a holding company, Botany Consolidated Mills, had been incorporated in Delaware, the creation of which seemed to largely have benefited its major shareholders ("Low Wages, High Profits" 1926, 333). On April 15 at a meeting of 1500 people in Wallington, New Jersey, near to the Passaic line, Flynn told the strikers not to give in to the company management ("Anniversary of Passaic Sees Strike On" 1927; "Minister Who Tested Riot Act is Freed on Bail" 1926). Using money from the Garland Fund, also known as the American Fund for Public Service, a million-dollar inheritance donated by radical free love advocate Charles Garland, a student at Harvard, she hired Mary Heaton Vorse to publicize the workers' cause (Camp 1995, 114; "Church Peace Lobby Financed by Red Money" 1929; Henning 1927a, 1927b; Witt 2022). Unable to come to an agreement with the employees, the Botany vice president, Charles F. Johnson, claimed the stoppage was over, but as Vorse would argue in the *Daily Worker* after the conclusion of the strike, referring to a demonstration that had been held in nearby Belmont Hill Park, this was not at all true:

> There has never been a strike like this. Never in the history of this country or any other, can you find a strike where the workers would stand secure and laughing in face of an offensive like today's, made after seven months. They have the serenity of the invincible.
> VORSE 1927

On March 11, at a meeting in Newark, New Jersey that raised $179 for the strike, the speakers were Flynn and Benjamin Gitlow, who, accused in 1919 of "criminal anarchy," had eventually had his conviction upheld by the US Supreme Court in *Gitlow v. US* (1925) before being pardoned by Al Smith, the governor of New York. Gitlow would eventually become an opponent of communism ("Newark Labor Defense Aids Passaic Strikers" 1926). On July 2, a much larger conference of labor unions in New York pledged $300,000. At that gathering, Elizabeth also spoke of the surprising solidarity of the Passaic employees:

> The workers will rather starve on the picket lines than starve slaving in the mills. This strike is demonstrating that the unorganized in America can be organized. It is demonstrating that the textile workers are capable of dealing with the textile barons. It is demonstrating that the unorganized are again stirring.
> "New York Holds Big United Conference for Passaic Relief" 1926

Other speakers included Gitlow, who, as he had done in Newark, urged participants to join the ILD, and Susan Brandeis, the daughter of US Supreme Court justice, Louis Brandeis. Meanwhile, an attempt to hold a similar street demonstration in Cincinnati was resisted by police and city authorities and did not take place. While she was at the ILD's annual meeting in Chicago, Flynn found time to address a September 6 rally on behalf of the Passaic strikers at the Ashland Auditorium, in which Ruthenberg, Albert Weisbord, the Passaic union leader, and James P. Cannon also spoke. However, on September 10, Elizabeth was asked to end her participation in the dispute by other strike leaders because she was now seen as being sympathetic to communism, and the mill owners refused to negotiate with communists. She and Weisbord, with whom at the time she was romantically involved, ceded control of the strike to the United Textile Workers of America, an American Federation of Labor (AFL) affiliated union, and an agreement was achieved on November 12, 1926. The settlement accepted the right of the employees to engage in collective bargaining and the use of arbitration in the event of future conflict with the owners, and all the strikers were allowed to return to work (Brite 1926; Camp 1995, 117–118, 120; "Flynn Will Speak at Mass Meeting of Labor Defense" 1926; "New York Holds Big United Conference for Passaic Relief" 1926; "Ranks of Pasaaic [sic] Bosses Broken as Big Mill Gives In" 1926; "Strike Leader Will Speak at I.L.D. Meeting" 1926). Thus, when Camp (1995, 114) writes that "Passaic was the first mass strike under communist leadership," it is worth remembering that communist leadership was not from the perspective of the textile employees the factor that produced an acceptable agreement. Rather, Passaic might be seen as a steppingstone in Flynn's path toward abandoning the interests of the working class in favor of an ideology that has tended to oppress ordinary people as it at the same time claims to represent them.

On an ILD promotion trip to western states, Flynn spoke at a joint ILD-ACLU meeting held in the Music-Art Hall in Los Angeles on December 13, 1926, and on the following January 11, she returned to Spokane, the scene of her activist success, where she praised Weisbord and the Passaic strikers as an example for others to follow. On January 21, she appeared at the Moose Temple in downtown Seattle, giving her speech with musical accompaniment, and dramatizing some of the incidents that had happened in Passaic ("Gurley Flynn Draws Big Crowd in L.A.; Hits Syndicalist Law" 1926; "Gurley Flynn Greeted Warmly by Spokane in Tour for Mill Strike" 1927; "Gurley Flynn Talks Passaic to Capacity Crowd of Seattleites" 1927).

6   Flynn the Communist

During her Smith Act trial, Flynn would give an explanation for the change in her political views in 1926 as follows:

> I came to the conclusion that Socialism could be achieved not by one splurge of violence, but by persistent political activities of the workers and the people. And so in order to participate in political activities, in the effort to achieve Socialism, I joined the Communist Party. I had become convinced that the Communist Party was the logical inheritor of all the best traditions, history and struggles of the older Socialist movement and the IWW.
>
> FLYNN, quoted by BAXANDALL 1987a, 35; FLYNN 1952a, 10–11; FLYNN 1952b

Previously, sounding rather like *Pravda*, the official newspaper of the Soviet Union, she had emphasized the reasons for being impressed not only by the party as a whole and its intellectual founders, but by some of its most important leaders:

> The living realization of the scientific truths discovered by Marx and Engels almost a century ago and brilliantly advanced by the genius of Lenin and Stalin is embodied in the glorious achievements of the Soviet Union and in the whole world Communist movement.
>
> FLYNN 1939a

Elsewhere, she wrote of "the feelings of love and devotion which the European people have today towards the Communists of their countries" (Flynn 1946, 5), and claimed that "On May Day we salute the Soviet Union – land of socialism – land of peace and plenty, the great ideal of labor since time immemorial, the cooperative commonwealth of all who toil" (Flynn 1941). On trial, she persisted with the myth:

> Other students and writers took up where they [Marx and Engels] left off, particularly V. I. Lenin, a giant intellect and a great man who suffered exile and imprisonment under the Russian Czar.
>
> He returned to his beloved country to lead the workers and peasants to free themselves form Czarist tyranny and exploitation. Lenin enriched Marxism by his studies, especially his analyses of new social conditions brought about by the rise of imperialism and the advent of socialism.
>
> FLYNN 1952b

As is pointed out with respect to Tom Barker, the attractiveness to many Western radicals of the new regime in Russia appears to have blinded them to oppressions taking place in that location that were far worse than the exploitation that motivated them in their own countries, where their union activism, journalistic endeavors, and ability to make legal arguments were often successful channels for lessening or at least demonstrating misery (Conquest 1986, 5). In the case of Barker, it seems amazing that he was unaware of the despotism of Lenin, even though it was publicized not only by those critical of communism, but by Kropotkin, Goldman, Berkman, Steimer, and others who were initially convinced and had genuinely wanted to support the new polity to which they journeyed, but were soon confronted by the appalling evil that it represented in fact. In defense of Elizabeth, Lynn (2016, 308) writes that "Despite repeated revelations about the abuses within the Soviet Union, Flynn blamed Stalin and not the Soviet system." However, by speaking out loudly in favor of communism, she helped Stalin continue to do damage. Stalin, who is reported to have said, "We will make soup of kulaks" (Haven 2010) actually murdered as many as twenty million people, killed in executions, worked to death and otherwise eliminated in concentration camps, and deliberately starved to death in a famine to which he refused to respond (Grimes 2015; Keller 1989). Among his many crimes, Stalin also used "show trials" of falsely accused persons and groups, such as the mainly Jewish doctors vilified in *Pravda* for having instigated a "Doctors' Plot" for "wrecking, espionage and terrorist activities against the active leaders of the Soviet Government" (Clarfield 2002, 1487), two of whom died in jail before the rest were released shortly after Stalin's death. As Robert Conquest noted in his book, *The Harvest of Sorrow: Soviet Collectivization and the Terror-Famine* (1986):

> We may perhaps put this in perspective in the present case by saying that in the actions here recorded about twenty human lives were lost for, not every word, but every letter, in this book.
> CONQUEST 1986, 1

While Stalin launched and perpetuated the purge of "kulaks" ("kurkuls" in Ukrainian), the supposed counterrevolutionary country-dwellers he designated as "class enemies," claiming they were being eliminated through a kind of spontaneous ejection process performed by poorer peasants, he maintained this "dekulakization," a deliberate plan of agricultural collectivization that led to starvation and ethnic cleansing, mostly of Ukrainians, on a massive scale, was not organized by himself, and he specifically denied that the Terror-Famine of 1932–1933, known also by its Ukrainian language name, the "Holodomor," had even occurred (Conquest 1986, 5, 7, 322; "Holodomor – Famine in Soviet Ukraine 1932–1933, in Commemoration of the 75th Anniversary" 2008, 5). For some researchers, the starvation was a consequence that Stalin and other Soviet leaders had deliberately planned:

> Did the famine of 1932–33 constitute a genocidal attack upon Ukrainians? Evidence presented by a good many horrified witnesses suggests that it did. In their view, the famine occurred because the Soviet authorities ruthlessly collected grain for export, stripping bare one of the most productive agricultural regions of the U.S.S.R., and allowing the local inhabitants to starve, sometimes forcing them into Siberian exile or simply driving them into the wilderness to perish.
> MARRUS 1988, XV

This was a view that Conquest had shared, but eventually he revised his assessment as follows:

> That Stalin was fully informed does not quite prove that he had planned the famine from the first. His continuing to employ the policies which had produced the famine after the famine had clearly declared itself, and indeed to demand their more rigorous application, does however show that he regarded the weapon of famine as acceptable, and used it against the kulak-nationalist enemy.
> CONQUEST 1986, 326

Stalin and various members of the Politburo were aware of the starvation in Ukraine, as were people beyond the borders of the Soviet Union if they cared to inquire. Information about it was published in the West, as early as 1934 in Vienna, in a brief publication titled *The Famine: Authentic Documentation of the Mass Starvation in the Soviet Union*, and later in substantial detail in *The Black Deeds of the Kremlin: A White Book* (Pidhainy, ed. 1953–1955), which was published in North America in the early 1950s (Boriak 2001). Because the attempt to annihilate the kulaks, which he terms "the Soviet elimination of a social class," Norman M. Naimark (2010, 2, 8–9; Haven 2010), the author of *Stalin's Genocides*, argues that it should be considered to be an act of genocide, referring to a problem in the West, including in its academic institutions, that he describes as follows:

> Because Stalin killed in the name of the higher ideals of socialism and human progress, it is sometimes argued, his cannot be equated with the base motives of history's other twentieth-century genocidaires.
> NAIMARK 2010, 5

For Elizabeth Gurley Flynn, then, leadership of the communist faith in the US does not in any way entitle the government in a free country, as reflected in the ideals of the US Constitution, to take away her right to speak, write, associate, travel, publish, campaign, or run for office, but her attachment to the horrors taking place in the Soviet Union at the same time at the hands of allied communists, activities which may well be considered as genocide, do reflect negatively on the turn that her political opinions and activities had taken. On the other hand, what Flynn could say about the reality of capitalism in practice still constituted a legitimate assessment. She wrote:

> This is a beautiful, bountiful country, abounding in natural resources. *But they do not belong to the people.* They belong to the Morgans, Rockefellers, Mellons, du Ponts, and their associates, with their network of interlocking directorates – thousands of companies, big and small – railroads, mines, public utilities (gas, electricity, telephone, transit companies), lumber, rubber, chemicals, steel, auto, department stores, restaurants, amusements, radio, newspapers, insurance companies. There is the highest degree of trustification and monopoly of ownership of the resources of the country and its industrial and financial system by a numerically small group. There is also the highest degree of technical development and of industrial efficiency as well as productivity, possible in the great modern plants, mines and railroads. *But they do not belong to the people.*
> FLYNN 1946, 10

Here, Elizabeth maintained consistency with what she had been fighting for with the Wobblies and the ACLU, the quality of life of ordinary Americans against the domination of interests that prospered by undermining it. But as communist leaders held meetings and wrote articles designed to convince more people of their arguments, their opponents, including those who represented what Flynn saw as the real owners of the country, fought back, passing laws designed to eliminate the communist threat. In 1940, as mentioned, Congress passed the Smith Act, which made it a crime applying whenever anyone "knowingly or willfully advocates, abets, advises, or teaches the duty, necessity, desirability, or propriety of overthrowing or destroying the government of the United States or the government of any State, Territory, District or

Possession thereof, or the government of any political subdivision therein, by force or violence."

In 1948, eleven of the top twelve Communist Party, USA leaders were arrested for having violated the Smith Act. Surprisingly, the twelfth national committee member, Flynn, was not detained, and so she became the chair of the Smith Act Defense Committee and set about raising money for the defense. In 1951, the appeal of the case, *Dennis v. United States* (1951) was heard by the US Supreme Court. The communists were prosecuted for violating the Smith Act because they planned to teach that socialism was inevitable, and that therefore the US government should be forcibly overthrown. The four books that they planned to use were Stalin's *The Foundations of Leninism* (1924); Marx and Engels' *Manifesto of the Communist Party* (1848); Lenin's *The State and Revolution* (1917); and the *History of the Communist Party of the Soviet Union* (1939) (Barrett 1999, 238–239; Camp 1995, 209–210; Powe 1990, 88, fn 42). The Court was very divided in this case, showing divisions in US society that would become even more apparent during the Vietnam War. Here, the majority felt that the clear and present danger test which the Court had used for example in *Debs* was too lenient for dealing with Communists, whom they instead designated as being wicked. For example, Chief Justice Fred M. Vinson pointed out that communists use "aliases and double-meaning language." Justice Robert H. Jackson warned that if the conviction was overturned, the communists might plot and later it would be "too late" to stop a Red takeover. So, the majority felt that, if there is "substantial evil," the government need not prove clear and present danger. The two dissenters felt quite differently. In his opinion, Justice Hugo Black suggested another possible test, the preferred position. Black believed that the 1st Amendment should enjoy a privileged constitutional position, winning all arguments, and that it should be taken literally, meaning that no speech or writing should ever be considered illegal. Thus Black argued that the Constitution allows people to advocate the forcible overthrow of the government, and that the Smith Act is therefore unconstitutional. He wrote: "[T]he First Amendment is the keystone of our government, [its] freedoms ... provide the best insurance against destruction of all freedom." Also dissenting, Justice William O. Douglas went almost as far, arguing that speech by itself can never be conspiracy. He contended that the 1st Amendment actually protected the US from communism:

> Communists in this country have never made a respectable or serious showing in any election. I would doubt that there is a village, let alone a city or county or state, which the Communists could carry. ... Communism has been so thoroughly exposed in this country that it has been crippled

as a political force. Free speech has destroyed it as an effective political party.

Dennis v. United States, 341 U.S. 494 (1951)

In 1950, the McCarran Internal Security Act of 1950 (often referred to simply as the McCarran Act, the Internal Security Act, or, based on the title of one of the latter's subchapters, the Subversive Activities Control Act) was also passed, over the veto of President Harry S Truman, barring communists and fascists from immigrating to the United States, and creating the Subversive Activities Control Board, which was empowered to investigate organizations and determine whether they were communist, and if they were, order them to provide information about their activities and membership to the federal government. In June 1952, Elizabeth was interviewed at the United States Court House in Foley Square, Manhattan (today known as the Thurgood Marshall United States Court House), by a two-member panel of this board, federal Justice Department lawyer Peter Campbell Brown, and Kathryn McHale, who had formerly led the American Association of University Women. The board had the goal of determining the nature of the Communist Party, USA. Its two other members at the time were Watson B. Miller and David J. Coddaire; each of the four received a salary of $12,500 a year. Although Flynn expressed her veneration for the Soviet Union, she denied that the party received financing or was told what to do by agencies based outside the US ("Board Decision Near On Soviet Domination Of U. S. Communists" 1952; "Board on Subversives to Await Return of Congress for Funds" 1950; Camp 1995, 166, 216–217; "Miss Flynn Denies Anti-U. S. Attitude" 1952; "Richardson Predicts Fair Enforcement of Communist Controls" 1950; "Soviet Aid to Reds in U.S. Denied Here" 1952; Vapnek 2015, 152–153).

At the time, Elizabeth had been included as one of a "second string" of thirteen party leaders, having being arrested in June 1951, and she stood out as being the most notable of the group. Representing herself at the 1952 trial before US District Court Judge Edward J. Dimock, as did Pettis Perry, another of the accused, and being one of the witnesses for the defense, she spoke for several weeks, providing an extensive portrait of her own personal biography as well as an overview of the perspective of the Communist Party, USA. It was an occasion for her to engage in what today might be considered "free media," although that participation meant she could not complete her testimony before the Subversive Activities Control Board. The Board decided that the party was a so-called "Communist action" group, which meant that it must register with the Justice Department and reveal the names of its members (Beveridge 1952; "Miss Flynn Ends Testimony" 1952; "Red Leader Testifies" 1952; Roper 1954).

On November 19, 1952, she was twice cited for contempt by the trial judge for refusing to answer some questions, receiving a penalty of two concurrent thirty-day sentences of imprisonment, which she would serve at the end of the trial ("Elizabeth Gurley Flynn Faces Jail After Double Contempt at Red Trial" 1952; Flynn 1952b; "Term for Contempt Ends" 1953; Vapnek 2015, 156). Even so, Flynn liked Judge Dimock, and considered he had gone out of his way to make the trial fair. He imposed sentences that were significantly less than what was proposed by prosecutors (Flynn 1963a, 14–15). He took an active part in the case, asking Elizabeth what was meant by "the dictatorship of the proletariat," and whether the Communists would wait to set up their ideal form of government until they had sufficient popular support to be able to amend the US Constitution. Reluctant at first to provide an answer, eventually she confirmed that they would wait ("Jurist Queries Witness" 1952). Of course, the history of communist parties taking power around the world does not suggest that she answered him with any expectation of accuracy. On the other hand, the judge's questions, though they were configured like an introductory American Government text, suggest he had perhaps forgotten that prior revolutionists in the US did not wait for constitutional change before they removed King George III, and that the Founders, when they instituted the US Constitution that formed the backbone to the ideas that undergirded Dimock's probing, had not felt a need to follow the rules under the existing charter, the Articles of Confederation, when they replaced it.

On January 20, 1953, following an eight month long trial, the defendants were found guilty of violating the Smith Act by their actions in organizing the Communist Party. Following a two-year-long appeals process in which the defendants argued among other claims that the desire to overthrow the government was being "imputed" to each of them severally, the Second Circuit Court of Appeals ruled:

> To permit such declarations to be considered on the issue of the "intent" of a particular defendant, a *prima facie* case of conspiracy among the appellants and others having been made out, was not to impute to such defendant the intent of others, but was simply to include such declarations among the circumstances which the jury might consider in determining the individual intent of that particular defendant.
>
> United States v. Flynn et al., 131 F. Supp. 742 (S.D.N.Y. 1955)

The issue of imputation of intent had not been considered by the US Supreme Court in *Dennis* ("Post-Dennis Prosecutions Under the Smith Act" 1955, 109–110). Consequently, the ability of any major Communist Party leader to establish his or her innocence at this time in history on the charge of seeking to overthrow the government became severely limited.

During the appeals process, while she was out of jail on bail of $25,000, Elizabeth ran for Congress as a People's Rights Party candidate to represent the East Bronx seat that was currently held by a Democrat, Charles J. Buckley. Eventually, the US Supreme Court declined to hear a further appeal, and Flynn, sentenced to a three-year term, and following her good behavior, serving twenty-four months' imprisonment at the Federal Women's Reformatory at Alderson, was released on May 25, 1957 (Camp 1995, 250; "Elizabeth Flynn Freed" 1957; Flynn 1963a, 21; "Red Candidate to File" 1954). During the original trial, Judge Dimock had asked Flynn and the other defendants whether they would be willing to be relocated to the Soviet Union if that settlement of the case could be obtained, which she and a few of the others quickly declined (Flynn 1963a, 184–185).

Out of jail, she again ran for election under the People's Rights Party banner, this time for a seat on the Manhattan City Council. The Marxist Discussion Club, a student organization at City College, invited her to meet with them, but she was barred from doing this by an agreement between the five area community colleges because of her Smith Act violation ("City College Bans Miss Flynn's Talk" 1957; "Miss Flynn a Candidate" 1957). Elizabeth also recalled having not been allowed to lecture at Brown University back when she was what was termed "an agitator of the IWW" (Flynn 1987, 251). Apparently, the tortured logic of the administrators in question was that the enemies of "democracy" should not be allowed to participate in elections or be protected by the First Amendment, the antithesis of Justice Douglas' view. On the other hand, Flynn's gravitation toward and eventual embrace of communism made longtime *Chicago Tribune* reporter, Walter Trohan, balk when she was introduced to students at an Illinois college "as a steadfast advocate of freedom of speech and one of the great ladies of the American left. ... It might have been better if the college official had chosen to introduce her by her correct title, which is national chairman of the Communist Party of the United States of America" (Trohan 1963).

Indeed, on March 13, 1961, the National Committee of the Communist Party, USA, announced that Flynn had been chosen as national chairman, succeeding Eugene Dennis, who had died on January 31 ("Miss Flynn Heads Reds" 1961). The same year, the US Supreme Court, in *Scales v. US* and *Communist Party of America v. Subversive Activities Control Board*, which were decided on the same day, June 5, upheld respectively the constitutionality of the Smith Act and the authority of the Board to determine the status of organizations as being "Communist," thus requiring their registration with the Justice Department.

Four justices, Black, Douglas, Justice William J. Brennan, Jr., and Chief Justice Earl Warren, dissented (Flynn 1961a, 3–4, 15). In *Scales*, in which the conviction was upheld of Junius Irving Scales, the chairperson of the North and South Carolina districts of the Communist Party, for being a communist, Justice Douglas wrote:

> We legalize today guilt by association, sending a man to prison when he committed no unlawful act. Today's break with tradition is a serious one. It borrows from the totalitarian philosophy.
> *Scales v. United States*, 367 U.S. 203 (1961)

In the fall of 1961, Flynn participated in Moscow at the 22nd Congress of the Soviet Communist Party in Moscow where on the opening day, October 17, the premier, Nikita S. Khrushchev delivered a six and one half hour speech that included an attack on the more strongly anticapitalist approach of China and its supporter, Albanian leader, Enver Hoxha, denigrating the latter's personality cult style, a criticism that Elizabeth echoed when she also spoke. From a Western perspective, the conference was viewed as a sign that Khrushchev was willing to embrace a more tolerant and peaceful line on foreign policy as some of the more offensive aspects of Stalin's rule were being publicly identified and jettisoned. It was apparent from his speech that he saw both China and Albania as instead clinging to those now heterodoxical tenets, although it was mainly Albania that he discussed. One of the Chinese leaders, Chou En-lai, who was present at the conference, defended Albania and criticized Khrushchev for his attack ("Albanians Pledge 'Fight to the End' 1961; Buchalla 1961; Communists Wind Up Congress in Moscow" 1961; "German Treaty Deadline Eased by Khrushchev" 1961; Gulick 1961; Gwertzman 1961; "More Time for Berlin Solution" 1961).

The conference also declared that Stalin had been a mass murderer, ordering his corpse removed from the Lenin Mausoleum on Red Square where it had resided since shortly after his death in 1953, providing Western Marxists and other radicals who had denied the starvation in Ukraine and the many other political killings perpetrated by Stalin with new authority to finally admit they had been wrong ("Communists Wind Up Congress in Moscow" 1961; Grover 1961). Flynn now openly embraced the less warlike revisionism that Khrushchev was imposing.

Attention to the 22nd Congress on the part of US journalists led to some failed attempts by Americans partaking of the political activity in Moscow to portray the Soviet Union as a much better place to live. Flynn, for example, reported on a television show that she was putting on weight, implying that people who went hungry in the US would be better fed in Moscow, an unfortunate denigration of her rhetorical approach ("Russians Get American Red Views of U.S." 1961). Meanwhile, the segregationist opponent of civil rights legislation, US Senator James "Big Jim" Eastland from Mississippi no less absurdly claimed that Flynn had returned to the US with a plan for Soviet domination of the globe (Moore 1961).

A few weeks earlier, when Flynn was already in Moscow, fellow US communist leader, William Z. Foster, who had gone to the Soviet Union for medical treatment, passed away, and she appeared as the principal speaker at his poorly attended funeral at the Lenin Mausoleum, the ashes later being taken for placement in the wall of the Kremlin. Bill Haywood was also a participant in the proceedings. In her oration, Elizabeth praised Foster for having "fought hard to unify our party as a Marxist-Leninist party and rid it of revisionists" ("Foster Buried at Kremlin" 1961), an indication perhaps that, notwithstanding the death of Stalin and the modifications it was leading to, she was, as demonstrated too by her rejection of Albanian-style communism, still committed only to a single template of "correct" belief, even if its guidelines changed from time to time. This was a spectacularly different pose for a woman who, in the first half of her life had symbolized so many dimensions of the quest for human liberty, including an absolute commitment to freedom of speech and conscience (Barrett 1999, 271; "Foster Buried at Kremlin" 1961).

Back in the US in January 1962, Elizabeth received a passport revocation letter from the State Department, which had begun to interpret the McCarran Act as empowering it to deny communist leaders the right to travel, a circumstance that would persist until June 22, 1964 when the US Supreme Court, in *Aptheker v. Secretary of State*, disallowed it, having two weeks earlier overturned the party's requirement to register with the government. Herbert Aptheker was another Communist Party, USA leader who had had his passport revoked; Flynn was the other appellant. The Court provided several rationalizations for the decision. For Chief Justice Arthur Goldberg, the law violated the due process clause of the Fifth Amendment, while Black found three different reasons for overturning the law. Like Douglas, he saw it as breaching the protections of the First Amendment ("High Court to Review Ban on Reds' Passports" 1963; Laursen 1981, 904–905, 908; "Mrs. Flynn Hearing Put Off Until May 3" 1962; Vapnek 2015, 172–175; Vile 2009; Voss 1962). In his concurring opinion, Justice Douglas wrote:

> Free movement by the citizen is, of course, as dangerous to a tyrant as free expression of ideas or the right of assembly, and it is therefore controlled in most countries in the interests of security. That is why riding

boxcars carries extreme penalties in Communist lands. That is why the ticketing of people and the use of identification papers are routine matters under totalitarian regimes, yet abhorrent in the United States.

Aptheker v. Secretary of State, 378 U.S. 500 (1964)

Today, Douglas might find there is much less distinction to be made between traveling in the United States and in other places, that the individual liberty that he and Black and, in the earlier part of her life, Flynn vigorously endorsed, has in many ways disappeared. As White (2022, 229) notes, Douglas was rewarded for having eloquently defended the constitutional rights of communists by himself becoming the subject of FBI surveillance ("F.B.I. Kept Close Watch on Douglas" 1984).

Having arrived back in Moscow at the beginning of August 1964, and suffering again with heart trouble, her pulse rate very low, Flynn was admitted to a hospital, the Central Clinic of the Soviet Health Ministry at the end of the month and, on September 5, she died. One of her last acts had been to criticize the Communist leaders of China in an article that appeared in *Pravda*. She received a state funeral in Red Square, at which 25,000 people were present, Khrushchev participating in the event. Following her cremation, her ashes were sent to Chicago's Waldheim Cemetery, where the bodies of many anarchists have been laid to rest ("Elizabeth Gurley Flynn is Dead: Head of U.S. Communist Party" 1964; "Miss Flynn is Cremated: Tribute in Moscow Today" 1964; "Russian Tribute to U.S. Leader" 1964; "Top U.S. Communist Succumbs in Moscow" 1964; "U.S. Communist Leader Ill" 1964).

PART 2

Internationalists

CHAPTER 4

Tom Barker: a Wobbly Who Wobbled

Tom Barker was a radical union activist who moved from England to New Zealand, and on to Australia, Chile, and Argentina; then, in later years, he spent time in the Soviet Union and worked in the US before returning to his original home. He is often mentioned in scholarly works, with the conversation that occurred near the end of his life in 1963 with historian Eric Fry (Barker 1965; Fry 1965) by far the most cited source for his activities, and often the only reference that is used, one that forms much of the basis for conventional interpretations of Barker's life and its impact. However, notwithstanding the great value of that contribution to understanding Barker's significance, there is a wealth of available alternative resources, including many articles published by Barker in radical journals, as well as an abundance of newspaper reports of his activities as he moved around the world, commencing quite early in his life as an Industrial Workers of the World (IWW) leader, and becoming eventually a more predictable, though less consistent, advocate of socialism. Moreover, Fry's article presents biographical information from the perspective of the interviewee, most of it based on the latter's memory of events that had occurred many years in the past; while there is no reason to doubt the accuracy or honesty of Tom's observations or the way they were recorded by Fry, there are many other possible standpoints available for recording Barker's life. The purpose of this chapter, therefore, is to illuminate other characteristics of his intensely remarkable existence that are quite frequently acknowledged, but today seldom documented in any significant detail. In particular, inconsistencies between the varying ideological commitments evinced at different times by Barker, including his role, such as it was, as an apologist for the violations of human rights that occurred in the early years of the Soviet Union, remain largely unexplored.

Beginning in Chicago in 1905, the IWW, known also as the Wobblies, presented a challenge to the more conservative and much more traditional American Federation of Labor (AFL), which approached unionization as a domestic activity and discriminated against less-skilled employees, women, and minorities. Instead, the ambassadors of the IWW traveled the world, embracing more militant and globally cognizant perspectives, ones which have often been identified as anarchist and syndicalist in nature, and their philosophy of direct action and dedication to the interests of those whom they viewed as a working class, especially those laboring for industrial concerns, earned their operatives the ire of governments, employers, and property-owners wherever they were active. The transference of a Wobbly mindset was aided by sailors, including those who were members of New Zealand's Seamen's Union or of the Marine Transport Workers Union (MTW), on behalf of which Barker acted in Argentina and then in Europe, as the ships on which they worked journeyed to faraway ports (Davidson 2015, 28; De Angelis 2012, 1–2, 2014, 8–9; Gómez 2017, 7–8; Rosenthal 2015, 73). Speaking of the Wobblies in Australia, where Barker would move and assume a major role in their activities, Burgmann writes:

> Based on a premise fundamentally different from both Communism and Laborism, the IWW represented a revolutionary working-class politics intent upon self-emancipation, dedicated as it was to the principle that there are none better to break the chains than those who actually wear them.
>
> BURGMANN 1995, 1

1 New Zealand

Thomas "Tom" Barker, ubiquitously known as "Tom Barker," was born in Crosthwaite in Westmoreland in northwest England in 1887 to Thomas Grainger Barker and Sarah Trotter. As a boy he worked on farms, joining the 8th King's Royal Irish Hussars, a British Army cavalry regiment, which was presently housed in Aldershot, Hampshire in 1905, and becoming a lance corporal, until heart problems including rheumatic fever forced him to end his military service after three years. In 1908, he started to work on the tram system in Liverpool (Barker 1965 6–7; Burgmann 1995, 70; Olssen 1996p; Turner [1967] 1969, 14).

The prevailing view is that Barker arrived in New Zealand in 1909 (Burgmann 1995, 70; Cain 1993, 72; Fry 1965, 1; Turner [1967] 1969, 14), although Olssen (1988, 114) writes that "Tom Barker ... arrived in Auckland from Manchester [rather than from Liverpool] in 1911" and Weiss (2021, 39) says also that he emigrated in 1911. This was a country to which his sister, Jenny Connor, had also relocated. Tom had been making 25s [£1 5s] working 60 hours a week in Liverpool, a situation much improved when he relocated to a similar position in Auckland which paid £4 10s for a 48-hour week (Barker 1965, 7; Harrison 1961). He quickly became involved with and rapidly emerged as an organizer for the Auckland Electric Tramways Union, as well as the New Zealand Socialist Party and the New Zealand Federation of Labor (NZFL), an employee organization which was known as the "Red Feds." He befriended Red Fed leaders Canadian-born John Benjamin "J.B." King, and gifted orator, Harry Scott Bennett, who was originally from Australia (Cain 1993, 7; Olssen 1988, 133, 138; Shor 2005, 155). Despite the improvement in his salary, Barker was by no means a fan of his Auckland employer:

> In 1911 Tom Barker emerged as the revolutionary leader of the unskilled. Here as elsewhere an influx of new members demanded new strategies for dealing with old grievances. In September 1911 the men voted to affiliate with the Red Federation, and then seceded from the arbitration system. For the moment the trammies shared Barker's belief that an 'ounce of Direct Action is worth a ton of Parliamentary string-pulling, and Trades Council chin wag.'
> OLSSEN 1988, 139

By 1912, Barker was occasionally attracting attention with articles he wrote for the radical Wellington-based NZFL paper, the *Maoriland Worker*, using the moniker "Spanwire," a name derived from a type of cable that protects tramways (Cain 1993, 72). In the first of these pieces (Barker 1912a), he reported on events in Auckland, including recent lectures by Bennett, one of which, titled the "Eureka Stockade," had an audience of 1700. The talk described events in Ballarat, Victoria known as the "Battle of the Eureka Stockade," a fight between gold miners and the colonial authorities which had taken place on December 3, 1854. Bennett and Barker viewed Eureka, where the miners were led by an Irish immigrant called Peter Lalor, as an important event in the fight by workers to develop democratic practices in the Antipodes at the expense of those Tom described in his article as "the hired thugs of the autocratic rulers of Australia at that time" (Barker 1912a). After he had moved to Sydney, he would later complain about the imprisonment of a Eureka veteran, Montague "Monty" Miller in the Perth jail (Barker 1916a), an event which is discussed later in this chapter. Bennett, much admired as a teacher, had also on other occasions talked in Auckland about "The Tragedy of Calvary and the Tragedy of Toil" and "The Opium Traffic in Melbourne," and, further to the north in Dargaville, on "Socialism" (Barker 1912a). Revealing some of the influences and allegiances that were presently competing for his attention, Barker wrote:

> We of the Socialist Party are indeed in a quandary. We are attacked by the Labor Party because we are against political action, and we are challenged by the I.W.W. because we are a political party. By the way, an I.W.W. club

> has been formed in Auckland. ... It has already got a large and increasing membership, and is doing sterling work, spreading the doctrines and gospel of Industrial Unionism. Good luck to it, say I.
>
> BARKER 1912a

In other articles that Barker published as "Spanwire" in the *Maoriland Worker* in 1912, he described the strike being conducted by the Waihi Trade Union of Workers, which would ultimately fail and be considered a letdown for the "Red Feds," an organization which had been formed in 1909 after another strike in 1908 at Blackball. Following a work stoppage in September 1913 at the Huntly mine, conditions on the waterfront led to an out-and-out confrontation in which Barker was more actively involved.

On October 11, 1912, Barker reported that, notwithstanding the fact that some of the Waihi strike leaders had been jailed, they were winning their fight, and, in response, a general strike was being planned (Barker 1912b):

> The workers of Waihi are winning gloriously – there are four scabs out of 700 men. Bravo, men and women of Waihi; you have the mine and its owners in the palm of your hands. According to the lying [Auckland newspapers] "Herald" and "Star," they are getting defeated but telegrams from the scene of action gives the lie.
>
> BARKER 1912b

When the Red Fed leadership actually declined to call a general strike following the failure at Waihi, which ended in violence, they lost the support of some of its more militant members, including that of Barker, who became more oriented toward the approach of the IWW (Derby 2006; Nolan 2006; Olssen 2006; Shor 2005, 154). In early November, Tom and a colleague took a train to Waihi, where he stayed for five days, and observed the solidarity of strikers he encountered at the Miners' Union Hall, praising J.B. King's work with the union, but being offended by the sight of people on the other side of the argument who were still laboring, and describing the divergence in terms of a class war that, he felt, must inevitably now be fought (Barker 1912c):

> These spindle-shanked vacuous youths are not diggers! Nay, nay, Orlando – these are the paragons of pressdom, they are the boon companions of the Blowflies, they are the patriots, yea, they are the scabs. Of all the contemptible forms of life that infest our earth to-day the scab is the most detestable. Can you wonder that honest men hold their noses, that women pull their children away?
>
> BARKER 1912c

Soon afterwards, the situation was much changed for the worse, and the strikers were attacked, directly or indirectly at the instigation of the Reform Party government of prime minister William Ferguson "Farmer Bill" Massey, the police, and the mineowners, with the assistance of "a horde of drunken criminals, Maoris drunk on nethylated [methylated] spirits, thugs, and wasters" who had "terrorised and brutally maltreated and murdered men and women of our own class in Waihi" (Barker 1912d). Fellow Red Fed leader, Bob Semple, a future member of the New Zealand parliament and Labour minister, had echoed the less than assuaging language, complaining that the "scabs" included "thugs, toughs, and half-castes" (Olssen 1988, 159). In the assault, just one man, Frederick G. "Fred" Evans – trying to remember his name half a century later, Barker (1965, 11) said, "I think his name was Timothy Evans" – had been killed when the Red Feds were evicted from their Union Hall on November 12, 1912 with shots being fired as rival union members, police, and their supporters raised the British flag and sang "God Save the Queen," an event since known as "Black Tuesday" (Barker 1912d, 1912f, 1915n, 1965, 11; Nolan 2006; Olssen 1988, 159; Rainford 2015).

After becoming an IWW organizer in 1913, Tom was soon being listed in an IWW directory of its Antipodean officials as the Secretary-Treasurer of the Auckland local ("I.W.W. Directory (Australasian Locals)" 1913). By August, he was traveling around the country, and visited Wellington, where, together with the Latvian-born tailor and anarchist pamphleteer, Philip Josephs, he held "11 propaganda meetings in 14 days" (Barker 1913a) with the goal of setting up a local office there. In an advertisement in the Wellington *Evening Post* about a planned talk on Sunday, August 10 at the Socialist Rooms on Manners Street, Barker was now identified more expansively as "the New Zealand organiser of the I.W.W." (Untitled 1913a), while his appearance at a weekly meeting of the Wellington Freedom Group, an anarchist collective founded by Josephs a few weeks earlier, which met at his business, was similarly reported by the *Maoriland Worker*, noting that "Comrade Barker" was the "organiser of the I.W.W." ("Wellington Notes" 1913a, 1913b). A few weeks later, the *Littleton Times* printed a letter from Tom in which he too described himself as a "Dominion Organiser" for the I.W.W. (Barker 1913f). On August 19, he headed to Christchurch, where he gave a speech about "Anti-militarism" (Barker 1913a). On September 6, he held an IWW meeting at the Clock Tower in Christchurch with Sid Kingsford, a local area letter writer, opponent of militarism, and defender of the IWW (Kingsford 1912), which led to a court appearance for Tom, who was charged with "obstruction," for which he was fined 10s, with 7s costs (Barker 1913a; Moriarty-Patten 2012, 108–109; "Round the Clock Tower: "Labour Agitators" Fined" 1913). Characteristically misinterpreting the meaning of public speaking regulations, a tactic he would later use when explaining an anti-conscription poster as actually endorsing involvement in the First World War, Barker told the magistrate that "The City Council told me that they only had power to grant permission to speak in Cathedral Square, and so I thought I was quite free to speak anywhere else" ("Round the Clock Tower: "Labour Agitators" Fined" 1913). In Christchurch that month, Barker set up a branch of the IWW, even though there was already an existing group, which had been formed in 1910, and which saw its function as being to support the NZFL and its embrace of political involvement as a means of representing employees. Working with King, a member of the "Chicago IWW," which had in 1908 revised the preamble adopted by the Wobblies' 1905 conference to remove commitments to cooperative activity with political parties and legislatures, Barker had also set up the IWW branch in Auckland (Cain 1993, 72; Kingsford 1911; Milburn 1966, 675, 675 fn 12; Moriarty-Patten 2012, 10; Prebble 1999).

Later, Tom spoke to gatherings across the Buller District in the northwest area of the South Island, including coal mining towns such as Millerton, Runanga, Denniston, and Burnett's Face, Ngakawau (where Stockton Mine employees lived), Westport (where gold and coal were mined), Waiuta (a gold mining settlement which today is a ghost town), and the aforementioned Blackball, which is now the home of the Blackball Museum of Working Class History [*Mahi Tupuna*]. Meeting with the Paparoa Miners' Union, he gave a talk on "Industrialism and Sabotage"; the advocacy of "sabotage" by IWW members in New Zealand, Australia, and, as discussed in Chapter 3, the United States, would over the next few years lead to much controversy. On October 9, 1913, he met with the Westport Watersiders, where he was much impressed by what he found out about this union of waterside workers, who shared work hours and pay equally among its members (Barker 1913d; P.R. 1913b; Untitled 1913b).

Debate in the United States between advocates of (i) the independent and more antigovernmental direct action approach of the Chicago IWW which was endorsed by William Dudley "Big Bill" Haywood (who would later be involved with Barker at the Kuzbas project in Russia and, as described in Chapter 3, with Elizabeth Gurley Flynn), and (ii) the more mainstream approach of the dissident "Detroit IWW" (later called the Workers' International Industrial Union) that was set up as an alternative by Daniel De Leon and other supporters of the Socialist Labor Party of America (SLP), and who sought to work through the use of political association with groups such as the SLP, was now reflected amidst Wobbly activity in New Zealand. The Detroit IWW was arguably more socialist than the Chicago IWW, which, despite its use of the concepts of class, surplus value, and other aspects of Marxist economics, was essentially anarchist and syndicalist in character (Barker 1965, 18; Cain 1993, 15, 112; Moriarty-Patten 2012, 9–11; Van der Walt and Schmidt 2009, 159–160, 162). In a letter to the *Littleton Times*, Tom showed his sympathy with the Chicago IWW approach when, in typical fashion, he referenced the need for direct action based on the existence of what he viewed as class differences (Derby 2006), writing that:

> The question is a bread and butter one. It can only be solved by those concerned, by their own direct participation in that struggle, and not by any bunch of well-intentioned, easy-going people who have never struggled on the long-handled shovel, or racked their brains what excuse to give to the landlord.
> BARKER 1913f

Starting on February 1, 1913, the Auckland branch of the IWW began publishing its monthly paper, the *Industrial Unionist*, which appeared much more frequently as the country's full-blown 1913 strike developed, folding after the issue of November 29 the same year. Tom soon started writing provocative articles that were published in its pages, some of which again were credited to "Spanwire," as would occasionally be commentaries he wrote later on in Australia (Barker 1914d, 1965, 13).

On August 1, 1913, the *Industrial Unionist* published Barker's article, "Parliament and its Relationship to Economics" (Barker 1913e), in which he elaborated, from his Chicago IWW perspective, the need to reject working with political parties and legislatures, referring to the relationship between the NZFL and that country's United Labour Party, an antecedent of today's Labour Party (Findlay 2019, 32–33, 144). Viewing the New Zealand Parliament as the site of "class warfare," he argued that:

> Parliament is a reflection of economic power on the industrial field. ... Whether Conservatives, Liberals, Reformers or Socialists grace the plush seats of the class parliament, it matters not one iota. ... Let us distinctly understand that all political legislation is controlled by industrial change.
>
> Therefore, the Capitalist class who own and control the basic Industries must, by the very nature of that ownership, control the Parliamentary institution.
> BARKER 1913e

If anyone needed proof of the above statements, they would only need to look at Australia, Barker notes, where the Labor Party came to power driven by the demands of many radical activists, but then it did not fulfil the goals of many of its supporters. In fact, the significance of this issue to the development of socialism in Australia has long been debated by historians (see Shone 2022, 70–73). Instead of expecting legislators to implement the desired change, Tom advocates, consistently with mainstream IWW doctrine, creation of One Big Union and use of militant direct action, rather than the current situation whereby "there are 50 craft unions, with 50 secretaries, 50 offices, 50 telephones, 50 little narrow outlooks and 50 agreements with the bosses – all expiring at 50 different times" (Barker 1913e; De Angelis 2017, 259).

On March 1, 1913, in a piece in the *Industrial Unionist*, Barker condemned the "half-hearted methods" and "servility" of the Auckland tramway union (Barker 1913v). Criticizing its effectiveness, Tom again advocated the IWW's solutions of creating One Big Union, which would be much more able to negotiate with employers, and direct action to have the power to lessen the numbers of hours and days per week that the employees worked:

> There is not a doubt that, unless the Tramway Workers assert themselves, their wages and working conditions will remain much the same.
> BARKER 1913V

Here, Barker advocated a particular tactic of the direct action philosophy that he would often encourage: employees slowing down the pace of their jobs in order to put pressure on employers to make concessions, which included "obeying the rule book in every minute detail," thereby taking longer to do their work (Barker 1913v), the consequence of which would be a redistribution of the balance of power between owner and union. Tom's views at this point are already strongly reflective of the IWW canon, as are his comments almost a year before in two of his contributions to the *Maoriland Worker*, where he was similarly critical of the union's slow road to what he considered progress and maybe also its plodding steps in a backward direction:

> If the opinions of some of its prominent officials are an index, the Tramway Union has anything but a clear grasp of the principles of Industrial Unionism, and if it is to make progress it will have to follow the example of the miners of Old England, and push fossilised officials and their colleagues and their retarding influence right clean out of the way. The Union, however, is moving, albeit rather slowly, but God knows its members will have to shake themselves a good deal before they will be fit to be in the forefront of the fighting division of the One Big Union of New Zealand.
> BARKER 1912a

Elsewhere, dismayed by the decision of the Tramway Union's members not to pay a levy to support the waterside workers if they should decide to strike:

> This Union has fallen from greatness. After milking the Federation [the NZFL], all it can, it decides to remain neutral in a general strike; that is to say, that if the Watersiders Union is out on strike, the tramwaymen will carry blackleg labor on the cars to take the lumpers' places. Tramwaymen of Auckland! There is no neutral position in a fight between organised Labor and organised Capital.
> BARKER 1912e

Of course, Barker did not stay in New Zealand for very long, and this limited his ability to be the catalyst for much local change. Here the rationalization for his choice of approach perhaps not only explains what was going on in less radical unions and in the respective Labour/Labor parties in New Zealand and Australia at the time, but also predicts some of the failures that would occur in the future:

> Better a small, compact organization, class-conscious, imbued with the courage born of fighting the class war, than a loose, disjointed, indecisive, reactionary mob, led first one way and then another by the spur of the moment and the prospect of immediate gain.
> BARKER 1912a

On April 1, 1913, the *Industrial Unionist* published Barker's article titled "Machine Slavery" (Barker 1913c). In it, he referred to the IWW's preamble, with its statement that "The working class and the employing class have nothing in common" (Turner [1967] 1969, 8), a situation currently exacerbated by what he saw as "the ever-increasing multitude of paupers and social outcasts contrasted with the concentration of wealth and power in correspondingly fewer hands" (Barker 1913c), and he also elaborated on the significance of his organization's commitment to the One Big Union idea as follows:

> We must organise, educate, and agitate ... when the One Big Union holds universal sway, and the "Internationale" rings the wide world over, the Working Class will no longer be the slaves of the machine; their shackles will snap like twigs before the storm.
> BARKER 1913c

The June 1, 1913 issue of the *Industrial Unionist* carried Barker's article, "The Worker and the "Backbone"" (Barker 1913h), in which Tom looked at recent events in Australia and New Zealand, including the 1912 Brisbane General Strike, which had developed out of a dispute by tramway employees fired for wearing their union badges at work, raising issues about the purpose of unionists wanting to identify their membership, amid more general concerns about protecting the rights to unionize and withdraw labor. While the strike was tolerated for a couple of weeks, it soon, on February 2, led to "Black Friday," when police, some of them on horseback, attacked gatherings of strikers who were meeting on the streets in a demonstration for which a permit had not been approved. The same day, as part of the protest, septuagenarian Emma Miller led a women's march to Parliament House, the home of Queensland's unicameral legislature; the procession was also attacked by mounted officers, the women responding by battling the men and horses using their hatpins and umbrellas as weapons ("Peace at Brisbane" 1912; "The Truth about the Strike" 1912; Young 1991, 173, 180–186). A report in the Sydney-area *Worker*, partially reprinted a month later in the Melbourne *Labor Call*, commented on the violence as follows:

> We know from world-wide experience that the exercise of violence transforms men into wild animals. That is what happened in Brisbane on Friday. The Cossacks of the Czar, with the instincts of the jungle bred in them, could not have been more ravenous in the pursuit of blood than Brisbane's "civilised" police.
> "Madness of Moneybags" 1912; "The Truth about the Strike" 1912

In his article, Barker uses this 1912 walkout to illustrate the phenomenon of farmers with conservative ideas who read about strikes in reactionary newspapers, and who then volunteer to become "scabs," replacing strikers, and attempt to undermine the goals of labor unions:

> The interests at stake in this strike were not the interests of the farmers themselves, but of a Yankee dividend-grinding company headed by the notorious [Joseph Stillman "J.S."] Badger [an American], and of the various monopolies and trusts controlling the food supply and transportation facilities in Brisbane and vicinity.
> BARKER 1913h

Although farmers at present enjoy tolerable conditions that allow them to follow the injunctions of "the journalistic prostitutes of the capitalist daily press"

(Barker 1913h), and undermine unions' actions trying to improve the conditions experienced by transportation, sugar, and waterside workers, butchers, and sailors, each of whom had recently in New Zealand fallen victim to farmer scabbery, those conditions will not, Tom predicts, last for ever. Of course, as Young (1991, 173) notes, the fact that other participants in disputes, such as J. S. Badger, who was also known as "Bully Badger," "had a deep-seated hatred of unionism" did not suggest that improvement in labor relations would be straightforwardly achieved. In the future, Tom warns, China, Argentina, and Russia will be able to expand their underused farming industries, and the era of, for example, New Zealand dominating the market for butter, will come to an end. Then, perhaps, the agriculture worker will begin to appreciate the perspective of the IWW, and start to see him or herself as a wage earner similar to others who survive or prosper by selling their labor (Barker 1913h). In the meantime, however, he issues a warning to anyone influenced by less progressive notions and driven to undermine the union cause: "[I]f you value your stock, your herds, and your house, mind your own business and stay at home" (Barker 1913h).

In a letter published in the *Littleton Times* around this time, Barker (1913f) emphasized many of the themes he was discussing in his contributions to the *Industrial Unionist*, calling again for the development of One Big Union and denying that morality is a set of fixed criteria that operates regardless of which group of citizens is in charge. Instead, he claims, virtue could transmute when a stronger movement of working people allowed them to take over and institute "the social values created by them" (Barker 1913f). The present way that society is organized is thus not only unfair, but, from the point of view of labor, it is actually immoral:

> Just so long as the few own and control the socially created values produced by labour, just so long will that system be wrong from a working class standpoint, and the workers are quite justified in using any and every means that will help them in their struggle for equal opportunity, whether it agrees with the ethics and morals of the owning class or not.
> BARKER 1913f

Sounding like Lois Waisbrooker (1897) and other anarchists in his zeal to reject the use of political or electoral activity by union activists, he asks whether "starving working men, frail, worn-out women, and underfed, are going to amuse themselves with nose-counting in parliamentary campaigns" (Barker 1913f). Writing about plans for Barker's upcoming visits to Wellington and Christchurch in the August 1, 1913 issue of the *Industrial Unionist*, correspondent

"P.R." gives a similar indication as to the latter's aversion to voting as a solution to political problems, writing that "Tom Barker will soon go South, accompanied by a formidable bluey-full of dynamite (mental), guaranteed to blow up some iron-bound notions *re* emancipation by ballot paper" (P.R. 1913a).

In his article "'Mad Mullahs' and Blind Alleys," which appeared on July 15, 1914 in *Direct Action*, the newspaper of the Australian IWW which was funded by its Sydney chapter, a publication which he would later edit (Barker 1914b, 1915b), Tom Barker denied that dismissing the value of voting to democracy was the way it was sometimes seen, as the foolish objective of a Mad Mullah, contending instead that "it does not necessarily mean that the ballot box is useful because the majority of Radical workers in N.Z., or any other country, deem it to be useful. Majorities are very seldom right, and the Labour movement itself, is by no means an exception to this rule" (Barker 1914b). Citing the example of Peter Kropotkin, another critic of parliamentary systems, he concluded that "I don't think that anyone, who has read the valuable works of the eminent Russian scientist, would call him a Mad Mullah, just because he has no use for the ballot box" (Barker 1914b). Kropotkin had written:

> As to parliamentary rule, and representative government altogether, they are rapidly falling into decay. The few philosophers who already have shown their defects have only timidly summed up the growing public discontent. It is becoming evident that it is merely stupid to elect a few men, and to entrust them with the task of making laws on all possible subjects, of which subjects most of them are very ignorant. It is becoming understood that Majority rule is as defective as any other kind of rule; and Humanity searches, and finds, new channels for resolving the pending questions.
>
> KROPOTKIN 1887

For voting to be able to achieve noteworthy results, Barker continued, there would need to be significant change to the political and economic environment within which it operates at present:

> The I.W.W. bases its organisation upon the fact that all social questions have been, are and will be settled by might – that is, while Capitalism exists
>
> BARKER 1914b

In the next few years, a few supporters of Tom would threaten to employ a more physical kind of dynamite as they agitated for his release from jail, while a larger number would be accused of having done so and be imprisoned on the basis of false "evidence." However, in response to the union activity of 1913, including the advocacy of "sabotage," workers were greeted by accounts in the *Industrial Unionist*, that suggested more conservative organs, specifically the *New Zealand Herald* and the *Auckland Star*, were plotting to perform their own sabotage upon the union side with their stories about an attempt to plant another form of nitroglycerine, gelignite, on an Auckland-area express train. That suspicion, raised in editorials that may have been written by Barker himself, who had happened to be traveling on the train in question, might have been substantiated by the fact that some of the *Herald*'s reporting derived from the interests of its editorial writer, who was reappointed as the paper's editor in 1913: he was William Lane, the one-time socialist founder of the New Australia Co-Operative Settlement Association, and leader of its communes in Paraguay called New Australia and Colonia Cosme, both of which, like many of his prior opinions (though not his racism), he had eventually abandoned. In his new employment, he became well-known as a jingoistic critic of labor unions and a passionate advocate of the First World War, someone who probably did not approve of Barker or of his activities (Shone 2022, 102).

One of the editorials in the *Industrial Unionist* referenced the Bread and Roses Strike in Lawrence, Massachusetts the previous year, where similarly devious tactics had been resorted to by employers seeking to undermine the industrial involvement of IWW activists, who, in Lawrence, included Bill Haywood and the subject of Chapter 3, Elizabeth Gurley Flynn, and imprison or execute them. In that case, leaders of the strike against the American Woolen Company, Joe Ettor and Arturo M. Giovannitti, were arrested and tried as accessories to murder on the ground that their speeches had incited the otherwise unrelated murder of Anna "Annie" Lopizzo, which happened during a riot. Nonetheless, as he would later explain, Barker viewed the Lawrence strike as an illustration of "[t]he power of the working class ... to control hamper or interrupt industry," since it "aimed a vital blow at the exploiters, and compelled them to give better conditions" ("Fighting Conscription: Views of Tom Barker" 1916). Moreover, the trial attracted attention throughout the world ("Ateo Rivolta" 1912; "Have 350 Veniremen" 1912; "Hit "American Plutocracy"" 1912; "Make Auditors Cry" 1912; Shone 2019, 239–240; "Socialists to Steer Clear Union Fights" 1912; "Solidarity Still Spreading" 1913; "Woollen Trust Faces Inquiry by Congress" 1912; Young 1991, 173). One *Industrial Unionist* editorial, comparing the 1912 strike with the 1913 Auckland train incident commented as follows:

> If the Lawrence plot had not been discovered and exposed by a fortunate accident it is certain that several innocent I.W.W. organisers would now

be doing life sentences – if they escaped the electric chair. It is equally certain that if the local plot had not been so ridiculously amateurish the daily papers would have made great capital against the strikers, and that many staunch men of the working class would now be in jail on "circumstantial evidence."

"Solidarity Still Spreading" 1913

In another piece, the IWW paper amplified its concerns, suggesting that at least one of the newspapers might have been involved in the anti-union project:

The statement of the "New Zealand Herald" that "There is ample evidence that the plan was deliberately designed," recalls the fact, also, that in the case of the Lawrence "discovery" the "Boston American," a capitalist paper, had the news of the "discovery" on sale in the streets before the incident had actually happened.

"Capital and Gelignite" 1913

A few days later, another *Industrial Unionist* editorial asked, "Who Will Bring Them to Account?" continuing its suspicions that the appearance of the gelignite was a plot designed to undermine union activity:

It is pertinent to ask who will bring the plotters to account seeing that "authority" function[s] chiefly in the interest of the owning class.

"Who Will Bring Them to Account?" 1913

On November 15, 1913, the *Auckland Star* had reported the "singularly fortunate discovery of a heavy charge of gelignite which had been placed on the line" ("A Sensational Report: Find of Gelignite Charge" 1913), which had been turned in to the railway's district manager by a resident near the Greenlane station [often referred to in 1913 articles as Green Lane], who claimed that he had found the explosive and a detonator on a rail near a signal box. However, although the report noted that the honesty of the person reporting his discovery of the explosive had not yet been determined, it made no connection to labor unions or to the IWW, and in fact neither were mentioned. A report in the *Herald* the same day much more confidently accepted the account given by the alleged discoverer of the gelignite, and bore subheadings such as "Express in Peril," "Removed Just in Time," and "Outrage Near Green Lane," each of which would have been designed to sell more copies. It announced:

> By a fortunate accident the gelignite was discovered and was removed from the line a few moments before the train passed over the spot.
> "Train Sensation: Express in Peril" 1913

Even so, the report again made no reference or implication that unions or the IWW were involved. On November 20, the *Herald* and the *Star* each announced a second discovery, the previous day, of gelignite at the Greenlane station. This time, a smaller amount was noticed on the floor of a staff bathroom ("More Gelignite Found" 1913; "Promiscuous Gelignite" 1913). Neither paper's report made any connection to union activity.

Subsequently, police investigations revealed that the person who had "discovered" the explosive, an aged veteran named Joseph Davis, was responsible for both incidents, a small quantity of gelignite and other evidence connecting him to the crimes having been found by a detective at Davis's home. The *Herald*'s reporting of these developments on November 29 again made no reference to unions or to the IWW ("Gelignite Sensation: Green Lane Incidents" 1913); similar stories in the *Star* about the court's charging of Davis on November 21, and his trial on November 28, also contained no links to unions or the Wobbles ("Gelignite Sensation: Sequel to Greenlane Story" 1913; "The Green Lane Gelignite: Aged Prisoner Remanded" 1913).

On December 8, 1913, the *Star* reported that Davis, who was 75, had been sentenced to up to five years' imprisonment. In court, his lawyer, W.D. Glaister, explained that his client had been affected by the ongoing strike, which "had been too much for him" ("The Gelignite Scare: Davis Sentenced" 1913). Thus a connection to union activity was now revealed to explain his actions, but there was no suggestion that Davis was working on behalf on any commercial, government, or law enforcement interest. Perhaps, then, the perspective of Barker's periodical, the *Industrial Unionist*, on the matter is best understood as being unnecessarily fearful of the degradation of the "respectable British community like New Zealand, where relations between Labour and capital are really brotherly" ("Capital and Gelignite" 1913), the implication of the biting irony in this editorial from that paper, a common feature of many of Barker's spoken and written utterances, suggesting the truth to be the opposite. Another article from the *Industrial Unionist* contains a more cynical perspective on the matter following the announcement of Joseph Davis being the actual villain:

> If those interested in breaking the strike concocted the plot it is almost certain that they would not have the courage to carry it out personally.
> "Who Will Bring Them to Account?" 1913

Maybe the old man, in poor health and denied an opportunity to become a special constable and police the strikers, which was the case, was just a patsy.

Among his other IWW activities, Barker started to advise the waterside workers in Wellington, and it was claimed that he had advocated "sabotaging" imported goods by dropping them in the Wellington harbor. The watersiders, along with many miners, went out on strike on October 22 following a stoppage on October 18 by the Wellington shipwrights, who were affiliated with their union. The miners at the Taupiri Coal Mines Company in Huntly had also struck, on October 19, prompting their employers to lock them out, these groups becoming the first participants in what would become the 1913 general strike, which expanded as dock area employees in Auckland on October 28, Westport on October 29, and Greymouth on November 3, joined in, commitment to industrial action being stronger in those places than in many others. Yet, despite the significance traditionally attributed by historians to the strike, it should be noted that, undermined by government and the employment of police specials and "scab" labor, it quickly fizzled out, being essentially over by the end of the year, some miners being the last to stay out. An editorial in the *Southland Times* on October 25, 1913, was highly critical of Barker's line on unionism, seeing it as an approach more fitted to the home of the IWW, the United States:

> We ... believe that the adoption of I.W.W. tactics in New Zealand would be visited by such severe penalties that they could never be continued on a large scale. The cause of labour will never be advanced by extremists of the Barker type, and industrial content will never come from I.W.W. methods.
> "A Choice Suggestion" 1913

As pickets arrived at the docks in Wellington on October 23, Tom had given a speech in which he in fact advocated the use of IWW tactics, including "sabotage," by which he meant disrupting business activity by deliberately doing professionally inappropriate things, such as tram workers not collecting fares. As noted above. another aspect of this kind of sabotage, often advocated by Barker, was for employees to do their work much more slowly than usual or expected. Reports in the *Lyttleton Times* told what Barker had said in Wellington, though they did not include in their descriptions anything about dumping goods in the water. The prime minister, William Massey, blamed non-New Zealanders for this industrial action, although, as Roth (1956) points out, he was himself an immigrant born in Limavady, County Londonderry, in what is now Northern Ireland. At that time, there were immigrants everywhere in New Zealand and Australia, so it is not surprising that they were involved, among other activities, with the unions; moreover, many, like the prime minister and Barker, were then viewed as British subjects, and not as aliens, which perhaps is the subtext to Massey's statement, an attempt to alter conventional categorizations. Although the police in Auckland were sympathetic to the unions, by the next month, "Massey's Cossacks" would arrive there, and strike leaders, including future Labour Minister for Public Works, Bob Semple, and future leader of the Labour Party, Harry Holland, were arrested a day after the declaration of a general strike on November 10 ("Auckland Scenes: End Not in Sight" 1913; "Beware of Seadogs!" 1913; "General Strike: Work Being Resumed" 1913; "New Zealand Strike" 1913b; Olssen 1988, 227, 228; Prebble 1999; Roth 1956; "Wellington Strike: Waterside Strikers Out" 1913; "Wharfside Orators" 1913). For Barker, the prime minister was "Iron Heel Massey, the Cowyard Premier, who had graduated from the shippons [cattle sheds] of Pukekohe," who, "with the executive of the Farmers' Union, called on the country districts for special constables, mounted and armed with yard long bludgeons" (Barker 1914d).

The next day, on November 12, 1913, Barker was also arrested in Auckland, accused of using seditious language when he was in Wellington. He posted bail of £250 ("Auckland Arrest" 1913; Barker 1914d; "General Strike: Work Being Resumed" 1913; "New Zealand Strike" 1913b; "Still Another: Barker Arrested" 1913; "Strike Weakening: Many Seeking Work" 1913). In a letter to the editor of the *Industrial Unionist*, a correspondent named E. Toy asked, "Are we drifting back to the dark ages when freedom of speech was a crime?" (Toy 1913).

The strike by now also included farmers, carters, and the Hotel and Restaurant Employees' Union; the action by the latter group meant that hotels in Auckland were closed. At this point, the Waterside Workers' Union was content with the situation, knowing that to the extent that ships were still being loaded in Auckland – apparently, on November 12, eighteen boats on the Auckland waterfront were worked on – that labor would be ineffective because dockers in Australia and the UK, who were supporting the unions, would refuse to unload them. A few days later, Barker, now described as the head of the "Auckland Strikers Executive," was arrested again in Wellington with others on a charge of sedition. This time, he was not allowed bail ("Arrested Men Remanded" 1913; "New Zealand Strike" 1913a; Prebble 1999; "The Auckland Position" 1913; "The Strike" 1913). Interviewed during his stay in the Terrace Jail in Wellington, where Holland, Semple, and others were also imprisoned, and following his release on January 15, 1914, he was reported to be upbeat, happy that he had been able to wear his own clothing during the ordeal, and had been well-fed, at least some of his meals being supplied to him from outside, and he had been allowed to exercise ("Terrace Gaol, Wellington" 2013; "Tom

Barker: Released from Jail" 1914; W.R. 1913). However, in some ways his release was a Pyrrhic victory, because having been bound over to keep the peace for a year, and to submit recognizances to guarantee such behavior, he was freed only because a shoe merchant named George Higgins lent him some of the money with the expectation that Tom would honor his agreement with the state. Concerned that he would be unable to do this, with his supporter having similar misgivings, that he would lose the amount of the bond that he had guaranteed, Barker moved on to Australia, sailing to Sydney on the *Maheno* (Cain 1993, 72; Barker 1965, 15).

In his April 2, 1914, article, "New Zealand General Strike," Tom Barker (1914d) traces the history of militant unionism in New Zealand back to the unsuccessful 1890 Maritime Strike (which also involved Australia and Fiji) and passage of the Industrial Conciliation and Arbitration (IC&A) Act of 1894, which might seem to constitute a positive development because it banned strikes in New Zealand for a while, creating an orderly process for labor dispute compromise using a Conciliation Board whose members were chosen by both factions, employers and unions. However, from the standpoint of Barker and his allies, the Act was not a positive development, because it also put an end to labor union militancy. This situation had changed in Auckland in 1907 and 1908, when the tramworkers went on strike and won that battle with the Tramway Company (Barker 1914d). Elsewhere, in one of his "Spanwire" pieces, Tom makes fun of "the long-nosed public spirited gentry who in Auckland and Europe live and luxuriate upon exploitation" (Barker 1913b), volunteering as "scabs" to keep businesses running while a strike is underway. He notes that in the earlier dispute, that involvement by outsiders of this sort was not necessarily successful, evidence of which was provided "when a certain official won his spurs by taking 20 minutes to bring a car down Wellesley Street, while small boys placed stone on the line" (Barker 1913b).

After the failed 1913 strike was over, Barker wrote a column in which he suggested it would be good to return to England and demonstrate how life in New Zealand was even worse than they might have imagined:

> To make a lecture effective a lantern and slides would be necessary. The late strike furnished many striking photos and pictures, which, if converted into slides would be very interesting, and give the would be immigrant some idea of how capitalism rules in N.Z.
>
> BARKER 1914e

Ironically, he decided, presumably because of the legacy of feudalism that still tinged the divisions between the classes, "slavery in England is better than peonage under the iron heel of capitalistic New Zealand" (Barker 1914e).

2   Australia

In Australia in 1914, Barker would soon become involved with that country's IWW publication, *Direct Action*, having taken over by October 1 as its editor, replacing Irish-born Thomas "Tom" Glynn, a person who had a significant influence on Barker's thinking who had lived in South Africa where he had served as a Transvaal police constable and become involved with the IWW there; Glynn would be one of the Twelve arrested and imprisoned for a long time, accused of fire-bombing businesses to pressure the government to release Barker, who was currently incarcerated and accused of violating the War Precautions Act. Barker had once considered himself a Christian, but Glynn's views on such matters differed substantially (Burgmann 1995, 115; Cain 1993, 64, 66; Olssen 1988, 140). On May 15, 1914, Tom Glynn's article "Mission of Churches" appeared in *Direct Action*. It ends:

> Yes, we are afraid the mission of the Church is pretty well now what it was in the beginning, and ever shall be: To induce the workers to accept a blank cheque on eternity.
> THEY'LL GET PIE IN THE SKY WHEN THEY DIE
> BURGMANN 1995, 72; GLYNN 1914

On August 22, 1914, Tom Barker's article "WAR and the Workers" appeared in *Direct Action* (Barker 1914g). It is perhaps illustrative of occasions when Tom took his argument far beyond what was necessary, arriving in territory that raised many issues about the logic of what he wrote. As an opponent of military conscription, he would enjoy much support from workers, political radicals, and veterans alike. But in siding with the enemies, he would surely lose much of that assent. In this article, for instance, discussing not only the present conflict, but also the Boer War (in which Glynn had fought against the Boers), he writes as follows:

> Remember: That the Australian Workers had no quarrel with the Boers, neither have they with the German Workers.
> BARKER 1914g

Later in the piece he continues, providing a more generally acceptable rationale for his approach:

> Don't be fooled with jingoism: The workers have no quarrel with Austria, Germany or Japan. The workers in those countries are as ruthlessly robbed and exploited as the workers of Australia. All European crowned heads are large investors in armament firms, and the Steel Trust [a consolidation of steel companies controlled by the United States Steel Corporation – see Cain 1993, 4; Hessen 1972; Meade 1901]. Therefore they want war in order to create a demand for steel, guns and munitions.
> BARKER 1914g; BURGMANN 1995, 183

However, in an article titled "The Cavel [sic] Case" (Barker 1915k), which appeared in *Direct Action* a little more than a year later, he again suggested his insensitivity to conventional feelings when he discussed the death of Edith Cavell, an English nurse whom the Germans had executed in Belgium for spying; here Barker rejected sentimental portrayals of Cavell's fate, "the blubber and lamentation" (Barker 1915k) employed to criticize Germany, pointing out that spies everywhere else are seldom treated well when discovered. Instead, he asks, why not lament the fates of "thousands of girls in Sydney and Melbourne [who] are working for wages that are not sufficient to house and feed them"? (Barker 1915k):

> [T]wo scenes pass before my eyes. The first one is in Belgium. A woman stands facing a file of German soldiers. A word of command rings out sharply, the rifles speak. The woman falls with a smile upon her lips. The second scene is in Hyde Park, Sydney. ... A woman approaches. Her boots are down at heel. Her clothes are dirty, bedraggled and torn. An old straw hat is perked jauntily upon a frowsy head of hair. She staggers as she walks. Her face is a tragedy, bruises, and cuts and dirt. Eyes that once may have been beautiful are now blackened by the blows of some blackguard. As she shuffles past, the respectable women pull their skirts away, and put their noses in the air. The children are playing on the grass. They stop for a moment or two. A boy calls out, "She's a moll!" And then they resume their playing again.
> BARKER 1915k

On October 1, 1914, Tom's article, "The Boss's Nightmare" (Barker 1914f) appeared in *Direct Action*, in which he addressed the perspective of Ernest Arthur "E.A." Craig, the president of the Auckland Employers' Association, a staunch opponent of the IWW. Craig had argued that businesses and most workers have a common interest; unfortunately, however, unions have become dominated by extremists who seek industrial action rather than to live in peace. Therefore, according to Craig, the solution lies in more moderate workers showing up at union conferences and giving voice to that outlook which is shared by employers and Godfearing employees, challenging the claims of "the fanatical element, which, as a rule dominates workers' meetings" (Barker 1914f; "Mental Suggestion" 1915). Businesses should try to distribute their own literature, in which they would interpret labor problems from their own allegedly more moderate perspective. Furthermore, Craig claimed, strikes should be replaced by what had now become the traditional approach in New Zealand, using legally mandated arbitration procedures.

Here, Barker attempted to pull apart the assumption that workers and owners shared a common interest, pointing out that the kinds of locale where employers and employees resided tended to differ significantly, with bosses living off the labor of their workers inhabiting one type of area, and the employees themselves, though more healthy due to the hard work they had put in, at times close to starvation in a completely different type of neighborhood (Barker 1914f). Nonetheless, Tom concludes, workers share the belief of Craig that strikes are not the best way to achieve industrial peace:

> Yes, Mr. Craig, some strikes are futile, but the ever successful one is that which takes place on the job, the slow down process, and a hundred and one little tricks and actions of the red hot worker, who cuts a hole in the purse that nourishes the "sponge." And the beauty of it is, Mr. Craig, that the boys are drawing their wages, and there are no starving wives and children.
> BARKER 1914f

From Barker's perspective working more slowly was always more likely to put pressure on employers to compromise. That type of argument was perhaps a motivation for a speech E.A. Craig gave at the annual meeting of the Auckland Employers' Association in July 1915, where, clearly indicating that he meant the IWW, he announced that there was a local chapter of a group which saw "scientific sabotage as being the most powerful weapon of the militant minority" ("Auckland Employers' Association: Annual Meeting" 1915; Kneen 1915a; "Scientific Sabotage" 1915; a slightly different version of the quoted remarks appears in "N.Z. Troubles" 1915).

John Payne, the M.P. for Grey Lynn, was a natural ally of Barker with respect to opposing E.A. Craig and the latter's hostile approach to unionism, and he also wanted to repeal the compulsory elements of the 1909 Defence Act, which initially had required all males aged 12 to 21 to undergo military training ("The Defense Act of 1909" 1966; "Mr. Payne's Price" 1912). However, although Payne was opposed to conscription, and had complained in a parliamentary debate that military preparation included teaching potential recruits how to kill, he was nonetheless in favor of the First World War effort, being an opponent of German and Austro-Hungarian expansionism (Findlay 2019, 54, 54 fn 218; "Points on the Estimates" 1913).

Like Barker, Payne blamed the failure to resolve the 1913 strike on the intransigence of the Auckland Employers' Association. He was a critic of the new, essentially antiunion policies being championed by Craig, whom, he claimed, had become president of the employers' group in a coup, with David Goldie, its former president, who had held the office since 1902, not actually wanting to be replaced, Payne argued, for the reason given by the organization, that he was exhausted and sick; in fact, he was pushed out because he disapproved of what Craig wanted to do, which, in Payne's view was "to starve the people into subjection" ("A Denial" 1913; "Employers' Association" 1913; "Mr Payne Bowled Out" 1913; "Pressure Required" 1913). Payne had also criticized the 1912 arrest of the leaders of the Waihi Trade Union of Workers' strike committee. That conflict had started when the Waihi Goldmining Company tried to create a rival, more moderate union to undermine the miners' solidarity (Holland, "Ballot Box," and Ross 1913, 42–46). As Tom Barker noted in one of his *Direct Action* articles:

> In 1912 the miners of Waihi refused to be lowered by engine drivers who had been financed by the mining companies to form a scab union of engine drivers. The intention was, of course, to separate the powerful union of mine workers into a dozen small unions, which would advantage the employers, so that they might introduce the old time competitive contract system, which had been abolished by the advent of the miners [punctuation sic] industrial union.
>
> BARKER 1915d

McAloon (2006) writes that "the bitter dispute at Waihi during 1912 was directly caused by employers sponsoring an arbitrationist union in competition with the majority union." This was generally the kind of approach which Craig sought to stimulate (Belcher 1915; Kneen 1915a, 1915b). A member of the Federated Seamen's Union, one of the tactic's victims, observed that, as of August 1915, Craig had already "created several unions which were brought into existence for the deliberate purpose of trying to choke the neck of bona fide organisations" (Belcher 1915).

Craig also argued, in agreement with Alfred Walter "A.W." Averill, the Anglican Bishop of Auckland, that employers should favor married men as employees, putting pressure on those who were single to enlist in the military. Meeting with James Allen, the Minister of Defence, on November 23, 1915, Craig told the minister that "the employers of Auckland ... would do everything they could to stimulate and assist recruiting" ("The Recruiting Problem" 1915). Both Craig and Averill believed there were many "shirkers" in New Zealand who refused to perform their natural duty, and making it difficult for them to find or keep non-military employment was a line of attack that could be garnered to oblige them to be less "selfish" ("Shirkers and Cowards" 1915). One of these "shirkers," Tom Barker, who when arrested for opposing (or, he insisted disingenuously, for advocating) conscription in Australia had been asked to show documentation that he was a military veteran, which he was ("The "To Arms" Poster" 1915).

Where Barker and Payne differed substantially was in their view of Germans of all kinds, the Kaiser and other leaders of that nation, and persons of German descent, who had come to make a home in New Zealand, or who were the children of those who had emigrated, often with "German" last names. Barker, as was noted above, perhaps somewhat recklessly, identified with the people of the First World War enemy nations, seeing them as other workers like himself, part of a class that was perpetually victimized by those in power. Payne, on the other hand, for a few months at the beginning of 1916, even published his own journal, *New Zealand Philistine*, in which he railed against Germans of all stripes, whether or not in the military. His ally, the Women's Anti-German League (WAGL) and its president, Lady Anna P. Stout – the suffragist founder of the country's Women's Franchise League, a person much involved in charitable works for soldiers and poor people alike, a defender of Māori interests, and, like Payne, hardly a jingoistic fanatic – nevertheless advanced the claim that the New Zealand-born sons of German immigrants might, if serving in the military, be prone to sabotaging the war effort. Thus Payne and the WAGL did much to demonize Germans of all kinds, almost all of whom were entirely innocent (Francis 2016, 296, 296, fn 26; Hucker 1979, 41; Johnson 1975, 87; Stout 1914; "Une Femme" 1913). A letter published in the Wellington paper, the *Dominion*, written by the WAGL's secretary, E. J. Moore, perhaps suggests a sincere attempt to balance conflicting issues underlying the organization's philosophy, even as it revealed a somewhat restricted understanding of the nature of nationality and of the character of patriotism:

> The league is constantly urging on the Government the necessity of not allowing Germans, naturalised or non-naturalised, to go with the troops or hold positions in our Defence Forces. Yet they still allow it to go on. We do not blame the deserter; he is only fighting for his country.
> MOORE 1916

Although at first he continued to write about the labor situation in New Zealand, Barker was living in Sydney, where he was fined £50 for issuing a poster discouraging military recruiting in violation of the War Precautions Act, and £20 for violating the Printing Act by making the poster (Barker 1965, 25; "Barker in Melbourne" 1915; Cain 1993, 233; "The "To Arms" Poster" 1915; "Tom Barker's Case: Application for Release" 1915). It read:

> To Arms! Capitalists, Parsons, Politicians, Landlords, Newspaper Editors, and Other Stay-at-Home Patriots, Your Country Needs You in the Trenches! Workers, Follow Your Masters!
> "Prussianising Australia: Tom Barker's Experience" 1915

For many union members, the prosecution and the initial denial of bail were seen as being vindictive, because any attempt to oppose military conscription was being interpreted as undermining recruiting; a similar approach was used in the United States when it became involved in the First World War in April 1917: it passed the Espionage Act of 1917 and its even more restrictive 1918 amendments, outlawing criticism of the war. President Woodrow Wilson, also in April 1917, created the Committee on Public Information (CPI), which circulated false information about Germans and German culture, even publishing insulting cartoons, promoting racist misinformation to a much greater extent than Payne and the WAGL (Neumann 2009; Shone 2019, 268; Stone 2006, 35).

Over in New Zealand, four copies of Tom's poster appeared near Wellington's Supreme Court where they were quickly removed. On September 14, 1915, Barker appeared in the Central Police Court in Sydney to face four charges, two of which were dismissed. Police gave evidence that toward the end of July they had seen the notice displayed in public on a number of occasions, and that they had responded by defacing or removing it (Barker 1915l; Burgmann 1995, 190; Davidson 2011, 46; "Prussianising Australia: Tom Barker's Experience" 1915; "The "To Arms" Poster" 1915; "Tom Barker's Case: Application for Release" 1915). As noted above, Barker denied that he had produced "an anti-recruiting poster. The poster was to stimulate recruiting among the parsons, politicians, capitalists, etc. I am patriotic enough to send every parasite out of the country to the trenches" (Barker 1915g). Of course, as Turner (1962, 127 fn 18, [1967]

1969, 3, 16–17) points out, the announcement was in reality promoting Barker's actual opinion, as displayed on the front page of an issue of *Direct Action*, that ordinary Australians should not "go to Hell in order to give piratical, plutocratic parasites a bigger slice of Heaven" (Barker 1914g). It was suggested in a column by "Otus" in the *Maoriland Worker* (Otus 1915) that Barker's deceitfulness could be interpreted as a way of backing down, and Tom conceded that "the boys got legal advice for me, and I became thereby through some mysterious mode of reasoning a Parliamentarian" (Barker 1915g). While the *International Socialist* criticized the prosecution, arguing as Barker had done, that the poster was not anti-recruitment, and noting that many organizations had campaigned for the sentence to be overturned, its editorial also revealed a striking lack of support for Barker in general:

> With this protest we Socialists can heartily join. We can do so all the more readily when we recollect that as editor of "Direct Action" Tom Barker has always been an opponent of Socialism and Socialists. Even when Socialists have been fighting in the Courts for free speech, and when they have been jailed for their opinions, Tom Barker has never printed a word of protest.
> "Tom Barker's Case" 1915; "Wanted – A Moratorium" 1915

On October 13, 1915, Barker's appeal was heard, and the £50 part of the fine was overturned, but not the £20 ("The Barker Appeal" 1915). However, the magistrate also ordered Tom to deposit bonds to guarantee his future behavior:

> Magistrate: Barker, you are convicted. ... I order you to enter into sureties, self in £100 and one surety in a similar sum, or two sureties each in £50, to OBSERVE THE REGULATIONS of the War Precautions Act during the currency of the war in which Great Britain is at present engaged, in default six months' imprisonment.
> "The "To Arms" Poster" 1915

Despite the time Tom spent in jail waiting to go to court, publishing the poster was very successful in mobilizing people against conscription and the war in general. In response to Barker's imprisonment due to the denial of bail, which was later rescinded, and in order to prevent approval of conscription, the Labour Volunteer Army was formed in June 1915; one of its members was the suffragist, Adela Pankhurst (Bloodworth 2015). Partially because of the attention given to Barker's case, the arguments against having a draft were quickly becoming associated with the activity of the IWW, and consequently politicians of many stripes attacked the organization. On August 15, 1915, Tom Barker's article, "Politicians, the i.w.w. & the War" (Barker 1915i) appeared in *Direct Action*, in which he pointed out that a reciprocal association was also developing, with politicians, often revealing ignorance about the geography of Europe or the psychology of the modern electorate, lecturing audiences on the need for war, but finding few of those listening wished to volunteer to fight it (Barker 1915i). Of course, Tom himself and his constant activity on behalf of his IWW agenda did much to bring about this situation. Visiting Melbourne, on September 25, 1915, he spoke at the Trades Hall about his prosecution at a meeting of the Amalgamated Conference of Unions, and as a result delegates passed a motion condemning his experience, which they telegraphed to politicians. The next day, he repeated the performance at a meeting of the Socialist Party of Victoria held at the city's Bijou Theatre. In Geelong, on September 28, he talked to the Trades and Labor Council, and following a number of similar promotional and fundraising appearances, on October 1, he addressed a meeting of the local area IWW (Barker 1915f, 1915h; "Barker in Melbourne" 1915; Laidler 1915)

In another piece, "The Loyalty of Labor Politicians" (Barker 1915l), Tom turned his attention onto the activities of the politicians who were now attacking the IWW, questioning their own allegedly patriotic motives. For example, he criticized Labor leader John Daniel "Jack" Fitzgerald, a longtime supporter of union activity going back to the 1890 maritime strike and the current NSW Vice President of the Executive Council, a body that formally adopts decisions made by state's Cabinet, who was currently involved in promoting conscription in Australia through his involvement with the Universal Service League. Fitzgerald had been reported as saying that the persons responsible for the poster "ought to be placed in a German internment camp" (Barker 1915l). However, Tom notes, Fitzgerald and other salaried government "pseudopatriots" had "also received their recruiting expenses for their arduous and strenuous work in getting other people to do what they are not game to do themselves" (Barker 1915l). He concluded:

> In drawing conclusions from the recent prosecution, one can only infer that I was given twelve months, not because I prejudiced recruiting, but simply because I did not draw recruiting expenses. In short, I got twelve months for scabbing on … Fitzgerald and their ilk, for doing for nothing what they got paid handsomely for.
> BARKER 1915l

Toward the end of 1916, the Labor Party would expel all 18 of its members of the NSW Legislative Assembly who had endorsed conscription (Cain 1993, 190; "P.L.L. Expulsions: 18 Members of Parliament" 1916).

On February 15, 1915, Barker's article, "War on Capitalism: The Reduction of the Output" (Barker 1915n) had appeared in *Direct Action*, in which he turned his attention to growing unemployment in Australia, citing Nietzsche but misspelling his name, and arguing that "Industrial Unionism," by which he referred to the policies of the IWW, was the solution to present economic problems: in particular, educating working people to see the folly of listening to politicians, including the Labor Party, or of expecting arbitration decisions that purported to solve disputes to be complied with by employers. Again, he emphasized his view that, if everyone slowed down the rate at which they were laboring, they would create increased demand for employees (Barker 1915n):

> By this slowing down process, and the reduction of the hours of labour, he is meeting with conscious and awakened power, the baneful effects of each new labor-saving device; he is reducing the amount of unpaid labor time, which provides the ruling class and their lackies with their means of life and their power; he is weakening the power of the State, and every other institution that binds him down to present-day slavery, that jail, starve and persecute him, he is strengthening himself by weakening his masters, and by developing his controlling power over the means of wealth production.
> BARKER 1915n

Here Tom expressed his fervent hope, but while this tactic might well have achieved a reduction in unemployment, and would be popular among IWW supporters, probably few other participants in the economy, including employers and the interest groups that represented them, the politicians, and many conservative workers, would wish to endorse its use.

In a subsequent piece, "The A.W.U. in the Northern Territory," Barker (1915j) perhaps provided an explanation why others would reject the IWW's "solution" to unemployment, arguing that the IWW "is organised upon the basis of the class struggle" (1915j). On the other hand, he continues, its rival, the Australian Workers' Union (AWU) has traditionally favored white employees, often excluding minorities from membership and its benefits. In the Northern Territory, for example, he notes that around 2,500 workers of Asian origin have, against their wishes, been excluded from the AWU, which, he says, currently represents only six or seven hundred white employees, in support of whom, the union has even campaigned to have workers of color fired from jobs they did manage to find. Attempting to rectify the situation, Barker says that the IWW has now printed recruiting literature in Chinese (Barker 1915j; Burgmann 1995, 89–90). Here, of course, from a contemporary perspective, Tom correctly categorizes as racist the White Australia policy, which was long endorsed by the AWU and members of the Labor Party, and which would continue until Gough Whitlam became prime minister in 1972 ("AWU Timeline" 2020). In pursuit of the policy, the AWU undermined its own efforts to improve the conditions under which Australians labored.

For Barker, the imminent collapse of the Second International, an organization of many European socialist groups, over disagreement about whether or not to favor the First World War, was, from his generally anti-war perspective a positive development. In his article, "May Day, 1915" (Barker 1915e), he complains that many leftist organizations in their zeal for war have missed the real need exemplified by the policies of the IWW, to represent and institute reform that benefits the workers of the world:

> We see them traitorously betraying the very class they claim to represent, by acting as bell wethers in reuniting working class fodder for the guns of the ruling class.
> BARKER 1915e

Barker was often critical of radical perspectives that differed from his own IWW approach. For example, in an article called "A Good "Reason"" (Barker 1915a), he noted that *Direct Action*, the publication in which the piece appeared, was not technically allowed in New Zealand, although it still managed to find its way into the country, providing an opportunity for readers to grasp the IWW viewpoint (Barker 1915a, 1915d). When he criticized "the William-Joseph Fusion, of Maoriland," who had "vetoed its admission," he was referring to William Massey, the leader of the Reform Party, and Joseph Ward, the leader of the Liberal Party, whose parties had formed a wartime coalition government; Massey was the prime minister, and former prime minister Ward (until 1912), notwithstanding the alliance, was formally titled the Leader of the Opposition (Barker 1915a). Perhaps, Barker continues, it was the kind of radical ideas that *Direct Action* embraced that prompted Massey and Ward to remove it from the panorama of political debate: "maybe we are too prone to leave the clouds of Fabianism and the worship of G.B. Shaw, and get down to the mundane prosaic work of organising on the job" (Barker 1915a). The first leftist publication for which Tom had written, the *Maoriland Worker*, which was not suppressed, was also a target now for Tom's criticism, due to its ability to attract corporate advertising and agitate for reform, rather than, like the IWW, centering its activities around seeking industrial revolution and worker control (Barker 1915a).

In his article, "Coming Trouble in New Zealand," Barker (1915n) expanded his analysis of union activity and political leadership. Here, he presented an account of the Arbitration Court that since the end of the 1890 strike had been operating in New Zealand to negotiate settlements between employers and laborers and thus prevent strikes; the latter had often been a goal of unions and Labour politicians, although the perspective of Barker and the IWW differed substantially, viewing acceptance of Court decisions as being a sell-out of the working class and its true interests. Here, Tom caustically dismisses the idea of New Zealand having in recent history been the "land without strikes" (Barker 1915d). Not only have union members throughout that time been unhappy with settlements imposed by the Court, he writes, but the strikes at Blackball and Waihi had shown that the era of formal conflict regulation was now over, an opinion that is today generally accepted by labor historians (Derby 2010). Moreover, strikes in themselves were a valuable means of lessening the profits earned by employers, and thereby hastening the final undoing of capitalist control of industrial enterprises:

> The next strike will cost them about twenty times as much; in fact, we hope that it will cost them every cent of surplus value that they have purloined from the workers. Carry the strike on to the job, and make every day a strike for the control of the job, and a day nearer the time when the boss will get into copper riveted overalls and hobnail boots.
> BARKER 1915d

On January 8, 1916, in *Direct Action*, Barker presented some details of successful local IWW activities, including the setting up of two new locals, one in Perth, and another in Mount Morgan, Queensland, a mining town, where he reported that "[a]n incipient revolution is impending ..., where the I.W.W. is beginning to take a growing interest in the mineowners' little games, and the impotency of the A.W.U." (Barker 1916i). In the Boulder area in the goldfields region of Western Australia, Tom reported that workers of Italian origin were fans of *Il Proletario*, the Pittsburgh, Pennsylvania Italian-language paper that had been started in 1896 and which later affiliated with the IWW; consequently some literature had been ordered by the Sydney Wobblies from that source (Barker 1916i; Bencivenni 2011, 28).

Just as *Il Proletario* was targeted in the United States during the Red Scare, and Mollie Steimer and others were arrested for distributing leaflets in New York that opposed the First World War (Shone 2019, ch. 9) Barker now found himself once again prosecuted due to a cartoon drawn by Sydney "Syd" Nicholls that Tom had published in *Direct Action* at the end of 1915, creative work which was clever enough to be syndicated in *Syndikalisten* in Sweden and *Darbininkų Balsas* in Lithuania, but which the government viewed, once again, as undermining recruitment. Barker was fined £100, but failure to pay the fine exposed him to a year's imprisonment, and he was again jailed ("An Anti-Recruiting Journal: I.W.W. Publisher Fined" 1916; Barker 1965, 27; Burgmann 1995, 192; Cain 1993, 70–71, 234–235; Foyle 2000; Glynn 1916; "Red Fed. Paper Fined" 1916; Turner [1967] 1969, 18–19).

Following Tom's sentencing in April 1916, an appeal was heard on May 4 (*Report of Mr. Justice Street, the Commissioner Appointed by the Act* 1919; "Sydney Propaganda: The Barker Case" 1916). Many unionized workers, including bricklayers, carpenters, plumbers, packers, miners, sheet metal workers, clerks, and insurance agents, complained about the conviction, raising funds for Barker's defense, and sending details of their dissatisfaction to the Minister of Defence, Senator George Pearce, frequently stressing the opinion that the prosecution violated the traditionally accepted liberty of Australians to say what they thought without restriction. Another IWW member, Ken Leslie, who had distributed a pamphlet criticizing conscription that had then been published in a London paper, the *Labour Leader*, and elsewhere, received a £50 fine or six months' imprisonment in lieu of payment. Pressure from Labor members of parliament led to Leslie's release on May 8 or 9 (sources differ), after he submitted bonds to guarantee his future behavior. Then Barker's sentence was reduced at the end of June to a £25 fine or three months' imprisonment, and he was released on August 3, a partial reprieve that was a political rather than a legal solution improvised by Hugh Mahon, the federal Acting Attorney General, in response to intense lobbying, one that changed a court ruling that had been upheld on appeal ("Barker and Klausen: To be Released" 1916; "Barker Defence Committee" 1916; Cain 1993, 194; Hogan 2008, 438–439; "I.W.W. Cases: Tom Barker Released" 1916; "Ken Leslie Released" 1916; "Mahon[,] Hugh" N.d.; "Release of Leslie" 1916; *Report of Mr. Justice Street, the Commissioner Appointed by the Act* 1919; "Set Barker Free" 1916; "The Barker Case" 1916; "The Barker Case: Further Protests" 1916; "The Barker Case: More Protests" 1916; "Tom Barker's Release" 1916; Untitled 1916).

On June 30, 1916, the Melbourne-based *Socialist* drew attention to debate in New Zealand, where a similar fight by progressives to resist military conscription was underway. Among the arguments being made was that of Victoria University professor T. A. Hunter, who argued that to prevent the war having a negative effect on birth rates, men over 35 should constitute the first group of draftees taken. However, when New Zealand's Military Service Act was passed on August 1, 1916, its "First Division" target, those who would be called up initially, were single men aged between 20 and 45 without dependents ("Conscription in Maoriland" 1916; Davidson 2015, 32; "Military Service Act 1916" 2016).

In the first half of September, freed from jail, Barker set off on a speaking tour, promoting the aspirations of the IWW and also, at other meetings, making the case against conscription, although he clearly believed the two issues shared the same ultimate goal, writing that "A thousand determined direct actionists can smash conscription in this country" ("Fighting Conscription: Views of Tom Barker" 1916). He visited the Broken Hill mining area before moving on to Adelaide, and then to Melbourne, where he also found time to address meetings of the Socialist Party (Barker 1916b, 1916c). In a meeting at the Trades Hall in Broken Hill, Barker gave a succinct outline of the reason why he opposed conscription and the war in general:

> The burning question before the working class movement to-day is the question of conscription. Not long since it was the boast of the British race that conscription, [punctuation sic] would never be forced upon the people. But a great-European war has plunged the working classes of half the world into a cataclysm of blood and horror. We are not here to-night to discuss which is right or wrong among the various nations involved, nor as to the cu[l]pability of the big business interests that really brought the war about, and are to-day responsible for its continuance.
> "Fighting Conscription: Views of Tom Barker" 1916

Additionally, Barker warned of the possibility of forced enlistment being used to break a strike ("Fighting Conscription: Views of Tom Barker" 1916), something that would occur in the future, as happened when such a specification was included in the Smith-Connally Act of 1943 in the United States and then implemented in the Philadelphia Transit Company strike of 1944. Although President Roosevelt had vetoed the provision, Congress overturned the veto, and the next year, the federal government made use of the power, threatening to allow workers currently exempt from military service to be drafted if they did not return to work. Of course, since this particular work stoppage had been implemented by white officials of the Philadelphia Rapid Transit Employees' Union who were seeking to block the promotions of black employees to positions they had not previously held, Barker, given his commitment to labor unions serving persons of all races, might have approved of the US government's tactic in this specific case (Roosevelt 1943; "What: The Philadelphia Transit Strike of 1944" N.d.; Winkler 1972, 74, 81, 84–89).

At this point, conflict between the IWW and the Australian government in all its forms started to become a more substantial battle. On September 4, J.B. King, who had moved to Sydney in 1912 and become involved with *Direct Action* from its founding in 1914, appeared in Sydney's Central Police Court accused of printing the paper without first securing a bond as required by section 10 of the Newspapers Act of 1898. He was fined £20 or £25 (sources differ) ("News Summary" 1916; "Publisher Fined" 1916; Shor 2005, 154; "The Newspaper Act." 1916; "War on the I.W.W." 1916).

On the same date, September 4, 1916, three IWW speakers, Peter Larkin, a sailor who would soon deliver a lecture on "The Historical Basis of the Irish Rebellion" at Sydney's Town Hall; Donald Grant, a man born in Inverness, Scotland who would later serve on the Sydney City Council and in the upper house of the NSW parliament, the Legislative Council; and Charles Reeve, whose name was often given in reports as being Reeves, a bricklayer who earlier in the year had been heading up IWW activity advocating "sabotage" in Fremantle and Perth in Western Australia; appeared in the same court as King, charged with having directed "abusive words" at the prime minister, "Billy" Hughes, in their speeches in the city's open-air Domain area on Sunday, August 27. When they spoke in the courtroom, they were at first applauded by a group of supporters who, sitting at the back, decorated the adjacent walls with political slogans; the magistrate threatened to clear the court if they did not quiet down ("Irish Meeting" 1916; "I.W.W. Premises Raided" 1916; "New South Wales" 1916; Rushton 1973, 54 fn 12; "Sydney Domain Speakers in Court" 1916; "The Hon. Donald McLennan Grant (1890–1970)" N.d.; "The I.W.W.: Reeves in the West" 1916; "War on the I.W.W." 1916).

Larkin, Grant, and Reeve were each found guilty and fined £5 for making statements that might cause disaffection, a violation of the War Precautions Act. Additionally, Peter Larkin was sentenced to three months' imprisonment and ordered to either post a £100 bond for the duration of the war or serve an additional six months in jail. Donald Grant and Charles Reeve were ordered to post a similar financial guarantee of their future good behavior. However, Grant's conviction would be overturned on December 16, 1916, at which time he was in jail charged with treason ("Domain Orators" 1916; "I.W.W. Appellants" 1916; "I.W.W. Premises Raided" 1916; "New South Wales" 1916; "Peter Larkin Fined" 1916).

Indeed, the government's war against the IWW became much more serious with a series of arrests, including those of Grant, Larkin, and Reeve, that began on September 23, 1916, and which attracted public attention as newspapers started, on October 10, to report the charges and court appearances of twelve IWW members subsequently known as "the Twelve" and "the Sydney Twelve," who were initially charged with treason, but whose alleged misdeeds revolved around a series of attempted firebombings in Sydney government buildings, stores, and warehouses that had commenced in June; some fires failed to start, and fortunately no one had been killed. The fate of these individuals, as determined in the case, *R. v. Reeve and Others*, would become a major event in the life of Tom Barker, since not only were many of the incidents purportedly staged to prompt his own release from imprisonment and the government's agreement not to institute conscription, but because he would lead the long assault, after each of the Twelve were convicted on at least one charge, to have those convictions overturned; at the end of the process, the last incarcerated member of the Twelve, Reeve, was finally released from jail on license on September 27, 1921, as the result of an election promise by the NSW Labor government amid arguments that he alone had not had his convictions overturned in order for the police and the government to save face. Though John Benjamin King's sentence for advocating sabotage had been ruled excessive, he was also convicted of forging banknotes on December 15, 1916, and so had not been released until August 31, 1921 ("At Last" 1921; "A Welcome Forestalled" 1921; Burgmann 1995, 205; "Charges of Treason" 1916; "Donald Grant Arrested" 1916; "Forged Bank Notes" 1916; "I.W.W.: Sabotage in Sydney" 1916; Rushton 1973, 53, 54).

The Twelve accused of involvement in what would come to be referred to as "Barker's fires" included five persons discussed above: King (aged 46 at the time of the trial, originally from Canada); Larkin (46, Ireland); Grant (27, Scotland); Reeve, (30, England); and Glynn (35, Ireland). The others were John Hamilton (42, Australia); Bernard Bob Besant (25, England); Donald McPherson (29, Scotland); William Teen (30, Australia); William Beatty (30, England); Morris Joseph Fagin (40, Russia); and Thomas Moore (34, New Zealand) (Burgmann 1995, 207; "Treason Case: Trial in Sydney" 1916).

At the beginning of November, the charge was reduced from treason to conspiracy, for a reason or reasons that are unclear, possibly because of the fear that a jury would be less willing to convict the accused if faced with the possibility of the death penalty being applied (Cain 1993, 216; Mack 1916; Rushton 1973, 53–54). Perhaps the flowery, emotional, judgmental language of the arrest warrant, that the members of the Twelve had acted by "wholly withdrawing the love, obedience, fidelity, and allegiance, which every true and faithful subject of our lord the King does, and it is right, ought to bear" ("Treason Case: Trial in Sydney" 1916; Turner [1967] 1969, 36) would have turned off more persons reading it than just Barker, fellow IWW members, and other assorted radicals – maybe a certain percentage of those toiling hopelessly and dejectedly for unjustifiably inadequate remuneration on wharves and in mines or factories, those condemned by disadvantage always to be poor, never able to afford to feed their children adequately, might find in the designation of IWW resistance as "treason" a certain smug denigration of themselves as serfs. After all, a substantial number of those living "within his dominions, to wit, the State of New South Wales" ("Treason Case: Trial in Sydney" 1916) had made it perfectly clear that they had no desire or intention to serve that "lord the King" by fighting for him in Europe. Following the revision, there were three charges: firstly, conspiracy to set fire to various businesses with intent to injure people who happened to be on the premises; secondly, conspiracy to unlawfully actuate Barker's release from his prison sentence; and thirdly, seditiously attempting to create discontent and disaffection among the population, including persons in the military (*Report of Mr. Justice Street, the Commissioner Appointed by the Act* 1919; *R. v. Reeve and Others* 1917).

More appropriately, the prosecutor, Ernest Lamb, K.C., stressed to the judge, Justice Robert Pring, the doctrine of "sabotage" that had been promoted in some Domain speeches, and the costs to businesses of the fires that did ignite (£250,000), the danger to innocent persons, even though no one was actually killed, the employment lost by some who worked in damaged buildings, the lessened profits earned as a result by targeted businesses, and the attempt to force the state government to release Tom Barker, were all reasons why the Twelve should be found guilty. All were convicted of at least one of the charges and they received sentences of five, ten, or fifteen years in prison, to be served concurrently (Burgmann 1995, 213–214; Cain 1993, 218).

In February and March 1917, an appeal was heard by the Court of Criminal Appeal, a three-judge panel consisting of NSW Chief Justice Sir William Cullen, Justice Richard Meares Sly, and Justice Alexander Gordon. Many arguments were made against the convictions, including the fact that some persons who had given evidence against the Twelve were in fact accomplices, and that therefore much of what they had claimed was false, lies encouraged by the Sydney police. However, the Court did little to assuage the angst of Barker and his many allies in the labor movement, almost entirely upholding the convictions and sentences, stating repeatedly in its determination that sufficient evidence had been admitted at the original trial to support the jury's decision. The sole exception was as follows: Glynn's and McPherson's convictions on the second charge were overturned, and their sentences reduced from fifteen to ten years. Although Glynn had spoken at one of the IWW's meetings in the Domain, he had made no reference to releasing Barker; there had been no evidence submitted indicating that McPherson had discussed Tom's imprisonment prior to the latter's release ("Barker's Fires: The I.W.W. Criminal" 1917; Head 2016, 167; "I.W.W. Cases: Tom Barker Released" 1916; "I.W.W. Cases: Two Sentences Reduced" 1917; "I.W.W. Plotters: The Sydney Trial Concluded" 1916; Mack 1916;

R. v. Reeve and Others (1917); "The I.W.W.: Further 'Startling' Evidence" 1916; "Treason Case: Trial in Sydney" 1916); Turner [1967] 1969, 80. Thus the process to have the Twelve released would prove to be extensive, prolonged, and frustrating, although it afforded Tom Barker, who did everything he could to be the champion of that cause, greater opportunities to demonstrate his leadership ability and intellectual skill.

On September 29, 1916, the Governor General of Australia, Sir Ronald Munro Ferguson, issued a Compulsory Service Proclamation, signed by the Minister of Defence, George Pearce, which ordered, effective October 2, every male aged between 21 and 34, and being unmarried and childless, to enlist. As of November 18, the Defence Department revealed that 190,254 men had registered, 178,749 of them had been medically examined, and 106,111 of those had been declared fit. In the federal parliament, the Labor Party asked that the proclamation be withdrawn, and any soldiers enlisted be allowed to leave their camp, with those prosecuted for refusing to participate being treated compassionately. On November 22, following a Cabinet meeting, the proclamation was revoked due to widespread disagreement about its appropriateness. The conscripted soldiers were then sent home, and the government indicated its intention to commute the sentences of anyone punished for not complying with its instructions, though they also said that annulment might not be applied to anyone who had evaded arrest. Three days later, the Governor General issued another proclamation, this time ordering the release of all draft resisters who had been incarcerated ("Compulsory Service: Proclamation Withdrawn." 1916a, 1916b; "Defaulters Released." 1916; "For Home Defence: Proclamation" 1916; "Home Service Proclamation" 1916a, 1916b; "The Defence of Australia" 1916). On December 9, 1916, Tom Barker's article, "Spasms" (Barker 1916j), appeared in *Direct Action*. He congratulated Pearce for backing down, noting that prior to the overturning of the original announcement, some conscription opponents in the state of Victoria had been sentenced to terms of three or six months for failing to register.

Why did the Australian government's attempt to implement conscription fail? In another Barker column, he noted that Senator Myles Ferricks had stood up against attempts to involve the country in the First World War and to authorize conscription to fight it, and thus Ferricks must be one of the people congratulated for the present achievement:

> At one of his [Ferricks'] election campaign speeches, delivered in 1915, he stated that the war would soon be settled if the people who had made the war had been made to fight it, and the working class had been standing by as referees. During the conscription campaign, Ferricks chased the

> frantic and noisy Hughes from one end of the country to the other, and denounced the infantile Welshman to the people, and exposed his notorious machinations.
>
> BARKER 1917O

However, he wrote, in general a class conscious working class and a militant, educative activity such as that demonstrated by the IWW, are the only ways to avoid war and achieve progress. Thus, Tom continued, Ferricks' current interest in starting to elect ambassadors would be unlikely to be successful. Replacing old-fashioned gentlemen diplomats with members of the political class, characters such as – Barker names the following four – Billy Hughes, Leader of the Opposition Joseph Cook, the NSW premier William Holman, or the NSW attorney general David Hall – would never end war or improve the condition of ordinary people.

> Take the same William, elect him as a diplomat. Send him to play the game at the Courts of Europe. Do you think he would have made a better job of it than [Sir Edward] Grey [the British foreign secretary] or [M.] Sasonof [the Russian secretary of foreign affairs]? Or any of the majority of Australian politicians? You would get war just the same.
>
> Diplomats are pawns in the game. So are politicians. They are the screen for big business, the profit monger, the armament maker, the shoddy manufacturer, the market cornerer and the territory grabber.
>
> BARKER 1917O

At the beginning of October, rotten eggs were thrown at the anti-conscription activist and opponent of Billy Hughes, Adela Pankhurst, in Katamatite in Victoria, damaging her dress ("A Sample of Prussianism" (1916); Barker 1916j; Jordan 2018, 1, 13; "Miss Pankhurst Assaulted" 1916). On October 17, the prime minister threw an oratorical missile at Pankhurst during a speech at Bendigo, Victoria, in which he attacked Tom Barker and the IWW in general. Hughes said that he possessed a copy of a letter that Adela had written to Tom, in which she argued that it was IWW activity that had forced the Labor Party to reject conscription ("Miss Pankhurst and Tom Barker" 1916).

Indeed, as the attempt to impose involuntary military service in Australia failed due to the efforts of its opponents, who of course included the IWW, the government now concentrated its attention on undermining the IWW itself. In Ballarat, Victoria, on October 9, 2016, Hughes had given a similar speech, in which the argument leaders of the Auckland Employers' Association had previously used against Barker in New Zealand was again put to use against the activities he was now leading and inspiring in Australia. The prime minister condemned the IWW as "to a man anti-conscriptionists. ... They are all anarchists and enemies of society" (Barker 1916h). In response, flyers now appeared in support of the Twelve, but the Crimes Prevention Act of 1916, which prohibited publishing written materials that stirred up the commission of crimes, was passed in NSW, followed at the federal level by the Unlawful Associations Act of 1916, which made membership in the IWW punishable by six months' imprisonment (Burgmann 1995, 215–216; Olssen 2006; Rushton 1973, 56–57).

Barker's article, "An I.W.W. explains" which appeared in the Scottish paper, *Forward*, on August 14, 1920, looked back to the events of 1917 and the prime minister's near obsession with blaming the IWW for anything negative that happened (Barker 1920b). After the steamship, *Cumberland*, was damaged by an explosion, and another steamer, the *Matunga* disappeared, Hughes said, "If it is a coincidence, that two vessels should be lost in that way, it is a very remarkable one" ("Was Matunga Blown Up?" 1917). In response, Tom commented:

> There was never a time that Hughes took the platform that he did not accuse me in particular and the I.W.W. in general for the disappearance of the "Matunga" and the "Cumberland."
> BARKER 1920b

It later turned out that the *Matunga* had been torpedoed and sunk by a German surface raider, the *Wolf*, and most of its crew and passengers were taken prisoner. Initially, reports of the damage to the *Cumberland* speculated about whether there had been one or two internal explosions, and whether the ship had been hit by a torpedo or by a mine; although the *Cumberland* survived for five weeks as repairs were attempted, it eventually sank. A report later in the year by the federal Superintendent of Navigation still concluded that the damage "was caused by an explosion the origin of which is not known" ("Cumberland Explosion: Navigation Department Findings" 1917). Minefields laid by the *Wolf* are now known to have been the source of the *Cumberland*'s demise, so the prime minister was correct that the loss of both steamboats was not a coincidence: they were casualties of the fact that Australia was at war with Germany (Burgmann 1995, 215; Cain 1993, 120; "*Cumberland* Shipwreck 1917" 2003; "Matunga's Crew" 1918, 1919; "Matunga's Passengers: Experiences in Captivity" 1918; "Matunga Victims" 1918; Robinson 2002; "Steamer Cumberland: Damaged by Explosion" 1917; "Steamer Cumberland Founders" 1917; "Story of the Matunga" 1918; "The Matunga" 1918a, 1918b; "The Steamer Cumberland: Story of the Explosion" 1917; "Was Matunga Blown Up?" 1917).

In Western Australia, a number of IWW members, conscription opponents, and writers for *Direct Action* and other radical papers were arrested and charged for the dubiously applicable crimes of "conspiring ... to carry into execution an enterprise having for its object to raise discontent and disaffection, and promote feelings of ill-will and enmity among the subjects of the King" ("A Charge of Conspiracy" 1916; Burgmann 1995, 212; "I.W.W. Conspiracy" 1916; "I.W.W. Methods" 1916). Most were denied bail. Two state employees were also victims of the new anti-IWW zeal, being suspended from their positions. H. M. Leighton, a clerk in the statistical department and president of the Clerks' Union, was punished because he had distributed anti-conscription materials. William W. Siebenhaar, the deputy-registrar general, had disputed the appropriateness of the new arrests (Barker 1916a). One of those charged was the much venerated 85 year-old Eureka veteran, advocate of a Detroit IWW perspective, and avid freethinker, Montague "Monty" Miller, whose incarceration in Perth jail, Barker (1916a) pointed out, was completely inappropriate. Siebenhaar was accused of soliciting money to help Miller during work time, but even though he showed that he had not done this, he still eventually lost his job (Turner [1967] 1969, 47). Later, after his conviction under the Unlawful Associations Act for being an IWW member, Miller was released from imprisonment on account of his age; nonetheless, in 1918, he would be barred from speaking in public (Barker 1965, 32; Burgmann 1995, 222; "Imprisonment of Montague Miller" 1917; "Montague Miller: In Gaol at Eighty-Five" 1917; "Montague Miller Released" 1917). In an elegy printed in the *Westralian Worker*, Siebenhaar, a Dutch-born anarchist who was also a poet, eulogized Miller's constancy and other achievements at the time of the latter's death in 1920, following which he had been buried in a red coffin draped with a Red Flag ("Montague Miller's Funeral" 1920). One of the verses was:

> By false mirage and hope too oft misled,
> Our progress slowly finds the upward track;
> But by your march our vanguard was outsped:
> For you no halt, no pause, no looking back;
> For you no base recoil!
> SIEBENHAAR 1920

In an article called "Australian Brutality" in the Sydney publication, the *Communist*, on August 5, 1920, dedicated also to memorializing the life of Monty Miller, Tom Barker (1920c) wrote:

> Well may we lift our hats to such men! There is no finer spur for us younger men than the example of that greatest and oldest and most venerable pioneer of the Proletarian Revolution.
>
> BARKER 1920C

Another arrestee, Alexander Horrocks, a one-time member of the miners' union who had been injured in an accident at work, and a subscriber to *Direct Action*, had been found in possession of two chests of IWW papers, which convinced authorities he was the leader of the IWW affiliate based in Boulder, WA, and he too was charged with conspiracy. However, Horrocks claimed he had merely been asked to take care of the papers, which had been found in his home. In court, it was pointed out that among the haul was a letter written to Horrocks by Wobbly activist Pat Daly, urging him to advocate a general strike the moment conscription began ("An I.W.W. Case: Horrocks Before the Court" 1916; Burgmann 1995, 77, 212–213; Cain 1993, 242–243; "I.W.W. Case: Fresh Charge Against Horrocks" 1916; "Mr. Walker Cross-Examines" 1916; "Sabotage Scourge: Prosecutions in the West" 1916; "The Conspiracy Charges: Aid for Horrocks" 1916; "The I.W.W.: Case in the West." 1916; "The Kalgoorlie Arrest" 1916; "The Kalgoorlie Arrest: Accused Before the Police Court" 1916; "To-Day's Proceedings" 1916). On December 15, 1916, the jury deliberated for about four hours in the case, finding many of the accused guilty. However, with one exception, the judge, Nassau, Bahamas-born Justice Robert Bruce Burnside, who was contemporarily also a member of the Supreme Court of Western Australia, did not sentence anyone accused of conspiracy to imprisonment, releasing Miller on his own recognizance due to his advanced years, and requiring Horrocks and the others to post two £25 sureties to guarantee their good behavior in the next two years (Burgmann 1995, 213; Cain 1993, 244–245; Staples 1979; "The I.W.W. and the Conspiracy Charges: Lenient Treatment" 1916). Explaining his sentencing decision, Burnside told the court:

> I am prepared to let you go upon your entering into recognisances to be of good behavior to keep the peace, and to obey the laws of the land. You will see, therefore, that justice may be tempered with mercy. If you desire to make martyrs, as you term it, of yourselves, and experience the undesirable atmosphere of prison, then you may do so for any period up to two years. If you desire to continue to break the law, you must remain where that desire must, to some extent, be curtailed.
>
> JUSTICE ROBERT BURNSIDE, quoted in "The I.W.W. and the Conspiracy Charges: Lenient Treatment" 1916; TURNER [1967] 1969, 75

The most significant of the arrests, and the exception to the judge's apparent forbearance, was that of Michael "Mick" Sawtell, who had written a letter titled "An Injury to Me is an Injury to All," adjudged by state authorities as having been threatening to Senator Patrick "Paddy" Lynch, an Irish-born advocate of conscription and ally of Billy Hughes, due to Sawtell's reference to sabotage and the claim that if Barker were not released, the senator's farm would be attacked. In the past, Sawtell had in a piece in *Direct Action* praised "such men as Marx, Engels, Shaw, Ibsen, Kropotkin and Tom Mann" for having "given the world new and better ideas; they have fought for the overthrow of capitalism" (Sawtell 1915). Mann was one of the British labor union leaders who managed the successful London Dock Strike of 1889; he lived in Australia from 1902 to 1910, where he was an organizer for the Victorian Labor Party (Mann 1923, 82–92, 170). Eventually Sawtell, who unsurprisingly complained in court that his "crime" constituted the defense of a class, rather than being an individual action, and more creatively argued that his use of the term "sabotage" was an inducement to the farm's employees to go on strike, was sentenced to six months' hard labor. For about nine months in 1915–1916, the Boulder local, to which Sawtell belonged, had rented its headquarters from Paddy Lynch, though the senator was probably not aware of the transaction when it occurred (Barker 1916a; Burgmann 1995, 213, 222; Cusack 2002, 3, 5, 47, 138, 144–145, 147–149, 155, 166, 174; ""I.W.W." 1916; "I.W.W. Methods." 1916; The I.W.W." 1917).

In December 1916, Barker pressed for a new trial for the Twelve, none of whom, he insisted, had ever been convicted of what he referred to as a criminal offense, criticizing the government in public and participating in strikes being excluded from his characterization of lawbreaking as they would be by many other people. He encouraged labor unions to pass resolutions calling on the government to release his IWW colleagues. He met personally with the Coal Lumpers' Union on December 9, while he reported in *Direct Action* that the Sydney Wharf Laborers' Union and branches of the Seamen and Firemen's Union, the Municipal Employees' Union, and the Carpenters' Society, along with Labor Party local branches in two suburbs of Sydney, East Woollahra and Forest Lodge, had all passed motions of this kind (Barker 1916k). Chairing a well-attended meeting of the Twelve's supporters in the Domain on Sunday, December 17, Tom responded to Hughes' denigration of the IWW as a criminal organization, commenting that the prime minister had illegally influenced the trial of the Twelve by asserting the guilt of the accused in advance of the jury's decision (Barker 1916e). At the event, a participant called Miss Jago recited lines from Percy Bysshe Shelley's "Masque of Anarchy": this was not the first time that the poem had been used by labor activists in Sydney to represent their cause: another union leader, Rose Summerfield, had referred to it at the beginning of her "Master and Man" speech at Leigh House on Castlereagh Street in Sydney on July 17, 1892 (Barker 1916e; Shelley 1819; Shone 2022, 13–18; Summerfield 1892, 3).

Elsewhere on Castlereagh Street, at the Southern Cross Hall on December 25, a concert was held by a newly formed Women's Committee that had as its goal securing funds for the families of the imprisoned Twelve; the evening generated about £50 for that purpose (Barker 1916d). With the same need in mind, on January 11, 1917, Tom addressed a meeting at the Blackall Fountain, a memorial that celebrates Queensland's second governor, Samuel Blackall, ironically an opponent of employing Kanaka workers. At the time of Barker's visit, the monument stood at the corner of Brisbane and Nicholas streets in Ipswich, Queensland. In his speech, Barker emphasized the lack of correspondence between advocacy for the interests of labor, which was legitimate, and the accusations against the Twelve of criminality, prosecutions that had been designed to undermine the campaign against conscription. In addition to the need for funds to support the wives and children of those now imprisoned, the IWW required £800 to finance an appeal ("Address by Tom Barker" 1917; Kovac 2021). Three days earlier, Barker had spoken to a meeting of the Builders' Labourers Union at the Trades Hall in Brisbane. There he explained why he had decided to visit the area, which was not only to let people know about what had happened to the Twelve, but to try and strengthen ties between unions in New South Wales and those in Queensland ("Builders' Laborers: Address by Tom Barker" 1917; Cade 1917). At another meeting, in the Market Square in Brisbane, Tom repudiated the idea that the IWW was engaged in conspiracy, instead arguing that "the politicians who have attempted to force conscription on this country" had met "behind closed doors," but since they were viewed as being "respectable members of society," their own intrigue would be tolerated while the Twelve remained in jail ("Tom Barker in Brisbane" 1917).

At the same time, Barker was watching similar events in New Zealand, noting the imprisonment in January for twelve months of Sidney "Sid" Huguenot Fournier d'Albe, a wanderer for labor union causes in much the same manner as Tom. A man of Huguenot ancestry who had worked with striking miners battling police and soldiers in Wales's Rhondda Valley at the time of the Tonypandy Riots in 1910–1911, Fournier had now been prosecuted for seditious speech for addressing a crowd on behalf of Wellington's Conscription Repeal League and advising them to resist the Military Service Act (Barker 1917i; G.K. 1960–1961; Richardson 2020, 134–135; Roth and Beardsley 1960–1961, 21–22; "Seditious Utterance: Conscription Opposed" 1917; "Seditious Utterances: Man Sentenced to Gaol" 1917). Somewhat optimistically, given the way that courts and politicians tended to view the IWW and its associates, Barker wrote:

> He is a born fighter, and I know him well. The sleuths found a rifle, cartridges, I.W.W. book, anarchist literature, a bludgeon, a machine gun manual, and a MAN in his premises. His crime is NOTHING.
>
> BARKER 1917i

Not surprisingly, Tom was aware of a current event in the United States, the strike for higher rates of pay and more equitable task assignment practices by forty thousand iron ore miners on the Mesabi Iron Range near Duluth, Minnesota, an event that allowed him to express again his dislike of the Steel Trust. When the American Federation of Labor (AFL) declined to assist, the IWW sent Carlo Tresca, Joe Schmidt, and Sam Scarlett to represent the workers and coordinate their Central Strike Committee; later, Elizabeth Gurley Flynn, the subject of Chapter 3, would also arrive to help the effort. In a display of the same government tactics that had been used in the Lawrence strike, the three IWW leaders and others were briefly arrested for having "defamed" the company by displaying a banner that claimed a striker had been killed by the employer, the USS subsidiary, the Oliver Mining Company; later, the principals were charged with murder as authorities declared their speeches had prompted violence when two persons were killed in a house twelve miles away as police attempted to make an arrest. The miners eventually returned to work, some of their demands having been achieved, including a 10% raise (Barker 1917d; Elef 1988, 63–72; Ronning 2003, 359, 364–369, 376). For Barker, the story was a familiar one:

> Police methods in America are the most disgraceful in the world, and the administration of justice, or whatever you like to call it, in that country comes second only to the sunny State of New South Wales.
>
> BARKER 1917d

On February 4, 1917, Barker returned to Brisbane's Trades Hall to give a lecture titled "Proletarian Treason." Defending and attempting to explain the role of the IWW, he emphasized that the capitalist system tended to make some wealthy by keeping the majority poor, and argued that the goal of some contemporary developments, which included the introduction of new machinery, was actually "to make the workers unskilled, and to bring them down to the one dead level" (Barker, quoted in "The I.W.W.: Address by Mr. Tom Barker" 1917). Despite the fact that, due to the war, 300,000 Australians had enlisted in the military, there were still many unemployed, which indicated that the function of capitalism was not to benefit society but to exploit labor and maximize profits. As a solution, he again suggested that employees should pursue a policy of working more slowly, which would have the effect of lessening the amount of money that business owners would make ("The I.W.W.: Address by Mr. Tom Barker" 1917).

In a Barker column published on February 24, 1917, Tom turned his attention more specifically to why the organizational abilities of the IWW were much needed in Australia. The Australian Workers' Union (AWU) had come about through mergers of smaller unions, a process pioneered by W.G. (William Guthrie) Spence, the founder of the Australian Shearers' Union (ASU) in 1886, who had also sought to achieve One Big Union, and therefore to eliminate the negative consequences inflicted on workers when they withdrew their labor (Burgmann 1995, 89, 165; Shone 2022, 3, 5–6; Svensen 1995, xiv). However, Barker writes, the AWU, which he presently sees as being the IWW's rival, is unable to properly assist Queensland shearers and shed hands in a continuing dispute because of its commitment to an arbitration system that discourages strikes and secures support for Labor Party candidates, rather than prioritizing an increase in the shearers' piece rate and the goal of £3 per week for the shed hands (Barker 1917c; Hanson 1917; "Shearers' Strike" 1917; "Shearers' Strike: Position in Queensland" 1917):

> And we say, quite dispassionately, and without malice, that if the A.W.U. continues hindering its membership from taking advantage to force better conditions and more wages, that "disruption" will become widespread and general. And there seems to be a very discernible flaw in the "one big unionism" that signs an agreement for 28s, when the men have already established 30s per hundred. And more than I.W.W. men will see its shortcomings quite easily.
> BARKER 1917C

In such circumstances, On Big Union is not an ideal goal, because a conglomerate in the shape of the AWU and its ally, the Australian Labor Party – some of whose members today, Barker writes, seem more conservative than their apparent opponents such as Sir Joseph Cook, the recent Liberal Party prime minister, and Sir William Irvine, the current Australian attorney general, who, as premier of Victoria, had in 1903 crushed a strike by railroad workers – inadequately represent the interests of their unionized members and supporters (Barker 1917c; Bennett and Smith 1983).

> "One Big Unions" are mooted everywhere, and every day, but they come to nothing. Just because they fail to understand that the workers must be educated in economics and the social struggle. "One Big Union" of the

> Amalgamation type is like trying to put a roof on before the walls are built. ... You can't build a mansion on the top of slum tenements, and you cannot make an industrial union by merely amalgamating obsolete and outgrown craft unions.
>
>   BARKER 1917C

In a *Direct Action* article that appeared on March 17, 1917, Barker described the conflict between IWW and AWU activists among the gold, silver, and copper miners whom he visited at Mount Morgan, Queensland, where the large amount of gold generated made fortunes for Mount Morgan Gold Mining Company shareholders (Barker 1917k; "The I.W.W. is After the Works" 1917):

> When the Mount Morgan wealth producer has had his last breath coined into dividends, they plant him with much ceremony. And he sleeps within sight of the most unsightly dump that I ever saw in my life. And Fat only makes about three-quarters a million a year out of the hides and muscle and sinew of the wage workers in that town. Every quid is reddened with a human sacrifice, and the verdant cemetery is a tragedy, a tragedy of broken bodies, and crushed limbs, of miners' complaint, and of young and vigorous manhood murdered by the plundering profit-ghouls, at the portals of manhood. Mount Morgan is hell. It is hell, so that Park Lane may be heaven. But the I.W.W. is also here.
>
>   BARKER 1917k

During his visit, Tom described the current state of the fight to free the Twelve, taking note of the sympathy afforded the IWW by most of those who attended meetings with him, and arguing that his union would soon be able to eclipse the influence of the AWU, which, clinging to its outdated philosophy, was presently opposing its own members' wage demand at Mount Morgan to receive 14 shillings a day, as being too high. "The I.W.W.," he noted, "is after the works." Meanwhile, local AWU officials were pointing out that any dues they collected were not being used to defend the Twelve, whom they characterized as "murderers" (Barker 1917a, 1917k; "The I.W.W. is After the Works" 1917).

In one of his reports, Barker announced that "Three National Industrial Unions of the Industrial Workers of the World will be brought into existence within the next few months" (Barker 1917k), in the areas of metals mining, waterside labor, and sheep farming and shearing. This news generated a response from the Secretary of the AWU's Western Branch, Arthur Blakeley, who, in a letter to the *Australian Worker*, damned the proposal as an attempt to create a "scab union" or a "bogus union," formed not to improve conditions or pay or to improve the organization of the industries in question, but rather to create the means for promoting the IWW's extremist political goals. Instead, what was wanted, he maintained, was consolidation with his own "sane union" (Blakeley 1917). Paradoxically, despite Blakeley's advocacy of the AWU's particular version of One Big Union structure, he also played into Tom's hands by mentioning his group's customary rejection of non-white workers as members (Cain 1993, 87):

> If this bogus union follow the footsteps of their confreres at Port Darwin, where, in 1915, a band of Chows, blacks, and, nondescripts were organised to break an A.W.U. strike on the waterside, they will soon have their hands full. The fact that this organisation [the IWW] will take in black, brown, or brindle, will no doubt account for a few members.
> BLAKELEY 1917; BARKER 1917k also reports much of these comments

In response to the letter in his column published on April 7, 1917, Barker questioned the accuracy of Blakeley's description of events in Port Darwin, where he said that both in the past and at present, AWU and IWW members worked together harmoniously. Rejecting "the tortuous reasonings of our well paid friend, ... we would find that everything that did not agree exactly with his conclusions should be lumped together under the category of "scab"" (Barker 1917b).

To his credit, Barker wanted the IWW to represent everyone, while Blakeley and not only the AWU, but also the Labor Party for whom he was at the time a candidate for the federal House of Representatives to serve the Darling area, actively sought perpetuation of the "White Australia" policy mentioned above. Though Blakeley was not the most obvious target for Barker's criticism, since he was campaigning for political office on the basis of his opposition to conscription, and, after his election he supported the campaign to reexamine the convictions of the Twelve ("Darling Selection: Mr. Blakeley the Labor Candidate" 1917; Marshall 1979; "Mr Blakeley's Thanks" 1917), the situation nevertheless gave Tom plenty of opportunity to engage in satire, writing, for instance, that "I can not miss this opportunity of congratulating Mr. Blakeley upon his remarkable sagacity in selecting two white people for his parents" (Barker 1917b). Reflecting on the inevitable lack of precision inherent in racial categorization, he continued:

> And, where in the name of Mike, is Mr. Blakeley going to draw the territory line between the white and the coloured[?] Is the Siberian to be

> called a white or a yellow? Is a Syrian to be called a black or a white. Is the Maltese to be considered as a Latin or an Arab?
>
> I can't, for the life of me, see why all the workers of all colours can't be in the one union.
>
> BARKER 1917b

A few days later, Tom reported that his trip to Queensland had succeeded in providing a reliable source of funds to be able to agitate for the release of the Twelve and provide some assistance to their families, pay for campaign expenses, and fund opposition to the imprisonment of Mick Sawtell and other allies (Barker 1917l). Visiting Rannes, a small town in Queensland, during a storm, he had ridden a horse through the rain, getting lost before he reached his destination, where he held meetings at a ballast pit. Once again, he spread the story of the Twelve and the wrong done to them, returning by train to Mount Morgan, and continuing on to Baree, another small town in Queensland, and then to gatherings in Rockhampton, Gympie, and Brisbane (Barker 1917a).

On June 3, 1917, a letter written by Tom Barker was seized pursuant to regulations instituted under the War Precautions Act. A private Japanese ship, the *Nikko Maru*, was intercepted and written material was confiscated, either because it contained radical content, or if it was in a language other than English. At the same time persons of Russian origin believed to have been involved in demonstrations where Red Flags may have been waved were being targeted for deportation; one who went under the name Frank Madorsky (or Madorski) was identified as possessing correspondence from Barker when the *Nikko Maru* was searched, but since he was leaving the country, he was allowed to continue on (Curtis 2010, 114–115; Evans 1988, 164–165; "Long Live Free Russia" 1917; "Queensland Organisers' Reports" 1917). Ultimately, this continuing surveillance would lead to Barker being deported to Chile.

At the end of August, Barker was arrested at the IWW office in Sydney, and charged with being a member of an illegal organization, pursuant to amendments made in July 1917 to the Unlawful Associations Act; the original law in 1916 had already, as mentioned, specifically identified the IWW as being illegal, stating that "The following are hereby declared to be unlawful associations, namely:— (a) The association known as the Industrial Workers of the World," but, as Barker (1965, 31) later noted, "We kept functioning after we had been declared illegal. They didn't take the offices away from us; once we'd paid our rent we were safe there." Now the law was toughened, the situation changed, and along with seven other IWW members, he was quickly sentenced to six months' imprisonment; this time, there was no possibility of avoiding jail by paying a fine. For Wobblies unlike Barker, who were not British subjects, similar penalties could also be applied under the authority of the Alien Restriction Order, which had been passed in 1915. There was no basis to challenge any decision to deport, which could be made by either the defense minister or attorney general of the recently elected ruling Nationalist Party (in May 1917, with Hughes assuming its leadership and continuing as prime minister) without giving any reason, and the secrecy of the process as a whole meant that people disappeared without any newspaper coverage; however, Adela Pankhurst was able to take advantage of being on bail to fight back, getting married, and ultimately avoiding removal (Burgmann 1995, 217–218; Cain 1993, 263; Evans 2000, 36; "I.W.W. in Sydney" 1917; "I.W.W. Men Sentenced" 1917; "I.W.W. Suppression: Mr Tom Barker Arrested" 1917; Nicholls 2007, 42, 54–56, 59; "Out of the Way" 1917; "The War on the I.W.W." 1917; "Tom Barker Arrested" 1917; "Unlawful Associations Act: Deportation Regulation" 1917).

In New Zealand, the coalition government that Barker had described as "the William-Joseph Fusion, of Maoriland" (Barker 1915a) passed the Undesirable Immigrants Exclusion Act of 1919, seeking to permanently extend restrictions passed for the duration of the First World War, ostensively to punish the citizenry of recent enemies, Germans and Austro-Hungarians, but arguably actually enacted to mainly limit the presence and speech of people arriving from any other country, since it allowed the attorney general to expel anyone who was "disaffected" or "disloyal" ("An Undesirable" 1925; Robb 2020). For example Moses Baritz, originally from Manchester in England, who considered himself a Marxist, was followed around by government officials as he lectured, his comments being recorded. He was then deported under the Act to Australia, where he was nevertheless allowed to land, for allegedly working with well-known anarchist Emma Goldman and the IWW, questionable claims that he had denied ("Baritz Barred" 1920; "Moses Baritz: Deported from New Zealand" 1920). The Labour Party leader, Harry Holland, condemned the new law, arguing that "the idea of autocratically delivering sentence without any semblance of trial is repellent to fair-minded people" ("A Deported Alien" 1920). In another case the next year, he pointed out that "It is neither unlawful nor seditious to advocate the wildest forms of socialism or communism" ("An Undesirable" 1925).

Following Australia's multiple attempts to deport Paul Freeman in 1918 and 1919, he became known as "the human shuttlecock," bouncing around the Pacific Ocean. Freeman had registered as an alien in 1916 as required by the War Precautions Act, saying he had been born to German parents in the United States. Identified by the government as a disloyal IWW troublemaker, he was twice deported to the United States, which refused to let him land, unconvinced that he was an American, partly because he did not have a passport. Arriving back in Sydney from San Francisco on the *Sonoma*, and unable to land in Australia following the Americans' second refusal to admit him, he went on hunger strike; his weakened health and the support of demonstrators and ship employees eventually persuaded the authorities to let him in. After receiving medical treatment, he was placed in an internment camp for Germans called the Holdsworthy Concentration Camp, where, having been sentenced to 14 days on bread and water for breaking camp rules, he responded by again refusing all food. He was then deported again, this time to Germany, along with about 500 Germans ("500 Germans Deported" 1919; "An Undesirable Alien: Reasons for Deportation" 1919; "Australia Gets Excited over One-Man Hunger Strike" 1919; "Australian Deportee's Journeyings" 1919; "Four Times across the Pacific: Strange Case of Paul Freeman" 1919; "Freeman Interned" 1919; "Landing Permitted: Freeman Denies I.W.W. Connection" 1919; Nicholls 2007, 54–55; "Paul Freeman" 1919; "The Human Shuttlecock" 1921).

In a letter he wrote on April 2, 1920 from Stettin, Germany [a city that in 1945 would become Szczecin, Poland] to former merchant sailor Percy "Jack" Brookfield, a radical member of the NSW Legislative Assembly, Freeman gave his perspective on what had happened so far. He complained that he had been transferred to the internment facility too quickly: "The military dragged me out of the hospital in a very bad physical condition. I could just barely move about, and that was all" (Freeman 1920).

At the end of 1920, Paul met with Tom Barker when both were in Stettin (Barker 1921q). Present along with Tom at the first conference of the Red International of Labor Unions (RILU) in Moscow in July 1921, a meeting which is discussed below, Freeman went with other delegates to visit a coal mine at Kursk, but was killed, along with five others in a train accident (Barker 1921f). In his obituary of Paul, Barker recalls activities that they had engaged in together and reveals that the latter was certainly an active member of the IWW, although he says he has no idea where he was born, which made Paul's political opinions a source of vulnerability to government extremism, even though he could not speak German (Barker 1921f). Eulogizing his friend in the following way, Barker might have been speaking of himself:

> Paul Freeman was one of that great army of the tireless, world-tramping, universal I.W.W. He passed from land to land and continent to continent with as little care as some men cross the street.
> BARKER 1921f

3   Chile

When he had finished his prison sentence, serving more than the allotted term of six months, Tom Barker was deported on July 8, 1918, one of a number of foreign-born members of the IWW who were expelled, with the secrecy of the process creating a variety of guesses as to what the total number might be. The ship on which he left, the *Mineric*, landed in Valparaíso on August 13. Tom arrived with seven other deportees whom the local newspaper, *El Mercurio*, listed as being Sam Kipling, Carl Tudland, Karl Petersen, George Andersen, Hyman Issermann, Alexander "Alec" Rosenthal, and Thomas "Tom" Dillon (Cain 1993, 265–266; "Los ocho deportados de Australia y su presencia en Chile" 1918). Australian authorities had planned that they would later be joined by Frank Bilboa, Peter Villalabetia, and John Burtovich, but when the latter's ship, the *Boveric*, arrived in March 1919, the Chileans refused to allow the three Wobblies to land, although Barker (1923a, 1965, 34) notes that Julius Muhlberg, who, like his fellow-Wobbly, John H. Randolph, the fiancé of the feminist and pacifist teacher, Kathleen Hotson, had arrived on an earlier ship, the *Jeseric*, succeeded in helping Bilboa briefly leave the vessel, and in consequence was arrested. Apparently, Barker and the deportees who arrived with him had planned on trying to continue onward on the *Mineric*, but before they disembarked, they also encountered Muhlberg, who recommended the group stay because the local atmosphere would be friendly to them. Having left the ship, Barker connected with the IWW's branch in Valparaíso, which was active on the waterfront. It had been established by Juan Onofre Chamorro, a sailor and butcher who kept two revolvers on his meat-cutting table to protect himself from any potential enemy. Chamorro was also the president of la Sociedad de Estibadores y Gente de Mar de Valparaíso (SEGEM) [the Valparaíso Stevedores and Seafarers Society] and involved with the syndicalist labor federation, la Federación Obrera Regional Chilena [the Regional Workers' Federation of Chile] (FORCh or FORCH). The deportees arrived with little money or clothing, but some were able to find work, and some support was received from local workers' groups and the British Consul in Valparaíso, and also from a Mr. Holm, the head of the local Salvation Army, on whose roof the deportees had lodged (Araya Saavedra 2008, 26, 27, 32–33, 34, 2016; Barker 1920b, 1965, 34–35; Basaez and Cerda 2015, 81; Cain 1982, 59, 60, 1993, 269; Damousi 1991, 12, 14; Evans 2000, 35–38; Mason 2018, 65; Nicholls 2007, 54–56; Rosenthal 2015, 77; Savala 2019, 151; Turner [1967] 1969, 215; Weiss 2021, 54). Even though he was now in South America, the Australian government continued to monitor Barker, being particularly concerned to prevent him from communicating by mail with people back there (Cain 1982, 61–62). In the minds of his political enemies, his prowess as a revolutionary leader was awesome.

As with the Ley de Residencia in Argentina that was discussed in Chapter 1 in connection with Virginia Bolten, the presence of Barker and other IWW deportees would now persuade Chile to approve a similar law ("Armando Jaramillo Valderrama" N.d.; Armijo and Cortés 2013, 119–120, 126; Chile Congreso Nacional. Cámara de Diputados. 1917, 619; Sepúlveda 2016, 74–75). Introducing the measure in the lower house of the National Congress, the Cámara de Diputados [Chamber of Deputies, which is today called the Cámara de Diputadas y Diputados] on December 5, 1917, Deputy Armando Jaramillo Valderrama referred to the fact that other countries had seen the wisdom of denying access to troublemakers:

> Los Estados Unidos de Norte América, esa gran República modelo de democracia í libertades, al ver que la Europa espulsaba de su seno los elementos corrompidos, se apresuró a dictar una lei de residencia, leí que indujo a los previsores estadistas de Brasil, la República Arjentina el Uruguai i de otros paises sud americanos a seguir el mismo ejemplo a fin de evitar que se convirtieran sus territorios en un albergue de individuos que sólo representan una carga pesada i peligrosa para la sociedad.
>
> La lei de residencia en Chile se impone por esta razon i será una consecuencia lójica i obligada de las leyes dictadas en otros paises americanos.
> CHILE CONGRESO NACIONAL: CÁMARA DE DIPUTADOS 1917, 619

> [The United States of North America, that great model republic of democracy and liberties, seeing that Europe was expelling corrupt elements from its bosom, hastened to dictate a law of residence; I read that it induced the far-sighted statesmen of Brazil, the Argentine republic, Uruguay, and other South American countries to follow the same example in order to prevent their territories from becoming a shelter for individuals who only represent a heavy and dangerous burden for society.
>
> The law of residence in Chile is imposed for this reason and will be a logical and necessary consequence of the laws enacted in other American countries.]

In fact, the United States, as well as being an inspiration to other nations, was using its law to deport Australian Wobblies back to their own country. Additionally, Sepúlveda places the inspiration for Chile's legislation with European leaders:

> Una vez construida esta imagen negativa de los anarquistas por las clases dominantes de América Latina, se dieron al trabajo de copiar las *leyes de residencia* implementadas en Europa, especialmente cuando estos "degenerados agitadores profesionales" – según su discurso de clase – principalmente "inmigrantes" o "extranjeros," azuzaban los conflictos entre el capital y el trabajo y criticaban públicamente el orden burgués y los pilares del sistema de dominación sin titubeos ni ambages. En otras palabras, la clase dominante se dotó de instrumentos jurídicos y legales que le permitieron legitimar la represión legal-institucional contra el mundo libertario.
>
> SEPÚLVEDA 2016, 74–75

> [Once this negative image of the anarchists was built by the ruling classes of Latin America, they took to the job of copying the residency laws implemented in Europe, especially when these "professional degenerate agitators" – according to their class discourse – mainly "immigrants" or "foreigners," fueled the conflicts between capital and labor and publicly criticized the bourgeois order and the pillars of the system of domination without hesitation or ambiguity. In other words, the ruling class provided itself with juridical and legal instruments that allowed it to legitimize the legal-institutional repression against the libertarian world.]

For a while, Barker's location and the details of what happened to him were concealed from most of his friends and allies. Then, in the *Maoriland Worker* on June 11, 1919, a letter from his sister, Jenny Connor, dated May 21, reported that Tom, "recently deported by the War Lords and Capitalists of Australia" was in Santiago, and it gave an address where he could be contacted (Connor 1919). However, following passage of Chile's residency law, he was deported to Argentina (Burgmann 1995, 271). Exactly how the expulsion process took place is described in a letter Barker sent to Tom Glynn, by then the editor of the *Australian Communist*; portions of the missive were published in that Sydney periodical on January 14, 1921:

> The Australian wobblies left a big trail across Chile and Argentina in our peregrinations. They showed [Julius] Muhlberg ... a gun on the Cordilleras [the mountainous border area between the two countries], 13,000 feet up, and told us that was our reception if we showed our faces there again. We went across into the hands of la policia Argentina, who described us as "undeseables, revoltosos y bolshevikis" [undesirables,

rioters, and Bolsheviks]. However, it doesn't matter what they call you if they only let you go and they did that.

>   BARKER 1921r

4 Argentina

In Argentina, Barker continued his radical activities on behalf of the IWW in the La Boca dock area of Buenos Aires, where in 1919, he founded the Marine Transport Workers Industrial Union (MTW), which catered to sailors from around the world (Araya Saavedra 2016; De Angelis 2017, 253, 256). Tom's account of this time, which was published in the *Industrial Pioneer*, suggests that, although he did not reside there for long, his influence was considerable:

> In Buenos Aires we recognized the members of other oversees unions. We transferred them free. If a man was in good standing overseas, he merely registered at the union office for his next job and he paid nothing. All we required was that he should act according to the union rules in the port. This system smashed the shanghaiers out of their business and made it impossible for them to operate. When the dockers boycotted a ship at the behest of our union, they did not return to work until they had been paid for the time they had not worked, a fact that was not appreciated by the shipping companies.
>
> BARKER 1921n, 46

According to Barker, organization of labor in the port area now reflected his oft-stated concerns that working too fast would benefit owners of ships at the expense of employees, and that the hours available should be allocated equitably among those who sought them (Barker 1921o):

> The second shift would be from 12 noon till 6 P.M., with another half-hour for "smoke-oh." No more work would then be done until the following day, when the men would go on the alternative shifts. The work for one day's pay would therefore amount to five and one-half hours. The men were to be engaged at the Union "stand" by rotation. It was considered better for everyone to have some work than for the "royals" to do it all and keep other men out of job.
>
> BARKER 1921o

Some three months after Barker had departed Argentina, the Hobart, Tasmania newspaper, the *World*, reprinted a report from the MTW's own publication that gave a colorful description of Barker's activities in Buenos Aires, in particular his relationship with the British vice-consul in that city. From the style of the writing, with its somewhat exaggerated emphasis on class struggle in the context of English culture, and given Tom's important role as the secretary of the MTW, it seems likely that it was penned by Barker himself:

> The British vice-consul in Buenos Aires does not like the secretary of the Marine Transport Workers (Tom Barker.) [punctuation sic] They are fellow countrymen, but are on different sides of the social fence. The secretary went to work when he was nine years of age on a Westmoreland farm. At that period the vice-consul was qualifying in a middle class school to become a public servant. The education that was imparted in those days in English grammar schools was directed towards teaching the students how to be servile and humble before their superiors, and intolerant and tyrannical towards their alleged inferiors.
> "The Secretary and the Consul: News of Tom Barker" 1920

The article also reveals a suspicion that the two-faced vice-consul, who is believed to have asked Australian authorities for information about Tom's background, had also told local authorities "that the secretary, Barker, is an "estafador" [swindler] from Australia. The fact is that Barker never needed to steal, as he has two hands, and is not afraid to lift them in gaining his own living. He commenced to earn his living at an age when you were learning the rudiments of arithmetic" ("The Secretary and the Consul: News of Tom Barker" 1920). To the extent that this characterization reflects actual events, it perhaps provides some of the reasoning for Barker's quick departure. By August 1920, looking back, he was also providing an explanation in terms of a current crackdown on union activity:

> According to the communications just received from Buenos Aires, the Argentine ruling class are having another periodical attack of blue funk. In the good old style, they seize all union officials upon whom they can lay hands, gaol them, and then seal up their union offices. Working-class papers are suppressed, and the editors thrown in gaol.
> BARKER 1920d

The next year, Tom developed a more generally apposite critique of consuls, and presumably vice-consuls, the world over that reflected his encounters in

Argentina, as well as further suggesting that "The Secretary and the Consul: News of Tom Barker" was his own account:

> With regard to consuls, I find from an extensive experience that they do not care a damn about their fellow countrymen who earn a living on ships. ... I have seen them in Buenos Aires deliberately keep a seaman on the beach by refusing to give him a passport, without which he could not get a ship. If you venture into their offices they bawl, "Take off yer hat," and from thence on you are doomed. They hate unions, and conspire against officials of the unions in foreign ports, and are not above making false accusations and complaints in order to cover their own malpractices.
> BARKER 1921k, 58

When he left, resigning as MTW secretary in February 1920, he headed for London on a Norwegian ship, working to pay for the cost of his ticket, taking with him paperwork supplied by the Federación Obrera Regional Argentina (FORA), which, along with other credentials, including those of the MTW, would allow him to participate in a number of conferences in Europe, one of the first being a meeting of unions that took place in Oslo later the same year. Fellow-deportee from Australia to Chile, Julius Muhlberg, also served as an MTW delegate (Araya Saavedra 2016; Barker 19210, 50, 1965, 36; Burgmann 1995, 271; Cain 1982, 62; De Angelis 2012, 5, 2017, 253, 256).

Before he exited Argentina, Barker wrote an article which appeared in the *Worker's Dreadnought* on January 31, 1920, in favor of the cereal growers and other agricultural employees in that country. He argued that in general, two groups of workers, sailors and farm employees, had been fated to fall behind those in other industries in terms both of rewards for their labor and of union representation (Barker 1920a):

> The isolation that divides the workers in both industries is largely responsible for this state of disorganisation. But the need of the hour, the greed and rapacity of their masters – for no other workers are so underpaid and overworked as the workers on the ships and on the land – and the desire for a more attractive life, act as the motive springs for these workers forming unions in their industry.
> BARKER 1920a

Surprisingly, Tom pays tribute to his old rival, the Australian Workers' Union (AWU), which he credits for becoming "the largest pastoral organization in the world. ... Its success has been phenomenal, and its staff of voluntary delegates is in every wheat field, fruit orchard, and cattle station. It is the consolodisation of the hitherto neglected force of the country worker" (Barker 1920a). In Argentina, on the other hand, up to the present time, the conditions faced by farm workers are much more exploitative. Mosquitos of two types exact their price: not only mordacious insects, but ones of the human kind, "whose richness and idleness is contrasted with the squalid and sordid slaves of the pampa" (Barker 1920a):

> [T]he sweating reaper knows the gnawing bites of hunger, even while surrounded by the very fruits of his labour. ... His clothes are still damp with the salty sweat of the previous day's slavery. Still half asleep, he tends the rattling, noisy machine, felling the slender stalks. He has sixteen or more long hours of slavery, and for the sum of three and a half pesos a day.
> BARKER 1920a

Barker continues, optimistically identifying many details of ways that the conditions of harvest workers might be upgraded by the setting up of the Agricultural Workers' Union, which now has its headquarters in Rosario, and is staffed with organizers from the big cities and ports more familiar with improvements and inspired by the goal of One Big Union. However, since farm workers remain exploited in many areas of the world today, it is not clear to what extent his objectives had at that point been achieved, and to what degree he is presenting only a pious hope that will electrify fellow attendees at upcoming conferences but not come to pass (Barker 1920a).

5 Europe, Conferences, and the Twelve

Barker spent part of April and May 1920 in Norway and Sweden, where, in addition to participating in a transport workers' conference in Oslo, he was able to publicize the case of the Twelve, printing 18,000 copies of leaflets that made the argument that they were innocent, and talking to labor unions and to the Norwegian Labour Party [*Det Norske Arbeiderparti*], which is today known as *Arbeiderpartiet*. On May Day (May 1), the flyers were distributed throughout Norway, and the information was later published in *Syndikalisten* in Stockholm, which changed its name in 1922 to *Arbetaren* [The Worker], and another syndicalist paper, Copenhagen [København]-based *Solidaritet* (Barker 1920f, 1921b, 1921r; Burgmann 1995, 271; Walker 1970).

Having returned to London, Barker became the secretary of the local office of the Australian Workers Defence Committee at 28 East Road, and continued to focus on the imprisonment of the Twelve. An article he published in the empathetic and widely read national newspaper, the *Daily Herald*, on May 14, 1920 offered to send speakers out to organizations to provide the details of the Wobblies' imprisonment, and asked unions to become active about the matter and send donations to his new address, at 34 Baxter Road in Islington. A few days later, he sent a letter to fellow opponent of conscription, Jack Brookfield, informing him where he was now living. He informed Brookfield that few people in England had any awareness of the existence of the Australian prime minister, Billy Hughes, although members of the British Labour Party did plan to discuss the continued imprisonment of the Twelve and see what it could do to secure their release. He told of his plans to host a meeting on Wednesday, May 9 in the hall at the Australian Workers Defence Committee, a gathering at which another of the Wobblies sent to Chile on the *Mineric* with him, Alec Rosenthal, would be the chair. Because of his power in the Legislative Assembly, Brookfield was subsequently able to push the Australian Labor Party to support the release of the Twelve. (Barker 1920f; Bloodworth 2015; De Angelis 2012, 5; "I.W.W. Prisoners: Committee's Call for Help" 1920).

A letter writer in the Melbourne paper, the *Socialist*, had suggested that someone summarize the details of the circumstances of the Twelve for readers, and Barker, citing his familiarity with the issues, responded in another letter, titled "The Australian Sedition Cases" in the edition of June 17. Pointing out the London address of the Australian Workers Defence Committee, he announced that a 52-page pamphlet called "Guilty or Not Guilty" had been written by Harry Boote, and was available by mail from his office (Barker 1920e). He continued:

> It is a wonderful story, so wonderful, in fact, that one who reads it can only come to the conclusion that these men are the victims of a political and judicial conspiracy.
> BARKER 1920e

An announcement in the *Daily Herald* on Friday, July 16 promoted a speech at the Communist League in London: "Not Guilty. A Defence by Tom Barker of the Australian I.W.W. prisoners, to-night at 8.30." On the following Sunday he appeared at two British Socialist Party meetings in Hampstead (Red Feather 1920).

Pursuant to the Police Inquiry Act of 1918, Justice Philip Street was appointed by the NSW government as a commissioner to conduct a formal inquiry into questions raised about the way that the police had behaved in connection to the prosecution of the Twelve in the case of *R. v. Reeve*, some of the more critical comments having come from members of the Legislative Assembly itself.

However, in the report of the Street Commission, which was printed on August 28, 1919, Street did not find convincing evidence that any of the convictions were flawed:

> I have to report that no fresh facts have been elicited before me raising any doubt in my mind as to the guilt of the convicted men. I am, of course, discriminating between fresh facts, on the one hand, and, on the other hand, criticism of the credibility of the evidence before the jury.
> *Report of Mr. Justice Street, the Commissioner Appointed by the Act* 1919, 57; TURNER [1967] 1969, 140

Many members of the Labor Party believed that, with this decision, Justice Street had sold out to other interests. The report produced by the annual conference of the NSW Labor Party that year commented as follows on the need for yet another, and more appropriate, review of the trial:

> The reservations and guarded report of Mr Justice Street will serve as an everlasting monument to the servility for which even Judges can be remarkable, though the result of such servility involves the liberty and perhaps the very lives of fellow citizens.
> "Mr Justice Street's Commission on Police Methods" 2008, 97

The Royal Commission of Inquiry into the Matter of the Trial and Conviction and Sentences Imposed on Charles Reeve and Others, known as the Ewing Commission, headed by Justice Norman Ewing of Tasmania, the holder of a number of legislative appointments over the years and a former Supreme Court of Tasmania judge, was next tasked, this time by a new NSW Labor Party government, to address the convictions of the twelve IWW prisoners. The Ewing Commission produced an entirely different result to that of Street. It met in Sydney, reviewed evidence and heard from many witnesses, generating a report, which was published on July 31, 1920. It concluded that six of the Twelve (Bernard Bob Besant, Morris Joseph Fagin, John Hamilton, Donald McPherson, Thomas Moore, and William Teen) were completely innocent, while much of the evidence against them in general was tainted by police informers, who had extensively lied (Burgmann 1995, 242–244; Cain 1993, 223; "Conclusion of I.W.W. Inquiry" 1920; Connolly 1920; "Death of Mr. Justice Ewing" 1928; Gray 2018, 424; "I.W.W. Case: Royal Commission's Report" 1920; *Report of the Royal Commission of Inquiry into The Matter of the Trial and Conviction and Sentences Imposed on Charles Reeve and Others*. 1920; "The Report" 1920). Justice Ewing wrote:

> Since the trial it has been made quite clear, by the evidence given before Mr. Justice Street, and also adduced before me, that [three of the witnesses] are persons of such a character that they may justly he described as liars and perjurers, and men who, whenever it served their own ends, and irrespective of the consequences to other persons, would not hesitate to lie, whether upon oath or otherwise.
>
> "The Report" 1920

Nevertheless, the Ewing Commission found that there was a conspiracy to burn down businesses, in which some IWW members were involved, and also took the position that, while it was permissible to possess a copy of the book *Sabotage* [It is not clear whether the opinion was referring to Émile Pouget's work of that name, Artruro M. Giovannitti's translation of it, or the different version written by Elizabeth Gurley Flynn, which is discussed in Chapter 3], "a man becomes responsible for the doctrines of the author enunciated in the book when he sells or distributes copies of it in large quantities, and either expressly or in effect enjoins members of the public to read, mark, learn, and inwardly digest its contents and practice the methods therein advocated" ("The Report" 1920). Ewing noted that while William Beatty had possessed approximately a thousand copies of *Sabotage*, he had been sufficiently but also appropriately punished for "seditious conspiracy." In so noting, the judge provided a somewhat bizarre rationalization for his view, commenting:

> This is a vastly different thing from having one copy, which any ordinary and innocent vendor might have. It indicates, to my mind, an approval of the doctrines therein preached, and I think he must be held responsible for them. Although this fact does not connect him with these fires, it is certainly strong evidence that he was an approver of the illegal and in some directions the criminal methods advocated in that book. Had he been a person selling the book for gain, such as a bookseller, that fact would have had little influence upon me. But, seeing that he was a voluntary worker in the cause, he must, to my mind, be taken to incur responsibility for the doctrine that he chooses to disseminate voluntarily. Some of these doctrines are distinctly seditious.
>
> "The Report" 1920

Among the six members of the Twelve who were not exonerated, most of their convictions were also dismissed by the Commission as being inappropriate or excessive, which left just two persons in jail, Charles Reeve and John Benjamin

King, the latter being still required to finish serving an earlier sentence (Barker 1921b; "I.W.W. Case: Royal Commission's Report" 1920; "The Report" 1920).

In October 1920, Tom appears to have found time to pay homage to the body of the Lord Mayor of Cork, Terence MacSwiney, at Southwark Cathedral, a propaganda triumph in Sinn Féin's campaign for Irish independence, which he described as "a magnificent sight in London, and about two miles of Self-Determination Leagues marching in military style behind. The Sinn Fein colors had a glorious airing that day through the streets of London. The hard-bodied British bonehead, with a celluloid Union Jack in his coat lapel, writhed in torment on the sidewalk, and waited in vain for tanks, black and tans, and the R.I.C. [Royal Irish Constabulary]" (Barker 1921r). MacSwiney had been on a hunger strike in Brixton Prison in London, which, after 74 days, resulted in his death (Maume 2009; Power 2020; Windle 2005, 214, fn 56).

In a letter mailed from Scotland that was published in the Brisbane *Daily Standard* on February 1, 1921, Barker congratulated the myriad individuals, labor unions, publications, and left-leaning political parties that had contributed to the release of the ten imprisoned Wobblies, and he urged further attempts to free the remaining two ("Tom Barker Welcomes his Mates from Gaol" 1921). In another note, dated January 1, 1921, and published in the *Socialist* on Friday, March 4, 1921, Barker reflected on what he saw as the irony that "In Germany there is full liberty of the press, organisation, speech and assembly, which is more than we can say of the land of Hughes, Lloyd George and those who WON the war" (Barker 1921q).

The previous December, Tom had been in Germany, attending the Freie Arbeiter Union Deutschland (FAUD)-organized Syndicalist Conference in Berlin with other Wobblies, together with US IWW leader George Hardy making two visits to the Zentralfriedhof Friedrichsfelde [Friedrichsfelde Central Cemetery] in the Lichtenberg borough of Berlin, and placing wreaths on the graves of Karl Liebknecht and Rosa Luxemburg, socialists killed in mysterious but clearly murderous circumstances (Barker 1921i, 1921q, 1965, 36; Burgmann 1995, 271; Plievier 1921). At the meeting, the new Russian government's plan to set up the Red International of Labor Unions (RILU), which it would do in 1921, was hardly welcome news to FAUD, the publisher of *Der Syndikalist*, or to other like-minded unions, identifying a problem in which Barker would become tangled when he went to Moscow, and which would prompt criticism by a South American union he was representing; syndicalism and communism make unhappy bedfellows (Thorpe 2000, 212, 213; Weiss 2021, 39–40).

In 1922, there was another conference sponsored by the FAUD that met in Berlin, at which growing awareness of the oppressive tendencies of Lenin and of Russian communism in general led to the International Working Men's

Association (IWMA) being founded as a non-authoritarian syndicalist alternative to the RILU, inspired by Bakunin's First International of 1864–1876, and which bore the similar title of the International Workingmen's Association (IWA) (Shapiro 1933, 5–6; Thorpe 2000, 210, 213).

6   Russia

In a letter dated January 17, 1923 and published on February 24, Barker recalls that, traveling east from Germany:

> I was held in a box car at Yamburg [in Russia] for 10 days awaiting for the permit to travel on. It was 20 below zero, and as I had only the clothes I stood in, and after about 10 years in Aussy, Argentina, Chile, and other sub-tropical joints, it was a wonder I didn't freeze to death.
> BARKER 1923a

At a gathering that took place on January 23 and 24, 1921, he delivered a speech in Moscow to the All-Russian Industrial Union of Miners at an event known as the Second All-Russia Congress of Miners, in which he asked:

> And bad as things are, are you not a thousand times better off now than the mining slaves of the great capitalist countries, who toil to enrich their masters, contract pthisis [phthisis], lead-poisoning, and all the other ills and evils of the capitalist system?
> BARKER 1921h

Unfortunately, Barker's commitment to the changes taking place in Russia rested on an assumption that they would continue, and that the country's new leaders would not themselves turn out to be "masters," or the workers become "slaves." Few observers looking back at that country's experiment with what was called "communism" would agree that it was anything like as successful as Tom here assumes that it will be. In fact, the two speeches Lenin gave at the meeting perhaps suggest in themselves reasons why the revolution might fail, since he was critical of the idea that labor unions, comprised of "proletarians, who may not be class conscious, [and] are often ignorant, backward and illiterate" (Lenin [1921] 1965b), were capable of acting outside the tutelage of the Communist Party:

> Marxists have been combating syndicalism all over the world. We have been fighting in the Party for over twenty years, and we have given the workers visual proof that the Party is a special kind of thing which needs forward-looking men prepared for sacrifice; ... The workers and the peasants are two distinct classes. Let us talk about vesting the rights in the trade unions when electricity has spread over the whole country – if we manage to achieve this in twenty years it will be incredibly quick work, for it cannot be done quickly.
>
> LENIN [1921] 1965b

In July 1921, Barker represented the FORA-V, the "V" referring to the group's fifth congress, a group that had now started to call itself the FORA-C or FORA-Comunista, at the first conference of the RILU in Moscow, at which, as Tosstorff (2004, 383) notes, much of the activity "predominantly revolved around the discussions with the syndicalists over the broad strategic and programmatic orientation of the organization." Here, Barker promoted the idea of founding an international union of seafarers. He also explained his ideas in his work, *The Story of the Sea*, which appeared in serial form in the Chicago *Industrial Pioneer*, and was then released in a number of IWW pamphlets; what he wrote was substantially based on his experience working with the MTW in Buenos Aires. The FORA-C had specifically delineated the terms under which he was to represent them, stressing the need for the RILU to be independent of the Russian state apparatus, and to maintain its anarcho/a-communist philosophy, an objective which was inherently challenging. At the conference, there was much debate about whether RILU should be subsumed under the political authority of the Comintern, also known as the Third International, which advocated a more mainstream form of communism. Consequently, the syndicalists at the conference published a response rejecting affiliation. Thus some elements of the FORA-C leadership came to regard Barker's representation of their interests as having been a mistake (De Angelis 2012, 2–4, 2017, 256–260; Jeifets 2021; Jeifets and Jeifets 2014, 77; Martínez 2018, 69–71; Tosstorff, 2004, 277, 278, 345; Weiss 2021, 39–40). Even though Barker had spoken against formal association with the Comintern, an article in the Argentinian paper, *La Protesta*, on July 4, 1922, argued that when it became clear that the goal of the FORA-C's mandate was not going to be achieved, Tom should have walked out:

> Y es curioso que, al votarse la moción centralista y al quedar supeditado el moviemento sindical al partido bolsheviqui, Tom Barker haya quedado en su asiento, olsidándose de tan terminantes "instrucciones." ¿Es así como compiló com un mandato?
>
> "El "secretariado" y el delegado Tom Barker" 1922

[And it is curious that, when the centralist motion was voted and the trade union movement was subordinated to the Bolshevik party, Tom Barker was left in his seat, forgetting such strict "instructions." Is this how he complied with a command?]

Tom Mann was also at the RILU gathering, representing London unions, supporting Comintern involvement, and being similarly impressed with what he believed was happening in Russia:

> In Russia I had the opportunity of conferring with the delegates of over forty nationalities. I was confirmed in the conviction that the Russian Revolution has taught us many things. Perhaps the most important of these is that the administration or management of industry must be by councils of workers and not by parliaments.
> MANN 1923, 323

However, what reads like a syndicalist commitment seems to have been sited mistakenly in an organization that, as Alexander Berkman pointed out, was ultimately designed to serve Lenin:

> As you see, the alleged dictatorship of the proletariat was only the dictatorship of Lenin. He dictated to the politbureau, the politbureau to the Central Committee, the Central Committee to the Party, the Party to the proletariat and the rest of the people. Russia counted a population of over a hundred millions; the Communist Party had less than fifty thousand members; the Central Committee consisted of several score; the politbureau numbered about a dozen; and Lenin was one. But that one was *the* proletarian dictatorship.
> BERKMAN [1929] 2005, 162)

In August 1921, Barker addressed the Convention of the All-Russian Union of Transport Workers in Moscow. In his speech, he encouraged Russia's miners and people in the transportation industry to work hard, reminding them that "The greatest friend that the bourgeoisie," who wanted the new government and social system to fail, "can hope for is another year of famine" ("Tom Barker's Address to the Workers in Moscow" 1921). He also gave the audience some details of his mariners' organization project:

> I have come to Russia in company with Fellow-worker Muhlberg for the purpose of interesting the marine and water section of your Union in the

necessity of creating ONE union for all the workers of the seas, rivers and harbours. All nationalities meet upon the sea. The present form of organisation of the workers of the sea in all countries is purely upon a nationalist basis. We have the marine workers of one country strike-breaking and scabbing upon the workers of other countries.

"Tom Barker's Address to the Workers in Moscow" 1921

Despite the tension between syndicalist and communist approaches to unionization and his own allegiance with the former kind, Barker's presence in Russia had an influence upon him that at times obscured the evidence around him of the many failings of Lenin and Trotsky's new system. He wrote to Tom Glynn as follows in a letter that was published on September 9, 1921:

The banners and the decorations of public squares, the demonstrations, the parades, and the dressing of the children, the preparation of their food, the sunshine, and the glorification of the proletariat, all these have far-reaching effect upon the children. Every year now brings a gigantic army to the Communist side of youth and strength. Each year sees the disappearance of the older and more puerile types, with their bourgeois ideas, religion and parish patriotism, with their vermin and stupidity.

BARKER 1921b

When he heard news of the February Revolution, he had written the following in a column published in *Direct Action* on March 31, 1917:

A single night may divide the gloomy eve of Wrong, and the rosy dawn of Right. The Red Flag of the Proletarian has supplanted the ensign of despotism on the ivory tinted towers of the Winter Palace. From the icy dungeons of the Siberian tundras, comes cries of joyous deliverance from the nightmare, of lives that have been almost hopeless vigils.

BARKER 1917n

In that piece, he credits technological progress, and specifically the inventions of George Stephenson, Thomas Edison, Richard Arkwright, and Rudolf Diesel for making the continuance of Czarism impossible. Perhaps here he had in mind Kropotkin's (1907, 206–207) view that technological innovation came out of the experiences of ordinary laborers and not from any plans of the elite.

This century will see the last of Czarism. All gaols and prison fortresses will go the way of the Bastille and St. Peter and St. Paul [a fortress prison

in St. Petersburg from which Kropotkin had escaped]. The maudlin fairy tales of the pastor of the eternal Nirvana fades before the practical possibilities of Heaven on Earth. The Industrial Democracy grows and strengthens as the old political superstition of the State dies.
BARKER 1917n

A couple of weeks later, Barker gave a lecture titled "The Russian Revolution" at the Trades Hall in Lithgow, NSW, where he told the audience that in Russia, murderers in general were not executed, but sentenced to life imprisonment, which was a superior situation compared to that of Australia ("Tom Barker in Lithgow" 1917); unfortunately, once the Bolsheviks had cemented control, this did not continue to be the case. Notwithstanding the criminals who now became victims of capital punishment, either immediately or postponed by toil in labor camps at Lenin's directive, Zimmer (2010, 344) suggests it is likely that, of all the anarchists who returned to Russia at this time, about 90% would end up being killed by the Russian authorities. In his veneration, Tom emphasized that Russia tolerated more free speech than Australia, and suggested its model of One Big Union was something to emulate ("Tom Barker in Lithgow" 1917).

How aware was Barker at the time of his letter to Glynn four years later of all the people being killed by the new government, or how many anarchists, pacifists, Ukrainian nationalists, and others were now suppressed, or in jail, or working themselves to death in concentration camps in the Solovetsky Islands, Archangel, Turkestan, and other places? How did he respond to the comments of Alexander Berkman and Emma Goldman, who left the new "workers' paradise" in December 1921 and as soon as January 7, 1922 wrote a letter listing the names of ten anarchists who had been executed the previous year? Did Tom know that Kropotkin had met with Lenin as early as May 10, 1919 to complain about the murderous intolerance of dissent and to appeal for the life of a friend, or that he had also written several letters, two of which were dated March 4, 1920 and December 21, 1920, similarly attempting to reduce the government's violence, which included the taking of hostages? Did he know of the conflict that began in March 1921, when the Kronstadt sailors, along with their families, were imprisoned as counter-revolutionaries for trying to choose their own representatives to the local soviet, often afterwards being executed or sent to camps from which they would never emerge; Berkman's book (1922) about the Kronstadt murders would soon be published by *Der Syndikalist*. In 1921, Western periodicals for whom Barker wrote articles and where he knew the principals, such as the Victoria Socialist Party's the *Socialist*, which had been published by Glynn, the *Australian Communist*, later renamed the *Communist*, which was briefly edited by Glynn after his release from jail during the time he helped found the Australian Communist Party, and the *Workers' Dreadnought*, edited by Adela Pankhurst's sister, Sylvia, each initially denied that any anarchists had been imprisoned in Russia (Avrich 1973, 145–149; Berkman 1922, 5–38; Dixson 1966, 21–23; Durham 1985, 204–206, 209–210, 213, 216; Rocker et al. 1924, 47; Shone 2013, 166, 169–170, 173–175, 2019, 276; Shub 1953, 227, 231–233; "The Persecutions in Russia" 1924, 39; Wexler 1989, 32, 46–48).

On July 8, 1921, the *Communist* reported on a debate about "Bolshevism" that had taken place between A.D. Kay, the president of the Citizens' Democratic Association, and A.S. Reardon, a supporter of the Bolshevists, at the Sydney Town Hall. There was little doubt about which side of the argument was favored by the *Communist*'s editors, as the title referred to Kay as a "Charlatan," and subtitles read "Lying About Russia" and "A Clown at the Town Hall" ("A.D. Kay, Charlatan" 1921). The paper continued:

> After hearing A.D. Kay, of the Citizens' Democratic Association debate with A.S. Reardon on "Bolshevism," we are satisfied that he is what we always thought he was – a charlatan.
>
> "A.D. Kay, Charlatan" 1921

Calling Kay also "an ignoramus" and many other unflattering names, the piece continued by referring to "Kay's blustering, bluffing, ignorant, lying attack upon Russia" ("A.D. Kay, Charlatan" 1921). The article claimed that Kay had either lied about many aspects of contemporary Russia or was ignorant of the facts, giving some details from his speech which it attempted to repudiate by stating the opposite opinion.

Thus the paper reported that Kay had claimed "That Emma Goldman was a Socialist; that she was now in gaol in Russia; that she was opposed to Bolshevism; that she desired to return to free America" ("A.D. Kay, Charlatan" 1921). In response, it wrote: "Emma Goldman is not a Socialist; she is not in gaol in Russia; she is not opposed to Bolshevism; she does not want to return to the U.S.A." ("A.D. Kay, Charlatan" 1921). Later in the piece, however, the writer confusingly claimed that Goldman was an anarchist (which of course was true) and was opposed to Bolshevism (which had not always been the case, but by now was also true), before in a contradictory statement concluding:

> Both Goldman and Berkman are to-day giving their lives to aid the Russian Communists in their fight against the capitalist world, and they will continue to help them until the end.
>
> "A.D. Kay, Charlatan" 1921

Admittedly, there was confusion at the time about the overall character of the revolution in Russia, and consequently many of the radical papers fairly quickly reversed their positions when some more negative aspects of Lenin and Trotsky's regime came to light (Durham 1985, 2013). However, the article in the *Communist*, despite its dogmatic insistence on the "facts," displays little insight into what Goldman and Berkman were actually doing in the Soviet Union. Considering that they had been deported from the US with other anarchists on the *Buford*, leaving New York City on December 21, 1919 and arriving in Russia about a month later, any intention by Emma to return at the present time would be extremely difficult to achieve, even if she did want to do so. Except for a brief, three-month stay by Goldman to deliver lectures which was precisely approved in 1934, she and Berkman did not return. Spending two years in the Soviet Union allowed them to note its many illogicalities: the death penalty had not been eliminated, the Kronstadt sailors had been crushed, and in the absence of a legitimate continuing threat to overthrow the new regime, there had been no attempt by the Bolsheviks to relax their oppressive control or that of the Cheka, Lenin's anti-counterrevolutionary police (Dirlik 1991, 220). Goldman and Berkman left Russia legally, going through Latvia, having received passports to attend a conference in Germany, but it seems that Lenin allowed these well-known anarchists who had been openly critical of what was happening under his dictatorship to leave in order to help perpetuate the fiction that, in Russia, anarchists would be safe, rather than what was the truth, that they were mostly being imprisoned or killed. If Goldman had decided to stay, or if she had been less important, and she had not been murdered yet, she would eventually have been in jail. This was also the reprieve option given to another prominent deportee from the US, Mollie Steimer, and to her partner, Simon (Senia) Fleshin, in their case specifically to avoid being sent to Solovetsky, after they were released from other Soviet prisons for giving their opinions and defending less fortunate anarchists (Shone 2013, 165–175, 2019, 277–278; Wenzer 1996, 103; Wexler 1989, 58). Shub writes:

> It is an indisputable fact ... that the greatest of all the anarchists – Peter Kropotkin – opposed Lenin from the start and considered the Bolshevik ideology more hostile to anarchism than so-called "bourgeois liberalism."
> SHUB 1953, 227

Why, then, did Tom, who came to have personal access to Lenin (Barker 1965, 37; Burgmann 1995, 271), take such a different tack? Partly, it seems to be because, like many other radicals, he viewed the Russian Revolution as a very positive accomplishment for humankind. In the light of that conviction, though he concedes the irony of this, he seems to reassess his commitment to the interests and welfare of the ordinary worker when he writes in a way that will cause some former allies to doubt that this is the same person who masterminded strikes in New Zealand and Australia:

> And, it seems funny, Tom [Glynn], ... when we see here [in Russia] the introduction of [the Frederick W.] Taylor [scientific management] system, to teach the unqualified workers how to dispense with unwanted motions and get better results. It will not hurt the Russian to do so, and a leaf from the bosses [sic] book is good when it goes towards settling the vital food and transport questions of the day.
> BARKER 1921C

Gone now is the ideal of working as slowly as possible in order to expand the number of positions available, weakening management authority and helping to lessen unemployment. He no longer critiques the toil and exhaustion and psychological damage attendant upon sweated labor. Up to this point, it is not hard to imagine Tom heaping scorn on the oppressive nature of time and motion studies to make laborers function more "efficiently," but suddenly under Lenin's rule he now approves of their value. Inconsistently, the same year, in "The Story of the Sea," he wrote about the 1913 New Zealand Strike from his typical perspective, expressed in his characteristically combative manner:

> When, in 1913, the workers ... struck thruout [sic] New Zealand, the N. Z. Government, headed by the cow-punching Massey, filled the jails, cells and corridors, with striking seamen and laborers from the wharves.
> BARKER 1921k, 54

Barker's account of his presence at Kropotkin's funeral and of encountering Emma Goldman and Alexander Berkman makes no reference to the fate of the anarchists who glimpsed just a segment of the funeral procession through the bars of Butyrka prison where they were jailed. Moreover, Tom's rather facile account misses the point that Lenin, relieved that he could now avoid any additional criticism from the mouth or pen of Kropotkin, had suddenly decided to embrace the significance of his "ally's" life (Avrich [1967] 1971, 227–228, 1973, 26; Goldman [1931] 1970, 865, 869; Harrison 1921, 92; Wexler 1989, 31; Wenzer 1996, 97). Tom wrote:

> I was at Kropotkin's funeral. It was an anarchist ceremony, and quite impressive. The old man was very thin and very old, and his beard nothing liqe [like] so luxuriant as the pictures. The Soviet Administration did everything for him, doctors and whatever was possible. ... Black flags were everywhere, and Emma Goldman and Berkman were both present.
> BARKER 1921C

Sadly, the legacy of Lenin, Stalin, and Putin has been nothing like what Barker (or Berkman, Goldman, or Kropotkin) hoped for, and throughout the world today, wage slavery, corrupt politicians and incompetent government, ethnic cleansing, poverty, war, and the continual generation of new refugees continue, without much hope for improvement. Unfortunately, to some extent, Barker was impressed with Lenin's arguments about the dangers of counterrevolutionaries who would spoil the new society much as independent unions would undermine communism. In a letter dated February 1, 1921 that was published in the April 1921 issue of *Industrial Pioneer*, he vents his suspicions of such elements in both Eastern Europe and in Russia itself, commenting:

> So, undoubtedly, the efforts will come thru [sic] agents, smuggled in, to re-organize the counterrevolutionary elements still existing to some minor extent in Russia. These trouble-making gentry who could well spare themselves for some other much worthier cause – say, the white slave traffic – will find their work both hard and dangerous.
> BARKER 1921h

In a directive that was issued on March 2, 1921, and signed by Lenin and Trotsky, the Kronstadt sailors, arguably more committed to the emancipatory values articulated at the advent of the Revolution than its leaders, were condemned as "the tools of former Tsarist generals who together with Socialist-Revolutionist traitors staged a counter-revolutionary conspiracy against the proletarian Republic" (Berkman 1922, 14–15). At the Tenth Congress of the Russian Communist Party, which was held in Moscow from March 8–16, 1921, Lenin had rejected the "expression of petty-bourgeois and anarchist wavering" because it might "actually weaken the consistency of the leading line of the Communist Party and help the class enemies of the proletarian revolution." Consequently, he felt he was entitled "to wage an unswerving and systematic struggle against these ideas" (Lenin [1921] 1965a). In his letter, Barker was less obviously threatening, but for someone who had spent his adult life fighting governments and their authority, his tone is nonetheless surprising:

> "War on the Bourgeoisie" is not a platitude, and the person – whatever his label – who works to bring more war, misery and hunger upon the Russian workers and peasants will thereby probably receive more attention than he bargains for.
> BARKER 1921h

Reporting on a visit to St. Petersburg, at the time called Petrograd, in July of 1921, Tom continues to demonstrate the optimism of his earlier (Barker 1917n) piece. But by the point when he is writing, July 29, perhaps his viewpoint is better understood as naïveté in the face of Lenin's paranoid goals, evidence of which is already widespread. Barker writes:

> In once royal parks about the feet of the statues, in the gorgeous Palace of Labor grounds, around the precincts of the once dreaded prison of Peter and Paul, in the courtyard before the Winter Palace, everywhere the humble potatoe [sic] is obtruding himself, demonstrating the superiority of use over ornament or tradition. And the city so lately ringed with trench and barbed wire entanglements, is now ringed with green potatoe [sic] beds, well designed to resist as deadly an enemy as the worst of the white armies and their ally, famine.
> BARKER 1921g

In a piece titled "One Union for All of Us," Tom announced that "in Petrograd, on the 7th of August, 1921, there will be seen the founding of the Marine Transport Workers' Union" (Barker 1921d). Here, he demonstrated his earnest concern for sailors around the world and the challenging conditions they experienced:

> The worker who follows the deep water is the most isolated of the sons of men. His home is a stinking hole, the food he eats is small in quantity and poor in quality. The shore world conspires against him, from the shanghaier and the harlot down to the policeman. His officers maltreat and cheat him, and the shipowners – arrogant, bloated and stingy – buy up the union leaders and their scurvy, roughhouse myrmidions [myrmidons].
> BARKER 1921d

Unfortunately, while Barker was no longer in Russia, but back in England planning what would take place at the meeting, the International Trade Union Council (ITUC), which had been founded in 1920 with the aim of steering the commitments of syndicalists and other independent unions in the direction of Bolshevik goals, turned against creating a global sailors' union, replacing it with a less ambitious organization to be based in Moscow. As Tosstorff (2004, 346) notes, "The Russians ... soon started to get ideological 'belly ache', in view of the dominance of the syndicalist element." Thus at the August conference, Barker and other syndicalists found themselves outvoted 10–5 as, instead of securing the independent union he had planned, the meeting merely expanded the scope of the International Propaganda Committee for Transport Workers (IPC-TW) to include ship and waterfront labor (Tosstorff 2004, 346; Weiss 2021, 35, 40–41).

7   New York City

While in Russia, Barker became interested in Bill Haywood's project, a commune south of Tomsk in Central Siberia called the Kuzbas Autonomous Industrial Project [or the Autonomous Industrial Colony; also Kuzbass, in the Kuznetsk (or Kousnetzk) Basin, Kuzbas being created from the Kuz in Kuznetsk and the Bas in Basin], the stated purpose of which was to demonstrate modern mining and manufacturing techniques to people in the region, which contained rich deposits of coal and iron. Tom would spend the next five years in New York organizing and inspiring skilled workers to join the scheme, which in its first two years was run locally by Haywood and Mann, and which also involved timber mining and the processing of animal hides, as well as developing cement, brick, and glass production. Tom's new wife, Bertha (or Berta) Isaakovna, a ballet dancer originally from Poland, whom he had met in Russia in 1921, accompanied him to the US at the end of that year; they stayed in New York until about April 1926 (Barker 1965, 38; Burgmann 1995, 271; De Angelis 2012, 6, 2017, 259–260; Olssen 1996; "Socialisation: Experiment in Siberia" 1922).

A party of Kuzbas-bound workers left Seattle in April 1922, the Society for Technical Aid to Soviet Russia, a group founded in 1919 to promote and assist Kuzbas and similar colonies, having opened a branch there, viewing the port as geographically best-centered for moving people to Siberia (A.F. 1922; "Kuzbas Colony: Formation of Brisbane Organisation" 1923). However, many trips went via alternate routes. On October 4, 1922, an article in the *Australian Worker* ("Russia" 1922) reported the sailing of Kuzbas recruits and their families, totaling 135 persons from New York on the *Rotterdam* liner, transferring in Rotterdam to the *Warzawa*, which would take them to Petrograd. It continued:

> The workers represented many nationalities, including American, Finnish, Russian, Lithuanian, German, Croatian, Austrian, Jugo-Slav, Swiss, Swedish, Cuban, Polish, and Hungarian. Besides their own

equipment of tools and clothing they are taking with them more than two tons of clothing for the use of the Russian workers in the districts to which they are going, as well as other gifts.

"Russia" 1922

An initial problem was how workers from the US, Canada, Australia, and other countries would be able to enter Siberia, since Western countries did not necessarily issue visas to Russia, the Soviet Union not at this point being completely recognized as having a legitimate government. In fact, Barker advised Australians to instead secure a passport which authorized someone to visit China or Japan, since they would likely be traveling to Kuzbas through both those nations. On the other hand, the Russians also wanted to see documents, and Tom advised that if his office in New York were sent the photographs of new hires, they would make a "passport" of sorts and mail it to the company that owned the ship on which the person would be traveling to Siberia. Tom also felt it necessary to advise recruits about the freezing temperatures they would encounter, the poor housing currently available, and the dangerous nature of the mining being undertaken (Barker 1923b). Also suggesting the work was appropriate only for those who were willing to make a serious initial investment in the project, but noting that Kuzbas was not seeking to import any "agitators" (1923b), he continued:

> Each worker must be able to secure his own own fare and expenses to Kuzbas, and he must possess an ample supply of the best clothing to stand the most severe weather. He should also deposit fifty dollars ... for the purchase of additional foodstuffs, although we are prepared to waive that if he is short and we need his services. We are also prepared here to secure goods unprocurable in Australia, and ship them with our usual shipments to Russia, free of duty and imposts, upon receipt of the value at this office.
>
> BARKER 1923b

In a letter to Harry Holland, a Russian named P. Artemiev who had lived in New Zealand and returned to Petrograd, described many of the details of how Kuzbas was being organized, and suggested that individuals "with working-class minds and who are sincerely desirous of helping the workers of Russia to consolidate their victory over capitalist ownership" write to Bill Haywood at his Moscow address ("A Voice from Russia" 1923):

> The conditions are that every immigrant must bring with him 100 dollars worth of tools, 100 dollars worth of provisions, and sufficient boots, clothing, and necessary domestic utensils. He must also pay his passage up to the Russian boundary. The Soviet Government will pay 100 dollars per immigrant and this money will be expended in purchasing, from other countries, farming and other machinery for the settlers.
>
> "A Voice from Russia" 1923

It was clear from Artemiev's report as from Barker's that the organizers of the Kuzbas project were seeking from those it hired an ideological commitment to contributing positively to the changed Russian environment, although, as noted above, there was already disagreement between observers of the Soviet Union about what exactly Lenin and Trotsky and their Revolution had brought into being. While news of the letter received by Holland was reported in a matter-of-fact way in the *Maoriland Worker*, a writer for another New Zealand paper, the *Pahiatua Herald*, presented it with rather more skepticism, pointing out the negative accounts of life in Russia that had become increasingly abundant, and thus assigning the news from Artemiev "to the long tally of evidence against the Soviet Communist system which our Labour politicians are now finding it convenient to repudiate" ("Labour and the Soviet" 1923).

Advertisements in Western publications sought more recruits, again warning that "Only men who thoroly [sic] know their work, who can stay by their work, and who have patience to start in what is going to take 20 years, should apply" ("The New Proletarian Pennsylvania Kuzbas" 1925). Since, in 1923, the Communist government had taken control of the project, an advertisement at the beginning of 1925 now described Kuzbas as "A Russian State Industry Operated by a Combination of Russian and American Workers and Engineers" ("The New Proletarian Pennsylvania Kuzbas" 1925). Barker (1923a) saw Kuzbas as an opportunity for the working class to prove it could manage a major industrial project, although many of those hired outside Russia were motivated by political goals and possessed professional expertise in engineering, manufacturing, or mining; the ordinary workers were mostly represented by the local, less-skilled population. At times, Tom's rhetoric seemed to exaggerate the degree to which the project would be likely to succeed:

> We will have steel plants there in 10 years three times bigger than Newcastle ever will be. When we get the Trans-Siberian railway burning coal, and block her up with coal, then she will have to improve and shed many of the old saboteurs who have tried pretty hard to strangle Russia.
>
> BARKER 1923a

Not everyone on the left felt that Kuzbas was a positive development. In an issue of the *Workers' Dreadnought*, a piece titled "Kuzbas or Communism?" criticized Barker's defense of the fact that Russian workers would be paid less than those coming from outside which he had rationalized, pointing out that the Westerners had invested their own money at the outset in the project. Moreover, the article asked what type of new economic system was really being implemented by the strategy.

> What is the difference between Kuzbas and an ordinary productive cooperative society? What is the difference between Kuzbas and an ordinary capitalist co-partnership firm, each employee having a share and therefore a vote in the concern?
> "Kuzbas or Communism" 1922

Certainly, its writer felt able to answer his or her own question, with no less commitment than Barber to exaggerated dogma:

> Under Communism everyone will be entitled to make free use of social products without any sort of payment. Tom Barker does not seem to have grasped that. His ideas of Communism seem to be mere petty capitalism. Moreover, observe that the Committee is to fix wages and bonuses, without reference to the workers.
> "Kuzbas or Communism" 1922

In another article in the *Workers' Dreadnought* a few days later, Barker was blasted by its editor, E. Sylvia Pankhurst, as now not even trying to be a communist, but rather being a kind of capitalist (Pankhurst 1922). While praising the Russian Revolution, Pankhurst (1922) complained that with its authorization of the Kuzbas endeavor, "now the Soviet Government sells piece-meal the victory won by the blood of Russia's millions." Moreover, she continues, there is a sexist and classist aspect to the financial requirements that people recruited outside Russia must satisfy, in that:

> Doubtless it is realised that the proletarian woman able to contribute upwards of £100 is practically non-existent, and that, of single women, only the middle class are likely to apply.
> PANKHURST 1922

Unfortunately, Pankhurst concludes, expanding on the point made above concerning the relative salary levels, there is also a colonial component in the project which, she says sarcastically, will necessitate another revolution in order to finally liberate the locals from capitalism:

> The little foreign capitalists of Kuzbas will employ the native Russian workers as wage labourers, giving them no share in the management of the enterprise or that of the colony.
> PANKHURST 1922

By the end of 1922, reports on developments at Kuzbas revealed a range of additional problems. The concessions agreed to by the Soviets had been misunderstood by the project's leadership and later arbitrarily altered, with the consequence that coal and steel were being produced, but it did not under the agreement belong to the Kuzbas project. Skilled workers had been recruited for specific positions, but when they arrived in Siberia, they were assigned different work; management was inefficient and chaotic. Living conditions were poor, there was not enough food, the river water was undrinkable, and many people became sick. People lacked money to buy what they needed or to leave the colony and return home. Meanwhile, Bill Haywood, freezing and despondent, had returned to Moscow ("American Colony Fails under Russian Control" 1923; "Haywood's Colony is Ghastly Failure" 1922). A report at the end of 1923 indicated some upgrades had taken place, but adequate amounts of food remained a problem even though 60% of workers' salaries was being deducted to pay for it. The article, in the Brisbane *Daily Standard*, a paper which had, to the satisfaction of Barker (1923a), generally drawn attention to and published positive stories about Kuzbas, concluded:

> Living and social conditions at the colony are still far from ideal, it was admitted, but there has been a tremendous improvement during the past summer, so much so that this typical American was now entirely content to stay and see the thing through, even after the expiration of his contract. Much friction at first was declared to be due to the indefinite status of the whole enterprise, the Russian management had not let go, and the American could not take hold. Then many types were attracted through decidedly mixed or mistaken motives. Nationalistic divisions also existed. Above all, the ill-prepared state in which the first groups of colonists found matters, as well as the lack of discrimination in choosing the personnel, caused serious trouble. This has been smoothed out almost entirely, and many hundreds of Russian miners who migrated when the Americans came in have now returned to work.
> KRUSO 1923

By August of 1924, the *Standard* was citing the July issue of a source called "Russian Information," which, it stated, "clearly indicates that the colony is now well established and affords an encouraging example of working class co-operative enterprise" ("Kuzbas Colony: Satisfactory Progress." 1924). Perhaps the most significant evidence of disagreement between different observers and volunteers' perceptions of their experience at Kuzbas was illustrated by the accusations made by Thomas B. Doyle and his wife, who returned disappointed to Louisiana following their participation in the commune. The Doyles claimed that another Kuzbas returnee, Noah Lerner, an electrician now living in Brooklyn, N.Y., had openly confessed to them that he hired the vehicle, a red wagon, that transported the explosives used in the September 16, 1920 Wall Street bomb attack outside the offices of J.P. Morgan and Co., which had killed more than thirty people. Lerner had been arrested when the attack occurred but was soon released ("A New York Sensation" 1920; "Boasted of Share in Wall St. Blast" 1923; "Bomb Suspect Held; Hired Wagon That Carried Death into Wall St., Police Say" 1923). Apart from telling their account of Lerner's apparent confession, the Doyles also accused members of the Kuzbas organizing committee of theft, though most of those charges were quickly dismissed in court. Describing that event, Barker (1923c) implied that Wobbly rival, Samuel Gompers, the American Federation of Labor (AFL) president, was involved in pursuing the claim, and noted that the failure of the Lerner accusations put an end to plans for Mrs. Doyle to embark on "an anti-Russian crusade" (1923c). Thomas Reese, one of the members of the Kuzbas organizing committee who was charged, argued that the Doyles had framed Lerner to undo confidence in any testimony he might give in the other case (Cain 1993, 3; "Electrician Framed in Bomb Plot, Charge" 1923).

8 England

After a few months spent in Russia, Barker returned to Britain with his wife at the end of 1926, where he started to write about labor union issues in that country. Discussing the end of a national strike by coal miners, which had also had the effect of closing down most production of steel due to the need for coal to produce pig iron, Tom concluded that "The men have literally been starved back to work" (Barker 1926b). The settlement of the dispute was viewed by the miners as a failure because they were obliged to settle for terms they did not want to accept. Here, in the context of the present strike, Tom reiterated his oft-stated IWW belief that acceptance of people working eight hours a day would lead to putting "300,000 men on the industrial scrap heap" (Barker

1926b). He returned to the view he had suspended when considering what was wanted at Kuzbas, that slowing down the industrial process would always create more jobs and lessen the employers' profits. Unfortunately, what seemed to be happening from the perspective of A. J. Cook, the secretary of the Miners' Federation of Great Britain, Barker reported, was that, influenced by US methods and US companies, mining in the UK was being mechanized, leading to more work, not less, spread over more hours, using fewer and fewer employees (Barker 1926a, 1926b). Quoting statistics that had been presented to the House of Commons by Frank Varley, the M.P. for Mansfield, Tom pointed out that more efficiency in coal mines was being accompanied by a reciprocal reduction in wages and loss of jobs: "In Durham the 72,024 miners working in May, 1924, had fallen to 31,324 in May 1927" (Barker 1927a).

In an article dated November 13, 1927, Barker discussed a report in the *Cocoa Workers Magazine*, a communication vehicle used by the confectioners, Rowntree & Co., that reflected the Quaker values of Joseph Rowntree that had led to the company's enlightened approach to employment of working people, which included provision of affordable, attractive housing. Written by his son, Benjamin Seebohm Rowntree, the sociologist and parallel advocate of improving the lives of the poor, the account described the sorry state of housing for "the unfortunate cotton workers of British India" (Barker 1927d) in Bombay [Mumbai], where two families of workers would often be lodged in a single windowless and furniture-less room measuring about 10 feet by 12 feet, with everyone having to sleep on the floor (Barker 1927d; "Cocoa Works Magazine" N.d.).

Over the years, there was less and less awareness of Tom Barker, whose exuberance had inspired radicals the world over and terrified many important personages in New Zealand, Australia, Chile, and Argentina. In 1930, he was living in London representing the Russian Oil Products Company. That was the year that the Australian government told him that he was now allowed, if he wished, to return to that country. For a time he worked for a utility, the London Electricity Board (LEB), which was formed in 1948 when UK electricity supply was nationalized under the Labour Party government's Electricity Act of 1947. As such, his employer would likely have been viewed positively by Barker, although he would probably have been dismayed when the industry was reprivatized in 1990 (Burgmann 1995, 271; "London Electricity goes to France." 1998; "Reflections in our Mirror: Tom Barker" 1930).

On May 24, 1949, the *Daily Herald* published a letter from Barker concerning the ornithological writer, William Henry Hudson [Guillermo Enrique Hudson], denying a columnist's attribution to Hudson of being an English author. Hudson, who was born in Argentina and had moved to London, where he became a British citizen, nevertheless, according to Tom, "belongs to the pampas of the Rio Plata" (Barker 1949). He continued:

> Hudson was a poet and writer the English countryside could never have produced. He belongs to the constellation of the Southern Cross – and to Argentina! They do him greater honour than ever England did.
> BARKER 1949

Also in 1949, Barker was elected as a member of the Labour Party to the borough council in the St. Pancras area, on the north side of London, and from 1958 to 1959 he was also its mayor. Local government reorganization merged St. Pancras into the borough of Camden in 1965, where he continued to serve. As a St. Pancras councilor in 1958, Tom was one of 23 elected officials who were obliged by the national government to pay a surcharge of £1,400 when an audit determined they had made payments that exceeded their authority; they had lowered the rents of public housing tenants. Living on a retirement pension, the payment was a struggle for Barker to comply with (Burgmann 1995, 271; Harrison 1961; Mitchell et al. 1979, 70; Olssen 1996; "Rutland Boughton on Music Today" 1958). In the 1980s, the government of Margaret Thatcher imposed a similar surcharge on Liverpool councilors it viewed as having engaged in unjustified "overspending" in 1984–1985 when the city's Labour Party majority decided to operate with a budget deficit, claiming its 1983 election victory had justified following such a policy. It sought to expand the public sector, including building public housing and parks, at the time the national Conservative Party government was committed to greater privatization. Ultimately, 47 members of the council were surcharged, as were those in some other areas such as the London Borough of Lambeth, who had pursued similar left-wing policies (Marqusee 2013; Parkinson 1985 37–40 130–134; Tonge 2019; Waddington 2013). On May 1, 1958, at the suggestion of Tom, who was serving as the deputy mayor, the Red Flag was flown over the St. Pancras Town Hall. That day, 142 police officers were assigned to the immediate area, and the demonstration resulted in 19 people being arrested as political opponents also congregated around the building seeking to have the flag removed (Butler 1958; "Labour Party Suspend Councillor" 1958; "London Borough Flies a Red Flag" 1958; Mathieson 2016).

Tom Barker died following stomach surgery on April 6, 1970, his wife, Bertha, surviving him. He was 83. In 1973, a musical written by Arnold Hinchcliffe and directed by Cliff Fenn, titled "Tom Barker of Camden – and the World," to which Burgmann (1995, 271) refers as "a documentary play about his life" debuted at the Unity Theatre as part of the 1973 Camden Festival. A review in *Stage and Television Today* on June 21 of that year was not at all impressed by what its writer saw as the amateurish production and its "incredibly naive polemics" (M.A.M. 1973), feeling that Barker's story could be told more successfully in a different format:

> Somewhere, under the infantile dialogue, halting acting, over-ambitious staging, inadequate lighting, halting music, ineffectual stage management and costuming of Arnold Hinchcliffe's "Tom Barker of Camden – and the World," there is an interesting story about a notable man. Unfortunately, nothing in the Unity contribution to this year's Camden Festival, manages to dig deep enough to unearth such gold.
> M.A.M. 1973

Nevertheless, even if this attempt at portrayal was a failure, the real life of Tom Barker was something quite extraordinary. Burgmann writes:

> To Barker, the nomadic male worker, in the fact that he really had nothing to lose, epitomised strength not weakness, steadfastness not wobblyness.
> BURGMANN 1995, 61

At the end of his life, despite his involvement in political activity around the world Tom remained poor, living on a pension, needing donations from his old friends in New Zealand to pay the fine imposed due to his political activity, still steadfastly committed to his working class principles, but in terms of political ideology, he had, over the years, wobbled. Frank Cain notes:

> Many commentators have remarked that the IWW was a syndicalist and at sometimes an anarcho-syndicalist body. These claims were never made by the IWW itself. It never referred to itself as an anarcho-syndicalist organisation and rarely discussed syndicalism in its journal.
> CAIN 1993, 107

On the other hand, viewing Barker's time in New Zealand as an example of syndicalist activism, Shor writes as follows:

> Open-air meetings, in particular, provided a forum for revolutionary syndicalism while creating a proletarian public sphere. At the same time, Auckland trammies, Barker's union, revolted against the disciplinary regime of companies that tried to enforce strict regulations on the job. Increasing militant action, including secession from the arbitration

system and wildcat strikes, reinforced the revolutionary syndicalist message articulated by Barker and King.
SHOR 2005, 153–154

As the representative of the IWW in Australia, it is certainly true that *Direct Action*, which was edited by Barker, was particularly concerned with the daily fights for unionization, release of imprisoned confederates, higher pay, and worker control of industries, as well as constant criticism of politicians and their parties and negative coverage of rival union leaders and their intentions. However, in its pages, there are references to anarchist thinkers that suggest their philosophical approach lies at the core of the project, even if writers working for One Big Union lacked a substantial degree of knowledge about their works. On October 15, 1914, the presence of quotations from Max Stirner and Herbert Spencer might indicate *Direct Action*'s support for individualistic libertarian ideas, although they are accompanied by two phrases attributed to Marx, and the piece also includes an atypically phrased formulation of Marx's well-known statement in *Theses on Feuerbach*, that "Philosophers have hitherto only interpreted the world in various ways; the point is to change it" (Marx [1845] 2002), which it credits to Engels ("Dug Up and Still Sound" 1914).

The paper's listings of publications available for purchase from its offices included many of the writings of Marx as well as IWW bulletins, but they also had a pamphlet version of Kropotkin's 1880 piece, "An Appeal to the Young" that had originally been published in French in *Le Révolté* ("Literature in Stock" 1914). On May 5, 1917, an article by Harry Melrose that celebrated the advent of the Russian Revolution, albeit cautioning that "If the Russian Revolution has not gained freedom from wage slavery, it should, at least, prove to the working class what can be gained by sudden concerted action" (Melrose 1917), referred also to Kropotkin's opinion that "it is only after the overthrow of the old constitution, that the real work of revolution can be said to begin" (Melrose 1917). Melrose did not cite the source of the quotation, which is *The Conquest of Bread* (Kropotkin [1906] 2011, 22).

The beginning of a piece published in *Direct Action* on May 15, 1915 written by someone identified as "Ajax" noted at its beginning that "Property's robbery (Proudhon)," again using an unfamiliar format for a well-known quotation that perhaps suggests Ajax's awareness of the anarchist thinker was based only on what he or she had heard someone say. Ajax did not discuss Proudhon's ideas any further, apart from saying that Marx's opinion, which the article was mainly interested in endorsing, "confirms" the theories of Proudhon and Henry George (Ajax 1915). In another article, with the title, "Sabotage," Walker C. Smith (1914) had earlier written in the pages of *Direct Action* somewhat tentatively:

> "Property is robbery," said Proudhon. If this means that reverence for "property rights" is the basis of all exploitation, then Proudhon was right.
>
> SMITH 1914

On January 15, 1915, the paper included a skeptical reference to Bakunin: "One "Direct Action" in the hands of a man who has paid for it, will do more good than fourteen philosophers discussing the referenda and Michael Bakunin" (Untitled 1915), suggesting the authors might be more interested in elaborating their own theories than those most commonly identified with an anarchist perspective, and again indicating only a very tentative familiarity with the subject matter. On May 1 of the same year ("Michael Bakounine: In 1868" 1915), however, an extensive quotation from a Bakunin essay from the December 19, 1868 issue of *Égalité* was included in the IWW publication, although the title of the piece was not given: it is "Bourgeois Socialism," which, interestingly, had been reprinted in February 1915, in the London-based anarchist journal, *Freedom* (Bakunin 1915), and this was perhaps the Australian author's source. On July 7, 1917, *Direct Action* included a quotation from Voltairine de Cleyre that for many today will retain its inspirational quality:

> Make no laws whatever concerning speech, and speech will be free; so soon as you make a declaration on paper that speech shall be free, you will have a hundred lawyers proving that "freedom does not mean abuse, nor liberty license"; and they will define and define freedom out of existence. Let the guarantee of free speech be in everyman's determination to use it, and we shall have no need of paper declarations. On the other hand, so long as the people do not care to exercise their freedom, those who wish to tyrannize will so do; for tyrants are active and ardent, and will devote themselves in the name of any number of gods, religious and otherwise, to put shackles upon sleeping men.
>
> DE CLEYRE 1909, 390, 1917

Its source is the second installment of de Cleyre's essay, "Anarchism and American Traditions," which was published in two parts in Emma Goldman's publication, *Mother Earth*. Interestingly, although it otherwise printed the quoted passage as it appeared in 1909, *Direct Action* deleted its title and the first two words of the paragraph, which had begun, "Anarchism says." (De Cleyre 1909, 390). Probably not too much should be made of this, but in the light of Cain's (1993, 107) point noted above that *Direct Action* "rarely discussed syndicalism in its journal," here two explanatory references that would help the reader situate de Cleyre's argument – "Anarchism says" and "Anarchism and American Traditions" – were left out.

Perhaps in the case of Tom Barker, this commitment to the IWW cause made him more amenable to floating around between different ideological perspectives, abandoning some, such as Christianity and the Red Feds, but open to other influences, so that, while not officially joining up with the Soviet Communist Party, he was able to work for the Kuzbas project, which others dismissed as just an example of capitalist exploitation of workers. Despite his fiery IWW past, he could serve as an elected representative of the British Labour Party and – once again, drawing attention by doing something outlandish such as raising the Red Flag on the roof of the town hall – expect to create a sensation. Yet that determination to be controversial, a characteristic that also defined J.B. King, Paul Freeman, and other members of the IWW, may to some extent have undermined his chances of success. As Shor comments:

> The language deployed by King and the Wobblies, especially in the campaign to free Barker, was used against them by the state and federal governments to prosecute and repress the IWW leadership.
> SHOR 2005, 162, fn 31

The tremendous variety of activities at which Tom Barker was able to demonstrate his rhetorical and organizational skills, and the multiplicity of places in which he managed to cause trouble for bosses and police and, in particular, for politicians and other "authorities," dismissing with a few sarcastic words their power and any claims they might employ to justify its exercise, indicate that, notwithstanding any wobbling exhibited here or there, he may still have been the finest of the soldiers of the IWW, the greatest Wobbly of all.

CHAPTER 5

Kōtoku, Shūsui: the Ringleader

On June 22, 1908, anarchist and Marxist demonstrators, many of whom were intellectuals, with some being Buddhist priests, gathered to celebrate the release from prison of one of their number, Yamaguchi, Koken. [Japanese persons are identified here with their family names being given first, followed by a comma; that practice is not followed with respect to non-Japanese persons who have names of Japanese origin.] A group of thirty-eight marched through Tokyo carrying three red flags, each of which bore a slogan celebrating their perspectives: "Anarchy" (*Museifushugi*), "Revolution" (*Kakumei*), and "Anarchist Communism" (*Museifu Kyōsanshugi*). The demonstrators were soon arrested and their banners seized. This event became known as the *Akahata jiken*, the Red Flag Incident. The apparent commitment to a Kropotkinist version of anarchism displayed on one of the flags reflected the ideological development of Kōtoku, Shūsui, who was not himself present, and of other, younger radicals who were influenced by him, and who made use of the protest to emphasize the extent to which they felt more radicalized than some of their socialist allies. Among this faction were Arahata, Kanson; Ōsugi, Sakae; and Yamakawa, Hitoshi, who now received relatively harsh sentences of imprisonment of approximately two years; Sakai, Toshihiko, who was not a participant, but who was assumed to be the protest's leader, was given a similar sentence. Ironically, their incarceration saved the four of them from becoming involved in the conspiracy that came to be known as the High Treason Incident, which would lead to Kōtoku's execution (Chang 1976, 97; Crump 1980, 413, 1993, 25, 31; Mackie 1994, 140–141; Sen 1918, 132–133; Sievers 1969, 100–101, 102; Tsuzuki 1966, 35–36; Vizetelly 1911, 291).

Those arrested were charged under Article 16 of the *Chian keisatsu hō* (Public Order and Police Law) of 1900. Two female colleagues of the apprehended demonstrators, Kanno, Suga (or Kanno, Sugako), and Kamikawa, Matsuko, visited the police headquarters to find out what had happened, where they witnessed some of their colleagues being beaten by police and were themselves arrested, a similar experience to that of persons elsewhere who visited authorities to ask after anarchists, such as Albert Parsons following the Haymarket Tragedy in Chicago in 1886, a tactical error which led to his eventual execution, and Marie-Anne "Marianne" Michel, the mother of Louise Michel, after the collapse of the Paris Commune in 1871 (Shone 2013, 61, 2019, 61). Kanno and Kamikawa, who admitted they were anarchists, were acquitted, although they had spent two months in jail waiting for the trial; two other women, Ōsuka, Satoko and Ogure, "Rei" Reiko, received suspended sentences for their involvement in the protest (Hane 1988, 53–54; Mackie 1994, 140–141; Sievers 1983, 155, 221 fn 20; Uchiyama 1908, 5, 5 fn 8).

Following the trial, police began an intensive campaign of surveillance of socialist and anarchist leaders. Kōtoku himself found his house routinely surrounded by four police officers who questioned each of his visitors about why they were there (CIRA-Nippon 1975; Notehelfer [1971b] 2010, 162; Sen 1918, 133–134; Sievers 1983, 221 fn 26; "Socialism in Japan: Kotoku's Work" 1911; Tierney 2015, 123–124). More importantly, the Red Flag affair caused Prime Minister Saionji, Kinmochi's cabinet to resign, having been seen by its critics, who included many newspaper editors and journalists, as too lenient in dealing with radical elements. As a result, Katsura, Taro was returned to power, and his pursuit of a more aggressive posture included a ban on using words such as "strike," "labor union," "socialism," and "revolution." Radical newspapers and meetings were themselves also prohibited (Notehelfer [1971b] 2010, 159; Tierney 2015, 123). For example, *Sekai fujin* [Women of the World], which was edited by Fukuda, "Hide" Hideko and contained contributions from Kōtoku, was soon fined and prevented from publishing following its inclusion of a piece called "Saisho no teki" ["The First Enemy"] written by someone writing under the name Kakuda, Meisaku, an appellation that suggested the word for revolution, *Kakumei* (Kaku ... Mei) (Horimoto 1999, 3–4; Sievers 1983, 126; Yang 2017, 78).

The same year, dismayed by the government's reaction to the Red Flag Incident, the Buddhist priest, Uchiyama, Gudō, published *In Commemoration Of Their Imprisonment: Anarcho-Communism* [*Nyūgoku Kinen: Museifu Kyōsan*], a "booklet to commemorate the imprisonment" (Uchiyama 1908, 5) of the anarchists in question, in which he took criticism of the Japanese emperor to a new extreme, denying the latter's god-like status and authority to rule, describing the ruling class as "vermin that sucks people's blood" (Uchiyama 1908, 2; Crump's translation (1980, 372) is similar):

> To destroy the present government and establish a free country without an emperor is not treason but an action appropriate to heroes who love justice. Why is this so? The boss of this government, the emperor, is not the son of a god, as the schoolteachers deceivingly tell you. The ancestors of the present emperor came from a remote corner of Kyushu; murdering and stealing.
> UCHIYAMA 1908, 4

Back in 1905 in a letter to the Brisbane socialist paper, the *Worker*, Shūsui had drawn attention to the fact that use of words such as "revolution" and "strike" in Japan was enough to cause police to close down a public meeting, complaining:

> In this respect the Japanese Government is certainly fifty years or a century behind the Governments of Western Europe. The ruling power of Japan is, on this point at least, no less barbarous than that of Russia. The Csar is merely the head of the religious organisation of his country, but the Mikado pretends to be GOD HIMSELF.
> KŌTOKU 1905b

Eventually, the intensive police scrutiny of dissident activity led to the "*Taigyaku jiken*" [High Treason Incident, which has also been referred to as the Great Treason Affair and the Lèse Majesté Incident], in which 26 radicals would be tried and convicted, all but two of whom would initially be sentenced to death, with twelve of them eventually receiving life imprisonment, the remaining twelve being hanged. In addition to Kōtoku and his erstwhile significant other, Kanno, who identified with Sophia Perovskaya, one of the 1881 assassins of Tsar Alexander II, and the aforementioned Uchiyama; Furukawa, Rikisaku; Matsuo, Uichita; Miyashita, Takichi; Morichika, Umpei; Naruishi, Heishirō; Niimi, Uichirō; Niimura, Tadao; Ōishi, Seinosuke; and Okumiya, Kenshi were all executed. The concept of *taigyaku* [High Treason] had not previously been utilized, and was only introduced into the legal system in 1908 (Crump 1980, 375; Hane 1988, 55; Tierney 2015, 70).

Police in Matsumoto, in Nagano Prefecture, an inland area of Honshū, discovered that Miyashita, a sawmill worker, was manufacturing dynamite, but initially responded only by warning him to abandon anarchism and bomb-making. They continued to monitor Miyashita's activities, and, with the assistance of his friend, Shimizu, Taichiro, who betrayed him, discovered that he was continuing to pursue his revolutionary activity. In fact, he had sent some cans containing explosives to Kōtoku who, having second thoughts about the project, returned them. On May 25, 1910, Miyashita was arrested along with Niimura and Furukawa. Other arrests followed, including that of Kōtoku about a week later, Uchiyama and Kanno being already in jail serving prior sentences. Kanno and some of the other plotters saw their plan, an attempt to kill the Japanese emperor that was not so far fully developed, as a way to demonstrate to the public that, as Uchiyama had written, he was not divine, but was merely another human being. Kōtoku, on the other hand, unlike Kanno, who remained actively involved, had removed himself from the plot, being convinced that assassination would, far from assisting the radicals to make their case, actually undermine their political goals. She remained enthusiastic about carrying out the plan, hoping to emulate Perovskaya (Crump 1980, 377; Filler 2009, 87, fn 17; Hane 1988, 55; "How They Plotted to Kill Emperor" 1911; Notehelfer [1971b] 2010, 191; Sievers 1969, 104–105, 1983, 157; Victoria 1996, 134–135). Kōtoku's withdrawal thus raises the question: If someone leaves a conspiracy and then stays silent about its existence, do they thereby become innocent; or, on the other hand, was the Japanese government justified in still considering him to be its ringleader, since his anarchist theories had exacted an educative influence upon his colleagues who continued to take part? (Sievers 1969, 110). Moreover, does it make any difference if the conspiracy in question was, as Filler (2009, 61) notes, "[a] loose-knit plot"? For a contemporary observer of the ensuing trial, Kōtoku was "le seul "intellectual" de ce groupe de conjurés" (Maybon 1911, 494) [the only "intellectual" of this group of conspirators] implying also that his impact on the activities of others might be very powerful. The Ministry of Foreign Affairs filed its paperwork relating to the plot as "The Case of the Conspiracy of the Socialist, Kōtoku Denjirō [Kōtoku, Shūsui], and Twenty-Five Others" ["*Shakaishugisha Kōtoku Denjirō hoka nijūgomei no inbō ikken*"], suggesting that its officials saw Kōtoku as their most dangerous opponent; unfortunately, many details of the case have been lost or destroyed (Shone 2019, 195; Susumu 2013, 27; Tierney 2015, 5).

The attempted assassination of the Japanese emperor was a crime for which the Constitution allowed a possible sentence of death, even if a suspect had only an "intention" to harm a member of the royal household, which, for Vu (2022, 171) means that "Kotoku and several other anarchists were arrested for a thought-crime." Indeed, the trial, looked at from a contemporary perspective, appears particularly flawed, and to have reflected the government's abhorrence of socialist and anarchist theories that they perceived as being a threat to Japan's future (Tierney 2015, 125; Ueda 2008, 50; Victoria 1996, 135), rendering it thus a political enterprise rather than a legitimate legal proceeding, much like the prosecution in Australia of the alleged perpetrators of "Barker's fires" that were discussed in the previous chapter. For Lévy (2002, 65), the fate of the alleged anarchist plotters was to some extent contingent upon the absence of a noble Dreyfus type of character to point out its unfairness and inappropriateness. For fellow-socialist and one-time Kōtoku ally, Sen, Katayama, a Marxist whose original name was Yabuki, Sugatarō, there were many violations of due process committed by police and the courts:

> Now, these comrades were tried, mind you, in secret in the first and in the final court, from whose verdict there is no way to make appeal. And when condemned to death, they were strangled to death right after the verdict

was given, only three full days being allowed them instead of the usual sixty or more days. Even their remains were not yielded to their relatives. Why did they hasten in this particular case? We do not yet know the exact reasons. But I know that the court used false telegrams freely in order to compel the accused to confess.

SEN 1918, 138–139

On the other hand, Nobutaka Ike (1944, 224–225) disputes Katayama's perspective, pointing out that Kōtoku had once shared Kanno's desire to kill the emperor in order to show that the latter was human, and he may never have genuinely abandoned that cause:

It is true that verbally, at least, Kōtoku deplored violence; but then so did Bakunin who not only actively promoted numerous uprisings, but who also indirectly inspired some to undertake 'propaganda by the deed.'

IKE 1944, 225

Consequently, Ike continues, since assassination would be compatible with Kōtoku's commitment to direct action, the trial therefore needed to be kept secret.

Ike (222) also suggests that the era of anarchist influence in Japan might have soon petered out, but ironically the notoriety of Kōtoku that was achieved when his activities burst into historical significance due to the High Treason Incident meant that awareness of its doctrines would continue and spread. Nonetheless, in its aftermath, even the words for socialism and anarchism became difficult for Japanese publishers to print. In the case of Oscar Wilde's 1891 essay, "The Soul of Man under Socialism," the title was translated as "Wilde's Conception of Society" and as "Wilde's Philosophy" by the editors of *Kindai shisō* [Modern Thoughts], both of whom had been imprisoned following the Red Flag Incident: Kōtoku's protégé, Ōsugi, Sakae, and Kanno's common law husband, Arahata, Kanson. Over the next two decades, use of Kōtoku's name, and attempts to study his work, were similarly frowned upon and could potentially be dangerous. Attempts to dissect the prosecution and outcome of the trial of Kōtoku, Kanno, and their colleagues, or debate the merits of the imperial system, were taboo until the end of the Second World War when many changes became possible, some deriving from the United States' occupation of Japan. Release of all the surviving trial records only occurred in 1963 (Asukai 1978, 123; Chen 2011, 171–172; Crump 1998, 19; Tierney 2015, 71).

Even so, awareness of Kōtoku's life, philosophy, and fate persisted during the decades of its proscription. For instance, development of the poet and advocate of free love, Takamure, Itsue's (1894–1964) growing commitment to anarcho/a-feminist principles was influenced by knowledge of the *Taigyaku jiken* because some of those arrested had come from her own home environment of the Kumamoto Prefecture. Gradually, following a period when many socialists and anarchists withdrew to the countryside in order to draw less attention from the police and government, a reappearance of radical activity emerged after the end of the First World War (Carter 1982, 1–3, 31–32; Crump 1993, 30, 1998, 15–16; Hane 2015, 11; Tsurumi 1985, 13).

Trials and internment of anarchists and other presumed terrorists have often been conducted in less than open circumstances, and in ways that have not followed the traditional rules prescribed under law. The Wobblies in particular were victims of this tactic. As noted in the previous chapter, the trial of the various associates and allies of Tom Barker led to years of protest and in every instance to eventual acquittal and/or reduction of sentence, bringing the police and the court system in New South Wales into substantial disrepute. Similarly, some of the many accused (though never tried in an actual court) prisoners at the penal colony in Guantánamo Bay, such as Abd al-Rahim al-Nashiri, had been tortured by the Central Intelligence Agency (CIA) to obtain confessions before they arrived. Incarcerated without trial in a course of action that began on January 11, 2002, they were denied due process for base political motives and the convenience of government, rather than due to any concern for justice or fairness. Indeed, the Military Commissions Act of 2006 even took away the right of those at Guantánamo to seek *habeas corpus* review, although the US Supreme Court, in *Boumediene v. Bush* (2008), found this to be unconstitutional (Bayoumi 2022; Douglas 2013).

Israel's own version of Guantánamo, Camp 1391, keeps Palestinian, Lebanese, and other Arab prisoners who have not been convicted in court in solitary confinement at its secret facility that is erased from maps and photographs, while details of their whereabouts are also hidden from its detainees. At Camp 1391, concealed inside a military base in the north of the country, there have been many accusations of torture and rape of prisoners, and access to the Red Cross, lawyers, and elected members of the government is routinely denied (Elfström and Malmgren 2005; McGreal 2003). Why are those accused of terrorism, some of whom are often just assumed to be culpable, not brought to trial using the normal procedures, since if their guilt is so obvious, it would be reasonable to expect that conviction would ensue? Instead, a less than ideal process can result in both innocent and guilty people being found responsible, as though truth is unimportant, undermining the rule of law and confidence in its evenhandedness.

Also, it is interesting to consider the manner in which those accused of radical or terrorist killings have been held in custody in recent years, for example, subject to the "enhanced interrogation techniques" employed by the CIA, made to sit in stress positions, waterboarded, or forced to wear bags over their heads, as though their blameworthiness has been convincingly proven by government directive (Wofford 2014). In the past, this was not always the case. The sense that political dissidents, notwithstanding any violent activity in which they have been involved, maintain a right to be handled in a civilized way is no doubt unpopular, but perhaps it says much for the conduct of a society when it is able to achieve fair treatment of its opponents and enemies. Those accused in the Haymarket Tragedy were able to gather in their cells with reporters and friends. In the case of Kōtoku, he was allowed to meet his mother after he had been sentenced to be hanged – she would die before the sentence on her son was carried out – and reportedly she told him, "Die my son, like the Samurai of old" ("An Affecting Scene: Japanese Conspirators Sentenced" 1911; Sako 1911a, 382, 1911b). Although that permission did not allow them to meet in private, it was a much more humanitarian gesture than many other aspects of the trial process. None of the High Treason Incident convictions have ever been overturned, the last of those who was imprisoned, Sakamoto, Seima, having failed to convince the legal system that errors had been made (Tierney 2015, 5).

Beyond the world of the formally incarcerated, recent years have seen many "security" improvisations in the lives of ordinary people in the United States, Japan, and elsewhere, particularly in regard to their workplaces and travel arrangements. Routine background investigations now delay hirings, while marijuana and other drug convictions can render people permanently unemployable. Use of lie detectors, hand searching of workers when they go to lunch and leave at the end of the day, electronic surveillance, and regular drug testing have changed the nature of the business world, so that employees are often now routinely regarded as suspects, a development that has changed the nature of society as a whole. It is hardly surprising, then, that some citizens in a burgeoning police state, creation of which no voters have been asked to approve, may feel that they no longer live in a democracy, that they are no longer effectively its citizens, and that perhaps they ought to consider fighting back.

For the original trial of Kōtoku and the others accused of being involved in the *Taigyaku jiken*, which took place from December 10 to December 29, 1910, a special court was inaugurated, with the intention being to hold its proceedings in private, the accused not being allowed to have legal representation. Following criticism of this set-up, the formula was revised, with the public and the press allowed to be present, but only when the accused were being questioned; defense attorneys were permitted, but they had little time to prepare. Visitors were searched, and between thirty and forty members of the police were also stationed around the courtroom. A panel of seven justices was appointed, the chief judge being Tsuru, Joichirō. The trial and its conclusions were then reviewed and confirmed in a second process by the Supreme Court in January (Anderson 2010, 383–384; "Emperor of Japan: Alleged Conspiracy Plot" 1910; "Jack London And Others Protest Execution Of 26 Japanese" 1910; Kanno [1911] 1988, 58; Sievers 1983, 139; "Socialism in Japan: Kotuku's Work" 1911; Tierney 2015, 124–125). In her diary, which she wrote while imprisoned, Kanno revealed that she had doubted the ability of the trial court to conduct a process that was fair:

> I boarded the prison carriage just before noon. From the window of the carriage I could see in the dim sunlight saber-bearing figures solemnly standing guard en route. They seemed to presage the verdicts of the trial, and I waited impatiently for the court proceedings to start at 1:00 P.M.
> KANNO [1911] 1988, 58

At the conclusion of the second trial, the chief justice of the supreme court announced that, following a completely fair investigation process, the guilt of those on trial had been convincingly proven ("An Affecting Scene: Japanese Conspirators Sentenced" 1911; "Anarchists Given Death Sentences" 1911).

Despite its revised approach, many of the details of the trial court process were nevertheless kept secret. However, for some commentators, notably F.G. Notehelfer, the author of the first major work in English about the life of Kōtoku, Shūsui, the lack of openness is not disturbing:

> The critical attitude towards the closed trial which many contemporary scholars have adopted should perhaps be judged more precisely within the historical context in which the trial was held. There was certainly nothing illegal about the decision of the court to hold the trial *in camera*.
> NOTEHELFER [1971b] 2010, 186

Notehelfer (189) continues that, since there had been no actual attempt to kill the emperor, the case would focus on the intent of Kōtoku and the other accused, some of whom had admittedly been involved in procuring explosives; given the wording of the recent law, actual participation in violence would not be necessary to obtain conviction. However, Notehelfer's perspective raises the question whether "trials" conducted in Syrian jails in the present day, utilizing bureaucratic procedures and filing paperwork following extensive torture of prisoners, and often succeeded by execution, can be justified because the victims are opponents of President Bashar Hafez al-Assad, who has made the law (Wainwright 2016). More typical is the evaluation of Elison that Kōtoku died not for his intent, but for his anarchist beliefs. He writes:

> The ensuing trial utilized dubious and inconclusive evidence, and resulted in the execution of twelve "conspirators," including the purported ringleader Kōtoku. Miyashita's plans had been heavily influenced (if not inspired) by Kanno Sugako, who was Kōtoku's mistress. Kōtoku's own involvement may, cautiously, be described as peripheral at best.
> ELISON 1967, 437, fn 2

In an article in the Vermont-based Italian-language anarchist newspaper, *Cronaca Sovversiva*, Alexandra Kropotkin, the daughter of Peter Kropotkin, pointed out the unfairness of the supposedly legal process:

> Arrestati, Kotoku e i suoi compagni, gettati in un carcere, torturati, esaminati in un sembiante d'istruttoria, condannati da un tribunale di eccezione, senza neppure le garanzie costituzionali, privati di ogni valida difesa, furono messi a morte come si trattasse di banditi volgari, peggio, come fossero dei cani lebbrosi.
> A. KROPOTKIN 1911

> [Arrested, Kotoku and his companions, thrown into a prison, tortured, examined with a semblance of investigation, sentenced by an extraordinary court, without even the constitutional guarantees, deprived of any valid defense, were put to death as if it were a question of vulgar bandits – worse, as if they were leprous dogs.]

At the time of the Great Treason Affair and the executions of those convicted, there was tremendous interest around the world in what was taking place. A report sympathetic to the convicted "socialists" in the *Tacoma Times* reported the hangings in this way:

> Disregarding a stream of protests from all over the world, the Japanese government today wiped out, by means of the gallows, the lives of Denjiro Kotoku, his mistress, Suga Kanno, and ten other Japanese socialists convicted by star chamber sessions of the secret court of having conspired against the life of the mikado.
> "12 Jap Socialists Executed" 1911

At the time, George Madgwick, the secretary of the South Australian Socialist Party, wrote a letter that was printed in two Adelaide newspapers criticizing the trial and what he saw as its purpose, attempting also to explain that Kōtoku was a decent person who should not have been executed. In 1909, Madgwick had been involved in a dispute over whether Tom Mann should be able to give a speech at the city's Central Market, a location that required a permit, which the Adelaide mayor, Alderman Frank Johnson, had not approved because Mann, who, as pointed out in the previous chapter, had been an organizer for the Victorian Labor Party, left the organization, earning him the disapproval of Adelaide Labor leaders ("Mann and the Mayor" 1909; "Mr. Tom Mann in Adelaide" 1909; Rancie 1911; "Socialists Blocked" 1909). With respect to the alleged Japanese plot, Madgwick now also came to the defense of Kōtoku, asking:

> If they were guilty of "conspiring to kill the Mikado" why was it necessary to have a secret trial? Socialists throughout the world know that "conspiring to kill" is a trumped-up charge which the Japanese Government is using as an excuse to suppress the entire working class movement in that country. Kotoku's real crime was that he translated into the Japanese language the writings of revolutionary Socialists such as Karl Marx, also Leo Tolstoy, Peter Kropotkin, and others, and that he always stood on the side of the working class as against the ruling class.
> MADGWICK 1911a, 1911b

As the trial and executions were reported around the world, the suspects were described both as socialists and anarchists, often a competition between editors with regard to the way Kōtoku and his allies were to be denigrated, matched by attempts of similarly inclined radicals to claim them as being like themselves. In New Zealand, the *Gisborne Times* described the event as "the trial of the participants in the recently discovered anarchist conspiracy against the Throne" ("An Affecting Scene: Japanese Conspirators Sentenced" 1911), while the *San Francisco Call*, a newspaper based in a city where Kōtoku had spent several months and engaged in a variety of activities with the local area population, referred to "the investigation leading to the arrest of the anarchists" ("Anarchists Given Death Sentences" 1911). The New York *Sun* noted that while Kōtoku was "an avowed anarchist," its significance "means nothing to the mass of the populace, which knows nothing about anarchy and would consider a red flag merely an ornament to be carried on a pole at holiday time" ("Kotoku, Japan's Anarchist" 1911). In Emma Goldman's publication, *Mother Earth*, fellow anarchist Hippolyte Havel unabashedly made the identification clear:

> The government of the Mikado has evidently played what it thought a trump card by characterizing the condemned as Communist Anarchists. But it has merely succeeded in proving itself barbaric and brutal; nay, more – very stupid. We have never asserted the contrary regarding our condemned comrades; indeed, in our original appeal we clearly stated that Denjiro Kotoku was an Anarchist, known in Japan as the leader of the "Kropotkinists."
>
> HAVEL 1911, 354–355

Kōtoku himself identified the plotters as anarchists, suggesting a reason for the confusion during the trial and elsewhere:

> It must be stated ... that the views held by us anarchists concerning revolution, the character of our movement, and other such matters have not come clear at all, not in preliminary interrogations nor in the public prosecutor's examination. Rather, the facts have been subjected to guesses, twists, and interpretations, until the truth about this incident has, I fear, been completely obscured.
>
> KŌTOKU [1910b] 1967, 468

The *Mataura Ensign*, a paper in New Zealand, referred to Kōtoku as "the Socialist leader" but noted also that "he published translations of the works of Kropotkin, a leading light of Anarchism, and other advocates of Anarchistic principles" ("Executed: the Japanese Plotters" 1911). On the other hand, the Sydney, Australia-based publication, *Truth*, presented the ideological affiliation very differently, denying any association between Kōtoku and anarchism:

> Dr. Kotoku, "the Tolstoy of the East," a most distinguished scholar, and the leader of the Militant Socialist movement in Japan, has been executed under the guise that he is an "Anarchist."
>
> "The Jap Socialists: Murder of Dr. Kotoku" 1911

Similarly. the *New Zealand Herald*, spoke of "Dr. Kotoku, the Socialist leader" ("Japanese Plotters: Twelve Executed" 1911). For other commentators, Kōtoku's translation and publication of Marx and Engels' *Communist Manifesto* in 1904 was a key element in the reaction against him and his cohorts by the Japanese government (Ike 1957, 242–243; W.R.W. 1911). An editorial in *Mother Earth* expressed this concern:

> His "crime" consists in spreading radical ideas, and in translating the works of Karl Marx, Leo Tolstoy, Peter Kropotkin, and Michael Bakunin. As a leader of the "Left" in the social revolutionary movement of Japan, he was called the "head of the Kropotkinists." We are convinced that the charge of conspiracy against the Emperor is false.
>
> "Observations and Comments" 1910

An editorial in the Spanish newspaper, *El Pais*, saw the real plot as having been the attempt to fabricate an assassination attempt on the emperor:

> El gobierno japonés temió el despertar de su pueblo y decidió suprimir de cualquier inodo á los abnegados propagandistas.
>
> "La barbarie japonesa" 1911

> [The Japanese government feared the awakening of its people and decided to suppress the self-sacrificing propagandists in any way.]

In much the same fashion, the *Hawaiian Star* emphasized that those of a socialist persuasion in California believed the trial to be an attack on those who were not anarchists, but who had engaged in "merely the translation of Socialist literature into the Japanese language and the attempt to carry on a Socialist propaganda" ("Jack London And Others Protest Execution Of 26 Japanese" 1910). In an editorial in the West Virginia paper, the *Wheeling Majority*, publisher Walter B. Hilton defended Kōtoku in no uncertain terms, comparing what he described as the latter's murder with that of Francisco Ferrer y Guardia, the founder of Barcelona's Escuela Moderna, whose progressive pedagogical approach was disparaged by the Catholic Church as a form of terrorism (Hilton 1911; Shone 2019, 195 fn 1):

> Kotoku is described as a anarchist, sometimes, and at others as an [sic] Socialist. In our conception of the words, he was neither. He could hardly, from the occidental view, be classed as an extremist. We would regard him here as a reformer. Indeed, the capitalist system is not developed sufficiently in Japan, and the slavish conditions of the feudal system still too prominent to admit of a Socialist agitation or an understanding of Socialism. ... Kotoku taught the truth that human beings, born into this world without their consent, were entitled to bread if they were willing to work for it – and this truth is always unpalatable to those who have more bread than they can eat and who never worked for a single loaf.
>
> HILTON 1911

To some extent, details of the trial and its conclusion remain unclear, and the executions were kept quiet until they occurred. A report in the Brisbane newspaper, the *Daily Standard*, a decade later indicates that Kanno was executed a day following the hanging of the men:

> What the course was the reader will know from the fact that on January 24, 1911, 11 men (including Kotoku) were executed, and the following day a woman (Kanno Suga, a prominent Anarchist Communist) suffered the same fate for complicity in a bomb plot.
> "Labor Movement in Japan" 1921

Similarly, Racel points out that "Kanno was executed on 25 January 1911, one day after the male conspirators" (Racel 2011, 246 fn 16), as Tierney (2015, 125) confirms. Meanwhile, while Bowen Raddeker (1988, 10) in one place writes that "she was hanged along with eleven of her comrades, some of whom were socialists or state socialists, some of whom were anarchists," elsewhere she points out that:

> As a woman she could be, and was, lawfully executed. This was together with eleven male comrades, anarchists and other socialists – or, not quite together, since Suga was garrotted separately from them, one day later.
> BOWEN RADDEKER 2002

However, this is not the picture to be gleaned from initial wire-based accounts, which reported that Kanno died at the same time as Shūsui. ("Jap Anarchists Executed" 1911; "Japanese Anarchists: Executions Carried Out" 1911; "Japanese Executions" 1911). In some cases, descriptions of the two former lovers dying together presented a range of apparent detail. The *Tacoma Times*, for instance, reported as follows:

> The most affecting incident, according to one of the officials who saw the socialists die, was when Kotuku and the little woman who had shared his fortunes to death, stood on the trap together. No black cap is used in the executions in Japan, and the pair, unlike the others condemned, were permitted to stand face to face onthe trap.
> "Courage!" said Kotuku as the rope was adjusted. "We die for liberty." Suga Kanna [sic] spoke no word, but she smiled, and with their eyes fastened on each other and utterly disregarded the grim surroundings, the two plunged downward to death.
> "12 Jap Socialists Executed." 1911

The subtitle of a report in the *Daily Capital Journal*, an Oregon paper, said that "Suga Kanno, the Only Woman in the Lot, Was Hanged Along With Her Lover, They Smiling [sic] at Each Other as the Ropes Were Tightened Around Their Necks." ("Twelve Japanese Socialists are Hanged at Tokio Japan Today" 1911). This more colorful version of what had happened may have contributed to the notoriety of Shūsui and Kanno.

1   Kanno, Suga, "Wife," and Other Wives

When newspapers around the world reported the *Taigyaku jiken* and Kōtoku's demise in the early days of 1911, Kanno, Suga, the woman he had been involved with both romantically and in his revolutionary endeavors, was often referred to as his "wife" ("An Affecting Scene: Japanese Conspirators Sentenced" 1911; "Anarchists in Japan: Short Shrift for the Prisoners" 1911) although that was not technically the case, since they were never officially married, giving their relationship common law status. Sievers (1983, 141, 151) writes that Kanno was only ever legally married to Kamiya, Fukutarō, for approximately two years commencing in 1898, with the eventual divorce taking place in 1902. Even the report in the *San Francisco Call* that said "[t]he wife of Kotoku was the only woman in the band" ("Anarchists Given Death Sentences" 1911) seems by implication to lessen the extent of Kanno's participation in the plot, but in reality, she was one of its leaders, while Kōtoku had gradually withdrawn from the ideas that it embodied. Although she was acquitted of the Red Flag Incident charges, Kanno's frustration with the weeks she spent in jail following that arrest and the contemporaneous discovery that she was suffering from tuberculosis, drove her to want to commit "un acte de violence qui ferait trembler la nation entière sur ses fondations symboliques" (Godin 2022) [an act of violence that would shake the entire nation to its symbolic foundations]. While norms of propriety in many locations at the time may have suggested to writers the benefit of making no reference to "common law," the expectation that women should adopt a submissive role quite probably influenced the portrayal of her as an also-ran, rather than as one of the masterminds of the project. In the *Heraldo de Madrid*, for instance, a report pictured Kanno as Kōtoku's eager assistant:

> El aima do la conspiración era el célebre Kotoku Denjiro, ex profesor y ex periodista, entusiasta de las doctrinas de Kropotkine. Las persecuciones de que era objeto hicieron de Kotoku un apóstol; su amante, Sugano Suga [Kanno], le ayudaba con ardor.
>
> "El anarquismo japonés" 1911

[The soul of the conspiracy was the celebrated Kōtoku Denjiro, a former professor and former journalist, enthusiastic about Kropotkin's doctrines. The persecutions to which he was subjected made Kōtoku an apostle; his lover, Sugano Suga [Kanno], ardently assisted him.]

Vizetelly's book, *The Anarchists: Their Faith & Their Record*, however, reported that he "lived with a woman who passed as his wife, but who was legally the wife of another person" (Vizetelly 1911, 290) and referred to "Kotoku and his mistress" (292). Kanno was additionally romantically involved with fellow-radical, Arahata, Kanson, who had also been imprisoned for participating in the Red Flag Incident. This exposed Kōtoku to criticism from socialist colleagues for linking up with her to the detriment of Arahata, and negative reports about the affair, which began in June 1909, were published in Japanese newspapers (Notehelfer [1971b] 2010, 174; Sievers 1983, 156; Tsuzuki 1966, 36). Sievers writes:

> What Kanno had in common with other literary women who were her contemporaries was a sense of outrage about the sexual double standard, social constraints on female sexuality generally, and the hypocrisy of the family system – something these women shared with many of the male writers of their day.
> SIEVERS 1999, 202

Like her contemporaries, Victoria Woodhull, Lois Waisbrooker, Elizabeth Cady Stanton, Emma Goldman, Margaret Sanger, Voltairine de Cleyre, and Lucy Parsons, Kanno also argued that women were, due to the nature of traditional marriage, slaves, pointing out that "For us women, the most urgent task at hand is to develop our self-awareness. In accordance with longstanding customs, we are seen as a form of property. Women in Japan are in a state of slavery" (Hane [1982] 2003, 247; Kanno [1911] 1988, 52–53).

Another Madrid publication, *La Correspondencia de España*, saw Kanno as being under the influence of Kōtoku, but also credited her with having developed the scheme:

> Esta ciudadana ... había entablado relaciones amorosas con Kotoku, y éste convirtióla á su ideas extremas. ... Durante su encierro imaginó matar al Soberano, y, una vez en libertad, comunicó su plan á Kotoku.
> "¿Han sido ya ejecutados les terroristas japoneses?" 1911

[This citizen ... had entered into a love affair with Kōtoku, and she converted him to her extreme ideas. ... During her confinement she imagined killing the Sovereign, and, once released, she communicated her plan to Kōtoku.]

Kōtoku's first wife became Kōtoku, Asako when they married in 1896; she was seventeen and he was twenty-six. Her original family name is not known, but she had a samurai warrior household background. The marriage having apparently been arranged by his mother and Asako's parents, he had been impressed by a photograph of her, but when he saw her in the flesh he was disappointed. Kōtoku then behaved in dishonorable and disingenuous way. After two months, he pleased her by suggesting she should pay a visit to her family, taking her to the train station, but then mailing her a letter of divorce (CIRA-Nippon 1975; Notehelfer [1971b] 2010, 36, 37; Tierney 2015, 24; Yada 1972, 156).

Kōtoku, Shūsui's second wife was Morooka (or Morōka), Chiyoko, who became Kōtoku, Chiyoko. In theory, the fact that Chiyoko, or "Chiyo," was accomplished in art and poetry, and competent in English, French, and classical Chinese, made her a more suitable partner for the highly educated Shūsui. However, he also rapidly found his new wife to be unsuitable, partly again due to her physical appearance. This time, in place of mailing a letter of divorce, he scheduled a trip to the Yoshiwara, a red light district, hoping that the fact he had consorted with prostitutes there would incite Chiyoko to divorce him. He spent a couple of days in Yoshiwara but his second wife did not abandon him, although they would eventually separate. When Kōtoku's political philosophy developed into a form of anarchism, Chiyoko disapproved, remaining committed to socialism ("Kotoku's Correspondence with Albert Johnson (Conclusion)" 1911, 286 fn **; Notehelfer [1971b] 2010, 47, 48, 166; Tierney 2015, 24, 222 fn 27).

Unsurprisingly, despite Kōtoku, Shūsui's endorsement of women's rights, some of the details of his personal life have been portrayed by modern writers as being inconsistent. However, when Notehelfer ([1971b] 2010, 166) writes that "Neither Asako nor Chiyoko, the products of a traditional upbringing, possessed the intellectual and emotional daring necessary to earn Kōtoku's respect, and consequently neither was capable of providing him with the psychological support," it may be pointed out that such rationalizations, although still utilized by marriage arrangers and admirers of matrimony today, nonetheless employ gender-based stereotypes about what is or is not appropriate. Thus those around Kōtoku who pushed him to wed two women whom he had not met on the basis of photographs and listings of so-called personal attributes can be criticized for their sexist assumptions, while Shūsui himself can be lambasted for evaluating women obsessively on the basis of their physical appearance. However, with respect to some other issues, the criticism of

Kōtoku's apparent variation on matters of gender is by no means unquestionable. Explaining the denunciation, Hane writes:

> By early 1909 he had divorced his second wife and was living with Kanno. Despite his ideological belief in equality for women, Kōtoku often treated women as mere sexual objects and was a frequenter of the brothels. Like many male reformers of this era, he saw no contradiction in his professed humanitarian ideals and his visits to, and hence support of, publicly sanctioned brothels, prewar Japan's most inhumane exploitation of impoverished young girls. In her personal life, Kanno too had affairs with a number of men.
> HANE 1988, 54

Similarly, Mackie (1994, 104, fn. 30) argues that "Kōtoku's often liberal views on women's issues in print were not matched by his private conduct." Sievers (1983, 221 fn 16) comments that "he was well known for his chauvinist attitudes toward women, but his views probably differed only in degree from those of many other men in the socialist movement." But is it appropriate to dismiss a person's written and spoken opinions in favor of women's rights by implying that the use of prostitutes, or opposition to banning prostitution, is somehow evidence of male chauvinism? Not all feminists favor restrictions on prostitution, which limit people's choices about how to live, and deny opportunity to those who have few options for obtaining an adequate living; not all see curbs on prostitution as being a solution to human trafficking. The criticism that is to be found in Hane's and Mackie's statements seems to include a supposition that women should be more limited than men in the types of sexual behavior in which they are permitted to engage, an assumption that is in contemporary society increasingly disdained, as it was by Kanno. In fact, Kōtoku himself addressed this issue in an article in *Yorozu Chōhō* [The Complete Morning Report]:

> There are people calling for the abolition of prostitution, waxing indignant over the depravity of the gentry, advocating the reform of popular customs urging that morality be improved ... and so on. Yet, it seems to me that at times like these, when money is needed even to get hold of a volume dealing with the subject of morality or to gain admission to a halfday course of lectures, all the endless chatter of their sermonising is utterly futile.
> Nobody willingly becomes a prostitute. Nobody willingly sells their honour. There is nobody who does not want popular customs to be

reformed or who does not want morality to be improved. Yet the reason why things work out differently is simply because of money.

KŌTOKU [1900] 2009, 4

Notehelfer also approaches the issue of Shūsui's morality from a different perspective:

> Most of his [Kōtoku's] biographers claim that this incident [his rejection of Asako] reflects his 'feudal' attitudes towards women and the institution of marriage. Such an assertion may not be incorrect, but it glosses over more fundamental personal problems.
>
> NOTEHELFER [1971b] 2010, 37

For many feminists, including those who were writing at the same time as Kōtoku, marriage was an institution that oppressed women, forcing them to abide by the decisions of, and be formally represented by their husbands. Thus it is unsurprising to find that Shūsui would say of himself in an article he wrote in 1907 called *"Fujin shokan"* ["Women's Jurisdiction"], that he was "in love with love, but not with marriage" (Kōtoku 1907a; Sievers 1983, 221 fn 16). Perhaps a more accurate criticism of what are seen as Kōtoku's inconsistencies in this area, and which may apply to other aspects of his life, is Notehelfer's additional comment that:

> Such behavior was not conducive to harmonious relations at home and, despite Kōtoku's stress on humanism and moral piety in his writings, one is frequently left with the impression of a man seriously lacking in human warmth.
>
> NOTEHELFER [1971b] 2010, 48

Like his colleagues, Kinoshita, Naoe and Sakai, Toshihiko, Kōtoku wrote articles about the limitations imposed on women, in particular their formal and legal exclusion from politics, and the absurdity that despite this exclusion, they were supposed to actively approve Japan's involvement in warfare and even to volunteer to work as nurses to the injured (Mackie 1994, 104, 123, 124). In 1904, Kōtoku and Sakai translated part of August Bebel's *Woman Under Socialism* (Mackie 1994, 136, fn 157).

Kōtoku approved of the Article 5 Campaign, which, by repealing Article 5 of the Public Order and Police Law of 1900, would have given women political rights. He had supported the lobbying effort in the Diet to change the law, an effort with which Kōtoku, Chiyoko was involved, but which was not supported by all women's groups. However, by 1907, Shūsui had become more of an anarchist, and now criticized that campaign in a September 1, 1907 *Sekai fujin* leader titled "Women and Socialism," and in a column called "Women's Liberation and Socialism" (Horimoto 1999, 3–4; Mackie 1994, 139; Sievers 1983, 127–132; Yang 2017, 75–76), in which he made reference to Emma Goldman's essay, "The Tragedy of Women's Liberation," where she had written:

> All these busybodies, moral detectives, jailers of the human spirit, what will they say? Until the woman has learned to defy them all, to stand firmly on her own ground and to insist upon her own unrestricted freedom, to listen to the voice of her nature, whether it call for life's greatest treasure, love for a man, or her most glorious privilege, the right to give birth to a child, she cannot call herself emancipated.
> GOLDMAN 1910, 227–228; LARGE 1977, 444

The essay would be translated and published in the Japanese Bluestockings' [Seitōsha] journal, *Seitō*, in 1913 (Large 1977, 444; Shone 2019, 189–191). Sievers writes:

> Kōtoku indicated that for women to use parliamentary tactics, as they were doing in the Article 5 campaign, was useless: working men in Europe and America had the vote, but were still treated like draft animals and slaves in the capitalist system; moreover, women had the vote in some parts of the United States, but that had certainly not freed them from bondage.
> SIEVERS 1983, 131; MACKIE 1994, 139 is similar

Nonetheless, as Mackie (1994, 139) notes, "under present conditions, the repeal of those regulations which limited women's political activities was necessary for women to participate fully in the socialist movement." Given his recent embrace of the use of direct action over legislative and interest group approaches, Kōtoku was demonstrating his commitment to that conviction in this ongoing debate between Japanese socialist factions, one which reflected the fundamental disagreement also dividing the Chicago and Detroit factions of the IWW. However, that did not mean he had turned against women's rights – just the best means to achieve them. Although Article 5 would be repealed in 1922 following a campaign by the New Women's Association [Shin fujin kyōkai], which was founded in 1919, voting and participation in political parties were still denied to women until after the Second World War (Coutts 2012, 325–326, 326 fn 3; Mackie 1997, 35–36, 57).

Born in Osaka in 1881, and the victim of a rape at the age of fifteen, Kanno's political beliefs would become more radical over the years; by 1908, she was identifying herself as an anarchist. Ironically, given her personal connections to Kōtoku, in 1903 she had written articles in support of the Fujin Kyōfūkai [Women's Moral Reform Society], expressing opposition to the legal brothels that existed in Japan. Gradually, she involved herself with Heiminsha [the Commoners' Society], which, to attract the attention of women who were not supposed to take an interest in political matters, held "academic lectures" that discussed socialist and women's rights issues. Later, Kanno became Kōtoku's secretary and started to work with him on some of his writings. By 1909, she had become the first (and last) editor of their paper, *Jiyū shisō* [Free Thought], but following the release of its first two numbers in May and June, the publication was banned and she was prosecuted, and hence she was already in prison at the time of the High Treason Incident trial ("Anarchists Given Death Sentences" 1911; Chang 1976, 97; "Freethought in Japan" 1909, 69–70; Hane 1988, 19, 51–52; Horimoto 1999, 37; Sievers 1983, 139, 156–157; "Socialism in Japan: Kotoku's Work" 1911).

As noted above, Kanno's extensive diary that she compiled while incarcerated has survived, and it has been translated into English by Mikiso Kane (Kanno [1911] 1988). From her perspective, the accused were victims rather would-be terrorists:

> I tend to get dizzy easily, so I felt a bit faint, having climbed many stairs and because of the stifling presence of the crowd in the courtroom. After I calmed down, I looked around at my fellow defendants. They were all sitting circumspectly, looking worried. They looked as if they were afraid to smile at each other. A pride of hungry lions. Their nails and teeth had been filed and smoothed down. There they sat before me. Twenty-five sacrificial lambs.
>
> KANNO [1911] 1988, 58

Ultimately, however, she felt that the unfairness directed at the accused, most of whom, unlike herself, had not been involved in the plot (Hsu 2016, 204 fn 195), had been predictable:

> However, it should not have surprised me. My past experiences should have prepared me to expect this as a matter of course. We initiated our plot precisely because this kind of outrageous legal system and despotic political authority exist. It was absurdly foolish to hope, even for a moment, that the wielders of power – whose authority I do not

acknowledge – might save my comrades simply because the court hearings were meticulously carried out.

KANNO [1911] 1988, 60

2   Kōtoku's Trajectory toward Anarchism

For Crump (1993, 21), Kōtoku was "the most influential socialist of his generation." Pelletier (2002, 93) calls him "l'un des éminents fondateurs du socialisme japonais qui a évolué de la social-démocratie à l'anarchisme" [one of the eminent founders of Japanese socialism who evolved from social democracy to anarchism]. But in his early years, he was attracted to liberal ideas, and references to classical Confucianism are to be found in his writings and speeches. In his socialist phase, many of his allies came from Japan's minority Christian community, while Kōtoku himself developed into one of the most severe critics of the Christian faith.

Kōtoku's life began shortly after the start of the Meiji Restoration of 1868, which replaced the Tokugawa period (1600–1867). Much social change was taking place, including the abandonment of the nation's caste system, a development which inspired young Japanese to think in more modern, individualistic political terms, although the new system in practice, due to its flaws and corruption, gradually inspired very different sentiments such as those which Kōtoku came to embrace. He was born on September 22, 1871, in Nakamura, a town where he is buried, in today's Kōchi Prefecture, which was then known as Tosa, on Shikoku, the smallest of Japan's four main islands, an area that was sympathetic to the ongoing reforms (Crump 1993, 21–22, 1998, 8–9; Notehelfer 1971a, 31, [1971b] 2010, 4; Tierney 2015, 15; Tsuzuki 1966, 30).

His father, Kōtoku, Atsuaki, was a pharmacist who died when Shūsui, whose original name was Denjirō, was one year old. The latter's consequent informal scientific training acquired from working in the family business, which sold herbal remedies and sake, caused him to become known as "Dr." Kōtoku, a title to which García [1976] 2013, 40, 2000, 1) argues, he was technically never entitled to use. His mother was Ono, "Taji" Tajiko, who took over the pharmaceutical enterprise from her husband, dying shortly before Shūsui was executed in 1911, having visited him in prison after his death sentence was announced, causing him to wonder if she had committed suicide (Ike 1944, 225; Sievers 1969, 5–6; Tierney 2015, 19).

Kōtoku's elementary school education remained influenced by Confucian ideas that to some extent were being challenged by the Meiji changes, but it allowed him to become familiar with classical Chinese and to learn how to write in that language, as well as to read the works of its foremost advocates, Confucius, Mencius (or Menzi or Meng Ke), and Xunzi (or Hsűn Tzu). Later, in 1888, he attended a school owned by Nakae, Chōmin, who had translated Rousseau's *Du Contrat Social; ou, Principes du Droit Politique* [*The Social Contract; or, The Principles of Political Rights*] into Japanese, an experience that exposed Denjirō to contemporary European political ideas. Nakae encouraged his pupil to learn English, and it was he who gave Kōtoku the name of "Shūsui," which means "autumn water" or "autumn flood"; that is also the title of the seventeenth chapter of the classical Taoist text the *Zhuangzi* (or *Chuang Tzu*), which has been translated as "autumn floods" (Asukai 1978, 126; García [1976] 2013, 33; Racel 2011, 240–242; Notehelfer [1971b] 2010, 4 fn 1; Sievers 1969, 23–24; Tierney 2015, 21, 22). Kōtoku's association with Taoism and Confucianism, and the degree to which it may or may not be of importance, is discussed later in the chapter.

In the new Japanese environment, the ideas of Rousseau and other modern Western thinkers became conducive to the development of capitalism, but eventually the opening up of society to more opportunity to make money led to resentment as the burgeoning economy, which included postwar inflation and the setting up of monopolies protected by the government, created a gulf between the living standards of rich and poor. Consequently, thinkers such as Kōtoku came to view socialist restrictions on the economy favorably and he, in particular, alarmed by the social and cultural transformation away from traditional and apparently more gentlemanly and respectful Confucian *mores*, came to see the Meiji Restoration as itself being a mistake. Even when he was a reporter, working for the *Yorozu Chōhō* newspaper from 1898 to 1903, and being a supporter of the Jiyūtō [Liberal Party], which had been founded in 1881 amid hopes for political reform, only to be disbanded in 1900, he was already convinced that the new system was flawed. Following the Jiyūtō's demise, Kōtoku wrote a piece in the *Yorozu Chōhō* titled "*Jiyūtō o matsuru bun*" ["A Requiem for the Liberal Party"] commemorating its fall. Not surprisingly, these concerns led to the 1898 formation of the Shakai-shugi kenkyūka [the Society for the Study of Socialism], most of whose members were Christians, a group with which Kōtoku was involved that met at Tokyo's Unitarian Church, and a more ideologically focused successor to the Shakai-mondai kenkyūka [the Society for the Study of Social Problems]. At their meetings, they discussed the writings of European socialists (Asukai 1978, 132; Duus and Scheiner 1998, 152–153; Notehelfer [1971b] 2010, 61–62; Tierney 2015, 32).

On May 20, 1901, with support from the Nippon Railroad Workers' Union and the Iron Workers' Union, members of the reformulated Shakai Shugi Kyōkai [Socialist Society], which had developed in 1900 out of the Shakai-shugi kenkyūka, formed the the Shakai Minshutō [Social Democratic Party], which was immediately banned by the government as soon as it published its platform, which was essentially liberal in nature, advocating universal adult suffrage and relegalization of labor union activities that had been outlawed the previous year. It also backed some public ownership. To the horror of the government, the manifesto was printed in several newspapers, mostly ones based in Tokyo (Asukai 1978, 132; Elison 1967, 440 fn 14, 441; Ichioka 1971, 2; Ike 1944, 226–227; Kublin 1950, 326–328; Nishida 1978, 71; Notehelfer [1971b] 2010, 12; Sen 1918, 60–62; Sievers 1969, 4, 44, 1983, 117–118; Takeuchi 1967, 727; Totten 1966, 23–24, 26; Tsuzuki 1966, 33; Wakabayashi 1998, 10).

Eventually, Notehelfer (1971a, 31) comments, "the cumulative experiences of childhood and adolescence, which had been capped by his educational experience in the home of Nakae, were being transformed into a coherent picture of his society and the future he envisioned for it." Nevertheless, the presence in Kōtoku's world view of various contradictions and dissatisfactions might instead be seen as making it difficult for him to grant the existence of such coherence. Indeed, in his early years as a "socialist," he was slow to begin reading books about socialism, and the extent of his actual familiarity with the works of Marx has been questioned (Asukai 1978, 138; Duus and Scheiner 1998, 154 fn 9). Later, during his time in prison, which afforded him a great deal of time to overcome that deficit, he exposed himself to many different perspectives, including learning more about Marx and Kropotkin, both of whom he tended to regard as all examples of the same "socialist" phenomenon. However, as Takeuchi (1967, 729, 730) notes, by 1905, Kōtoku reached a point where he was advocating direct action instead of parliamentary reform along with certain aspects of Marxist theory, such as class and production of surplus value. Interestingly that combination of commitments is surprisingly similar to those of the Industrial Workers of the World (IWW) approach adopted by Tom Barker, the subject of the previous chapter. During the few months that Shūsui would spend in the Bay Area in California in 1905–1906, he would meet with representatives of the IWW. His views had changed sharply since 1899, when, as the secretary of the Alliance for Tax Abatement in Shikoku, he had seen success at achieving reform as perhaps lying in his own election to the Diet (Elison 1967, 441).

In 1901, Kōtoku, and fellow *Yorozu Chōhō* journalist, Uchimura, Kanzō, set up a group called the Risōdan (Band of Idealists), which aimed to promote societal reform, a goal in favor of which they were able to employ their newspaper. Uchimura was a critic of the belief that the emperor was divine, and had refused to bow before an edict known as the Imperial Rescript of Education, an action that led to much criticism of him as a Christian, and caused him to be fired as a teacher (Bamba and Howes 1978, 20; Tierney 2015, 68–69). Kōtoku also in that year published *Imperialism: Monster of the Twentieth Century* [*Nijū-seiki no kaibutsu: teikoku shugi*], a work that has received recent attention due to its advocacy of what is seen as a modern perspective on foreign relations, one that spurns nationalism. In *Imperialism*, Kōtoku defended Uchimura and others who had been victimized in a surge of what passed for patriotism:

> When Uchimura Kanzō refused to bow in worship before the Imperial Rescript of Education, he was dismissed from his job as teacher. When Ozaki Yukio pronounced the word "republic" in a speech, he lost his post as government minister. All of these men were condemned for the crime of lèse majesté and antipatriotism. So much for the manifestations of patriotism of the Japanese people in this holy period of Meiji Japan.
>
> This is what the patriotism of the people leads to: anyone who challenges the conventional wisdom of the day is muzzled and forcibly restrained.
>
> KŌTOKU [1901a] 2015, 150

For Shūsui, Japan's involvement in China's Boxer Rebellion, an anti-foreign and anti-Christian reaction in 1900 that was crushed by an Eight Nation Alliance of global powers that included Japan, made him rethink his previously more supportive attitude to external involvement, which he had connected to his own country's modernization, favoring liberal and universal ideas over traditional Confucian norms. However, he now came to view Japanese nationalism as having swiftly turned into militarism, and believed that a noble effort to improve society had become contaminated by the aspirations of those who desired to become wealthy, while wars led to many different negative consequences for ordinary people, an argument that could be interpreted as a return to Confucian morality. News of the Boer War in South Africa helped convince him of the justness of his own position. The ideas in some of the articles that he wrote for different papers to make his arguments against patriotism and its illusory nature later became a part of his book. Already at this point, he views the legislature as being unable to solve the ongoing contamination of society by greed and lust for war, an opinion that will lead to his call for direct action in place of political persuasion (Anderson 2010, 371–372; Asukai 1978, 133, 134–135; Notehelfer 1971a, 36–37, 42–43, [1971b] 2010, 90; Sievers 1969, 53–54; Tierney 2015, 9–10, 30). In one of the articles, "Kokumin no mahi" ["The Paralysis of the People" or "National Paralysis"] Kōtoku writes:

> Following the excitement of the Sino-Japanese War our people have fallen into a troubled sleep of exhaustion, and have reached a state where they are completely unaware of anything. In the meantime thieves are plundering their warehouses and robbers are about to rob them of their lives, but they remain paralyzed and unaware, dreaming idly of price rises in the stock market.
>
> KŌTOKU, quoted by NOTEHELFER 1971a, 43

In *Imperialism: Monster of the Twentieth Century*, Kōtoku ([1901a] 2015, 137–138; Tierney 2015, 33) makes a point of describing his argument as emanating not from his own calculations, but instead owing much to European thinkers, of whom he mentions Tolstoy, Zola, Bebel, and John Morley. As noted above, he would later become involved in the translation of Bebel's book, *Woman Under Socialism*. Morley was a British journalist and Liberal Party MP who wrote a biography of prime minister William Gladstone; like Kōtoku, he was opposed to imperialism and to the Boer War. Because empire-building has swept around the world and has now infected Japan, Shūsui argues, he has no choice but to try and alert readers to its dangers (Kōtoku [1901a] 2015, 139, 141):

> Imperialism spreads like a wildfire in an open field. All nations bow down to worship this new god, sing hymns to praise it, and have created a cult to pay it adoration.
>
> KŌTOKU [1901a] 2015, 139

For Kōtoku, a fundamental flaw in the rationales that are used to justify foreign invasions is that there are no lands devoid of people or where governments do not already exist. Thus peaceful conquest is not possible, and the expenditure of military force inevitably leaves bodies and unwilling victims of conquest, as demonstrated by recent decades of European and United States colonialism (Kōtoku [1901a] 2015, 186–187):

> Like the spread of plague, imperialism is truly a horrible disease that infects everything that it touches. Indeed, so-called patriotism is the microbe that causes the disease while militarism is the means by which the microbe is transmitted.
>
> KŌTOKU [1901a] 2015, 206

Ultimately, Kōtoku argues, imperialism also inflicts damage on those nations that practice it. For example, establishing a colony is expensive, since developing a market system and maintaining law and order impose costs that will for a long time mainly be incurred by the colonial power; in the case of Japan, he writes, given the absence of money to support an empire, the expenditures for operating abroad will impose restrictions on the size of the home economy, impoverishing the Japanese people. Anyway, only a minority of citizens will profit from such a process, whereas the purpose of government should be to benefit everyone at home and abroad, even though warmongers tend to invent or exaggerate the need for conquests (Kōtoku [1901a] 2015, 140, 149, 199, 202; Tierney 2015, 48–49). Consequently, "the justice and humanity of world civilization must not permit patriotism to spread" (Kōtoku [1901a] 2015, 162).

Shūsui cites the well-known classical Confucian argument of Mencius that someone who sees that a child has fallen into a well will respond by risking his or her own life to try and save the victim. The point for Mencius is to demonstrate that such behavior is in no way self-serving, but rather results from an innate knowledge of virtue possessed by every human being, and not "out of sympathy for the parents, or to be thought well of by friends and neighbours, or from a sense of dislike at not being thought a feeling person" (Mencius 1963, 113, 132; Shone 2013, 258–259). In Kōtoku's hands, the passage is turned to support the struggles of Afrikaners fighting against British imperialism in South Africa and the Filipino/as attempting to free themselves from the yoke of American conquest.

> [A] human being moved by such selfless love and charity does not pause to think whether the child is a family member or a close relative. When he rescues the child from danger, he does not even ask himself whether the child is his own or belongs to another. For the same reason, righteous and benevolent men in every nation in the world pray that the people of the Transvaal will win their freedom and that the people of the Philippines will gain their independence. There are many such men even in England and the United States, even though their countries are belligerents in these wars. How is it possible for a patriot to adopt such a stance?
> KŌTOKU [1901a] 2015, 143

Thus, Kōtoku argues, the majority of the population, for example the supporters of colonialism in the UK and the US, are committing themselves to values that are alien to the deep-seated human awareness of the correct way to behave (143). Here, he notes that veterans of such wars are changed by their personal experiences in military service, returning home where they will often gather together with former comrades and mentally reenact battles and other experiences and the way they felt at that time for their rest of their lives. Yet they are victims themselves. "They are filled with pride and self-satisfaction when they recall these events. What foolishness!" (Kōtoku [1901a] 2015, 147). Not only is this affection for warlike pursuits condemned by Confucian teachings, but also by Buddhist and Christian texts (148).

Even as Shūsui demonstrates his familiarity with Confucianism, in *Imperialism* he also displays a dissatisfaction with some of its teachings, dismissing the extremes to which the principle of filial piety, *xiao* (*hsiao*; in Japanese, *kō*) can lead its advocates. Linking an unthinking obedience to the needs and wishes of one's parents to the desire of Japanese soldiers to serve their emperor in military conflict, he points out that there must be limits to such theories of obligation:

> People who claim that they act from a spirit of loyalty and for the sake of the emperor but know nothing of justice and humanity display the patriotism of a barbaric country and a superstitious loyalty. It is not unlike the filial piety that leads others to theft and prostitution.
> KŌTOKU [1901a] 2015, 160

As noted above, the issue as to how far Kōtoku's political ideas were or were not influenced by Confucianism will be explored later in the chapter.

Additionally, Kōtoku continues, warmongering makes violence seem more and more acceptable psychologically, threatening those who might at first have profited from colonialism. He gives the example of the Peterloo Massacre that took place at St. Peter's Field in Manchester, England on August 16, 1819, a protest by citizens seeking expansion of the franchise that was attacked by the cavalry, killing eighteen and injuring hundreds (Kōtoku [1901a] 2015, 152, 152 fn 29, 153). The reference to Peterloo here connects him with its literary anarchist critic, Percy Bysshe Shelley, who wrote his political poem "Masque of Anarchy" following the massacre (Shelley 1819; Shone 2022, 66). Even in 1901, Kōtoku, too, displays some anarchist similarities:

> The patriotic troops, who had defeated the enemy army at Waterloo, now turned their arms against their own people and massacred them at Peterloo. Is such patriotism truly a love of one's fellow citizens? What benefits do the sacred union and great patriotic concord of the nation confer upon the citizens once the foreign enemy has been defeated? The blade of the bayonet that cuts off the enemy's head serves just as well to spill the blood of one's fellow countrymen.
> KŌTOKU [1901a] 2015, 152–153

As noted in Chapter 1, the treatment of Albert Dreyfus in France and Émile Zola's defense of the military officer falsely imprisoned for treason raised issues of great concern to radical thinkers around the world, not only, as previously described, far away in Uruguay and Argentina, but also in Japan. For Kōtoku in *Imperialism* ([1901a] 2015, 177–178), the Dreyfus Affair signifies the potential for excessive military involvement in civilian life by spreading corruption and undermining public confidence in society:

> The reason is that the internal organization of the army is a world of oppression, a world where might makes right, a world of rigid hierarchy and blind obedience. Those who enter this world must leave all thoughts of righteousness and morality behind.
> KŌTOKU [1901a] 2015, 177

Zola, on the other hand, is to be praised for his perseverance in standing up for what is right, and Shūsui again finds support for moral uprightness in the words he attributes to Mencius that "I refuse to yield even when millions oppose me if to yield is to betray my conscience" (Kōtoku [1901a] 2015, 177; Tierney 2015, 94). For Tierney, Kōtoku's point in referencing Zola is as follows:

> Forced to flee France to protect his life, he [Zola] created the persona of the modern intellectual who follows his own conscience and uses his authority as a writer to attack powerful institutions in the name of universal values.
> TIERNEY 2015, 94

However, the allusion to Mencius, and the widespread admiration of Zola among radicals such as himself chiefly relate to those same "universal values": they are not necessarily evidence of Kōtoku's commitment to Confucianism in general. Thus, when Tierney (2015, 68) writes, "Kōtoku ... implicitly contrasted patriotism with *hakuai* (compassion or benevolence), another term with rich Confucian connotations," he seems to want to commit Shūsui to beliefs that have little to do with the socialist and increasing anarchist obligations that will dominate his life for the next decade, resulting in his judicial murder by the Japanese government for being the ringleader of a dangerous group. Indeed, Mencius' perspective requires no grounding in classical Confucianism to make sense, and many contemporary anarchists and libertarians would view its sentiments as being their own.

In 1903, Kōtoku published *Essence of Socialism* (*Shakaishugi-Shinzui*, which has also been translated as the *Quintessence of Socialism*). Zhang Ji, a member of

Tokyo's Socialist Study Group, an organization of Chinese students and others, would later translate both *Essence of Socialism* and *Imperialism* into Chinese, as well as some works of Malatesta (Tierney 2015, 118–119, 122; Tsuzuki 1966, 33). At the beginning of the *Essence of Socialism*, Kōtoku writes that many people in Japan are interested in hearing about socialism and what it represents, and that is the reason why he has written his new book. As in *Imperialism*, he makes reference to writers who have influenced him. Here, they are Marx; Engels; Thomas Kirkup, the author of *An Inquiry into Socialism*; Richard T. Ely, the Social Gospel advocate; the Christian Socialist, William Dwight Porter Bliss; William Morris, the architect and writer; and Ernest Belfort Bax, the English lawyer and socialist who was also an advocate of men's rights, and whose book, *The Legal Subjection of Men* (1896) was a critical response to John Stuart Mill's arguments in "The Subjection of Women" (1869), although there is no evidence that Kōtoku was aware of that work. Despite their various other interests, all of those mentioned had studied and written about socialism. The list is to some extent evidence of the change in Shūsui's thought, as well as of the works he had been reading, but it is unclear how extensive was his familiarity with the writers mentioned, and his view of "socialism" encompasses a wide range of perspectives, from revolutionary to quite passive advocacy of piecemeal social change (Kōtoku [1903] 1969, 128, 129–130; Tsuzuki 1966, 33).

Notwithstanding his acknowledgement of various other authors, Kōtoku ([1903] 1969, 131) reserves his praise of "the greatest revolutionary" for James Watt, about whom he comments:

> Once he had roused his subtle mind, seized upon the secrets of creation, and unfolded them before the eyes of the world, was there not then a complete and sudden change in the material conditions of every nation? The consequences of this "Industrial Revolution" have been enormous.
>
> KŌTOKU [1903] 1969, 131

Here, either Kōtoku ([1903] 1969, 131 fn 1) or his translator Sharon Lee Sievers cite Kirkup's *Inquiry into Socialism*, saying that it also indicates that Watt was "the greatest revolutionist and inventor the world has ever seen." Kirkup's statement in the third edition of his book is actually slightly different, calling Watt "the greatest innovator and revolutionist the world has ever seen" (Kirkup [1887] 1909, 40). Although the Industrial Revolution that started in England certainly had very profound social effects, it might be asked whether it was a revolution of the kind that Marx and the other thinkers Shūsui mentions would consider to have much connection to their philosophies, apart from its creation of exploitation and misery the world over that socialists have attempted since that time to ameliorate (and which some Marxist rulers have made even worse). As Kropotkin pointed out in *The Conquest of Bread*, a work that Kōtoku would read in English in 1907 and then in 1909 translate completely into Japanese with the title *Pan no ryakusbu* (Chang 1976, 97; Crump 1980, 274–276, 1993, xii; Kōtoku 1909, 70):

> And if Watt, Stephenson, Jacquard, etc., could only have foreseen what a state of misery their sleepless nights would bring to the workers, they would probably have burned their designs and broken their models.
> KROPOTKIN [1906] 2011, 251

As of 1903, Kōtoku's familiarity with Kropotkin is somewhat limited, so he probably does not know at this point that the Russian anarchist had a similar respect for the ingenuity of Watt, the steam engine pioneer, French loom developer Joseph Marie Jacquard, locomotive designer George Stephenson, and others inventors who worked with their hands, whom he viewed as the real scientists – informally credentialed, but more successful in achieving technological change than persons dressed in white coats pontificating in universities (Kropotkin 1907, 207; Shone 2013, 99).

Kirkup, too, was aware of the irony of industrial improvements becoming an instrument for the oppression of ordinary working people:

> If the triumphs of mechanical invention are only to be weapons for more effectually subjecting and exploiting the masses of mankind, better that James Watt had never succeeded with the steam-engine.
> KIRKUP [1887] 1909, 46

Meanwhile, in Japan, the recent development of capitalism, insofar as it had been accomplished, had significantly expanded the wealth of the country, but Kōtoku points out that many of its citizens lack even a sufficient quantity of rice to eat. Many are denied access to education and to medical care. People who are willing to work and earn the salaries that would allow them to benefit from this affluence lack the opportunity to labor, and may even starve as a result (Kōtoku [1903] 1969, 134, 135, 136, 145).

> Without the means of livelihood, what sort of freedom can there be? What progress, what sort of virtue or learning can there be?
> KŌTOKU [1903] 1969, 135

Here, Kōtoku addresses the "social question," which was discussed in Chapter 1 with reference to Virginia Bolten. Like other thinkers who apprehended the negative consequences of the much heralded development of capitalism, he could see that there was in Japan, as elsewhere, a large class of people unable either to take care of themselves or to avail themselves of the opportunities that had developed. In particular, events at the Ashio Copper Mine would typify this concern and, as discussed later in this chapter, Kōtoku would be called upon to respond to the mine's striking employees in the midst of a continuing environmental disaster (Pyle 1975, 348).

Like Virginia Bolten and the other anarchists in Argentina and Uruguay with whom she associated, and like Kropotkin, Kōtoku was inspired by the example of the Paris Commune, and he saw its form of government as an ideal for which radicals in Japan should hope to aim:

> Such great things were accomplished during the Rising of the Paris Commune! Though it be impossible for us to accomplish their equal, still we should try at least temporarily to clothe the poor warmly, to feed them till they are satisfied. This, of course, is not simply to be accomplished straightway; but if the present economic depression continues unabated for another three or five years, reaching the condition where the starved will be littered by the waysides, then the need will arise to save them, be it by launching an uprising.
>
> KŌTOKU [1910b] 1967, 479; [1910a] 1979, 100 has a
> similar translation, as does CRUMP 1980, 371

Accordingly, in the *Essence of Socialism*, Sievers (1969, 48–49) notes that "Kōtoku turned to a blend of early socialist theory and Marxian economic analysis to explain that the poverty and moral degeneration of society had its roots in the loss of distributive justice." Unfortunately, in that work, Kōtoku ([1903] 1969, 147–160) reviews the arguments of Marx and Engels in *Capital* and elsewhere as though their predictions are necessarily true and do not need to be questioned. Surprisingly, then, the policies that he advocates in succeeding pages seem inconsistent with those more radical prognostications. For example, Shūsui makes the argument that *some* areas of an economy can be successfully incorporated into a system of partial "national ownership" (165). Moreover, he insists:

> The principles of socialism clearly do not aspire to centralized power; ownership should be by the nation, the towns, or prefectures and villages, according to the nature of machinery and enterprises.
>
> KŌTOKU [1903] 1969, 165–166

If this still sounds like a system of communism, or a scheme that could be quickly centralized into such a regime in the manner of Lenin, it next transpires that private companies and individuals would still be involved in Kōtoku's ideal approach, so he is in fact advocating a kind of social democracy, a rather different type of socialism, one where most people would be "middle class," rather than "wage slaves" (Kōtoku [1903] 1969, 184). It seems he has in mind a system such as that of modern Sweden or Germany, where capitalism continues but is successful within the parameters imposed by substantial state supervision. Yet, like Kirkup, he is happy to incorporate the ideas of Marx and Engels into a blanket understanding of what socialism would signify.

> Even though the land and capital which represent the means of production would revert to public ownership, the management of many enterprises would continue to remain in individual hands. For example, though the public owns such enterprises as railroads and telegraph lines, their management is entrusted to private companies. Such enterprises as sake, salt, and tobacco operate as government monopolies, but a part of the production and exchange remain – as always – an individual enterprise. Publicly owned cultivated land is turned over to private individuals for farming. The aim of private management by individuals or companies is always to get market profits for themselves.
>
> KŌTOKU [1903] 1969, 167

More specifically, Shūsui says of Marx and Engels, that they were not anarchists or nihilists, that they eschewed violence as a means of achieving social change, seeking reform through the ballot box with universal suffrage (Kōtoku [1903] 1969, 198). He presents their ideas as being rather more compatible with those of mainstream socialists than they would generally appear to be, and he recommends that in Japan, socialists should at first start to work on policies that would attract more considerable support, such as allowing all adults to vote, lessening work hours, and fully legalizing labor unions (199). For Tsuzuki (1966, 33), the range of thinkers subsumed under the banner of socialism in Kōtoku's *Essence of Socialism* "illustrated his eclecticism." Notehelfer ([1971b] 2010, 76, 80) suggests that Kōtoku may have begun by reading writers such as Kirkup and Ely, and later moved on to works by Marx and Engels, but that his familiarity with the specifics of their ideas when he was writing the *Essence of Socialism* was poor. He had, though, by 1897 digested the work of Albert Schäffle, who had given his own book the title *The Quintessence of Socialism* [*Die Quintessenz des Sozialismus*] (Notehelfer [1971b] 2010, 61; Sievers 1969, 34). Interestingly, in that work, Schäffle ([1874] 1890, 6, 11–12) refers to the need for Marx to focus on his criticism of capitalism, and not to say too much about what socialism will be like when it is actually achieved. Unlike Kōtoku, Schäffle's description of "socialism" refers exclusively and in considerable detail to the views of Marx, and it may be from this source that, as of 1903, Shūsui had obtained most of his knowledge of Marxism. For Schäffle, socialism is Marxism. However, it can be argued that, for Kōtoku, Marxism is really a much more democratic and conventional form of socialism. As Sievers writes:

> But when it came to the fundamental questions of how the new age would come into being, who would lead the forces of change, and for that matter, what constituted the good society which would result, Kōtoku revealed himself to be a Japanese with ideas quite different from many of his European and American counterparts. There is in Kōtoku no call for a violent revolution, led by an urban proletariat, proceeding on the basis of dialectical processes. In *Shakaishugi shinzui*, violent revolution is replaced by the same gradualist, perhaps LaSallean views Kōtoku had entertained in earlier days. The leadership of the urban proletariat is replaced by the same progressive intelligentsia he had called upon so many times before.
> SIEVERS 1969, 50

An important development in Kōtoku's career was his reaction to the Russo-Japanese War of 1904–1905, a battle between the two large nations for control of Korea. Up until the Fall of 1903, articles and editorials about war in *Yorozu Chōhō* spanned a range of political viewpoints. When the publisher of the *Yorozu Chōhō*, Kuroiwa, Ruikō, became pro-war and, in October, the publication turned in the same direction, Kōtoku and two other writers, Sakai, Toshihiko, and Uchimura, Kanzō, resigned. Kōtoku and Sakai then founded the Heiminsha [the Commoners' Association] and its new, weekly paper, the *Heimin Shimbun* [The Common People's Newspaper, also transliterated in Western characters as *Shinbun*], which openly criticized the war, advocating global disarmament. At the same time, the Shakai Shugi Kyōkai [Socialist Society], of which Shūsui was a leader, passed a resolution opposing the war. Kōtoku and Sakai wrote the manifesto for the Heiminsha, which promoted pacifism and began with the statement, "Liberty, Equality, Fraternity: these are the three great principles that make human life worth living in this world," indicating its authors' familiarity with French history. The new paper's subtitle was "A Weekly Journal of Socialist Propaganda," although its anti-war activities appealed also to other segments of the population, including a wider swath of Japanese Christians. On its first appearance, on November 15, 1903, the *Heimin Shimbun* included some of Tolstoy's folk tales and sold 8,000 copies. Subsequent issues, which averaged sales of 3,500 to 4,000, became a major irritant to the Japanese government, which constantly resisted its activities, eventually closing the weekly down (Anderson 2010, 119–121, 375; Asukai 1978, 124, 130, 138, 139; Bamba and Howes 1978, 261; Crump 1998, 9; Howes 1978, 107; Kublin 1950, 328; Mackie 1994, 100–101; Okamoto 1970, 93; Powles 1978, 153; Sievers 1983, 119).

When Tolstoy wrote his anti-war article, "Bethink Yourselves!," a piece that opposed the Russo-Japanese War and war in general from a Christian and Buddhist perspective, beginning with a citation from the bible's book of Luke, Kōtoku and Sakai printed it in the *Heimin Shimbun* in August 1904:

> [H]ow can a believing Christian, or even a skeptic, involuntarily permeated by the Christian ideals of human brotherhood and love which have inspired the works of the philosophers, moralists, and artists of our time, how can such take a gun, or stand by a cannon, and aim at a crowd of his fellow-men, desiring to kill as many of them as possible?
>
> TOLSTOY [1904] 2021, 5

However, in the next issue, Kōtoku published a response denying the need to resort to theological authority to make an argument that the war was wrong (Anderson 2010, 123, fn 69, 378–379). On March 28, 1904 (Ike gives an alternative date of March 17), the paper published a piece by Shūsui that opposed plans to increase taxation to pay for the war, titled "Aa zōzei" ["Ah, Increased Taxation"], following which its editor, Sakai, was jailed for three months, although the government's closing down of the publication was overturned in court, and its activities continued for a while (Ike 1944, 231; Kublin 1950, 329, 329 fn 36; Tierney 2015, 98).

3 Sugamo Prison and Six Months in the United States

At the start of the the Russo-Japanese war, Kōtoku was fined 80 yen for publishing Marx and Engels' *Communist Manifesto*, translated into Japanese by himself and Sakai, Toshihiko, in the *Heimin Shimbun* edition dated November 13, 1904, and he then received a five-month prison sentence for publishing an essay by the Christian radical journalist, fellow former *Yorozu Chōhō* writer, Ishikawa, Sanshirō, titled "Appeal to Elementary School Teachers," which opposed ultranationalism. At the end of this first period in its publication history, *Heimin Shimbun* also became involved with promoting the Article 5 campaign, and in its January 15, 1905 issue, appearing when the journalists were appealing the paper's forced closure, they included a petition in favor of that proposal. The last number appeared on January 29 and its presses were seized, although the facilities of another paper, *Chokugen* [Straight Talk] remained available for the *Heimin Shimbun* reporters' use until September 10, 1905, when it was also ordered closed (Crump 1998, 9; Elison 1967, 445; Ike 1944, 231, 1957, 242–243; Konishi 2013, 194; Lévy 2002, 61–62; Notehelfer [1971b] 2010, 106–107, 109; Okamoto 1970, 93, 140; Racel 2011, 244–245; Schnick 1995, 5–7; Sen 1918, 95; Sievers 1969, 65–66, 1983, 122–123; Tierney 2015, 98).

Following his stay in Sugamo prison, Kōtoku's poem, "A Red Flag" appeared in *Chokugen*:

> Coldness of the jail situated in the north of a city is to cut the skin.
> The clothes become like a stone, food is, too.
> It is impossible to endure for a delicate constitution.
> Soon the stomach and bow[e]ls are destroyed,
> He groans with a dose of medicine.
>   KŌTOKU [1905a] 1979, 107

He continues, suggesting the success of either the assassination of Alexander II who, dying, was carried to the Winter Palace in 1881, or possibly of the first Russian Revolution of 1905, or perhaps the inevitability of the future (1917) Russian Revolution, but also predicting the fears and emotions that will culminate with the High Treason Incident:

> Do you not see the black clouds gathered
> Over Winter Palace in the dusk,
> Then the Crown will be cut off and crushed in a dripping blood?
>   KŌTOKU [1905a] 1979, 108

In Ichigaya Prison in 1910, where the next year he would be hanged, Kōtoku included a poem called "From Prison" in a letter he sent to his second wife, Chiyoko, displaying similar sentiments about the demoralizing effects of his incarceration:

> For thirty years I have passed in reading books,
> To-day I spend in vain supporting my sick body.
> Through the high stone wall, I glimps[e] a healthy bird flying
> Through the iron window the cold wind blows in
> I pity for a hungry fly.
>   KŌTOKU [1910c] 1979, 110

Although as indicated in his extant poetry, imprisonment predictably made Shūsui depressed at times, the ability to spend much of his time reading caused him to tell Sakai that the five months in Sugamo was going quickly. Jail gave him some space where he was able to read John William Draper's *History of the Conflict Between Religion and Science*, Friedrich Engels' *Ludwig Feuerbach: The Roots of the Socialist Philosophy*, Ernst Heinrich Haeckel's *Riddle of the Universe*, Parish B. Ladd's *Commentaries on Hebrew and Christian Mythology*, Ernest Renan's *Life of Jesus*, and Michael A. Lane's lesser-known volume, *The Level of Social Motion* (Elison 1967, 446; Notehelfer [1971b] 2010, 110–112, 116; Sievers 1969, 68–69, 69 fn 4). These choices reflect an interest in the underlying faith of his many Christian socialist allies, but also his own dissatisfaction with Christianity, a perspective that would find culmination in his final work, *Kirisuto Massatsuron* [On the Obliteration of Christ], which was published after his life, and would have some influence in spreading anticlerical ideas, particularly in China (Notehelfer [1971b] 2010, 111).

When he was released from Sugamo in November 1905, Kōtoku decided to visit the United States. Many reasons have been suggested for his eagerness to do this, including his poor health, his desire to meet radical thinkers from beyond Japan, and the need simply to move out of the range of police surveillance. However, the view that it was the six months he subsequently spent in the Bay Area of California that brought about his transformation from socialist to anarchist has been disputed because during the time he had been in jail, he was corresponding with Albert Johnson, a San Francisco anarchist, and Shūsui himself felt that he had already made the transformation, as he revealed to Johnson in a letter he wrote to him on August 10, 1905, saying that he had entered the jail "as a Marxian Socialist and returned as a radical Anarchist," a quotation much cited as evidence of his ideological makeover (Chang 1976, 95; Crump 1998, 9, 1980, 223; Elison 1967, 446; García [1976] 2013, 40; Ichioka 1971, 3; Kublin 1950, 338; Tsuzuki 1966, 34). During his imprisonment, Johnson had sent him a copy of Kropotkin's *Fields, Factories And Workshops*, and also given him the latter's address in England (Crump 1980, 222). Indeed, finding out more about Kropotkin may have steered Kōtoku in the direction of the typical anarchist perspective that crime is social, writing in that August 10 letter "that the governmental institutions – court, law, prison – are only responsible for ... poverty and crime" (Kōtoku, letter to Johnson, cited by Tsuzuki 1966, 34). Now, taking with him Kropotkin's *Memoirs of a Revolutionist* to read on the trip, he sailed for Yokohama on the *Iyo Maru* on November 14, arriving in San Francisco on December 5 following a four day stay in Seattle that had commenced on November 29. He was still in California at the time of San Francisco's Great

Earthquake of April 18, 1906 (Crump 1998, 10; Elison 1967, 448, 449; Ichioka 1971, 3–4).

While he was in California, Kōtoku held meetings with members of the recently founded Industrial Workers of the World (IWW), who impressed him with their syndicalist approach to labor issues and their endorsement of direct action, and he gave a speech at one of the IWW gatherings he attended, which included some Americans who would later, as the Wobblies' philosophy developed, become its members (Crump 1980, 224, 240, 1998, 10; Duus 1999, 23–24; Elison 1967, 450–451; Ichioka 1971, 4; Notehelfer [1971b] 2010, 128; Racel 2011, 245; Totten 1966, 29; Tsuzuki 1966, 34). Notehelfer comments:

> On the fifteenth of December he was visited by three members of the Industrial Workers of the World (I.W.W.), who asked him to speak at a meeting of their organization. This was to be his first introduction to American 'syndicalism', whose formula of 'direct action' he was to take back to Japan.
> NOTEHELFER [1971b] 2010, 125

Notehelfer is the Kōtoku scholar who most tries to explain his subject's beliefs in terms of having a classical Chinese underpinning, a view that may be considered to exaggerate the connection. It is perhaps ironic, then, that his comment that Kōtoku learned about direct action from the IWW (which also seems to preclude him from already being familiar with syndicalist ideas) does not address the concept of direct action within that history of ideas in China and Japan – specifically, Andō, Shōeki's (1703–1762) deployment of *chokkō*, a kind of direct action. These issues will be explored later in the chapter.

In San Francisco, and in Oakland, where Kōtoku participated in a meeting on January 21, 1906 to commemorate "Bloody Sunday," the shooting of unarmed demonstrators by Tsar Nicholas II's Imperial Guard, an atrocity which had taken place in St. Petersburg a year before, on January 9, 1905, he became acculturated to some extent into the burgeoning IWW perspective that sought reform using the configuration of strong industry-based labor unions who would be willing to withdraw their labor to achieve their goals. He saw the police in the Bay Area violently crushing local strikes, and he began to read Emma Goldman's journal, *Mother Earth*; as Goldman sought to spread the influence of her publication and of anarchism around the world, she would make use of her connections to Shūsui and to her admirer, Itō, Noe, the lover and intellectual ally of Ōsugi, Sakae, both of whom would also be killed, essentially by their own government. Not surprisingly, *Mother Earth* would devote much attention to Kōtoku's trial and subsequent execution. Kōtoku was also influenced by the arguments of his landlady, Mrs. Rose Fritz, an émigrée from Kiev who was a critic of voting, and her seventeen year-old daughter, Anna, who helped Kōtoku improve his English. The bedroom that he rented contained photographs of Kropotkin and of Mikhail Bakunin, and Fritz sent Kropotkin a letter that Shūsui had written to which he replied (Camfield 1999, 35–38; Crump 1980, 226, 240, 243–244, 245, 273–274, 1993, 23; Elison 1967, 450–451; Hsu 2016, 10, 10 fn 26, 195; Konishi 2013, 198 fn 85, 231; Notehelfer [1971b] 2010, 124, 126–127, 129; Shone 2019, 197–198; Sievers 1969, 79). In response to what he was seeing and hearing, he wrote:

> America is the country of democratic government. It is the country of liberty. But even now the freedoms of speech, of assembly, of the press are day by day being scraped away, being robbed. Suppose there were persons who attempted violent opposition to the present government of a gentlemen's clique, to religion, to manners and customs – one and all, they would be subjected to ruthless persecution. Some days ago, at a great demonstration held by the workers in San Francisco, very many comrades were beaten up by the police and were dragged off to jail.
> KŌTOKU, *Nikki to shokan*, quoted by ELISON (1967, 450–451)
> and partly by NOTEHELFER ([1971b] 2010, 129)

As Elison (1967, 452–454) notes, even though it is clear that Shūsui had substantially accomplished his transformation toward anarchism during or before his imprisonment in Japan, the edifying adventure in Northern California and his experience of encountering first-hand the San Francisco Earthquake and the consequent imposition of martial law made him view that period of his life as part of the metamorphosis. The disaster itself, he regarded as having temporarily created a condition of anarchist communism, of which he completely approved:

> I had a most enlightening experience connected with this terrible disaster in San Francisco. It was nothing else but this: since the eighteenth day of this month the whole city of San Francisco has entirely been under the condition of Anarchist Communism.
> Commerce at a complete standstill ... the mails, trains, steamships (to the vicinity) completely free of charge ... foodstuffs distributed daily by a relief committee ... All able-bodied men as a matter of duty are working on the transport of foodstuffs, the accommodation and care of the sick and injured, the clearing of fire ruins and the construction of shelters. Even if one wanted to buy, there are no goods for sale, so money has

> become completely extinct. Is this not of greatest interest?! But this ideal paradise will only continue for a few more weeks, and then again will revert to the original capitalist system of private property. This I lament.
>
> KŌTOKU, *Nikki to shokan*, quoted by ELISON (1967, 453–454); a similar translation can be found in NOTEHELFER ([1971b] 2010, 131) and in YANG (2005, xxxiii)

When he returned to Japan, he reported the change to his world view in a speech in Tokyo he delivered on June 28 1906 called "Sekai Kakumei Undō Nō Chōryū" ("The Tide Of The World Revolutionary Movement"), in which he denied the usefulness of obtaining change through electoral means. Then, in a now fairly well-known article titled "Yo Ga Shisō No Henka" ("The Change In My Thought") on February 5, 1907 (Chang 1976, 96; Crump 1980, 224–225, 275, 290, 384, 1998, 11; Elison, 1967, 454–457; Ike 1944, 232; Kōtoku [1907c] 1980, 428; Notehelfer [1971b] 2010, 141), he wrote:

> I want to make an honest confession. My views on the methods and policy to be adopted by the socialist movement started to change a little from the time that I went into prison a couple of years ago. Then, during my travels last year, they changed dramatically. If I recall how I was a few years back, I get the feeling that I am now almost like a different person.
>
> KŌTOKU [1907c] 1980, 428; KŌTOKU, cited by CRUMP 1980, 225

He continued:

> El sufragio universal y el parlamentarismo no conducen a una revolución social verdadera y no hay más solución, para el logro de esta revolución, que la acción directa a través de la unión de todos los trabajadores.
>
> KŌTOKU, cited by GARCÍA [1976] 2013, 41

> [Universal suffrage and parliamentarism do not lead to a true social revolution and there is no other solution, to achieve this revolution, than direct action through the union of all workers.]

Ike (1944, 234–235) points out that Kōtoku realized that implementation of a direct-action strategy would be dangerous. However, he responded, if the government used the army to suppress strikes, there would indeed be casualties, but industrial workers already risked similar dangers due to the nature of their employment, making it worthwhile to attempt to improve the conditions under which they labored.

In "The Change In My Thought," Kōtoku now emphasized that the goals he and his colleagues had been seeking, what he had understand as a socialist system, could not be achieved by giving all adults the vote and expecting parliament then to miraculously reflect the wishes of the majority of Japanese citizens (Kōtoku [1907c] 1980, 429). Even if the people who ran for office as candidates started out aiming to do this, they would rapidly be corrupted by interaction with other elements of the political process.

> People change with their circumstances and as MPs they would by no means be the same individuals as when they first put themselves forward as candidates. As politicians living in the capital, they would be different again from the public-spirited people they first were when still in their home districts. One wonders if there really can be any who genuinely remain true to the values they held before they were elected. Isn't prestige what invariably comes first in the lives of all MPs (or, at any rate, the vast majority of them)? And next comes power, followed by profit. Isn't their field of vision restricted to themselves, their families, or at most – and even this applies to only the very best among them – to their parties?
>
> KŌTOKU [1907c] 1980, 429–430; [1907b] 1979, 79 has a similar translation

While Kōtoku was in California, Sakai, Toshihiko had set up the Japanese Socialist Party (Nihon Shakaitō). At its second convention on February 17, 1907, Kōtoku spoke for one hour in favor of amending a committee's resolution which summarized the party's agenda, adding a phrase that agreed with his own ideas, referring to "the inefficacy of the policy of working through the Diet." Shūsui was partly motivated by the ongoing Ashio Copper Mine controversy, which had resulted in a riot (and which is discussed later in the present chapter). Although his proposal was rejected by the conference, he succeeded in preventing more moderate members from inserting "within the limits of the law" into the document. The speech was published two days later in a new version of *Heimin Shimbun*, which lasted for the first four months of 1907, and which resulted in the Saionji Cabinet shutting down both the paper and the Socialist Party itself; the publication was also under attack for having published Kropotkin's "Appeal to the Young." At this point, Kōtoku's influence was considerable, which meant that it was thought to be dangerous, a circumstance not at all helped by the fact that this was the first time the party had debated the details of its platform in public. In his criticism of using parliamentary methods to achieve change, Kōtoku had cited the work of the Ashio area's representative in the Diet, Tanaka, Shōzō, as having failed to achieve significant redress that would benefit the local citizenry (Crump 1993, 24–25; "El socialismo en el

Japón" 1907; Ichioka 1971, 2; Ike 1944, 232 fn 35; Lévy 2002, 75; Mackie 1994, 103; Nimura 1997, 198, 199; Notehelfer [1971b] 2010, 145. 146, 146 fn 2; Sen 1918, 113–116; Sievers 1983, 124; Stone 1975, 399; Totten 1966, 30; Tsuzuki 1966, 34; Vu 2022, 169). At the conference, he had said:

> Old Tanaka Shōzō is a man worthy of the greatest respect. In the next ten years or so, we are likely to see half a dozen of his caliber in the Diet. But what has actually resulted from 20 years of Tanaka Shōzō raising his voice over there. None of you was able to raise a finger at Furukawa's Ashio copper mine. But look what the workers of Ashio were able to achieve in the past three days! They sent shivers down the spines of the entire ruling class! (applause) Yes, violence is evil, but we must recognize that what could not be achieved in twenty years was achieved by just three days of direct action. I am not saying that we should all go out on strike right away, but the working class must build up strength through solidarity and experience.
>
> Kōtoku's speech, reported in *Heimin Shimbun*, no. 28
> (February 19, 1907), quoted in NIMURA 1997, 199

This was a criticism that was probably not appropriate, because Tanaka was an effective politician who had worked tirelessly to address the problems faced by his constituents. However, the fact that he resigned from his seat in the Diet to work full time on behalf of the farmers whose land had been polluted by the Ashio copper mine could be interpreted as support for Kōtoku's argument that parliamentary service was ineffective compared to direct action (Asukai 1978, 135).

Crump (1980, 290–291) points out that, not long before the convention, in a letter published in *Heimin Shimbun* on February 1, 1907, Kōtoku had applied his new argument to the lack of success achieved by the Social Democratic Party of Germany (SDP; Sozialdemokratische Partei Deutschlands) via its traditional pursuit of electoral success:

> What the European working class needs is not to elect a majority of MPs but to gain the assurance of food and clothes and shelter. It does not need the eloquent phrases of Bebel or [French socialist leader, Jean] Jaurès. What it does need is to achieve the social revolution. It is not laws which produce food and clothes, any more than it is votes which can be the means of revolution.
>
> KŌTOKU, quoted by CRUMP 1980, 291

Here, the apparent rejection of the ideas of one of the SDP leaders, August Bebel, whom he had mentioned in *Imperialism* as being a contributor to the development of his own thought, gave emphasis to his new anarchist affiliation. In pursuit of converting others to anarchism, he had recently written a letter to Albert Johnson in which he said he planned to utilize the reconstituted *Heimin Shimbun* for that purpose (Crump 1980, 309–310, 436 fn 12; Kōtoku, letter to Albert Johnson, December 18, 1906, in "Kotoku's Correspondence with Albert Johnson (Continuation)" 1911, 208). Even so, as he advocated direct action, Shūsui did not say that voting lacked any utility at all:

> Although I have been talking in this way, I certainly do not think it would be a bad thing to gain the right to vote. Nor am I by any means vehemently opposed to the movement for reforming the election laws. Should universal suffrage be achieved, then the workers' views would at least to some extent have to be borne in mind as parliament went about its business of law making. No one could deny that at least there would be a certain amount of advantage to the workers in this. But, all the same, it still has to be said that whatever the workers gained from this would be nothing more than the advantages accruing to them from such schemes as projects for social reform.
> KŌTOKU [1907c] 1980, 438; [1907b] 1979, 83 provides a similar translation

In another note to Albert Johnson, Kōtoku, in his less than perfect English, informed him of a new project:

> Now that our daily has been suppressed and our many comrades have gone to the prison, I have no work, no business, so I got leisure to write. I am now alone, at an inn in Yugawara, a famous watering place, one day's ride from Tokio. I came here to improve my health and am now translating a pamphlet, Arnold Roller's "Social General Strike."
> KŌTOKU, letter to Albert Johnson, May 3, 1907, in "Kotoku's Correspondence with Albert Johnson (Continuation)" 1911, 208

The Social General Strike was a pamphlet written by German anarchist Siegfried Nacht, who used the pseudonym, Arnold Roller. Some commentators have pointed to Kōtoku's 1907 translation of it as a sign that, like Roller, Kōtoku viewed direct action primarily in terms of a general strike orchestrated by strong labor unions, resulting in revolution (Crump 1993, 25–26). But as Lévy (2002, 75–76) points out, in his February 17 speech, Kōtoku was connecting the concept to the activities of those protesters in the Ashio area who, even though they lacked union leadership, were able to create a local disturbance. He viewed their activity as having potential for success, much more than Tanaka's attempts to represent his constituents. Such activities were certainly less expansive than those theoretical undertakings envisaged by Roller in *The Social General Strike*, where he wrote:

> The profoundest conception of the General Strike ... , the one pointing to a thorough change of the present system: a social revolution of the world; an entire new reorganization; a demolition of the entire old system of all governments – is the one existing amongst the proletarians of the Roman race (Spain and Italy). For them the General Strike is nothing less than an introduction to the social revolution. Therefore, we call this the General Strike, to distinguish it from General Strikes for higher wages, or for political privileges (political mass strikes) "The Social General Strike."
> ROLLER 1905, 5–6

For Shūsui, on the other hand:

> L'action directe est celle des ouvriers qui se lancent dans une lutte sans l'intermédiaire de chefs ou de représentants, elle est la manifestation du degré de la force et de la volonté ouvrières. Elle peut donc, selon les circonstances, recourir à diverses formes d'action.
> LÉVY 2002, 75

> [Direct action is that of workers who throw themselves into a struggle without the intermediary of leaders or representatives; it is the manifestation of the degree of workers' strength and will. It can therefore, depending on the circumstances, have recourse to various forms of action.]

While Roller shows his support for the the kind of employee tactics advocated by Tom Barker, which were described in the previous chapter, such as slowing down the pace of work or tram employees not collecting fares, this seems to be a strategy that goes well beyond anything advocated by Kōtoku, who, after all, was reluctant to proceed with the plot at the heart of the Great Treason Affair, viewing it as counterproductive:

> In Barcelona and Belgium a few sympathizers of the General Strike forced all workers in factories to give up work by injuring the machinery; secretly throwing emery into the oil boxes of the machines; or by loosening or

tightening a screw thus causing the largest machinery to get out of order, or even to break. In machine shops pieces of iron were thrown in the cog wheels, which were thus broken.
ROLLER 1905, 10

García ([1976] 2013, 6) writes that "pesar de la original figura de Andō Shōeki" [notwithstanding the original figure of Andō, Shōeki], anarchists in Japan, including Kōtoku and Ōsugi, immersed themselves in the theories of their allies in Europe to the exclusion of their own country's advocate of direct action. Indeed, as noted above with reference to Notehelfer, it would seem surprising that commentators who emphasize the Confucian, Neo-Confucian, or Taoist connections that they believe might lie in Kōtoku's thought, make no reference to Andō, Shōeki (1703–1762).

Little is known about the life of Andō, a doctor and philosopher who was the opponent of hierarchy, including the religious pecking order imposed on thinking by Buddhism, Confucianism, Taoism, and Shinto, and their quasi-sacred or otherwise authoritative texts, and thus by teachers, a knowledge he viewed as a kind of false consciousness advocated by, and benefiting those with power. Instead, he sought authority in the natural world (*shizen*), and interestingly found in the culture of the Ainu (Ezo), a subgroup in Japan who were often viewed by the majority as being inferior, a way of life that came closer to the more authentic, natural identity he prized, the details of which he believed were accessible to him in the form of innate knowledge. For Andō, unlike the Ainu, the apparently more sophisticated people such as samurai and their underlying Confucian philosophy were disconnected from engagement in agricultural labor, an aspect of natural living, which instead was confined to peasants, who sometimes, despite their interaction with Nature and the food they produced, died of starvation (Nelson 2022, ii, 1, 30, 45, 70; Ombrello 2010, 85–87; Tucker 2009, 132, 143, 2013, 55–56, 58–59).

With his rejection of many kinds of knowledge, Andō's generally skeptical attitude to authority can be likened to Sartre's argument in *Nausea*, that "Every existing thing is born without reason, prolongs itself out of weakness and dies by chance" (Sartre [1938] 1964, 133). In that novel, one of the characters, the Self-Taught Man, turns out not to be "self-taught" at all because he accepts the order that someone else has imposed upon reality – in this case, perhaps, the compiler of an encyclopedia's (or a librarian's, a journalist's, or a professor's, etc.) ideas about who or what is important and who or what is not (Sartre [1938] 1964, 30; Shone 2013, 230). While Sartre's underlying argument was that every person is in fact free to make what they want out of their lives, Andō is perhaps more concerned about the need for liberty to interpret the natural world from his or her own perspective or own knowledge. In that respect, he perhaps resembles to a greater extent, the German anarchist, Max Stirner (Shone 2013, 234–235), who wrote:

> Whether I am in the right or not there is no judge but myself. Others can judge only whether they endorse my right, and whether it exists as right for them too.
> STIRNER [1907] 2005, 187

Another aspect of Andō's approach that perhaps connects with Kōtoku, as mentioned above, is his advocacy of *chokkō*, a kind of direct action, which some scholars have felt links the ideas of the two thinkers. For example, Littler writes:

> In the late-Meiji period, Kōtoku Shusui utilised *chokkō* as a call to direct action in mutual aid, in reference to the Chokkōdan.
> LITTLER 2017, 20 fn 52

The Chokkōdan (Direct Action Group) was a small socialist network that was formed in 1903, which expanded its activities following the commencement of the Russo-Japanese War in February of the next year. Kōtoku and Sakai were members, and it was the Chokkōdan that produced the publication, *Chokugen*. As was noted earlier, the interrelationship between *Heimin Shimbun* and *Chokugen* and its editors and contributors, allowed Shūsui to utilize *Chokugen* when the first *Heimin Shimbun* was closed down by the government (Konishi 2013, 194).

For Konishi, even if Andō himself was not directly an influence on Kōtoku's later beliefs and embrace of direct action, Chokkōdan, rather than European influences such as the IWW and Kropotkin, certainly was:

> Kōtoku's participation in Chokkōdan suggests that historians' focus on his supposed conversion to Western anarchist "direct-action" theory after his trip to the United States misrepresents his adoption of anarchism. Kōtoku's declaration of his turn to anarchism and his call for "direct action" in his famous speech calling Japanese socialists to turn to anarchism, "My Change in My Thought," in 1907 after his return from the United States is often used to demonstrate the influence of the Western anarchist movement on Kōtoku. However, Kōtoku's "direct action" was a reference as much to the local direct action of mutual aid promoted by

the Chokkōdan as to the labor-union strikes of Euro-American anarchist direct-action theory.

KONISHI 2013, 196

Notwithstanding Konishi's point, it should perhaps also be noted that "mutual aid" is one of the key concepts in Kropotkin's writings, one of his books being titled *Mutual Aid: A Factor of Evolution* (Kropotkin [1902] 1904), while the idea that the more affluent should be willing to engage in a community's agricultural toil is a concern voiced long before the existence of the Chokkōdan by Andō, Shōeki. Since *chokkō* has also been translated as "direct cultivation," there is often ambiguity about whether he was advocating humanity's moral or physical improvement (Ombrello 2010, 85–87). In fact, Tucker (2013, 55) notes that the translation of *chokkō* as "direct tilling of the soil" rendered his ideas anathema to many of the more educated leisure class of his age. For those beyond Japan, he argues the value of Andō's approach has been no more successful:

> Rather egregiously, Shōeki's interpreters frequently assume that Japanese contexts are sufficient for fathoming his philosophy. When that approach yields few insights, the conclusion too often has been that Shōeki was an eccentric thinker, and at worst, an inscrutable paradox quickly to be put aside.
>
> TUCKER 2013, 55–56

Fortunately, the more Kropotkin-like meaning that might attach to *chokkō* remains available for selection by those unwilling to embrace its more extreme Moist (Mohist) – the ideas of Mo Tzu (Mozi) – or Maoist implications: forcing, say, attorneys and physicians, perhaps wearing their Gucci shoes, to dig up beets. Tucker concludes in his article:

> After all, Shōeki was a physician. While he might have tilled the soil, it is doubtful that he would have turned away patients who needed medical attention to go weed his fields. Shōeki must have understood "direct tilling" (*chokkō* ...), not in a literal sense, but in a manner that engaged all in work that could be shared, to one degree or another, by all. If so, then his philosophical system stands as one emphasizing the need for mutual respect and recognition of the integrity, as living creatures in productive process, of all together, without arrogance or condescension.
>
> TUCKER 2013, 83

In 1897, two more moderate Socialists, Takano, Fusatarō, and his deputy, Sen, Katayama visited California and returned to set up more traditional forms of craft-based unions that would be less willing to strike, such as the Tekko Kumiai (the Ironworkers' Union), having been influenced on their trip by the ideas of Samuel Gompers, with whom Takano had corresponded. Additionally, to promote unionization of that sort, they organized the Rodo Kumiai Kiseikai (the Association for the Formation of Labor Unions), which was based on the model of the American Federation of Labor (AFL) of which Gompers was the first and longtime president (Abrams 1987, 45; Gordon 1983, 25; Marsland 1989, 46, 49; Tierney 2015, 31–32). Unfortunately, passage of the Public Order and Police Law in 1900 made it more difficult for unions to operate in a conventional and law-abiding way (Ichioka 1971, 2; Kublin 1950, 325–326; Miyata 1988, 120; Sievers 1969, 43). After Kōtoku's execution, another Christian socialist (like Takano and Sen), Suzuki, Bunji, the leader of the Yūaikai labor movement he had founded, which enjoyed prominence between 1912–1919, would attempt to develop unionism in Japan with more peaceful consequences (Gordon 1991, 79; Large 1970, 559, 578; Maki 1992, 71–72).

Imprisoned in 1910 and seeking to explain the significance of direct action for employees and organizations that represented them, Kōtoku wrote in a manner that is now closer to that of Roller:

> [T]he advancement of the welfare of labor unions as a whole will make little headway if the matter is entrusted to a parliament – the workers must take action themselves; rejecting the indirect action of enlisting members of parliament as intermediaries, the workers should themselves take action directly; without electing representatives, the workers should all press forward themselves. And now to speak concretely: in order to perfect equipment in the factories, and to achieve a limitation of working hours, rather than take action to get the industrial laws reformed through parliamentary intermediaries, the workers must negotiate directly with the factory owner – and, if he does not listen, they must go on strike. So that term "direct action" for the most part is used in reference to a strike. Or, again, there are those who argue that during a time of extreme depression, when the starved are littered along the roadsides, it is perfectly proper to break into the houses of the rich and seize food. And one cannot maintain that to seize food is not yet another form of direct action.
>
> KŌTOKU [1910b] 1967, 476–477; [1910a] 1979, 98 has a similar translation

In an article he wrote titled "The Labour Movement in Japan," which was published in the Australian paper, the *Socialist*, he reported on a successful three-day work stoppage by 10,000 workers in "Moji port" (today, part of the city of Kitakyūshū), where the need to continue moving a large amount of coal had prompted the employer to settle (Kōtoku 1908):

> At present, the labour movement in Japan is growing in a very sound direction. Since the Russo-Japanese war the ideas of direct action has spread as a contagion. And great or small strikes are bursting every day at the mines and factory towns all over the country. Being prohibited by the law, there is no union nor syndicate in the modern sense, and the workers go on strike always without any preparation, but most of them end with the tolerable success.
> KŌTOKU 1908

4   Ashio Copper Mine

At the Ashio Copper Mine located in Tochigi prefecture in the center of Japan, the firm, which had originally belonged to the Japanese government, but which had been purchased by Furukawa, Ichibē, became the focus of many labor and environmental issues that caught the attention not only of Kōtoku, but of a wide range of concerned farmers, journalists, socialists, and students. For many of those on the left, including Kōtoku, Ashio, where 40% of Japan's copper was produced, signified the failure of recent political and economic changes in the direction of installing capitalism (Stone 1975, 385; Tierney 2015, 92).

Area farmers numbering 300,000 were affected by the industrial pollution caused by the mine, which dispersed its waste products, including copper, chromium, and arsenic into the Watarase River, affecting not only the water, the color of which changed, and its fish, most of which died, but also the rice that was grown in the area. Logging activity by the mining company to obtain timber used in the mine had also increased flooding of the agricultural area, which became a major problem by 1896. Although the farmers, whose property and income were also damaged as a result of the mine runoff had marched several times to Tokyo to complain, and interest groups were formed to draw attention to the situation, little was done to alleviate the environmental problems throughout the decade of the 1890s. In 1897, the mine was ordered to close or to restore the area to its prior condition, removing the pollution, but cleanup efforts were not a success. Supporting the farmers, Kōtoku wrote most of the articles presenting their side that appeared in the *Yorozu Chōhō*, up until he resigned from the paper in 1903. Aware of Shūsui's endorsement as well as of his writing proficiency, Tanaka asked him to write a *jikiso* (direct appeal) to the emperor on behalf of the pollution victims. In response to the various meetings and other measures adopted by the mine's opponents, the government promised more remedial action. Tanaka and Kōtoku shared the concern that, under present circumstances, the government catered much more to the interests of Furukawa, who was often seen as a successful entrepreneur, rather than to its farmers, who were at times referred to as peasants, their land, the river, and the forest area (Asukai 1978, 135–136; Crump 1998, 15; Littler 2017, 5; Notehelfer [1971b] 2010, 65, 66, 1975, 361–362, 381; Stone 1975, 385, 387, 388, 392, 394, 399; Tierney 2015, 91–92). That perspective was presented by Tanaka in a speech to the Diet in which he complained:

> The government has abandoned the people whom it is its constitutional duty to protect. To destroy the people is to destroy the nation. Does the so-called 'government' realize what it is doing?
>
> TANAKA, quoted by NOTEHELFER 1975, 381

On February 13, 1900, farmers again marched to Tokyo to protest the failure to resolve the pollution problems, an event since named the Kawamata Incident (Stone 1975, 390). The campaigners gathered at their starting point, the Unryu-ji Temple, and on the way, they may have numbered 2,500 or 3,000, with other estimates of the participants being as high as 12,000. At Kawamata, the site of a floating bridge, where they were ordered to end the march, some protesters may have thrown stones at police and it appears they tried to push the police back, which resulted in a counter charge, which then led to beatings of demonstrators and some arrests, although eventually all charges were dropped (Stone 1975, 395).

In February 1907, the Ashio miners went on strike, an event that would prove to be the largest organized work stoppage in the country's history, and one that influenced the government to adopt a more restrictive policy toward unions, socialists, and the press (Duus and Scheiner 1998, 166–167). Beginning on February 4, the strike became a riot as the miners cut the electricity supply to their workplace, and destroyed sixty-five company buildings, most of which they burned down, and damaged other property, with the dispute finally only being ended by the army. Despite the existing restrictions on unionization, an activist called Minami, Sukematsu had begun toward the end of 1906 to attract the support of the miners for his organization, the Greater-Japan Society of Devotion to Japanese Labor (Dai Nippon Rōdō Shiseikai). Soon, Shiseikai was campaigning for increases in salaries and food rations, including improvement in the quality of the rice supplied to the men, which was of less quality than that supplied to their supervisors. Although Minami and his fellow strike leaders were aware that the Public Order and Police Law of 1900 did not allow their agitation of worker grievances, they had repeatedly called for union solidarity to achieve their goals. Reportedly, when Kōtoku heard of the riot, he was overjoyed (Mikio 1966, 507–508; Nimura 1997, 67–68, 69, 71, 200, 262 fn 13). The *Cronaca Sovversiva* subtly connected the Ashio strike to the later execution of Kōtoku and the other alleged plotters:

> Nelle miniere del rame di Ashio i lavoratori vi guadagnavano da un franco a un franco e mezzo al giorno, per uu lavoro estenuante presto convertito in agonia. Nella primavera del 1907 un grande sciopero scoppiò a Ashio e la truppa tosto chiamata sul luogo, come nei nostri paesi, si cinse a portare una solida garanzia di sfruttamento alla classe capitalista.
> G.S. 1911

> [In the copper mines of Ashio the workers earned from one franc to one and a half francs a day, for a grueling work soon turned into agony. In the spring of 1907 a great strike broke out in Ashio and the troops soon called up there, as in our countries, girded themselves to bring a solid guarantee of exploitation to the capitalist class.]

Similarly, the Sydney, Australia-based *International Socialist* argued that Kōtoku "incurred the displeasure of the government by his anti-military ideas and by taking up the cause of the northern rice farmers whose farming was being ruined by the impositions of great copper mining interests in Ashio in turning the poison water from the mines on the rice fields" (W.R.W. 1911).

5 Kōtoku and the Japanese Language

Commitment to creation of a standard written national language (*kokugo*), which would be used in all areas of Japan, grew as the country ventured further beyond its borders as part of the conquest of foreign territory that Kōtoku criticized in his book, *Imperialism*. Thus, that work was written in *kundokubun* (vernacular reading register) by taking the language of classical Chinese in which the works of Confucius and Mencius had been scribed, and adapting it to Japanese, creating a hybrid idiom. While *kundokubun* transposition had been used for many centuries, for example to convert Buddhist sutras, the development of *kokugo* can be viewed as an instance of imperialism, especially once the Russo-Japanese War had commenced (Bundschuh 2021, ii, 4–5; Essertier 2017, 16; Tierney 2015, 11).

Although the style of *kokugo* made it easier for Shūsui's readers in China and Korea to understand his work as printed, later modernization of the Japanese language rendered his books less accessible, and, as a consequence, Tierney (2015, 11) notes, *Imperialism* has recently been retranslated into modern Japanese. Nonetheless, the ideology of *kokugo* encourages modern textbook publishers to promote works that are written in it as contributing to patriotism (Yoshii 2014, 2–3). Perhaps ironically, in his discussion of the language of Japanese newspapers, Kōtoku argues that they should be composed in a colloquial form that more people would understand, rather than in *kundokubun* or classical Japanese styles. As a member of the Genbun Itchi Kai (the Society for the Unification of Speech and Writing), he was demonstrating his commitment to *genbun itchi*, communication employing a unified vernacular, a change that would soon be implemented in newspapers and by book publishers (Essertier 2017, 28–29). He pointed out its benefits for businesses and individual readers alike:

> The number of readers would surely double or triple if all newspaper articles were written in a *genbun itchi* style and even readers without training in classical and elegant styles were able to read them. Journalists would have a far greater impact on society – it would be two or three times greater than the impact they now have – and newspaper companies would enjoy far greater profits. Even those who are fully trained in reading classical styles and who can appreciate their elegance would spend less mental energy and less time reading newspapers. They would spend half or even less than half what they currently spend.
>
> KŌTOKU [1901b] 2017, 34

Here, it might be asked whether Kōtoku's goal is that people should spend less time reading or to be able to read more content, since the two arguments seem to be mutually contradictory. However, it is clear that he sees greater educational value in using words that many will understand, rather than focusing on writing to earn academic plaudits:

> If you are only going to write something for your own pleasure or show what you have written to a few intellectuals, then any kind of style is fine, but if you want to inform and teach millions of people you have to use the most effective style, i.e., the colloquial style of the period.
>
> KŌTOKU [1901b] 2017, 36–37

Kōtoku's call for simplicity to aid the novice's understanding bears some surprising similarity to the arguments of the increasingly disenchanted Catholic, Auberon Waugh, who, although he opposed making the substance of church services more understandable to the average worshipper such as himself, preferring them to remain difficult to understand or analyze, took a similar position to Kōtoku insofar as he stressed the importance of choosing a specific delivery style. Waugh wrote:

> True zealots, especially on the liberal side, would probably assume that the indifferent center constitutes the greatest threat to Catholicism's rebirth, that the Church should be prepared to shed it and concentrate on a nucleus of enthusiasts who might yet win the world to their thinking.
> As a self-appointed spokesman for the unenthusiastic center one is bound to find this attitude rather hurtful. Certainly the role of pig-in-the-middle is not the most dignified, and calls for a certain humility.
> We pigs cannot claim to be better Catholics, nor more knowledgeable, nor more inspired by love, than the enthusiasts; nor can we appeal to the first principles of democracy in such a transcendental matter and claim that because we represent the majority we must be right. Catholics believe that their Church's mystical body includes its saints in heaven, whose votes are impossible to collect, and its Chairman's vote overrides the lot. Quite possibly we are quite wrong in everything we say or do. Our only claim to be heard is that we exist.
> WAUGH 1970

For Kōtoku, on the other hand, allowing a preference for traditional religious rituals to obscure the enlightenment of the majority is the wrong approach:

> If Christian hymns were sung in 31 syllables, it would be like a Christian priest wearing the pre-modem clothing of a Japanese aristocrat. Each period has its own style and if one does not use the colloquial style of the period it is difficult to persuade the people.
> KŌTOKU [1901b] 2017, 36

6 Kōtoku the Atheist

In March 1910, bothered by the constant surveillance of his activities while he was in Tokyo, Kōtoku again relocated about seventy miles away to Yugawara, accompanied by Kanno. In the last letter that he wrote to Albert Johnson, which bore the date April 11, 1910, he reminded his correspondent that he was working on a new book, which would be called *Kirisuto Massatsuron* [*On the Obliteration of Christ*] (García [1976] 2013, 44, 2000, 3; Tsuzuki 1966, 37, 37 fn 11, 37 fn 12). Kōtoku wrote:

> I am writing a book in which I mean to assert that Christ never existed, but was a myth; that the origin of Christianity is found in pagan mythology, and that most of the Bible is forgery.
>
> KŌTOKU, letter to Albert Johnson, April 11, 1910, in "Kotoku's Correspondence with Albert Johnson (Conclusion)" 1911, 286

When he returned from the United States, Shūsui had been surprised to find Christian missionaries were actively trying to convert people to their beliefs, an occurrence he attributed to the government's desire to promote its new imperialism (García [1976] 2013, 45; Hsu 2016, 210; Racel 2011, 267–268):

> Christian priests, taking advantage of the weakness of the government, got a great monetary aid from the State, and under its protection they are propagating in full vigor the Gospel of Patriotism. Thus Japanese Christianity, which was before the war the religion of poor, literally now changed within only two years to a great bourgeois religion and a machine of the State and militarism!
>
> KŌTOKU, letter to Albert Johnson, December 18, 1906, in
> "Kotoku's Correspondence with Albert Johnson (Continuation)"
> 1911, 208; GARCÍA [1976] 2013, 45 is similar

However, this seems an exaggerated conclusion given the fact that many of his fellow socialist activist opponents of the Russo-Japanese conflict were Christians, though of course there were some Christians who were fiercely patriotic.

In *Kirisuto Massatsuron*, Kōtoku took the position that there had never been a person called Jesus, an argument that has been made in other countries at different times. The book, which was published in Japan following his execution in 1911, became influential in China where, in the 1920s, the Anti-Christian Movement, which also dismissed other religions as examples of naïve superstition, used it, along with similar texts, to spread the view that the stories of Jesus were fictional (Hansen 2020, 104–105; Zheng 2019, 135, 139–140). The Chinese version appeared in print in 1924, and was translated by someone using the name "Lidiaopi," who has subsequently been identified as probably being Liu

Wendian (1891–1958), a Peking University professor who had once studied in Japan (Zheng 2019, 136–138).

Zheng (2019, 136, 147) notes that Kōtoku's dismissal of religious authority allowed him also to shrewdly unseat the quasi-religious myths that justified the existence of the Japanese emperor, but, as Notehelfer ([1971b] 2010, 193) points out, few of his fellow-citizens cared or dared to make that argument even if they found it convincing. Kōtoku's commitment to atheism was not a last-minute event in response to his circumstances at the end of his life. When he departed for Sugamo Prison on February 28, 1905 to begin his sentence, he took a bible with him, telling Kinoshita, Naoe he wanted to spend some time investigating its shortcomings (Notehelfer [1971b] 2010, 109). Pelletier (2002, 104) writes that "Kōtoku Shūsui s'est toujours méfié de cette religion" [Kōtoku Shūsui was always suspicious of this religion]. Notehelfer concludes:

> While he [Kōtoku] cooperated with Uchimura Kanzō, Kinoshita Naoe, Katayama Sen, and some of the other Christians and Christian-Socialists, he always felt their values to be somehow foreign and dangerous.
> NOTEHELFER [1971b] 2010, 71

7 Kōtoku's Chinese Influences

Kōtoku's teacher, the scholar of Rousseau, Nakae, Chōmin, encouraged him to be familiar with the classical writings of Chinese thinkers, including early Confucian and Taoist works. Asukai (1978, 131–132) writes that this time in Shūsui's life was thus one where he attempted "to internalize modern French thought by using the Confucian concept of *jin*, virtue." However, over the centuries, the main ethical concepts of Confucianism changed, with the consequence that *jin* no longer indicated exactly the same kind of virtue that it did back in the days of Confucius and Mencius, who understood *jen* (pronounced "ren") as goodness or benevolence. Benedict (1946, 118) points out that "In fact jen became in Japan an outlaw virtue and was entirely demoted from the high estate it had in Chinese ethics."

Accordingly, the frequent scholarly interpretation of Kōtoku, a socialist who became an anarchist, as being hidebound by his classical Oriental education raises a number of questions and ultimately perhaps damages the understanding we have of a rather profound, though not necessarily consistent thinker nor one well-versed in the theories he promoted. For example, his biography is changed by Lévy and some other scholars to the extent that it needs to be asked whether in fact Kōtoku has become a victim of cultural stereotyping:

> L'anarchisme de Kōtoku, à notre avis, était essentiellement lié au nouveau courant révolutionnaire qui se dessinait dans le mouvement ouvrier à l'échelle mondiale, mais son attachement, jusqu'à la fin de sa vie, à une éthique politique, basée sur les notions de solidarité, et d'entraide, reflète son univers mental et intellectuel lié au confucianisme, acquis au cours de son enfance, transformé dans un sens démocratique par la référence à Mencius et à Zhuang zi au cours de sa vie de disciple auprès de Nakae Chōmin.
>
> LÉVY 2002, 79

[Kōtoku's anarchism, in our view, was essentially linked to the new revolutionary current that was taking shape in the workers' movement on a world scale, but his attachment, until the end of his life, to a political ethic, based on the notions of solidarity, and mutual aid, reflects his mental and intellectual universe linked to Confucianism, acquired during his childhood, transformed in a democratic sense by the reference to Mencius and Zhuangzi during his life as a disciple with Nakae, Chōmin.]

Similarly, Notehelfer contends that, hobbled by his ancestry and his "Asian" samurai/ Confucian/ Taoist influences, Kōtoku, was unable to achieve his radical potential:

> As a product of the *shishi* [gentlemanly] tradition, there was inherent in Kōtoku a potential for revolutionary action. There was even a potential for revolutionary thought. But such action, and such thought, had their roots within traditional, not modern values.
>
> NOTEHELFER [1971b] 2010, 3

This seems to be a somewhat distorted evaluation of a man who was one of the major revolutionary campaigners of the late nineteenth and early twentieth centuries. It can also be asked whether, although Kōtoku was familiar with many icons of Chinese and Japanese culture, he was any more rigorously familiar with their minutiae than he was with socialism when he advocated that doctrine before he had really read much about it, in *Imperialism* viewing many thinkers, including Marx, as essentially making the same argument. Then he gravitated to anarchism, and certainly, having become a translator of Kropotkin, to whom he referred as "the anarchists' prime authority" (Kōtoku [1910b] 1967, 469), he was very familiar with what the latter believed. He was a friend of Albert Johnson, with whom he corresponded, and while he was in San Francisco visiting Johnson, he learned something from Rose Fritz, who was an admirer of Bakunin. He also had some contact with Emma Goldman and Hippolyte Havel at *Mother Earth*. But when he became an anarchist, was his knowledge of anarchist theory as full of holes as his familiarity with many diverse aspects of socialism had been when he declared himself a socialist? Did he know of the individualistic approach of Max Stirner, or his contemporaries Benjamin R. Tucker, the editor of "Liberty," or Tucker's friend, the promoter of the ideas of Stirner, John Henry Mackay? In His "The Tide Of The World Revolutionary Movement" address on June 28, 1906, Kōtoku lauded the work of, among others, Proudhon, Johann Most, and Malatesta (Elison 1967, 458), but had he read them?

Murthy (2011, 186 fn 45) argues that "Kōtoku was deeply trained in the classical Chinese texts from a young age and supported the reviving of Confucius and Lao Zi. ... In his famous work on imperialism, Kōtoku invoked Mencius's analogy concerning helping other people's parents as if they were one's own to break down the barriers of states." But when various leading lights of classical Chinese thought are clustered in this fashion, the analysis is open to criticism that it ignores the conflicts between two very different religions, Confucianism and Taoism, and between rival schools of Confucianism, between Mencius and Xunzi as to whether or not human nature is good or bad, or whether, even if human nature is naturally good, people will have the necessary skills or wish to choose to follow its guidance, or if their ability to behave appropriately might be determined by the environment in which they live or the rituals they have learned. The conflict is perpetuated in Neo-Confucianism through the rival interpretations of Wang Yang-ming and Chu Hsi and their followers (Chong 2003, 219–210, 226–227; Kim 2011, 375; Schofer 1993, 117–119, 131–132; Shih 1969, 397–398; Tucker 2009, 144–145; Yearley 1980, 465–466, 477). Moreover, Nakae wanted Kōtoku to *read* the classics, and to be able to write in a form of classical Chinese: he did not necessarily want him to apply their teachings in every situation. Tierney comments:

> Chōmin had his students read Mencius and Zhuangzi: "Unless one understands the rules of Chinese writing, how can one compose a text? One who aspires to write well needs to read many Chinese texts."
> TIERNEY 2015, 22, 222 fn 18; the cited quotation is from KŌTOKU 2001, 31–32

Notehelfer emphasizes Nakae's purpose when giving his advice:

> For while Nakae shared his student's commitment to such Confucian values as sincerity, honesty, single mindedness of purpose, and a concern for reason and justice, he did not share Kōtoku's disdain for the commercial

world and commercial ethics. The realistic side of Nakae told him that business ethics, while far from Confucian, was very much a part of the Meiji reality, and that a person who wanted to succeed in the Meiji world would have to compromise with the system as it stood.

NOTEHELFER [1971b] 2010, 33

Moreover, Notehelfer's own roughly hewn stereotype of "Confucian values" contains elements that are not necessarily compatible with "a concern for reason and justice": the advocacy of filial piety (which Kōtoku disdained and, as noted above, in *Imperialism*, mocked), and respect for authority, which he dedicated his adult life to undermining. The reverence for the great weight of the various pronouncements of Confucius and Mencius that is found in the *Analects* (the main source for information about Confucius) and in the *Mencius*, for example, is not necessarily rational or ideal from every perspective, especially in the age of capitalism and revolution. Indeed, Notehelfer to some extent undercuts his own statement when he writes:

> One cannot help but wonder on occasion what Kōtoku meant by 'love' and 'benevolence', but it seems clear that these, like harmony, purity, single-mindedness of purpose, filial piety, and other concepts that had come to him out of the Confucian tradition, were abstractions that rarely reflected themselves in his daily actions.
>
> NOTEHELFER [1971b] 2010, 49

Thus, Shūsui's familiarity with ancient Chinese texts as alluded to in his writings is not inescapably an affiliation that distorts his commitment to socialist and later to anarchist thought, and it is also hard to agree with Notehelfer (1971a, 33) that "Kōtoku had come to identify the universals of the Confucian tradition with the ideals of the French Revolution." Rather, it seems, Tierney (2015, 66) is correct that, in scorning the value of *Imperialism*, "Notehelfer treats Confucianism as an ossified dogma that interferes with and distorts Kōtoku's reception of Western thought." Ward (2019, 407) offers a similar assessment that "Notehelfer ... reduced the nuances of Kōtoku's politics to an attempt to translate premodern Confucian ethics into a modern political idiom, rendering Kōtoku and Japanese anarchism more generally as cultural anachronisms inadequate to political modernity."

Similarly, when Sievers (1969, 46) writes that "In the period from 1901 to 1903, Kōtoku's socialism consisted of a series of broad assumptions which owed as much or more to his Confucian upbringing as to his conversion to a Marxian revolutionary ethic," it is judicious to consider that *Imperialism*, a work widely considered to have anticipated the theories of contemporary international relations scholars, was published in 1901. It might also be noted here that Albert Johnson was praised by Kōtoku in a poem he wrote in his diary during the time he was visiting California as being open-minded about the teachings of religions other than Christianity:

> Though he was born in the West, not received a baptism of Christ,
>   But recites the teachings of Lao Tsu [Lao Zi] and be pleased with self-renunciation of Buddha.
>   KŌTOKU [1906] 1979, 108–109

Fortunately, this scholarly endorsement has not so far led to the anarchist ideas of Johnson being portrayed as watered down or compromised by his familiarity with Taoism and Buddhism.

Kōtoku was nonetheless familiar with his cultural heritage, so it is unsurprising that he would from time to time make reference to it. In his attempt to define anarchism near the end of his life, he makes mention of the presumed authors of classical Taoist texts, claiming a similarity between their teachings and those of his newest belief system, but typically he presents no detail that ought to convince the reader of the thoroughness of his analysis:

> There are many who simply take the anarchist revolution to mean attempts by pistol or bomb upon the life of the sovereign. This is due to the universal failure to understand just what anarchism is. As you, our defenders, already know, the doctrines of this movement constitute a type of philosophy which is greatly similar to the thought of Lao Tzu [Lao Zi] and Chuang Tzu [Zhuangzi] in the Orient. Anarchism consists of the following belief: It is the manifest trend of the nature of human society that the present-day system of coercive rule by authoritarianism and force of arms will cease to exist and a society of communal life and mutual assistance welded by bonds of morality and love will appear. To perfect our freedom and happiness we must advance in accordance with this trend.
>   KŌTOKU [1910b] 1967, 469; [1910a] 1979, 92 has a similar translation

On the other hand, in the case of Mencius and the latter's example of how a person would feel and react to seeing that a child had fallen into a well, there is a direct connection to anarchism that lies in the recognition, common to both perspectives, that human beings possess innate knowledge of virtue (Shone 2013, ch. 10). Additionally, recent Mencius scholarship has addressed the idea of naturalizing his philosophy, bypassing religious references, including the Confucian use of the word for heaven (*tian*; *T'ien*), and understanding his argument on this topic instead in terms of the effect of evolution in managing to perfect human experience, whereby the theory now becomes that people learn from errors that were made in the past, new information being passed on genetically from generation to generation (Behuniak 2011, 492–493).

Thus for Kōtoku to cite Mencius in this fashion seems to run consistently with what he had learned later in his life from Kropotkin, and can be understood as an anarchist perspective. As Kōtoku realized, he was not a great thinker, and much of his influence lay in communicating the radical ideas of other more profound and systematic socialists and anarchists and other critics of government, as he strived to undermine the reactionary and contradictory political culture in which he found himself living in the Meiji age. Moving gradually in the direction of pacifism and opposition to colonialism and imperialism, and seeking redress from the excesses he now saw in contemporary capitalist development, he embraced many potentially incompatible perspectives at different periods of his life. However, his compassion for the majority of people inadequately served by conventional notions of democracy as somehow being a system of indirect and occasional representation by a class of political candidates or "leaders," led him instead to embrace direct action, a method by which he thought the masses might achieve some measure of immediate input and relief from neglect, rather than just piously waiting in misery, perhaps with the right to vote this year or next, but probably not, hoping and hoping for some kind of change that would never transpire.

Conclusion

In the Introduction to the present work, a list of concepts, commitments, and names occurring among the beliefs of the five thinkers discussed in the preceding chapters was given: anarchism, syndicalism, the Industrial Workers of the World, industrial unionism, the general strike, and militant labor union activism in general, direct action, creating One Big Union, anxiety about "the social question," support for people and soldiers of "enemy" nations, and opposition to military conscription, to the First World War, and to the sending of Western troops at the end of that conflict to interfere disruptively in the Soviet Union. Many of these ideas have been misunderstood, and in view of their interrelationship, perhaps there is too much focus on the putative differences between them, and less on the more fundamental objectives that Virginia Bolten, Tom Barker, Kōtoku, Shūsui, Helen Armstrong, and Elizabeth Gurley Flynn hoped to achieve. As Emma Goldman wrote, linking some of the ideas noted above:

> Syndicalism is, in essence, the economic expression of Anarchism. That circumstance accounts for the presence of so many Anarchists in the Syndicalist movement. Like Anarchism, Syndicalism prepares the workers along direct economic lines, as conscious factors in the great struggles of to-day, as well as conscious factors in the task of reconstructing society along autonomous industrial lines, as against the paralyzing spirit of centralization with its bureaucratic machinery of corruption, inherent in all political parties.
> GOLDMAN 1913, 7

At the heart of the endeavors of the thinkers described in the present book and those of others with similar viewpoints was a desire to see ordinary people rewarded fairly for the work they did, and to achieve some admittance to the so-called finer things in life, including provision of basic needs and services, such as adequate housing and access to education and healthcare. They also wanted to have the ability to talk and write about their needs and experiences, and to form labor unions and other organizations that would help them achieve relief from exploitation that caused misery and death. Yet, faced with a demand for freedom of speech or the ability to bargain collectively or, in a world of great differences in wealth and opportunity that divides the rich and poor, presenting an improved imagining of how society might rightly be organized, the response of government and its police and the owners of capital who profited from the existing set-up was generally to seek to undermine or even crush the criticism that they considered dangerous to their effective dominion.

To this day, thinkers who call themselves anarchists are presumed to advocate anarchy, to be bomb-throwers, or absurdly to be Bolsheviks, a confusion that has never been helped by the fact that some anarchist thinkers have used the words anarchism and anarchy interchangeably and because, during the era of IWW prominence and the brief apparent success of Bolshevism in Russia, mainstream newspaper reports and editorials accused the Wobblies and Bolsheviks of having the same agenda. As Jensen points out:

> The truth, however, is that the I.W.W. philosophically stands poles apart from the Communists. True, a few who were "wobblies" shifted ground and later appeared in the Communist camp or became its followers. But the vast majority of the I.W.W. could not make the jump. As believers in the value of the individual and in the integrity of his personal being, they had built an organization without strong central authority, which allowed freedom to the individual member. The "wobblies" hated authoritarians in any form.
> JENSEN 1967, 108

Moreover, the fact remains that no anarchist philosopher has ever desired the complete absence of government, and the original classical Greek word, *anarkhiā*, stands for the absence of leadership, but does not mean "no government at all." From this confusion has arisen a specious contemporary conclusion often to be found in online sources that "anarchists" believe in no government, while "libertarians" believe in "less government." While it is of course true that modern right-libertarians such as the Libertarian Party, USA advocate less government, the argument misrepresents the opinions of left-libertarians, i.e., of anarchists, who have also throughout the history of anarchism, labeled themselves libertarians, the concept of liberty being fundamental to the beliefs of both camps. Furthermore, despite the designations of "right" and "left" that at times appear to signify an enormous difference between two factions, right-libertarians and left-libertarians share a commitment to letting individuals, rather than governments or religious leaders and others who enjoy psychological domination over portions of the population, make many of the decisions that confront human beings as a whole. Thus it is prudent to deemphasize overreliance upon the categorization of ideological or organizational distinctions if for no other reason than because there is disagreement as to which labels are best suited to which example. In the case of syndicalism, different understandings of the concept can, as with anarchism, lead to additional confusion. In his contemporaneous study of the IWW, Paul F. Brissenden illustrates the potential contradictions when he comments:

> Syndicalism is the most modern phase of the revolutionary movement. It can with perfect safety be dubbed revolutionary, but to call it socialistic would elicit the protests of many syndicalists to whom "socialism" is mere middle-class reform, and to call it anarchistic would also be unwise, as an even larger number of them believe syndicalism to be the only true socialism. However, it is unquestionably revolutionary and seems really to be the most startling manifestation of the proletarian unrest that the world has yet seen. In syndicalism there is a synthesis of elements: the Socialist indictment of capitalism and part of the Socialist programme; the anarchist method and ideal; and the unionist idea of organization in trade or industry.
> BRISSENDEN 1913, 1

Similarly, with regard to the potential for misunderstanding, Petersen concludes:

> Most historians of the IWW have labelled it "syndicalist," despite the fact that Wobbly leaders consistently called themselves industrial unionists and distinguished themselves from syndicalists; indeed, the most dedicated syndicalists, like William Z. Foster, left or drifted away from the IWW because of differences of opinion over organization and tactics. ... The major historians of the Canadian OBU repeatedly call this union a Canadian version of syndicalism, but nowhere do they show how the OBU was syndicalist or why this term is specifically relevant in this case.
> PETERSON 1981, 53

O'Connor (1956, 165) writes of "the semi-anarchism of the wobblies," and Donner (1982, 535) designates the IWW as "an authentic expression of American radicalism" and as possessors of an "anarcho-syndicalist ideology." Nevertheless, underlying the theoretical tags, IWW, anarchist, and syndicalist pursuits are, and were, largely activities related to speech, writing, publication, and association with others, including the offering of assistance to low-paid employees, particularly if on strike.

Thus, Virginia Bolten's significance can be better explained in terms of speeches like the ones she made to inaugurate the Cerro Social Studies Center, while protesting Argentina's Residence Law, and at Maciel Pier when participating in the FORU's Congress. Alternatively, her actions can be understood from her involvement with publications such as *Emancipación, La Nueva Senda*, or *Regeneración*; or her association with others in the setting up in Montevideo of the women's group, "Emancipación"; or by considering some of her articles, such as "Preguntas y respuestas"; or from analyzing her involvement in the strike at Zárate. What is important here is that, while such activities provoked concern on the part of governments in Argentina and Uruguay, they were essentially examples of the exercise of rights which citizens are generally, or officially, or at least ideally, considered to possess.

Similarly, the importance of Helen Armstrong is illustrated by her extensive radical participation, not only in the difficult, most contentious weeks of the Winnipeg General Strike, but also from the social objectives she sought to achieve over a years-long period as the leader of the Women's Labor League where she emphasized the needs of women, the poor, prisoners, and immigrants, and highlighted the importance of free speech and collective bargaining. Although, unlike the other four persons discussed in the present work, Helen did not write books and articles, her many spoken contributions to gatherings of labor, local government, and social organizations, including her participation as one of the delegates to the Western Labour Conference in Calgary, Alberta, an event that was a major influence on the thinking of the strikers as well as the source of much criticism by their opponents such as the Committee of One Thousand, constitute significant evidence of what she believed and what she accomplished. Her presence is documented repeatedly in newspaper accounts, not only in radical publications like the *Voice* and the *Western Labor News*, but also in the area's mainstream media.

Elizabeth Gurley Flynn's half century of energetic public speaking on behalf of left-wing causes was supplemented by books and articles in which, like her statements in court when she was on trial, emphasized her commitment to open discourse and in detail presented her own understandings of the nature of her prominent activist life, as did her choices about which victims of government discrimination or oppression she would support. As she redeployed from a Wobbly perspective to a communist one, her activities around the United States were followed in many *Daily Worker* reports.

Tom Barker wrote many articles for the local IWW publications that he edited, the *Industrial Unionist* in New Zealand, and *Direct Action* in Australia, and many more in radical newspapers such as the *Daily Worker*, in scholarly radical journals, and in the Wobblies' Chicago-based magazine, *Industrial Pioneer*. He sent letters that demonstrated his sarcastic temperament to sympathetic listeners and to the press, and gave public lectures as he raised funds for union activities and tried to obtain his colleagues' release from jail. He was a participant in a number of important revolutionary political conferences in

Europe and, from New York, he worked to promote the Kuzbas Autonomous Industrial Project in Siberia.

There is a wealth of material that illustrates the importance Kōtoku, Shūsui to the history of radical thought, including the articles and editorial columns he wrote as a newspaper journalist, his translations of some of the key works of major European thinkers, his speeches at political party conferences, the poetry he wrote when incarcerated, letters he wrote to Albert Johnson, Peter Kropotkin, and others, and his own books that endorse socialism, and criticize patriotism, colonialism, imperialism, capitalism, and Christianity.

When a person is an anarchist or a person of similar beliefs, then the reaction to palpable criticism of those in power contained in what you say or do often leads to violent attacks from police who serve the power of authorities, lies and exaggerations spread by politicians, strike-breaking, censorship, deportations, flawed trials, imprisonment, and even executions. This double standard seems to reflect, at least to some extent, the very effectiveness of the campaigns for political change that Wobblies and other anarchists and syndicalists have achieved. In the case of the IWW, of which for a substantial part of their lives, Tom Barker and Elizabeth Gurley Flynn were prominent leaders, they were trying to expand labor unions to include the less skilled, minorities, and women, and to achieve One Big Union, which were also the goals of Helen Armstrong and her fellow radicals in the Winnipeg General Strike of 1919, and was something the like of which Kōtoku, Shūsui sought to achieve in Japan, and which Bolten promoted in southern South America. The IWW were also seen as a threat to preexisting, much more conservative craft-based approaches to organizing workers which consequently developed into rivals with an interest in avoiding the changes the Wobblies desired (Cannon 1928, 14).

Today, in a domain understood increasingly in terms of worldwide problems and proposed global solutions, it might be imagined that many of the difficulties confronted by Virginia Bolten, Helen Armstrong, Elizabeth Gurley Flynn, Tom Barker, and Kōtoku, Shūsui would by now be to a substantial extent resolved. The tremendous affluence of Western nations might cause a naïve observer to expect the termination of the near-enslavement of laborers denied participation in workplace rule-making as they toil to obtain the ability to feed themselves and their dependents, or of their lack of access to medical and pharmaceutical products and services, education, whereby they might improve their position in society, and availability of transportation, even to get to work. Yet nothing like that accomplishment has in any way been achieved, even in the wealthiest nations of North America and Western Europe. As airlines escort prosperous vacationers around the globe, the rickety boats of starving emigrants from elsewhere collapse in rather less courtly circumstances.

Refugees wander the globe, escaping disasters natural and man-made, desperately seeking a place where their families can survive, abandoning the dictators who continue to rule with tacit permission from less offensive political authorities, who are afraid to challenge the imagined authority of crooks and tyrants, focusing instead on keeping as many refugees as possible beyond the shores of their own realms. Not only are there human beings without a place to live, but there are some who lack the citizenship of any country, and many more whose passports will allow them access only to a restricted number of locations, mostly ones where they would never wish to go. As noted in Chapter 3, when Elizabeth Gurley Flynn and Carlo Tresca spoke to strikers at the Hillcrest Silk Mills in New Jersey, the employer was threatening to move the firm to North Carolina. Today, businesses still redeploy to places where the pay and benefits and civil rights protections will be less. Competition with products made in other, cheaper locations with fewer safety standards also helps undermine the work and remuneration and future availability of employment in the nations where better conditions exist. Meanwhile, as discussed in Chapter 5, the great success of big government, its modern ability to observe and chronicle and regulate almost every activity of human beings has proceeded apace, generally without those in charge having asked for permission from the members of society to approve the positioning of the controls and therefore to allow themselves to be spied upon.

At the same time, academic political science, particularly in the United States, which has excessively focused on techniques of political participation such as, in particular, voting, registration requirements, levels of participation in elections, the names and backgrounds of candidates, and how much support they may have, has reduced the character of "democracy" to its most inadequate, most simplistic, most procedural definition, avoiding consideration of the contribution of continued problems like poverty and denial of the most basic needs and services that would lead to a more appropriate inventory.

While in the United States, Alexis de Tocqueville, wanting to account for the new political system he would labor to describe, included a visit to the prison in Wethersfield, Connecticut. Surely, a reasonable calculation of how democratic a nation might be, rather than just counting how many people are enfranchised or bother to vote, would be to ask, how many people are in its jails, and which groups are most likely to be there? In the US, for example, at the end of 2020, there were 1,691,600 persons incarcerated, and a total of 5,500,600 under the control of the courts, including those on parole or probation (Kluckow and Zeng 2020, 4). Approximately 38% of those presently in jail are African-Americans, although that group constitutes only about 12% of the US population (Sawyer and Wagner 2023). In Xinjiang, in western China, more than a million Uyghurs and other Muslim minorities per year have been imprisoned in detention camps identified by the government as skills training facilities, but designed to impose ideological compliance with the views of the Communist Party (Kao et al. 2021; Kuo 2019). Almost every country in the world, including the ones with the most objectionable governments, employ voting, which, to paraphrase Tocqueville when he wrote about the old Mexican Constitution of 1824 (Cockell 2022, Tocqueville [1835–1840] 1899, 162–163, 174 fn 38), suggests that voting may not have too much to do with whether or not a nation is truly democratic:

> The Constitution of the United States is like those exquisite productions of human industry which insure wealth and renown for their inventors, but which are profitless in any other hands. The truth is exemplified by the condition of Mexico at the present time. The Mexicans were desirous of establishing a Federal system, and they took the Federal Constitution of their neighbours the Anglo-Americans as their model, and copied it with considerable accuracy. But although they had borrowed the letter of the law, they were unable to create or to introduce the spirit and the sense which give of life.
> TOCQUEVILLE [1835–1840] 1899, 162–163

On the other hand, many of the changes sought by the five thinkers discussed in the present work and their allies, strong labor unions able to bargain collectively, universal access to basic needs such as housing, healthcare, and education, and a universal right to travel, with far fewer people in jail, free speech, and a free press, and governments having much less power: success in these areas would perhaps constitute a more substantive understanding of democracy, regardless of whether there was any need for choosing leaders or much interest in voting.

Bibliography

"9 Meetings Held as Protest for Labor Leaders." 1919. *Winnipeg Evening Tribune* [MAN], September 8.

"12 Jap Socialists Executed." 1911. *Tacoma Times* [Wash.], January 24.

"248 Delegates Set 300,000 Members as Goal For Second Year of Activity of I.L.D." 1926. *Daily Worker* [Chicago], September 9.

"500 Germans Deported." 1919. *Aberdeen Daily Journal* [U.K.], October 15.

"600 Jitneys in City This Year, Organizer Says." 1917. *Winnipeg Evening Tribune* [MAN], March 10.

"7,500 Pack Labor Church." 1919. *Western Labor News* [Winnipeg, MAN], June 2.

"10,000 Crimes are Charged to the I.W.W." 1917. *Chicago Tribune*, September 30.

"$18,000 Here to Aid Sacco and Vanzetti." 1921. *New York Herald*, November 18.

"60,000 Electors Fail to Register." 1920. *Winnipeg Evening Tribune* [MAN], May 12.

Abrams, Bruce A. 1987. "A Muted Cry: White Opposition to the Japanese Exclusion Movement, 1911–1924." Ph.D. diss. City University of New York.

"A Charge of Conspiracy." 1916. *Chronicle* [Adelaide, SA], November 4.

"A Choice Suggestion." 1913. Editorial. *Southland Times* [Invercargill, N.Z.], October 25.

"A Crime to Strike." 1919. Editorial. *Western Labor News* [Winnipeg, MAN], June 20.

"A Deported Alien." 1920. *Southland Times* [Invercargill, N.Z.], January 14.

"Address by Tom Barker." 1917. *Queensland Times* [Ipswich, QLD], January 13.

"Add 10,000 New Members, Labor Defense Plan." 1926. *Daily Worker* [Chicago], October 10.

"A Denial." 1913. *Evening Post* [Wellington, N.Z.], November 24.

"A.D. Kay, Charlatan." 1921. *Communist* [Sydney, NSW], July 8.

A.F. 1922. "Skilled Workers for Russia." *Northern Standard* [Darwin, NT], July 18.

"A Few Frank Words Concerning Agitators." 1919. Advertisement. *Winnipeg Citizen* [MAN], June 16.

Ajax. 1915. "The Myth of Ownership, or The Sanctity of Private Property." *Direct Action* [Sydney, NSW], May 15.

"Albanians Pledge 'Fight to the End.'" 1961. *Belfast Telegraph* [U.K.], October 23.

Albornoz, Martín, and Diego Antonio Galeano. 2016. "El momento beastly: la policía de Buenos Aires y la expulsión de extranjeros (1896–1904)." *Astrolabio: Nueva Época* [Córdoba, Argentina] 17:6–41.

Albornoz, Martín, and Diego Antonio Galeano. 2019. "Los agitadores móviles: trayectorias anarquistas y vigilancias portuarias en el Atlántico Sudamericano, 1894–1908."*Almanack* [Guarulhos, Brazil] 21:310–357.

"A las mujeres." 1910. *La Nueva Senda* [Montevideo, Uruguay], January 7.

Alexander, Robert J., with the collaboration of Eldon M. Parker. 2005. *A History of Organized Labor in Uruguay and Paraguay*. Westport, Conn.: Praeger.
"Aliens' Release Asked by Labor." 1919. *Winnipeg Evening Tribune* [MAN], June 21.
"All Loaves of Bread Must Weigh 20 Ozs." 1917. *Brandon Daily Sun* [MAN], July 4.
"All Postal Workers in West Ordered to Strike." 1919. *Winnipeg Evening Tribune* [MAN], May 26.
"Almazoff is Released by Probe Board." 1919. *Winnipeg Evening Tribune* [MAN], August 16.
"Almazoff Says He is Opposed to Bloodshed." 1919. *Winnipeg Evening Tribune* [MAN], August 15.
Alonso, Cecelia. 2021. "Virginia Bolten: feminismo anárquico en la casa y la fábrica." *Reveladas* [Rosario, Argentina], May 1.
"American Colony Fails under Russian Control." 1923. *Sunday Star* [Washington, D.C.], August 12.
"An Affecting Scene: Japanese Conspirators Sentenced." 1911. *Gisborne Times* [N.Z.], February 1.
"An Anti-Recruiting Journal: I.W.W. Publisher Fined." 1916. *Colonist* [Nelson, N.Z.], March 31.
"Anarchists Given Death Sentences." 1911. *San Francisco Call* [Calif.], January 10.
"Anarchists in Japan: Short Shrift for the Prisoners." 1911. *Poverty Bay Herald* [Gisborne, N.Z.], January 25.
Andersen, Jake. 2020. ""Rebel Girls" Reevaluated: Gender in the Lives of Three Wobbly Women." *Thetean* 49:55–74.
Anderson, Emily. 2010. "Christianity in the Japanese Empire: Nationalism, Conscience, and Faith in Meiji and Taisho Japan." Ph.D. diss. University of California, Los Angeles.
Andrew, Hayley. 2019. "Helen (Ma) Armstrong." *The Canadian Encyclopedia*. https://www.thecanadianencyclopedia.ca/en/article/helen-ma-armstrong (December 9, 2022).
"A New York Sensation." 1920. *Murchison Times and Day Dawn Gazette* [Cue, WA], September 24.
"Anniversary of Passaic Sees Strike On." 1927. *Daily Worker* [New York], January 25.
"An I.W.W. Case: Horrocks Before the Court." 1916. *Evening Star* [Boulder, WA], October 18.
"Antis Ask Aliens to Meeting." 1917. *Manitoba Free Press* [Winnipeg, MAN], June 30.
"An Undesirable." 1925. *Ashburton Guardian* [N.Z.], June 5.
"An Undesirable Alien: Reasons for Deportation." 1919. *Age* [Melbourne, VIC], June 4.
Araya Saavedra, Mario. 2008. "Fundación e ideología en la Región chilena de la Industrial Workers of the World – IWW (1919–1927)." B.A. thesis. Universidad de Artes y Ciencias Sociales [Santiago, Chile].

Araya Saavedra, Mario. 2016. "La Presencia de anarquistas australianos en Valparaíso (1918)." *Periódico Anarquista: La Boina* [Chile], July 28.
"Argentina." 1902. *Vida Nueva* [Montevideo, Uruguay], November 15.
"Armando Jaramillo Valderrama." N.d. Biblioteca del Congreso Nacional de Chile: Reseñas biográficas parlamentarias. https://www.bcn.cl/historiapolitica/res enas_parlamentarias/wiki/Armando_Jaramillo_Valderrama (June 19, 2022).
Armijo, Camilo Plaza, and Víctor Muñoz Cortés. 2013. "La ley de residencia de 1918 y la persecución a los extranjeros subversivos." *Revista de Derechos Fundamentales* [Valparaíso, Chile] 10:107–136.
Armstrong, Helen. 1917a. "The Alternative." Letter to the Editor. *Voice* [Winnipeg, MAN], August 10.
Armstrong, Helen. 1917b. "Two Blacks do not Make White." Letter to the Editor. *Voice* [Winnipeg, MAN], November 30.
Armstrong, Helen. 1918. "The Girl's Budget." Letter to the Editor. *Voice* [Winnipeg, MAN], March 1.
Armstrong, Helen [as D. Helen Armstrong]. 1935. "The Behavior of Women; Are the Men to Blame?" Letter to the Editor. *Winnipeg Free Press* [MAN], September 21.
Armstrong, Helen. 1943. "Visiting States." Letter to the Editor. *Winnipeg Evening Tribune* [MAN], May 12.
"Arrested Men Remanded." 1913. *Industrial Unionist* [Auckland, N.Z.], November 20.
"Arrest of Two Awes Strikers." 1912. *Newark Evening Star* [N.J.], January 31.
"Arrests Follow Riot at Mine." 1919. *West Virginian* [Fairmont, W.Va.], August 28.
"Arthur Percy Chew" N.d. https://ancestors.familysearch.org/en/K2QF-42H/art hur-percy-chew-1887-1967 (March 9, 2023).
"Artist's Bride Drowns from Honeymoon Launch." 1920. *Evening Public Ledger* [Philadelphia, Penn.], September 13.
"A Sample of Prussianism." 1916. *Evening Echo* [Ballarat, VIC], October 20.
"A Sensational Report: Find of Gelignite Charge." 1913. *Auckland Star* [N.Z.], November 15.
"Ask Appointment of Policewoman to Local Force." 1915. *Winnipeg Evening Tribune* [MAN], November 27.
"Ask Immediate Resignation of Labor Minister." 1919. *Winnipeg Evening Tribune* [MAN], June 20.
"Ask Release of Winnipeg Strike Men." 1920. *Hamilton Daily Times* [ONT], April 17.
"Assert They are Tricked on Petition." 1918. *Manitoba Free Press* [Winnipeg, MAN], February 6.
Asukai, Masamichi. 1978. "Kōtoku Shūsui: His Socialism and Pacifism." In *Pacifism in Japan: the Christian and Socialist Tradition*, eds. Nobuya Bamba and John F. Howes. Vancouver: University of British Columbia.
"Ateo Rivolta." 1912. Editorial. *Cronaca Sovversiva* [Barre, Vt.], September 28.
"At Last." 1921. *Socialist* [Melbourne, VIC], December 2.

"Auckland Arrest." 1913. *Industrial Unionist* [Auckland, N.Z.], November 13.
"Auckland Employers' Association: Annual Meeting." 1915. *Wanganui Herald* [Whanganui, N.Z.], July 22. [The spelling of Wanganui was later altered to comport with the Māori spelling].
"Auckland Scenes: End Not in Sight." 1913. *Star* [Christchurch, N.Z.], November 12.
"Australia Gets Excited over One-Man Hunger Strike." 1919. *Evening Telegraph and Post* [Dundee, U.K.], June 4.
"Australian Deportee's Journeyings." 1919. *Westminster Gazette* [U.K.], June 4.
Avery, Donald. 2006. "The Radical Alien and the Winnipeg General Strike of 1919." In *Canadian Working-Class History: Selected Readings*, 3rd. ed., ed. Laurel Sefton MacDowell and Ian Radforth. Toronto: Canadian Scholars' Press.
"A Voice from Russia." 1923. *Maoriland Worker* [Wellington, N.Z.], February 14.
Avrich, Paul. [1967] 1971. *The Russian Anarchists*. Princeton: Princeton University Press.
Avrich, Paul, ed. 1973. *The Anarchists in the Russian Revolution*. London: Thames and Hudson.
Avrich, Paul. 1980. "Introduction." In *The First Mayday: the Haymarket Speeches 1895–1910* by Voltairine De Cleyre. Sanday, Orkney, UK: Cienfuegos.
Avrich, Paul. 1984. *The Haymarket Tragedy*. Princeton: Princeton University Press.
Avrich, Paul. 2004. *Voces anarquistas: Historia oral del anarquismo en Estados Unidos*, trans. Antonia Ruiz Cabezas. Madrid: Fundación de Estudios Libertarios Anselmo Lorenzo.
"A Welcome Forestalled." 1921. *Northern Star* [Lismore, NSW], September 1.
"AWU Timeline." 2020. The Australian Workers' Union, National Office, Granville, NSW. https://www.awu.net.au/our-union/history/ (December 14, 2020).
Baer, James A. 2015. *Anarchist Immigrants in Spain and Argentina*. Urbana: University of Illinois Press.
"Bail Refused to Mrs. Armstrong et al." 1919. *Western Labor News* [Winnipeg, MAN], June 27.
Bakunin, Mikhail. 1915. "Bourgeois Socialism." *Freedom* [London], February.
Balawyder, A. 1967. *The Winnipeg General Strike*. Vancouver, BC: Copp Clark.
Baldwin, Roger N., Norman Thomas, Elizabeth Gurley Flynn, John Haynes Holmes, and Wilbur Thomas. 1926. "In Horthy's Hungary." Letter to the Editor. *Nation*, September 29.
Baldwin, Roger N. 1956. "Early Years of a Radical." Review of *Speak My Own Piece* by Elizabeth Gurley Flynn. *Nation*, May 12.
Bamba, Nobuya, and John F. Howes. 1978. *Pacifism in Japan: the Christian and Socialist Tradition*. Vancouver: University of British Columbia.
Bangarth, Stephanie D. 2002. "The Co-operative Committee on Japanese Canadians and the American Civil Liberties Union: Engaging Debate, 1942–1946." *Princeton University Library Chronicle* 63:496–533.

Bantman, Constance, and Bert Altena, eds. 2017. *Reassessing the Transnational Turn: Scales of Analysis in Anarchist and Syndicalist Studies*. Oakland, Cal.: PM Press.
"Bar Gurley Flynn, Even as a "Guest."" 1915. *Newark Evening Star* [N.J.], November 12.
"Baritz Barred." 1920. NZ *Truth* [Wellington, N.Z.], January 17.
"Barker and Klausen: To be Released." 1916. *Australian Worker* [Sydney, NSW], July 13.
"Barker Defence Committee." 1916. *Barrier Miner* [Broken Hill, NSW], June 13.
"Barker in Melbourne." 1915. *Direct Action* [Sydney, NSW], October 2.
Barker, Tom. 1912a. [as "Spanwire"]. "Auckland Activities." *Maoriland Worker* [Wellington, N.Z.], April 19.
Barker, Tom. 1912b. [as "Spanwire"]. "Auckland in the Van." *Maoriland Worker* [Wellington, N.Z.], October 11.
Barker, Tom. 1912c. [as "Spanwire"]. "A Visit to Waihi." *Maoriland Worker* [Wellington, N.Z.], November 15.
Barker, Tom. 1912d. [as "Spanwire"]. "Doings at Auckland." *Maoriland Worker* [Wellington, N.Z.], November 29.
Barker, Tom. 1912e. [as "Spanwire"]. "Dominion Doings." *Maoriland Worker* [Wellington, N.Z.], June 14.
Barker, Tom. 1912f. [as "Spanwire"]. "Fowlds will not Debate." *Maoriland Worker* [Wellington, N.Z.], September 17.
Barker, Tom. 1913a. "Around N.Z.: Organiser's Notes." *Industrial Unionist* [Auckland, N.Z.], October 1.
Barker, Tom. 1913b. [as "Spanwire"]. "A Suggestion." *Industrial Unionist* [Auckland, N.Z.], November 8.
Barker, Tom. 1913c. [as "Spanwire"]. "Machine Slavery." *Industrial Unionist* [Auckland, N.Z.], April 1.
Barker, Tom. 1913d. "N.Z. Organizer." *Industrial Unionist* [Auckland, N.Z.], November 1.
Barker, Tom. 1913e. "Parliament and its Relationship to Economics." *Industrial Unionist* [Auckland, N.Z.], August 1.
Barker, Tom. 1913f. "Practical Politics." Letter to the Editor. *Littleton Times* [N.Z.], September 1.
Barker, Tom. 1913g [as "Spanwire"]. "The Auckland Tramway Union." *Industrial Unionist* [Auckland, N.Z.], June 1.
Barker, Tom. 1913h [as "Spanwire"]. "The Worker and the "Backbone."" *Industrial Unionist* [Auckland, N.Z.], June 1.
Barker, Tom. 1914a. "His Master's Voice." *Direct Action* [Sydney, NSW], October 1.
Barker, Tom. 1914b. ""Mad Mullahs" and Blind Alleys." *Direct Action* [Sydney, NSW], July 15.
Barker, Tom. 1914c. "New Zealand and its Federation." *Direct Action* [Sydney, NSW], August 1.

Barker, Tom. 1914d. "New Zealand General Strike." *Voice of the People* [New Orleans, La.], April 2.

Barker, Tom. 1914e. "Open Column." *Maoriland Worker* [Wellington, N.Z.], February 11.

Barker, Tom. 1914f. "The Boss's Nightmare." *Direct Action* [Sydney, NSW], October 1.

Barker, Tom. 1914g. "WAR and the Workers." *Direct Action* [Sydney, NSW], August 22.

Barker, Tom. 1915a. "A Good "Reason."" *Direct Action* [Sydney, NSW], October 23.

Barker, Tom. 1915b. "A Weekly Paper." *Direct Action* [Sydney, NSW], November 6.

Barker, Tom. 1915c. "Another Victory for the I.W.W." *Direct Action* [Sydney, NSW], February 1.

Barker, Tom. 1915d. "Coming Trouble in New Zealand." *Direct Action* [Sydney, NSW], November 27.

Barker, Tom. 1915e. "May Day, 1915." *Direct Action* [Sydney, NSW], May 1.

Barker, Tom [as "Spanwire"]. 1915f. "Melbourne Notes." *Direct Action* [Sydney, NSW], October 9.

Barker, Tom. 1915g. "More Trouble." *Direct Action* [Sydney, NSW], December 11.

Barker, Tom. 1915h. "My Visit to Melbourne." *Direct Action* [Sydney, NSW], October 9.

Barker, Tom. 1915i. "Politicians, the I.W.W. & the War." *Direct Action* [Sydney, NSW], August 15.

Barker, Tom. 1915j. "The A.W.U. in the Northern Territory." *Direct Action* [Sydney, NSW], April 1.

Barker, Tom. 1915k. "The Cavel [sic] Case." *Direct Action* [Sydney, NSW], October 30.

Barker, Tom. 1915l. "The Loyalty of Labor Politicians." *Direct Action* [Sydney, NSW], October 30.

Barker, Tom. 1915m. Untitled. *Direct Action* [Sydney, NSW], January 1.

Barker, Tom. 1915n. "War on Capitalism: the Reduction of the Output." *Direct Action* [Sydney, NSW], February 15.

Barker, Tom. 1916a. "Another Batch of Arrests." *Direct Action* [Sydney, NSW], November 4.

Barker, Tom. 1916b. "A Word from Barker." *Direct Action* [Sydney, NSW], September 9.

Barker, Tom. 1916c. "Barker's Tour." *Direct Action* [Sydney, NSW], September 23.

Barker, Tom. 1916d [as "T.B."]. "Concert." *Direct Action* [Sydney, NSW], December 30.

Barker, Tom. 1916e. "Domain Protest: Enormous Gathering." *Direct Action* [Sydney, NSW], December 23.

Barker, Tom. 1916f. "General Strike." *Direct Action* [Sydney, NSW], November 11.

Barker, Tom. 1916g. "How "No" Was Carried in S.A." *Direct Action* [Sydney, NSW], November 4.

Barker, Tom. 1916h. "Hughes at Ballarat." *Direct Action* [Sydney, NSW], October 21.

Barker, Tom. 1916i. "Propaganda News." *Direct Action* [Sydney, NSW], January 8.

Barker, Tom. 1916j. "Spasms." *Direct Action* [Sydney, NSW], December 9.

Barker, Tom. 1916k. "Spasms." *Direct Action* [Sydney, NSW], December 16.

Barker, Tom. 1916l. "The New Gospel of Industrial Control." *Direct Action* [Sydney, NSW], November 4.

Barker, Tom. 1917a. "Around Central Queensland." *Direct Action* [Sydney, NSW], March 24.

Barker, Tom. 1917b. "A Scab Union." *Direct Action* [Sydney, NSW], April 7.

Barker, Tom. 1917c. "A.W.U. Conference: Ex-President Bailey on Politics." *Direct Action* [Sydney, NSW], February 24.

Barker, Tom. 1917d. "International Unionism: the Tresca Agitation." *Direct Action* [Sydney, NSW], March 10.

Barker, Tom. 1917e. "I.W.W. Disclaimer." *Sun* [Sydney, NSW], January 4.

Barker, Tom. 1917f. "Queensland: Weekly Report." *Direct Action* [Sydney, NSW], February 10.

Barker, Tom. 1917g. "Queensland: Weekly Report." *Direct Action* [Sydney, NSW], February 17.

Barker, Tom. 1917h. "Spasms." *Direct Action* [Sydney, NSW], February 17.

Barker, Tom. 1917i. "Spasms." *Direct Action* [Sydney, NSW], March 3.

Barker, Tom. 1917j. "Spasms." *Direct Action* [Sydney, NSW], March 10.

Barker, Tom. 1917k. "Spasms." *Direct Action* [Sydney, NSW], March 17.

Barker, Tom. 1917l. "Spasms." *Direct Action* [Sydney, NSW], March 24.

Barker, Tom. 1917m. "Spasms." *Direct Action* [Sydney, NSW], August 18.

Barker, Tom. 1917n. "The Russian Revolution." *Direct Action* [Sydney, NSW], March 31.

Barker, Tom. 1917o. "To Avert War." *Direct Action* [Sydney, NSW], February 10.

Barker, Tom. 1920a. "Agricultural Workers in Argentina." *Workers' Dreadnought* [London], January 31.

Barker, Tom. 1920b. "An I.W.W. Explains." *Forward* [Glasgow, U.K.], August 14.

Barker, Tom. 1920c. "Australian Brutality." *Communist* [Sydney, NSW], August 5.

Barker, Tom. 1920d. "Reaction in Argentine." *Workers' Dreadnought* [London], August 28.

Barker, Tom. 1920e. "The Australian Sedition Cases." Letter to the Editor. *Socialist* [Melbourne, VIC], June 17.

Barker, Tom. 1920f. "Tom Barker in London." *Socialist* [Melbourne, VIC], July 9.

Barker, Tom. 1921a. "Address to the Convention of the All-Russian Union of Transport Workers, Moscow." *Industrial Pioneer* [Chicago], July.

Barker, Tom. 1921b. "Another Letter from Tom Barker." *Communist* [Sydney, NSW], September 9.

Barker, Tom. 1921c. "From Moscow to the Boys in Australia." *Communist* [Sydney, NSW], February 29.

Barker, Tom. 1921d. "One Union for All of Us." *Industrial Pioneer* [Chicago], August.

Barker, Tom. 1921e. "Panama and Marine Transport Workers." *Industrial Pioneer* [Chicago], November.

Barker, Tom. 1921f. "Paul Freeman." *Industrial Pioneer* [Chicago], November.

Barker, Tom. 1921g. "Petrograd in July, 1921." *Industrial Pioneer* [Chicago], October.

Barker, Tom. 1921h. "Red Russia and the I.W.W.: A Letter from Tom Barker." *Industrial Pioneer* [Chicago], April.

Barker, Tom. 1921i. "The German Martyrs and the I.W.W." *Industrial Pioneer* [Chicago], March.

Barker, Tom. 1921j. "The Story of the Sea," chs. 1 and 2. *Industrial Pioneer* [Chicago], January.

Barker, Tom. 1921k. "The Story of the Sea," chs. 3 and 4. *Industrial Pioneer* [Chicago], February.

Barker, Tom. 1921l. "The Story of the Sea," chs. 5 and 6. *Industrial Pioneer* [Chicago], March.

Barker, Tom. 1921m. "The Story of the Sea," ch. 6. *Industrial Pioneer* [Chicago], April.

Barker, Tom. 1921n. "The Story of the Sea," ch. 7. *Industrial Pioneer* [Chicago], May.

Barker, Tom. 1921o. "The Story of the Sea," chs. 8 and 9. *Industrial Pioneer* [Chicago], July.

Barker, Tom. 1921p. "The Story of the Sea," chs. 10, 11, 12, and 13. *Industrial Pioneer* [Chicago], August.

Barker, Tom. 1921q. "Tom Barker in Germany." *Socialist* [Melbourne, VIC], March 4.

Barker, Tom. 1921r. "Tom Barker in London." *Australian Communist* [Sydney, NSW], January 14.

Barker, Tom. 1923a. "Making History: Kuzbas Colonists." *Daily Standard* [Brisbane, QLD], February 24.

Barker, Tom. 1923b. "Men Wanted for Kuzbas." *Workers' Weekly* [Sydney, NSW], August 3.

Barker, Tom. 1923c. The Trial of the Kuzbas Committee: Prosecution Fails. *Workers' Weekly* [Sydney, NSW], December 14.

Barker, Tom. 1926a. "Miners of U.S. are Warned by British Leader." *Daily Worker* [New York], December 28.

Barker, Tom. 1926b. "Starved Miners Return to Pits in Battle Mood." *Daily Worker* [New York], December 15.

Barker, Tom. 1927a. "Commons Hears Britain Facing New Mine Crisis." *Daily Worker* [New York], July 27.

Barker, Tom. 1927b. "Foreign Concessions Can Do Profitable Business in Soviet Union." *Daily Worker* [New York], August 31.

Barker, Tom. 1927c. "Great Trade of U.S.S.R. Going to New Markets." *Daily Worker* [New York], July 15.

Barker, Tom. 1927d. "Indian Workers Live Miserably in Mill Towns." *Daily Worker* [New York], November 14.

Barker, Tom. 1927e. "Russian Oil Firms Cut Gasoline Price in English Markets." *Daily Worker* [New York], July 12.

Barker, Tom. 1949. "W. H. Hudson." Letter to the Editor. *Daily Herald* [London], May 24.

Barker, Tom. 1965. "Tom Barker's Story." In *Tom Barker and the I.W.W.*, ed. Eric C. Fry. Canberra, ACT: Australian Society for the Study of Labour History.

"Barker's Fires: the I.W.W. Criminal." 1917. *Kyogle Examiner* [NSW], March 21.

Barrett, James R. 1999. *William Z. Foster and the Tragedy of American Radicalism.* Urbana: University of Illinois Press.

Bartram, James K. 2018. "I Can't Speak: Social Control and the IWW Free Speech Movement." M.A. thesis. California State University, Fresno.

Basaez, María Belén García, and Nicolás Valentín Muñoz Cerda. 2015. "Crisis social, relocalización de mano de obra y politización popular, Valparaíso 1918–1922." Universidad de Chile Facultad de Filosofía y Humanidades, Departamento de Ciencias Históricas, May.

Basham, Ardythe, ed. 2000. *Rising to the Occasion: A Community History of Wolseley, West Broadway and Armstrong's Point.* Winnipeg, MAN: Robert A. Steen Memorial Community Centre.

Baxandall, Rosalyn Fraad. 1987a. "Introduction." In *Words on Fire: the Life and Writing of Elizabeth Gurley Flynn* by Elizabeth Gurley Flynn, ed. Rosalynn Fraad Baxandall. New Brunswick, N.J.: Rutgers University Press.

Baxandall, Rosalyn Fraad. 1987b. "Pioneer or Aunt Tom? Elizabeth Gurley Flynn's Feminism." In *Words on Fire: the Life and Writing of Elizabeth Gurley Flynn* by Elizabeth Gurley Flynn, ed. Rosalynn Fraad Baxandall. New Brunswick, N.J.: Rutgers University Press.

Bayoumi, Moustafa. 2022. "Journey to Guantánamo." *Nation*, July 25-August 1.

Behuniak, James, Jr. 2011. "Naturalizing Mencius." *Philosophy East and West* 61:492–515.

Belcher, W. 1915. "Preference to Unionists." *New Zealand Times* [Wellington, N.Z]. August 27.

Bellamy, Edward. 1887. *Looking Backward: 2000–1887.* Boston: Houghton Mifflin.

Bellucci, Mabel. 2003. "Virginia Bolten la comunera Libertaria." *DLa Tapa* https://www.nodo50.org/dlatapa/2002archivosdlt/sin_hist_12.htm (October 2, 2021).

Bencivenni, Marcella. 2011. *Italian Immigrant Radical Culture: the Idealism of the Sovversivi in the United States, 1890–1940.* New York: New York University Press.

Benedict, Ruth. 1946. *The Chrysanthemum and the Sword: Patterns of Japanese Culture.* Boston, Mass.: Riverside.

Bennett, J. M., and Ann G. Smith. 1983. "Irvine, Sir William Hill (1858–1943)." *Australian Dictionary of Biography.* https://adb.anu.edu.au/biography/irvine-sir-william-hill-6801 (June 11, 2022).

Bercuson, David Jay. 1971. *Confrontation at Winnipeg: Labour, Industrial Relations, and the General Strike.* Montréal, QUE: McGill-Queen's University Press.

Berkman, Alexander. [1912] 1970. *Prison Memoirs of an Anarchist.* New York: Schocken.

Berkman, Alexander. 1922. *The Kronstadt Revolution.* Berlin, Germany: *Der Syndikalist.*

Berkman, Alexander. [1929] 2005. *The ABC of Anarchism.* Mineola, N.Y.: Dover.

Berzish, Murphy. 2010. "Suppressing the Winnipeg General Strike: Paranoia or Preserving the Peace?" *Manitoba History*, Fall.

Betten, Neil. 1967. "Strike on the Mesabi – 1907." *Minnesota History* 40:340–347.
Beveridge, George. 1952. "Tedious First Phase of Battle to Smoke Out Reds Is Winding Up." *Sunday Star* [Washington, D.C.], June 29.
"Beware of Seadogs!" 1913. *Star* [Christchurch, N.Z.], October 28.
"Big Legal Fight over Killing During Strike." 1922. *Bermidji Daily Pioneer* [Minn.], May 17.
"Biographical Note." 2021. Guide to the Elizabeth Gurley Flynn Papers. Tamiment Library and Robert F. Wagner Labor Archive, Elmer Holmes Bobst Library, New York University.
Blakeley, Arthur. 1917. "Proposed Bogus Unions: What the I.W.W. Threatens." Letter to the Editor. *Australian Worker* [Sydney, NSW], March 29.
Bloodworth, Sandra. 2015. "Broken Hill: A Radical History." *Red Flag* [Melbourne, VIC], October 1.
"Bloody Shirt; Two Teeth Knocked Out." 1909. *Spokane Press* [Wash.], November 17.
"Blumenberg to Lecture." 1916. *Winnipeg Evening Tribune* [MAN], September 30.
"Board Acts to Oust Communist Member." 1940. *Butler County Press* [Hamilton, Ohio], June 7.
"Board Decision Near On Soviet Domination Of U. S. Communists." 1952. *Sunday Star* [Washington, D.C.], June 15.
"Board on Subversives to Await Return of Congress for Funds." 1950. *Evening Star* [Washington, D.C.], October 28.
"Board Orders Alien Deported." 1919. *Winnipeg Evening Tribune* [MAN], July 18.
"Board Orders Deportation of Blumenberg." 1919. *Winnipeg Evening Tribune* [MAN], August 13.
"Boasted of Share in Wall St. Blast." 1923. *Sunday Star* [Washington, D.C.], May 13.
"Bolshevism in Winnipeg: "One Big Union" Assumed Entire Control of City But Was Ousted by a Bourgeois Committee." 1919. *New York Times*, June 22.
Bolten, Virginia. 1900a. "Comunicado." *La Protesta Humana* [Buenos Aires, Argentina], Juily 8.
Bolten, Virginia. 1900b. "Preguntas y respuestas." *La Protesta Humana* [Buenos Aires, Argentina], April 29.
Bolten, Virginia. 1900c. "Varias." *La Protesta Humana* [Buenos Aires, Argentina], May 13.
Bolten, Virginia. 1901. "Discurso pronunciado en el acto de repudio al asesinato de Cosme Budislavich, 24 de octubre de 1901." *El Municipio* [Rosario, Argentina], October 25.
Bolten, Virginia. 1905a. "A los obreros en huelga." *El Obrero* [Montevideo, Uruguay], March 6.
Bolten, Virginia. 1905b. "En la rusia Americana." *El Obrero* [Montevideo, Uruguay], April 15.
Bolten, Virginia. 1905c. "La mazorca." *El Obrero* [Montevideo, Uruguay], August 4.

Bolten, Virginia. 1905d. "¿Por qué se lucha?" *El Obrero* [Montevideo, Uruguay], January 6.
Bolten, Virginia. 1905e. "¿Qiénes son?" *El Obrero* [Montevideo, Uruguay], June 17.
Bolten, Virginia. 1905f. "¡Trabajadores!" *El Obrero* [Montevideo, Uruguay], May 20.
Bolten, Virginia. 1905g. "Una idea." *El Obrero* [Montevideo, Uruguay], April 22.
Bolten, Virginia. 1905h. "Los gobiernos y la cuestión social." *El Obrero* [Montevideo, Uruguay], October 6.
Bolten, Virginia. 1906. "Las dos clases." *El Obrero* [Montevideo, Uruguay], June 16.
Bolten, Virginia. 1908a. "Alerta!" *La Acción Obrera* [Buenos Aires, Argentina], May 6.
Bolten, Virginia. 1908b. "Dios." *La Acción Obrera* [Buenos Aires, Argentina], April 20.
Bolten, Virginia. 1909a. "¿Justicia?" *La Nueva Senda* [Montevideo, Uruguay], September 18.
Bolten, Virginia. 1909b. "Nuestras agitaciones" *La Nueva Senda* [Montevideo, Uruguay], November 19.
Bolten, Virginia. 1909c. "Oíd, vosotros!" *La Nueva Senda* [Montevideo, Uruguay], December 4.
Bolten, Virginia. 1910a. "Enseñanzas del pasado." *La Nueva Senda* [Montevideo, Uruguay], March 18.
Bolten, Virginia. 1910b. "La organización se impone." *La Nueva Senda* [Montevideo, Uruguay], March 5.
Bolten, Virginia. 1911. "Para los niños." *Tiempos Nuevos* [Montevideo, Uruguay], January 15.
"Bomb Suspect Held; Hired Wagon That Carried Death into Wall St., Police Say." 1923. *Atlanta Tri-Weekly Journal* [Ga.], May 15.
"Booze Project Splits Women's Labor League." 1918. *Winnipeg Evening Tribune* [MAN], September 13.
Bordagaray, María Eugenia. 2011. "Las anarquistas argentinas y el voto femenino (1946–1951)." In *Sufragio femenino: Prácticas y debates políticos, religiosos y culturales en Argentina y América*, ed. Carolina Barry. Buenos Aires, Argentina: EDUNTREF.
Boriak, Hennadii. 2001. "The Publication of Sources on the History of the 1932–1933 Famine-Genocide: History, Current State, and Prospects." *Harvard Ukrainian Studies* 25:167–186.
Botelho-Urbanski, Jessica. 2019. "Strike! A Century Later." *Winnipeg Free Press* [MAN], May 11.
Bowen Raddeker, Hélène. 1988. "Women and Treason in Pre-war Japan: the Prison Poetry of Kanno Sugo and Kaneko Fumiko." *Lilith: A Feminist History Journal* 5:9–25.
Bowen Raddeker, Hélène. 1997. *Treacherous Women of Imperial Japan: Patriarchal Fictions, Patricidal Fantasies*. Abingdon-on-Thames, U.K.: Routledge.

Bowen Raddeker, Hélène. 2002. "Resistance to Difference: Sexual Equality and its Lawful and Out-law (Anarchist) Advocates in Imperial Japan." *Intersections: Gender, History and Culture in the Asian Context*, March.

Bowman, Sam. 1914. "Optimism and Socialism." Letter to the Editor. *Voice* [Winnipeg, MAN], May 15.

"Bresci." 1901. *El Rebelde* [Buenos Aires, Argentina], January 19.

"Bride Drowns; "Dill Pickle" Chief Saved." 1920. *Chicago Tribune*, September 13.

Brite, Mary D. 1926. "Free Speech (?) in Cincinatti." *Nation*, October 13.

Brissenden, Paul F. 1913. "The Launching of the Industrial Workers of the World." *University of California Publications in Economics* 4:1–82.

"British Born Men Given Freedom but Must Stay Inactive." 1919. *Winnipeg Telegram* [MAN], Strike Edition, June 20.

Buchalla, Carl. 1961. "Albania, Feuding with Moscow, Turns to Red China." *Sunday Star* [Washington, D.C.], October 22.

"Builders' Laborers: Address by Tom Barker." 1917. *Daily Standard* [Brisbane, QLD], January 13.

Bundschuh, John Adikes. 2021. "Tense, Aspect, and Modality in the Creation of Narrative Structure: Early Heian Japanese Translations of Sinitic Buddhist Texts." Ph.D. diss. Ohio State University.

Burgmann, Verity. 1995. *Revolutionary Industrial Unionism: the Industrial Workers of the World in Australia*. Cambridge, U.K.: Cambridge University Press.

Burrows, Paul. 2008. "'Apostle of Anarchy:" Emma Goldman's First Visit to Winnipeg in 1907." *Manitoba History*, February.

Burton, H.P. 1912. "Says 'Justice Itself is on Trial at Salem.'" *Day Book* [Chicago], October 30.

Butler, R.A. 1958. *May Day Celebrations, St. Pancras*. Hansard, vol. 587, May 8.

Byington, Steven T. 1908. "Translator's Preface." In *Anarchism: Exponents of the Anarchist Philosophy*. New York: Benjamin R. Tucker.

Cade, Jack. 1917. "Tom Barker: A Striking Personality." *Direct Action* [Sydney, NSW], January 27.

Cahill, Barry. 1996. "*Howe* (1835), *Dixon* (1920) and *McLachlan* (1923): Comparative Perspectives on the Legal History of Sedition." *University of New Brunswick Law Journal* 45:281–307.

Cain, Frank. 1982. "The Industrial Workers of the World: Aspects of Its Suppression in Australia 1916–1919." *Labour History* 42:54–62.

Cain, Frank. 1993. *The Wobblies at War: A History of the IWW and the Great War in Australia*. Melbourne, VIC: Spectrum.

Calzetta, Elsa. 2014. *Nuestra tribuna: hojita del sentir anárquico femenino 1922–1925*. Bahía Blanca, Argentina: Universidad Nacional del Sur.

Camfield, Graham. 1999. "From Tolstoyan to Terrorist: the Revolutionary Career of Prince D.A. Khilkov, 1900–1905." *Revolutionary Russia* 12:1–43.

Campbell, Lyndsay. 2019. "The War-Time Elections Act and Women Voters in 1917." Active History. https://activehistory.ca/2019/11/the-war-time-elections-act-and-women-voters-in-1917/ (February 19, 2023).

"Campbell Says Laurier Avoids Main Question." 1917. *Winnipeg Evening Tribune* [MAN], December 12.

Camp, Helen C. 1995. *Iron in Her Soul: Elizabeth Gurley Flynn and the American Left.* Pullman: Washington State University Press.

"Canadian Labor War is Spreading over Entire Country." 1919. *Chicago Tribune*, May 30.

"Candidates State Position on Vital Issues." 1923. *Winnipeg Evening Tribune* [MAN], November 17.

Cannon, James P. 1926. "Protest Against the Roumanian Terror!" *Daily Worker* [New York], October 21.

Cannon, James P. 1928. "W.D. Haywood: A Pioneer of Revolutionary Unionism." *Labor Unity* [New York], June.

Cano, Luis C. 2006. Review of *Las Anarquistas Rioplatenses 1890–1990* by Cristina Guzzo. *Hispania* 89:890–891.

Capetillo, Luisa. 1924. "La mujer." *Nuestra Tribuna* [Montevideo, Uruguay], June 15.

"Capital and Gelignite." 1913. Editorial. *Industrial Unionist* [Auckland, N.Z.], November 18.

"Capitalist Courts Condone Murder of Men and Women." 1919. *Butte Daily Bulletin* [Mont.], September 29.

Cappelletti, Ángel. 1990. *Anarchism in Latin America.* Chino, Cal.: AK. https://libcom.org/library/anarchism-latin-america (October 3, 2021).

"Captives Released." 1919. *Western Labor News* [Winnipeg, MAN], Special Strike Edition No. 30 Extra, June 20.

Carlson, MariFran. 1988. *¡Feminismo! The Woman's Movement in Argentina from its Beginnings to Eva Perón.* Chicago: Academy Chicago.

Carter, Patricia. 2017. "Guiding the Working-Class Girl: Henrietta Rodman's Curriculum for the New Woman, 1913." *Frontiers: A Journal of Women Studies* 38:124–155.

Carter, Rosalie Gaye. 1982. "Takamure Itsue: Social Activist and Feminist Theorist: 1921–1931." M.A. thesis. University of British Columbia.

Cartwright, R.L. 2020. "Mesabi Iron Range Strike, 1907." Minnesota Historical Society. https://www.mnopedia.org/event/mesabi-iron-range-strike-1907 (May 13, 2023).

"Cases of Disability of Wage Earners May Be Under Scope of Mothers' Allowance Act." 1920. *Winnipeg Evening Tribune* [MAN], March 29.

"Cases in Court." 1919. *Enlightener* [Winnipeg, MAN], June 26.

Cassidy, Christian. 2021. "The History of the Wolseley Bus." https://westenddumplings.blogspot.com/2021/04/the-history-of-wolseley-bus.html (February 27, 2023).

"Causes of the Winnipeg Strike: Royal Commission Appointed." 1919. *Mail* [London], June 30.

Cawen, Inés Cuadro. 2017. "Anarquismo e identidades de género en el Uruguay del Novecientos." *Claves: Revista de Historia* [Montevideo, Uruguay] 3:213:248.

Chang, Chia-ning. 1976. "A Study of the Response of Japanese *Bungakusha* toward Social Reality in the Meiji-Taishō Period." M.A. thesis. University of Hong Kong.

Chaplin, Ralph. 1948. *Wobbly: the Rough-and-Tumble Story of an American Radical.* Chicago: The University of Chicago Press.

"Charges of Treason." 1916. *New Zealand Herald* [Auckland], October 12.

"Charitinoff's Deportation is Ordered." 1919. *Winnipeg Evening Tribune* [MAN], August 14.

Chen, Qi. 2011. "Oscar Wilde and East Asia: Empire, Nation-State, and the Globalisation of Aestheticism." Ph.D. diss. Royal Holloway University of London.

Chew, A. Percy. 1909a. "Benefactors of Humanity." *Voice* [Winnipeg, MAN], July 30.

Chew, A. Percy. 1909b. "Cancer and its Cure." *Voice* [Winnipeg, MAN], September 10.

Chew, A. Percy. 1909c. "Prophecy." *Voice* [Winnipeg, MAN], July 30.

Chew, A. Percy. 1909d. "Social Fungi." *Voice* [Winnipeg, MAN], July 23.

Chew, A. Percy. 1909e. "Surplus Value." *Voice* [Winnipeg, MAN], July 23.

Chew, A. Percy. 1909f. "The Patriots of Bermondsey." *Voice* [Winnipeg, MAN], November 5.

Chew, A. Percy. 1909g. "The Tellers of Tales." *Voice* [Winnipeg, MAN], September 10.

Chew, A. Percy. 1910a. "Election Smiles." *Voice* [Winnipeg, MAN], May 6.

Chew, A. Percy. 1910b. "Socialism." *Voice* [Winnipeg, MAN], March 25.

Chew, A. Percy. 1910c. "The Beam in Our Own Eye." *Voice* [Winnipeg, MAN], May 6.

"Chief of Dill Picklers Sues Socialist Wife." 1920. *Chicago Tribune*, June 15.

Chile Congreso Nacional: Cámara de Diputados. 1917. Sesión 22 extraordinaria. December 5. Biblioteca del Congreso Nacional de Chile, 599–622. https://www.bcn.cl/historiapolitica/corporaciones/periodo_detalle?inicio=1915-06-01&fin=1918-05-31&periodo=1891-1925&cam=Diputados (June 19, 2022).

Chong, Kim-Chong. 2003. "Xunzi's Systematic Critique of Mencius." *Philosophy East and West* 53:215–233.

Christie, Nancy, and Michael Gauvreau. 1996. *A Full-Orbed Christianity: the Protestant Churches and Social Welfare in Canada, 1900–1940.* Montréal: McGill-Queen's University Press.

"Church Peace Lobby Financed by Red Money." 1929. *Chicago Tribune*, May 5.

CIRA-Nippon. 1975. "Kōtoku Shūsui: Founder of Modern Anarchism in Japan." https://theanarchistlibrary.org/library/cira-nippon-kotoku-shusui (September 28, 2022).

"City College Bans Miss Flynn's Talk." 1957. *New York Times*, October 26.

Cives, Diego. 2019. "*La Protesta* (*Humana*): la voz escrita del anarquismo argentino (1897–1910)." M.A. thesis. Universidad Nacional de San Martín.

"Civic Committee Retires." 1918. *Voice* [Winnipeg, MAN], March 22.

"Civic Employees Returning to Work Repudiating Sympathetic Strike." 1919. *Manitoba Free Press* [Winnipeg, MAN], May 30.

Clarfield, A. Mark. 2002. "The Soviet "Doctors' Plot" – 50 Years On." *British Medical Journal* 325:1487–1489.

"Cleveland Workers Hear Ruthenberg Speak at May Day Celebration." 1924. *Daily Worker* [Chicago], May 8.

Cleverdon, Catherine L. [1950] 1974. *The Woman Suffrage Movement in Canada*, 2nd. ed. Toronto: University of Toronto Press.

Cockell, Charles. 2022. "Liberty Lies in the Heart." *Kyiv Post* [Ukraine], April 26.

"Cocoa Works Magazine." N.d. https://www.rowntreesociety.org.uk/explore-rowntree-history/rowntree-a-z/cocoa-works-magazine/ (April 5, 2022).

"Collazo, Maria." 2020. *Dictionnaire international des militants anarchistes*, January 12. http://www.militants-anarchistes.info/spip.php?article9397 (November 10, 2021).

Collette, Christine. 1989. *For Labour and for Women: the Women's Labour League, 1906–18*. Manchester: Manchester University Press.

"Committee to Help Unemployed Gets Job Without Least Delay." 1922. *Winnipeg Evening Tribune* [MAN], December 6.

"Communists Wind Up Congress in Moscow." 1961. *Evening Star* [Washington, D.C.], November 1.

"Compañeros de "El Rebelde."" 1899. *El Rebelde* [Buenos Aires, Argentina], September 17.

"Compulsory Service: Proclamation Withdrawn." 1916a. *Birchip Advertiser and Watchem Sentinel* [Birchip, VIC], November 29.

"Compulsory Service: Proclamation Withdrawn." 1916b. *Nagambie Times* [VIC], November 24.

"Conclusion of I.W.W. Inquiry." 1920. *Sunday Times* [Sydney, NSW], July 18.

Connolly, Roy. 1920. "The I.W.W. Commission: Last Week's Investigation." *Worker* [Brisbane, QLD], July 15.

Connor, Jenny. 1919. "Tom Barker." *Maoriland Worker* [Wellington, N.Z.], June 11.

Conquest, Robert. 1986. *The Harvest of Sorrow: Soviet Collectivization and the Terror-Famine*. New York: Oxford University Press.

"Conscription in Maoriland." 1916. *Socialist* [Melbourne, VIC], June 30.

""Conspiracy" Cases Before Judge Stocker." 1909. *Spokane Press* [Wash.], December 1.

"Contending Parties in the Steel Strike are Optimistic." 1919. *Norwich Bulletin* [Conn.], September 27.

"Council Will Support Claim of Unemployed." 1923. *Winnipeg Evening Tribune* [MAN], December 4.

"Country Before Politics Urged." 1925. *Winnipeg Evening Tribune* [MAN], April 25.

Coutts, Angela. 2012. "Imagining Radical Women in Interwar Japan: Leftist and Feminist Perspectives." *Signs* 37:325–355.

Craton, Ann Washington. 1927. "With Women Workers in Shop, Factory, Home, and on the Picket Line." *Daily Worker* [Chicago], March 14.

"Crimes and Criminals." 1910. *Justice* [London], February 12.

Crippen, Carolyn L. 2004. "Three Women Pioneers in Manitoba: Evidence of Servant-Leadership." Ph.D. diss. University of North Dakota.

Crump, John. 1980. "A Critical History Of Socialist Thought In Japan To 1918." Ph.D. diss. University of Sheffield.

Crump, John. 1993. *Hatta Shūzō and Pure Anarchism in Interwar Japan*. Basingstoke, U.K.: St. Martin's.

Crump, John. 1998. "The Anarchist Movement in Japan, 1906–1996." Anarchist Communist Editions, Pamphlet No. 8. http://libcom.org/library/anarchist-movementjapan (April 20, 2018).

"Cumberland Explosion: Navigation Department Findings." 1917. *Sunday Times* [Sydney, NSW], September 30.

"*Cumberland* Shipwreck 1917." 2003. Information Sheet, NSW Heritage Office.

Cunha, Eduardo Augusto Souza. 2018. "Editar a revolta: Edição e circulação de impressos anarquistas em Buenos Aires (1890–1905)." M.A. thesis. Universidade de São Paulo.

Curtis, Louise Ann. 2010. "Red Criminals: Censorship, Surveillance and Suppression of the Radical Russian Community in Brisbane during World War I." Ph.D. diss. Griffith University [Queensland].

Cusack, Danny. 2002. "With an Olive Branch and a Shillelagh: the Political Career of Senator Paddy Lynch (1867–1944)." Ph.D. diss. Murdoch University [Western Australia].

Dalmau i Ribalta, Antoni. 2011. "El conflicte de "La Neotípia" (1905–1911). Un episodi clau en la pugna entre lerrouxistes i anarquistes." *Recerques* [Barcelona, Spain] 62:95–116.

Dalmau i Ribalta, Antoni. 2016. "Sobre el anarquista Paulí Pallàs, La Patagonia y algunas confusiones." *Historia Social* 84:23–37.

Damousi, Joy. 1991. "Socialist Women and Gendered Space: the Anti-Conscription and Anti-War Campaigns of 1914–1918." *Labour History* 60:1–15.

"Darling Selection: Mr. Blakeley the Labor Candidate." 1917. *Australian Worker* [Sydney, NSW], March 22.

Davidson, Jared. 2011. *Remains to be Seen: Tracing Joe Hill's Ashes in New Zealand*. Wellington, N.Z.: Rebel.

Davidson, Jared. 2015. "Wobbly Driplines: Strikes, Stowaways & the SS Manuka." *Labour History Project Bulletin*, April.

Davidson, Jared. 2016. *Fighting War*. Wellington, N.Z.: Rebel.

Davis, Mike. 1983. "The Stop Watch and the Wooden Shoe: Scientific Management and the Industrial Workers of the World." In *Workers' Struggles, Past and*

Present: A "Radical America" Reader ed. James Green. Philadelphia, Penn.: Temple University Press.

De Angelis, Paula. 2012. "Tom Barker and the Syndicalism of the Sea: the Underground Influence of the IWW." https://www.academia.edu/3488237/_Tom_Barker_and_the_Syndicalism_of_the_Sea_The_Underground_Influence_of_the_IWW_ (May 9, 2022).

De Angelis, Paula. 2017. "Tom Barker and Revolutionary Europe." In *Wobblies of the World: A Global History of the IWW*, eds. Peter Cole, David Struthers, and Kenyon Zimmer. London: Pluto.

"Death of Mr. Justice Ewing." 1928. *West Australian* [Perth, WA], July 20.

"Declares State Should Assume Care of Fatherless Children." 1921. *Winnipeg Evening Tribune* [MAN], October 6.

De Cleyre, Voltairine. 1909. "Anarchism and American Traditions (Conclusion)." *Mother Earth* 3:386–393.

De Cleyre, Voltairine. 1917. "Free Speech." *Direct Action* [Sydney, NSW], July 7.

"Defaulters Released." 1916. *Argus* [Melbourne, VIC], November 28.

Defense Committee. 1920a. *"Saving the World from Democracy": the Winnipeg General Sympathetic Strike*. Winnipeg, MAN: Defense Committee.

Defense Committee. 1920b. *W.A. Pritchard's Address to the Jury in the* Crown vs. Armstrong, Heaps, Bray, Ivens, Johns, Pritchard, and Queen. Fall Assizes, Winnipeg, MAN, 1919–1920. Winnipeg, MAN: Defense Committee.

DeLamotte, Eugenia C. 2004. *Gates of Freedom: Voltairine de Cleyre and the Revolution of the Mind*. Ann Arbor: University of Michigan Press.

De la Rosa, María Fernanda. 2010. "La propaganda por el hecho dentro del discurso anarquista en la Argentina del Centenario." *Temas de Historia Argentina y Americana* [Buenos Aires, Argentina] 17:75–98.

Delgado, Leandro. 2010. "La participación del anarquismo en la formación del intelectual autónomo en el Río de la Plata (1900–1930)." *A Contra corriente* [Buenos Aires, Argentina] 8:163–197.

"Deputies Indicted for Killing Woman in Strike." 1922. *St. Louis Star and Times* [Mo.], February 15.

"Deputies on Trial." 1923. *San Antonio Light* [Tex.], March 5.

"Deputy Sheriffs Not Guilty in Slaying Miss Sellins." 1923. *Daily Kennebec Journal* [Augusta, Me.], June 9.

Derby, Mark. 2006. "The case of William E. Trautmann and the role of the 'Wobblies.'" In *Revolution: the 1913 Great Strike in New Zealand*, ed. Melanie Nolan. Christchurch, N.Z.: Canterbury University Press.

Derby, Mark. 2010. "Strikes and Labour Disputes." *Te Ara – the Encyclopedia of New Zealand*. http://www.TeAra.govt.nz/en/strikes-and-labour-disputes (May 30, 2022).

"Desde el Rosario." 1900. *La Protesta Humana* [Buenos Aires, Argentina], April 15.

De Shazo, Melvin Gardner. 1925. "Radical Tendencies in the Seattle Labor Movement as Reflected in the Proceedings of Its Central Body." M.A. thesis. University of Washington.

De Souza, Ingrid Souza Ladeira. 2019. "Salimos a la lucha ... sin Dios y sin jefe. O periódico *La Voz de la Mujer* como experiência feminina do anarquismo na Argentina. (1896–1897)." M.A. thesis. Universidade Federal do Estado do Rio de Janeiro.

"Desperate Riot at McKees Rocks." 1909. *Brownsville Daily Herald* [Tex.], August 23.

"Desperate to Get Ettor." 1912. *Barre Daily Times* [Vt.], November 22.

"Detective is Expert on Writing." 1910. *Spokane Press* [Wash.], February 15.

Devine, Jason. 2009. ""You understand we are radical": the United Mine Workers of America, District 18 and The One Big Union, 1919–1920." Honours thesis. University of Calgary.

Diez, Xavier. 2007. *El anarquismo individualista en España (1923–1938)*. Barcelona, Spain: Virus.

Dirlik, Arif. 1991. *Anarchism in the Chinese Revolution*. Berkeley: University of California Press.

"Disputes Act is Sought by Labor Council." 1922. *Winnipeg Evening Tribune* [MAN], October 11.

"Dixon Begins Appeal to Jury." 1920. *Winnipeg Evening Tribune* [MAN], February 13.

"Dixon under Arrest on Sedition Charge." 1919. *Manitoba Free Press* [Winnipeg, MAN], June 28.

Dixson, Miriam. 1966. "The First Communist 'United Front' in Australia." *Labour History* 10:20–31.

"Domain Orators." 1916. *Daily Telegraph* [Launceston, TAS], September 14.

Domínguez Rubio, Lucas. 2012/2013. "Las publicaciones periódicas libertarias argentinas en el acervo del CeDInCI: "una hemerografía local esmerada."" *Políticas de la Memoria* [Buenos Aires] 13:23–48.

"Donald Grant Arrested." 1916. *Barrier Miner* [Broken Hill, NSW], September 27.

Donner, Frank. 1982. "Workers and Wobblies." *Nation*, May 1.

Douglas, Lawrence. 2013. "A Kangaroo in Obama's Court: Will the Guantanamo Tribunal Execute a Man We Tortured?" *Harper's*, October.

"Down and Out: Agitator Jones is a Little Shy on Cash." 1908. *Ely Miner* [Minn.], February 7.

"Dragged at Horses [sic] Heels." 1909. *Monte Vista Journal* [Colo.], August 28.

"Dramatic Incident at Trial of Russell." 1919. *Manitoba Free Press* [Winnipeg, MAN], December 3.

"Dug Up and Still Sound." 1914. *Direct Action* [Sydney, NSW], October 15.

Duncan, James A. 1918. Resolution to Senator Miles Poindexter regarding the Tom Mooney case, April 13. https://digitalcollections.lib.washington.edu/digital/collection/pioneerlife/id/19173 (February 6, 2023).

Dupuis, Michael. 2005. "The Toronto Star and the Winnipeg General Strike." *Manitoba History*, June.
Dupuis, Michael. 2014. *Winnipeg's General Strike: Reports from the Front Lines*. Charleston, S.C.: History Press.
Durham, Martin. 1985. "British Revolutionaries and the Suppression of the Left in Lenin's Russia, 1918–1924." *Journal of Contemporary History* 20:203–219.
Duus, Masayo Umezawa. 1999. *The Japanese Conspiracy: the Oahu Sugar Strike of 1920*. Berkeley: University of California Press.
Duus, Peter, and Irwin Scheiner. 1998. "Socialism, Liberalism, and Marxism, 1901–31." In *Modern Japanese Thought* ed. Bob Tadashi Wakabayashi. Cambridge, U.K.: Cambridge University Press.
Edmund, Jayme. 2017. "Protests, Pageants, and Publications: Narratives of Labor Agitators, 1913–1914." M.A. thesis. University of Northern Iowa.
"Efficiency and Character of Hotel Workers." 1917. *Voice* [Winnipeg, MAN], July 13.
Ehrick, Christine. 2004. *The Shield of the Weak: Feminism and the State in Uruguay, 1903–1933*. Albuquerque: University of New Mexico Press.
"E. Jacob Crull of Elkhart, Blames Suffrage for Suicide." 1917. *Chicago Tribune*, May 6.
"El anarquismo en el Río de la Plata." 1901. *Caras y Caretas* [Buenos Aires, Argentina], August 11.
"El anarquismo japonés." 1911. *Heraldo de Madrid* [Spain], January 9.
"Elect Engdahl Head of I.L.D." 1929. *Daily Worker* [Chicago], August 21.
"Election Bill Before House Will Bar Alien Born Voters from Polls." 1917. *Winnipeg Evening Tribune* [MAN], September 7.
"Electrician Framed in Bomb Plot, Charge." 1923. *Birmingham-Age Herald* [Ala.], May 15.
Elef, Robert M. 1988. "The 1916 Minnesota Miners Strike against U.S. Steel." *Minnesota History*, Summer.
Elfström, Birgitta, and Arne Malmgren. 2005. "'Facility 1391" - a secret prison." Report from the Second Hearing in the High Court of Justice, Jerusalem, December 15, 2004. International Commission of Jurists, Swedish Section.
Elison, George. 1967. "Kōtoku Shūsui: the Change in Thought." *Monumenta Nipponica* 22:437–467.
"Elizabeth Flynn Freed." 1957. *New York Times*, May 26.
"Elizabeth Flynn Held." 1921. *Birmingham Age-Herald* [Ala.], March 7.
"Elizabeth Flynn Speaks Saturday." 1917. *Daily Missoulian* [Missoula, Mont.], February 6.
"Elizabeth Gurley Flynn, 8 Others, Seized as Radicals." 1921. *Chicago Tribune*, March 7.
"Elizabeth Gurley Flynn Arrested in Philadelphia." 1921. *New York Tribune*, March 7.
"Elizabeth Gurley Flynn Faces Jail After Double Contempt at Red Trial." 1952. *New York Times*, November 20.
"Elizabeth Gurley Flynn is Dead: Head of U.S. Communist Party." 1964. *New York Times*, September 6.

"Elizabeth Gurley Flynn Ill." 1927. *Daily Worker* [New York], January 17.

"Elizabeth Gurley Flynn, Noted Fighter, Will Speak in Cleveland." 1924. *Daily Worker* [Chicago], May 8.

"Elizabeth Gurley Flynn Sentenced for Conspiracy." 1909. *Montana News* [Helena], December 16.

"Elizabeth Gurley Flynn Warns of Fascist Menace." 1924. *Daily Worker* [Chicago], April 14.

"Elizabeth Gurley Flynn Will Speak on Sunday." 1909. *Spokane Press* [Wash.], December 11.

"El movimiento obrero: La huelga en Barracas." 1902. *Caras y Caretas* [Buenos Aires, Argentina], November 22.

"El "secretariado" y el delegado Tom Barker." 1922. *La Protesta* [Buenos Aires, Argentina], July 4.

"El socialismo en el Japón" 1907. *El Día* [Madrid, Spain], May 24.

Eltzbacher, Paul. 1908. *Anarchism: Exponents of the Anarchist Philosophy*, trans. Steven T. Byington. New York: Benjamin R. Tucker.

"Emperor of Japan: Alleged Conspiracy Plot." 1910. *Evening Express* [Cardiff, U.K.], December 31.

"Employers' Association." 1913. *Auckland Star* [N.Z.], November 11.

"Ending of Paterson Strike Angers I.W.W." 1913. *Sun* [New York], July 21.

"En el Cerro." 1903. *La Rebelión* [Montevideo, Uruguay], January 18.

"En el Rosario de Santa Fe." 1899. *La Protesta Humana* [Buenos Aires, Argentina], April 1.

Engle, Nancy Arlene Driscol. 2003. "Benefiting a City: Women, Respectability and Reform in Spokane, Washington, 1886–1910." Ph.D. diss. University of Florida.

"En Zárate." 1902. *Caras y Caretas* [Buenos Aires, Argentina], November 22.

Essertier, Joseph. 2017. "Kotoku Shusui and Japanese Linguistic Imperialism." *New Directions* 35:15–43.

"Ettor Addresses Jury." 1912. *Evening Star* [Washington, D.C.], November 23.

"Ettor and His Companions are Freed by Jury." 1912. *Prescott Daily News* [Ark.], November 27.

"Ettor, Giovannitti and Caruso Acquitted." 1912. *Day Book* [Chicago], November 26.

"Ettor Here To-Night Giovannitti Says." 1913. *Sun* [New York], January 15.

"Ettor Interest Mounts Higher." 1912. *Wheeling Majority* [W.Va.], July 18.

Evans, Arthur M. 1919. "Profiteers Help "REDS" Agitate Winnipeg Strike." *Chicago Tribune*, June 20.

Evans, Raymond. 1988. *The Red Flag Riots: A Study of Intolerance*. St. Lucia: University of Queensland Press.

Evans, Raymond. 2000. ""Tempest Tossed": Political Deportations from Australia and the Great War." In *Alien Justice: Wartime Internment in Australia and North America*, eds. Kay Saunders and Roger Davies. St. Lucia: University of Queensland Press.

"Executed: the Japanese Plotters." 1911. *Mataura Ensign* [Gore, N.Z.], January 25.
"Exit Miss Flynn." 1940. Editorial. *New York Times*, May 10.
Fairplay. 1919. "Lest We Forget." Letter to the Editor. *Western Labor News* [Winnipeg, MAN], July 11.
Farmer, Seymour J. 1911. "Single Tax v. Malthus." *Voice* [Winnipeg, MAN], December 15.
Farmer, Seymour J. 1912. "Malthus or George?" *Voice* [Winnipeg, MAN], January 5.
Farmer, Seymour J. 1919. "Labor Day at the Twin Cities." *Western Labor News* [Winnipeg, MAN], September 5.
"Fascism is Real Menace in U. S. Labor Movement." 1924. *Daily Worker* [Chicago], June 10.
"Fatal Strike Riot." 1909. *Reporter and Farmer* [Webster, S.D.], August 26.
"Favor Second Winnipeg Strike." 1920. *New York Times*, January 22.
"F.B.I. Kept Close Watch on Douglas." 1984. *New York Times*, July 22.
Fernández, Gustavo. 2010. "Orígenes del Movimiento Sindical Uruguayo (1865–1919)." *Periódico Rojo y Negro* [Montevideo, Uruguay], April.
Fernández Cordero, Laura. 2006/2007. Review of Nuestra Tribuna: *Hojita del sentir anárquico femenino (1922–1925)* by Elsa Calzetta. *Políticas de la Memoria* [Buenos Aires, Argentina] 6/7:245–247.
Fernández Cordero, Laura. 2015. "The Anarchist Wager of Sexual Emancipation in Argentina, 1900–1930." In *In Defiance of Boundaries: Anarchism in Latin American History*, eds. Geoffroy de Laforcade and Kirwin Shaffer. Gainesville: University Press of Florida.
Fernández Cordero, Laura. 2017. *Amor y anarquismo: Experiencias pioneras que pensaron y ejercieron la libertad sexual*. Buenos Aires, Argentina: Siglo Veintiuno.
Fernández Cordero, Laura. 2019. "Bolten, Virginia." *Diccionario Biográfico de las Izquierdas Latinoamericanas*. https://diccionario.cedinci.org/bolten-virginia/ (January 25, 2022).
"Fighting Conscription: Views of Tom Barker." 1916. *Daily Standard* [Brisbane, QLD], September 16.
Filler, Stephen. 2009. "Going beyond Individualism: Romance, Personal Growth, and Anarchism in the Autobiographical Writings of Itō Noe." *U.S.-Japan Women's Journal* 37:57–90.
Findlay, Quentin. 2019. "The Relationship between the Early New Zealand Labour Party and Socialism 1900–1935." Ph.D. diss. Lincoln University [Canterbury, N.Z.].
"Five Men to Come Out." 1919. *Western Labor News* [Winnipeg, MAN], Special Strike Edition No. 31, June 21.
Fleming, Marie. 2019. *The Anarchist Way to Socialism: Elisée Reclus and Nineteenth-Century European Anarchism*. Abingdon-on-Thames, U.K.: Routledge.
Flynn, Elizabeth Gurley. 1909. "Story of My Arrest and Imprisonment." *Industrial Worker* [Seattle, Wash.], December 15.

Flynn, Elizabeth Gurley. 1914. "The Truth About the Paterson Strike." Speech at the New York Civic Club Forum, January 31, 1914. Iowa State University, Archives of Women's Political Communication. https://awpc.cattcenter.iastate.edu/2020/10/15/the-truth-about-the-paterson-strike-january-31-1914/ (October 7, 2021).

Flynn, Elizabeth Gurley. 1916. "Do You Believe in Patriotism?" *Masses*, March.

Flynn, Elizabeth Gurley. 1917a. *Sabotage: the Conscious Withdrawal of the Workers' Industrial Efficiency*. Chicago: I.W.W. Publishing Bureau.

Flynn, Elizabeth Gurley. 1917b. "The Minnesota Trials." *Masses*, January.

Flynn, Elizabeth Gurley. 1939a. "Defend the Civil Rights of Communists!" *Communist*, December.

Flynn, Elizabeth Gurley. 1939b. "Mine Eyes Have Seen the Glory." *New Masses*, May 2.

Flynn, Elizabeth Gurley. 1940. "Why I Won't Resign from the ACLU" *New Masses*, March 19.

Flynn, Elizabeth Gurley. 1941. "May 1st: the Sun of Tomorrow." *New Masses*, May 6.

Flynn, Elizabeth Gurley. 1946. *Meet the Communists*. New York.: Communist Party, U.S.A.

Flynn, Elizabeth Gurley. 1950. "Freedom to Advertise." Letter to the Editor. *Nation*, December 30.

Flynn, Elizabeth Gurley. 1952a. *Elizabeth Gurley Flynn Speaks to the Court, Opening Statement to the Court and Jury in the Case of the Sixteenth Smith Act Victims in the Trial at Foley Square, New York*. University of Pittsburgh: American Left Ephemera Collection. https://digital.library.pitt.edu/islandora/object/pitt:31735061658054 (May 2, 2023).

Flynn, Elizabeth Gurley. 1952b. "Statement at the Smith Act Trial." New York City, N.Y., April 24, 1952. Iowa State University, Archives of Women's Political Communication. https://awpc.cattcenter.iastate.edu/2017/03/21/statement-at-the-smith-act-trial-april-24-1952/ (October 7, 2021).

Flynn, Elizabeth Gurley. 1961a. *Freedom Begins at Home*. New York: New Century.

Flynn, Elizabeth Gurley. 1961b. "Penalizing Communists." Letter to the Editor. *New York Times*, November 16.

Flynn, Elizabeth Gurley. [1962] 1977. *Memories of the Industrial Workers of the World (IWW)*. Transcript of a speech at Northern Illinois University, DeKalb on November 8, 1962. Occasional Papers Series, No. 24. New York: American Institute for Marxist Studies.

Flynn, Elizabeth Gurley. 1963a. *The Alderson Story: My Life as a Political Prisoner*. New York: International Publishers.

Flynn, Elizabeth Gurley. 1963b. *The McCarran Act, Fact and Fancy*. New York: Gus Hall-Benjamin J. Davis Defense Committee.

Flynn, Elizabeth Gurley. 1973. *The Rebel Girl: An Autobiography. My First Life (1906–1926)*. New York: International Publishers.

Flynn, Elizabeth Gurley. 1987. *Words on Fire: the Life and Writing of Elizabeth Gurley Flynn*, ed. Rosalynn Fraad Baxandall. New Brunswick, N.J.: Rutgers University Press.
"Flynn Goes West to Speak on International Labor Defense Tour." 1926. *Daily Worker* [New York], December 2.
"Flynn in Nation Wide Tour for Labor Defense." 1926. *Daily Worker* [New York], October 23.
"Flynn Starts East on Sacco-Vanzetti Tour." 1926. *Daily Worker* [New York], December 29.
"Flynn Will Speak at Mass Meeting of Labor Defense." 1926. *Daily Worker* [New York], September 2.
"Flynn Woman Acquitted, To Keep Up Work." 1915. *Newark Evening Star* [N.J.], December 1.
Foner, Eric. 2023. "War Fever: the Crusade Against Civil Liberties During World War I." *Nation*, February 20–27.
Foner, Philip S. 1970. "The IWW and the Black Worker." *Journal of Negro History* 55:45–64.
Foner, Philip S. 1991. *History of the Labor Movement in the United States*. 10 vols. New York: International Publishers
Fones-Wolf, Ken. 1996. Review of *Iron in Her Soul: Elizabeth Gurley Flynn and the American Left* by Helen C. Camp. *Pennsylvania History: A Journal of Mid-Atlantic Studies* 63:284–285.
Forbes, Tara. 2021. "Singing Solidarity: Class Consciousness, Emotional Pedagogy, and the Songs of the Industrial Workers of the World." Ph.D. diss. Wayne State University.
"Forged Bank Notes." 1916. *Sun* [Sydney, NSW], December 15.
"For Home Defence: Proclamation." 1916. *Australian Town and Country Journal* [Sydney, NSW], October 4.
Forster, Merna. 2011. *100 More Canadian Heroines: Famous and Forgotten Faces*. Toronto: Dundurn.
"Foster Buried at Kremlin." 1961. *Evening Star* [Washington, D.C.], September 6.
"Four Times across the Pacific: Strange Case of Paul Freeman." 1919. *Press* [Christchurch, N.Z.], June 13.
Foyle, Lindsay. 2000. "Nicholls, Sydney Wentworth (Syd) (1896–1977)." *Australian Dictionary of Biography*. https://adb.anu.edu.au/biography/nicholls-sydney-wentworth-syd-11235 (July 9, 2022).
Francis, Andrew. 2016. "From 'Proven Worthy Settlers' to 'Lawless Hunnish Brutes': Germans in New Zealand in the Great War." In *Germans as Minorities during the First World War: A Global Comparative Perspective*, ed. Panikos Panayi. Abingdon-on-Thames, U.K.: Routledge.
"Francisco Ferrer." 1909. *El Surco* [Montevideo, Uruguay], September 10.
Francis, Daniel. 2010. *Seeing Reds: the Red Scare of 1918–1919, Canada's First War on Terror*. Vancouver, B.C.: Arsenal Pulp.

Frankenstein, Alfred V. 1924. "Show How Big Bosses Choke Free Speech." *Daily Worker* [Chicago], June 9.

"Free Admission Parlor Closed by Magistrate." 1924. *Winnipeg Evening Tribune* [MAN], November 18.

"Free in Murder Case." 1923. *Evening Star* [Washington, D.C.], June 9.

"Freeman Interned." 1919. *Evening Post* [Wellington, N.Z.], July 21.

Freeman, Paul. 1920. "From Paul Freeman." Letter. *Socialist* [Melbourne, VIC], June 4.

"'Free Speech is on Trial – Not I" Says Elizabeth Gurley Flynn." 1915. *Day Book* [Chicago], December 1.

"'Free Them All!' is Slogan at I.L.D. Meeting." 1926. *Daily Worker* [New York], September 10.

"Freethought in Japan." 1909. *Blue-Grass Blade* [Lexington, Ky.], July 11.

Friedheim, Robert L., and Robin Friedheim. 1964. "The Seattle Labor Movement, 1919–20." *Pacific Northwest Quarterly* 55:146–156.

Frugoni, Emilio 1902. "Á los obreros." *Pro-Zola* [Montevideo, Uruguay] 1:1–18.

Fry, Eric. C. 1965. *Tom Barker and the I.W.W.* Canberra, ACT: Australian Society for the Study of Labour History.

Fudge, Judy, and Eric Tucker. 2010. "The Freedom to Strike in Canada: A Brief Legal History." *Canadian Labour & Employment Law Journal* 15:333–353.

Galleani, Luigi. [1925] 1982. *The End of Anarchism?*, trans. Max Sartin and Robert Attilio. Sanday, Orkney, UK: Cienfuegos.

García, Víctor. [1976] 2013. *Museihushugi: El anarquismo japonés*. Madrid, Spain: La Neurosis o Las Barricadas Ediciones.

García, Víctor. 2000. *Three Japanese Anarchists: Kotoku, Osugi and Yamaga*, trans. Paul Sharkey. Berkeley, Cal.: Kate Sharpley Library.

Gavigan, Shelley A.M., and Dorothy E. Chunn. 2007. "From Mothers' Allowance to Mothers Need Not Apply: Canadian Welfare Law as Liberal and Neo-Liberal Reforms." *Osgoode Hall Law Journal* 45:733–771.

"General Strike: Work Being Resumed." 1913. *Telegraph* [Brisbane, QLD], November 13.

"Gelignite Sensation: Sequel to Greenlane Story." 1913. *Auckland Star* [N.Z.], November 28.

George, Harrison. 1918. *The I.W.W. Trial: Story of the Greatest Trial in Labor's History by One of the Defendants*. Chicago: IWW.

"German Treaty Deadline Eased by Khrushchev." 1961. *Evening Star* [Washington, D.C.], October 17.

"Girl Leads Labor War." 1909. *Ekalaka Eagle* [Mont.], October 22.

"Girl to Discuss Labor Problem." 1908. *Detroit Times* [Mich.], March 27.

Glynn, Thomas. 1914. "Mission of Churches: the Same Yesterday, To-day and Forever." *Direct Action* [Sydney, NSW], May 15.

Glynn, Thomas. 1916. "Tom Barker Again "Up": Valuable Help from I.W.W." Letter to the Editor. *Socialist* [Melbourne, VIC], March 17.

Godin, Noël. 2022. "La liberté ou rien." *CQFD* [Marseille, France] no. 208 (April).

Goldman, Emma. 1907. "On the Road (Continuation)." *Mother Earth* 2:128–135.

Goldman, Emma. 1910. *Anarchism and Other Essays*. New York: Mother Earth Publishing Association.

Goldman, Emma. 1913. *Syndicalism: the Modern Menace to Capitalism*. New York: Mother Earth Publishing Association.

Goldman, Emma. [1931] 1970. *Living My Life*. 2 vols. New York: Dover.

"Goldman Wrote 'Dear Fred Howe'; Had Friend Freed." 1919. *New York Times*, November 27.

Goldsborough, Gordon. 2018a. "Memorable Manitobans: William Boad "Billy" Simpson (1877–1952)." https://www.mhs.mb.ca/docs/people/simpson_wb.shtml (March 8, 2023).

Goldsborough, Gordon. 2018b. "Memorable Manitobans: William H. "Bill" Hoop (1876–1928)." https://www.mhs.mb.ca/docs/people/hoop_wh.shtml (March 9, 2023).

Goldsborough, Gordon. 2020. "Memorable Manitobans: Katherine Ross Queen (1885–1934)." https://www.mhs.mb.ca/docs/people/queen_kr.shtml (March 8, 2023).

Golin, Steve. 2020. Review of *Radical Seattle: the General Strike of 1919* by Cal Winslow. https://newyorklaborhistory.org/web/?page_id=1840 (February 7, 2023).

Gómez, Francisco Fernández. 2017. "Factores del desorden: La nacionalización de los anarquistas hasta la Gran Guerra." *Rubrica Contemporanea* [Barcelona, Spain] 6:67–94.

"Good Speakers at State Labor Convention." 1917. *Northwest Worker* [Everett, Wash.], February 1.

Gordon, Andrew. 1983. "Les rapports sociaux et le mouvement syndical dans l'industrie lourde japonaise au XIXe siècle." *Le Mouvement social* 122:3–31.

Gordon, Andrew. 1991. *Labor and Imperial Democracy in Prewar Japan*. Berkeley: University of California Press.

Gori, Pietro. 1909. "La cuestión social y los anarquistas." *El Surco* [Montevideo, Uruguay], September 10.

Gori, Pietro. 1927. *La donna e la famiglia*. Lecture presented at the Teatro Iris, Buenos Aires, November 25, 1900. Buenos Aires, Argentina: Culmine.

"Government Warned Against Reducing Mothers' Allowance." 1923. *Winnipeg Evening Tribune* [MAN], March 15.

"Governor Johnson Will Not Order Troops to the Range." 1907. *Bermidji Daily Pioneer* [Minn.], August 7.

Grant, Adrian. 2011. "Workers to the Rescue": Workers' International Relief in Ireland, 1925. https://www.historyireland.com/workers-to-the-rescueworkers-international-relief-in-ireland-1925/ (April 30, 2023).

"Grants Habeas Corpus Writ in Test Trial Case." 1919. *Winnipeg Evening Tribune* [MAN], July 28.

Gray, Stephen. 2018. "Protest Law and the First World War: the Case of the Industrial Workers of the World (IWW)." *Monash University Law Review* 44:402–427.

Greening, E.W. 1965. "The Winnipeg Strike Trials." *Relations Industrielles / Industrial Relations* 20:77–85.

Grimes, William. 2015. "Robert Conquest, Historian Who Documented Soviet Horrors, Dies at 98." *New York Times*, August 4.

Grover, Preston. 1961. "Stalin's Body Now Lies in Grave Near Kremlin." *Evening Star* [Washington, D.C.], November 1.

G.S. 1911. "Perche' li hanno assassinati?" *Cronaca Sovversiva* [Barre, Vt.], March 11.

Gulick, Lewis. 1961. "Soviet-Albania Break Viewed as Omen by U. S." *Evening Star* [Washington, D.C.], December 11.

"Gurley Flynn Arrested." 1921. *Pioneer Express* [Pembina, N.D.], March 11.

"Gurley Flynn, Coyle and Hayes to Speak at Cleveland Protest." 1926. *Daily Worker* [New York], June 4.

"Gurley Flynn Draws Big Crowd in L.A.; Hits Syndicalist Law." 1926. *Daily Worker* [New York], December 15.

"Gurley Flynn Free; Plans to Keep On Talking." 1915. *New York Times*, December 1.

"Gurley Flynn Greeted Warmly by Spokane in Tour for Mill Strike." 1927. *Daily Worker* [New York], January 13.

"Gurley Flynn Sends Bid to Bill Shannon." 1909. *Spokane Press* [Wash.], December 30.

"Gurley Flynn Speaks for Labor Defense in Detroit Sunday." 1924. *Daily Worker* [Chicago], May 17.

"Gurley Flynn Speaks in Pittsburgh, Will Expose Queen Marie." 1926. *Daily Worker* [New York], November 24.

"Gurley Flynn Talks Passaic to Capacity Crowd of Seattleites." 1927. *Daily Worker* [New York], February 1.

"Gurley Flynn Visits City." 1910. *Coeur d'Alene Evening Press* [Ida.], February 25.

Gutkin, Harry, and Gutkin, Mildred. 1997. *Profiles in Dissent: the Shaping of Radical Thought in the Canadian West*. Edmonton, ALB: NeWest Press.

Gwertzman, Bernard. 1961. "Soviet Communists in 22nd Congress." *Sunday Star* [Washington, D.C.], October 15.

Hajo, Cathy Moran. N.d. "Armstrong, Mrs. (?-?)" Jane Addams Papers Project. Digital Edition. https://digital.janeaddams.ramapo.edu/items/show/17787 (March 12, 2023).

Hane, Mikiso. [1982] 2003. *Peasants, Rebels, Women, and Outcastes: the Underside of Modern Japan*, 2nd. ed. Lanham, MD.: Rowman & Littlefield.

Hane, Mikiso, ed. 1988. *Reflections on the Way to the Gallows: Rebel Women in Prewar Japan*, trans. Hane Mikiso. Berkeley: University of California Press.

Hane, Mikiso. 2015. "Introduction." In *The Prison Memoirs of a Japanese Woman* by Kaneko, Fumiko, trans. Jean Inglis. Abingdon-on-Thames, U.K.: Routledge.

Hansen, Christopher M. 2020. "The Christ and the Discourse: A Critique of the Historiographical and Rhetorical Trends in the Christ Myth Debate." *Northern Plains Ethics Journal* [Fargo, N.D.] 8:97–123.

"¿Han sido ya ejecutados les terroristas japoneses?" 1911. *La Correspondencia de España* [Madrid, Spain], January 5.

Hanson, R.J. 1917. "Shearers' Strike at Hughenden." *Truth* [Brisbane, QLD], July 29.

Harding, L.D. 1909. "Inciting to Riot." *Jeffersonian* [Atlanta, Ga.], September 23.

Harmon, Jim. 2020. "Harnois Theater was the Pride of Missoula ... Albeit Briefly." *Missoula Current* [Mont.], October 19. https://missoulacurrent.com/harnois-theater/ (April 22, 2023).

Harrison, George. 1961. "They Hadn't Forgotten." *Liverpool Echo* [U.K.], November 25.

Harrison, Marguerite E. 1921. *Marooned in Moscow*. New York: George H. Doran.

"Have 350 Veniremen." 1912. *Richmond Palladium* [Va.], September 30.

Havel, Hippolyte. 1911. "Justice in Japan." *Mother Earth* 5:354–358.

Haven, Cynthia. 2010. "Stalin Killed Millions: A Stanford Historian Answers the Question, Was it Genocide?" *Stanford News*, September 23.

"Haywood's Battle for Patterson [sic] Silk Mill Workers." 1913. *United Labor Bulletin* [Denver, Colo.], May 29.

"Haywood's Colony is Ghastly Failure." 1922. *Idaho Recorder* [Salmon City, Ida.], December 8.

Haywood, William D. 1913, "The Rip in the Silk Industry." *International Socialist Review* [Chicago] 13:783–788.

Haywood, William D. 1929. *Bill Haywood's Book: the Autobiography of William D. Haywood*. New York: International Publishers.

Head, Michael. 2016. *Crimes Against the State: From Treason to Terrorism*. Abingdon-on-Thames, U.K.: Routledge.

Heads, Wendy. 1997. "The Local Council of Women of Winnipeg 1894–1920: Tradition and Transformation." M.A. thesis. University of Manitoba.

"Hears Soviet Resolutions: Canadian Labor Congress Applauds Sponsor, Under Sedition Charge." 1919. *New York Times*, September 24.

"Helios Manrique Bolten." 2021. https://ancestors.familysearch.org/en/9XBJ-ZWF/helios-manrique-bolten-1908-2004 (March 2, 2022).

Helquist, Michael. 2015. *Marie Equi: Radical Politics and Outlaw Passions*. Corvallis: Oregon State University Press.

Henning, Arthur Sears. 1927a. "Central Fund Links Agency Aiding Pacifism." *Chicago Tribune*, July 14.

Henning, Arthur Sears. 1927b. "Present United Front for "New Social Order."" *Chicago Tribune*, July 15.

"Here is the "Disorderly Conduct.""" 1909. *Spokane Press* [Wash.], November 6.

Hermida, Ariane. 2016. "Wobbly Wheels: the IWW's Boxcar Strategy." IWW History Project: the Industrial Workers of the World 1905–1935, University of Washington. https://depts.washington.edu/iww/wobbly_trains.shtml (May 6, 2023).

Hessen, Robert. 1972. "Charles M. Schwab, President of United States Steel, 1901–1904." *Pennsylvania Magazine of History and Biography* 96:203–228.

"High Court to Review Ban on Reds' Passports." 1963. *New York Times*, December 3.

Hilton, Walter B. 1911. "Editorials." Editorial. *Wheeling Majority* [W.Va.], February 23.

"Hit "American Plutocracy."" 1912. *Star* [Washington, D.C.], November 24.

Hogan, Michael, ed. 2008. *Labor Pains: Early Conference and Executive Reports of the Labor Party in New South Wales*. Volume IV: 1918–1925. Annandale, NSW: Federation.

Holland, H. E., "Ballot Box," and R. S. Ross. 1913. *The Tragic Story of the Waihi Strike*. Wellington, N.Z.: The "Worker" Printery.

Holleman, Joe. 2022. "History Professor Fights to Shine Light on St. Louis Labor 'Martyr.'" *St. Louis Post-Dispatch* [Mo.], August 19.

Holling, Mrs. Luther. 1917. "Doesn't Want to Vote at Price of Honor of Nation." Letter to the Editor. *Winnipeg Evening Tribune* [MAN], September 11.

"Holodomor – Famine in Soviet Ukraine 1932–1933, in Commemoration of the 75th Anniversary." 2008. Exhibit in the Ralph J. Bunche Library, United States Department of State, Washington, D.C., September 16 – October 31, 2008.

"Home Service Proclamation." 1916a. *Ararat Chronicle and Willaura and Lake Bolac Districts Recorder* [Ararat, VIC], November 17.

"Home Service Proclamation." 1916b. *Warrnambool Standard* [VIC], November 23.

Horimoto, Fumiko. 1999. "Pioneers of the Women's Movement in Japan: Hiratsuka Raichō and Fukuda Hideko Sen Through Their Journals, *Seitō* and *Sekai Fujin*." M.A. thesis. University of Toronto.

Horn, Michiel. 1999. "Students and Academic Freedom in Canada." *Historical Studies in Education / Revue d'histoire de l'éducation* 11:1–32.

Horodyski, Mary. 1986. "Women and the Winnipeg General Strike of 1919." *Manitoba History*, Spring.

"Hotel and Houseworkers are Opposed to Liquor." 1918. *Manitoba Free Press* [Winnipeg, MAN], September 13.

"Housemaids Lay Plans for Union at Initial Meet." 1918. *Winnipeg Evening Tribune* [MAN], April 12.

"Housemaids Pick Union Officials." 1918. *Winnipeg Evening Tribune* [MAN], April 19.

"Housemaids' Picnic." 1918. *Manitoba Free Press* [Winnipeg, MAN], June 28.

"Housemaids to Ask for a 10-Hour Day." 1918. *Winnipeg Evening Tribune* [MAN], October 11.

"Housemaids' Union Formed." 1918. *Manitoba Free Press* [Winnipeg, MAN], April 12.

"Housemaids Want 10 Hour Day." 1918. *Manitoba Free Press* [Winnipeg, MAN], October 11.

Howerth, Ira W. 1906. "The Social Question of Today." *American Journal of Sociology* 12:254–268.

Howes, John F. 1978. "Uchimura Kanzō: the Bible and War." In *Pacifism in Japan: the Christian and Socialist Tradition*, eds. Nobuya Bamba and John F. Howes. Vancouver: University of British Columbia.

"How They Plotted to Kill Emperor." 1911. *Hawaiian Gazette* [Honolulu], February 7.

Hsu, Rachel Hui-Chi. 2016. "Beyond Progressive America: *Mother Earth* and its Anarchist World (1906–1918)." Ph.D. diss. Johns Hopkins University.

Hucker, Graham. 1979. "When the Empire Calls: Patriotic Organisations in New Zealand During the Great War." M.A. thesis. Massey University.

"Huge Meeting Lauds Fight on Frame-Up." 1926. *Daily Worker* [Chicago], November 30.

Ichioka, Yuji. 1971. "A Buried Past: Early Issei Socialists and the Japanese Community." *Amerasia Journal* 1:1–25.

Idiong, Uduak. 1997. "The Third Force: Returned Soldiers in the Winnipeg General Strike of 1919." *Manitoba History*, Autumn.

Ike, Nobutaka. 1944. "Kotoku: Advocate of Direct Action." *Far Eastern Quarterly* 3:222–236.

Ike, Nobutaka. 1957. *Japanese Politics: An Introductory Survey*. New York: Alfred A. Knopf.

"Imprisonment of Montague Miller." 1917. *Socialist* [Melbourne, VIC], October 5.

"Indications of Business Activity." 1925. *Commercial and Financial Chronicle*, November 28. Federal Reserve Bank of St. Louis. https://fraser.stlouisfed.org/title/1339/item/518340?start_page=26 (May 30, 2023).

"Informal Reception Tendered: Five Released Strike Leaders." 1921. *Manitoba Free Press* [Winnipeg, MAN], March 2.

"International Labor Defense (1925–1946): Organizational History." N.d. https://www.marxists.org/history/usa/eam/other/ild/ild.html (May 30, 2023).

"International Notes." 1913. *Freedom* [London], July.

"Intense Interest in Elizabeth Flynn Trial." 1909. *Spokane Press* [Wash.], December 8.

"Investigation of Strike Asked." 1909. *Bisbee Daily Review* [Ariz.], August 24.

"Irish Meeting." 1916. *Socialist* [Melbourne, VIC], September 22.

"Irish Peasants Facing Plague Thru Starvation." 1925. *Daily Worker* [New York], April 15.

Isitt, Benjamin. 2003. "The Search for Solidarity: the Industrial and Political Roots of the Cooperative Commonwealth Federation in British Columbia, 1913–1928." M.A. thesis. University of Victoria.

Isserman, Maurice. 1988. "Threads of Conspiracy." *Nation*, October 10.

"I.W.W." 1916. *Northern Miner* [Charters Towers, QLD], October 28.

"I.W.W. Appellants." 1916. *Sun* [Sydney, NSW], December 21.

"I.W.W. Case: Fresh Charge Against Horrocks." 1916. *Evening Star* [Boulder, WA], October 30.

"I.W.W. Case: Royal Commission's Report." 1920. *Daily Advertiser* [Wagga, NSW], July 31.

"I.W.W. Cases: Tom Barker Released." 1916. *Sun* [Sydney, NSW], November 21.

"I.W.W. Cases: Two Sentences Reduced." 1917. *Sydney Morning Herald* [NSW], March 10.

"I.W.W. Conspiracy." 1916. *Evening Telegraph* [Charters Towers, QLD], December 18.

"I.W.W. Directory (Australasian Locals)." 1913. *Industrial Unionist* [Auckland, N.Z.], June 1.

"I.W.W. Here and Russ Bolshevik Shown as Allies." 1918. *Chicago Tribune*, May 10.

"I.W.W. in Sydney." 1917. *Evening Post* [Wellington, N.Z.], September 1.

"I.W.W. Leader Charges Billy Sunday Broke Unions." 1915. *Day Book* [Chicago], March 18.

"I.W.W. Men Sentenced." 1917. *Warrnambool Standard* [VIC], September 1.

"I.W.W. Methods." 1916. *Albury Banner and Wodonga Express* [Albury, NSW], November 17.

"I.W.W. Plotters: the Sydney Trial Concluded." 1916. *Gisborne Times* [N.Z.], December 4.

"I.W.W. Premises Raided." 1916. *Barrier Miner* [Broken Hill, NSW], September 24.

"I.W.W. Prisoners: Committee's Call for Help." 1920. *Daily Herald* [London], May 24.

"I.W.W.: Sabotage in Sydney." 1916. *Evening Star* [Dunedin, N.Z.], October 11.

"I.W.W. Suppression: Mr Tom Barker Arrested." 1917. *Sun* [Christchurch, N.Z.], August 31.

"Jack London And Others Protest Execution Of 26 Japanese." 1910. *Hawaiian Star* [Honolulu], December 20.

"Jail is Crowded with I.W.W. Men." 1909. *Spokane Press* [Wash.], November 3.

"Jailer of 'Reds' at Ellis Island Their Samaritan." 1919. *Chicago Tribune*, November 27.

James, Henry. [1886] 1980. *Henry James: Novels 1886–1890: the Princess Casamassima, The Reverberator, The Tragic Muse*. New York: The Library of America.

"Jap Anarchists Executed." 1911. *Prescott Daily News* [Ark.], January 25.

"Japanese Anarchists: Executions Carried Out." 1911. *Daily Herald* [Adelaide, SA], January 26.

"Japanese Executions." 1911. *Mullumbimby Star* [NSW], January 26.

"Japanese Plotters: Twelve Executed." 1911. *New Zealand Herald* [Auckland, N.Z.], January 26.

Jeifets, Victor. 2021. "La derrota de los "Lenins argentinos": La Internacional Comunista, el Partido Comunista y el movimiento obrero de Argentina, 1919–1922." *Pacarina del Sur* [Mexico City] 12:46–47.

Jeifets, Victor, and Lazar Jeifets. 2014. "La Internacional Comunista y la izquierda argentina: primeros encuentros y desencuentros." *Archivos de historia del movimiento obrero y la izquierda* [Buenos Aires, Argentina] 3:71–92.

Jensen, Vernon H. 1967. "The "Legend" and the "Case" of Joe Hill." *Dialogue: A Journal of Mormon Thought* 2:97–109.

"Jitney Drivers to Form Union; to Call Meeting." 1916. *Winnipeg Evening Tribune* [MAN], July 10.

"Jitneys." 1915. *Voice* [Winnipeg, MAN], July 2.

"John Archibald Jones." 1940. *New York Times*, December 13.

"John Beffel Dead; Aided Sacco Defense." 1973. *New York Times*, September 18.

Johnson, C.L. 1919. "Revolution or Strike in Winnipeg?" *The Public: A Journal of Democracy* [New York], June 21.

Johnson, Jeffrey A. 2020. "Aliens, Enemy Aliens, and Minors: Anti-Radicalism and the Jewish Left." In *Historicizing Fear: Ignorance, Vilification, and Othering* eds. Travis D. Boyce and Winsome M. Chunnu. Boulder: University Press of Colorado.

Johnson, Oakley C. 1957. *The Day is Coming: Life and Work of Charles E. Ruthenberg 1882–1927*. New York: International.

Johnson, Simon. 1975. "The Home Front: Aspects of Civilian Patriotism in New Zealand during the First World War." M.A. thesis. Massey University.

Jonasson, Stefan. 2022. "Freyja's Legacy: Margrét J. Benedictsson and the Struggle for Equality." https://lh-inc.ca/component/content/article/604-freyja-s-legacy-margret-j-benedictsson-and-the-struggle-for-equality?catid=11&Itemid=101 (March 15, 2023).

Jones, Esyllt Wynne. 2003. "Searching for the Springs of Health: Women and Working Families in Winnipeg's 1918–1919 Influenza Epidemic." Ph.D. diss. University of Manitoba.

Jordan, Deborah. 2018. "Adela Pankhurst, Peace Negotiator: World War 1, Queensland." *Outskirts* 39:1–20.

"Judge Mann Dismisses Free Speech Case." 1909. *Spokane Press* [Wash.], November 2.

"Jurist Queries Witness." 1952. *New York Times*, November 26.

"Jury from Next County." 1913. *Ogden Standard* [Ogden City, Utah], June 13.

"Jury Gets Case of Miss Flynn in Paterson Strike." 1913. *Newark Evening Star* [N.J.], July 2.

Kanno, Sugako. [1911] 1988. "Reflections on the Way to the Gallows," trans. Mikiso Hane. In *Reflections on the Way to the Gallows: Rebel Women in Prewar Japan* ed. Mikiso Hane. Berkeley: University of California Press.

Kao, Jeff, Raymond Zhong, Paul Mozur, and Aaron Krolik. 2021. "How China Spreads Its Propaganda Version of Life for Uyghurs." ProPublica, June 23. https://www.propublica.org/article/how-china-uses-youtube-and-twitter-to-spread-its-propaganda-version-of-life-for-uyghurs-in-xinjiang (June 19, 2023).

Kaunonen, Gary. 2018. "The Minnesota Miners' Strike That Brought Immigrant Workers Together." https://www.whatitmeanstobeamerican.org/places/the-minnesota-miners-strike-that-brought-immigrant-workers-together/ (May 13, 2023).

Kealey, Gregory S. 1992. "State Repression of Labour and the Left in Canada, 1914–20: the Impact of the First World War." *Canadian Historical Review* 73:281–314.

Kealey, Gregory S., and Christina Burr. 2003. "Jury, Alfred Fredman." In *Dictionary of Canadian Biography*, vol. 14. Toronto: University of Toronto/Université Laval. http://www.biographi.ca/en/bio/jury_alfred_fredman_14E.htm (February 15, 2023).

Keller, Bill. 1989. "Major Soviet Paper Says 20 Million Died As Victims of Stalin." *New York Times*, February 4.

Kelly, Paula. 2016. "Looking for Mrs. Armstrong." *Canada's History*, January 9. https://www.canadashistory.ca/explore/women/looking-for-mrs-armstrong (September 8, 2021).

"Ken Leslie Released." 1916. *Australian Worker* [Sydney, NSW], May 11.

Kershner, Jim. 2009. "A Fight for Free Speech." *Spokesman-Review* [Spokane, Wash.], November 1.

Kim, Sungmoon. 2011. "Confucian Constitutionalism: Mencius and Xunzi on Virtue, Ritual, and Royal Transmission." *Review of Politics* 73:371–399.

Kingsford, Syd. 1911. "I.W.W. Clubs." Letter to the Editor. *Maoriland Worker* [Wellington, N.Z.], June 23.

Kingsford, Syd. 1912. "Industrial Workers of the World." Letter to the Editor. *Lyttleton Times* [Christchurch, N.Z.], September 19.

Kirkup, Thomas. [1887] 1909. *An Inquiry into Socialism*, 3rd. ed. London: Longman, Green.

Kizer, Benjamin H. 1966. "Elizabeth Gurley Flynn." *Pacific Northwest Quarterly* 57:110–112.

Kluckow, Rich, and Zhen Zeng. 2020. *Correctional Populations in the United States, 2020 – Statistical Tables*. U.S. Department of Justice: Bureau of Justice Statistics, March.

Kneen, J. R. 1915a. "Mr Craig and Seamen's Union." *New Zealand Times* [Wellington, N.Z]. August 30.

Kneen, J. R. 1915b. "Preference Clause: Mr E. A. Craig's Complaint." *New Zealand Times* [Wellington, N.Z]. August 4.

Knowles, Valerie. 2019. "When Winnipeg Erupted." *Legion Magazine*, May 15.

Konishi, Sho. 2013. *Anarchist Modernity Cooperatism and Japanese-Russian Intellectual Relations in Modern Japan*. Cambridge, Mass.: Harward University Press.

Kornbluh, Joyce L. 1964a. "Paterson 1913." In *Rebel Voices: An IWW Anthology*, ed. Joyce L. Kornbluh. Ann Arbor: University of Michigan Press.

Kornbluh, Joyce L. 1964b. "Soapbox Militants: Free Speech Campaigns 1908–1916." In *Rebel Voices: An IWW Anthology*, ed. Joyce L. Kornbluh. Ann Arbor: University of Michigan Press.

Kornbluh, Joyce L. 1964c. "With Folded Arms: the Tactics of Direct Action." In *Rebel Voices: An IWW Anthology*, ed. Joyce L. Kornbluh. Ann Arbor: University of Michigan Press.

"Kotoku, Japan's Anarchist." 1911. *Sun* [New York], March 8.

"Kotoku's Correspondence with Albert Johnson (Conclusion)." 1911. *Mother Earth* 6:282–287.

"Kotoku's Correspondence with Albert Johnson (Continuation)." 1911. *Mother Earth* 6:207–209.

Kōtoku, Shūsui. [1900] 2009. "Abolish Money." *Yorozu Chōhō* [Tokyo], February 9. https://www.katesharpleylibrary.net/s4mxdq (July 3, 2022).

Kōtoku, Shūsui. [1901a] 2015. *Imperialism: Monster of the Twentieth Century*, trans. Robert Thomas Tierney. In *Monster of the Twentieth Century: Kōtoku Shūsui and Japan's First Anti-Imperialist Movement* by Robert Thomas Tierney. Oakland: University of California Press.

Kōtoku, Shūsui. [1901b] 2017. "Genbun Itchi and Newspapers" (Genbun itchi to shinbun shi), trans. Joseph Essertier. In "Kotoku Shusui and Japanese Linguistic Imperialism" by Joseph Essertier. *New Directions* 35:34–43.

Kōtoku, Shūsui. [1903] 1969. *The Essence of Socialism*, trans. Sharon Lee Sievers. In "Kōtoku Shūsui, *The Essence of Socialism*: A Translation and Biographical Essay" by Sharon Lee Sievers. Ph.D. diss. Stanford University.

Kōtoku, Shūsui. [1905a] 1979. "A Red Flag." In *A Short History of The Anarchist Movement in Japan*, ed. Le Libertaire Group. Tokyo: Idea Publishing House.

Kōtoku, Shūsui. 1905b [as "D. Kotoku"]. "'Progressive" Japan! Listen to a Japanese Socialist Editor." Letter to the Editor. *Worker* [Brisbane, QLD], April 1.

Kōtoku, Shūsui. [1906] 1979. "20 Lines Dedicated to Mr. Johnson or An American Comrade." In *A Short History of The Anarchist Movement in Japan*, ed. Le Libertaire Group. Tokyo: Idea Publishing House.

Kōtoku, Shūsui. 1907a. "Fujin shokan" [Women's Jurisdiction]. *Sekai fujin*, January 2.

Kōtoku, Shūsui. [1907b] 1979. "Why I Have Changed My Thought (Of Universal Suffrage)," In *A Short History of The Anarchist Movement in Japan*, ed. Le Libertaire Group. Tokyo: Idea Publishing House.

Kōtoku, Shūsui. [1907c] 1980. "The Change In My Thought (On Universal Suffrage)," trans. John Crump. In *"A Critical History Of Socialist Thought In Japan To 1918"* by John Crump. Ph.D. diss. University of Sheffield.

Kōtoku, Shūsui. 1908 [as "D. Kotoku"]. "The Labour Movement in Japan." *Socialist* [Melbourne, VIC], July 24.

Kōtoku, Shūsui. 1909. Letter to Albert Johnson, May 25. *Blue-Grass Blade* [Lexington, Ky.], July 11.

Kōtoku, Shūsui. [1910a] 1979. "A Letter from Prison." In *A Short History of The Anarchist Movement in Japan*, ed. Le Libertaire Group. Tokyo: Idea Publishing House.

Kōtoku, Shūsui. [1910b] 1967. "Discussion of Violent Revolution: From a Jail Cell," trans. George Ellison. *Monumenta Nipponica* 22:468–481.

Kōtoku, Shūsui. [1910c] 1979. "My Sentiments at Cell." In *A Short History of The Anarchist Movement in Japan*, ed. Le Libertaire Group. Tokyo: Idea Publishing House.

Kōtoku, Shūsui. [1910d] 1979. "To My Mother." In *A Short History of The Anarchist Movement in Japan*, ed. Le Libertaire Group. Tokyo: Idea Publishing House.

Kōtoku, Shūsui. [1911a] 1979. "From Prison." In *A Short History of The Anarchist Movement in Japan*, ed. Le Libertaire Group. Tokyo: Idea Publishing House.

Kōtoku, Shūsui. 1911b. *Kirisuto massatsu ron* (On the Obliteration of Christ). Tokyo: Hinoeuma Shuppansha.

Kōtoku, Shūsui. 2001. *Chōmin sensei: Chōmin sensei gyōjōki.* Tokyo: Iwanami Shoten.

Kovac, Caroline. 2021. "Council to Investigate Return of Blackall Monument to Rightful Spot." https://www.ipswichfirst.com.au/council-to-investigate-return-of-blackall-monument-to-rightful-spot/ (June 9, 2022).

Kramer, Reinhold, and Tom Mitchell. 2010. *When the State Trembled: How A.J. Andrews and the Citizens' Committee Broke the Winnipeg General Strike.* Toronto: University of Toronto Press.

Krieger, Nancy. 1983. "Queen of the Bolsheviks: the Hidden History of Dr. Marie Equi." *Radical America*, September-October.

"Kronika Miejscowa" 1919. *Czas* [Winnipeg, MAN], July 12.

Kropotkin, Alexandra [as "Sacha Kropotkine Lebedeff"]. 1911. "La Tragedia di Tokyo." *Cronaca Sovversiva* [Barre, Vt.], February 11.

Kropotkin, Peter. 1887. "The Coming Anarchy." *Nineteenth Century*, August.

Kropotkin, Peter. 1898a. "Lo que entendemos por revolución" *El Rebelde* [Buenos Aires, Argentina], November 11.

Kropotkin, Peter. 1898b. "Lo que entendemos por revolución (Conclusión)." *El Rebelde* [Buenos Aires, Argentina], November 27.

Kropotkin, Peter. [1902] 1904. *Mutual Aid: A Factor of Evolution*, revised ed. New York: McClure Phillips.

Kropotkin, Peter. [1906] 2011. *The Conquest of Bread.* Garden City, N.Y.: Dover.

Kropotkin, Peter. 1907. *Fields, Factories and Workshops.* New York: G.P. Putnam's Sons.

Kropotkin, Peter. 1909. *The Commune of Paris.* London: Freedom.

Kropotkin, Peter. [1927] 1970. *Kropotkin's Revolutionary Pamphlets: A Collection of Writings by Peter Kropotkin*, ed. Roger N. Baldwin. New York: Dover.

Kruso, William F. 1923. "Kuzbas Digs in for the Winter." *Daily Standard* [Brisbane, QLD], December 28.

"Krwawe zajścia uliczne: Wojsko strzela do tłumów." 1919. *Czas* [Winnipeg, MAN], July 25.

Kublin, Hyman. 1950. "The Japanese Socialists and the Russo-Japanese War." *Journal of Modern History* 22:322–339.

Kuo, Lily. 2019. "'If You Enter a Camp, You Never Come Out': Inside China's War on Islam." *Guardian*, January 11.

"Kuzbas Colony: Formation of Brisbane Organisation." 1923. *Grey River Argus* [Greymouth, N.Z.], May 12.

"Kuzbas Colony: Satisfactory Progress." 1924. *Daily Standard* [Brisbane, QLD], August 26.

"Kuzbas or Communism." 1922. *Workers' Dreadnought* [London], April 15.

"La barbarie japonesa." 1911. *El Pais* [Madrid, Spain.], January 8.
Labor and the War: American Federation of Labor and the Labor Movements of Europe and Latin America. 1918. Washington, D.C. American Federation of Labor.
"Labor Asks $12 Wage Minimum for Women: Commission Scheme is Condemned." 1919. *Winnipeg Evening Tribune* [MAN], February 6.
"Labor Bound to Face Steady Immigration Next Fifteen Years." 1922. *Winnipeg Evening Tribune* [MAN], December 20.
"Labor Convention Asks Six-Hour Day for Miners." 1918. *Lethbridge Daily Herald* [ALB], January 7.
"Labor Church Protests Cut in Allowances." 1923. *Winnipeg Evening Tribune* [MAN], March 28.
"Labor Congress Has Auspicious First Session." 1919. *Manitoba Free Press* [Winnipeg, MAN], September 23.
"Labor Debaters Chosen for Next Friday Night." 1920. *Manitoba Free Press* [Winnipeg, MAN], July 30.
"Labor League Meets." 1923. *Winnipeg Evening Tribune* [MAN], May 7.
"Labor Men Asking Six Hour Day and a Five Day Week." 1918. *Manitoba Free Press* [Winnipeg, MAN], August 30.
"Labor Movement in Japan." 1921. *Daily Standard* [Brisbane, QLD], February 26.
"Labor Objects to Immigration." 1923. *Winnipeg Evening Tribune* [MAN], September 19.
"Labor Repeats Protest Against Immigration." 1923. *Winnipeg Evening Tribune* [MAN], March 21.
"Labor Urges Changes in Humane Laws." 1923. *Winnipeg Evening Tribune* [MAN], January 2.
"Labor Women in Clash as Booze Issue Re-Opens." 1918. *Winnipeg Evening Tribune* [MAN], September 12.
"Labour and the Soviet." 1923. *Pahiatua Herald* [N.Z.], February 22.
"Labour Party Suspend Councillor." 1958. *Glasgow Herald* [U.K.], May 22.
"La crisis obrera." 1897. Editorial. *La Protesta* [Buenos Aires, Argentina], June 27.
Laidler, P. 1915. "Barker's Case." *Direct Action* [Sydney, NSW], October 1.
Lamont, Corliss. 1968a. "Introduction." In *The Trial of Elizabeth Gurley Flynn by the American Civil Liberties Union*, ed. Corliss Lamont. New York: Monthly Review.
Lamont, Corliss, ed. 1968b. *The Trial of Elizabeth Gurley Flynn by the American Civil Liberties Union*. New York: Monthly Review.
"Landing Permitted: Freeman Denies I.W.W. Connection." 1919. *Singleton Argus* [NSW], June 5.
Langston, Donna. 2002. *A to Z of American Women Leaders and Activists*. New York: Facts on File.
Large, Stephen S. 1970. "The Japanese Labor Movement, 1912–1919: Suzuki Bunji and the Yuaikai." *Journal of Asian Studies* 29:559–579.

Large, Stephen S. 1977. "The Romance of Revolution in Japanese Anarchism and Communism during the Taishō Period." *Modern Asian Studies* 11:441–467.

Larsen, Norm, ed. 2017. *Notable Trials from Manitoba's Legal History – Including – Sedition Trials from the Winnipeg General Strike*. Altona, MAN: Friesens.

"La situacion." 1897. Editorial. *La Protesta* [Buenos Aires, Argentina], August 1.

"Laurier is Heard by Huge Crowd." 1917. *Winnipeg Evening Tribune* [MAN], December 11.

Laursen, Thomas E. 1981. "Constitutional Protection of Foreign Travel." *Columbia Law Review* 81:902–931.

Lavrin, Asunción. 1995. *Women, Feminism, and Social Change in Argentina, Chile, and Uruguay, 1890–1940*. Lincoln: University of Nebraska Press.

Lawrence, Tayla. 2020. "A Defence of Plantinga's Response to the Omnipotence Paradox and Free Will." *Simon Fraser University Undergraduate Journal of Philosophy* 2:3–15.

Lay, H. G. 1999. "Réflecs d'un gniaff: On Emile Pouget and *Le Père Peinard*." In *Making the News: Modernity and the Mass Press in Nineteenth Century France*, eds. Dean de la Motte and Jeannene M. Przyblyski. Amherst: University of Massachusetts Press.

"Leaders of the Unemployed." 1908. *Fargo Forum and Daily Republican* [N.D.], October 14.

Leal, Claudia Feierabend Baeta. 2006. "*Pensiero e Dinamite*: Anarquismo e repressão em São Paulo nos anos 1890." Ph.D. diss. Universidade Estadual de Campinas [Brazil].

Leeder, Elaine. 1993. *The Gentle General: Rose Pesotta, Anarchist, and Labor Organizer*. Albany: State University of New York Press.

Lefeaux, Wallis Walter. 1921. *Winnipeg, London, Moscow: A Study of Bolshevism*. Winnipeg, MAN: Canadian Workers Defense League.

"Le Forche." 1913a. *Cronaca Sovversiva* [Barre, Vt.], July 12.

"Le Forche." 1913b. *Cronaca Sovversiva* [Barre, Vt.], July 19.

Le Libertaire Group, ed. 1979. *A Short History of The Anarchist Movement in Japan*. Tokyo: Idea Publishing House.

"L'Émeute à Winnipeg." 1919. *La Liberté* [Winnipeg, MAN], June 24.

Lenin, V.I. [1921] 1965a. "Preliminary Draft Resolution of the Tenth Congress of the R.C.P. on The Syndicalist and Anarchist Deviation in our Party" in *The Tenth Congress of the R.C.P. Verbatim Report, March 8–16, 1921*, 1st English Edition. Moscow: Progress Publishers. https://www.marxists.org/archive/lenin/works/1921/10thcong/ch04.htm (February 17, 2018).

Lenin, V.I. [1921] 1965b. "The Second All-Russia Congress of Miners." https://www.marxists.org/archive/lenin/works/1921/jan/23.htm#fw01 (June 29, 2022).

Levi, Charles. 2006. "Sex, Drugs, Rock & Roll, and the University College Lit: the University of Toronto Festivals, 1965–69." *Historical Studies in Education / Revue d'histoire de l'éducation* 18:163–190.

Levy, Carl. 2019. "American Anarchisms?" *Anarchist Studies* 27:103–107.

Lévy, Christine. 2002. "Kōtoku Shūsui et l'anarchisme." *Ebisu* 28:61–86.

Lewis, Thurber. 1926a. "Police Club Workers for Queen Marie; Monarch Shudders at Cries of "Cotzofanesti.""" *Daily Worker* [New York], November 16.

Lewis, Thurber. 1926b. "The Queen of Terrorland." *Daily Worker* [New York], October 21.

Lewycky, Dennis. 2019. *Magnificent Fight: the Winnipeg General Strike*. Halifax, NS: Fernwood.

"Liberal Members Contest Budget in Wednesday Debate." 1921. *Winnipeg Evening Tribune* [MAN], May 19.

"Liberals Plan Party Advantage: Caucus on Bill." 1917. *Brandon Daily Sun* [MAN], September 7.

Liquor, Gaming and Cannabis Authority of Manitoba. N.d. "History of Liquor Regulation: 1916." https://lgcamb.ca/timeline/1916-1/ (January 25, 2023).

"Literature in Stock." 1914. *Direct Action* [Sydney, NSW], September 15.

"Lithuanian Fascist Atrocities Rousing World Wide Protest; Authors Send Cable." 1927. *Daily Worker* [New York], February 21.

"Little Local Stories." 1908a. *Detroit Times* [Mich.], March 27.

"Little Local Stories." 1908b. *Detroit Times* [Mich.], April 6.

Littler, J. 2017. "The Making of an Alternative Religion in Late-Meiji Japan (1899–1912): A Study of Arai Ōsui (1846–1922)." M.Sc. thesis. Oxford University.

"Local Council Protests Cut in Mothers' Allowance Act." 1923. *Winnipeg Evening Tribune* [MAN], March 24.

"Local News." 1908. *Olneyville Times* [Providence, R.I.], March 20.

"Local News." 1917. *Voice* [Winnipeg, MAN], May 25.

"Locals." 1910. *Voice* [Winnipeg, MAN], December 23.

"London Borough Flies a Red Flag." 1958. *New York Times*, May 2.

"London Electricity Goes to France." 1998. BBC News, November 30. http://news.bbc.co.uk/1/hi/business/the_company_file/224583.stm (July 9, 2022).

"Long Live Free Russia." 1917. *Herald* [Melbourne, VIC], March 31.

Lopes, Milton. 2009. "Elisée Reclus e o Brasil." *Revista Geographia* [Niterói, Rio de Janeiro, Brazil] 11:160–175.

"Los ocho deportados de Australia y su presencia en Chile." 1918. *El Mercurio* [Valparaíso, Chile], August 24.

Lowe, Graham S. 1982. "Class, Job and Gender in the Canadian Office." *Labour / Le Travail* 10:11–37.

Lowell, Esther. 1924. "Overworked Manicurists Form Independent Union to Carry on Drive for Good Conditions." *Daily Worker* [Chicago], September 23.

"Low Wages, High Profits." 1926. Editorial. *Nation*, March 31.

Lozza, Arturo Marcos. 1985. "Tiempos de huelgas: Los apasionados relatos del campesino y ferroviario Florindo Moretti sobre aquellas épocas de fundaciones, luchas y serenatas." Buenos Aries, Argentina: Anteo.

Lynn, Denise. 2016. Review of *Elizabeth Gurley Flynn: Modern American Revolutionary* by Lara Vapnik, *Labour / Le Travail* 77:306–308.
Mack, A. 1916. "The Conspiracy Charges: I.W.W. Men Sentenced." *Direct Action* [Sydney, NSW], December 9.
Mackie, J. L. 1955. "Evil and Omnipotence." *Mind* 64:200–212.
Mackie, Vera. 1994. "Creating Socialist Women in Japan, 1900–1937." Ph.D. thesis. University of Adelaide.
Mackie, Vera. 1997. *Creating Socialist Women in Japan: Gender, Labour and Activism, 1900–1937*. Cambridge, U.K.: Cambridge University Press.
MacKinnon, Peter. 1977. "Conspiracy and Sedition as Canadian Political Crimes." *McGill Law Journal* 23:622–643.
Macoc, Lucía. 2011. "Feminismo e Identidades políticas a principios del siglo XX en la Argentina. Construcciones discursivas sobre la Mujer en el socialismo y el anarquismo." *Cuadernos del Ciesal* 9:151–173.
Madgwick, G. 1911a. "Socialism in Japan." Letter to the Editor. *Daily Herald* [Adelaide, SA], February 11.
Madgwick, G. 1911b. "Japanese Executions." Letter to the Editor. *Register* [Adelaide, SA], February 13.
"Madness of Moneybags." 1912. *Labor Call* [Melbourne, VIC], March 21.
"Mahon[,] Hugh." N.d. Legal Opinions. Australian Government: Attorney-General's Department. https://legalopinions.ags.gov.au/opinionauthor/mahon-hugh (August 2, 2022).
"Make Auditors Cry." 1912. *Star* [Washington, D.C.], November 24.
Maki, Wilma Jane. 1992. "The 1921 Mitsubishi Kawasaki Strike: the Past and Present World of the Kobe Shipyard Strikers." M.A. thesis. University of British Columbia.
M.A.M. 1973. "Unity." Review of "Tom Barker at Camden – and the World" by William Hinchcliffe, a play at the Camden Festival, London. *Stage and Television Today* [London], June 21.
"Manicurists Join Hairdressers in Organizing Union." 1924. *Evening Star* [Washington, D.C.], September 11.
"Mann and the Mayor." 1909. *Evening Post* [Wellington, N.Z.], July 28.
Mann, Tom. 1923. *Tom Mann's Memoirs*. London: Labour Publishing.
"Many Hurt as Strikers Riot." 1913. *Perth Amboy Evening News* [N.J.], April 18.
"Many Join with Workers Party in Relief for Irish." 1925. *Daily Worker* [New York], March 19.
Manzoni, Gisela Paola. 2009. "Antimilitaristas y libertarias: La postura de las mujeres anarquistas ante el militarismo." First Conference of the Interdisciplinary Center for Gender Research, October 29 and 30, 2009, La Plata. La Plata, Argentina: En Memoria Académica.

Marrus, Michael R. 1988. "Foreword." In *The Foreign Office and the Famine: British Documents on Ukraine and the Great Famine of 1932–1933*, eds. Marco Carynnyk, Lubomyr Y. Luciuk and Bohdan S. Kordan. Kingston, ONT: Limestone.

Marqusee, Mike. 2013. "We Could Have Won!" *Red Pepper*, July 4.

Marshall, Norma. 1979. "Blakeley, Arthur (1886–1972)." *Australian Dictionary of Biography*. https://adb.anu.edu.au/biography/blakeley-arthur-5268 (June 16, 2022).

Marsland, Stephen E. 1989. *The Birth of the Japanese Labor Movement: Takano Fusatarō and the Rōdō Kumiai Kiseikai*. Honolulu: University of Hawai'i Press.

Martínez, María Migueláñez. 2018. "Más allá de las fronteras: El anarquismo Argentino en el periodo de entreguerras." Ph.D. diss. Universidad Autónoma de Madrid.

Martin, Louis C. 2007. "Tin Plate Towns, 1890–1910: Local Labor Movements and Workers' Responses to the Crisis in the Steelworkers' Union." *Pennsylvania History: A Journal of Mid-Atlantic Studies* 74:492–528.

Martins, Angela Maria Roberti, and Ingrid Souza Ladeira de Souza. 2018. "Feminine Voices of Anarchism in Argentina of the XIX and XX Centuries." *LexCult* [Rio de Janeiro, Brazil] 2:210–244.

Marx, Karl. [1845] 2002. *Theses On Feuerbach*, trans. Cyril Smith. https://www.marxists.org/archive/marx/works/1845/theses/index.htm (May 5, 2022).

Mason, Robert. 2018. *The Spanish Anarchists of Northern Australia: Revolution in the Sugar Cane Fields*. Cardiff: University of Wales Press.

Masters, Donald C. 1950. *The Winnipeg General Strike*. Toronto: University of Toronto Press.

Mathieson, David. 2016. *Radical London in the 1950s*. Stroud, U.K.: Amberley.

"Matunga's Crew." 1918. *Maitland Daily Mercury* [NSW], March 11.

"Matunga's Crew." 1919. *Sydney Morning Herald* [NSW], January 23.

"Matunga's Passengers: Experiences in Captivity." 1918. *Argus* [Melbourne, VIC], March 2.

"Matunga Victims." 1918. *Sun* [Sydney, NSW], July 2.

Maume, Patrick. 2009. "MacSwiney, Terence James." *Dictionary of Irish Biography*. https://www.dib.ie/biography/macswiney-terence-james-a5297 (June 24, 2022).

Maybon, Albert. 1911. "Socialistes et Regicides en Japon." *Mercure de France*, February 1.

"Mayor and Chief are "Marked Men."" 1909. *Yakima Herald* [Wash.], December 22.

McAloon, Jim. 2006. "The Making of the New Zealand Ruling Class." In *Revolution: the 1913 Great Strike in New Zealand*, ed. Melanie Nolan. Christchurch, N.Z.: Canterbury University Press.

McCallum, Todd. 1998. "'Not a Sex Question'? The One Big Union and the Politics of Radical Manhood." *Labour / Le Travail* 42:15–54.

McCormack, A. Ross. 1977. *Reformers, Rebels and Revolutionaries: the Western Canadian Radical Movement 1899–1919*. Toronto: University of Toronto Press.

McGreal, Chris. 2003. "Facility 1391: Israel's Secret Prison." *Guardian*, November 13.

Meade, Edward Sherwood. 1901. "The Genesis of the United States Steel Corporation." *Quarterly Journal of Economics* 15:517–550.

Meagher, Meredith. 2013. "The Girl Orator of the Bowery: Elizabeth Gurley Flynn, Ireland and the Industrial Workers of the World." *History Ireland* 21:28–30.

"Meeting in Warren, Ohio." 1924. *Daily Worker* [Chicago], May 8.

Melrose, Harry. 1917. "From Revolution to Revolution." *Direct Action* [Sydney, NSW], May 5.

"Memorable Manitobans: Isaac Campbell (1853–1929)." 2018. https://www.mhs.mb.ca/docs/people/campbell_i.shtml (February 22, 2023).

Mencius. 1963. *Mencius*, trans. W.A.C.H. Dobson. Toronto: University of Toronto Press.

"Mental Suggestion." 1915. *Poverty Bay Herald* [Gisborne, N.Z.], February 12.

"Metal Trade Employers are Ready for Mediation." 1919. *Manitoba Free Press* [Winnipeg, MAN], May 30.

"Michael Bakounine: In 1868." 1915. *Direct Action* [Sydney, NSW], May 1.

"Mighty Protest in N.Y Against Roumania Terror." 1926. *Daily Worker* [New York], October 16.

"Mike Sokolowski Innocent." 1919. *Enlightener* [Winnipeg, MAN], June 26.

Mikio, Sumiya. 1966. "The Development of Japanese Labour-Relations." *The Developing Economies* [Chiba, Japan], 4:499–515.

"Military Service Act 1916." 2016. New Zealand Ministry for Culture and Heritage. https://nzhistory.govt.nz/media/photo/military-service-act-1916 (June 2, 2022).

Milburn, Josephine F. 1966. "Trade Unions in Politics in Australia and New Zealand." *Western Political Quarterly* 19:672–687.

Millán, Márgara. 2012. "De la périphérie vers le centre: Origines et héritages des féminismes Latino-Américains." *Revue Tiers Monde* 209:37–52.

Miller, David. *Anarchism* 1984. London: J.M. Dent & Sons.

Miller, Nicola. 2008. *Reinventing Modernity in Latin America: Intellectuals Imagine the Future, 1900–1930*. New York: Palgrave Macmillan.

Mills, Allen. 1980. "Single Tax, Socialism and the Independent Labour Party of Manitoba: the Political Ideas of F.J. Dixon and S. J. Farmer." *Labour/Le Travailleur* 5:33–56.

"Miners Give $500 to Gurley Flynn." 1909. *Spokane Press* [Wash.], December 11.

"Miners Rally to Aid of Women." 1909. *Medford Mail Tribune* [Ore.], December 12.

"Minimum Wage Law Gaining Advocates." 1919. *Manitoba Free Press* [Winnipeg, MAN], June 7.

"Minimum Wage Law Violated, Labor Men Say." 1929. *Winnipeg Evening Tribune* [MAN], February 6.

"Minister Who Tested Riot Act is Freed on Bail." 1926. *Chicago Tribune*, April 16.

"Miss Flynn a Candidate." 1957. *New York Times*, August 23.

"Miss Flynn Denies Anti-U. S. Attitude." 1952. *New York Times*, June 27.

"Miss Flynn Ends Testimony." 1952. *New York Times*, November 8.
"Miss Flynn Heads Reds." 1961. *New York Times*, March 14.
"Miss Flynn Hits Klan Menace at Federation Meet." 1924. *Daily Worker* [Chicago], June 3.
"Miss Flynn is Cremated: Tribute in Moscow Today." 1964. *New York Times*, September 8.
"Miss Flynn on Trial." 1913. *New York Tribune*, July 1.
"Missoula Police Wage Brutal War on Free Speech." 1909. *Montana News* [Lewiston, Mont.], October 14.
"Miss Pankhurst and Tom Barker." 1916. *Barrier Miner* [Broken Hill, NSW], October 20.
"Miss Pankhurst Assaulted." 1916. *Labor Call* [Melbourne, VIC], October 19.
Mitchell, Jeanette, et al. 1979. *In and Against the State*. https://theanarchistlibrary.org/library/london-edinburgh-weekend-return-group-summer-in-and-against-the-state?v=1629438866 (July 10, 2022).
Mitchell, Tom. 1996. "'Repressive Measures': A.J. Andrews, the Committee of 1000 and the Campaign Against Radicalism after the Winnipeg General Strike." *Left History* 4:133–167.
Mitchell, Tom. 2004. "'Legal Gentlemen Appointed by the Federal Government': the Canadian State, the Citizens' Committee of 1000, and Winnipeg's Seditious Conspiracy Trials of 1919–1920." *Labour / Le Travail* 53:9–46.
Mitchell, Tom. 2019. "Strike or Revolution? H.A. Robson's Inquiry and the Winnipeg General Strike." *Manitoba Law Journal* 42:56–84.
Mitchell, Tom, and James Naylor. 1998. "The Prairies: In the Eye of the Storm." In *The Workers' Revolt in Canada, 1917–1925* by Craig Heron. Toronto: University of Toronto Press.
Miyata, Mami. 1988. "Deguchi Nao: Modernization and New Religions." M.A. thesis. University of British Columbia.
Molgat, Anne. 1988. "*The Voice* and the Women of Winnipeg, 1894–1918." M.A. thesis. University of Ottawa.
Molinaro, Dennis. 2015. "State Repression and Political Deportation in Canada, 1919–1936." Ph.D. diss. University of Toronto.
Molnar, Donald. 1987. "The Winnipeg General Strike: Class, Ethnicity and Class Formation in Canada." m.a. thesis. McGill University
Molyneux, Maxine. 1986. "No God, No Boss, No Husband: Anarchist Feminism in Nineteenth-Century Argentina." *Latin American Perspectives* 13:119–145.
"Montague Miller: In Gaol at Eighty-Five." 1917. *NZ Truth* [Wellington, N.Z.], October 20.
"Montague Miller Released." 1917. *Truth* [Melbourne, VIC], October 6.
"Montague Miller's Funeral." 1920. *Evening News* [Sydney, NSW], November 22.
Moore, E. J. 1916. "German Deserter." Letter to the Editor. *Dominion* [Wellington, N.Z.], September 16.
Moore, William. 1961. "Uncover New Red Plan to Destroy U.S." *Chicago Tribune*, April 8.

"More Gelignite Found." 1913. *New Zealand Herald* [Auckland], November 20.

"More Time for Berlin Solution." 1961. *Sunday Star* [Washington, D.C.], October 22.

Moriarty-Patten, Stuart. 2012. "A World to Win, A Hell to Lose: the Industrial Workers of the World in Early Twentieth Century New Zealand." M.A. thesis. Massey University.

Morse, Chuck. 2009. "Anarchism in Argentina." https://theanarchistlibrary.org/libr ary/chuck-morse-anarchism-in-argentina (January 8, 2022).

Mortin, Jenny. 1979. "General Strike." *Winnipeg Tribune* [MAN], June 21.

"Moses Baritz: Deported from New Zealand." 1920. *Socialist* [Melbourne, VIC], January 30.

"Most Orderly Strike on Record." 1919. *Western Labor News* [Winnipeg, MAN], Special Strike Edition No. 1, May 17.

"Mountie Tells Court Almazoff Urged Revolt." 1919. *Winnipeg Evening Tribune* [MAN], August 9.

"Movimiento Social: Montevideo." 1903. *La Rebelión* [Montevideo, Uruguay], January 18.

Moya, José C. 2004. "The Positive Side of Stereotypes: Jewish Anarchists in Early-Twentieth-Century Buenos Aires." *Jewish History* 18:19–48.

Moya, José C. 2008. "What's in a Stereotype? The Case of Jewish Anarchists in Argentina." In *Rethinking Jewish Latin-Americans*, ed. Jeffrey Lesser and Raanan Reín. Albuquerque: University of New Mexico Press.

"Mr Blakeley's Thanks." 1917. *Western Age* [Dubbo, NSW], May 15.

"Mr Justice Street's Commission on Police Methods." 2008. In *Labor Pains: Early Conference and Executive Reports of the Labor Party in New South Wales*. Volume IV: 1918–1925, ed. Michael Hogan. Annandale, NSW: Federation.

"Mr Payne Bowled Out." 1913. *Pahiatua Herald* [N.Z.], November 26.

"Mr. Payne's Price." 1912. *Manawatu Herald* [Foxton, N.Z.], June 29.

"Mrs. Armstrong Committed for Trial." 1919. *Manitoba Free Press* [Winnipeg, MAN], June 25.

"Mrs. Armstrong Gets Bail." 1919. *Winnipeg Telegram* [MAN], Strike Edition, June 28.

"Mrs. Armstrong is to Face Charge." 1919. *Manitoba Free Press* [Winnipeg, MAN], June 6.

"Mrs. Armstrong Released on Bail." 1919. *Manitoba Free Press* [Winnipeg, MAN], June 28.

"Mrs. Armstrong to Stand Trial." 1919. *Winnipeg Evening Tribune* [MAN], June 25.

"Mrs. Flynn Hearing Put Off Until May 3." 1962. *New York Times*, April 25.

"Mrs. Helen Armstrong Will Be Candidate." 1923. *Winnipeg Evening Tribune* [MAN], September 5.

"Mrs. Sellins was Shot During Riot." 1919. *West Virginian* [Fairmont, W.Va.], September 27.

"Mr. Tom Mann in Adelaide." 1909. *Advertiser* [Adelaide, SA], July 14.

"Mr. Walker Cross-Examines." 1916. *Daily News* [Perth, WA], November 15.

Muñoz, Pascual. 2020. "La Sociedad Tipográfica Montevideana y los orígenes del Sindicato de Artes Gráficas." *El Obrero Grafico* [Montevideo, Uruguay], December 20.

"Murder Trial in Progress at Salem." 1912. *Alexandria Gazette* [Va.], October 1.

Murthy, Viren. 2011. *The Political Philosophy of Zhang Taiyan: the Resistance of Consciousness*. Leiden Series in Comparative Historiography, vol. 4. Leiden, Netherlands: Brill.
"Mutilation of Body to Assist 'Reds' Alleged." 1919. *Pine Bluff Daily Graphic* [Ark.], October 17.
Myers, Ronald A. 2020. "The Battle for Spokane." *Inlander* [Spokane, Wash.], December 21.
Naimark, Norman M. 2010. *Stalin's Genocides*. Princeton: Princeton University Press.
Naylor, James. 2016. "Dixon, Frederick John." In *Dictionary of Canadian Biography*, vol. 16. Toronto: University of Toronto/Université Laval. http://www.biographi.ca/en/bio/dixon_frederick_john_16E.html?print=1 (March 23, 2023).
Naylor, James, and Tom Mitchell. 2019. "The Speech Bill Pritchard Never Gave." *Labour / Le Travail* 84:279–302.
Nelson, Andrew. 2022. "Two Tokugawa Era Skeptics: Tominaga Nakamoto and Andō Shōeki." M.A. thesis. University of Hawai'i at Mānoa.
Nettlau, Max. 1972. "Viaje libertario a través de la América latina, part 1." *Reconstruir* [Buenos Aires, Argentina], January-February.
Neumann, Caryn E. 2009. "Committee on Public Information." https://www.mtsu.edu/first-amendment/article/1179/committee-on-public-information (July 15, 2022).
"Newark Labor Defense Aids Passaic Strikers." 1926. *Daily Worker* [New York], March 13.
"Newly Arrived Harvesters Apply for Relief." 1923. *Winnipeg Evening Tribune* [MAN], August 17.
"New South Wales." 1916. *Townsville Daily Bulletin* [QLD], September 6.
"News Summary." 1916. *Daily Telegraph* [Launceston, TAS], September 5.
"New York Backs Sacco-Vanzetti in Life Fight." 1925. *Daily Worker* [New York], March 7.
"New York Holds Big United Conference for Passaic Relief." 1926. *Daily Worker* [New York], July 4.
"New York Joan and Husband Beat Freights All Way to Chicago." 1908. *Spokane Press* [Wash.], October 7.
"New York Shudders in Fear of Salt and Pepper Attack." 1913. *Laramie Republican* [Wyo.], February 15.
"New York United Textile Union Protests Police Interference in Hillcrest Silk Mill Strike." 1925. *Daily Worker* [New York], November 18.
"New Zealand Strike." 1913a. *Armidale Chronicle* [NSW], November 15.
"New Zealand Strike." 1913b. *Week* [Brisbane, QLD], November 21.
Ngai, Mae M. 2012. "Promises and Perils of Transnational History." *Perspectives on History*, December.
Nicholls, Glenn. 2007. *Deported: A History of Forced Departures from Australia*. Sydney: University of New South Wales Press.
"Night Meeting Fails to Settle Winnipeg Strike." 1919. *Chicago Tribune*, May 24.

Nimura, Kazuo. 1997. *The Ashio Riot of 1907: A Social History of Mining in Japan*, ed. Andrew Gordon, trans. Terry Boardman and Andrew Gordon. Durham, N.C.: Duke University Press.

Nishida, Takeshi. 1978. "Kinoshita Naoe: Pacifism and Religious Withdrawal." In *Pacifism in Japan: the Christian and Socialist Tradition*, eds. Nobuya Bamba and John F. Howes. Vancouver: University of British Columbia.

"No Bail will be Allowed in Case of Red Leaders." 1919. *Winnipeg Telegram* [MAN], Strike Edition, June 18.

"Noble Mentions Bolshes at Blumenberg Hearing." 1919. *Winnipeg Evening Tribune* [MAN], August 2.

"No Girl Need Want for Food." 1919. *Western Labor News* [Winnipeg, MAN], Special Strike Edition No. 8, May 26.

Nolan, Melanie. 2006. "Introduction." In *Revolution: the 1913 Great Strike in New Zealand*, ed. Melanie Nolan. Christchurch, N.Z.: Canterbury University Press.

Noone, Val. 2014. "Class Factors in the Radicalisation of Archbishop Daniel Mannix, 1913–17." *Labour History* 106:189–204.

Notehelfer, F.G. 1971a. "Kōtoku Shūsui and Nationalism." *Journal of Asian Studies* 31:31–39.

Notehelfer, F.G. [1971b] 2010. *Kōtoku Shūsui: Portrait of a Japanese Radical*. Cambridge, U.K.: Cambridge University Press.

Notehelfer, F.G. 1975. "Japan's First Pollution Incident." *Journal of Japanese Studies* 1:351–383.

"N.Z. Troubles." 1915. Editorial. *Direct Action* [Sydney, NSW], September 1.

"Observations and Comments." 1910. Editorial. *Mother Earth* 5:305–309.

O'Connor, Harvey. 1956. "Saga of the Wobblies." *Nation*, August 25.

"Offers the Strike as Negro's Weapon." 1919. *New York Times*, December 1.

"Office Workers' Guild Perfects Organization." 1920. *Winnipeg Evening Tribune* [MAN], September 8.

"Office Workers to Form a Union." 1920. *Labor World / Le Monde Ouvrier* [Montréal], August 14. https://numerique.banq.qc.ca/patrimoine/details/52327/3305004 (April 2, 2023).

"Officials Try to Force Confessions." 1909. *Spokane Press* [Wash.], December 2.

Okamoto, Shumpei. 1970. *The Japanese Oligarchy and the Russo-Japanese War*. New York: Columbia University Press.

"Old Men Lose Cleaning Jobs." 1923. *Winnipeg Evening Tribune* [MAN], August 2.

Olssen, Erik. 1988. *The Red Feds: Revolutionary Industrial Unionism and the New Zealand Federation of Labour 1908–14*. Auckland [N.Z.]: Oxford University Press.

Olssen, Erik. 1996. "Barker, Tom." In *Dictionary of New Zealand Biography*. https://teara.govt.nz/en/biographies/3b7/barker-tom (July 26, 2021).

Olssen, Erik. 2006. "The Lessons of 1913." In *Revolution: the 1913 Great Strike in New Zealand*, ed. Melanie Nolan. Christchurch, N.Z.: Canterbury University Press.

Ombrello, Mark. 2010. "Ogyū Sorai and Andō Shōeki as "Modern" Thinkers: An Historiographical Overview." Kyoto, Japan: Kyoto Notre Dame University, Departmental Bulletin Paper, March 30.

"On Getting Together." 1919. *Western Labor News* [Winnipeg, MAN], Special Strike Edition No. 27, June 17.

"Opposes Chinese Hiring White Girls." 1919. *Winnipeg Evening Tribune* [MAN], February 6.

"Organizational History." N.d. https://www.marxists.org/history/usa/eam/cpa/ldc.html (May 30, 2023).

"Organizzatrice Operaia Uccisa." 1919. *Patriot* [Indiana, Penn.], September 6.

Otta. 1909. "Un foco apagado: Francisco Ferrer." *El Surco* [Montevideo, Uruguay], August 10.

Otus. 1915. "The Moving Finger." *Maoriland Worker* [Wellington, N.Z.], November 24.

"Out of the Way." 1917. *Wanganui Chronicle* [Whanganui, N.Z.], September 1. [The spelling of Wanganui was later altered to comport with the Māori spelling].

Pandolfi, Serena. 2021. "Né Dio, né padroni, né marito: donne tra lotta sindacale e anarchismo." *Lo Spigone* [Rome, Italy], April 6.

Pankhurst, E. Sylvia. 1922. "Kuzbas or Communism: Questions that Must be Answered." *Workers' Dreadnought* [London], March 18.

Panzner, John. 1964. "The Spokane Free Speech Fight – 1909." In *Rebel Voices: An IWW Anthology*, ed. Joyce L. Kornbluh. Ann Arbor: University of Michigan Press.

Parfitt, Steven. 2016. "The Justice Department Campaign Against the IWW, 1917–1920." IWW History Project: Industrial Workers of the World, 1905–1935. Seattle, University of Washington. https://depts.washington.edu/iww/justice_dept.shtml (April 11, 2023).

Parkinson, Michael. 1985. *Liverpool on the Brink: One City's Struggle against Government Cuts*. Hermitage, U.K.: Policy Journals.

"Part of McGrath's Report Tabled." 1918. *Voice* [Winnipeg, MAN], February 8.

"Paterson Ceases to be Field for Labor Agitators." 1915. *Newark Evening Star* [N.J.], September 4.

"Paterson Silk Strike." 1913. *Hamilton Daily Times* [ONT], February 26.

"Paul Freeman." 1919. *Australian Worker* [Sydney, NSW], September 25.

"Peace at Brisbane." 1912. Editorial. *Greymouth Evening Star* [N.Z.], March 8.

Pelletier, Philippe. 2002. "Ōsugi Sakae, Une Quintessence de l'anarchisme au Japon." *Ebisu* 28:93–118.

Pellicer, Eustaquio. 1900. "Sinfonia." *Caras y Caretas* [Buenos Aires, Argentina], August 11.

Penner, Anna. 2000–2001. "Politics in the Park: Winnipeg's Victoria Park During the General Strike." *Manitoba History*, Winter.

Perez, Juan Bautista. 1900. "La emancipación de la mujer," *El Rebelde* [Buenos Aires, Argentina], January 7.

"Peter Larkin Fined." 1916. *Tweed Daily* [Murwillumbah, NSW], September 14.

Peterson, Lars. 2015. "From Anarchists to 'Anarcho-Batllistas': Populism and Labor Legislation in Uruguay." In *In Defiance of Boundaries: Anarchism in Latin American History*, eds. Geoffroy de Laforcade and Kirwin Shaffer. Gainesville: University Press of Florida.

Peterson, Larry. 1981. "The One Big Union in International Perspective: Revolutionary Industrial Unionism 1900–1925." *Labour/ Le Travailleur* 7:41–66.

Petit, Víctor Pérez. 1902. "Zola." Lecture given at the "Vida Nueva" Club, October 24, 1902. Montevideo, Uruguay: Imprinta Artística de Dornaleche y Reyes.

"Philadelphia to Clean-Up "Reds."" 1922. *Evening Journal* [Wilmington, Del.], July 22.

Pidhainy, Semen O., ed. 1953–1955. *The Black Deeds of the Kremlin: A White Book*, 2 vols. Detroit: Globe.

Plantinga, Alvin. 2008. *God, Freedom and Evil*. Grand Rapids, Mich.: William B. Eerdmans.

Plievier, Theodor. 1921. "At the Grave of Karl Liebknecht." *Industrial Pioneer* [Chicago], March.

"P.L.L. Expulsions: 18 Members of Parliament." 1916. *Sydney Morning Herald* [NSW], November 7.

"Points on the Estimates." 1913. *Dominion* [Wellington, N.Z.], September 20.

""Poison Threat" Has About Passed Away." 1913. *Day Book* [Chicago], January 13.

"Police Frame-Up, Defense in Trial of Miss Flynn." 1913. *Newark Evening Star* [N.J.], July 1.

"Police Prevent Meetings and Bar Agitators from Paterson, N. J." 1915. *Solidarity* [Cleveland, Ohio], September 11.

"Police Prohibit "Antis" Meeting." 1917. *Manitoba Free Press* [Winnipeg, MAN], June 16.

"Police Replaced by Thugs." 1919. *Western Labor News* [Winnipeg, MAN], Special Strike Edition No. 22, June 11.

Pollack, Sylvan A. 1926. "Sacco, Vanzetti Must Not Die, is N.Y. Demand." *Daily Worker* [Chicago], May 23.

Porrini, Rodolfo Carlos. 2013. "Anarquistas en Montevideo: ideas y prácticas en torno al "tiempo libre" de los trabajadores (1920–1950)." *História: Debates e Tendências* [Passo Fundo, Brazil] 13:357–371.

"Possession of Trotzky Paper Prevents Bail." 1919. *Winnipeg Evening Tribune* [MAN], July 19.

"Post-Dennis Prosecutions Under the Smith Act." 1955. *Indiana Law Journal* 31:104–119.

Pouget, Émile. [1898] 1912. *Sabotage*, trans. Arturo M. Giovannitti. https://theanarchist library.org/library/emile-pouget-sabotage (May 18, 2023).
Powe, L.A., Jr. 1990. "The First Amendment and the Protection of Rights." In ""He Shall Not Pass This Way Again": the Legacy of William O. Douglas," ed. Stephen L. Wasby. Pittsburgh: University of Pittsburgh Press.
Power, Ed. 2020. "What Terence MacSwiney's Body Went Through during his 74-day Hunger Strike." *Irish Times* [Dublin], October 21.
Powles, Cyril H. 1978. "Abe Isoo: the Utility Man." In *Pacifism in Japan: the Christian and Socialist Tradition*, eds. Nobuya Bamba and John F. Howes. Vancouver: University of British Columbia.
Poy, Lucas, and Daniel Gaido. 2011. "Under German Eyes: Germán Avé-Lallemant and the Origins of Marxism in Argentina." *Science & Society* 75:480–505.
P.R. 1913a. "New Zealand Notes." *Industrial Unionist* [Auckland, N.Z.], August 1.
P.R. 1913b. "N. Z. Organizer." *Industrial Unionist* [Auckland, N.Z.], October 1.
Prebble, Frank. 1999. "The I.W.W. and the General Strike in Aotearoa." http://www.tak ver.com/history/nz/tm/tm09.htm (April 19, 2022).
"Pressure Required." 1913. *New Zealand Times* [Wellington, N.Z], November 27.
"Priest Fails to End Silk Strike in Jersey; Owners to Move Mills to North Carolina." 1925. *New York Times*, November 18.
Prieto, Agustina, Laura Fernández Cordero, and Pascual Muñoz. 2013/2014. "Tras los pasos de Virginia Bolten." *Políticas de la Memoria* [Buenos Aires, Argentina] 14:207–219.
Pritchard, William A. 2019. "The State Trials: Address to be Delivered by William A. Pritchard." In "The Speech Bill Pritchard Never Gave" by James Naylor and Tom Mitchell. *Labour / Le Travail* 84:282–302.
"Proceedings of the Third Annual Convention, Industrial Workers of the World, Held at Chicago, Ill." [1907] 2011. Stenographically reported by W.S. McDermutt. Transcribed and edited by Robert Bills. New York: Socialist Labor Party of America.
"Program and Organization of the International Working Men's Association." [1884] 2014. In *The Method of Freedom: An Errico Malatesta Reader*, by Errico Malatesta. ed. Davide Turcato, trans. Paul Sharkey. Oakland, Cal.: A.K.
"Progresando." 1899a. *La Protesta Humana* [Buenos Aires, Argentina], January 21.
"Progresando." 1899b. *La Protesta Humana* [Buenos Aires, Argentina], August 6.
"Project Early End of Winnipeg Strike." 1919. *New York Times*, May 25.
"Promiscuous Gelignite." 1913. *Auckland Star* [N.Z.], November 20.
"Protest Parade." 1919. *Western Labor News* [Winnipeg, MAN], September 5.
"Prussianising Australia: Tom Barker's Experience." 1915. Editorial. *Maoriland Worker* [Wellington, N.Z.], September 29.
"Prussianism in Winnipeg." 1917. *Voice* [Winnipeg, MAN], June 22.

"Publiaciones recibidas." 1899. *La Protesta Humana* [Buenos Aires, Argentina], December 10.

"Publisher Fined." 1916. *Urana Independent and Clear Hills Standard* [Urana, NSW], September 8.

Pyle, Kenneth B. 1975. "Symposium: the Ashio Copper Mine Pollution Case: Introduction: Japan Faces Her Future." *Journal of Japanese Studies* 1:347–350.

"Queen Marie Visits Roumanian Synagog While in Chicago." 1926. *Intermountain Jewish News* [Denver, Colo.], November 25.

"Queensland Organisers' Reports." 1917. *Direct Action* [Sydney, NSW], June 16.

"¿Que es política?" 1902. *El Rebelde* [Buenos Aires, Argentina], October 24.

"Quinlan is Given Long Sentence." 1913. *Newark Evening Star* [N.J.], July 3.

"Quinlan to Prison." 1913. *Daily Kennebec Journal* [Augusta, Me.], July 4.

Racel, Masako N. 2011. "Finding their Place in the World: Meiji Intellectuals and the Japanese Construction of an East-West Binary, 1868–1912." Ph.D. thesis. Georgia State University.

Rago, Margareth. 1997. "A liberdade entre a utopia e a história: Luce Fabbri e o anarquismo na América do Sul." *Cadernos PAGU* (Campinas, Brazil) 8/9:279–317.

Rainford, John. 2015. *A Short History of Social Democracy From Socialist Origins to Neoliberal Theocracy*. Sydney, NSW: Resistance.

Rama, Carlos M. 1957. "La Revolución mexicana en el Uruguay." *Historia Mexicana* 7:161–186.

Rama, Carlos M. 1968–1969. "Obreros y anarchistas." *Enciclopedia Uruguaya*, book 32. Montevideo, Uruguay: Editores Reunidos y Editoria Arca.

Rama, Carlos M. 1990. *El Anarquismo en América Latina*. Caracas, Venezuela: Biblioteca Ayacucho.

Ramsden, Sarah, and Nathan Kramer. 2022. "Memorable Manitobans: May Edith Lunn Lazier Pitblado (c1871–1950)." https://www.mhs.mb.ca/docs/people/pitblado_mell.shtml (February 2, 2023).

Rancie, N. 1911. "The Passing of George Madgwick." *International Socialist* [Sydney, NSW], May 6.

"Ranks of Pasaaic [sic] Bosses Broken as Big Mill Gives In." 1926. *Daily Worker* [New York], November 14.

Rea, J. E. 1973. *The Winnipeg General Strike*. Toronto: Holt, Rinehart and Winston of Canada.

Reclus, Elisée. 1914. *Correspondance: Tome 2: Octobre 1870 – Juillet 1889*. Paris: Librairie Schleicher Frères. https://gallica.bnf.fr/ark:/12148/bpt6k832346/f211.item (November 30, 2021).

Reclus, Elisée [translated as Eliseo]. 1943. *Correspondencio (de 1850 a 1905)*, ed. Luce Fabbri, trans. Horacio E. Roqué. Buenos Aires, Argentina: Imán.

"Red Candidate to File." 1954. *New York Times*, September 27.

Red Feather. 1920. "Hampstead." *Call* [London], July 22.
"Red Fed. Paper Fined." 1916. *Taranaki Herald* [New Plymouth, N.Z.], March 30.
"Red Leader Testifies." 1952. *New York Times*, October 4.
"Reflections in our Mirror: Tom Barker." 1930. *Daily Standard* [Brisbane, QLD], January 28.
"Regulations Govern Women Employees." 1919. *Manitoba Free Press* [Winnipeg, MAN], August 1.
Reilly, Nolan, and Sharon Reilly. [1986] 2019. *Winnipeg General Strike: Driving & Walking Tour*. 100th Anniversary Edition. Winnipeg: Manitoba Federation of Labor.
"Release of Leslie." 1916. *Sun* [Sydney, NSW], May 11.
"Relief Body is Criticized." 1923. *Winnipeg Evening Tribune* [MAN], March 21.
Renshaw, Patrick. 1968. "The IWW and the Red Scare 1917–24." *Journal of Contemporary History* 3:63–72.
Report of Mr. Justice Street, the Commissioner Appointed by the Act. 1919. Ordered by the Legislative Assembly to be printed, August 28. Sydney, NSW: William Applegate Gulick.
Report of the Royal Commission of Inquiry into The Matter of the Trial and Conviction and Sentences Imposed on Charles Reeve and Others. 1920. State of New South Wales, Parliamentary Papers, Second Session, vol. 1.
"Restaurants to Fight Minimum Wage Order." 1919. *Manitoba Free Press* [Winnipeg, MAN], October 7.
"Retains Miss Milholland." 1913. *New York Times*, June 20.
"Review Spirit of Fight to Save Sacco, Vanzetti." 1926. *Daily Worker* [New York], November 17.
Richardson, Len. 2020. "6 Beyond the 1960s I: Literary Reflections" In *People and Place: the West Coast of New Zealand's South Island in History and Literature*, ed. Len Richardson. Canberra, ACT: ANU Press.
"Richardson Predicts Fair Enforcement of Communist Controls." 1950. *Evening Star* [Washington, D.C.], October 24.
"Riots Mark Paterson Strike." 1913. *Washington Herald* [D.C.], April 18.
"Riot Victims Buried." 1909. *Evening Star* [Washington, D.C.], August 24.
Robb, James. 2020. "Harry Holland, Leon Trotsky, and 'Undesirable Immigrants.'" https://convincingreasons.wordpress.com/2020/08/09/harry-holland-leon-trotsky-and-undesirable-immigrants/ (July 19, 2022).
Robinson, Geoff. 2002. "The Political Economy of Maritime Industry Non-Reform in Interwar Australia: the Establishment of the Maritime Services Board of New South Wales." *Eras Journal* [Melbourne, Australia], December. https://www.monash.edu/arts/philosophical-historical-international-studies/eras/past-editions/edition-four-2002-december/the-origins-of-the-maritime-services-board-of-new-south-wales-a-study-of-micro-economic-non-reform-in-interwar-australia (August 4, 2022).

"Robochyi narod." [1993] 2001. Internet Encyclopedia of Ukraine, Canadian Institute of Ukrainian Studies. http://www.encyclopediaofukraine.com/display.asp?linkpath =pages%5CR%5CO%5CRobochyinarodIT.htm (April 2, 2023).

Rocker, Rudolf, Augustin Souchy, Emma Goldman, and Alexander Berkman. 1924. "The Persecutions in Russia." *Freedom* [London], September.

Rogers, Geraldine. 2008. *Caras y Caretas: cultura, política y espectáculo en los inicios del siglo XX argentino*. La Plata, Argentina: Universidad Nacional de La Plata.

Roller, Arnold. 1905. *The Social General Strike*, trans. F.K. Chicago: Debating Club No. 1.

Ronning, Gerald. 2003. "Jackpine Savages: Discourses of Conquest in the 1916 Mesabi Iron Range Strike." *Labor History* 44:359–382.

Roosevelt, Franklin D. 1943. "Veto of the Smith-Connally Bill." *The American Presidency Project*, June 25. http://www.presidency.ucsb.edu/ws/?pid=16420 (January 27, 2018).

Roper, James E. 1954. "Red Ban Is Law, but Action Under it is a Long Way Off." *Evening Star* [Washington, D.C.], August 26.

Rosenthal, Anton. 1995. "The Arrival of the Electric Streetcar and the Conflict over Progress in Early Twentieth-Century Montevideo." *Journal of Latin American Studies* 27:319–341.

Rosenthal, Anton. 2015. "Moving between the Global and the Local: the Industrial Workers of the World and their Press in Latin America." In *In Defiance of Boundaries: Anarchism in Latin American History*, eds. Geoffroy de Laforcade and Kirwin Shaffer. Gainesville: University Press of Florida.

Roth, Herbert. 1956. "General Strike in Auckland." *Here and Now*, November.

Roth, Herbert, and E.G. Beardsley. 1960–1961. "Sidney Huguenot Fournier d'Albe." *New Zealand Monthly Review*, December–January.

"Round the Clock Tower: "Labour Agitators" Fined." 1913. *Press* [Christchurch, N.Z.], September 18.

Rushton, P. J. 1973. "The Trial of the Sydney Twelve: the Original Charge." *Labour History* 25:53–57.

"Russell is Witness in Own Behalf." 1919. *Winnipeg Evening Tribune* [MAN], December 17.

Russell, Phillips. 1913. "The Arrest of Haywood and Lessig." *International Socialist Review* [Chicago] 13:789–792.

"Russia." 1922. *Australian Worker* [Sydney, NSW], October 4.

"Russians Get American Red Views of U.S." 1961. *Chicago Tribune*, October 16.

"Russian Tribute to U.S. Leader." 1964. *Birmingham Post* [U.K.], September 9.

"Rutland Boughton on Music Today." 1958. *Stage* [London], December 4.

R. v. Reeve and Others. 1917. New South Wales, State Reports, vol. XVII. [NSWStRp 9; (1917) 17 SR (NSW) 81 (10 March 1917)].

Ryder, Walter Scott. 1920. "Canada' Industrial Crisis of 1919." M.A. thesis. University of British Columbia.

"Sab. Cat Yowls." 1918. *Chicago Tribune*, May 10.

"Sabotage Scourge: Prosecutions in the West." 1916. *Register* [Adelaide, SA], November 11.
"Sacco-Vanzetti Conference in Intensive Drive." 1926. *Daily Worker* [New York], November 20.
"Sacco-Vanzetti Defense Body is Ended; Reports." 1927. *Daily Worker* [New York], December 20.
Sako. F. 1911a. "Barbarous Japan." *Mother Earth* 5:379–382.
Sako. F. 1911b. "Il Giappone Barbaro." *Cronaca Sovversiva* [Barre, Vt.], March 4.
Sampert, Shannon. 2019. "A Champion of Workers' Rights." *Winnipeg Free Press* (MAN), December 2.
Sanbonmatsu, Kira. 2003. "Gender-Related Political Knowledge and the Descriptive Representation of Women." *Political Behavior* 25:367–388.
Sanger, Margaret. 1931. *My Fight for Birth Control*. New York: Farrar & Rinehart.
Sangster, Joan. 1984. "Canadian Women in Radical Politics and Labour, 1920–1950." Ph.D. thesis. McMaster University.
Sartre, Jean-Paul. [1938] 1964. *Nausea*, trans. Lloyd Alexander. New York: New Directions.
Savala, Joshua. 2019. "Beyond Patriotic Phobias: Connections, Class, and State Formation in the Peruvian-Chilean Pacific World." Ph.D. diss. Cornell University.
Sawtell, M. 1915. "Mr Scadden, Worker." *Direct Action* [Sydney, NSW], August 1.
Sawyer, Wendy, and Peter Wagner. 2023. "Mass Incarceration: the Whole Pie." Northampton, Mass.: Prison Policy Institute. https://www.prisonpolicy.org/reports/pie2023.html (June 19, 2023).
"Says O.B.U. Men Try to Destroy Organized Labor." 1919. *Winnipeg Evening Tribune* [MAN], June 2.
"Says She Did Not Incite Riot." 1913. *Perth Amboy Evening News* [N.J.], July 2.
"Says Steel Trust Stole Inventions." 1908. *Detroit Times* [Mich.], April 9.
"Says Sunday Is Paid to Oppose Workers." 1915. *New York Times*, March 17.
Schäffle, Albert. [1874] 1890. *The Quintessence of Socialism*, trans. Bernard Bosanquet. 2nd. ed. London: Swan Sonnenschein.
Schnick, Daniel William. 1995. "Walking the Thin Line: Ishikawa Sanshirō and Japanese Anarchism." M.A. thesis. University of British Columbia.
Schofer, Jonathan W. 1993. "Virtues in Xunzi's Thought." *Journal of Religious Ethics* 21:117–136.
"Schoppelrei to be Deported This Week." 1919. *Winnipeg Evening Tribune* [MAN], September 22.
Schutzer, Arthur. 1969. Review of *The Trial of Elizabeth Gurley Flynn by the American Civil Liberties Union* by Corliss Lamont. *Science & Society* 33:375–377.
Schwartz-Shea, Peregrine. 2001. "Curricular Visions: Doctoral Program Requirements, Offerings, and the Meanings of 'Political Science.'" Presented at the annual meeting of the American Political Science Association, San Francisco.

Schwartz-Shea, Peregrine, and Dvora Yanow. 2002. "'Reading' 'Methods' 'Texts': How Research Method Texts Construct Political Science." *Political Research Quarterly* 55:457–486.

"Scientific Sabotage." 1915. *Daily Telegraph* [Sydney, NSW], July 24.

"Second Red Funeral in Paterson Strike." 1913. *Sun* [New York], July 6.

"Seditious Utterance: Conscription Opposed." 1917. *New Zealand Herald* [Auckland, N.Z.], January 17.

"Seditious Utterances: Man Sentenced to Gaol." 1917. *Marlborough Express* [Blenheim, N.Z.], January 17.

"Seeks Work for Sightless Typists." 1920. *Winnipeg Evening Tribune* [MAN], April 28.

Segall, Marcelo. 1972. "En Amerique latine: Developpement du mouvement ouvrier et proscription." *International Review of Social History* 17:325–369.

Sen, Katayama. 1918. *The Labor Movement in Japan*. Chicago: C. H. Kerr.

Sepúlveda, Eduardo A. Godoy. 2016. "Discurso y Práctica sobre la Violencia en el Anarquismo Argentino a comienzos del Siglo XX." *Palimpsesto* [Santiago, Chile] 6:69–89.

"Set Barker Free." 1916. Editorial. *Direct Action* [Sydney, NSW], June 10.

Shapiro, Alexander. 1933. "The Policy of the International." *Vanguard* [New York] 6:5–8.

"Shearers' Strike." 1917. *Daily Herald* [Adelaide, SA], July 14.

"Shearers' Strike: Position in Queensland." 1917. *Inverell Times* [NSW], July 6.

Shelley, Percy Bysshe. 1819. "The Mask of Anarchy: Written on the Occasion of the Massacre at Manchester." http://knarf.english.upenn.edu/PShelley/anarchy.html (January 28, 2021).

"Sheriff Refuses to Evict Strikers." 1909. *New York Times*, August 13.

Shields, Art. 1986. *On the Battle Lines: 1919–1939*. New York: International Publishers.

Shih, Joseph. 1969. "Secularization in Early Chinese Thought: A Note on Hsün Tzu." *Gregorianum* 50:391–404.

"Shirkers and Cowards." 1915. *Evening Post* [Wellington, N.Z.], May 28.

Shone, Steve J. 2010. *Lysander Spooner: American Anarchist*. Lanham, Md.: Lexington.

Shone, Steve J. 2013. *American Anarchism*. Leiden, Netherlands: Brill.

Shone, Steve J. 2019. *Women of Liberty*. Leiden, Netherlands: Brill.

Shone, Steve J. 2022. *Rose Summerfield: Australian Radical*. Lanham, Md.: Lexington.

Shor, Francis. 2005. "Left Labor Agitators in the Pacific Rim of the Early Twentieth Century." *International Labor and Working-Class History* 67:148–163.

Shub, David. 1953. "Kropotkin and Lenin." *Russian Review* 12:227–234.

"Sidelights from Other Cities in Washington." 1910. *Colfax Gazette* [Wash.], January 7.

Siebenhaar, W. 1920. "Montague Miller." *Westralian Worker* [Perth, WA], November 26.

Sievers, Sharon Lee. 1969. "Kōtoku Shūsui, *The Essence of Socialism*: A Translation and Biographical Essay." Ph.D. diss. Stanford University.

Sievers, Sharon Lee. 1983. *Flowers in Salt: the Beginnings of Feminist Consciousness in Modern Japan.* Stanford, Cal.: Stanford University Press.
"Siguranza Admits Murder of Workers' Leader in Roumania." 1926. *Daily Worker* [New York], October 15.
"Silk Strikers Draw Crowds at Mass Meeting." 1925. *Daily Worker* [New York], December 19.
"Silk Strikers Insist upon Full Demands." 1925. *Daily Worker* [New York], November 22.
Simeoni, Alicia. 2007. "En San Luis se filmará la película de las anarquistas rosarinas." *Pagina 12* [Buenos Aires, Argentina], October 3.
Simon, S. Fanny. 1946. "Anarchism and Anarcho-Syndicalism in South America." *Hispanic American Historical Review* 26:38–59.
Siracusa, Gloria. 2014. "Un "germinalista" en la escana neuquina: Joaquín Dicenta." In *La dramaturgia de Neuquén en la memoria: El teatro español a comienzos del siglo XX*, ed. Margarito A. Garrido. Neuquén, Argentina: Universidad Nacional del Comahue.
"Six Strikers Denied Free Speech." 1913. *Day Book* [Chicago], February 25.
Smith, Doug. 1994a. "The Winnipeg General Strike." *Manitoba Social Science Teacher* 20:3–7.
Smith, Doug. 1994b. *The Winnipeg Labour Council 1894–1994: A Century of Labour Education, Organization and Agitation.* Winnipeg, MAN: Manitoba Labour Education Centre.
Smith, Walker C. 1914. "Sabotage." *Direct Action* [Sydney, NSW], August 10.
"Social Board Hears Reports of Privations." 1922. *Winnipeg Evening Tribune* [MAN], December 9.
"Socialisation: Experiment in Siberia." 1922. *Daily Standard* [Brisbane, QLD], November 8.
"Socialism and Women." 1907. *Justice* [London], June 8.
"Socialism in Japan: Kotoku's Work." 1911. *People* [Sydney, NSW], April 1.
"Socialist Held as Suspect at Biwabik." 1908. *Minneapolis Tribune* [Minn.], January 24.
"Socialist Party and Bolsheviki." 1918. *Voice* [Winnipeg, MAN], February 22.
"Socialists Blocked." 1909. *Register* [Adelaide, SA], July 15.
"Socialists to Hear Elizabeth Gurley Flynn." 1915. *Washington Times* [D.C.], April 4.
"Socialists to Steer Clear Union Fights." 1912. *Medford Mail Tribune* [Ore.], May 16.
"Solidarity Still Spreading." 1913. Editorial. *Industrial Unionist* [Auckland, N.Z.], November 18.
Soltis, John Gabriel. 1918. "Taxation and the Working Class." *Voice* [Winnipeg, MAN], July 5.
"Some of the Women." 1917. *Voice* [Winnipeg, MAN], August 31.
"Soviet Aid to Reds in U.S. Denied Here." 1952. *New York Times*, June 26.
"Soviet Republic Here Certain, 'Reds' Predict." 1919. *New York Tribune*, April 6.

"Speakers Call on Labor to Destroy the Ku-Klux Klan." 1921. *Birmingham Age-Herald* [Ala.], February 10.

"Speakers for Jobless Men Invade Council with New Griefs." 1923. *Winnipeg Evening Tribune* [MAN], January 3.

"Speaker Terms Domestic Work as "Humiliating."" 1921. *Winnipeg Evening Tribune* [MAN], January 26.

"Speech Fight Appeals Grow." 1909. *Spokane Press* [Wash.], November 17.

Spencer, Nicole. 2010. "Charity or Job: the Examination of the Ontario Mothers' Allowance." M.A. thesis. Carleton University.

"Split in Ranks of Women's Societies over "Scab Troop."" 1918. *Winnipeg Evening Tribune* [MAN], October 2.

"S. P. of C. Election Funds." 1915. *Voice* [Winnipeg, MAN], October 15.

Spooner, Lysander. [1867] 1971. *No Treason, No. II. The Constitution*. In *The Collected Works of Lysander Spooner*, by Lysander Spooner, ed. Charles Shively. 6 vols. Weston, Mass.: M & S Press.

"Spokane Convicts I.W.W." 1910. *Newport Miner* [Wash.], March 3.

Stanton, Elizabeth Cady. [1895] 1999. *The Woman's Bible*. Amherst, N.Y.: Prometheus.

Staples, G. T. 1979. "Burnside, Robert Bruce (1862–1929)." *Australian Dictionary of Biography*. https://adb.anu.edu.au/biography/burnside-robert-bruce-5434/text9219 (June 7, 2022).

"Start Trial of Woman Leader of Silk Strike." 1913. *Newark Evening Star* [N.J.], June 30.

Stavisky, Sebastián. 2017. "La primera víctima del movimiento obrero: El discurso anarquista sobre la Muerte en los albores del siglo XX en Argentina." *Conflicto Sociale* [Buenos Aires, Argentina] 10:168–195.

Stavisky, Sebastián. 2020. "Manuel Costa-Iscar y el anarquismo individualista en Buenos Aires." *Izquierdas* [Santiago, Chile], July.

"Steamer Cumberland: Damaged by Explosion." 1917. *Newcastle Morning Herald and Miners' Advocate* [NSW], July 9.

"Steamer Cumberland Founders." 1917. *Australian Town and Country Journal* [Sydney, NSW], August 15.

"Stenographers Working in Offices." 1917. *Manitoba Free Press* [Winnipeg, MAN], January 16.

"Still Another: Barker Arrested." 1913. *Star* [Christchurch, N.Z.], November 26.

Stirner, Max. [1907] 2005. *The Ego and His Own: the Case of the Individual Against Authority*, trans. Steven T. Byington. Mineola, N.Y.: Dover.

Stone, Alan. 1975. "The Japanese Muckrakers." *Journal of Japanese Studies* 1:385–407.

Stone, Geoffrey R. 2006. "Constitutions Under Stress: International and Historical Perspectives." *Bulletin of the American Academy of Arts and Sciences* 59:34–36.

Storm in Teacup. 1943. "Visits in Wartime." Letter to the Editor. *Winnipeg Evening Tribune* [MAN], May 24.

"Story of the Matunga." 1918. *Age* [Melbourne, VIC], June 13.
Stout, Anna P. 1914. "Lady Stout's Address." Letter to the Editor. *Manawatu Standard* [Palmerston North, N.Z.], December 9.
"Strike Heads Sought to Control Civic, Provincial and Federal Ships." 1919. *Manitoba Free Press* [Winnipeg, MAN], May 30.
"Strike Leader Will Speak at I.L.D. Meeting." 1926. *Daily Worker* [New York], September 4.
"Strike Leaders Sentenced." 1920. *New York Times*, April 7.
"Strike Parade in Defiance of the Mayor's Proclamation is Abruptly Discontinued." 1919. *Manitoba Free Press* [Winnipeg, MAN], June 7.
"Strikers Find National Plot to Herd Scabs." 1925. *Daily Worker* [New York], November 14.
"Strikers Fire on Constables." 1910. *Democratic Banner* [Mt. Vernon, Ohio], April 22.
"Strike Weakening: Many Seeking Work." 1913. *New Zealand Herald* [Auckland, N.Z.], November 13.
Strong-Boag, Veronica. 1979. "The Girl of the New Day: Canadian Working Women in the 1920s." *Labour / Le Travail* 4:131–164.
"Strong Protest is Made over Allowance Cut." 1923. *Winnipeg Evening Tribune* [MAN], March 22.
Stubbs, Roy St. George. 1954. *Prairie Portraits*. Toronto: McClelland and Stew Art.
"Successful Dance Held." 1918. *Manitoba Free Press* [Winnipeg, MAN], June 7.
"Sudden Change for the Worse." 1919. *Scotsman* [Edinburgh, U.K.], June 7.
"Suffragist Lawyer Defends Girl Strike Leader in Patterson [sic] Trial." 1913. *Rock Island Argus* [Ill.], July 7.
Summerfield, Rose. 1892. "Master and Man." Address to the Australian Socialist League, July 17. https://www.reasoninrevolt.net.au/bib/PR0000099.htm (August 27, 2020).
"Sunday Meetings." 1914. *Voice* [Winnipeg, MAN], February 27.
"Supplementary Estimates for $120,057 Passed." 1924. *Winnipeg Evening Tribune* [MAN], April 3.
Suriano, Juan. 1997. "Las practicas políticas del anarchismo Argentino." *Revista de Indias* (Madrid, Spain) 57:421–450.
Susumu, Yamaizumi. 2013. "The Significance of the Centennial of the High Treason Incident." In *Japan and the High Treason Incident*, eds. Masako Gavin and Ben Middleton. New York: Routledge.
Svensen, Stuart. 1995. *The Sinews of War: Hard Cash and the 1890 Maritime Strike*. Sydney: University of New South Wales Press.
"Sydney Domain Speakers in Court." 1916. *Barrier Miner* [Broken Hill, NSW], September 15.
"Sydney Propaganda: the Barker Case." 1916. *Direct Action* [Sydney, NSW], April 15.
"Sympathy Helped Clear Gurley Flynn; Filigno Will Appeal." 1910. *Spokane Press* [Wash.], February 25.

Szach, Jerry. 2009. "Playing in the Shadow of the Ukrainian Labour Temple." *Manitoba History*, February.

"Tailors of N. Y. Organizing to Battle Bosses." 1925. *Daily Worker* [New York], October 10.

Takeuchi, Yoshitomo. 1967. "The Role of Marxism in Japan." *The Developing Economies* [Chiba, Japan], 5:727–735.

Tarcus, Horacio. 2021. "Locascio, Santiago." Diccionario Biográfico de las Izquierdas Latinoamericanas. https://diccionario.cedinci.org/locascio-santiago/ (February 24, 2022).

"Ten Thousand More Join in Silk Strike." 1913. *Washington Times* [D.C.], May 3.

"Term for Contempt Ends." 1953. *New York Times*, January 1.

"Terrace Gaol, Wellington." 2013. New Zealand Ministry for Culture and Heritage/Manatū Taonga. https://nzhistory.govt.nz/media/photo/terrace-gaol (May 21, 2022).

"The Auckland Position." 1913. *Wairarapa Age* [Masterton, N.Z.], November 13.

"The Barker Appeal." 1915. *Direct Action* [Sydney, NSW], October 16.

"The Barker Case." 1916. *Socialist* [Melbourne, VIC], May 19.

"The Barker Case: Further Protests." 1916. Editorial. *Direct Action* [Sydney, NSW], May 6.

"The Barker Case: More Protests." 1916. *Direct Action* [Sydney, NSW], April 29.

"The Charge." 1919. *Western Labor News* [Winnipeg, MAN], Special Strike Edition No. 29, June 19.

"The Committee of 35,000." 1919. Editorial. *Western Labor News* [Winnipeg, MAN], Special Strike Edition No. 22, June 11.

"The Conspiracy Charges: Aid for Horrocks." 1916. *Kalgoorlie Miner* [WA], November 25.

"The Defence Act of 1909." 1966. *An Encyclopedia of New Zealand*. https://teara.govt.nz/en/1966/compulsory-military-training/page-2 (July 29, 2022).

"The Defence of Australia." 1916. *Barrier Miner* [Broken Hill, NSW], October 1.

"The End of the Strike: the Facts." 1919. Editorial. *Manitoba Free Press* [Winnipeg, MAN], June 26.

"The Fight for Free Speech in America." 1910. *Justice* [London], January 15.

"The Firemen's Union and the Proposed Compromise." 1917. *Voice* [Winnipeg, MAN], April 27.

"The Gelignite Scare: Davis Sentenced." 1913. *Auckland Star* [N.Z.], December 8.

"The Green Lane Gelignite: Aged Prisoner Remanded." 1913. *Auckland Star* [N.Z.], November 21.

"The Hon. Donald McLennan Grant (1890–1970)." N.d. https://www.parliament.nsw.gov.au/members/formermembers/Pages/former-member-details.aspx?pk=1499 (July 24, 2022).

"The Human Shuttlecock." 1921. *Evening Post* [Wellington, N.Z.], July 30.

"The I.W.W." 1917. *Daily Telegraph* [Launceston, TAS], March 12.

"The I.W.W.: Address by Mr. Tom Barker." 1917. *Daily Standard* [Brisbane, QLD], February 5.

"The I.W.W. and the Conspiracy Charges: Lenient Treatment." 1916. *Sunday Times* [Perth, WA], December 17.
"The I.W.W.: Case in the West." 1916. *Examiner* [Launceston, TAS], November 10.
"The I.W.W.: Further 'Startling' Evidence." 1916. *Stratford Evening Post* [N.Z.], October 12.
"The I.W.W. is After the Works." 1917. *Townsville Daily Bulletin* [QLD], April 5.
"The I.W.W.: Reeves in the West." 1916. *Sunday Times* [Perth, WA], October 15.
"The Jap Socialists: Murder of Dr. Kotoku." 1911. *Truth* [Sydney, NSW], March 5.
"The Kalgoolie Arrest." 1916. *West Australian* [Perth, WA], October 18.
"The Kalgoolie Arrest: Accused Before the Police Court." 1916. *Western Mail* [Perth, WA], October 20.
"The Matunga." 1918a. *Sun* [Sydney, NSW], February 27.
"The Matunga." 1918b. *Sydney Morning Herald* [NSW], February 27.
"The Newspaper Act." 1916. *Inverell Times* [NSW], September 8.
"The New Proletarian Pennsylvania Kuzbas." 1925. *Daily Worker* [New York], January 20.
"The Persecutions in Russia." 1924. *Freedom* [London], July–August.
"Theo. Stefanik Loses Vote under New Franchise Act." 1917. *Winnipeg Evening Tribune* [MAN], October 3.
"The Recruiting Problem." 1915. *Auckland Star* [N.Z.], November 24.
"The Report." 1920. *Sydney Morning Herald* [NSW], July 31.
"These Are the Friends of Our Enemies." 1919. *Winnipeg Telegram* [MAN], Strike Edition, May 31.
"The Secretary and the Consul: News of Tom Barker." 1920. *World* [Hobart, TAS], May 27.
The Shame of Pennsylvania. 1928. New York: American Civil Liberties Union.
"The Steamer Cumberland: Story of the Explosion." 1917. *Advertiser* [Adelaide, SA].
"The Strike." 1913. *Horowhenua Chronicle* [Levin, N.Z.], November 13.
"The "To Arms" Poster." 1915. *Direct Action* [Sydney, NSW], October 1.
"The Trades and Labor Council." 1917a. *Voice* [Winnipeg, MAN], July 6.
"The Trades and Labor Council." 1917b. *Voice* [Winnipeg, MAN], September 7.
"The Truth about the Strike." 1912. *Worker* [Wagga, NSW], February 8.
"The War on the I.W.W." 1917. *Dominion* [Wellington, N.Z.], August 31.
"The Winnipeg General Strike." 1994. Editorial. *Manitoba Social Science Teacher* 20:2.
"The Winnipeg General Strike: 100 Years Later." 2019. *Winnipeg Free Press* [MAN], May 11.
"The Winnipeg Revolutionary Strike." 1919. Editorial. *Winnipeg Citizen* [MAN], June 9.
"The Winnipeg Strike." 1919. Editorial. *Chicago Tribune*, June 25.
"The Winnipeg Strike Trial: Evidence of Eleven Witnesses Heard." 1919. *Hamilton Daily Times* [ONT], December 10.
"They Still Trifle with Human Rights up on the Mesaba Range." 1907. *Labor World* [Duluth, Minn.], August 24.

Thomas, A. Vernon. 1917. "Fired! What For?" Letter to the Editor. *Voice* [Winnipeg, MAN], February 16.

Thompson, David. 2020. "More Sugar, Less Salt." *Labour / Le Travail* 85:127–164.

Thompson Dorfman Sweatman LLP. 2012. 1887–2012: A Short History. Winnipeg, MAN: Thompson Dorfman Sweatman LLP. https://www.tdslaw.com/history/ (February 22, 2023).

Thorpe, Wayne. 2000. "The German Syndicalists in the First World War." *Central European History* 33:195–216.

"Threats of Terrorism." 1919. *Scotsman* [Edinburgh, U.K.], June 7.

"Thursday Evening Session." 1919. *Western Labor News* [Winnipeg, MAN], Special Strike Edition No. 7, May 24.

Tierney, Robert Thomas. 2015. *Monster of the Twentieth Century: Kōtoku Shūsui and Japan's First Anti-Imperialist Movement.* Oakland: University of California Press.

"To Bond Jitneys." 1917. *Voice* [Winnipeg, MAN], August 24.

Tocqueville, Alexis de. [1835–1840] 1899. *Democracy In America*, trans. Henry Reeve. 2 vols. New York: D. Appleton.

"To-Day's Proceedings." 1916. *Daily News* [Perth, WA], November 10.

"To Fight Against Re-Introduction of "Demon Rum."" 1919. *Winnipeg Evening Tribune* [MAN], January 25.

"Toledo Workers to Hear Gurley Flynn Speak Friday Night." 1924. *Daily Worker* [Chicago], June 11.

Tolstoy, Leo. [1904] 2021. "Bethink Yourselves!" trans. V. Tchertkoff. Boston: Ginn. https://www.marxists.org/archive/tolstoy/1904/bethink-yourselves.html (November 19, 2022).

"Tom Barker Arrested." 1917. *Singleton Argus* [NSW], September 1.

"Tom Barker in Brisbane." 1917. *Direct Action* [Sydney, NSW], January 20.

"Tom Barker in Lithgow." 1917. *Lithgow Mercury* [NSW], April 20.

"Tom Barker: Released from Jail." 1914. *Maoriland Worker* [Wellington, N.Z.], January 21.

"Tom Barker's Address to the Workers in Moscow." 1921. *Communist* [Sydney, NSW], August 5.

"Tom Barker's Case." 1915. Editorial. *International Socialist* [Sydney, NSW], October 2.

"Tom Barker's Case: Application for Release." 1915. *Daily Examiner* [Grafton, NSW], September 21.

"Tom Barker's Release." 1916. *Socialist* [Melbourne, VIC], June 30.

"Tom Barker Welcomes his Mates from Gaol." 1921. *Daily Standard* [Brisbane, QLD], February 1.

Tonge, Jon. 2019. "Militant's Rule Ended in Tears. But in Liverpool, Derek Hatton was Genuinely Popular." *New Statesman*, February 19.

Topp, Michael M. 2005. *The Sacco and Vanzetti Case: A Brief History with Documents.* Boston: Bedford/ St. Martin's.

"Top U.S. Communist Succumbs in Moscow." 1964. *Chicago Tribune*, September 6.
"To Reclaim Them." 1908. *Ely Miner* [Minn.], February 7.
Tosstorff, Reiner. 2004. *The Red International of Labour Unions (RILU) 1920–1937*, trans. Ben Fowkes. Leiden, Netherlands: Brill.
Totten, George Oakley, III. 1966. *The Social Democratic Movement in Japan.* Studies on Japan's Social Democratic Parties, Vol. I. New Haven, Conn.: Yale University Press.
Touroff, Anna B. 1910. *Report of the Socialist Women of Greater New York to the International Socialist Congress.* Copenhagen, Denmark, August 28-September 4.
Toy, E. 1913. "Hamilton Hustlers: Blocking Free Speech." *Industrial Unionist* [Auckland, N.Z.], November 18.
"Trades Council." 1918a. *Voice* [Winnipeg, MAN], May 17.
"Trades Council." 1918b. *Voice* [Winnipeg, MAN], June 21.
"Train Sensation: Express in Peril." 1913. *New Zealand Herald* [Auckland], November 15.
"Treason Case: Trial in Sydney." 1916. *Telegraph* [Brisbane, QLD], October 11.
"Trenton Ban on Elizabeth Gurley Flynn." 1913. *New York Times*, September 20.
Trohan, Walter. 1963. "Report from Washington." *Chicago Tribune*, January 7.
"Troopers Hold Rioters in Awe after Carnage." 1909. *Bisbee Daily Review* [Ariz.], August 24.
"Try to Link Dixon with 'Red' Coterie." 1920. *Winnipeg Evening Tribune* [MAN], January 30.
Tsurumi, E. Patricia. 1985. "Feminism and anarchism in Japan: Takamure Itsue, 1894–1964." *Bulletin of Concerned Asian Scholars* 17:2–19.
Tsuzuki, Chushichi. 1966. "Kotoku, Osugi, and Japanese Anarchism." *Hitotsubashi Journal of Social Studies* 3:30–42.
Tucker, Benjamin R. 1926. *Individual Liberty: Selections From the Writings of Benjamin R. Tucker.* Ed. C.L.S. New York: Vanguard.
Tucker, John A. 2009. "Disaster-Relief Confucian-Style: Ninomiya Sontoku's Philosophical Approach to Late-Tokugawa Poverty." *Japanese Studies Review* 22:131–148.
Tucker, John A. 2013. "Andō Shōeki's Agrarian Utopianism: An East Asian Philosophical Contextualization." *Taiwan Journal of East Asian Studies* 10:53–84.
Turcato, Davide. 2014. "Introduction." In *The Method of Freedom: An Errico Malatesta Reader*, by Errico Malatesta. ed. Davide Turcato, trans. Paul Sharkey. Oakland, Cal.: A.K.
Turner, Ian. 1962. "Industrial Labor and Politics: the Dynamics of the Labor Movement in Eastern Australia: 1900–1921." Ph.D. diss. Australian National University.
Turner, Ian. [1967] 1969. *Sydney's Burning.* Revised ed. Sydney, NSW: Alpha.
"Twelve Japanese Socialists are Hanged at Tokio Japan Today." 1911. *Daily Capital Journal* [Salem, Ore.], January 24.
"Two Flynn Dates." 1915. *Day Book* [Chicago], July 1.

"Two-Per-Cent. Beer Sales May Be Prohibited." 1916. *Brandon Daily Sun* [MAN], June 21.

Uchiyama, Gudō. 1908. "Anarchist Communist Revolution: In Commemoration of Imprisonment. Why Is Life So Hard for Tenant Farmers?" trans. Fabio Rambelli. https://theanarchistlibrary.org/library/uchiyama-gudo-anarchist-communist-revolution-in-commemoration-of-imprisonment (October 23, 2022).

Ueda, Kiyoshi. 2008. "Hiraizumi Kiyoshi (1895–1984): 'Spiritual History' in the Service of the Nation in Twentieth Century Japan." Ph.D. thesis. University of Toronto.

"Une Femme." 1913. "Beware Suffragette!" Letter to the Editor. *New Zealand Times* [Wellington, N.Z.], March 13.

"Unemployed Ask Continuance of Relief Grants." 1922. *Winnipeg Evening Tribune* [MAN], April 25.

"Union Combinations." 1910. *Washington Standard* [Olympia, Wash.], December 2.

"Unions Demand Minimum Wage." 1918. *Manitoba Free Press* [Winnipeg, MAN], February 7.

"Unlawful Associations Act: Deportation Regulation." 1917. Editorial. *Australian Worker* [Sydney, NSW], October 11.

"Unpolished Story of Cause and Struggle of Minnesota Miners." 1907. *Labor World* [Duluth, Minn.], August 31.

Untitled. 1913a. *Evening Post* [Wellington, N.Z.], August 9.

Untitled. 1913b. *Industrial Unionist* [Auckland, N.Z.], October 1.

Untitled. 1915. *Direct Action* [Sydney, NSW], January 15.

Untitled. 1916. *Maoriland Worker* [Wellington, N.Z.], June 14.

Untitled. 1916. *Voice* [Winnipeg, MAN], September 15.

Untitled. 1918. *Winnipeg Free Press* [MAN], April 6.

Untitled. 1919. *Winnipeg Evening Tribune* [MAN], April 12.

Untitled. 1920a. *Winnipeg Evening Tribune* [MAN], June 24.

Untitled. 1920b. *Winnipeg Evening Tribune* [MAN], September 22.

Untitled. 1920c. *Winnipeg Evening Tribune* [MAN], October 22.

"Urano Liber Manrique." 2019. https://www.geni.com/people/Urano-Manrique/6000000107110704852 (March 2, 2002).

"Urano Liber Manrique Bolten." 2021. https://ancestors.familysearch.org/en/L83K-7JS/urano-liber-manrique-bolten-1898-1980 (March 2, 2002).

"U.S. Communist Leader Ill." 1964. *Birmingham Post* [U.K.], September 5.

US House of Representatives. 1912. "The Strike at Lawrence, Mass." Hearings before the Committee on Rules of the House of Representatives on House Resolutions 409 and 433, March 2–7, 1912. Washington: Government Printing Office, April 4.

Valobra, Adriana. 2019. "Los niños proselitistas de las vanguardias obreras." In *Dora Barrancos: Devenir feminista. Una trayectoria político-intelectual*, eds. Ana Laura Martín and Adriana Valobra. Buenos Aires, Argentina: Consejo Latinoamericano de Ciencias Sociales.

Van der Walt, Lucien, and Michael Schmidt. 2009. *Black Flame: the Revolutionary Class Politics of Anarchism and Syndicalism.* Oakland, Cal.: AK.
Vapnek, Lara. 2015. *Elizabeth Gurley Flynn: Modern American Revolutionary.* Abingdon-on-Thames, U.K.: Routledge.
Vapnek, Lara. 2018. "The Rebel Girl Revisited: Rereading Elizabeth Gurley Flynn's Life Story." *Feminist Studies* 44:13–42.
Victoria, Brian Andre. 1996. "Zen and Japanese Militarism: A Critical Inquiry into the Roots of "Imperial Way-Zen.'" Ph.D. diss. Temple University.
"Victory at Spokane." 1910. *Wheeling Majority* [W.Va.], March 10.
Vidal, Daniel. 2012. "Ensayo y aborto de la primera revolución obrera en el Uruguay." *Periódico Rojo y Negro* [Montevideo, Uruguay], April 24.
Vidal, Daniel. 2014. "Intelectuales, periódicos y autoridad en el Centro Internacional de Estudios Sociales (Montevideo, 1897–1928)." https://anaforas.fic.edu.uy/jspui/handle/123456789/46370?mode=full (August 18, 2020).
Vidal, Daniel. 2017. "Intelectuales y autoridad en el Centro Internacional de Estudios Sociales (Montevideo, 1900–1913)." In *Territorios en disputa: prensa, literatura y política en la modernidad rioplatense,* ed. María Inés de Torres. Montevideo, Uruguay: Facultad de Información y Comunicación, Universidad de la República.
Viera, Marcelino. 2013. "Florencio Sánchez en su in-fidelidad anarquista." *Latin American Literary Review* 41:47–71.
Vile, John R. 2009. "*Aptheker v. Secretary of State* (1964)." The First Amendment Encyclopedia. https://www.mtsu.edu/first-amendment/article/698/aptheker-v-secretary-of-state (June 11, 2023).
"Visit of Queen Here Won't be a 'Royal' Success as ILD Exposes Regime and City Officers Balk." 1926. *Daily Worker* [New York], November 22.
Vizetelly, Ernest Alfred. 1911. *The Anarchists: Their Faith & Their Record.* London: John Lane.
Vorse, Mary Heaton. 1926. "Elizabeth Gurley Flynn." *Nation,* February 17.
Vorse, Mary Heaton. 1927. "Passaic Strikers' Reply to Mill Bosses." *Daily Worker* [New York], April 9.
Voss, Earl H. 1962. "U.S. Reds Face Passport Loss." *Evening Star* [Washington, D.C.], January 17.
Vu, Minh. 2022. "The Global Constitutions of Nation-States in China, Japan and Vietnam: Civilisations and Socialisms." Ph.D. diss. University of Queensland.
Waddington, Marc. 2013. "Liverpool's Militants Regroup 30 Years On." *Liverpool Echo* [U.K.], May 2.
Wainwright, Oliver. 2016. "'The Worst Place on Earth': Inside Assad's Brutal Saydnaya Prison." *Guardian,* August 17.
Waisbrooker, Lois. 1897. "Things as I See Them," *Lucifer,* December 22.

Wakabayashi, Bob Tadashi. 1998. "Introduction." In *Modern Japanese Thought* ed. Bob Tadashi Wakabayashi. Cambridge, U.K.: Cambridge University Press.

Walker, Bertha. 1970. "Tom Barker: One of the Greats Passes." *Tribune* [Sydney, NSW], June 3.

Walker, Bertha. 2016. *My Revolutionary Childhood*. Electronic ed.?:Alan Walker. https://www.solidarityforeverbook.com/mrc.html (August 24, 2011).

Walker, Jack, Q.C. 2004. *The Great Canadian Sedition Trials: the Courts and the Winnipeg General Strike, 1919–1920*, ed. Duncan Fraser, 2nd. ed. Winnipeg: University of Manitoba Legal Research Institute and Canadian Legal History Project.

Walter, Richard J. 1980. "The Socialist Press in Turn-of-the-Century Argentina." *The Americas* 37:1–24.

"Want Control of Storage Plants to Precede Pledges." 1917. *Winnipeg Evening Tribune* [MAN], September 29.

"Wanted – A Moratorium." 1915. Editorial. *Maoriland Worker* [Wellington, N.Z.], November 3.

"Want Woman as Juvenile Court Judge." 1916. *Winnipeg Evening Tribune* [MAN], April 14.

Ward, Max. 2019. Review of *Monster of the Twentieth Century: Kōtoku Shūsui and Japan's First Anti-Imperialist Movement* by Robert Thomas Tierney. *Journal of Japanese Studies* 45:406–411.

Ware, Norman J. 1932. "The Decline of the I.W.W." *Nation*, August 24.

"War on the I.W.W." 1916. Editorial. *Direct Action* [Sydney, NSW], September 2.

"Was Matunga Blown Up?" 1917. *Herald* [Melbourne, VIC], August 15.

Waters, Bob. 2010. *Four Generations That Walked the Walk*. Pittsburgh, Penn.: Dorrance.

Watt, Laura B. 1917. "Women to Boost Label." *Voice* [Winnipeg, MAN], September 21.

Waugh, Auberon. 1970. "A Catholic Criticizes the Pope." *New York Times*, November 9.

"W.D. Haywood is Indicted." 1913. *Madison Daily Leader* [S.D.], April 28.

Weir, Jo-Anne. 2007. "Undan Snjóbreiðunni (What Lies Beneath the Snow): Revealing the Contributions of Icelandic Pioneer Women to Adult Education in Manitoba 1875–1914." M.Ed. thesis. University of Manitoba.

Weiss, Holger. 2021. *A Global Radical Waterfront: the International Propaganda Committee of Transport Workers and the International of Seamen and Harbour Workers, 1921–1937*. Leiden, Netherlands: Brill.

"Wellington Notes." 1913a. *Maoriland Worker* [Wellington, N.Z.], July 18.

"Wellington Notes." 1913b. *Maoriland Worker* [Wellington, N.Z.], August 15.

"Wellington Strike: Waterside Strikers Out." 1913. *Lyttleton Times* [Christchurch, N.Z.], October 24.

Wenzer, Kenneth C. 1996. *Anarchists Adrift: Emma Goldman and Alexander Berkman*. St. James, N.Y.: Brandywine.

"Western Canada Conference of Typographical Unions." 1917. *Voice* [Winnipeg, MAN], June 22.
"Western Canada Labor Conference Held at Calgary, Alberta, March 13, 14, 15, 1919: Report of Proceedings." 1919. *Western Labor News*, Supplement. [Winnipeg, MAN], April 4.
Wexler, Alice. 1989. *Emma Goldman in Exile: From the Russian Revolution to the Spanish Civil War*. Boston: Beacon.
"Wharfside Orators." 1913. *Lyttleton Times* [Christchurch, N.Z.], October 24.
"What: the Philadelphia Transit Strike of 1944." N.d. http://northerncity.library.temple.edu/exhibits/show/civil-rights-in-a-northern-cit/collections/philadelphia-transit-strike-of/what--the-philadelphia-transit (July 24, 2022).
White, Ahmed A. 2007. "The Crime of Economic Radicalism: Criminal Syndicalism Laws and the Industrial Workers of the World, 1917–1927." *Oregon Law Review* 85:649–770.
White, Ahmed A. 2022. *Under the Iron Heel: the Wobblies and the Capitalist War on Radical Workers*. Oakland: University of California Press.
"'White Collar' Wearers Urged to Organize." 1920. *Winnipeg Evening Tribune* [MAN], September 21.
"Who is Responsible for the Outrage?" 1919. *Western Labor News* [Winnipeg, MAN], Special Strike Edition No. 27 Extra, June 17.
"Who Will Bring Them to Account?" 1913. Editorial. *Industrial Unionist* [Auckland, N.Z.], November 22.
"Who Will Wear Emma's Crown?" 1919. *Washington Herald* [D.C.], December 8.
Wiley, A. Terrance. 2014. *Angelic Troublemakers: Religion and Anarchism in America*. New York: Bloomsbury.
"Will Ask the Prince to Use His Influence." 1919. *Manitoba Free Press* [Winnipeg, MAN], September 8.
"Will Try Again to Organize the Mesabi Miners." 1908. *Daily Arizona Silver Belt* [Globe, Ariz.], February 9.
Windle, Kevin. 2005. "Standard-Bearer of the Australian Revolution: the Interrogation of Aleksandr Zuzenko by Special Branch: An Annotated Transcript." *New Zealand Slavonic Journal* 39:175–215.
Winkler, Allan M. 1972. "The Philadelphia Transit Strike of 1944." *Journal of American History* 59:73–89.
"Winning Denies Any Knowledge of Soviet." 1919. *Manitoba Free Press* [Winnipeg, MAN], August 1.
Winnipeg City Council. 1920. *By-Laws of the City of Winnipeg Dealt with by the Council During the Year 1919*. Winnipeg, MAN: Saults & Pollard.
"Winnipeg Counter-Terror Expert Denies Menace in Direct Action." 1986. *Winnipeg Free Press* [MAN], April 27.

"Winnipeggers to Register Names June 11 to 15?" 1917. *Winnipeg Evening Tribune* [MAN], May 22.

"Winnipeg Housemaids to Form Union at Meeting to be Held Thursday." 1918. *Winnipeg Evening Tribune* [MAN], April 10.

"Winnipeg Rioters are Shot by Police." 1919. *New York Times*, June 22.

"Winnipeg Strike Collapse: Causes of Men's Defeat." 1919. *Mail* [London], June 27.

"Winnipeg Strike Flames Anew." 1919. *New York Times*, June 11.

"Winnipeg Strike Head Found Guilty by Jury." 1919. *New York Times*, December 25.

"Winnipeg Strike Leader Released." 1920. *New York Times*, December 12.

"Winnipeg Strike Leader Sentenced." 1919. *New York Times*, December 28.

"Winnipeg Strike: Leaders of Last Year's Trouble Sent to Prison." 1920. *Shields Daily News* [Tynemouth, U.K.], April 7.

"Winnipeg Strike: Many Leaders Arrested." 1919. *Scotsman* [Edinburgh, U.K.], June 18.

"Winnipeg Strike Over." 1919. *Belfast News-Letter* [U.K.], June 9.

"Winnipeg Strike: Returned Soldiers in Separate Camps." 1919. *Nottingham Journal & Express* [U.K.], June 5.

"Winnipeg Strike Spreads Further." 1919. *New York Times*, May 18.

"Winnipeg Women Ask Federal Probe into Sugar Prices." 1923. *Winnipeg Evening Tribune* [MAN], May 2.

Witt, John Fabian. 2022. "Garland's Million; or, the Tragedy and Triumph of Legal History." *Law and History Review* 40:123–147.

Wofford, Taylor. 2014. "What CIA Torturers Did to Their Captives." *Newsweek*, December 9.

"Woman Agitator in Silk Strike on Trial at Paterson." 1913. *Evening World* [New York], June 30.

"Woman Claims Welfare Board is Home Wrecker." 1923. *Winnipeg Evening Tribune* [MAN], January 17.

"Woman's Quiet Influence." 1910. *Taranaki Herald* [New Plymouth, N.Z.], January 29.

"Woman Sues the Mayor." 1910. *Spokane Press* [Wash.], January 15.

"Woman Would Fill City's Prisons." 1909. *Daily Missoulian* [Missoula, Mont.], October 3.

"Women Gather Sugar Stocks in Pound Lots." 1917. *Winnipeg Evening Tribune* [MAN], December 5.

"Women Open Eating House in Strathcona Hotel, Cor. Main and Rupert." 1919. *Western Labor News* [Winnipeg, MAN], Special Strike Edition No. 6, May 23.

"Women Pickets Asked by Girl Leader." 1915. *Day Book* [Chicago], April 20.

"Women Resent Duty on Raisins." 1923. *Winnipeg Evening Tribune* [MAN], May 16.

"Women's Labor League." 1918a. *Voice* [Winnipeg, MAN], March 29.

"Women's Labor League." 1918b. *Voice* [Winnipeg, MAN], June 28.

"Women's Labor League." 1919. *Western Labor News* [Winnipeg, MAN], Special Strike Edition No. 15, June 3.

"Women's Labor League is Again Organized." 1925. *Winnipeg Evening Tribune* [MAN], March 4.
"Women's Labor League Objects." 1923. *Winnipeg Evening Tribune* [MAN], March 16.
"Women's Labor League Scores Draft Foes." 1917. *Winnipeg Evening Tribune* [MAN], July 4.
"Women's Wage Law Under Discussion." 1918. *Manitoba Free Press* [Winnipeg, MAN], March 2.
"Won't Re-Open Almazoff Case." 1919. *Winnipeg Evening Tribune* [MAN], August 18.
"Woollen Trust Faces Inquiry by Congress." 1912. *Sun* [New York], March 8.
"Workers are Murdered and Imprisoned by the Thousands in the Land of the Queen Marie." 1926. *Daily Worker* [New York], November 14.
W.R. 1913. "Word from Wellington." *Industrial Unionist* [Auckland, N.Z.], November 29.
W.R.W. 1911. "Freedom's Martyrs: Kotoku." *International Socialist* [Sydney, NSW], February 4.
Yada, Kinji, Ken. 1972. "Confucian Path to Meiji Socialism: Kōtoku Shūsui's Radical Reaction to Modernization." Ph.D. diss. University of Southern California.
Yanes Torrado, Sergio, Carlos Marín Suárez, and María Cantabrana Carassou. 2017. *Papeles de plomo: Los voluntarios uruguayos en la guerra de España*. Montevideo, Uruguay: Descontrol.
Yang, Manuel. 2005. "Yoshimoto Taka'aki, Communal Illusion, and the Japanese New Left." M.A. thesis. University of Toledo.
Yang, Qin. 2017. "Imai Utako and Her Contemporaries: A Survey into Intellectual Allegiance in the Early Feminist Movement in Late Meiji Japan, ca. 1900–1910." B.A. thesis. Haverford College.
Yanow, Dvora, and Peregrine Schwartz-Shea. 2010. "Perestroika Ten Years After: Reflections on Methodological Diversity." *Political Science and Politics* 43:741–745.
Yearley, Lee H. 1980. "Hsün Tzu on the Mind: His Attempted Synthesis of Confucianism and Taoism." *Journal of Asian Studies* 39:465–480.
Yeoman, James Michael. 2020. *Print Culture and the Formation of the Anarchist Movement in Spain, 1890–1915*. New York: Routledge.
Yerrill, P., and L. Rosser. 1987. *Revolutionary Unionism In Latin America: the FORA In Argentina*. London: ASP.
Yoshii, Ruri, 2014. "Language Skill Development in Japanese *Kokugo* Education: Analysis of the Television Program *Wakaru Kokugo Yomikaki No Tsubo*." M.A. thesis. Portland State University.
Young, Pam. 1991. *Proud to be a Rebel – The Life and Times of Emma Miller*. St. Lucia: University of Queensland Press.
Young, William, and David E. Kaiser. 1985. *Postmortem: New Evidence in the Case of Sacco and Vanzetti*. Amherst: University of Massachusetts Press.

Zaragoza, Gonzalo. 1996. *Anarquismo Argentino (1876–1902)*. Madrid, Spain: Editiones de la Torre.

Zheng, Xuejun. 2019. "Scientism, Nationalism, and Christianity: the Spread and Influence of Kotoku Shusui's *On the Obliteration of Christ* in China." *Cultura International Journal of Philosophy of Culture and Axiology* 16:135–149.

Zimmer, Kenyon. 2010. ""The Whole World is Our Country": Immigration and Anarchism in the United States, 1885–1940." Ph.D. diss. University of Pittsburgh.

Zola, Émile. [1894] 2005. *Germinal*, trans. Havelock Ellis. New York: Barnes & Noble.

Zola, Émile [identified as Zola, Emilio]. 1910. "La resolución." *La Nueva Senda*, March 18.

Zoratti, Jen. 2015. "Women Still Haven't Come Far Enough." *Winnipeg Free Press* [MAN], May 15.

Zubillaga, Carlos, and Jorge Balbis. 1986. *Historia del movimiento sindical Uruguayo*. Book II: *Prensa obrera y obrerista (1878–1905)*. Montevideo, Uruguay: Ediciones del la Banda Oriental.

Zubillaga, Carlos, and Horacio Tarcus. 2020. "Berri, Francisco." *Diccionario Biográfico de las Izquierdas Latinoamericanas*. https://diccionario.cedinci.org/berri-francisco/ (February 10, 2022).

"Zulema Manrique." 2019. https://www.geni.com/people/Zulema-Manrique/6000000107109084983 (March 3, 2022).

Index

Addams, Jane   114, 146
Ainu   295
Akahata jiken. See Red Flag Incident
alcohol   102–103, 107
Alderson Federal Prison, West Virginia   128
Alexander II (tsar of Russia)   254
Alien Restriction Order (1915) (Australia)   217
Allegheny Coal and Coke Company   145
al-Assad, Bashar Hafez (president of Syria)   259–260
Almazoff, Solomon Pearl   84, 86
al-Nashiri, Abd al-Rahim   257
American Civil Liberties Union (ACLU)   124, 144, 146, 147, 149, 150, 151, 161
American Federation of Labor (AFL)   91, 157, 171, 212, 245, 298
American Fund for Public Service. *See* Garland Fund
American Legion   151
American Political Science Association (APSA)   4
American Woolen Company   133, 183
anarcho/a-Batllism   9, 46–47
Anderson, Edward   99
Andō, Shōeki   288, 295–297
Andrews, A.J.   70, 71, 72, 73, 84
Andreytchine, George   148
Anthony, Susan B.   123, 124
Anti-Conscription League (Canada)   105
Apollo Hall, Spokane   119
Aptheker, Herbert   167
Aptheker v. Secretary of State (1964)   167, 168
Arahata, Kanson   252, 256, 266
Arkwright, Richard   233
Armstrong, George   68, 70–71, 73, 75, 76, 78, 79, 82, 83, 84, 85, 88, 89, 91, 104, 113, 115
Armstrong, Helen   68, 76, 79, 83, 87–115, 123, 144, 148
Artemiev, P.   241–242
Article 5 Campaign   269–270, 285–286
Articles of Confederation   164
Ashland Auditorium, Chicago   153, 157
Ashley, Jessie   135, 139

Ashio Copper Mine   282, 291–292, 293, 299–301
Auckland Electric Tramways Union   172, 178
Auckland Employers' Association   190–192, 206
Australian Communist. See Communist (periodical)
Australian Labor Party   177–178, 197–198, 205, 206, 210, 213, 215, 226, 227
Australian Shearers' Union (ASU)   213
Australian Workers' Union (AWU)   197, 199, 213, 215, 224
Averill, Alfred Walter "A.W."   193

Badger, Joseph Stillman "J.S." "Bully"   180–181
Bakunin, Mikhail   14, 19, 230, 250, 263, 289, 306
Baldwin, Roger N.   149, 155
Ballarat, VIC   173
Band of Idealists. *See* Risōdan
Baritz, Moses   217
Barker, Thomas Grainger (father of Tom Barker)   172
Barker, Tom   79, 83, 105, 140, 142, 148, 159, 171–249, 255, 274
Batlle y Ordoñez, José (president of Uruguay)   2, 46
Batllism   9, 46, 54
Bax, Ernest Belfort   280
Beatty, William   228
Bebel, August   124, 129, 269, 276, 292–293
Beffel, John Nicholas   150
Bellamy, Edward   124
Benedictsson, Margrét Jónsdóttir   83
Benedictsson, Sigfús Benedict   83
Bennett, Harry Scott   173
Berardelli, Alessandro   149
Berkman, Alexander   144, 146, 159, 232, 234, 235–236, 237–238
Berri, Francisco   54
Bilboa, Frank   219
Bimson, John   135, 137, 139
Bischev, Antonio   138
Blackall Fountain, Queensland   211
Blackall, Samuel   211

"Black Friday" (Brisbane) 180
Black, Hugo 162, 166, 167
"Black Tuesday" (Waihi, New Zealand) 175
Blakeley, Arthur 214–215
Bliss, William Dwight Porter 280
"Bloody Saturday" (Winnipeg) 71
"Bloody Sunday" (St. Petersburg) 56, 288
Bluestocking Society (Japan). *See Seitōsha*
Blumenberg, Samuel "Sam" 78, 79, 84, 85–86
Boer War (1899–1901) 189, 275, 276, 277
Bolten, Virginia 13, 24, 25–67, 120, 282
Boote, Harry 226
Borden, Robert (prime minister of Canada) 96
Botany Worsted Mills 155
Boumediene v. Bush (2008) 257
Boxer Rebellion (1899–1901) 275–276
Boyd, Frederick Summer 141
Brandeis, Louis 157
Brandeis, Susan 157
Bray, Roger E. 70–71, 75, 84, 111
Bread and Roses Strike (1912) 133, 183
Brennan, William J., Jr. 166
Bresci, Gaetano 24–25
Brisbane General Strike (1912) 180
Broken Hill, NSW 201
Brookfield, Percy "Jack" 218, 226
Brotherhood of Sleeping Car Porters 147–148
Brown, Peter Campbell 163
Brown University 165
Bruno, Giordano 74
Budislavich, Cosme 49
Buford (ship) 83, 236
Burnside, Robert Bruce 209–210
Butyrka Prison, Moscow 237
Buurmans, Victor 15
Byington, Steven T. 2
Byron, Lord George Gordon 121

Café de los Inmortales (coffee house) 20
Calvia, Maria 30, 32, 42–43
Calvin, John 74
Camp 1391 (Israel) 257
Campbell, Isaac 96
Cannon, James P. 153, 157
Capetillo, Luisa 44
capitalism 74, 75, 79, 91, 150, 188, 212, 281–282, 283

Capolaretti, Teresa 29, 44
Caras y Caretas (publication) 24, 41, 42
Caruso, Joseph "Joe" 133–134
Cassidy, Robert 72
Catholic Church 56, 263
Catholicism 13, 26–27
Cavell, Edith 190
Central Intelligence Agency (CIA) 257, 258
Cerro Social Studies Center, Montevideo 44
Chamorro, Juan Onofre 219
charity 78, 105, 193, 277
Charitinoff, Michael 78, 84, 86
Chew, A. Percy 90–91
Chian keisatsu hō. *See* Public Order and Police Law (1900)
Chicago anarchists. *See* Haymarket Tragedy
child labor legislation 133
Chinese immigrants 107, 198
chokkō 288, 296, 297
Chokkōdan 296
Chokugen (publication) 286, 296
Chou, En-lai (premier of China) 166
Chuang Tzu. *See* Zhuangzi
Chu, Hsi 307
Ciminaghi, Irma 31, 40
Citizens' Committee of One Thousand 69, 71, 74, 77, 80, 86, 92, 93–94, 104, 111
City College, New York 165
Civil Liberties Union. *See* American Civil Liberties Union (ACLU)
Claflin, Tennessee. *See* Claflin, Tennie C.
Claflin, Tennie C. 121
class 48, 52, 103, 176, 177, 197, 206, 274
clear and present danger test 144, 162
Cocoa Workers Magazine (publication) 246
Collazo, María 43, 44, 45
collective bargaining 68, 69, 70, 72, 76, 81–82, 157
Colonia Cosme 183
colonialism 276–277
Committee of One Thousand. *See* Citizens' Committee of One Thousand
Committee on Public Information (CPI) 194
Commoners' Society 271, 284
Communist Party of America v. Subversive Activities Control Board (1961) 165–166
Communist Party, USA 124, 147, 149, 162, 163–164, 165–166

INDEX 387

Communist (publication)   234–235
Compulsory Service Proclamation   205
Confédération Générale du Travail (CGT)   141
Confucius   273, 301, 305, 307, 308
Connolly, James   129
Connor, Jenny (sister of Tom Barker)   172, 221
conscription   96, 104–105, 189, 195–196, 200–201, 205–206, 211
Cook, A.J.   246
Cook, Joseph   206
Cook, Lady. *See* Claflin, Tennie C.
Copernicus   74
Craig, Ernest Arthur "E.A."   190–192, 193
Crimes Prevention Act (1916)   207
Cronaca Sovversiva (publication)   260, 301
Cullen, William   204
Cumberland (ship)   207

Daily Herald (publication)   226, 246
Daily Worker (publication)   147, 149, 156
Daskalud, Harry   86
Davis, Joseph   185–186
Debs, Eugene V.   144, 145, 151, 152, 155
Debs v. United States (1919)   144, 162
De Cleyre, Voltairine   250–251, 266
Dedham, Massachusetts Jail   150
Defence Act (1909) (New Zealand)   192
Degan, Mathias J.   17
De Leon, Daniel   176
Dennis, Eugene   165
Dennis v. United States (1951)   162, 164
Der Syndikalist (publication)   229, 234
Dick, Harriet   103, 107–108
Dick, Mrs. John. *See* Dick, Harriet
dictatorship of the proletariat   92
Diesel, Rudolf   233
Dill Pickle Club, Chicago   125
Dimock, Edward J.   163–164, 165
Diogenes   65–66
direct action   177, 178, 288, 290, 294, 296–297, 298, 310
Direct Action (publication)   182, 189, 190, 192, 195, 197, 198, 199, 200, 202, 205, 208, 209, 210, 233, 249–251
Direct Action Group *See* Chokkōdan
discontent, societal   58, 182, 204, 208

Disraeli, Benjamin (prime minister of the UK)   60
Dixon, Fred   75, 78, 82, 103
Dmietrieff, Elizabeth   18
Domain area, Sydney, NSW   204, 210
domestic workers   43, 90, 98, 111
Douglass, Frederick   123
Douglas, William O.   162–163, 165, 166, 167–168
Draper, John William   287
Dreyfus, Alfred   17–18, 255, 279
Duluth, Minnesota   130, 131, 142, 148, 212
Duncan, James Alexander "Jimmy"   91–92
Dunn, Michael   136
Dupont, Artur   54

Eastland, James "Big Jim"   167
Edison, Thomas   233
Égalité (publication)   250
elections. *See* voting
El Día (publication)   46, 63
El Municipio (publication)   49
El ObreroPanadero (publication)   54
El Obrero (the Montevideo publication)   51, 53–54, 56, 58, 59
El Perseguido (publication)   20
El Polo Bamba (coffee house)   20
El Rebelde (publication)   22–23, 25, 33–34
El Socialista (publication)   47
El Surco (publication)   24, 64
Ely, Richard T.   280, 283
Emancipación (publication)   44
"Emancipación" Women's Association   46
Emerson, Ralph Waldo   121
Engels, Friedrich   129, 158, 210, 249, 280, 282, 287
enhanced interrogation techniques   258
Equi, Marie   125–128, 153
Espionage Act of 1917 (U.S.)   146
Espionage Act, 1918 Amendments. *See* Sedition Act of 1918 (U.S.)
Ettor, Joseph "Joe"   129, 133–134, 142, 143, 144, 183
Eureka Stockade, Battle of the   173, 208
Evans, Frederick G. "Fred"   175
Ewing Commission   227–229
Ewing, Norman   227
Ezo. *See* Ainu

false consciousness 64
famine 152–153
farming 181, 224–225, 299–300
fashion 136–137
Faure, Sébastien 17, 23
Federal Women's Reformatory, Alderson, West Virginia 165
Federación Obrera Regional Argentina (FORA) 16, 45, 224, 231
Federación Obrera Regional Chilena (FORCh) 219
Federación Obrera Regional Uruguaya (FORU) 45, 46
Ferdinand I (king of Romania) 154
Ferguson, Ronald Munro (governor general of Australia) 205
Ferrer y Guardia, Francisco 56, 64, 263
Ferricks, Myles 205–206
Fifth Amendment (U.S.) 167
Fielden, Samuel 16
filial piety 278, 308
Filigno, C.L. "Charley" 122–123
First Amendment (U.S.) 146, 162, 165, 167
First International. *See* International Workingmen's Association (IWA)
First World War 83, 85, 87, 95, 103, 104, 144, 147, 176, 183, 192, 193, 194, 198, 199, 201, 257
Fitzgerald, John Daniel "Jack" 196
Fitzgerald, M. Eleanor "Fitzi" 144
Fleshin, Simon (Senia) 236
Flynn, Anna Katherine "Kathie" (sister of Elizabeth Gurley Flynn) 124, 126, 127
Flynn, Elizabeth Gurley 116–168, 176, 183, 212, 228
Flynn, Lucy Sabina "Bina" (sister of Elizabeth Gurley Flynn) 124, 125, 127
Flynn, Thomas (brother of Elizabeth Gurley Flynn) 124
Flynn, Thomas (father of Elizabeth Gurley Flynn) 124
FORA-C. *See* Federación Obrera Regional Argentina (FORA)
FORA-Comunista. *See* Federación Obrera Regional Argentina (FORA)
FORA-V. *See* Federación Obrera Regional Argentina (FORA)
Fort Quélern, France 15

Foster, William Z. 167, 313
Fournier d'Albe, Sidney "Sid" Huguenot 211–212
Freedom (publication) 250
free love 44, 120, 125, 156, 257
Freeman, Paul 217–218, 251
Freie Arbeiter Union Deutschland (FAUD) 229
French Revolution 2, 308
Freyja (publication) 83
Fritz, Rose 289, 306
Frugoni, Emilio 18
Fry, Eric 171
Fukuda, Hideko "Hide" 253
Fujin Kyōfūkai. *See* Women's Moral Reform Society
Furukawa, Ichibē 292, 299, 300

Galilei, Galileo 74, 75
Galleani, Luigi 56, 135
Garland, Charles 156
Garland Fund 156
gelignite 183, 184–185
Genbun Itchi Kai 302
general strike 148, 186, 293–294
genocide 160
George, Henry 76, 91, 121, 249
George III (king of the U.K.) 164
Germinal (publication) 19, 23
Germinal (Zola) 17, 19
Giovannitti, Arturo 129, 133–134, 189, 143, 144, 150, 183, 228
Gitlow, Benjamin 156–157
Gitlow v. U.S. (1925) 156
Gladstone, William Ewart (prime minister of the UK) 276
Glynn, Thomas "Tom" 189, 204, 221, 234–235
Gobley, A. 15
Godwin, William 2
Goldberg, Arthur 167
Goldie, David 192
Goldman, Emma 82–83, 144, 146, 148, 159, 217, 234, 235–236, 237–238, 250, 261, 266, 270, 288, 307
Gompers, Samuel 91, 245, 298
González, Vicenta 44
Gorbachev, Mikhail (president of the Soviet Union) 4

INDEX 389

Gori, Pietro (Pedro)   15, 20, 24, 26, 42, 45, 49
government by orders-in-council   78
Grant, Donald   202
Gray, Charles Frederick   68, 71
Great Treason Affair. *See* High Treason Incident
Greenstein, Abraham   139
Grijalbo, Alfonso   54
Grinius, Kazys (president of Lithuania)   155
Guantánamo Bay Detention Camp   257
Guerra, Pepita   26, 29, 30, 31, 32
Gurley, Annie (mother of Elizabeth Gurley Flynn)   123–124, 130
Gutiérrez, Rosalina   44

habeas corpus   83, 257
Haddock, William S.   145
Haeckel, Ernst Heinrich   287
Haledon, New Jersey   137, 138
Hall, David   206
Hancox, Edith   111, 112
Harding, Warren G. (president of the U.S.)   144
Harnois Theater, Missoula   132
Hart, Emma (mother of Helen Armstrong)   89
Havel, Hippolyte   261–262
Haymarket Tragedy   17, 23, 45, 49, 252, 258
Haywood, William "Bill"   133, 137, 138, 141–142, 144, 149, 167, 176, 183, 240, 241, 244
Heaps, Abraham A.   70, 73, 75, 82, 84, 103
Heiminsha. *See* Commoners' Society
Heimin Shimbun (publication)   284, 285, 286, 291, 292, 293, 296
Higgins, George   188
High Point, North Carolina   152
High Treason Incident   252, 254, 256, 257, 258, 260, 286, 294
Hillcrest Silk Mills   152
Hilton, Walter B.   263
Holdsworthy Concentration Camp   218
Holland, Harry   186, 217, 241–242
Holling, Mrs. Luther   95
Holman, William (premier of NSW)   206
Holodomor   159, 166
Hoop, William H. "Bill"   106
Horrocks, Alexander   209

Hotel and Housekeepers' Union (Winnipeg)   98, 102
Hotel and Restaurant Employees' Union (New Zealand)   187
Hotson, Kathleen   219
Housemaids and Hotelworkers' Union (Winnipeg). *See* Hotel and Housekeepers' Union (Winnipeg)
housing   241, 246, 247, 311, 317
Howe, Frederic C.   148
Hoxha, Enver (prime minister of Albania)   166
Hsün Tzu. *See* Xunzi
Hudson, Guillermo Enrique. *See* Hudson, William Henry
Hudson, William Henry   246–247
Hughes, William Morris "Billy" (prime minister of Australia)   202, 206, 210, 226
Hunter, T.A.   200
Hunzicker, Gustav A.   135

Ibsen, Henrik   121, 210
Ichigaya Prison, Tokyo   286
Ideas y Figuras (publication)   15
Il Proletario (publication)   134, 199
Immigration Act (1910) (Canada)   84
imperialism   158, 275, 276–279, 301–302, 308–309
imputation   164
Industrial Conciliation and Arbitration (IC&A) Act (1894)   188, 199
Industrial Pioneer (publication)   222, 231, 238
Industrial Unionist (publication)   177, 178, 179, 181, 183, 185, 186
Industrial Unionism. *See* Industrial Workers of the World (IWW)
Industrial Worker (publication)   116–117
Industrial Workers of the World (IWW)   70, 81, 116, 117, 118, 119, 122–123, 124, 129, 130, 131, 132, 133, 134, 135, 137, 138, 139–140, 141, 143–144, 146, 148, 161, 165, 171–172, 173–174, 175, 176, 178, 182, 183–184, 185, 186, 189 195, 196, 197–198, 199, 202, 204, 206–207, 208, 209, 210, 211, 213, 215, 216, 217, 248, 251, 257, 274, 288, 296
   Chicago IWW   176, 177, 270
   Detroit IWW   176, 208, 270

Ingersoll, Robert G.   74, 121
International Labor Defense (ILD)   149, 150, 152, 153, 154, 155
International Socialist (publication)   195, 301
International Trade Union Council (ITUC)   239
International Workers of the Amalgamated Food Industry   151–152
International Workingmen's Association (IWA)   14, 230
International Working Men's Association (IWMA)   229–230
Irvine, William   213
Isaakovna, Bertha (wife of Tom Barker)   240, 245, 247
Ishikawa, Sanshirō   285
Itō, Noe   288
Ivens, William   70–71, 73, 75, 76, 78, 82, 84, 90, 92, 109
Iyo Maru (ship)   287

Jackson, Robert H.   162
Jacquard, Joseph Marie   281
James, Henry   60–61
Japanese Christians   8, 284, 304
Japanese Socialist Party   291
Jaurès, Jean   292
Jeseric (ship)   219
Jewelry Workers' Union   139
jitneys   99–100
Jiyō shisō (publication)   271
Jiyūtō. *See* Liberal Party (Japan)
Johnson, Albert   287, 293, 303–304, 306, 309
Johnson, James Weldon   148
Johnson, John Albert   130
Johns, Richard J. "Dick"   70, 75, 76, 78
Jones, John Archibald "Jack" (husband of Elizabeth Gurley Flynn)   117, 121, 125, 129, 131–132
Josephs, Philip   175
J.P. Morgan and Co.   245
Jury, Alfred Fredman (father of Helen Armstrong)   89

Kamikawa, Matsuko   252
Kamiya, Fukutarō   265
Kanaka workers   211

Kanno, Suga   252, 254, 256, 259, 260, 264–267, 268, 271–272, 303
Kanno, Sugako. *See* Kanno, Suga
Katsura, Tarō (prime minister of Japan)   253
Kawamata Incident   300
Kay, A. D.   235
Khrushchev, Nikita S. (premier of the Soviet Union)   166, 168
Kindai shisō (publication)   256
King, John Benjamin "J.B."   173, 174, 176, 202, 203, 228–229, 249, 251
Kingsford, Sid   175
King, William Lyon "W.L." Mackenzie (prime minister of Canada)   110
Kinoshita, Naoe   269
Kirkup, Thomas   280, 281, 283
Kōtoku, Asako (first wife of Kōtoku, Shūsui)   267
Kōtoku, Atsuaki (father of Kōtoku, Shūsui)   272
Kōtoku, Chiyoko "Chiyo" (second wife of Kōtoku, Shūsui)   267, 269, 286
Kōtoku, Shūsui   124, 252–310
Kronstadt Rebellion   234, 236, 238
Kropotkin. Alexandra   260
Kropotkin, Peter   14, 16, 20, 22, 42, 52, 159, 182, 210, 234, 237–238, 249, 261, 263, 274, 281, 282, 287, 289, 296, 297, 310
Ku Klux Klan   147, 151
kulaks   159–160
kurkuls. *See* kulaks
Kuroiwa, Ruikō   284
Kushner, Jacob   135
Kuzbas project, Siberia   176, 240–245, 251

Labor Café (Winnipeg)   87–88, 98–99
Labor Call (publication)   180
Labor Defense Council (LDC)   149, 151
Labor Party (Australia). *See* Australian Labor Party
Labor World (periodical)   130
Labour Party (New Zealand). *See* New Zealand Labour Party
Labour Volunteer Army   195
Ladd, Parish B.   287
Lallemant, Germán Avé
Lalor, Peter   173
Lamb, Ernest   204

INDEX 391

Landis, Kenesaw Mountain   143
Lane, Michael A.   287
Lane, William "Will"   183
La Nueva Senda (publication)   18, 24, 41, 43, 57, 64
Lao Tzu. *See* Lao Zi
Lao Zi   307, 309
La Protesta. See La Protesta Humana (publication)
La Protesta Humana (publication)   21, 23, 35, 37, 47, 53, 231
La Questione Sociale (publication)   25, 56, 61
La Rebelión (publication)   44
Larkin, Peter   202
Las Proletarias   32, 34
Laurier, Wilfrid (prime minister of Canada)   96
La Voz de la Mujer (publication)   13, 26, 28, 31, 32, 33, 34, 35, 36, 37, 38, 42
Lawrence, Massachusetts   133, 150, 183–184, 212
Legislative Council (NSW)   202
Leigh House, Sydney, NSW   211
Leighton, H.M.   208
Lenin, Vladimir Ilich   158, 159, 162, 229, 230–231, 232, 233, 234, 236, 238, 239, 283
Léo, André   18
Le Révolté (publication)   249
Lèse Majesté Incident. *See* High Treason Incident
Leslie, Ken   200
Lessig, Adolph   137
Ley de Residencia (1902) (Argentina)   16, 22–23, 38–39, 45, 220
Ley de Residencia (1917) (Chile)   220, 221
Liberal Party (Australia)   96, 213
Liberal Party (Canada)   96
Liberal Party (Japan)   273
Liberal Party (New Zealand)   193
Liberal Party (U.K.)   276
Libertarian Party, USA   312
liberty   124, 167, 168, 264, 281
  freedom of speech   80, 92, 104, 116, 119, 122, 131, 134, 139, 141, 144, 146, 147, 163, 195, 234, 250, 314, 317
Liebknecht, Karl   79, 229
Littleton Times (publication)   175, 177, 181, 186

Local Council of Women (Winnipeg)   103, 109
Locascio, Santiago   23
London Dock Strike (U.K.)   210
Looking Backward: 2000–1887 (Bellamy)   124
Lopez, Frank   150
Lopizzo, Anna "Annie"   133, 183
Lucifer, the Light-Bearer (publication)   83
Luxemburg, Rosa   79, 22
luxury   65
Lynch, Patrick "Paddy"   210

Mackay, John Henry   307
MacDonald, Margaret   97
MacDonald, Ramsay (prime minister of the UK)   97
MacPherson, Donald   105, 107
MacSwiney, Terence   229
Madgwick, George   261
Madison Square Garden, New York   137, 153
Madonna, Vincenzo   138
Maheno (ship)   188
Mahon, Hugh   200
Majestic Theatre, Winnipeg   73, 79, 86
Malatesta, Errico   14, 25, 42, 61, 63, 135, 280, 307
Malthus, Thomas Robert   91
Manitoba Court of Appeal   72–73
Manitoba Association of Unemployed   111
Manitoba Temperance Act (1916)   102, 103
Mann, S.A.   116, 119
Mann, Thomas "Tom"   210, 232, 240, 261
Manrique, Manuel (partner of Virginia Bolten)   26, 34, 53
Maoriland Worker (publication)   173, 174, 175, 178, 195, 198, 221, 242
Marchisio, Teresa   30, 31, 32, 40, 42–43
Marelli, Henry   135–136
Marie (queen of Romania)   154
Marine Transport Workers Industrial Union (MTW)   172, 222, 229
Maritime Strike (1890)
Martin, Albert. *See* Lopez, Frank
Marx, Karl   14, 19, 121, 158, 210, 249, 261, 263, 274, 280, 282, 284, 306
Massey, William Ferguson (prime minister of New Zealand)   175, 186, 198, 257
Mattei, Ettore (Héctor)   14

Matunga (ship)   207
May Day   29, 45, 198
McCarran Internal Security Act
   (1950)   163, 167
McCormick Reaper Works
   (Chicago)   17
McHale, Kathryn   163
McMurray, Edward James   75
McNamara, Andrew T.   154
McPherson, Donald   203, 204, 227
Meighen, Arthur   69, 70, 84, 95
Meiji Restoration (1868)   272, 273
Melrose, Harry   249
Mencius   273, 277, 279, 301, 305, 306, 307,
   308, 309–310
Meng Ke. *See* Mencius
Menzi. *See* Mencius
Metcalfe, J.T.   72
Michel, Louise   14, 18, 33, 57, 252
Michel, Marie-Anne "Marianne"   252
Milholland, Inez   135
Military Service Act (New Zealand)   200–
   201, 211
Miller, David   2
Miller, Emma   180
Miller, Montague "Monty"   173, 208–209
Mill, John Stuart   60, 280
Mills, William B.   146
Minami, Sukematsu   300–301
Mineric (ship)   219, 226
minimum wage   97, 100–102, 103
Minnesota Iron Range   129
Missoula, Montana   117, 122, 129, 131–132
Miyashita, Takichi   254, 260
Morooka Chiyoko. *See* Kōtoku, Chiyoko
   "Chiyo"
Montevideo, Uruguay   15, 17, 18, 20, 24, 26,
   28, 41, 43, 44, 45, 46, 54, 56, 63, 64
Montjuich Prison, Barcelona   56–57
Mooney, Thomas J. "Tom"   91
Moore, E. J.   193
Moore, Fred H.   118, 150
Moose Temple, Seattle   157
Morley, John   276
Morris, William   60, 280
Most, Johann   307
Mother Earth (publication)   82, 83, 250, 261,
   262–263, 288, 307

Mothers' Allowances Act (1916)
   (Manitoba)   103, 107–109
Mo Tzu. *See* Mozi
Mount Morgan Gold Mining Company   214
Mozi   297
Muhlberg, Julius   219, 221, 224, 232

Nacht, Siegfried. *See* Arnold Roller
Nakae, Chōmin   273, 274, 306, 307–308
National Association for the Advancement of
   Colored People (NAACP)   148
National Association for the Promotion of
   Labor Unionism Among Negroes   147
Nebeker, Frank K.   143
New Australia Co-operative Settlement
   Association   183
New Australia Settlement   183
New Caledonia   14
New Castle, Pennsylvania   132, 133
New Women's Association   270
New Zealand Federation of Labor
   (NZFL)   172–173, 174, 177, 179
New Zealand Labour Party   177, 217
New Zealand Philistine (publication)   193
Nicholas II (tsar of Russia)   288
Nicholls, Sydney "Syd"   200
Nietzsche, Friedrich   187
Nihon Shakaitō. *See* Japanese Socialist Party
Nikko Maru (ship)   216
Noble, R.M.   85
Norris, Tobias (premier of Manitoba)   69
Novy Mir (publication)   86
Nuestra Tribuna (publication)   43–44

Odd Fellows' Hall, Spokane   118
Ogure, Reiko "Rei"   253
Oliver Iron Mining Company   129, 212
One Big Union   69–70, 79–80, 92, 94, 129,
   178, 179, 180, 213, 215, 234, 249
Ono, Tajiko "Taji" (mother of Kōtoku,
   Shūsui)   258, 267, 272
Ōsugi, Sakae   252, 256, 288, 295
Ōsuka, Satoko   253

Paine, Thomas "Tom"   121
Pankhurst, Adela   195, 206, 217, 235
Pankhurst, E. Sylvia   235, 243
Paparoa Miners' Union   176

Paraguay   20, 22, 61, 183
Paris Commune   13–14, 15, 17, 18, 57–58, 252, 282
Parnell, Charles Stuart   123
parliamentarism   290
Parsons, Albert   252
Parsons, Lucy   129, 266
Passaic Strike   149, 154, 155–157
passport revocation   167
Paterson, New Jersey   56, 119, 125, 135, 136, 137, 138, 139–140, 141, 155
Paterson Strike Pageant   137–138
patriotism   148, 193–194, 275, 278, 304
Pavilion, Coeur D'Alene, Idaho   119
Payne, John   191–192, 194
Pearce, George   200
Pellicer, Eustaquio   24–25
People v. Ruthenberg (1924)   151
Perdue, William Egerton (chief justice of Manitoba)   73
Perovskaya, Sophia   254, 255
Perry, Pettis   163
Pesotta, Rose   98–99, 150
Peterloo Massacre   278
Petit, Víctor Pérez   18
Petriella, Teofilo   129, 131
Philadelphia Transit Company Strike (1944)   201
Phillips, Hugh   76
Pitblado, Isaac   71, 72, 74, 100
Pitblado, May   100
Political Educational League (Winnipeg)   103
Pouget, Émile   140–141, 228
poverty   100, 115
Pratt, Nelson S.   122–123
Pravda (publication)   158, 159, 168
Pressed Steel Car Company, McKees Rocks, Pennsylvania   132
Pritchard, W.A. "Bill"   73, 74–75, 76, 81
Pring, Robert   204
prostitution   267–269
   marriage considered as prostitution   50, 120
Proudhon, Pierre-Joseph   19, 121, 249–250, 307
Pro-Zola (publication)   17
Public Order and Police Law (1900)   252, 269, 298, 301

Pugh, Fred C.   117, 188
Putin, Vladimir (president of Russia)   238
Puttee, Gertrude   100

Quakerism   246
Queen, John   70–71, 73, 75, 76, 82, 84, 103, 111
Queen, Katherine Ross   103–104
Quinlan, Patrick   135–136

Randolph, A. Philip   147
Randolph, John H.   219
Reardon, A.S.   235
Reclus, Elisée   15, 42
Red Feds. *See* New Zealand Federation of Labor (NZFL)
Red Flag Incident   252–253, 256, 265
Red International of Labor Unions (RILU)   218, 229, 231, 232, 251
Reed, John "Jack"   137
Reeve, Charles   202, 228
Regeneración (publication)   44
Reguera, José   23
Reguera, Manuel   23
religion   65, 189
Renan, Ernest   287
Retail Clerks' Union (Manitoba)   97
Risōdan   274
Robertson, Gideon   69–70
Robochyi narod (publication)   86
Rockhampton, QLD   216
Rodman, Henrietta   119
Roller, Arnold   293, 298
Roosevelt, Franklin Delano (president of the U.S.)   201
Rosario, Argentina   13, 26, 28, 32, 33, 35, 36, 37–38, 40, 42, 49, 53, 225
Rotterdam (ship)   240
Rouco Buela, Juana   24, 38–39, 40, 43, 44, 45, 64
Rousseau, Jean-Jacques   273, 305
Rowntree & Co.   246
Rowntree, Benjamin Seebohm   246
Rowntree, Joseph   246
Royal Commission of Inquiry into the Matter of the Trial and Conviction and Sentences Imposed on Charles Reeve and Others. *See* Ewing Commission
Royal Northwest Mounted Police (RNWMP)   71

Ruocco, Juana. *See* Rouco Buela, Juana
Russell, R.B. "Bob"   70–71, 72–73, 78, 84, 91, 111
Russian Oil Products Company   246
Russian Revolution   78, 83, 236–237, 249, 286
Russo-Japanese War (1904–1905)   284, 285, 296, 299, 302, 304
R. v. Dixon (1920)   75–76
R. v. Reeve and Others (1916)   203–205, 226
R. v. William Ivens, et al. (1920)   73–75
Ruthenberg, Charles Emil "C.E."   151, 157

sabotage   140–143, 176, 183, 186, 202, 228
  "scientific" sabotage   140, 142, 186, 196–197, 213, 294
Sacco, Nicola   134, 149, 150, 153
Saionji, Kinmochi (prime minister of Japan)   253, 291
Sakai, Toshihiko   124, 252, 269, 284, 285, 287, 291
Sakamoto, Seima   258
Salem, Massachusetts   134
Salvans, Baldomero   20
Salvation Army   116, 134, 219
San Francisco Earthquake   287–288, 289–290
Sanger, Margaret   100, 133, 137, 146
San Luis, Argentina   26, 38
Sartre, Jean-Paul   120, 295–296
Sawtell, Mick   210, 215
"scabs"   103, 138, 152, 174, 175, 180, 188, 215
Scales, Junius Irving   166
Scales v. United States (1961)   165–166
Scarlett, Samuel "Sam"   142, 212
Schäffle, Albert   283–284
Schmidt, Joseph "Joe"   142, 212
Schoppelrie, Oscar   84, 87
seamstresses' strike (Rosario)   13, 28
Seattle Central Labor Council (CLC)   91
Second World War   114, 256, 270
Sedition Act of 1918 (U.S.)   146
Seitō (publication)   270
Seitōsha   270
Seitō-sha. See Seitōsha
Sekai fujin (publication)   253, 270
Sellins, Frances "Fannie"   145
Semple, Robert "Bob"   175, 186
Sen, Katayama   298

Servetus, Michael   74
Shannon, Bill   119
Shaw, George Bernard   121, 198, 210
Shelley, Percy Bysshe   121, 210–211, 278
Shimizu, Taichiro   254
Shin fujin kyōkai. *See* New Women's Association
shizen   295
Siebenhaar, William W.   208
Siguranţă. *See* Siguranza
Siguranza   154
silk work   141, 152, 155
Sinclair, Upton   152, 155
Single Tax Movement   91
Smith Act (1940)   121, 158, 161–162, 164, 165
Smith Act Defense Committee   162
Smith, Alfred Emanuel "Al"   156
Smith-Connally Act (1943)   201
Social Democratic Party of Germany (SDP)   74, 78, 85, 90
Socialist Labor Party of America (SLP)   176
Socialist Party of Canada (SPC)   74, 78, 85, 90
Socialist Party (New Zealand)   172
Socialist Party (Uruguay)   18
Socialist (publication)   200, 226, 299
Socialist Women of Greater New York   129
social question, the   60–63, 282
Society for the Unification of Speech and Writing. *See* Genbun Itchi Kai
Sokolowski, Mike   71
Solidarity (publication)   133
Solovetsky Prison Camp   234, 236
Soltis, John Gabriel   90
Sonoma (ship)   218
Sozialdemokratische Partei Deutschlands. *See* Social Democratic Party of Germany (SDP)
"Spanwire." *See* Barker, Tom
Spencer, Herbert   249
Spence, William Guthrie "W.G."   213
Spokane, Washington   116–119, 122–123, 124, 131, 132
Spooner, Lysander   2, 55, 56
Stalin, Joseph   159–161, 166, 167, 238
Stanton, Elizabeth Cady   83, 119–120, 121, 266
Starzeleski, Joseph   145
Steel Trust. *See* United States Steel Corporation

INDEX395

Stefanik, Theodore 97
Steimer, Mollie 159, 199, 236
Stephenson, George 233, 281
Stirner, Max 16, 19, 50, 120, 249, 296, 307
Stony Mountain Penitentiary, Manitoba 70, 84, 85, 106
Stout, Anna P. 193
St. Pancras Town Hall, London 247
streetcars 45–46, 71, 99–100, 132–133
Street Commission 226–227
Street, Philip 226–227, 228
Subversive Activities Control Board 163
Sugamo Prison, Tokyo 285, 286, 287, 305
Summerfield, Rose 61, 100, 210–211
Sunday, Billy 140
surplus value, production of 79, 176, 274
Suzuki, Bunji 298
"Sydney Twelve" 189, 202–205, 210, 211, 212, 225, 226–229
Szczerbanowicz, Steve 71

Taigyaku jiken. *See* High Treason Incident
Takamure, Itsue 257
Takano, Fusatarō 298
Tanaka, Shōzō 291–292, 294, 300
Taylor, Frederick W. 237
Terrace Jail, Wellington 187–188
Terror-Famine (1932–1933). *See* Holodomor
Themis (Greek goddess) 65–66
Thompson, James P. 116
Thoreau, Henry David 121
Tkatchenko, Pavel 155
Tolstoy, Leo 261, 262, 263, 276, 285
Tocqueville, Alexis de 316–317
Touroff, Anna B. 129
Trades Hall, Melbourne 196
Tresca, Carlo 125, 126, 133, 135, 136, 138, 139, 142, 143, 144, 150, 212
Trohan, Walter 165
Trotsky, Leon 86, 233, 236, 238
Trotter, Sarah (mother of Tom Barker) 172
Truman, Harry S (president of the U.S.) 163
Tsuru, Joichirō 259
Tucker, Benjamin R. 56, 307
Turner Hall, Spokane 117
"Twelve." *See* "Sydney Twelve"

Uchimura, Kanzō 274–275, 284, 305

Uchiyama, Gudō 253, 254
Umberto I (king of Italy) 24
Undesirable Immigrants Exclusion Act (1919) (NewZealand) 217
United Mine Workers of America (UMWA) 145
United States Steel Corporation 132, 142, 145, 190, 212
United States v. Flynn et al.(1955) 163–164
United Textile Workers of America 157
Unlawful Associations Act (1916) 207, 208, 216

Vanderveer, George F. 143
Vanzetti, Bartolomeo 134, 149, 150, 153
Varley, Frank 246
Verenczuk, Mike 84
Vida Nueva Club, Montevideo 18
Vida Nueva (publication) 41
Vietnam War 162
Villard, Oswald Garrison 146
Vinson, Frederick M. "Fred" 162
violence 54, 55, 59
Vizetelly, Ernest 266
Voice (publication) 85, 89–90, 100
Vorse, Mary Heaton 116, 156
Vorwärts club, Buenos Aires 17, 20
voting 55–56, 182, 291, 292, 293

Waihi Goldmining Company 192
Waisbrooker, Lois 181, 266
Waldheim Cemetery, Chicago 168
Walker Theatre, Winnipeg 73, 78, 86
Wang, Yang-ming 307
Ward, Joseph 198
War Measures Act (Canada) 6, 78
War Precautions Act (Australia) 189, 194, 195, 202, 216, 218
Warren, Earl 166
War-Time Elections Act (Canada) 95–96, 97, 105
Warzawa (ship) 240
Watarase River, Japan 299
Watt, James 280, 281
Watts, Laura 104
Waugh, Auberon 303
Weisbord, Albert 157
Weller, C.E. 98

Western Federation of Miners 118, 129
Western Labor Conference, Calgary 73, 74, 79–80, 92, 94
Western Labor News (publication) 69, 70, 75, 77, 85, 89–90, 111
Wethersfield, Connecticut 316
"White Australia" policy 198, 215
Whitlam, Gough (prime minister of Australia) 198
Whitman, Walt 121
Wilde, Oscar 256
Wiley, A. Terrance 1
Williman, Claudio (president of Uruguay) 46, 63
Wilson, Woodrow (president of the U.S.) 194
Winning, James 106
Winnipeg Citizen (publication) 93
Winnipeg General Strike (1919) 68–72, 78, 80, 82, 84, 88, 89, 92, 100, 115
Winnipeg Political Equality League 95, 97
Winnipeg Social Welfare Commission 108
Winnipeg Street Railway Company 99–100, 112
Winnipeg Trades and Labor Council 68, 69, 78, 89, 97, 100, 101, 106, 107, 108, 109, 110
Wobblies. *See* Industrial Workers of the World (IWW)
Wolf (ship) 207
Wollstonecraft, Mary 50

Woman's Christian Temperance Union (WCTU) 109
Women's Anti-German League (WAGL) 193
Women's Franchise League 193
Women's Free Speech League 139
Women's Labor League (WLL) 87–88, 89, 92, 95, 96, 99, 100, 101, 103, 104, 106, 107, 110, 111
Women's Moral Reform Society 271
Woodhull, Victoria C. 121, 266
Workers' Dreadnought (publication) 224, 235, 243
Workers' International Industrial Union. *See* Detroit IWW
World War I. *See* First World War
Workers' Defense Union (WDU) 144, 145, 148, 149

Xunzi 273, 307

Yabuki, Sugatarō. *See* Sen, Katayama
Yamaguchi, Koken 252
Yamakawa, Hitoshi 252
Yorozu Chōhō (publication) 268, 273, 274, 284, 285, 299

Zárate, Argentina 41
Zhou, Enlai. *See* Chou, En-lai
Zhuangzi 273, 306, 309
Zhu Xi. *See* Chu, Hsi
Zola, Émile 17, 276, 279

www.ingramcontent.com/pod-product-compliance
Lightning Source LLC
Chambersburg PA
CBHW070608030426
42337CB00020B/3714